SYMBOLS AND ACRONYMS

1. Uppercase letters are used for asset prices, including currency values.
2. Lowercase letters are used for rates of change.
3. Superscripts indicate the currency units.
4. Subscripts indicate a point in time or a period of time.
5. Continuously compounded returns are in italics.
6. Return statistics are either in Greek letters or abbreviated in English (e.g., σ_j^2 or $Var(R_j)$).

P_t^d and P_t^f	Price of an asset at time t in the domestic and foreign currency, respectively
p^d and p^f	Domestic and foreign inflation (i.e. the rate of change in CPI), respectively
$S_t^{d/f}$	Spot exchange rate between currencies d (domestic) and f (foreign) at time t
$s_t^{d/f}$	Change in the spot exchange rate between currencies d and f during period t
$F_t^{d/f}$	Forward exchange rate between the domestic and foreign currencies priced at time 0 and for delivery at time t (sometimes denoted $F_{0,t}^{d/f}$)
$Fut_t^{d/f}$	Price in domestic currency of a futures contract on foreign currency priced at time 0 and for delivery at time t (sometimes denoted $Fut_{0,t}^{d/f}$)
i^d and i^f	Nominal interest rates in currencies d and f, respectively
ι^d and ι^f	Real interest rates in currencies d and f, respectively
$Call_t^{d/f}$	Value of a call option on foreign currency f at time t
$Put_t^{d/f}$	Value of a put option on foreign currency f at time t
$K^{d/f}$	The exercise (or striking) price of a currency call or put option
$X_t^{d/f}$	Real exchange rate at time t
$x_t^{d/f}$	Rate of change in the real exchange rate during period t
V	Value of an asset or security (e.g., $V_{Firm} = V_{Debt} + V_{Equity}$)
r_t^d and r_t^f	Rate of return during period t in currencies d and f, respectively
μ_j	Mean return on asset j
σ_j	Standard deviation of return on asset j (variance is denoted σ_j^2 or $Var(R_j)$)
$\rho_{j,k}$	Return correlation between assets j and k, such that $\rho_{j,k} = \sigma_{j,k} / (\sigma_j\sigma_k)$
$\sigma_{j,k}$	Return covariance between assets j and k, such that $\sigma_{j,k} = \rho_{j,k}\sigma_j\sigma_k$
β_j	Systematic risk of asset j (e.g., $\beta_j = \rho_{j,m}(\sigma_j/\sigma_m)$ for the one-factor market model)

Continuously compounded rates:

p	= $\ln(1+p)$	=	Continuously compounded inflation rate
i	= $\ln(1+i)$	=	Continuously compounded nominal interest rate
ι	= $\ln(1+\iota)$	=	Continuously compounded real interest rate
$s_t^{d/f}$	= $\ln(1+s_t^{d/f})$	=	Continuously compounded nominal spot rate change
$x_t^{d/f}$	= $\ln(1+x_t^{d/f})$	=	Continuously compounded real spot rate change

Multinational Finance

Third Edition

Kirt C. Butler

Michigan State University

THOMSON
™
SOUTH-WESTERN

Australia · Canada · Mexico · Singapore · Spain · United Kingdom · United States

Multinational Finance, 3e

Kirt C. Butler

VP/Editorial Director:
Jack W. Calhoun

VP/Editor-in-Chief:
Michael P. Roche

Executive Editor:
Michael R. Reynolds

Developmental Editor:
Jennifer E. Baker

Senior Marketing Manager:
Charlie Stutesman

Production Editor:
Starratt E. Alexander

Manufacturing Coordinator:
Sandee Milewski

Media Developmental Editor:
John Barans

Media Production Editor:
Mark Sears

Design Project Manager:
Bethany Casey

Production House:
Rebecca Gray Design

Cover Designer:
Bethany Casey

Cover Images:
© Digital Vision, Ltd.,
© PhotoDisc, Inc.,
© Artville, LLC.

Internal Designer:
Bethany Casey

Printer:
Transcontinental Printing, Inc.
Louiseville, QC

For My Family

Brief Contents

Contents

Preface

Everything should be made as simple as possible, but not simpler.

Albert Einstein

Multinational Finance assumes the viewpoint of the financial manager of a multinational corporation with investment or financial operations in more than one country. The book provides a framework for evaluating the many opportunities, costs, and risks of multinational operations in a manner that allows readers to see beyond the algebra and terminology to general principles.

KEY FEATURES

In its third edition, *Multinational Finance* keeps the major changes that were introduced in the second edition while continuing to refine the exposition. In particular, *Multinational Finance* retains the following features.

- **An emphasis on the basics of financial management.** *Multinational Finance* emphasizes the managerial aspects of multinational finance. Intended for MBA and advanced undergraduate classes, the text requires only a single preparatory course in finance. Chapters that extend material from the first course begin with a brief review of the fundamentals. Advanced material is placed in chapter appendices so that study can be tailored to each individual's objectives.
  - **A visual approach.** Graphs and figures are used to assist the reader in understanding key financial concepts and techniques.
  - **Numerous real-world examples.** Real-world examples are used to illustrate how the financial concepts and techniques are used in practice.
- **A reorganized table of contents.** Instructors that adopt *Multinational Finance* typically have a professional interest in one of two related areas:
  - International financial markets
  - International corporate finance

Detailed chapters on futures, options, and swaps will satisfy those instructors who insist on including derivatives in their courses. Because some instructors prefer that these topics be covered in a separate course in financial markets, the text is written so that the derivatives chapters can be skipped without loss of continuity. Chapter 11 provides an overview and comparison of the various derivative instruments for both types of course structures.

- **Comprehensive coverage of traditional topics.** Comprehensive coverage is provided on the traditional topics of multinational finance.
  - **International financial markets.** The text presents an in-depth treatment of the international financial environment, including currency and Eurocurrency markets and the international parity conditions.
  - **Derivative securities.** The text has detailed treatments of futures, options, and swaps because of the importance of these derivative instruments in currency risk management.

- **Risk management in the multinational corporation.** Entire chapters are devoted to managing the multinational treasury and its exposures to transaction, operating, translation, and country risks.
- **Valuation and the structure of multinational operations.** Valuing and structuring the corporation's international investments is at the heart of the text. The chapter on cross-border capital budgeting has far more depth than competing texts. Entire chapters are also devoted to multinational financing, taxation, valuation, and corporate governance.

- **Distinctive chapters on key topics.** Distinctive chapters are devoted to topics of special interest to practitioners of multinational finance.
  - Chapter 9 develops the rationale for hedging currency risk.
  - Chapter 18 takes a real options approach to valuing the flexibility provided by cross-border investments.
  - Chapter 19 describes cross-border differences in corporate governance and their implications for the international market for corporate control.
  - Part Six develops the international aspects of a traditional course in investments, with separate chapters devoted to international portfolio diversification (Chapter 20), asset pricing (Chapter 21), and portfolio management (Chapter 22).

Learning Aides

A number of learning aides are used to highlight the main points in each chapter.

- **Sidebars** run in the margins and highlight key concepts and definitions.
- **Market Updates** and **Applications** appear as boxed essays that provide real-world examples and practical applications of the conceptual material.
- **Web sites** appearing in the margins link the chapter topics to the real world.
- **Key Terms** appear in boldface the first time they are used. Key terms are listed at the end of each chapter and defined in a comprehensive **Glossary** in the text.
- **Conceptual Questions** at the end of each chapter summarize the key ideas in each chapter and allow students to test their understanding of the material.
- An expanded set of end-of-chapter **Problems** provides practice in applying the financial concepts, techniques, and strategies. Solutions are provided in a *Solutions Manual* that is available to instructors adopting *Multinational Finance* for classroom use.
- **Suggested Readings** are listed at the end of each chapter and are annotated to indicate the topics addressed by the articles.

Supplements

A comprehensive *Instructor's Manual* is available to adopting instructors.

- More than 600 **PowerPoint** slides review the key elements in each chapter and illustrate how to apply the material. The accompanying **NotesPages** provide additional insights and examples for classroom use.
- A *Solutions Manual* provides answers to the end-of-chapter questions and problems.

- A *Test Bank* includes nearly 1,100 test questions (and solutions) including true-false and multiple-choice questions, comprehensive numerical problems, and short essays.

The objective in providing these supplements is to reduce the burden of preparation and allow instructors to spend their time where it is most needed—in teaching the students.

ACKNOWLEDGMENTS

At my karate dojo in Michigan, we begin and end each class session with the Japanese phrase "onegai shimasu," which means "please teach me." This is appropriate for both students and teachers. Although I have learned a great deal from my own teachers and colleagues, I have learned at least as much from my students. Their varied backgrounds and approaches to learning have enriched my life and made me a better teacher, scholar, and student.

I am particularly grateful to the following scholars, whose thoughtful comments and suggestions helped me prioritize and execute changes to the third edition of *Multinational Finance*:

Louis K.C. Chan	University of Illinois, Urbana–Champaign
Joseph E. Finnerty	University of Illinois, Urbana–Champaign
Thomas Gjerde	Purdue University
Roger D. Huang	University of Notre Dame
Peter MacKay	Southern Methodist University
Rohan Williamson	Georgetown University

Other important contributors to this and previous editions include

Richard Ajayi	Wayne State University
Anne Allerston	Bournemouth University
Arindam Bandopadhyaya	University of Massachusetts, Boston
Jeffrey Bergstrand	University of Notre Dame
Rita Biswas	SUNY–Albany
Gordon Bodnar	John Hopkins University
G. Geoffrey Booth	Michigan State University
Donald J.S. Brean	University of Toronto
Louis K.C. Chan	University of Illinois
Robert A. Clark	University of Vermont
David B. Cox	University of Denver
Adri de Ridder	Stockholm University and Skandia Corporation
Miranda Detzler	University of Massachusetts, Boston
Thomas Grennes	North Carolina State University
Dora Hancock	Leeds Metropolitan University
Kwang Nam Jee	Korea Development Bank
Kurt Jesswein	Texas A&M International University
Jun-Koo Kang	Michigan State University
Andrew Karolyi	Ohio State University
H.S. Kerr	Washington State University
Naveen Khanna	Michigan State University
Yong-Cheol Kim	Clemson University
Paul Koch	University of Kansas

Theodor Kohers	Mississippi State University
C.R. Krishnaswamy	Western Michigan University
Chuck Kwok	University of South Carolina
Mya Maung	Boston College
Michael Mazzeo	Michigan State University
Richard M. Osborne	University of Colorado, Boulder
Barbara Ostdiek	Rice University
Terry Pope	Abilene Christian University
Mitchell Ratner	Rider College
Ashok Robin	Rochester Institute of Technology
Mehdi Salehizadeh	San Diego State University
Dorit Samuel	Capital University
Hakan Saraoglu	Bryant College
Anil Shivdasani	University of North Carolina
Richard R. Simonds	Michigan State University
Vijay Singal	Virginia Tech
Jacky C. So	Southern Illinois University, Edwardsville
Michael Solt	San Jose State University
Wei-Ling Song	Drexel University
Richard Stehle	Humboldt University
Chris Stivers	University of Georgia
Lawrence Tai	Loyola Marymount University
Dean Taylor	University of Colorado, Denver
Jon Vilasuso	Clarkson University

The Finance Team at South-Western College Publishing proved their worth in bringing this project to fruition. My thanks go to copyeditors Rebecca Roby and Sue Ellen Brown of Justified Left in Cincinnati, Ohio. Starratt Alexander and Jennifer Baker of South-Western College Publishing in Mason, Ohio, managed the editorial process under the guidance of Mike Reynolds and Mike Mercier. Rebecca Gray of Rebecca Gray Design in Chapin, South Carolina, managed production. Inspiration and direction were provided by my parents, Bruce and Jean Butler, and by my Sensei, Seikichi Iha.

Finally, and most importantly, I wish to thank my wife, Erika, and my children, Rosemarie and Vincent, for their tolerance and encouragement during many late nights, early mornings, and long weekends. My family is my inspiration and my refuge.

About the Author

Kirt C. Butler is an Associate Professor in the Department of Finance at Michigan State University, where he teaches multinational finance and global strategy in MSU's Eli Broad College of Business. He joined the faculty in 1985 after completing his doctorate in finance at Michigan State University. He also holds a M.S. degree in Computer Science from the College of Engineering and a B.A. in Psychology from the Honors College at Michigan State University.

Professor Butler's research has appeared in a variety of academic and practitioner journals including the *Journal of Finance, Journal of Accounting Research, Financial Analysts Journal, Journal of Portfolio Management, Journal of International Money and Finance*, and the *Journal of International Business Studies*, among others. His academic research has been profiled in *Time* and *Money* magazines, on the CNN and CNBC Web sites, and elsewhere. In 2001, he won the Withrow Teacher/Scholar Award in the Eli Broad College of Business at Michigan State University.

Professor Butler is also a Sensei of Okinawan Shido-kan (Shorin Ryu) Karate, with more than 25 years of experience and a rank of sixth degree black belt.

Overview and Background

part one

An Introduction to Multinational Finance

chapter 1

The more we learn of the possibilities of our world, and the possibilities of ourselves, the richer, we learn, is our inheritance.

H.G. Wells

1.1 • FINANCIAL MANAGEMENT OF THE MULTINATIONAL CORPORATION

In this book, we'll assume the viewpoint of the financial manager of a **multinational corporation (MNC)** with operations in more than one country.[1] As corporations extend their operations into international markets, they encounter new opportunities as well as new costs and risks. The challenge facing the multinational financial manager is to successfully develop and execute business and financial strategies in more than one culture or business environment.

MNCs have operations in more than one country.

At the heart of the opportunities, costs, and risks of multinational operations are the differences among the countries and peoples of the world. Local culture influences the conduct of business in profound and subtle ways, creating important cross-border differences in investment, financial, economic, political, regulatory, accounting, and tax environments. The multinational financial manager must be sensitive to these differences in the conduct of both professional and personal life.

Because of the far-reaching influence of local business environments on multinational operations, the multinational financial manager must be well versed in each of the traditional fields of business, including marketing, management of physical and human resources, law, regulation, taxation, accounting, and finance. Successful operation in each of these areas depends on knowing the local culture, and its written and unwritten conventions. Business problems are rarely the province of a single discipline, and the challenges facing multinational corporations are especially prone to be multidisciplinary.

---

1 The list of the world's largest corporations in Appendix 1-A is dominated by MNCs such as General Motors, or companies such as Wal-Mart that are rapidly becoming MNCs.

The multinational financial manager also must be an expert in several fields within finance. To be able to recognize and develop investment opportunities in foreign markets, the manager must understand the capabilities and limitations of traditional investment analysis, have a plan of attack for entry into and exit from foreign markets, and value the growth and abandonment options presented by foreign markets. The financial opportunities of the MNC also are richer than those of the domestic corporation because of cross-border differences in investors' required returns and hence the corporation's cost of capital. Multinational financial management requires a thorough knowledge of the international markets in interest rates and foreign currency, as well as derivative markets in interest rate and currency futures, options, and swaps. In many ways, today's financial manager must be a jack-of-all-trades as well as master of one—finance.

1.2 • THE OPPORTUNITIES OF MULTINATIONAL OPERATIONS

According to the **discounted cash flow** approach to valuation, the market value of an asset is equal to the present value of its expected future cash flows $E[CF_t]$ discounted at an appropriate risk-adjusted discount rate i.

$$V = \Sigma_t \, [E[CF_t] \, / \, (1+i)^t \,] \qquad (1.1)$$

This valuation equation has an important implication for the firm. If a corporate decision has no impact on the firm's expected future cash flows or discount rate, then the decision also has no impact on the value of the firm. Conversely, if a decision is to add value, then the decision must either increase expected cash flows or decrease the cost of capital.

Multinational Investment Opportunities

The set of investments available to the corporation is called its **investment opportunity set**. The corporation's investment objective is to identify, invest, and then manage the set of assets that maximizes the value of the firm to its stakeholders. In terms of Equation 1.1, the objective is to choose the set of investments that maximizes the present value of expected future cash flows. This means accepting projects with expected returns that exceed required returns and rejecting projects that do not meet this hurdle.

> The objective of invesment policy is to select those investments that maximize the value of the firm.

Operating cash flows can be increased by either increasing revenues or decreasing operating expenses. Multinational corporations can enhance revenues and reduce operating expenses in a number of ways that are not available to local firms.

Enhancing Revenues. Multinational corporations enjoy higher revenues than local firms by providing goods or services that are not readily available in local markets. Here are a few advantages that MNCs enjoy over domestic firms.

- *Global branding.* A global brand name can provide a competitive advantage over local competitors. For example, McDonald's and Coca-Cola have leveraged their internationally recognized brand names into marketing, production, and distribution efficiencies that are unavailable to local competitors.

- *The advantages of size.* Because of their size and scope of their operations, MNCs can exploit their competitive advantages on a larger scale and across a broader range of markets and products than domestic competitors. For example, Thailand is a relatively small country and might need a new power plant only once every several years. Rather than developing the necessary expertise locally, Thailand can employ a MNC with experience and expertise in power generation.

- *Flexibility in marketing and distribution.* MNCs have more marketing and distribution flexibility than domestic firms. In particular, they can more easily shift sales efforts toward markets willing to pay higher prices for their products. If Ford's Jaguar automobile is in high demand in the United States, then Ford can shift its marketing and distribution efforts toward the United States and away from regions of lower demand.

Here are a few strategies for preserving or enhancing revenues through multinational operations. Note that these strategies are often influenced by local factors.

- *Follow the customer.* Service firms, such as banks and accounting firms, often follow their customers into foreign markets. Parts suppliers in industries such as automobile manufacturing also follow this strategy. Once the nuances of operating in a foreign country have been mastered, these firms can begin to pursue foreign clients as well.
- *Lead the customer.* Service firms try to attract foreign companies into their domestic market. This lead-the-customer strategy is a way of solidifying relations with foreign companies before they establish relations with other local competitors.
- *Follow the leader.* When competitors are actively acquiring foreign assets, a common response is to acquire foreign assets to reduce the threat of falling behind in market share or production costs. This bandwagon phenomenon is especially common in industries enjoying high profitability.
- *Going local.* MNCs often build manufacturing capacity directly in foreign markets to avoid quotas or tariffs on imported goods. This reduces the risk of protectionism, as the MNC is seen as less of an outsider if it employs local workers. It may also increase sales, as people are more receptive to locally-produced goods.

Reducing Operating Costs. Multinational operations can reduce operating expenses in a number of ways that are not available to domestic firms.

- *Low-cost raw materials.* MNCs seek low-cost raw materials to reduce costs and ensure supply. The lure of low-cost resources can be powerful. In 1997, the French company Total secured a $2 billion deal with the Iranian government to develop Iran's South Pars gas field. Political opposition from Tehran—as well as from foreign governments—had prevented foreign investment in Iran since its 1979 revolution. When Iran sought outside investment to increase production and overcome a budget deficit, MNCs such as Total were quick to respond. In this case, economic necessity was strong enough to overcome two decades of political opposition.
- *Low-cost labor.* Many emerging economies attribute their growth to low labor costs. For example, Malaysia, Singapore, Thailand, and Vietnam have achieved double-digit GNP growth because of their low-cost but educated workforces. Shifting production to countries with low labor costs can greatly reduce operating costs. For example, labor accounts for as much as 75 percent of the cost of a new automobile. A corridor of *maquiladoras* investment along the U.S.–Mexican border has grown to accommodate the demand for the lower labor costs of Mexican workers.[2] The threat of low-cost foreign labor is one of the major fears of organ-

---

2 Established in 1966, the *maquiladoras* program allowed U.S. businesses to export from Mexico to the United States on a duty-free basis. Maquiladoras shipped $76.8 billion in goods during 2001, nearly half of Mexico's merchandise exports. Many maquiladoras have struggled since they lost their duty-free status in 2002.

ized labor in industrialized countries such as Germany and the United States. For this reason, labor unions are among the most vocal opponents of trade agreements such as the EU and NAFTA.

- *Flexibility in global site selection.* MNCs have greater flexibility than domestic firms in the location and timing of their investments. Competition between governments for capital investment allows MNCs to shop around for the most attractive deal. For example, Ford Motor Company announced in 1998 that it was building a $100 million assembly plant in the Philippines. In return, Ford was given a 6-year exemption from national and local income taxes, exemptions from import duties on equipment and machinery, and tax deductions for personnel training. Because of its size and international presence, Ford is in a much better position than local firms to be patient and pick its spots in its international site location decisions.

- *Flexibility in sourcing and production.* By having a diversified manufacturing base, MNCs can shift production to low-cost locations in response to currency movements or other factors. For example, if changes in currency values make parts components from some countries less expensive than others, Ford can use its global network of manufacturing facilities to increase production in low-cost countries and decrease production in high-cost countries. Local competitors do not enjoy this flexibility.

- *Economies of scale.* Companies possess **economies of scale** when size itself results in lower production costs. Economies of scale arise as fixed development or production costs are spread over a large output. For example, manufacture of integrated circuits requires high development costs and large fixed costs of investment. Once a manufacturing plant is set up, variable production costs can be quite low. High start-up costs serve to insulate large MNCs from local competition.

- *Economies of vertical integration.* Firms possess **economies of vertical integration** when they enjoy lower costs through their control of a vertically integrated supply chain. MNCs vertically integrate when it is costly to arrange the steps of a production process through external markets. Vertical integration is especially prevalent in industries that wish to protect their production processes and technologies. Mature MNCs often integrate their supply chains from labor and raw material inputs right through to the final marketing and distribution of their products.

Multinational Financing Opportunities

The objective of financial policy is to maximize the value of the firm by selecting the most appropriate mix of financing instruments, given the firm's investment decisions. Financial policy includes decisions regarding the mix of debt and equity, the currency of denomination of debt and equity, the maturity structure of debt, the markets in which capital is raised, the method of financing domestic and foreign operations, and financial risk management.

Many financial opportunities arise from financial market imperfections, so it is sensible to first define a perfect financial market.

> Financial policy sets the types of securities issued by MNCs.

The Perfect Market Assumptions and Concepts of Market Efficiency. The **perfect financial market assumptions** will prove useful at several points in the text.

> **In a perfect financial market, rational investors have equal access to market prices and information in a frictionless market.**

ttion has several components, as shown in Figure 1.1.

rictionless markets. Frictionless financial markets would have no transactions costs, taxes, government intervention, agency costs, or costs of financial distress.

- *Rational investors.* Rational investors price assets with a dispassionate eye toward their expected returns and risks. Although this sounds great in theory, investors are not always rational, and there are significant cross-border differences in investor behaviors. The study of the impact of psychological factors on behavior and asset prices is referred to as **behavioral finance**, and is an active area of financial research.

- *Equal access to market prices.* If all market participants have equal access to market prices, then no single party can influence prices. Although this is a convenient assumption, it does not always hold. There are many domestic and international actors that can influence prices. Governments influence interest rates, asset prices, and currency values through their fiscal and monetary policies. Cartels such as the Organization of Petroleum Exporting Countries (OPEC) influence oil prices through their control of production.

- *Equal access to costless information.* Equal access to costless information puts market participants on an equal footing. This assumption belies the fact that language serves as a very real barrier to the flow of information across (and sometimes within) national boundaries. Even with a common language, information is difficult to convey and can change in the telling. There are also wide differences in accounting measurement and disclosure requirements, and managers and other insiders benefit from their access to information in both developed and developing markets.

The assumption of frictionless markets is an assumption of operational efficiency in the financial markets. In an **operationally efficient** market, there are no drains on funds as they are transferred from one use to another. This does not mean that there are no opportunity costs in reallocating funds. Assets selling in perfect financial markets still have a competitively priced opportunity cost or required return that depends on their risk.

FIGURE 1.1
The Perfect Market Assumptions

Rational investors have equal access to market prices and information in a frictionless market.

1. Frictionless markets	No transactions costs
	No government intervention
	No taxes
	No agency costs
	No costs of financial distress
2. Rational investors	More return is good and more risk is bad
3. Equal access to market prices	Perfect competition
	No barriers to entry
4. Equal access to costless information	Everyone has instantaneous access to all public information

The last three assumptions are sufficient to ensure an informationally efficient market. Prices in an **informationally efficient** market fully and instantaneously reflect all relevant information. Informational efficiency does not require frictionless markets and operational efficiency. In the foreign exchange market, for example, prices can fully reflect information despite the existence of transactions costs. A bid-ask spread on currency transactions would simply preclude costless arbitrage, although currencies can still be correctly priced within the bounds of transactions costs. Similarly, efficient stock and bond markets can be informationally efficient despite relatively high transactions costs on foreign stock and bond transactions.

Operational efficiency and informational efficiency together promote **allocational efficiency.** In an allocationally efficient market, prices are determined in such a way that savings are optimally allocated to productive investments. Although financial market imperfections are becoming less important as domestic markets are progressively opened to foreign capital, financial market imperfections can still present formidable obstacles to international investment and portfolio diversification.

In a perfect financial market, there is no need for government regulators, bank auditors, or attorneys. With no taxes, there is no need for tax collectors or tax accountants. With equal access to market prices and no transaction costs, there is no need for financial intermediaries such as banks and brokers, nor any market for finance graduates. And, with costless information, there is no need for finance professors or this text. The net result is that the price of a particular asset is the same all over the world. This has important implications for the multinational corporation's financial policy.

The Implications of Perfect Financial Markets for Multinational Financial Policy.
The perfect market assumptions obviously omit most of what is interesting in the real world. Nevertheless, they provide a starting point for investigating many difficult issues in finance. In particular, the corporation's financial policy is irrelevant in a perfect financial market.[3] Individual investors can replicate or reverse any action that the firm can take in a perfect financial market, so the firm's financial policy cannot affect firm value. The converse must also be true.

> **If financial policy is to increase firm value, then it must increase the firm's expected cash flows or decrease the discount rate in a way that cannot be replicated by individual investors.**

This suggests that financial market imperfections can be sources of value for financial policy. Here are a few examples.

- *Financial market arbitrage.* Chapter 5 shows how market participants can take advantage of cross-border price differences.

- *Hedging policy.* Chapter 9 shows how financial managers can increase expected future cash flows through the firm's hedging policy.

- *MNC cost of capital when there are capital flow barriers.* Chapter 16 discusses how MNCs can lower their cost of capital by selling debt or equity securities to foreign investors that might be willing to pay higher prices than domestic investors.

- *Reducing taxes through multinational operations.* Chapter 17 shows how MNCs can reduce their tax bill by shifting production toward countries with

3 Franco Modigliani and Merton Miller have each won the Nobel Prize in Economics, largely for this insight. See Modigliani and Miller, "The Cost of Capital, Corporation Finance, and the Theory of Investment," *American Economic Review* (1958).

..ax rates or shifting ownership toward countries with high tax rates or
..elerated depreciation.

Barriers to the free flow of capital. Chapter 20 discusses vehicles for diversifying
across national boundaries when there are capital flow barriers.

- *Currency risk and the cost of capital.* Chapter 21 investigates whether investors care
about currency risk, and the impact of currency risk on the MNC's cost of capital.

Violations of any of the perfect financial market assumptions can lead to financial
opportunities for the multinational corporation with access to international markets.

Multinational Opportunities and Firm Value

Figure 1.2 illustrates the potential increase in firm value provided by multinational
investment and financial opportunities. The downward-sloping lines in Figure 1.2
represent the investment opportunity set of a hypothetical domestic firm and of a
comparable multinational corporation. Each firm accepts its most lucrative projects
first, so expected returns fall as more money is spent on investment. In Figure 1.2,
the expected return on the domestic corporation's first dollar of investment is 16 percent along the y-axis. With more attractive investment alternatives, the MNC's initial
investments are displayed with an expected return of 20 percent.

The upward-sloping lines represent each firm's required return or cost of capital on
investment. Firms draw on their lowest cost sources of funds first, so each firm's cost

---

FIGURE 1.2
The Potential Benefits of Multinationality

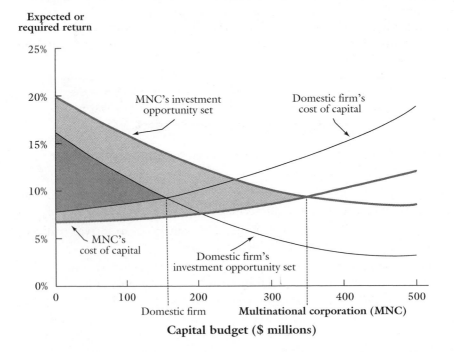

Key: The investment opportunities reflect expected returns on an incremental dollar of investment. The costs of
capital reflect investors' required returns on a given dollar of financing used to fund that investment.

Application

Que Hora Es?

Mexico City, September 12, 2004, 11:50 A.M.: You are a New Yorker working for AT&T on a satellite communications deal with Telmex, the Mexican telecom giant. You have scheduled a noon lunch with Miguel Rodriguez, your Telmex counterpart, at a fashionable restaurant in Mexico City. Conscious of the size and importance of the Mexican telecommunications market and of your part in the proposed venture, you arrive early and secure a private table.

12:20 P.M.: Twenty minutes have passed since your arrival and still no sign of Miguel. Could he have been caught in one of Mexico City's infamous traffic jams? Should you try to contact him on your cellular phone? The waiter doesn't seem concerned that you haven't begun to order. Should you order food for the two of you? Oh, dear.

12:35 P.M.: It has been over half an hour! Now you are really concerned. Your imagination starts to run away with you. Perhaps the deal has fallen through? No, you're just panicky. Perhaps he was overcome by smog? The delay is beginning to irritate you. You resolve to contact Miguel by phone—and just at that moment Miguel strolls calmly into the restaurant. Greeting you as if nothing is out of the ordinary, he takes a seat at your table and inquires how you have been. Doesn't he realize what an inconvenience he has caused?

Attitudes toward time differ widely across cultures, particularly in the precision with which time is measured. These businessmen are merely experiencing the difference between *hora Mexicana* (Mexican time) and *hora Americana* (American time).

---

of capital is an increasing function of the capital budget. The domestic firm has a cost of capital of 8 percent on the first dollar that it invests. With access to lower cost funds from international sources, the MNC in Figure 1.2 faces a required return of only 7 percent on its initial investments.

The expected return on the domestic firm's initial investment exceeds its cost of capital by 8 percent, so the first dollar invested by the domestic firm increases shareholder wealth by 8 cents. Successive investments yield diminishing marginal returns. The domestic firm will continue to invest until its required return on new investment exceeds its expected return. This occurs at a capital budget of around $150 million in Figure 1.2.

The MNC in Figure 1.2 earns an expected return of 20 percent at a required return of only 7 percent along the y-axis, so its first dollar of investment increases shareholder wealth by 13 cents. The MNC will continue to invest until its expected returns fall below its required returns. This occurs at a capital budget of approximately $350 million in Figure 1.2. With a larger and richer set of investments, the MNC in Figure 1.2 will have a higher value than comparable domestic firms.

The market values of multinational corporations will reflect these expanded investment and financing opportunities. Although these opportunities come with additional risks, the international experience of the MNC places it in a better position than its domestic rivals to evaluate and manage these risks. If the risks are too great, of course, the multinational corporation can choose to not invest in foreign operations. It is then no worse off than its domestic counterpart.

9

THE CHALLENGES OF MULTINATIONAL OPERATIONS

Recognizing and Overcoming Cultural Differences

An English aristocrat once said, "The only trouble with going abroad is that you have to leave home to do it." True enough. People and their cultural norms vary widely around the world. Managers and employees of the MNC must deal with unfamiliar business and popular cultures as they seek to extend the firm's competitive advantages into new and unfamiliar markets. Being able to understand, adapt to, and manage cultural differences can make the difference between a successful and an unsuccessful international venture.

The annals of international business are replete with anecdotes involving language differences, such as when General Motors introduced the Chevrolet Nova in Puerto Rico. Literally translated, "no va" means "it goes not." GM renamed the car Caribe for sale in Latin American countries. In another anecdote, a print advertisement for Coca-Cola in China used a set of Chinese characters that sounded like Coca-Cola but translated as "bite the wax tadpole." Coke's advertising slogan "Coke adds life" was literally translated into Chinese as "Coke brings you back from the dead."

Another way to categorize differences in national business environments is along the functional areas of business. The following list characterizes some of the differences that MNCs encounter in cross-border operations. The examples illustrate the challenges of international business, but are not intended to be exhaustive.

- *Differences in marketing.* Cross-cultural differences in marketing extend well beyond differences in language. For example, Walt Disney owns and operates the world's most successful theme parks. At the heart of Disney's success is their appeal to the entire family. Disney tried to retain this family orientation when it opened its EuroDisney theme park outside of Paris in the late 1980s. EuroDisney followed its U.S. practice and refused to sell alcoholic beverages at the theme park. This unfortunately ensured that no self-respecting Frenchman would visit the park ("No wine with dinner? Sacre bleu!"). EuroDisney was beset by other difficulties as well, including overoptimistic forecasts, labor strife, and political and popular opposition. Fortunately for Disney, its equity stake had been kept to a minimum by bringing in a variety of European debt and equity investors in a complex project finance arrangement. Disney's reputation did take a beating, along with several classes of foreign investors and the reputation of the French government of François Mitterrand.

- *Differences in distribution.* A prolonged stay in a foreign country inevitably means shopping for groceries. This can be an enjoyable experience because it allows the shopper to catch the "flavor" of the local culture. An observant shopper can detect many national differences in the ways foods are distributed. Residents of the United States are accustomed to large grocery chains that offer a wide selection of food and nonfood items. These large chains keep expenses low through economies of scale and efficient supply chain management. In many other parts of the world, groceries are sold in locally owned and operated mom-and-pop stores. Large discount stores are seen as impersonal and are not trusted by shoppers. The source of the local owners' advantage lies in their continuing relations with members of the local community. Because of these cultural differences in shopping habits, size can be seen as an advantage in one country and a disadvantage in another.

- *Differences in personnel management.* MNCs must adapt their human resource practices and organizational structures to accommodate the types of employees they will employ in their foreign operations. In many cases, personnel policies developed at home do not work in another culture.

- *Differences in legal, accounting, and tax systems.* For success in foreign cultures, multinational financial managers must learn unfamiliar tax laws, accounting and legal conventions, and business procedures. As an example, governments in developing countries sometimes offer tax benefits in the form of reduced tax holidays as an investment incentive. Negotiating these benefits and ensuring that they are not revoked subsequent to investment can be a delicate and time-consuming task.

- *Differences in financial markets.* Financial market operations vary across countries. Although the most obvious differences are in the volume and liquidity of trade, other differences can be profound. For example, banking practices in many Islamic countries are conducted according to the teachings of the prophet Mohammed as found in the Koran and other Islamic holy scriptures. According to these *Islamic banking customs*, depositors do not receive a set rate of interest but instead share in the profits and losses of the bank. Western banks opening branch banks in Islamic countries must be cognizant of local cultural and religious norms.

- *Differences in corporate governance.* Another difference between national business cultures lies in **corporate governance**—the mechanisms by which major stakeholders exert control over the corporation. The corporation is defined by a legal framework of contracts between customers, suppliers, labor, debt, equity, and management. Because each of these contracts is executed within the laws of the societies in which the firm operates, society itself helps determine the forms of these contracts and the rights and responsibilities of the various parties.

A foreign venture that does not respect local cultural sensibilities is destined for trouble. Multinational managers must learn new business systems and social behaviors, including what types of corporate behaviors are punished, what types are merely tolerated, and what types can lead to fruitful partnerships with foreign residents and their governments.

Application

Body Language

As if verbal language weren't enough of a barrier to communication, body language differs across cultures as well. In many settings, what we do with our bodies is even more important than what we say. (Voltaire wrote "Words were given to man to enable him to conceal his true feelings.") Although some body language is universal, a great deal of it is an accouterment of our culture.

Eye contact is a good example. In the Western world, direct eye contact conveys confidence. Avoiding eye contact is taken as a sign of weakness and may even convey untrustworthiness. In Western countries, subordinates show respect by meeting the eyes of their superiors. In some Asian countries, subordinates show their respect by avoiding eye contact. In some Arab countries, excessive eye contact between a man and woman is thought to be disrespectful to the woman. The eyes are the windows to the soul, but be careful which windows you look through.

̗ the Costs and Risks of Multinational Operations

̗ differences create additional costs for multinational operations. They also
̗se business risk. **Risk** exists whenever actual outcomes can differ from expectations.
̗e MNC has **exposure** to risk when its assets or liabilities can change in value with unexpected changes in business conditions. As individuals and businesses pursue cross-border
opportunities, they expose themselves to a wide variety of new risks.

̗k is the risk that
̗ness environment
̗ange unexpectedly.

An important new risk arising from cross-border operations is
country risk. **Country risk** is the risk that the business environment
in a host country will unexpectedly change. The MNC's most
important country risk exposures are to political and financial risks.

Political Risk. Political risk is the risk that the business environment in a host
country will change unexpectedly due to political events. Political risk is usually
determined within a country as political forces exert control over the business environment. Political sources of risk include unexpected changes in the operating
environment arising from repatriation restrictions, taxes, local content regulations,
restrictions on foreign ownership, business and bankruptcy laws, foreign exchange
controls, and expropriation.

Financial Risk. Financial risk refers more generally to the risk of unexpected
change in the financial or economic environment of a host country. Financial risk is
partly determined by political risk, but also by a myriad of financial and economic
factors that are outside the control of local political forces.

Currency risk is the risk of
unexpected changes in
currency values.

The MNC is exposed to **currency** (or **foreign exchange**) **risk** if
unexpected changes in currency values affect the value of the corporation's assets or liabilities. This is an important financial risk exposure for the MNC, as cash flows are paid and received in foreign currencies. Prior to 1970, the values of most currencies were fixed
against the U.S. dollar. In 1970–1971, this fixed exchange rate regime broke down,
and nearly all currencies floated against the dollar. This caused a global increase in
currency risk, as currency values fluctuated day-to-day.

The left-hand graphs in Figure 1.3 show the value of the U.S. dollar against the
Japanese yen, British pound sterling, and Swiss franc since the floating rate era began
in 1970. Sometimes the dollar moves in the same direction against all three currencies, such as during 1985. Sometimes it goes in one direction against one currency
and in another direction against the other currencies, such as in 1992 when England
chose not to adopt the euro. Changes in exchange rates are difficult to predict.

The right-hand graphs in Figure 1.3 show exchange rate volatilities measured by
absolute monthly changes in the spot rates. Exchange rate changes such as these
have a powerful effect on MNCs with cash flows in foreign currencies. If left
unhedged, foreign currency cash flows can change in value by 10 percent or more
over the course of a single month.

Volatility in currency markets can cause the value of the MNC to fluctuate in
unexpected ways. Profits on overseas transactions can quickly be wiped out by
changes in currency values. For this reason, financial risk management is essential for
both large and small firms competing in today's global marketplace.

1.4 • STRATEGIC ENTRY INTO INTERNATIONAL MARKETS

In the product life cycle, goods are often introduced in the home market and then marketed to foreign markets as the domestic market matures. This evolution proceeds at a

FIGURE 1.3

Value of the U.S. Dollar, 1970–2002

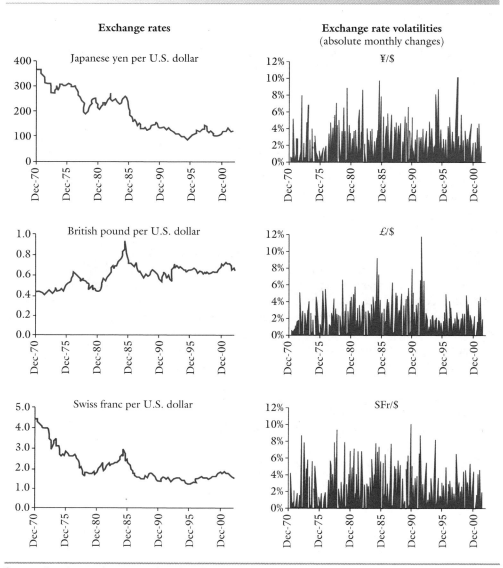

Source: Based on exchange rates from http://www.oanda.com.

different pace in different countries. New products tend to be distributed first in advanced countries and only later in less developed countries. Product evolution also proceeds at a different pace in different product markets. For example, new products are introduced more quickly in technology-intensive industries than in consumer durables because of technology's shorter product cycle.

> The form of market entry is determined by the particular markets and products.

Products that have reached maturity in their home markets may be ripe for sale elsewhere. But what is the best way to enter a foreign market? The choice of entry mode is the most important strategic decision made by the firm expanding into new markets. Once made, the choice of entry mode cannot be easily reversed.

.4 displays the risks of multinational operations as a decreasing function of
's knowledge of, or experience with, a foreign market. Unfamiliarity with a
market is the biggest obstacle to entry, so companies tend to begin their internalization process in countries that are culturally close. These markets are more
ly understood and offer more familiar operating environments than distant ones.
knowledge of foreign markets naturally increases with experience. As a MNC's knowledge of a foreign market grows, the real and perceived risks of dealing with the market
decrease. With this increasing familiarity comes an increasing ability and willingness to
take a more direct role in cross-border operations.

This section describes several modes of foreign market entry:

- Export-based
- Import-based
- Contract-based (e.g., licensing)
- Investment-based
- Through a strategic alliance or joint venture (that is, more than one of the
  above)

Table 1.1 summarizes the factors that influence the choice of foreign market entry.

An important difference among these foreign market entry modes is the resource
commitment of the parent firm. In exporting and licensing, production remains in
the home country, and few resources need be committed to international operations. In investment-based entry, production is transferred to the host country and
controlled by the parent company. This requires a substantially larger commitment in
capital, management time and effort, and other corporate resources. Required investment and ownership in a joint venture is negotiated between the partners.

FIGURE 1.4
The Risks of Foreign Operations as a Learning Curve

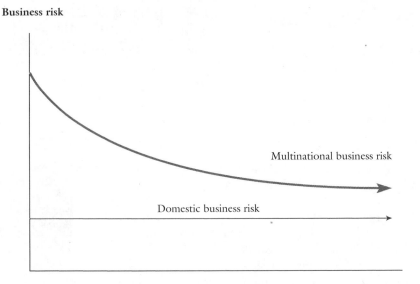

Business risk

Multinational business risk

Domestic business risk

Knowledge of the foreign country or market

TABLE 1.1

Factors Influencing the Choice of Entry Mode into Foreign Markets

	Export-based		Import-based	Contract-based	Investment-based		Strategic alliance
	Agents or distributors	Foreign sales branches or subsidiaries		Licensing or franchising	Foreign direct investment	Foreign acquisition or merger	Foreign joint venture
Resource commitment	Low	Moderate	Low	Low	High	High	Moderate
Speed of market entry	Fast	Moderate	Variable	Fast	Slow	Fast	Moderate
Sales potential	Low	High	Moderate	Moderate	High	High	High
Importance of trade barriers	High	High	High	Low	Low	Low	Low
Importance of investment restrictions	Low	Low	Low	Low	High	High	Moderate
Control of marketing and distribution channels	Low	High	High	Moderate	High	High	Moderate
Control over production	High	High	Low	Low	High	High	Moderate
Potential loss of production technology	Low	Low	Low	High	Moderate	Moderate	High
Problems in overcoming cultural distance	Low	Variable	Variable	Low	High	High	Variable
Political risk	High	High	High	Moderate	Moderate	High	Moderate
Political risk exposure	Low	Moderate	Variable	Moderate	High	High	Low

Another important difference between these foreign market entry modes is whether the parent maintains control of the production process. In exporting, the parent transfers the final good or service from the domestic to the foreign market while maintaining domestic production. In contract-based entry, the rights to the production process are usually transferred from the domestic owner to a foreign licensee for an agreed-on length of time. In investment entry, the parent preserves an ownership stake in the foreign assets but transfers control of the production process to the foreign market. In an investment-based joint venture, two or more partners share the benefits, costs, and risks of an investment by pooling their real, financial, and human assets.

Export-Based Foreign Market Entry

Exporting relies on domestic production and foreign sales. Exporters cannot count on the sympathy of the host government, so import barriers and foreign political risk can be high. On the other side of the coin, exporters do not have to worry about barriers to investment in the foreign market, and production technology is safely kept at home.

Firms that are just beginning to export their goods or services to foreign markets often make their initial sales through serendipity. Perhaps a foreign resident stumbled onto the company's product while on vacation and decided that it was just the thing she needed back home. These initial forays into international sales are more by chance than design.

The growth of worldwide package delivery services has made this form of export activity easier today than it was years ago. Some small companies never evolve beyond this passive approach to international

> Initial foreign sales usually come from direct contact between the manufacturer and buyers in the foreign market.

…ner companies, the decision not to actively pursue a foreign market is made …y after weighing the opportunities, costs, and risks of international sales.

…ie potential of a foreign market becomes apparent, producers begin to put …thought into the best way to gain entry to the market. Two effective approach- …o market entry are through (1) an agent or distributor and (2) a foreign sales …ranch or subsidiary.

Agents or Distributors. A relatively low-risk mode of export entry is to use a sales agent or distributor to handle marketing and distribution in the foreign market. Hiring a sales agent requires little commitment in time or capital on the part of the exporter. With little investment at risk, the exporter is relatively insulated from the costs and risks of foreign sales. The producer also retains control of production, ensuring that quality standards are maintained and that production technology stays at home.

A disadvantage is that the exporter cedes control of marketing and distribution channels to the sales agent. This prevents the exporter from gaining experience in the market. Also, the exporter has political risk exposure if there is a chance that the foreign government will change import quotas or tariffs in response to the exporter's entry.

For a successful partnership with the manufacturer, export agents should have

- Technical knowledge of the product
- Experience, expertise, and marketing contacts in the foreign country
- Experience and expertise in shipping, documentation, and trade credit
- Reliability and financial stability

Agents and distributors can be based in the domestic or foreign market. Exporters without international experience often are more comfortable dealing with domestic export agents. However, domestically-based agents might not be as familiar with the foreign market as a sales agent based in the foreign country. Agents already resident in the foreign market are familiar with the preferences and peculiarities of the market.

Key to the relationship between the manufacturer and the sales agent is the termination or cancellation clause in the sales contract. The termination clause is a double-edged sword. With a strong termination clause, the producer can exercise more control over the agent, terminate the contract if the contractual performance criteria are not met, or even exit the market. However, the sales agent must have some assurance of a continuing relation with the producer to fully commit to the sales arrangement. To avoid cross-border legal disputes, the contract must be legally binding in both countries and should identify the jurisdiction in which disputes are to be settled.

Foreign Sales Branches or Subsidiaries. As they become more familiar with foreign markets, exporters often take a more active role in marketing and distribution through a foreign sales branch or subsidiary. Foreign subsidiaries are incorporated in the host country, whereas foreign branches are treated as a part of the parent rather than as a separate legal entity. Because of this difference, the choice between a foreign sales branch and a foreign sales subsidiary is driven by liability and tax considerations.

This mode of entry can offer greater sales potential than a sales agent can. Establishing a sales branch or subsidiary in the foreign market allows exporters to manage the marketing and distribution channels and thereby reduce the agency costs involved in hiring a sales agent. Having a foreign branch also allows the manufacturer to be more aware of, and responsive to, changing conditions in the foreign market.

Foreign sales branches require a resource commitment.

On the other hand, establishing a foreign sales branch comes with bigger risks because of the greater resource commitment. With an increased commitment, the exporter can find itself facing more business and political risk on its foreign operations. Moreover, if the exporter is unfamiliar with the culture of the foreign market, establishing a foreign branch can lead to unexpected delays and costs as it deals with unfamiliar regulations. These costs and risks must be weighed against the higher sales potential when considering this mode of foreign market entry.

Import-Based Foreign Market Entry

Importing, the flip side of exporting, relies on foreign production and domestic sales. Importers buy goods from other countries because similar goods are costly, of poor quality, or simply unavailable in the domestic market.

For example, U.S.–based Nike Corporation is a multinational corporation that imports footwear, apparel, and sporting equipment from factories in Asia to markets around the world. The U.S. ($4.8 billion) and European ($2.6 billion) markets accounted for about 78 percent of Nike's 2001 revenues of $9.5 billion. China is a major supplier to Nike and other clothing manufacturers because of its low-cost labor. Indeed, imports from China to the United States grew from $15 billion in 1990 to more than $100 billion in 2001.

http://www. nikebiz.com

Rapid globalization and the quest for low-cost production have fostered poor working conditions in many developing countries, and importers such as Nike are frequently criticized for their overseas labor practices. The International Labor Organization, based in Switzerland, estimates that roughly 25 percent of children age 5 to 14 (250 million in total) are engaged in part-time or full-time work. Many of these children work in conditions that would not be tolerated in developed countries. This is a difficult social issue, as firing the children merely sends them out into the streets and even more difficult circumstances. In response to activist protests and media exposés, many MNCs have developed factory-monitoring programs to ensure compliance with international labor standards. Nike employs more than 50 people in its contractor compliance program.

Contract-Based Foreign Market Entry

In an international **license agreement**, a domestic company (the licensor) contracts with a foreign company (the licensee) to market the licensor's products in a foreign country in return for royalties, fees, or other compensation. The foreign licensee assumes the responsibility of producing, marketing, and distributing goods or services in the foreign market. To protect the licensor's reputation in both domestic and foreign markets, the licensing agreement is designed to ensure that a standardized product or service is delivered to the foreign market.

Licensing has several advantages for the multinational corporation. It provides rapid and relatively painless entry into foreign markets without a large resource commitment. Licensed products and services are produced in the host country, so import quotas or tariffs are not a hindrance and political risk is relatively low.

Although the resource commitment of the licensor is small, returns can be limited as well. Host governments sometimes impose a limit (such as 5 percent of revenues) on the amount of royalties that can be repatriated to the parent through an international license.

International licensing agreements come in many varieties. For example, an international **franchise agreement** is an agreement in which a domestic company licenses its trade name or business system to an independent company in a foreign market. Franchising is most often found in consumer service industries, such as fast-food restaurants (McDonald's), hotels (Hilton), and car rentals (Avis).

Licensing provides quick and relatively low-risk entry.

17

er variation on the licensing theme is a **reciprocal marketing agreement**, wo companies form a strategic alliance to co-market each other's products 1ome markets. Production rights may or may not be transferred. This form of entry is common in the pharmaceutical industry, where companies such as ck and DuPont have successful products in complementary market segments.

Management contracts are a form of licensing agreement in which a company licenses its organizational or management expertise to another company. Experienced employees of the parent firm usually are sent in to organize operations and manage the marketing, production, or distribution processes. For example, the EuroDisney theme park outside Paris is operated by Disney through a management contract.

Investment-Based Foreign Market Entry

Manufacturing firms typically use exports for their initial entry into international markets. Exporting is a low-risk way to acquire information about foreign markets. Unless the MNC already has experience exporting to a particular market, investment-based entry should come later in the product life cycle, usually when the product is in the mature stage in the domestic market. That is when the manufacturer begins to look for ways to extend the product life by penetrating new markets or reducing operating costs.

Investment-based entry into foreign markets can be accomplished in one of two ways:

- Foreign direct investment
- Mergers and acquisitions

The relative popularity of each entry mode is displayed in Figure 1.5, based on a sample of U.S. firms entering Europe. Cross-border mergers and acquisitions are by far the most popular methods of obtaining control over assets in another country.

Investment-based foreign market entry differs from exporting in that production is shifted to the foreign country, but ownership and control are retained by the parent corporation. Because this requires a large resource commitment, great care must

FIGURE 1.5
Market Entry Methods Chosen by U.S. Companies in Europe

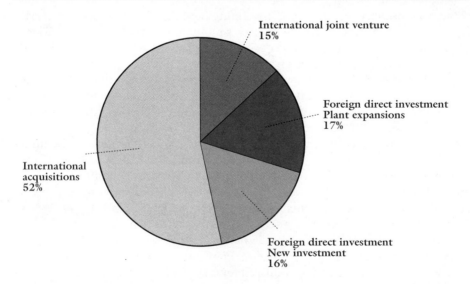

International joint venture
15%

Foreign direct investment
Plant expansions
17%

International acquisitions
52%

Foreign direct investment
New investment
16%

Source: Ernst and Young.

be taken before using one of these entry modes. The manufacturer must be far enough down the learning curve of Figure 1.4 to ensure that it can avoid the more obvious international marketing, production, and distribution blunders.

Foreign Direct Investment. Building productive capacity directly in a foreign country is called **foreign direct investment (FDI)**. An advantage of foreign market entry through FDI relative to export- or contract-based entry is that it provides a more permanent foothold in the foreign market.

Although foreign direct investment is evaluated in much the same way as domestic investment, it is exposed to additional currency, political, and cultural risks that may or may not be offset by higher revenues or lower costs. Because they entail substantial investments in capital and time, these investment proposals should be analyzed with great care. The consequences of failure for the stakeholders (especially managers) are high.

> FDI requires a large resource commitment.

Cross-Border Mergers and Acquisitions. In foreign direct investment, the parent company builds productive capacity in a foreign country. In a **cross-border acquisition**, a domestic parent acquires the use of an asset in a foreign country. A company can acquire productive capacity in a foreign country in one of two ways:

- Cross-border acquisition of assets
- Cross-border acquisition of stock

A cross-border **acquisition of assets** is the most straightforward way to acquire productive capacity, because only the asset is acquired. None of the liabilities supporting that asset are transferred to the purchaser. A major consideration in an asset acquisition is the purchase price. Buying an existing manufacturing plant in a foreign country is often less expensive than building a similar plant through foreign direct investment.

In a cross-border **acquisition of stock**, a MNC buys an equity interest in a foreign company. This is easiest to accomplish for publicly traded companies in countries with active equity markets. The purchaser can make either a friendly offer to management or a (possibly hostile) offer directly to stockholders through the financial markets.

In a cross-border **merger**, two firms pool their assets and liabilities to form a new company. Stockholders trade their shares in the original companies for shares in the new company according to a negotiated exchange ratio. For example, DaimlerChrysler was formed in a 1998 merger of Daimler-Benz (Germany) and Chrysler Corporation (United States).

Cross-border mergers can be difficult to consummate. Not only must a large proportion of stockholders in each company approve the merger (the proportion varies by company and country), but the merger must also be approved by governments in each country. Mergers often have antitrust implications, and government agencies in different countries can have widely divergent views on what is in the public interest.

Foreign Market Entry Through a Strategic Alliance

Although these entry modes have been presented as discrete, nonoverlapping categories, many international alliances have elements of more than one entry mode. The term **strategic alliance** refers to any collaborative agreement that is designed to achieve some strategic goal. In industries with heavy research and development requirements, strategic alliances can reduce the costs and risks of product development.

> Strategic alliances are collaborative agreements designed to achieve some strategic goal.

Strategic alliances are also used to penetrate foreign markets in which the domestic company has little expertise or experience. Firms that master the intricacies of partnering can

Market Update

Creating and Maintaining Competitive Advantage at Merck

...erck, & Co., Inc., is one of the world's largest producers and distributors of prescription pharmaceuticals, with annual sales of more than $10 billion. Although new prescription drugs require heavy investment in research and development (R&D), successful products can yield enormous returns on investment. Patent protection lasts 20 years in the United States, but about one-third of this time is needed to get FDA (Food and Drug Administration) approval. After a patent expires, other companies can market generic versions of the same drug.

Merck has used each of the investment-based entry modes as it builds its prescription drug portfolio and has been especially creative in forming international strategic alliances with its domestic and international competitors. Here is a chronology of Merck's most important strategic actions.

1970s   Merck *invests* heavily in R&D, spending 50 percent more on every dollar of sales than competitors in the prescription pharmaceutical industry. By 1990, this produced nearly 20 products with annual sales exceeding $100 million.

1983   Merck *acquires* a majority stake in Banyu Pharmaceuticals, the first foreign acquisition of a large Japanese company.

1986   Merck forms a *strategic alliance* with ICI Americas to co-market drugs for hypertension and diabetes.

1989   Merck forms a *joint venture* with Johnson & Johnson to market the dietary supplement Mylanta. Then, it forms a strategic alliance with ICI Americas to co-market Mylanta and ICI's antidepressant Elavil.

1991   Merck forms a *joint venture* with DuPont (Merck DuPont Pharmaceuticals Company) to develop DuPont's $700 million pharmaceuticals business.

1993   Merck *acquires* Medco Containment Services for $6.6 billion in cash. The new company—Merck-Medco Managed Care—vertically integrates Merck's R&D and production expertise with Medco's $2 billion distribution business. This initiates a wave of similar mergers in the pharmaceuticals industry.

reap the benefits of access to new products and technologies without having to develop their entire product line from scratch.

Strategic alliances have been elevated to perhaps their highest form in the Japanese *keiretsu* system. Non-Japanese firms trying to enter the Japanese market have discovered that a *keiretsu* can be awfully hard to penetrate. For example, by 1990 more than a thousand Japanese parts suppliers were operating in the United States, but only one U.S. parts supplier was operating in Japan. Japanese business practices are coming under increased criticism for their tendency to exclude foreign companies from Japanese markets and to create barriers to foreign investment in Japan.

In a joint venture, commitments and payoffs should be clearly defined.

A **joint venture** is an investment-based strategic alliance in which two or more companies pool their resources to execute a well-defined mission. A new company is usually created to accomplish the mission. Resource commitments, responsibilities, and earnings

Market Update (continued)

1994 Merck forms a *joint venture*—Astra Merck—with Sweden's Astra AB Inc. to develop and market prescription drugs that arise from Astra AB's research.

1995 Merck *divests* its Kelco specialty chemicals group to Monsanto for $1 billion as it refocuses on its core business in prescription pharmaceuticals.

1999 Merck *acquires* the portion of VWR Scientific Products (a laboratory products distributor) that it does not already own for $625 million.

2000 Merck forms a *joint venture* with Schering-Plough to develop therapies for cholesterol (Zocor-Ezetimibe) and allergy (Singulair-Claritin) management.

2001 Merck *acquires* Rosette Inpharmatics, a manufacturer of bioinformatics equipment that analyzes genetic information, for $615 million in stock.

2002 Merck *licenses* the U.S. rights to hypertension drugs Vasotec and Vaseretic to Biovail Corp for $250 million.

Through this network of investments and alliances and the fruits of its R&D efforts, Merck enjoyed annual earnings growth higher than 25 percent and profit on sales of more than 20 percent during the 1980s. This string of successes earned Merck the highest score in *Fortune* magazine's Corporate Reputations Survey for four consecutive years, from 1986 through 1989. Double-digit earnings growth continued throughout the 1990s.

In sports, you're only as good as your last game. Similarly, businesses cannot rest on past accomplishments. Patents on several of Merck's best-selling drugs expired in 1999–2002. Patent protection is a powerful force in the pharmaceutical industry. Industry giants Glaxo-Wellcome, AstraZeneca, and Pharmacia-Upjohn were formed when one or both partners faced expiring patents on key products. As of mid-2002, Merck is continuing to invest in R&D and participating in selective license agreements, acquisitions, joint ventures, and strategic alliances. Time will tell if Merck can continue its success.

are shared according to a contractual formula. Joint ventures are useful when companies in a single industry or in complementary industries want to share the risk of a large venture, such as development of a new product or market.

In a joint venture, the incentive to act opportunistically and violate the terms of the agreement is great once the foreign partner has acquired the production technology. Armed with the ability to produce the goods itself, the partner can become a competitor in other international markets and even in the parent's domestic market. Because of this threat, the multinational corporation using a joint venture must find the right partner and then structure the deal to their (mutual) advantage. When embarking on an international joint venture, companies in industries such as pharmaceuticals, electronics, and biotechnology must maintain control of their patents, trademarks, and production technologies. When the risk of technology loss is high, another mode of market entry might be preferred.

1.5 • THE GOALS OF THE MULTINATIONAL CORPORATION

Figure 1.6 presents the ownership and control structure that is typical of companies in market economies. In countries such as the United States, the primary goal of the firm is to maximize shareholder wealth. But shareholder wealth maximization is far from the only objective desired by those with a stake in the firm. The objectives of suppliers, customers, debtholders, managers, and employees are often in conflict with shareholder wealth maximization, especially during periods of financial distress. **Agency costs** are the costs of contracting and monitoring between the various stakeholders to reduce potential conflicts of interest. The presence of agency costs does not mean that management will not act in the best interests of shareholders, only that it is costly to encourage managers to do so. It is shareholders who ultimately bear these agency costs.

> Equity bears the agency costs of hiring managers to run the firm.

Viewing the firm as a pie is useful in a discussion of how one stakeholder's actions can affect the value of other stakeholders. Figure 1.7 represents the various claimants on the value of the corporation's expected future revenues. In this view, the value of revenues can be allocated to the values of operating expenses (labor and materials), the government (taxes), the suppliers of capital (debt and equity), and other claimants (e.g., potential litigants). **Stakeholders** are often narrowly defined as the owners of the firm's debt and equity securities. These marketed claims are paid out of operating income and are represented by V_{Debt} and V_{Equity} in Figure 1.7. Debtholders put their claims in writing through restrictive covenants in the bond indenture. As the residual owner, the value of equity's claim depends on the laws and legal conventions of the nations within which the multinational corporation operates.

Many other groups of individuals have a stake in the company, most but not all of whom have explicit claims on revenues. The objectives of these stakeholders are not identical with those of shareholders. For example, labor is more concerned with wages and job security than with shareholder wealth. The objective of "maximize shareholder

FIGURE 1.6
Corporate Governance

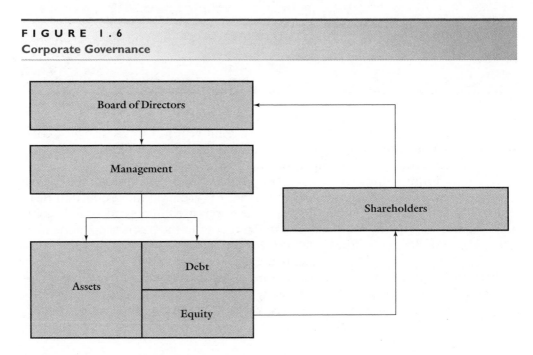

FIGURE 1.7

The Firm's Stakeholders and Their Claims on the Revenues of the Firm

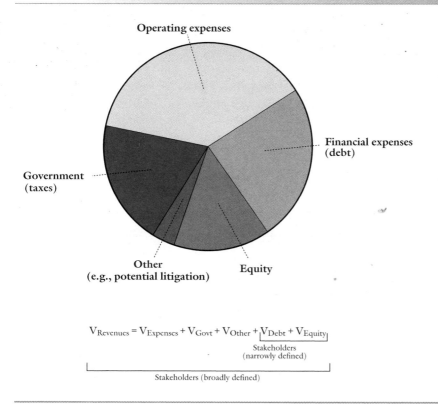

$$V_{Revenues} = V_{Expenses} + V_{Govt} + V_{Other} + \underbrace{V_{Debt} + V_{Equity}}_{\substack{\text{Stakeholders} \\ \text{(narrowly defined)}}}$$

Stakeholders (broadly defined)

wealth" can be in conflict with host countries' cultural, economic, political, social, ecological, or religious goals. By adopting a broad definition, stakeholders are taken to include the firm's customers, suppliers, and employees, represented by $V_{Expenses}$. Another set of stakeholders is the governments that have an explicit interest in the taxes paid by the firm (represented by V_{Govt}) and an implicit interest in all activities of the firm that influence the societies in which the firm operates (represented by V_{Other}). Although not all of these activities appear in the income statement, some of them can and do affect other stakeholders. For example, if the firm violates the laws of one or more of the countries in which it operates, it may be liable for civil or criminal penalties or both. Union Carbide's disaster at their plant in Bhopal, India (see the next Market Update), resulted in huge claims that adversely affected all stakeholders.

> MNCs have many stakeholders, each with their own objectives.

Countries differ in the extent to which they protect each of these stakeholders. Socialist countries place an emphasis on employee welfare. Some industrialized countries place a great emphasis on environmental concerns; others take a laissez-faire or hands-off attitude, allowing their industries to compete unfettered in the world marketplace. Most countries protect or subsidize key industries or selected sectors of their economies. These industries are deemed to be of vital importance to the nation's economy or national identity. Protected industries often include products related to agriculture, such as rice in Japan, beer in Germany, and wine in France. In the United States, various agricultural products that are vulnerable to foreign competition are protected through price supports and other subsidies.

Market Update

Union Carbide's Bhopal Disaster

Union Carbide Corporation is a diversified U.S. company with worldwide operations in a variety of industry segments. Union Carbide's 51%-owned subsidiary, Union Carbide India Limited, operated a chemical plant in Bhopal, India. In 1984, poisonous gases were inadvertently released from the plant, causing the death of more than 2,000 people and injuries to nearly a quarter of a million people. This disaster resulted in losses for nearly all of Union Carbide's major stakeholders (broadly defined). Debt and equity lost value in anticipation of a class action suit that was eventually held in Indian (rather than U.S.) courts. The careers and self-esteem of managers and employees involved in the Bhopal operation suffered directly. The biggest loss was suffered by the government (Union Carbide's equity partner in the deal) and people of India.

It is up to sovereign nations to determine the nature of the playing field on which companies operate within their borders. Chief executive and chief financial officers and their representatives must work within the rules and respect the sensitivities of the societies in which they operate.[4] Businesses ignoring the local rules of the game do so at their own peril.

1.6 • THE SECRET OF CORPORATE STRATEGY

At the root of the MNC's value are its core competencies. *Core competencies* are the things that the corporation does well. To sustain the growth and value of the company, the MNC must be able to leverage its core competencies into new products and technologies. Core competencies derive not from individual products or technologies, but from the people and processes that manage them. Investment in core competencies is a key strategic decision of the firm.

Management gurus Gary Hamel and C. K. Prahalad identify two different approaches to corporate strategy.[5] The first approach follows conventional wisdom.

"The secret of life is to be happy with what you have."

This approach focuses on maintaining strategic fit by trimming ambitions to match available resources, identifying unsatisfied market niches, allocating resources to profitable products, and ensuring conformity with industry practices.

The second approach extends this wisdom.

"The secret of life is to be happy with what you have, so make sure that you get enough!"

---

4 On this topic, Mark Twain wrote: "Always do right. This will gratify some people, and astonish the rest."

5 Hamel and Prahalad, "Strategic Intent," *Harvard Business Review* (1989).

The emphasis here is on investing in core competencies, not just profitable product lines, to ensure the continued growth and success of the corporation. Rather than just squeezing the most out of current products, cross-functional organizational learning is used to create new core competencies, new competitive advantages, and, eventually, new products. By going outside the lines of the current blueprint for success, the MNC can fully leverage its human and capital resources to create and achieve new goals.

1.7 • SUMMARY

An understanding of multinational financial management is crucial to success in today's, and inevitably in tomorrow's, marketplace. This is unquestionably true for firms competing directly with foreign firms, such as a domestic auto industry in competition with international automakers. It is also true for domestic firms whose suppliers, customers, and competitors are increasingly likely to be from foreign countries. In today's business environment, the success of firms in service and manufacturing industries depends on their ability to recognize and exploit imperfections in national markets for both products and factors of production and work effectively within the political and economic constraints imposed by foreign governments.

This book develops a framework for evaluating the risks and opportunities presented by the world's marketplaces. Although we usually take the perspective of the financial manager of a large multinational corporation, this framework works just as well for individuals, small businesses, or government entities. Along the way, we provide a tour of business environments in many countries around the world. Bon voyage.

KEY TERMS

acquisition of assets or stock	informational efficiency
agency costs	investment opportunity set
allocational efficiency	joint venture
behavioral finance	license agreement
corporate governance	management contracts
country risk	merger
currency (foreign exchange) risk	multinational corporation (MNC)
discounted cash flow	operational efficiency
economies of scale	perfect financial market assumptions
economies of vertical integration	political risk
exporting	reciprocal marketing agreement
financial risk	risk versus risk exposure
foreign direct investment (FDI)	stakeholders
franchise agreement	strategic alliance
importing	

CONCEPTUAL QUESTIONS

1.1   Describe the ways in which multinational financial management is different from domestic financial management.

1.2   What is country risk? Describe several types of country risk one might face when conducting business in another country.

1.3   What is foreign exchange risk?

1.4   What is political risk?

1.5   How can MNCs reduce operating expenses relative to domestic firms?

1.6   What are the perfect financial market assumptions and their implications for multinational financial management?

1.7   In what ways do cultural differences affect the conduct of international business?

1.8   Describe four broad modes of entry into international markets. Which of these modes requires the most resource commitment on the part of the MNC? Which has the greatest risks? Which offers the greatest growth potential?

1.9   What are the relative advantages and disadvantages of foreign direct investment, acquisitions/mergers, and joint ventures?

1.10   What is the goal of financial management? How might this goal be different in different countries? How might the goal of financial management be different for the multinational corporation than for the domestic corporation?

1.11   List the MNC's key stakeholders. How does each have a stake in the MNC?

PROBLEMS

1.1   You work in the Corporate Strategy Division of Motorola Corporation. Motorola manufactures mobile communications devices (cellular telephones, pagers, and support equipment) and semiconductors. Your division is considering entry modes into the fast-growing markets of Southeast Asia. Design an entry strategy into Southeast Asia that will eventually lead to direct investment in the region. (One way of answering this question is to examine what Motorola has actually done in the past. Use the Internet to investigate published reports of Motorola's international expansion strategy.)

SUGGESTED READINGS

The perfect financial market assumptions were introduced in

Franco Modigliani and Merton Miller, "The Cost of Capital, Corporation Finance, and the Theory of Investment," *American Economic Review* 48 (June 1958), pp. 261–297.

An interesting article on corporate strategy is

Gary Hamel and C. K. Prahalad, "Strategic Intent," *Harvard Business Review* 67, No. 3 (1989), pp. 63–76.

he World's Largest Corporations

ank	Company	Country	Industry	Sales ($m)	Assets ($m)	Income ($m)	Employees
1	General Motors Corp	USA	Automotive	173,215	274,730	388	6,002
2	Wal-Mart Stores	USA	Variety stores	165,013	70,349	1,140	5,377
3	Ford Motor Co	USA	Automotive	162,558	276,229	365	7,237
4	ExxonMobil Corp	USA	Petroleum refining	160,883	144,521	—	7,910
5	DaimlerChrysler AG	Germany	Automotive	151,035	175,889	467	5,785
6	Mitsui & Co LTD	Japan	Durable goods	128,162	62,097	11	346
7	Toyota Motor Corp	Japan	Automotive	119,656	154,884	215	4,540
8	General Electric Co	USA	Conglomerates	110,832	405,200	340	10,717
9	Royal Dutch/Shell Group	Netherlands	Petroleum refining	105,366	113,883	96	8,584
10	Nippon Tel & Tel	Japan	Telecom	97,956	180,201	224	2,821
	Int'l Business Machines	USA	Computers	87,548	87,495	307	7,712
	British Petroleum PLC	UK	Petroleum refining	83,566	89,561	80	5,008
	AXA	France	Insurance	82,742	511,032	92	2,035
	Citigroup Inc	USA	Financial services	82,005	716,937	115	9,867
	Hitachi LTD	Japan	Computers	75,483	92,804	338	160
	Siemens AG (ADR)	Germany	Conglomerates	72,996	65,453	443	1,719
	Allianz AG	Germany	Insurance	70,028	385,486	114	2,249
	Matsushita Electric	Japan	Electronics	68,862	72,518	290	941
	Royal Dutch Petroleum	Netherlands	Petroleum refining	63,220	68,330	58	5,150
	Sony Corp	Japan	Electronics	63,082	64,219	190	1,149
	United States Postal Service	USA	Trucking & courier	62,726	55,693	906	363
	AT&T Corp	USA	Telecom	62,391	169,406	148	3,428
	Philip Morris Cos Inc	USA	Cigarettes	61,751	61,381	137	7,675
	Boeing Co	USA	Aircraft	57,993	36,147	197	2,309
	Honda Motor LTD	Japan	Automotive	57,455	46,146	112	2,472
	Nissan Motor Co LTS	Japan	Automotive	56,388	61,709	142	(6,456)
	General Electric Cap Servs	USA	Financial services	55,749	345,018	130	4,443
	Toshiba Corp	Japan	Computers	54,239	53,794	191	(264)
	TIAA-CREF	USA	Insurance	52,566	289,248	—	911
	JP Morgan Chase & Co	USA	Commercial banks	51,852	667,003	—	7,501
	Prudential PLC	UK	Insurance	51,745	243,288	23	875
	Bank of America Corp	USA	Commercial banks	51,526	632,574	156	7,882
	Fiat SPA	Italy	Automotive	50,593	80,430	221	355
	Fujitsu LTD	Japan	Computers	49,576	48,440	188	403
	SBC Communications Inc	USA	Telecom	49,489	83,215	205	8,159
	E.ON AG	Germany	Transportation	48,729	52,134	132	2,656
	NEC Corp	Japan	Computers	48,461	44,747	155	101
	Deutsche Bank AG	Germany	Commercial bank	47,089	845,744	93	2,589
	Nestle SA	Switzerland	Foods	46,745	36,902	231	2,958
	Kroger Co	USA	Grocery stores	45,352	17,966	305	628
	Vivendi Universal SA	France	Conglomerates	43,879	83,356	276	1,441
	ING Groep NV	Netherlands	Insurance	43,826	471,821	86	4,712
	Unilever Combined	UK	Foods	43,595	27,998	255	2,947
	Citicorp	USA	Commercial banks	42,848	388,570	115	5,195
	Total Fina Elf SA	France	Petroleum refining	42,473	81,549	74	1,531
	Hewlett-Packard Co	USA	Computers	42,370	35,297	84	3,491
	Shell Tran & Trade	UK	Petroleum refining	42,146	45,553	41	3,434
	Sears Roebuck & Co	USA	Department stores	41,071	36,954	326	1,453
	American International Grp	USA	Insurance	40,656	268,238	55	5,055
	Enron Corp	USA	Petroleum wholesale	40,112	33,381	18	893

rce: Based on data from Standard & Poor's Compustat database.

27

World Trade and the International Monetary System

chapter 2

Overview

"History is almost always written by the victors."

Jawaharlal Nehru

This chapter begins with a discussion of world trade and the reduction of trade barriers in the world's goods, services, and financial markets. This is followed by a description of the balance-of-payments accounting system used to measure cross-border trade flows. The rest of the chapter is devoted to the international monetary system, the global network of governmental and commercial institutions within which exchange rates are determined. The international monetary system is influenced by national laws, policies, regulations, practices, and government intervention, and by supranational organizations, including the World Bank and the International Monetary Fund.

2.1 • INTEGRATION OF THE WORLD'S MARKETS

The world's markets for goods, services, and financial assets and liabilities have become increasingly integrated across national boundaries during the last several decades. International markets are **integrated** when assets sell for the same price in every country. In **segmented** markets, asset prices are not necessarily equal across markets. Factors that contribute to market segmentation include transactions costs, regulatory and institutional interference, informational barriers, and the immobility of labor. As barriers to trade progressively fall, foreign markets are playing an increasingly important role in the viability of domestic industries.

> Markets are increasingly integrated across national borders.

29

Cross-Border Integration of the Markets for Goods and Services

The pessimistic tone of daily news reports about efforts to integrate world trade highlights the substantial barriers to, and our halting progress toward, a truly global economy. Yet viewed through the long lens of history, trade barriers today are lower than ever. In the goods markets, the world's businesses are turning to foreign sales, foreign sourcing, foreign direct investment, and cross-border partnerships as paths toward expansion and consolidation. The markets for services have also seen an explosion of cross-border trade in telecommunications, information technology, and financial services.

The fall of barriers to international trade has been hastened by many trends and events, including

- Creation of the **World Trade Organization (WTO),** a global trade association, and the rise of regional economic linkages and trade pacts
- The emergence of China as a major trading partner, and China's entry into the WTO
- The global trend toward free-market economies
- The rapid industrialization of the Far East and Pacific Rim
- The emergence of a diverse set of central and eastern European economies
- Reunification of East and West Germany
- Hong Kong's 1997 return from British to Chinese control
- Adoption of the euro by Austria, Belgium, Finland, France, Germany, Greece, Ireland, Italy, Luxembourg, the Netherlands, Portugal, and Spain

Figure 2.1 lists the world's major trade pacts. There are ongoing discussions aimed at extending these pacts. The **European Union (EU)** has agreed to add countries from Central and Eastern Europe to its current members, which include Austria, Belgium, Denmark, Finland, France, Germany, Greece, Ireland, Italy, Luxembourg, the Netherlands, Portugal, Spain, Sweden, and the United Kingdom. Debate in North America is centered on extension of the **North American Free Trade Agreement (NAFTA)** among Canada, Mexico, and the United States to Latin America. There are active bilateral and regional trade talks in South America and Southeast Asia. A "Millenium Round" of WTO trade talks in Geneva, Switzerland, in 1999 included representatives from 160 countries. These types of multilateral trade agreements are gradually reducing the barriers to cross-border trade.

Foreign trade is a mainstay of industrialized economies, such as Japan and the United States, as they struggle for market share in a competitive global marketplace. Foreign trade is equally important to **less developed countries (LDCs)** as they strive to promote their industrial bases and increase the living standards of their citizens. The countries that have been most successful in nurturing their local manufacturing industries—such as Argentina, Brazil, Mexico, Singapore, South Korea, and Taiwan—are sometimes called **newly industrializing countries (NICs)** or **newly industrializing economies (NIEs).**

Newly industrializing countries undergo a "life cycle" of industrial growth. In their infancy, NIC growth is based on low labor costs. As these countries industrialize and labor costs increase, the labor-intensive industries that achieved early gains can lose their cost advantage. Industries such as clothing and footwear begin to migrate toward countries with even lower labor costs, and the NICs find themselves competing in the same products and markets as industrialized economies. This transition from a low-tech, labor-driven economy into a globally competitive, capital-intensive, high-technology economy is very difficult. These countries face vexing social and public policy issues as the work-

FIGURE 2.1
The World's Major Economic Cooperation and Free Trade Agreements

WTO—World Trade Organization	121 nations signed the Uruguay Round of the General Agreement on Tariffs and Trade (GATT) on April 15, 1994. GATT slashed tariffs globally by roughly 40%, established intellectual property protection, and created a dispute resolution process. The WTO oversees the trade agreement. The WTO had 145 members in February 2003, including China.
NAFTA—North American Free Trade Agreement	The United States, Canada, and Mexico.
EU—European Union	Austria, Belgium, Denmark, Finland, France, Germany, Greece, Ireland, Italy, Luxembourg, Netherlands, Portugal, Spain, Sweden, and the United Kingdom.
ASEAN—Association of South-East Asian Nations	Brunei, Cambodia, Indonesia, Laos, Malaysia, Myanmar, Philippines, Singapore, Thailand, and Vietnam.
APEC—Asia-Pacific Economic Cooperation	21 members including Australia, Canada, China, Japan, Korea, Russia, and the United States. APEC promotes open trade and economic cooperation in the region.
Mercosur—the "common market of the South"	Argentina, Brazil, Paraguay, and Uruguay. Bolivia and Chile are associate members.
Andean Community	Bolivia, Colombia, Ecuador, Peru, and Venezuela. In 1998, the Andean Community and Mercosur signed an agreement for the creation of a Free Trade Area. These countries are working with the UN Conference on Trade and Development (UNCTAD) to establish a Latin American common market.
OPEC—Organization of Petroleum Exporting Countries	Algeria, Indonesia, Iran, Iraq, Kuwait, Libya, Nigeria, Qatar, Saudi Arabia, United Arab Emirates, and Venezuela.
CIS—Commonwealth of Independent States	Armenia, Azerbaijan, Belarus, Georgia, Kazakhstan, Kyrgyz Republic, Republic of Moldova, Russian Federation, Tajikistan, Turkmenistan, Ukraine, and Uzbekistan.

force lays claim to the country's new-found wealth. Others suffer setbacks as governments attempt to match rising expectations with fiscal and monetary constraints.[1]

Cross-border trade is becoming increasingly important to the world economy. Figure 2.2 shows the growth in the United States' imports and exports of merchandise trade over 1972–2002. Many other countries have experienced similar growth in cross-border trade. Many newly industrializing countries have experienced even more rapid growth.

Globalization in the markets for goods and services has an enormous influence on individuals and societies, including

- An increase in cross-border investment in real assets (land, natural resource projects, and manufacturing facilities)

- An increasing interdependence among national economies leading to global business cycles that are shared by all nations

---

1 As Winston Churchill observed: "The problems of victory are more agreeable than the problems of defeat, but they are no less difficult."

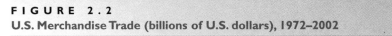

FIGURE 2.2
U.S. Merchandise Trade (billions of U.S. dollars), 1972–2002

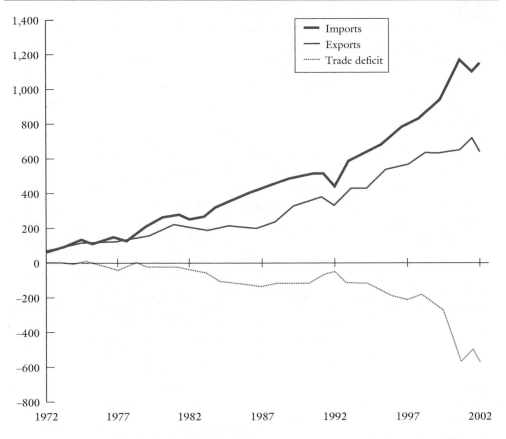

Source: U.S. Bureau of Economic Analysis (www.bea.gov).

- Changing political risk as nations redefine their borders and their national identities

These changes create many challenges for businesses. They also create opportunities to add value through cross-border operations.

Cross-Border Integration of the World's Financial Markets

Integration is proceeding at an even faster pace in the world's financial markets as advances in electronic communication and data processing reduce physical and institutional barriers to the flow of capital. Developments in information technology and telecommunications have been especially important in hastening the integration of international capital markets. Currency trading, in particular, has recently undergone explosive growth. Some of this growth is a consequence of the growth in import and export trade. But a considerable portion is due to the introduction of new financial markets and instruments that facilitate trade.

Integration is facilitated by advances in information technology.

Along with the reduction of barriers in the world's goods markets, the demise of capital flow barriers in international financial markets has had several consequences:

- An increase in cross-border financing as MNCs raise capital in whichever market and in whatever currency offers the most attractive rates

- Increasingly interdependent national financial markets
- An increasing number of cross-border partnerships, including many international mergers, acquisitions, and joint ventures
- An increasing number of cooperative linkages among securities exchanges

A striking example of the interdependence of the world's financial markets is the worldwide stock market crash that occurred on October 19, 1987. Beginning in Asian markets late in the afternoon of October 19, the crash followed the sun across Europe, the United States, and finally back to Asia, as each of these markets opened for trade. Nearly all of the world's major stock markets fell at least 20 percent in both local currency and in U.S. dollars during October 1987.[2] This historic event provided a powerful reminder that today, more than ever, we all live on the same small planet.

2.2 • BALANCE-OF-PAYMENTS STATISTICS

In July 1944, representatives of the allied nations convened at Bretton Woods, New Hampshire, to create a postwar financial system that would promote world trade and avoid a repetition of the worldwide depression of the 1930s. The **Bretton Woods Conference** created the International Bank for Reconstruction and Development, now known as the **World Bank**, to help in the reconstruction and development of its member nations. The World Bank Group has continued to evolve since its establishment at Bretton Woods and currently includes the following agencies:

http://www.bea.doc.gov

- *International Bank for Reconstruction and Development (IBRD)*—promoting development in poor-but-creditworthy countries through loans, guarantees, and advisory services
- *International Development Association (IDA)*—providing zero-interest loans or credits to the poorest countries
- *International Finance Corporation (IFC)*—promoting private sector investment in developing countries
- *Multilateral Investment Guarantee Agency (MIGA)*—promoting investment in developing countries by offering political risk insurance to investors and lenders
- *International Centre for Settlement of Investment Disputes (ICSID)*—facilitating the settlement of investment disputes between governments and foreign investors

Bretton Woods also created the **International Monetary Fund (IMF)** to provide assistance to countries trying to defend their currencies against temporary trade or supply/demand imbalances. The IMF is a huge supranational organization with 2002 funding of $275 billion. The IMF compiles statistics on each country's cross-border transactions and publishes a monthly summary of **balance-of-payments (BoP) statistics**. These statistics track each country's cross-border flow of goods, services, and capital. Table 2.1 presents balance-of-payments accounts for the United States on an annual basis since 1991. Balance-of-payments statistics show a country's inflows (+) and outflows (−) of goods, services, and capital. The accounts of most interest are (1) the trade balance, (2) the current account, and (3) the financial account.

> BoP statistics track cross-border trade in goods, services, and capital.

The **trade balance** measures whether a particular country is a net importer or exporter of goods. Exports are a positive number while imports are negative, so a *trade surplus* (a trade balance greater than zero) indicates that residents are exporting

---

2 See Roll, "The International Crash of October 1987," *Financial Analysts Journal* (1988).

TABLE 2.1

U.S. Balance of Payments (billions of U.S. dollars), 1991–2002

	1991	1992	1993	1994	1995	1996	1997	1998	1999	2000	2001	2002
Goods: Exports f.o.b.[1]	414	440	457	503	575	612	678	670	684	772	719	683
Goods: Imports f.o.b.	−491	−537	−589	−669	−749	−803	−876	−917	−1030	−1224	−1146	−1167
Trade Balance	**−77**	**−97**	**−132**	**−166**	**−174**	**−191**	**−198**	**−247**	**−346**	**−452**	**−427**	**−484**
Services: Credit	164	177	186	201	219	240	257	262	273	292	279	289
Services: Debit	−118	−116	−122	−132	−141	−151	−166	−183	−189	−219	−210	−240
Bal on Goods and Services	−31	−36	−69	−97	−96	−102	−108	−167	−262	−379	−358	−436
Income: Credit	149	132	134	165	212	226	261	259	291	353	284	245
Income: Debit	−125	−109	−110	−149	−187	−202	−240	−252	−272	−331	−269	−257
Bal on Goods, Serv and Inc	−7	−14	−45	−80	−72	−78	−88	−159	−244	−357	−344	−447
Current Transfers: Net	11	−35	−38	−38	−34	−40	−41	−45	−49	−53	−49	−56
Current Account	**4**	**−49**	**−83**	**−118**	**−106**	**−118**	**−128**	**−204**	**−293**	**−410**	**−393**	**−503**
Capital Account: Net	−4	1	0	0	0	1	0	1	−3	1	1	1
Direct Investment Abroad	−38	−48	−84	−80	−99	−92	−105	−143	−189	−178	−128	−124
Direct Invest from Abroad	23	20	51	46	58	87	106	179	289	308	131	30
Portfolio Investment Assets	−35	−50	−145	−97	−168	−236	−241	−174	−224	−278	−109	−26
Portfolio Invest Liabilities	51	81	115	93	228	304	408	208	333	552	482	388
Other Investment Assets	8	23	29	1	−86	−86	−142	−43	−65	−150	−134	−6
Other Investment Liabilities	37	70	116	167	152	161	193	36	120	156	140	213
Financial Account	**46**	**96**	**81**	**130**	**86**	**137**	**219**	**64**	**265**	**409**	**382**	**474**
Net Errors and Omissions	−46	−48	1	−11	19	−20	−91	139	31	0	11	29

[1] The term *f.o.b.* stands for "free-on-board" and indicates that the values of import and export goods are measured at the border of the exporting country.

Source: U.S. Bureau of Economic Analysis (http://www.bea.gov). Details may not add due to rounding.

more than they are importing. A *trade deficit* (a trade balance less than zero) means that residents are importing more goods than they are exporting. The trade balance is important to fiscal and monetary authorities because higher exports mean higher employment in the domestic economy. During 2002, U.S. imports and exports were $1,167 billion and $683 billion, respectively, for a trade deficit of $484 billion. As shown in Figure 2.2, the U.S. has run a trade deficit every year since 1978.

http://www.oecd.org

Table 2.2 provides 2002 trade balance estimates for the 30 members of the *Organisation for Economic Co-operation and Development (OECD)*. The population and 2002 gross domestic product (GDP) of each country are also shown for reference. The G-7 countries (Canada, France, Germany, Japan, Switzerland, the United Kingdom, and the United States) were net importers in 2002, with a combined trade deficit of −$336.6 billion. The remaining OECD countries were net exporters, with a combined trade surplus of $500.8 billion.

The **current account** is a broader measure of import-export activity that includes the trade balance on goods as well as services, royalties, payments for the use of patents, travel and tourism, employee compensation, individual investment and interest income, gifts, and grants. The United States has had a current account deficit every year since 1981. The U.S. current account deficit was $503 billion in 2002.

The **financial account** covers cross-border transactions associated with changes in ownership of financial assets and liabilities. Within the financial accounts, the "direct

TABLE 2.2
Trade Balances in OECD Countries, 2002

	Imports ($ millions)	Exports ($ millions)	Trade balance ($ millions)	2002 GDP ($ billions)	Population (millions)
Australia	69.4	64.9	−4.4	411.4	19.5
Austria*	71.7	72.4	0.6	202.0	8.2
Belgium*	191.8	209.9	18.1	246.1	10.3
Canada	222.5	253.1	30.6	715.0	31.9
Czech Republic	40.7	38.4	−2.3	68.9	10.3
Denmark	48.6	56.0	7.4	171.6	5.4
Finland	33.4	44.4	11.0	130.8	5.2
France	298.0	307.4	9.5	1,408.1	59.8
Germany	492.0	611.0	119.0	1,974.5	83.3
Greece*	28.2	11.0	−17.2	131.1	10.6
Hungary	37.7	34.4	−3.2	63.6	10.1
Iceland	2.3	2.3	0.0	8.7	0.3
Ireland*	52.9	89.0	36.1	116.0	3.9
Italy	239.0	247.6	8.5	1,167.3	57.7
Japan	336.7	416.0	79.3	3,935.6	127.0
Korea	152.2	162.5	10.3	470.4	48.3
Luxembourg	11.5	8.5	−3.0	20.3	0.4
Mexico	168.7	160.7	−8.0	633.5	103.4
Netherlands	192.7	221.0	28.3	416.8	16.1
New Zealand	15.0	14.4	-0.6	57.5	3.9
Norway	34.6	60.2	25.7	190.9	4.5
Poland*	54.3	40.0	−14.3	181.1	38.6
Portugal*	38.2	25.3	−13.0	119.7	10.1
Slovak Republic	16.6	14.4	−2.2	23.3	5.4
Spain	162.8	123.2	−39.6	639.3	40.1
Sweden	65.9	80.6	14.8	239.3	8.9
Switzerland	83.4	87.7	4.3	269.5	7.3
Turkey*	47.6	33.4	−14.2	186.8	67.3
United Kingdom	338.0	278.4	−59.6	1547.9	59.8
United States	1,202.6	693.5	−509.2	10,365.8	280.6
OECD countries	4,310.3	4,474.4	164.2	26,112.6	1,138.0
G7 countries	3,144.0	2,807.4	−336.6	21,114.2	649.5
Other OECD countries	1,166.3	1,667.0	500.8	4,998.4	488.5
World					6,233.8

Source: Cross-border trade and gross domestic product for calendar year 2002 from the Organisation for Economic Co-operation and Development (http://www.oecd.org). Estimates are indicated with an asterisk. Population estimates for 2002 are from the World Bank (http://www.worldbank.org).

investment" accounts include inflows and outflows of direct investment capital such as equity capital, reinvested earnings, and intercompany transactions between affiliated enterprises. The "portfolio investment" accounts include cross-border transactions associated with long-term debt and equity securities, money market instruments, and derivative instruments. The "other investment" accounts reflect other financial transactions, including foreign currency deposits, loans, and trade credits. The financial account is the net sum of these investment transactions. The United States has run a financial account surplus for many years, with more money being attracted into the United States than invested abroad.

As the name suggests, the IMF's balance of payments is a double-entry system that is intended to record both sides of every cross-border transaction. Because only one side of a transaction is typically reported to the monetary authorities, the balance of payments includes a "net errors and omissions" account to ensure that inflows equal outflows. This account is an attempt to infer short-term and long-term cross-border activity from imbalances elsewhere in the balance of payments. Illegal drug trafficking, for example, is seldom reported by the traffickers. Purchases and sales of short-term financial claims are also often unreported and can account for a sizable proportion of the "net errors and omissions" account. Errors and omissions were $29 billion in the United States during 2002, or less than 1/3 percent of the $10.4 trillion in U.S. gross domestic product.

2.3 • EXCHANGE RATE SYSTEMS

The range of possible exchange rate systems runs the gamut from floating rate systems in which currency values are determined in a competitive marketplace, to fixed rate systems in which governments set exchange rates and attempt to force their acceptance by buyers and sellers. As shown in Table 2.3, the IMF classifies exchange rate regimes into the following categories:

1. Exchange arrangements with no separate legal tender
2. Currency board arrangements
3. Other conventional fixed peg arrangements
4. Pegged exchange rates within horizontal bands
5. Crawling pegs
6. Exchange rates within crawling bands
7. Managed floating with no pre-announced path for the exchange rate
8. Independent floating

Exchange rates interact with monetary policy, so the IMF also categorizes national monetary policies along the following dimensions:

1. An exchange rate anchor (against a single currency or a composite, or within a grid)
2. A monetary aggregate target
3. An inflation targeting framework
4. IMF-supported or other monetary programs
5. Other

Rather than investigating the nuances of the various exchange rate regimes and their relation to monetary policy, we'll focus on the two textbook extremes of fixed and floating exchange rates.

Fixed or Pegged Exchange Rate Systems. In a **fixed exchange rate system**, governments set exchange rates and try to enforce their acceptance on buyers and sellers. If they can be maintained, fixed rate systems reduce foreign exchange risk for companies with cross-border trade. For instance, if a U.S. exporter agrees to supply goods to a foreign importer in exchange for an amount of foreign currency payable in two years, the U.S.

In fixed rate systems, governments determine exchange rates.

T A B L E 2 . 3
Exchange Rate Regimes

Exchange rate regime	Africa	Asia and Pacific region	Europe	Middle East	Americas
Exchange arrangements with no separate legal tender	*WAEMU:* Benin*, Burkina Faso*, Ivory Coast*, Guinea-Bissau*, Mali*, Niger*, Senegal*, Togo *CAEMC:* Cameroon*, C. African Rep.*, Chad*, Congo*, Equatorial Guinea, Gabon*	Kiribati, Marshall Islands, Micronesia, Palau,	*Euro Area:* Austria, Belgium, Finland, France, Germany, Greece, Ireland, Italy, Luxembourg, Netherlands, Portugal, Spain San Marino, Vatican		Ecuador*, El Salvador, Panama *ECCU:* Antigua & Barbuda, Dominica, Grenada, St. Kitts & Nevis, St. Lucia, St. Vincent & the Grenadines
Currency board or fixed peg arrangements	Botswana, Cape Verde, Comoros, Djibouti*, Lesotho*, Libya, Morocco, Namibia, Seychelles, Sudan, Swaziland, Zimbabwe	Bangladesh, Bhutan, Brunei Darussalam, China, Fiji, Hong Kong, Malaysia, Maldives, Nepal, Samoa, Taiwan, Vanuatu	Bosnia-Herzegovina*, Bulgaria*, Estonia*, Latvia*, Lithuania*, Macedonia*, Malta, Turkmenistan	Bahrain, Iran, Jordan*, Kuwait, Lebanon, Oman, Qatar, Saudi Arabia, Syria*, United Arab Emirates	Aruba, Argentina*, Belize, Bahamas, Barbados, Netherlands Antilles, Suriname
Crawling pegs or horizontal bands	Egypt	Solomon Islands, Tonga	Belarus, Cyprus, Denmark, Hungary*, Romania*	Egypt, Israel	Bolivia*, Costa Rica, Honduras*, Nicaragua*, Uruguay*, Venezuela
Managed floating with a preannounced path for exchange rates	Algeria, Angola, Burundi, Eritrea, Ethiopia*, Ghana*, Guinea*, Kenya*, Mauritania*, Mauritius, Nigeria*, Rwanda, Sao Tome*, Tunisia, Zambia*	Cambodia*, India, Indonesia*, Mongolia*, Myanmar (Laos)*, Pakistan*, Singapore, Sri Lanka*, Thailand*, Vietnam*	Azerbaijan*, Croatia*, Kazakhstan*, Kyrgyzstan*, Russian Fed.*, Serbia*, Slovak Rep., Slovenia, Ukraine*, Uzbekistan, Yugoslavia	Iraq*	Dominican Rep., Guatemala, Guyana*, Jamaica*, Paraguay, Trinidad & Tobago*
Independently floating	Congo, Gambia*, Liberia, Malawi*, Madagascar, Mozambique, Sierra Leone*, Somalia, S. Africa, Tanzania, Uganda	Afghanistan, Australia, Japan, New Zealand, Philippines*, S. Korea Papua West Guinea	Albania, Armenia, Czech Rep., Georgia, Iceland, Moldova, Norway, Poland, Sweden, Switzerland, Tajikistan, United Kingdom	Turkey*, Yemen*	Brazil, Canada, Chile, Colombia*, Haiti, Mexico, Peru*, United States

ECCU = Eastern Caribbean Currency Union. WAEMU = West African Economic and Monetary Union. CAEMC = Central African Economic and Monetary Union.
* indicates that a country has an IMF-supported or similar monetary program.

Source: Compiled from *International Financial Statistics*, a publication of the International Monetary Fund (www.imf.org), April 2003 issue. Exchange rate classifications are as of December 31, 2001.

exporter would know exactly how much the foreign currency will be worth in dollars in two years under fixed exchange rates.

Exchange rate changes in a fixed rate system are called **devaluations** when one currency falls in relation to another currency and **revaluations** when that currency rises in value against another currency. For example, if the Chinese government changes the official exchange rate from $0.1208/Ren to $0.1200/Ren, the Chinese renminbi has had a devaluation against the dollar. At the same time, the dollar has had a revaluation from Ren8.2781/$ (the reciprocal of $0.1208/Ren) to Ren8.3333/$ against the renminbi.

There are two major drawbacks to a fixed exchange rate system. First, fixed rates forge a direct link between domestic and foreign inflation and employment. Suppose Chinese inflation is high and U.S. inflation is zero. The prices of Chinese goods in renminbi will rise with Chinese inflation, while the prices of U.S. goods will remain constant in U.S. dollars. With a fixed exchange rate between renminbi and dollars, Chinese products become relatively more expensive than U.S. products for both Chinese and U.S. consumers. Consumers will shift their purchases away from high-priced Chinese goods and toward low-priced U.S. goods. This shifts employment away from China and toward the United States, resulting in rising unemployment in China and rising employment in the United States. As employment shifts toward the United States, Chinese wages will fall and U.S. wages will increase. In this way, a fixed exchange rate system links cross-country inflation differences to wage levels and employment conditions.

The second drawback is the difficulty of sustaining fixed exchange rates when they diverge from market rates. By standing ready to buy or sell currencies at official exchange rates, governments are attempting to preempt the function of the foreign exchange market. If an official rate differs from the market rate, the government will suffer a loss of value as counterparties buy the undervalued currency and sell the overvalued currency. If a government refuses to buy or sell at the official exchange rate, it impedes the cross-border flow of goods, services, and capital. Governments cannot indefinitely impose their will on financial markets; the markets ultimately prevail. When a devaluation arrives in a fixed rate system, it is usually a whopper.

Governments are most adamant about maintaining fixed rates when their fixed rate systems are under pressure. Devaluations typically come on the heels of claims that the government has full confidence in the value of their currency and will maintain the fixed rate system at all costs. This only encourages currency speculators to bet against the beleaguered currency. When fixed exchange rate systems collapse, government officials are then quick to blame currency speculators for precipitating the collapse. Because changes come infrequently but in large increments in a fixed exchange rate system, the apparent absence of currency risk is an illusion.

> The apparent absence of currency risk in a fixed rate system is an illusion.

Many governments nevertheless attempt to peg or manage their currency values in relation to another currency, such as the euro, U.S. dollar, or South African rand, or to a composite index. Denmark attempts to peg the value of the krone within a band around the value of the euro. Saudi Arabia tries to peg the value of the riyal to the dollar because oil—its major export—is globally priced in dollars. Other countries, such as Kuwait and Libya, try to maintain a peg to the value of a composite index such as the IMF's special drawing right. **Special drawing rights (SDRs)** are an international reserve account created by the International Monetary Fund and allocated to member countries to supplement their foreign exchange reserves. SDRs are not actual currencies. Rather, they are bookkeeping units of account that are traded only between central banks as they manage their balance of payments and foreign exchange positions.

Floating Rate Systems. **Floating exchange rate systems** allow currency values to fluctuate according to market supply and demand without direct interference by government authorities. In these systems, there are no official bounds on currency values. Nevertheless, government intervention in the foreign exchange markets can and does have an impact on currency values, especially in the short term. The United States and Japan are two countries that allow their currencies to float. An increase in a currency value under a floating exchange rate system is called an **appreciation** and a fall in a currency value is called a **depreciation**. As under fixed exchange rates, when one currency rises in value, the other must fall.

> Values are determined by supply and demand in a floating rate system.

The major advantage of a floating system is that changes in inflation, wage levels, and unemployment in one country are not forced on another country through currency values, as they are in a fixed exchange rate system. Consider our example of a rise in Chinese inflation. With floating exchange rates, the value of the dollar will tend to rise as both Chinese and U.S. consumers buy more of the lower-priced U.S. goods. As the dollar rises in value relative to the renminbi, U.S. goods will lose some of their price advantage over Chinese goods, and unemployment in China will not rise as rapidly as under a fixed rate system. Consumers in the United States will continue to buy Chinese goods because their dollars will buy relatively more goods in renminbi than in dollars as the dollar appreciates. In a freely floating system, the exchange rate adjusts for the inflation differentials between countries. In general, a freely floating system tends to insulate countries from changes in inflation, wage levels, and unemployment in other countries.

The major disadvantage of a freely floating system is the flip side of its major strength. Because exchange rates change continuously, it is difficult to know how much a future payment or receipt in a foreign currency will be worth. This means that investors and corporations that are exposed to currency risk must monitor their foreign exchange positions and, if necessary, hedge their currency risk exposures.

Exchange Arrangements with No Separate Legal Tender. Still other countries do not have a national currency of their own. The 12 members of **European monetary union (Emu)** are the most prominent countries following this system. Through 1998, the European *Exchange Rate Mechanism (ERM)* was a cooperative arrangement in which currency values were managed around a central rate called the *European Currency Unit (Ecu)*, a bas-

> The euro is used by 12 European countries.

ket of currencies weighted by each member's proportion of intra-European trade and gross national product. The dollar price of the Ecu was about the same as the weighted dollar values of the ERM's component currencies. In 1999, the Ecu was renamed the **euro**, and participating currencies were formally pegged to this central rate.

2.4 • A BRIEF HISTORY OF THE INTERNATIONAL MONETARY SYSTEM

The international monetary system refers to the global network of governmental and commercial financial institutions within which exchange rates are determined. Figure 2.3 highlights the key events in this system during the twentieth century. The system has evolved through several different exchange rate arrangements during this time. A review of this history will help you to understand how alternative exchange rate systems affect asset values across national borders. This is essential knowledge for managing the value and financial risks of an individual investment portfolio or a multinational corporation.

The International Monetary System Before 1944

Prior to 1914, the major countries of the world operated on what is known as the *classical gold standard*, in which gold was used to settle national trade balances. World War I

FIGURE 2.3
A History of the International Monetary System

Date	Event	Causes and repercussions
1914	Collapse of the classical gold standard	Prior to 1914, gold was used to settle trade balances in a pegged exchange rate system. Breakdown of the system led to a period of floating exchange rates.
1925	Gold exchange standard	U.K. and U.S. hold gold reserves. Other currencies are convertible into gold, dollars, or pounds in pegged system.
1930s	Global depression	Protectionist trade policies and a breakdown of the gold exchange standard lead to floating exchange rates and a global depression.
1944	Bretton Woods Conference	Price of gold set at $35/ounce. Other currencies convertible into dollars at pegged exchange rates. The IMF and the World Bank were also created at Bretton Woods.
1971	Smithsonian Agreement	Dollar devalued to $38/ounce of gold; G-10 countries agree to maintain their currency values within a 4.5% band around the dollar. Agreement quickly fell apart.
1972	European Joint Float Agreement	"The snake within the tunnel," a pegged system, adopted by the European Economic Community. The pound exits the system two months later.
1976	Jamaica Agreement	Floating rates declared acceptable, officially endorsing the system in place.
1979	European Monetary System (EMS) created	European Exchange Rate Mechanism (ERM) created to maintain currencies within a band around central rates. European Currency Unit (Ecu) created.
1985	Plaza Accord	G-10 agree to bring down the value of the dollar and cooperate in controlling exchange rate volatility.
1987	Louvre Accord	Dollar has fallen from its 1985 high. The G-5 agree to promote currency markets around current levels.
1991	Treaty of Maastricht	European community members agree to pursue a broad agenda of reform leading to European monetary union (Emu) and a single European currency.
1992	Exchange rate volatility leads to ERM breakdown	Uncertainty over the outcome of Emu ratification votes lead to a breakdown of the ERM. Bands widened to ±15 percent as England and Italy fall out of the system.
1995	Mexican peso crisis	The Mexican peso and Mexico's stock market head south.
1997	Asian crisis	Falling currency and asset values in Asian countries cause political upheaval in Indonesia and economic difficulties throughout the region.
1998	Russia's currency crisis	Value of the ruble plummets along with the values of other Russian assets.
1999	Euro replaces the Ecu	On January 1, 1999, the euro replaces the Ecu on a one-for-one basis. The currencies of participating Emu countries are pegged to the euro.
2002	Argentina's currency crisis	Peso is allowed to float against the dollar. The struggling Argentian stock market doubles in value.
2002	Euro replaces Emu-zone currencies	The euro begins public circulation on January 1, 2002, and replaces the national currencies of Emu participants on July 1, 2002.

upset this standard and threw the international monetary system into turmoil. In 1925, a *gold exchange standard* was instituted in which the United States and England held only gold reserves while other nations held gold, U.S. dollars, or pounds sterling as reserves. Reserves are used by central banks to manage their balance of payments and foreign exchange positions. The gold exchange standard lasted until 1931, at which time England withdrew from the system under pressure from massive demands on its reserves as a result of an unrealistically high pound sterling value. To maintain the competitiveness of their products on world markets, most other nations followed England in devaluing their currencies.

The global depression of the 1930s was fueled by this breakdown of the international monetary system and by the protectionist trade policies that followed. Currency speculation during this period was rampant, causing wild fluctuations in exchange rates. There was no way to hedge currency risk, because there was not an established forward exchange market at the time. Businesses were at the mercy of a very fickle monetary system.

Bretton Woods: 1944–1971

In addition to creating the International Monetary Fund and the World Bank, the Bretton Woods Conference created a fixed or pegged exchange rate system that lasted for 25 years. Under the Bretton Woods system, the price of an ounce of gold was set in U.S. dollars at $35 per ounce. Each nation agreed to maintain a fixed (or pegged) exchange rate for its currency in terms of the dollar or gold. For example, the German mark was set equal to 1/140 of an ounce of gold, or $0.25/DM. Under this form of gold exchange standard, only U.S. dollars were convertible into gold at the official par value of $35 per ounce. Other member nations were not required to exchange their currency for gold, but pledged to intervene in the foreign exchange markets if their currency moved more than one percent from its official rate.

The Bretton Woods system worked passably well until the late 1960s. Devaluations were common as the market periodically imposed its own values on the world's economies, but by-and-large the system facilitated cross-border trade and stimulated economic development. During the 1960s, U.S. inflation rose as the U.S. government borrowed money to finance the war in Vietnam. High U.S. inflation caused the market price of gold to rise above $35 per ounce and the market value of the U.S. dollar to fall below the official rate relative to foreign currencies. A run on the U.S. dollar ensued as speculators (investors, financial institutions, and governments) rushed to buy gold with dollars at the $35 per ounce price. Finally, on August 15, 1971, President Nixon surrendered to market forces and took the United States off the gold standard. Many currencies were already floating by this time. This date marked the end of the Bretton Woods system.

Exchange Rates After the Fall of Bretton Woods

Efforts to Resurrect a Pegged Exchange Rate System During the 1970s. After the collapse of Bretton Woods, several unsuccessful attempts were made to resurrect a gold exchange standard. The first of these, the *Smithsonian Agreement*, was signed in Washington, D.C., by the Group of Ten in December 1971.[3] This agreement devalued the U.S. dollar to $38 per ounce of gold and revalued other currencies relative to the dollar. A 4.5 percent band was established to promote monetary stability.

---

3 Also called the *Paris Club*, the Group of Ten included Belgium, Canada, France, Italy, Japan, the Netherlands, Sweden, the United Kingdom, the United States, and West Germany.

In April 1972, members of the **European Economic Community (EEC)** established a pegged exchange rate system known as "the snake within the tunnel" or "the snake."[4] The term *snake* refers to the fact that the pegged currencies floated as a group against non-EEC currencies. The tunnel refers to the band allowed around the central currency rates in the system.

Both the Smithsonian Agreement and the snake proved unworkable in the presence of continued exchange rate volatility. Countries were frequently forced to either devalue their currency or fall out of these pegged systems until an agreement could be reached on a new target price. Realignments were the rule of the day. The Bank of England allowed the pound sterling to float against other currencies in June 1972. The Swiss franc remained in the EEC's exchange rate mechanism until January 1973, at which time it, too, was allowed to float. In February 1973, the U.S. government devalued the dollar from $38 to $42.22 per ounce of gold. Currency values fluctuated even more severely following the 1973–1974 OPEC oil embargo.

This was a period of unprecedented financial risk. High volatility in floating exchange rates contributed to high levels of foreign exchange risk. Interest rate risk was on the rise as inflation grew in many countries. The OPEC oil embargo caused a great deal of oil price risk. Participants in the financial and goods markets faced a nemesis—financial price volatility—for which they were ill-prepared.

In January 1976, the IMF convened a monetary summit in Jamaica to reach some sort of consensus on the monetary system. Exchange rate volatility was still too high and policy objectives too diverse for governments to form an agreement on a fixed rate or pegged system. However, participants did agree to disagree. Under the Jamaica Agreement, floating exchange rates were declared acceptable, officially acknowledging the system already in place and legitimizing the basis for the floating rate system still used by many countries today.

In 1979, the European snake was replaced by the European Exchange Rate Mechanism (ERM). The ERM relied on central bank cooperation to maintain currency values within a ±2.25 percent band around ERM central rates. The United Kingdom (England, Northern Ireland, Scotland, and Wales) was subsequently admitted with a ±6 percent band around central rates. The ERM attempted to combine the best of the fixed and floating rate systems. First and foremost, currency risk was reduced because exchange rates tended to remain relatively stable within the ERM. The system did not require the highly restrictive monetary policies that accompany a fixed rate system, as the band allowed some movement around the central rate. Allowable currency movements varied in the ERM for different currencies and at different times. The German mark, historically the most stable of Europe's currencies, was usually kept within a band of ±2.5 percent around the central rate. If a currency fell below its ERM floor, European Union central banks would either cooperate in buying the currency to keep it within its ERM band or reset the allowable band around the central exchange rate.

The U.S. Dollar During the 1980s. During the mid-1980s, the dollar rose in value relative to other currencies. During this time, foreign governments complained that the high value of the dollar was causing inflation in their economies because of the high prices of U.S. imports. The U.S. government complained of a widening trade deficit due to the poor competitive position of high-priced U.S. goods. The dollar reached its high in early 1985, climbing to DM3.50/dollar against the German mark.

In September 1985, the Group of Ten met at the Plaza Hotel in New York and agreed to cooperate in controlling volatility in currency exchange rates. A principal

---

4 The European Economic Community was the predecessor to the European Union.

objective of the Plaza Accord was to bring down the value of the dollar. In fact, the dollar had already begun to fall during the spring and summer of 1985. By February 1987, the dollar had fallen to what many believed to be equilibrium. At that time, the Group of Five (France, Germany, Japan, the United Kingdom, and the United States) met in France and agreed in the *Louvre Accord* to promote stability in currency markets around current levels.

The 1991 Treaty of Maastricht and European Monetary Union. The most important international monetary development of the last half century is European monetary union (Emu), which aims for economic and monetary union within Emu countries. To achieve this objective, participating countries traded their currencies for the euro (€). Figure 2.4 displays the members of the European Free Trade Agreement (EFTA), the European Union (EU), and Emu.

The timetable for Emu was established in the 1991 *Treaty of Maastricht* and included the following dates:

- *January 1, 1999.* The euro replaced the Ecu in the European exchange rate mechanism, becoming a unit of account but not yet a physical currency. The exchange rates of participating countries were pegged to the euro at that time.

FIGURE 2.4
The European Union, Emu, EFTA, and EU Enlargement

As of May 2003, there were 19 members in the European Free Trade Agreement (EFTA). Fifteen of these were members of the European Union (EU) and 12 had adopted the euro as their currency through European monetary union (Emu).

EFTA member country	EU member	Emu member
Austria	✓	✓
Belgium	✓	✓
Denmark	✓	
Finland	✓	✓
France	✓	✓
Greece	✓	✓
Germany	✓	✓
Ireland	✓	✓
Iceland		
Italy	✓	✓
Liechtenstein		
Luxembourg	✓	✓
Netherlands	✓	✓
Norway		
Portugal	✓	✓
Sweden	✓	
Spain	✓	✓
Switzerland		
United Kingdom	✓	

Other candidates for EU enlargement are Bulgaria, Cyprus, the Czech Republic, Estonia, Hungary, Latvia, Lithuania, Malta, Poland, Romania, Slovakia, Slovenia, and Turkey.

- *January 1, 2002.* The euro began public circulation alongside national currencies.
- *July 1, 2002.* The euro formally replaced the currencies of participating countries.

Voters in Austria, Belgium, Finland, France, Germany, Ireland, Italy, Luxembourg, the Netherlands, Portugal, and Spain ratified the Maastricht Treaty. Voters in Denmark, Sweden, and the United Kingdom failed to ratify the treaty, but retained the option of joining Emu at a later date.

> Convergence criteria ensure similar economic and monetary conditions in Emu-zone countries.

A single-currency zone is only viable if the participating countries have similar economic and monetary policies. The Maastricht Treaty established the following **convergence criteria** for Emu entry to ensure relatively homogenous economic and monetary conditions in Emu countries:

1. Inflation rates within 1.5 percent of the three best-performing EU countries
2. Long-term interest rates within 2 percent of the three best-performing EU countries
3. Exchange rate stability within the ERM for at least two years
4. Budget deficits no higher than 3 percent of gross domestic product
5. Government debt less than 60 percent of gross domestic product

The two most important criteria are low inflation and low budget deficits.

By the end of 1997, there was convergence in inflation, interest rates, and budget deficits in the participating Emu countries. According to the European Commission, average EU inflation was 1.6 percent in 1997. The average budget deficit fell from 6.1 percent of GDP in 1993 to just 2.4 percent in 1997. Budget deficits were 3 percent or less in each participating country. There was less convergence in the amount of public debt outstanding. Only 3 of the 11 Emu participants met the 60 percent debt limit of the Maastricht Treaty, with Belgium (122.2 percent of GDP) and Italy (121.6 percent) the worst offenders. Greece did not meet any of the treaty's convergence criteria and was unable to join until 2001.

The largest impediments to European monetary union remain the divergent monetary, fiscal, political, and social conditions within participating countries. Member states are reluctant to surrender national sovereignty to the European parliament and the European Central Bank (ECB) in Brussels. Some countries, such as Germany, have historically enjoyed very high standards of living. Others have much lower mean incomes. Workers in high-wage countries are vulnerable to competition from elsewhere within Europe as monetary union equalizes wages across the continent. Workers in less well-to-do countries that have been protected from foreign competition by their national government are also at risk. The hope is that increased trade and general consumer welfare will more than compensate for these local losses.

The Emu zone is comparable to the United States in size and trading power. The trading block contains around 305 million people, compared to about 280 million in the United States and 127 million in Japan. Participating countries account for about 20 percent of the world's GDP, as well as about 20 percent of the world's cross-border trade. The United States accounts for approximately the same proportion of GDP and trade. Japan accounts for about 8 percent of GDP and about 8 percent of trade.

There are ongoing discussions regarding enlargement of European monetary union to include countries from elsewhere in Europe. In January 2001, Greece met the Emu convergence criteria and formally adopted the euro. The Czech Republic, Hungary, and Poland are on a fast track for EU membership, with Bulgaria and Romania close behind. Denmark, Sweden, and the United Kingdom are not participating in Emu, although they may join at a later date.

The European exchange rate mechanism had mixed success in maintaining exchange rate stability during the 1990s. The period immediately after the 1991 signing of the treaty was particularly troublesome. Government leaders were hopeful that the road to monetary unification would proceed smoothly, despite the warnings and protests of numerous euro-skeptics. However, Denmark failed to ratify the Maastricht Treaty in a close popular vote in May 1992. By early September, the success of the French referendum on the treaty, scheduled for September 20, 1992, was also in doubt. Turmoil hit Europe's currency markets in the week before the French referendum. On September 17, the British pound fell below its ERM floor. Despite increasing a key interest rate from 10 percent to 12 percent and threatening a boost to 15 percent, the English government could not keep the pound within its ERM range. Italy and then Spain suspended their currencies from the ERM after they too fell below their ERM floors. Italy and Spain eventually devalued their currencies before being readmitted to the ERM. The United Kingdom has remained outside the ERM since 1992.

Other countries in the region were affected as well. Finland and Sweden wished to share in European integration and had been maintaining informal links between their currencies and the Ecu. When the value of their currencies plummeted in September 1992, both countries intervened in an attempt to maintain their link with the Ecu. Finland quickly gave up resistance and allowed the Finnish markka to float, and ultimately adopted the euro as its currency in 1999. Sweden refused to give in and eventually raised its key lending rate to 500 percent per annum (inflation was less than 10 percent at the time) in an effort to defend the value of its currency. Another bout of currency volatility in August 1993 caused the ERM bands to be widened to ±15 percent around the central rate, making the ERM much more of a floating rate system on the fixed/floating continuum.

The Emerging Role of the International Monetary Fund

According to the Bretton Woods agreement, the mission of the International Monetary Fund is to make short-term loans to countries with temporary funds shortages. The IMF has come to the aid of many countries in times of stress, such as during the oil shocks of the 1970s, the debt crises of the 1980s, and the currency crises of the 1990s.

> The IMF has emerged as a lender of last resort.

Unfortunately, the IMF has not had a great deal of success in keeping their involvements short term. Only about 25 percent of the nearly 140 countries that have received IMF funding since 1965 have been able to repay their loans and emerge from IMF oversight. Nearly 40 countries have been receiving IMF aid for more than 25 years. On its January 2003 quarterly report, the IMF had a total of $69.1 billion in outstanding loans to countries including Algeria ($1.0 billion), Argentina ($10.6 billion), Brazil ($13.1 billion), Indonesia ($6.6 billion), Pakistan ($1.4 billion), Philippines ($1.3 billion), Russia ($5.0 billion), Turkey ($16.2 billion), Ukraine ($1.4 billion), and Uruguay ($1.3 billion).

http://www.imf.org

This section describes recent crises in Asia and Latin America that illustrate the role of the IMF in helping countries achieve economic stability. In each of these crises, conditions were triggered by

- A fixed or pegged exchange rate system that overvalued the local currency
- A large amount of foreign currency debt

In each case, the government depleted its foreign currency reserves in defense of the currency and was unable to maintain the fixed exchange rate.

The Mexican Peso Crisis of 1995. During December 1994 and January 1995, the Mexican peso lost 40 percent of its value against the U.S. dollar (see Figure 2.5). The Mexican stock market also fell 50 percent in local (peso) terms during this time.

FIGURE 2.5
The Mexican Peso Crisis

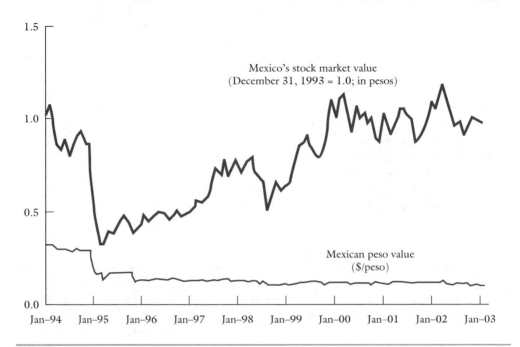

Source: http://www.msci.com and http://www.oanda.com.

The combined effect of the peso depreciation and stock market crash was a 70 percent drop in the dollar value of equity investments in Mexico.

The Mexican peso crisis caught many investors by surprise. The Mexican economy had been thriving during the 1980s and early 1990s as Mexico liberalized its economy in a series of economic and market reforms. The government had slashed its trade and investment barriers through agreements such as the North American Free Trade Agreement (NAFTA) and had privatized nearly 1,000 companies in industries including petroleum and telecommunications. The government had maintained a balanced budget since 1987, and inflation had been reduced from 150 percent in 1987 to 27 percent in 1994. Despite these positive trends, the Mexican government made two critical mistakes that precipitated the peso crisis:

- The government had maintained the value of the peso at artificially high levels by buying pesos on international markets. As a consequence, Mexico's foreign currency reserves fell from $30 billion in early 1994 to only $5 billion by November 1994.

- To appeal to international investors, commercial banks and the Mexican government had rolled over $23 billion of short-term peso-denominated debt into similar short-term securities called *tesebonos*, whose principal was indexed to the value of the dollar. The peso value of these obligations rose and fell with the value of the dollar.

With only $5 billion in foreign exchange reserves and $23 billion in short-term dollar-denominated liabilities, Mexico was deeply exposed to a fall in the value of the peso.

The peso came under increasing pressure in late 1994 as Mexico's foreign exchange reserves were depleted. Eventually, the government concluded that the exchange rate could not be sustained. On December 20, 1994, the government announced a 30 percent devaluation of the peso. The market value of the peso continued to fall as investors pulled out of Mexican assets. The resulting 50 percent fall of the peso against the dollar doubled the peso value of Mexico's short-term dollar-denominated tesebono obligations.

Mexico's crisis was aggravated by foreign currency debt.

The crisis in Mexico was essentially a crisis of short-term liquidity. The underlying economy was in relatively good shape. To assist Mexico in meeting its short-term tesebono obligations, the United States and the IMF assembled a standby credit of $40 billion. With liquidity ensured, the Mexican economy began to recover in 1995. Although 1995 GDP was 7 percent below 1994 levels, the relatively low value of the peso increased exports by 30 percent and decreased imports by 10 percent. As a result, the trade balance rose from a deficit of $18.5 billion in 1994 to a surplus of $7.4 billion in 1995. Although Mexico's crisis was severe, it was also relatively short-lived. The Mexican stock market and value of the peso have been fairly stable since the crisis. Mexico paid off its IMF loan in 2000.

The Asian Contagion of 1997. In May 1997, the Thai baht came under pressure as speculators bet against the currency, which was pegged to a currency basket that included the U.S. dollar. Foreign currency reserves were severely depleted as the Bank of Thailand defended the currency, falling from nearly $40 billion in December 1996 to less than $10 billion by July 1997. On July 2, 1997, Thailand allowed the baht to float. By the end of 1997, the baht had lost nearly 50 percent of its value against the dollar (see Figure 2.6).

Thailand suffered from several problems at the time of its crisis, including a current account deficit that was 8 percent of GDP, massive short-term foreign currency borrowings used to support speculative property ventures in Thailand, and declining competitiveness brought on by rising wages. Faced with these problems, investors lost confidence and Thailand's property and stock markets fell. By the end of the year, the Thai stock market had lost more than 50 percent of its value.

The "Asian contagion" soon spread to Indonesia. Like Thailand, Indonesia had a pegged exchange rate, a large current account deficit, massive short-term foreign currency debt used to support speculative property ventures, and declining competitiveness. The rupiah fell steadily throughout the second half of 1997. By the end of January 1998, the rupiah had lost more than 75 percent of its value against the dollar. Investors lost confidence in Indonesia's ability to repay its foreign debt, and Indonesia's stock market fell by 33 percent near the end of 1997.

South Korea's won was the next to fall. As in Thailand and Indonesia, South Korea's economic situation was undermined by a pegged exchange rate, a large current account deficit, and large short-term foreign currency obligations. In contrast to Thailand and Indonesia, the Korean economy was in relatively good shape. Much of the foreign currency debt had been invested in export industries that stood to gain from a drop in the won, as opposed to the speculative property ventures that were popular in Thailand and Indonesia. Despite the competitiveness of the Korean economy, the won lost nearly one-half of its value during the last several months of 1997, falling from $0.00104/W in October to $0.00059/W at year end. The Korean stock market lost more than 50 percent of its value between September 1997 and September 1998.

As in Mexico in 1995, the IMF came to the assistance of these troubled economies. With the support of the United States, Europe, and Japan, the IMF assembled standby credit arrangements of $58 billion for Korea, $43 billion for Indonesia, and $17 billion for Thailand. These packages were tied to structural reforms that included:

Some countries have followed IMF reforms, while others have not.

FIGURE 2.6
The Asian Contagion of 1997

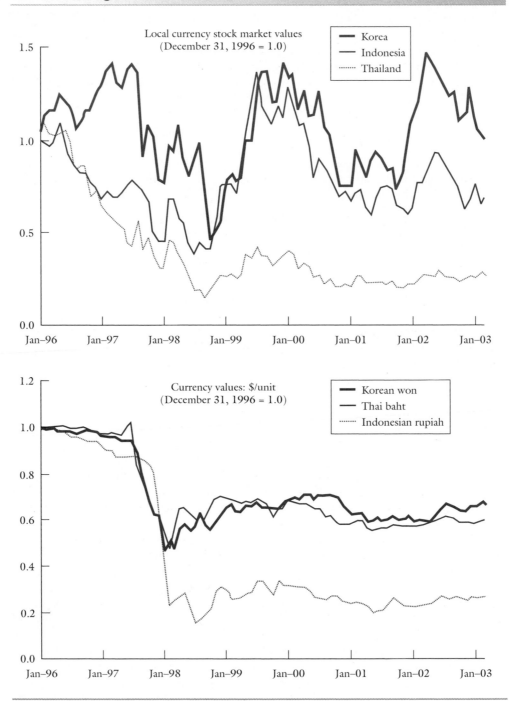

Source: http://www.msci.com and http://www.oanda.com.

- Fiscal and monetary restraint
- Liberalization of financial markets
- Increased competition, efficiency, and transparency

Korea and Thailand implemented significant reforms in banking and corporate governance. Indonesia agreed to some reforms, but has had less success in their implementation.

Korea was able to repay the balance of its IMF loan in 2001. As of the IMF's January 2003 quarterly report, Indonesia ($6.0 billion) and Thailand ($0.4 billion) were still indebted to the IMF. Commercial banks in all three countries continue to suffer from high proportions of nonperforming loans.

The Fall of the Russian Ruble in 1998. Russia embarked on a painful transition toward a market-based economy after the breakup of the Soviet Union in 1991. Russia's difficulties during this transition included hyperinflation, an undeveloped banking system, widespread tax avoidance, corruption, and huge budget deficits. The difficulties of the transition caused Russia's GDP to fall from $804 billion in 1991 to only $282 billion in 1998, with a budget deficit of nearly 10 percent of GDP.

In July 1993, Russia placed the ruble in a crawling peg. This stabilized the value of the ruble against the dollar (Figure 2.7) and reduced inflation from 1,700 percent in 1992 to 15 percent by 1997. It also resulted in high real (inflation-adjusted) ruble interest rates. Faced with declining tax revenues, the government financed its fiscal deficit by borrowing in the capital markets. In 1997, Russia began rolling over its ruble-denominated debt into dollar-denominated Eurobonds.

In 1998, the ruble came under speculative pressure as investors reassessed the viability of emerging market investments following the Asian crisis of 1997. By July 1998, Russia was finding it difficult to refinance its dollar debt as it matured. The IMF arranged a $23 billion loan package, but this was not enough to support the ruble. On August 17, 1998, Russia was forced to abandon its exchange rate peg and defaulted on more than $40 billion of debt. By April 1999, Russia owed the IMF nearly $13

FIGURE 2.7
Russia's Currency Crisis

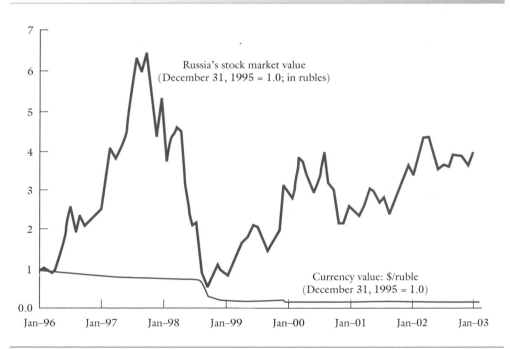

billion. As of March 2003, this amount was still more than $5 billion. These difficulties are expected to continue in the absence of meaningful reform within Russia.

Continuing Troubles in South America. Mexico's crisis presaged similar troubles elsewhere in South America.

- *Argentina.* In Argentina, a *currency board* had pegged the peso one-for-one to the dollar (see Figure 2.8) since 1991. Although the currency board cured the country's hyperinflation (inflation was 3,000 percent in 1989), the overvalued peso contributed to a severe depression beginning in 1998. To compound matters, the government had financed its large budget deficits with foreign currency debt, accumulating a balance of more than $150 billion.

   The government was forced to devalue the peso in January 2002 and eventually allowed the peso to float, despite an IMF-sponsored $40 billion standby line of credit. As its currency was devalued, Argentina added $3.6 billion to its existing IMF loans, bringing its total indebtedness to more than $6 billion. The stock market rebounded during this time, eventually climbing back to its previous high. Conditions in Argentina nevertheless remain dire. As of January 2003, 40 percent of Argentina's population was living in poverty, unemployment was approaching 20 percent, and Argentina owed $10 billion to the IMF.

- *Brazil.* Brazil experienced a currency crisis of its own beginning in 1998. Brazil is the world's fifth largest country both in population and landmass. Like Argentina, Brazil had massive foreign currency debt (more than $250 billion). The government was using a crawling peg that overvalued the Brazilian real. Brazil spent more than $50 billion in support of the real during 1998. The government ran

---

FIGURE 2.8
Argentina's Currency Crisis

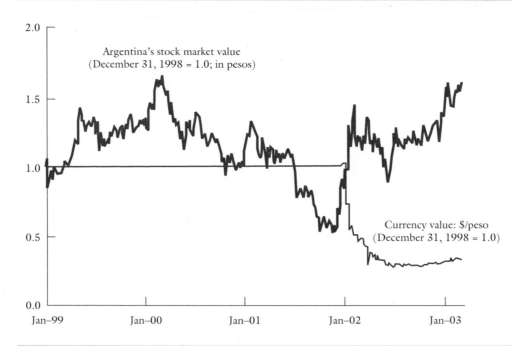

Source: http://www.msci.com and http://www.oanda.com.

out of foreign currency resources in November 1998 and negotiated a $42 billion IMF loan that called for fiscal and monetary restraint.

The Brazilian real was nevertheless devalued in November 1998 and allowed to float shortly thereafter. By 2000, Brazil had used $6.4 billion of its IMF line of credit. Although this had been reduced to $1.4 billion by 2001, continuing recession forced more borrowing. As of January 2003, Brazil's total IMF borrowings amounted to more than $13 billion.[5] As in Argentina, the resolution of this crisis will only reveal itself over time.

The IMF, International Lending, and Moral Hazard. The IMF's evolution from short-term lender into lender of last resort has sparked an active debate about the proper role of the IMF during currency crises. Both sides of this debate are interested in ensuring the stability of the international financial system. The sides differ in the means to this end.

> IMF loans can influence the expectations of borrowers and lenders.

Proponents of the IMF's policies believe that short-term loans can help countries overcome temporary crises, such as Mexico's 1995 peso crisis, and prevent the crises from spreading to other countries. Opponents argue the medicine prescribed by the IMF worsens these crises.[6] These critics believe that:

- Fiscal and monetary belt-tightening at the time of a crisis is counterproductive.
- Capital market liberalization exposes developing countries to even more risk.
- Providing loans so that a government can try to support an unsustainable exchange rate is throwing good money after bad.
- IMF loans can leave a legacy of debt that lasts for decades.
- IMF remedies tend to benefit developed countries and not the country in crisis.

Central to this debate is the notion of **moral hazard**—the risk that the existence of a contract will change the behaviors of parties to the contract. In the absence of IMF bailouts, lenders must assess the risks and expected returns of their investments and then bear the consequences. The expectation of an IMF bailout creates a moral hazard in that it changes the expectations and hence the behaviors of borrowers, lenders, and governments. The challenge for the IMF is in developing policies that both promote economic stability and ensure that the consequences of poor investment decisions are borne by investors and not taxpayers.

2.5 • SUMMARY

World trade is vitally important to the world's economy. This chapter began by describing the ongoing globalization and integration of the world's markets for goods, services, and capital. We then presented a description of the International Monetary Fund's balance-of-payments statistics that track the flow of goods, services, and capital into and out of each country. The balance-of-payments statistics allow multinational financial managers to identify opportunities as well as potential problem areas in the conduct of their foreign and domestic operations.

We then described the difference between fixed and floating exchange rate systems. Exchange rates under fixed rate and pegged systems have occasional large devaluations

---

5 The crisis in South America has spilled over into Uruguay, which owed the IMF $1.3 billion in October 2002 (about 7 percent of GDP).

6 See Stiglitz, *Globalization and Its Discontents* (2002).

and revaluations, while exchange rates under a floating rate system have smaller but more continuous depreciations and appreciations.

The chapter concluded with a history of the international monetary system. The currencies of many developed countries have floated since the currency crises of 1971. Attempts to limit exchange rate fluctuations through mechanisms such as the European Exchange Rate Mechanism have met with some success, although in the long run currency values are determined by market forces and not by government fiat. This was made painfully obvious in a series of currency crises in Asia, Russia, and Latin America.

The most significant monetary innovation of the last several decades is undoubtedly the 1999 introduction of the euro in Austria, Belgium, Finland, France, Germany, Ireland, Italy, Luxembourg, the Netherlands, Portugal, and Spain, and in Greece in 2001. The euro created a single-currency zone that includes roughly the population and market power of the United States and more than twice that of Japan.

KEY TERMS

appreciation
balance-of-payments (BoP) statistics
Bretton Woods Conference
convergence criteria
current account
depreciation
devaluation
euro
European Economic Community (EEC)
European monetary union (Emu)
European Union (EU)
financial account
fixed exchange rate system
floating exchange rate system

integrated versus segmented markets
International Monetary Fund (IMF)
international monetary system
less developed countries (LDCs)
moral hazard
newly industrializing countries (NICs) or
    newly industrializing economies (NIEs)
North American Free Trade Agreement
    (NAFTA)
revaluation
Special drawing right (SDR)
trade balance
World Bank
World Trade Organization (WTO)

CONCEPTUAL QUESTIONS

2.1   List one or more trade pacts in which your country is involved. Do these trade pacts affect all residents of your country in the same way? On balance, are these trade pacts good or bad for residents of your country?

2.2   Do countries tend to export more or less of their gross national product today than in years past? What are the reasons for this trend?

2.3   How has globalization in the world's goods markets affected world trade? How has globalization in the world's financial markets affected world trade?

2.4   What distinguishes developed, less developed, and newly industrializing economies?

2.5   Describe the International Monetary Fund's balance-of-payments accounting system.

2.6   How would an economist categorize systems for trading foreign exchange? How would the IMF make this classification? In what ways are these the same? How are they different?

2.7 Describe the Bretton Woods agreement. How long did the agreement last? What forced its collapse?

2.8 What factors contributed to the Mexican peso crisis of 1995 and to the Asian crises of 1997?

2.9 What is moral hazard, and how does it relate to IMF rescue packages?

PROBLEM

2.1 Update the history of the international monetary system (from Section 2.4) to the present. Have any new international treaties been signed? What currency or market crises have hit since the Asian contagion of 1997?

SUGGESTED READINGS

The 1987 global stock market crash is chronicled in

Richard Roll, "The International Crash of October 1987," *Financial Analysts Journal* 44 (September/October 1988), pp. 19–35.

Globalization and the role of the World Bank and the IMF are discussed in

Joseph Stiglitz, *Globalization and Its Discontents* (New York: Norton, 2002).

The International Financial Environment

part two

International Financial Markets

chapter 3

Overview

Toto, I've a feeling we're not in Kansas anymore.

Dorothy, *The Wizard of Oz*

At the center of the international financial markets is a set of commercial banks that make markets in foreign exchange and Eurocurrency deposits and loans.

- The foreign exchange market allows one currency to be exchanged for another.
  - The spot market is a market for immediate exchange of currencies.
  - The forward market is a market for future exchange of currencies.

- The Eurocurrency market is a market in bank deposits and loans that allows funds to be borrowed or invested over time within each currency.

This chapter describes the national and international financial markets in foreign exchange, Eurocurrencies, stocks, bonds, and derivatives, as well as the global network of commercial banks and financial exchanges that link these markets.

3.1 • FINANCIAL MARKETS

Characteristics of Financial Markets

Financial markets are markets for financial (as opposed to real) assets or liabilities. There are many ways to classify financial markets, each reflecting an important dimension of financial markets.

Perhaps the most important characteristic of a financial asset is its liquidity. **Liquidity** refers to the ease with which you can capture an asset's value. Liquid assets can be quickly converted into their cash value. Large publicly traded corporations in the United States enjoy a relatively liquid stock market. Many individuals and institutions participate in this market, and the market price of a share of stock can be quickly converted into cash. In contrast, it is much more difficult to sell a privately-held local business to a new owner. With few potential buyers, owners must shop around and often settle for much less than they think the company is worth.

> Liquidity is the ease of exchanging one asset for another of equal value.

Figure 3.1 displays another possible categorization of financial assets and markets. A dimension along which financial assets vary is according to maturity:

- **Money markets** are markets for financial assets and liabilities of short maturity, usually considered to be less than one year.

- **Capital markets** are markets for financial assets and liabilities with maturities greater than one year.

> Money markets are short term; capital markets are long term.

For many financial assets, the difference between short term and long term is an arbitrary distinction. In the domestic bond market, a 30-year Treasury bond is a long-term financial asset and is traded in the capital market at the time of its issue. But when a Treasury bond is three months from expiration, it is technically classified as a short-term instrument and is priced by market participants in the same way that 3-month Treasury bills are priced.

Despite the apparently arbitrary classification of financial markets according to maturity, the distinction is important because market participants tend to gravitate toward either short- or long-term instruments. Bond investors match the maturities of their assets to those of their liabilities, and so have strong maturity preferences. Commercial banks tend to lend in the short- and intermediate-term markets to offset their short- and

FIGURE 3.1
Financial Market Categories

Intermediated markets		
	Money markets	**Capital markets**
Internal	Domestic savings accounts Lines of credit with a domestic borrower	Domestic certificates of deposit (CDs) Long-term commercial loans to domestic borrowers
External	Eurocurrency deposits or loans	Long-term commercial loans to foreign borrowers

Nonintermediated (direct) markets		
	Money markets	**Capital markets**
Internal	Short-term commercial paper (CP) issued in domestic markets	Stocks or bonds issued in domestic markets
External	Eurocommercial paper (ECP) issued in international markets	Stocks issued in foreign markets Foreign bonds issued in foreign markets Eurobonds

intermediate-term liabilities. Life insurance companies and pension funds invest in long-term assets to counterbalance their long-term obligations. The distinctions between capital and money markets are also often encoded in national regulations governing public securities issues.

> External markets are outside national borders.

Financial markets also can be categorized according to whether or not they are regulated by a single country:

- Financial contracts in an **internal market** are issued in the currency of a host country, placed within that country, and regulated by authorities in that country.
- Financial contracts in an **external market** are placed outside the borders of any single country and can be regulated by more than one country or by none at all.

This is an important distinction because it determines regulatory jurisdiction; that is, the regulatory authority (e.g., a national government) with jurisdiction over the market.

Finally, financial markets can be classified according to whether or not a financial intermediary, such as a commercial bank, stands between borrowers and savers:

- In an **intermediated market**, a financial institution channels loanable funds from individual and corporate savers to borrowers.
- In a **nonintermediated** (or **direct**) **market**, borrowers such as governments or large corporations issue securities directly to the public without using a financial intermediary.

Nearly all borrowers—individuals, businesses, governments, and supranational institutions such as the World Bank—use financial intermediaries to some extent. Nations differ on the extent to which intermediated debt is augmented by debt issues sold directly to the public.

Commercial Banks as Financial Intermediaries

Financial intermediaries borrow from individuals and institutions with a desire to save and lend to those with a need for funds. Commercial banks are the most important financial intermediary in nearly every country. Commercial banks are active in the short- and intermediate-term deposit and loan markets. Banks and related financial institutions (thrifts, savings and loans) are also active in the long-term financial market through real estate loans. Insurance companies also play a role in long-term financial markets in some developed economies.

For domestic banks, the bulk of their transactions are with local depositors and borrowers in an internal credit market. Internal credit markets are markets for deposits and loans by local or domestic residents; hence, they are governed by the rules and institutional conventions of local authorities. These deposits and loans can be denominated in the domestic currency or in foreign currency. A U.S. resident depositing dollars with a U.S. bank is an example of an internal market transaction. Another example of an internal market transaction is a Korean subsidiary of a Japanese firm borrowing Korean won from a Korean bank. Local authorities regulate each of these transactions. Because of their foreign exchange activities, international banks are well positioned to serve as financial intermediaries in multiple credit markets.

> Internal credit markets are regulated by domestic authorities.

The need for international banking activities arose as commercial banks followed their local customers into foreign markets. As cross-border investment became more common early in this century, large banks developed financial services that facilitated the overseas trade of their customers. In addition to commercial credit, commercial banks provide a variety of ancillary services including collection, cash management, trade financing, market-making in foreign exchange and interest rate and currency derivatives, and risk management services.

External credit markets trade deposits and loans that are denominated in a single currency but are traded outside the borders of the country issuing that currency. Because external credit markets grew up in Europe, they are referred to as **Eurocurrency markets**. Dollar-denominated deposits held in a country other than the United States are called **Eurodollars**. As an example of a Eurodollar transaction, a Swiss bank with a branch in London might accept a dollar deposit from a Belgian dentist. Eurocurrency markets remain relatively unencumbered by government regulation because the government issuing the currency has no direct jurisdiction over the deposit, the lending bank, or the depositor.

> Eurocurrencies trade in an external credit market.

Figure 3.2 illustrates the linkages between the domestic credit markets of the United Kingdom, Japan, and the United States. The Eurocurrency markets provide competitively priced interest-bearing deposits and loans in each currency. The interbank spot and forward foreign exchange markets allow currencies to be exchanged at competitive rates. Because of the close association between the foreign exchange and Eurocurrency markets, international banks usually conduct trading in these markets out of the same trading room.

FIGURE 3.2
Linkages Between Credit and Currency Markets

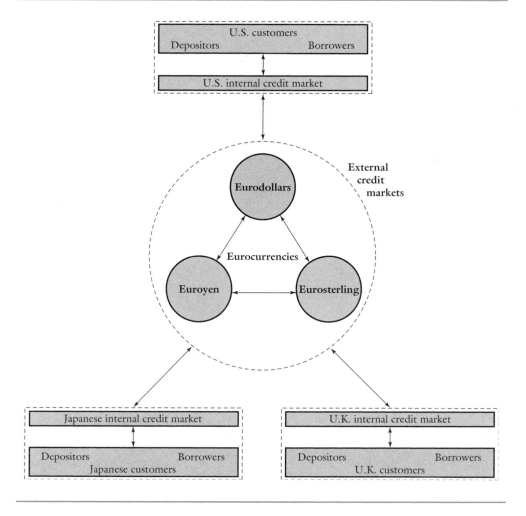

Table 3.1 ranks the world's largest banks by the percentage of their business conducted outside their country of incorporation. These globally diversified banks differ from domestic banks in the proportion of their business conducted with counterparties from other countries. Some of these global banks are relatively small. For example, American Express Bank has the highest percentage of international assets but is only the 456th largest bank worldwide. Others, such as UBS (Union Bank of Switzerland), are among the world's largest and most recognizable banks. HSBC Holdings (Hong Kong and Shanghai Banking Corporation), the world's 3rd largest bank, expanded during the 1800s and 1900s along with the growth of trade between the United Kingdom and Asia, with Hong Kong as the conduit. As international trade grew, so did HSBC's overseas lending and foreign exchange operations.

TABLE 3.1
World's Top Banks in International Activity

Rank		World ranking	Bank	Home country	Percent of assets overseas		Total assets ($ billions)	
2002	1996	2002			2002	1996	2002	1996
1	–	456	American Express Bank	United States	86.2	–	11.6	–
2	3	21	UBS	Switzerland	84.4	71.0	747.2	324.8
3	–	156	Arab Banking Corporation	Bahrain	83.5	–	26.6	–
4	2	36	Credit Suisse Group	Switzerland	79.6	74.2	609.6	389.3
5	1	70	Standard Chartered	United Kingdom	69.6	74.3	107.4	71.6
6	19	12	Deutsche Bank	Germany	66.6	46.5	809.2	569.9
7	14	22	ABN-AMRO	Netherlands	65.2	49.4	526.4	341.4
8	8	15	BNP Paribas	France	63.5	55.6	446.4	290.7
9	–	255	Investec	South Africa	63.3	–	23.3	–
10	–	56	KBC	Belgium	57.9	–	190.3	–
11	–	203	RZB Group	Austria	57.9	–	39.3	–
12	6	3	HSBC Holdings	United Kingdom	56.7	62.8	687.2	401.7
13	–	25	ING Bank	Netherlands	56.1	–	390.7	–
14	15	93	Allied Irish Banks	Ireland	52.6	48.8	78.3	43.9
15	11	163	Erste Bank	Austria	50.7	51.0	75.8	69.2
16	–	24	Santander Central Hispano	Spain	45.1	–	315.6	–
17	–	45	Scotiabank	Canada	43.5	–	184.6	–
18	18	46	National Australia Bank	Australia	43.4	46.7	205.1	124.0
19	–	105	Bank of Ireland Group	Ireland	41.5	–	72.0	–
20	–	38	Fortis Bank	Netherlands	40.8	–	333.1	–
21	23	33	Banco Bilbao Vizcaya	Spain	40.0	43.6	272.5	131.1
22	–	390	Anglo Irish Bank Corp	Ireland	38.9	–	19.1	–
23	–	47	Royal Bank of Canada	Canada	38.5	–	236.4	–
24	–	463	Bank of Cyprus	Cyprus	38.4	–	11.5	–
25	–	64	Toronto-Dominion Bank	Canada	38.3	–	173.2	–
26	24	43	Dresdner Bank	Germany	37.9	43.0	446.5	355.6
27	–	57	C.I.B.C.	Canada	37.4	–	170.7	–
28	21	61	Bank of Montreal	Canada	37.3	44.0	157.6	123.4
29	–	74	Bank of New York	United States	36.5	–	81.0	–
30	–	97	State Street Corporation	United States	35.5	–	69.9	–

Source: *The Banker*, February 1997 (p. 41) and February 2003 (p. 25).

Market Update

The New Basle Capital Accord

In 1988, the Bank for International Settlements convened a meeting of central bankers in Basle, Switzerland, and agreed upon a set of regulations governing the capital adequacy of international banks. The **Basle Accord** required that international banks set aside equity capital equal to 8 percent or more of their risk-weighted assets (loans) as a protection against credit risk. Banks with less than an 8 percent cushion had to raise capital or shed assets. The accord strengthened and harmonized international banking regulations, so that most big banks are much better capitalized today than they were in 1988.

Under the Basle Accord, banks allocate risk weights to their assets. A risk weight of 100 percent means that an asset is fully exposed to credit risk and requires an offsetting equity reserve of 8 percent. A risk weight of 25 percent requires a capital reserve of 2 percent. In the 1988 accord, risk weights depend on the type of borrower (government, bank, or corporate).

In January 2001, a New Basle Capital Accord was proposed to replace the 1988 accord. The "New Accord" is scheduled for implementation in 2004 and more broadly assesses the various risks faced by banks. The three elements or "pillars" of the New Accord are

- *Minimum capital requirements* that refine the framework set out in the 1988 accord
- *Supervisory review* of capital adequacy and internal assessment processes by regulatory bodies (such as the Federal Reserve Board in the United States)
- *Market discipline* through effective accounting disclosure requirements to encourage sound banking practices

> Under the Basle Accord, international banks retain equity capital according to their risk.

Under the New Accord, risk weights are based on external credit ratings (e.g., S&P or Moody's) or a bank's own internal ratings of credit risk.

Most international banks assess credit risk and identify risk-weighted assets using a method called value-at-risk. **Value-at-risk (VaR)** estimates potential losses with a certain level of confidence and over a certain time horizon due to adverse price movements in an underlying asset. For example, there might be a 5 percent probability of losing more than 20 percent of a loan portfolio's value over the next year. VaR has many critics because it fails to measure the probability or extent of losses beyond the 20 percent loss threshold. Nevertheless, it has become the accepted standard in the banking industry and forms the basis of bank capital adequacy requirements.

In response to the New Basle Accord's call for increased accounting disclosure, many financial institutions are beginning to report VaR numbers in their financial reports. There is preliminary evidence that these disclosures are informative in that they predict subsequent variability in revenues.[1]

The New Accord also requires an assessment of *operational risk*; that is, the risk of loss due to inadequate or failed processes, people or systems, or from external events. Operational risk includes such difficult-to-assess risks as computer failure, human error, and fraud. Although these risks are critical to a bank's health, operational risk assessment is still in its infancy.

---

1 Jorion, "How Informative Are Value-at-Risk Disclosures?" *Accounting Review* (2002).

Clearing and Settlement Mechanisms for International Transactions

Transfers between international financial institutions are accomplished through a cooperative network of telecommunication lines leased by the **Society for Worldwide Interbank Financial Telecommunications**, called **SWIFT**. SWIFT is an industry-owned cooperative with over 3,000 members from commercial banking, securities and asset management, and insurance. SWIFT ensures low-cost, secure transmission of interbank messages and funds transfers.

3.2 • THE FOREIGN EXCHANGE AND EUROCURRENCY MARKETS

The foreign exchange and Eurocurrency markets are linked through a set of international parity conditions that are discussed in Chapter 5. This section introduces these important international markets.

The Foreign Exchange Market

The foreign exchange market is largely an interbank market that deals in spot and forward currency transactions:

- In the **spot market**, trades are made for immediate delivery.
- In the **forward market**, trades are made for future delivery according to an agreed-upon delivery date, exchange rate, and amount.

Currencies are traded in spot and forward markets.

In the interbank currency market, spot transactions are settled within two business days for most currencies. Forward transactions are settled on the agreed-upon delivery date. The interbank market also trades currency swaps, which are forward market transactions involving more than one delivery date.

The foreign exchange market is at the heart of international trade and finance. The market links financial markets in various currencies. It is also an important tool for managing the currency risks faced by individuals, financial institutions, and multinational corporations. For these reasons, the foreign exchange market is discussed at length in Chapter 4.

The Eurocurrency Market

Eurocurrencies trade in an external market.

The Eurocurrency market, an external credit market in bank deposits and loans, resides outside the borders of the countries issuing the currencies in which the deposits or loans are denominated. Eurodollars, for example, are dollar-denominated deposits residing in non-U.S. banks. Similarly, the Eurosterling market resides outside the United Kingdom.

Eurocurrencies are generally in the form of variable-rate time deposits with maturities of less than one year. There is an active secondary market for large-denomination Eurocurrency certificates of deposit (CDs), with face values of $100,000 and up. These credit markets are operated outside of, or parallel to, national credit markets.

The primary function of the Eurocurrency markets, as with any market in deposits and loans, is to bring together savers and borrowers to transfer purchasing power over time. By acting through a financial intermediary, savers with excess funds can invest them profitably with borrowers willing to pay for the use of the funds.

Although Eurocurrency markets are conducted alongside national credit markets, they are not subject to the rules that governmental agencies impose on national credit markets. This allows the Eurocurrency markets to avoid domestic interest rate regulations (such as caps or floors), reserve requirements, and other barriers to the free flow of capital. Combined with high volume and high liquidity in the Eurocurrency markets, the absence of government restrictions means that Eurocurrency borrowing and lending rates are at least as favorable as domestic borrowing and lending rates. Corporations and financial institutions with access to the Eurocurrency market can typically obtain lower cost funds or store funds at higher interest rates than is possible in domestic credit markets.

The Eurocurrency market originated in London during the late 1950s. At that time, the Soviet Union held dollar-denominated deposits in U.S. banks to finance trade with the United States. The Soviet government was reluctant to leave these deposits in U.S. banks because of fear that the deposits would be frozen or seized for political reasons. Yet they did not want to convert these deposits into other currencies and expose themselves to fluctuations in the value of the dollar. The Soviet government requested that London banks hold dollar-denominated deposits. London bankers were only too happy to oblige, because the dollar-denominated deposits allowed them to make dollar-denominated loans to their customers and solidified their dominance of the international banking industry.

Table 3.2 lists outstanding Eurocurrency contracts for the dollar, euro, and pound sterling markets by country of issuer. Dollars and euros are by far the most active currencies,

TABLE 3.2
The World's Largest Eurocurrency Markets, by Country of Issuer (in U.S. dollars)

Rank	Eurodollar issuers		Euro issuers		Eurosterling issuers	
1	United States	805,797,151	Germany	584,898,553	Great Britain	72,861,488
2	Supranationals	98,201,016	France	169,601,599	Supranationals	30,385,692
3	Germany	78,953,610	United States	124,512,541	Germany	26,587,503
4	Mexico	44,155,424	Netherlands	79,476,899	United States	17,761,061
5	Great Britain	32,095,099	Great Britain	59,727,480	France	10,231,898
6	Netherlands	29,727,501	Supranationals	57,874,002	Netherlands	6,291,495
7	Italy	28,194,806	Spain	49,919,138	Italy	2,352,878
8	Japan	26,093,719	Italy	30,576,678	Canada	1,317,039
9	France	20,892,986	Sweden	18,048,142	Switzerland	1,288,845
10	Canada	19,564,442	Austria	10,472,872	Japan	1,036,576
11	Switzerland	16,779,787	Canada	10,148,028	Cayman Islands	804,604
12	Spain	16,715,132	Japan	8,957,821	Austria	723,639
13	Austria	12,084,301	Switzerland	8,205,901	Norway	645,445
14	Malaysia	7,780,693	Belgium	7,467,394	Spain	619,873
15	South Korea	5,985,336	Portugal	7,314,264	Finland	617,750
16	Sweden	5,761,833	Mexico	6,031,572	Poland	409,930
17	Singapore	4,415,527	Denmark	5,467,549	Australia	363,308
18	Hong Kong	3,802,508	Australia	4,668,701	Belgium	306,748
19	Finland	3,204,261	Finland	4,129,309	Portugal	212,030
20	Qatar	3,024,166	Poland	3,593,878	Ireland	117,810
	Others	18,501,125	Others	25,936,040	Others	0
	Total	1,281,730,423	Total	1,277,028,361	Total	174,935,609

* ECB is the European Central Bank.

** Supranationals include the IMF, the World Bank, and other international agencies.

Source: Compiled from MSCI Eurocurrency credit indexes (January 2003), http://www.msci.com.

with over one trillion dollars worth of Eurocurrencies outstanding in each currency. This is approximately the same as the amount of domestic deposits in the corresponding internal markets in dollars and euros. Eurocurrency markets are active in other major currencies as well. Domestic issuers dominate these markets, with the Eurosterling market being the most international.

3.3 • DOMESTIC AND INTERNATIONAL BOND MARKETS

Publicly traded bonds are an important source of capital for companies and governments. As shown in Figure 3.3, debt comprises about 70 percent of all publicly traded debt and equity securities in the world. National governments have issued $6.7 trillion or 18 percent of the $37 trillion in outstanding debt. Corporations and financial institutions issued the remaining $30.3 trillion.

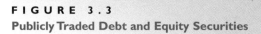
International bonds are traded outside the country of the issuer.

Bond issues can be categorized according to whether they are sold into domestic or international markets. International bonds can be further categorized as foreign bonds, Eurobonds, or global bonds.

- **Domestic bonds** are issued by a domestic company, traded within that country's internal market, and denominated in the functional currency of that country.

- **International bonds** trade outside the country of the issuer in an internal market, an external market, or both.
  - **Foreign bonds** are issued in an internal (domestic) market by a foreign borrower, denominated in domestic currency, marketed to domestic residents, and regulated by domestic authorities.
  - **Eurobonds** are denominated in one or more currencies, but are traded in external bond markets outside the borders of the countries issuing those currencies.
  - **Global bonds** trade in the Eurobond market as well as in one or more national bond markets.

Borrowers in the international markets include multinational corporations, national governments and their agencies, and supranational organizations such as the World

FIGURE 3.3
Publicly Traded Debt and Equity Securities

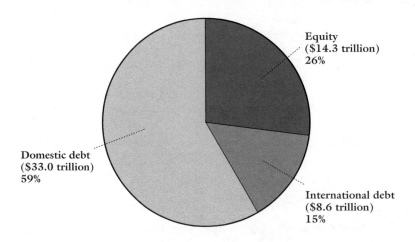

Equity ($14.3 trillion) 26%

Domestic debt ($33.0 trillion) 59%

International debt ($8.6 trillion) 15%

Source: Debt data from the Bank for International Settlements (December 2002).
Equity data estimated from the FTSE world index (December 2002).

Bank. These borrowers sometimes find their financing costs are lower in international markets than in their domestic market because of disequilibria in the international parity conditions, such as a cross-market difference in real borrowing costs. Borrowers from Emu-zone countries raise funds in the Eurobond market, most commonly in euros but also in dollars, yen, or pounds. Smaller borrowers from non-EU countries usually find borrowing costs are lower in their domestic bond market than in the international market, because of the higher information costs faced by international investors.

Table 3.3 and Figures 3.4 and 3.5 display the largest issuers into the domestic and international bond markets, based on data from the Bank for International Settlements (BIS). The $15.377 trillion U.S. market is by far the largest domestic bond market. Domestic bond markets in the 12 Emu-zone countries have a combined value of $5.226 trillion, slightly behind Japan's $5.847 trillion market. In the international bond market, issuers from North America ($2.433 trillion) and the 12 Emu-zone countries ($2.544 trillion) have each issued 34 percent of the entire market. The next

http://www.bis.org

TABLE 3.3
World's Largest Domestic and International Debt Markets, by Country of Issuer (in U.S. dollars)

Rank	Domestic debt	$ billions	Rank	International debt	$ billions
1	United States	15,834.1	1	United States	2749.3
2	Japan	6,663.5	2	Germany	1462.6
3	Germany	1,689.2	3	United Kingdom	793.7
4	Italy	1,587.6	4	France	511.3
5	France	1,215.3	5	Supranational agencies	438.5
6	United Kingdom	996.8	6	Netherlands	429.7
7	Canada	605.5	7	Italy	370.2
8	Spain	422.7	8	Japan	258.2
9	Netherlands	410.3	9	Spain	246.0
10	China	406.5	10	Canada	241.4
11	Belgium	360.1	11	Belgium	185.6
12	Korea South	350.5	12	Australia	138.2
13	Brazil	269.0	13	Sweden	131.1
14	Denmark	264.0	14	Switzerland	127.5
15	Australia	196.6	15	Austria	120.7
16	Switzerland	188.6	16	Argentina	83.7
17	Sweden	186.7	17	Brazil	70.4
18	Austria	175.8	18	Ireland	68.7
19	India	142.1	19	Portugal	67.1
20	Greece	114.8	20	Mexico	65.7
21	Mexico	89.4	21	South Korea	55.3
22	Turkey	81.1	22	United States	51.6
23	Portugal	80.1	23	Finland	50.8
24	Malaysia	78.2	24	Norway	49.6
25	Norway	75.1	25	Greece	49.3
	All countries	33,014.8		All countries	9,218.9

Source: Bank for International Settlements. Domestic debt values are as of June 2002. International debt values are as of December 2002. Includes issues by financial institutions, governments and government agencies, and corporations.

FIGURE 3.4
The World's Domestic Debt Markets by Issuer, $ Billions

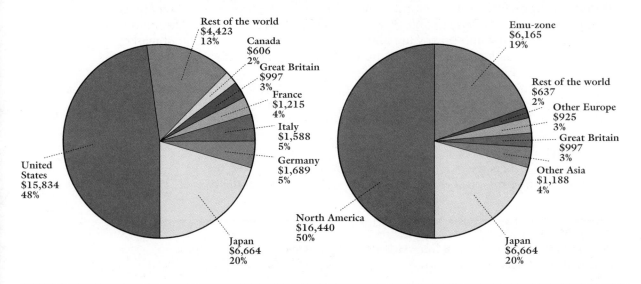

Source: Bank for International Settlements (December 2002).

FIGURE 3.5
The World's International Debt Markets by Issuer, $ Billions

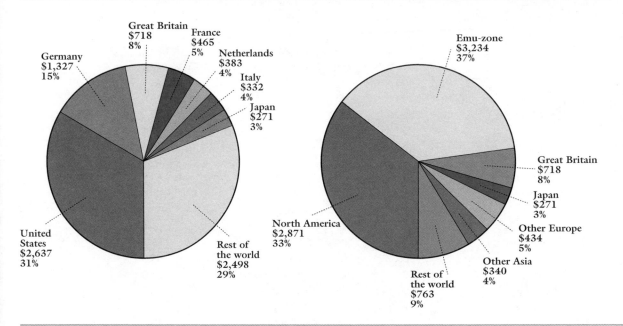

Source: Bank for International Settlements (December 2002).

most active issuers in the international market are from the United Kingdom ($623 billion) and Japan ($257 billion).

Domestic Bonds and Domestic Bond Markets—"When in Rome . . . "

In most national bond markets, the most prominent bonds are domestic bonds. Because they are issued and traded in an internal market, domestic bonds are regulated by the domestic government and are traded according to local conventions. Domestic investors typically face lower information costs than international investors in domestic firms because of their geographic proximity to the issuer. Lower information costs can lead to higher prices and lower capital costs for domestic issuers.

> Domestic bonds are regulated by the domestic government.

In the United States, government bonds are traded in an over-the-counter (OTC) market through commercial and investment banks. Corporate bonds are traded over the counter by commercial banks as well as on the bond-trading floor of the New York Stock Exchange. In other national markets, the publicly traded bonds of major corporations are either exchange-listed or traded over the counter by commercial and investment banks.

The "GMAC zr 15" listed as a domestic bond in Figure 3.6 is a zero-coupon dollar-denominated bond issued by General Motors Acceptance Corporation, maturing in the year 2015, and traded on the bond-trading floor of the New York Stock Exchange. The U.S. Securities and Exchange Commission regulates these domestic, internal, public (nonintermediated) bonds.

In most bond markets, prices are quoted as price-plus-accrued-interest. Bonds quoted with this convention do not necessarily fall in price on an ex-payment date. This makes it easier to compare prices across bonds with different coupons and payment dates. Bonds that do not conform to this convention include U.K. government bonds ("gilts") with a maturity of more than five years and some convertible and index-linked bonds. These bonds are quoted with coupons attached and fall in price on an ex-payment date in much the same way that common stock prices fall on an ex-dividend date. National bond markets vary along several other dimensions, some of which are listed in Table 3.4.

Registered Versus Bearer Issues. Corporate and government bonds in Canada, Japan, and the United States are issued as **registered bonds**. In countries requiring that bonds be issued in registered form, each issuer maintains a record of the owners of its bonds. Registration facilitates the calculation and payment of accrued interest, but it also imposes a recordkeeping burden on bond issuers. Registered bonds typically pay quarterly or semiannual interest.

FIGURE 3.6
Bond Market Taxonomy from a U.S. Perspective

Domestic bonds	International bonds	
	Foreign bonds	**Eurobonds**
GMAC zr 15 (NYSE)	Toronto Dominion 6.45 09 (U.S. OTC)	FNMA 7.25 30 (non-U.S. OTC)

TABLE 3.4
Bond Market and Eurocurrency Conventions

Type of bond	Ownership	Coupon payments	Day count
Domestic and foreign bonds			
Canada	Registered	Semiannual	Actual/365
Japan	Registered	Semiannual	Actual/365
France legacy bonds*	Bearer	Annual	Actual/365
Germany legacy bonds*	Bearer	Annual	30/360
Switzerland	Bearer	Semiannual	30/360
United Kingdom	Bearer	Semiannual	Actual/365
United States	Registered	Semiannual	30/360 - corporate bonds Actual/365 - Treasury bonds
Euro-denominated bonds	Bearer	Semiannual or annual	Actual/Actual
Eurobonds			
Fixed rate bonds	Bearer	Annual	30/360
Floating rate notes (FRNs)	Bearer	Quarterly or semiannual	Actual/360
Eurocurrencies			
e.g., LIBOR	Registered	Quarterly or semiannual	Actual/360

* Legacy bonds are domestic bonds that were issued before the 1999 introduction of the euro.

The convention in European countries is to use bearer bonds. **Bearer bonds** are not registered and can be redeemed by the holder. The principle advantage of bearer bonds is that they retain the anonymity of the bondholder. This can be impor-

> Bearer bonds retain the anonymity of the owner.

tant to some investors, such as those wishing to evade the local tax authorities. The bearer is assumed to be the legal owner of the bond, so bondholders must ensure that they do not lose the bonds or the bond coupons. Because it is inconvenient to present bond coupons for payment of interest, bearer bonds are usually issued with annual coupons.

Compounding and Yield Conventions. When bonds pay interest on a semiannual or quarterly basis, the U.S. convention is to multiply the periodic (semiannual or quarterly) yield times the number of compounding periods per year. For example, a 10 percent U.S. Treasury bond that pays 5 percent interest semiannually is quoted as paying 10 percent, which means 10 percent compounded semiannually. If the market price is 80 percent of par, then the effective periodic (semiannual) yield-to-maturity is the solution to

$$80 = \frac{5}{(1+i)^1} + \frac{5}{(1+i)^2} + \frac{5}{(1+i)^3} + \frac{105}{(1+i)^4}$$

or i = 11.518 percent per six months. This bond would be quoted in the United States with a yield of (2)(11.518%) = 23.036 percent compounded semiannually.

European bond dealers quote an **effective annual yield** that assumes annual com-

> Effective annual yields assume annual compounding.

pounding. For example, a 2-year bond paying 5 percent semiannually and selling at 80 percent of par value would be quoted as having an effective annual yield of $(1.11518)^2-1 = 0.24363$, or 24.363 percent per year. Effective annual yields make it easy to compare bonds with different payment schedules.

Bond yields in Japan are quoted according to a simple interest calculation that amortizes the bond's premium or discount to par value over the life of the bond:

$$\text{Yield} = \left(\text{Coupon rate} + \frac{100\% - \text{Price}}{\text{Years to maturity}}\right)\left(\frac{100\%}{\text{Price}}\right) \tag{3.1}$$

Consider a bond selling in the United States with a 10 percent coupon and semiannual payments (that is, 5 percent semiannually) with two years until maturity and selling at 80 percent of par value. A similar bond in Japan would be quoted as selling at a yield of $[0.10+(1.00-0.80)/2](1.00/0.80) = 0.25$, or 25 percent.

Day Count Conventions. Bond markets also differ in **day count** conventions that define the way in which interest accrues on the bond. Prices on U.S. Treasury notes and bonds are quoted as "Actual/365" assuming a 365-day year and interest that accrues according to the actual number of days that have passed since the most recent interest payment. Consider a Treasury bond with a 10 percent coupon. This bond pays 5 percent semiannually on June 30 and on December 31. If it is now February 6, then 36 days (January 1 through February 5) have elapsed since the last coupon interest payment. The price on this bond is quoted assuming the current bondholder is entitled to $0.05(36/182.5) \approx 0.00986$, or 0.986 percent of the principal as accrued interest.

> The day count defines the way in which interest accrues.

Corporate bonds in the Switzerland and the United States are quoted as "30/360" assuming a 360-day year with 30-day months. Under the 30-day convention, no interest accrues on the 31st of a month. A U.S. corporate bond paying 10 percent interest on a semiannual basis would be quoted on February 6 assuming the bondholder is entitled to 30 days of accrued interest from January plus 5 days of accrued interest from February for $0.05(35/180) \approx 0.00972$, or 0.972 percent of the principal as accrued interest. Accrued interest through the end of January would be $0.05(30/180) \approx 0.00833$, or 0.833 percent of the principal, since no interest accrues on January 31. The last day of February receives the last several days' worth of interest from February. Three days' interest is received on the 28th of February when this is the last day of the month. This simplification made it easy to calculate accrued interest across months before the advent of computers, as there were always 30 days of accrued interest during a month.

Foreign Bonds—Strangers in a Strange Land

Foreign bonds are issued in an internal (domestic) market by a foreign borrower, denominated in domestic currency, marketed to domestic residents, and regulated by domestic authorities. Foreign bonds are issued in the domestic currency and are priced according to domestic bond market conventions to make the bonds attractive to domestic residents. Foreign bonds are known as *Yankee bonds* in the United States, *Bulldog bonds* in the United Kingdom, *Samurai bonds* in Japan, and *Rembrandt bonds* in the Netherlands. By far the greatest value of foreign bonds is traded in Switzerland, followed by the United States and then Japan. In Emu-zone countries, foreign bonds have largely been supplanted by the euro-denominated Eurobond market.

> Foreign bonds are issued domestically by a foreign borrower.

The "Toronto Dominion 6.45 09" listed in the direct-internal-foreign bond category of Figure 3.6 is a dollar-denominated Yankee bond issued in the United States by Canada's Toronto Dominion Bank. This bond is sold over the counter through commercial and investment banks in the United States, pays a 6.45 percent semiannual coupon, and matures on January 15, 2009. This is a foreign bond issued in the U.S. internal market by a foreign borrower through a direct placement in the U.S. market.

For a foreign borrower to be able to place its debt at competitive prices, the issuer should be well known in the host country. One of the largest issuers of foreign bonds in the U.S. market is the World Bank, with more than 15 issues outstanding at maturities of 1 to 15 years. Less familiar names issue their bonds in the U.S. over-the-counter market, typically at lower prices and higher yields.

Eurobonds—Necessity Is the Mother of Invention

Eurobonds are issued and traded in the external bond market.[2] The "FNMA 7.25 30" bond issue in the Eurobond category of Figure 3.6 is a dollar-denominated bond issued by the Federal National Mortgage Association (called "Fannie Mae") with a 7.25 percent annual coupon and a maturity date in 2030. This Eurobond is issued directly to non-U.S. investors (in this case, by a U.S. borrower) in an external, public debt market.

> Eurobonds are external market bonds.

Origins of the Eurobond Market. As with many financial innovations, the Eurobond market was born and matured as borrowers and investors sought ways to circumvent government restrictions on cross-border capital flows. Governments constrain capital flows for a variety of economic and political reasons. Constraints on capital outflows are designed to protect the balance of payments from excessive capital outflows and to preserve the scarce long-term capital supplied by domestic savers. Constraints on capital inflows are designed to protect domestic businesses from foreign competition or ownership.

Two governmentally imposed barriers gave birth to the Eurobond market. In 1963, the United States levied an *interest equalization tax* on interest paid to U.S. investors by foreign borrowers. This put a tariff on non-U.S. borrowers attempting to issue foreign bonds in the U.S. market. Foreign bonds were not subject to interest withholding taxes within the United States, but the income tax on U.S. residents investing in foreign bonds made foreign bonds a costly way for foreign firms to raise dollar debt. Rather than go directly to the U.S. market, foreign borrowers began to issue dollar-denominated bonds in countries other than the United States. The interest equalization tax lasted until 1974, but by that time the Eurodollar bond market was firmly established.

The second barrier was an interest withholding tax that was imposed on domestic U.S. bonds through 1984. The interest withholding tax made it inconvenient for foreign investors to own dollar-denominated bonds. Eurobonds were an attractive alternative for investors wishing to avoid the interest withholding tax. When the United States dropped the withholding tax requirement on domestic bonds in 1984, the Eurodollar bond market and the domestic U.S. bond market became close substitutes for non-U.S. investors.

In the United States, the Securities Exchange Act of 1934 required that all new public securities issues be registered with the Securities and Exchange Commission (SEC). The SEC is responsible for ensuring that the registration statements accompanying the debt or equity issue disclose all material information about the issuer. There are no registration or disclosure requirements on private placements. The SEC has allowed a similar exemption on the Eurobonds of U.S. issuers that satisfy the SEC's criteria for private placement. This has helped to make Eurodollar bonds issued by U.S. firms competitive with those issued by foreign firms.

Once the benefits of Eurodollar bonds became apparent, Eurobonds denominated in other currencies soon followed. Several thousand Eurobond issues now trade in the secondary market. Borrowers include multinational corporations, commercial banks, national and regional governments, government agencies, and supranational organi-

---

2 Don't confuse the Eurobond market with the market for euro-denominated bonds. The Eurobond market trades euro-denominated bonds as well as Eurobonds denominated in other currencies.

zations such as the World Bank. The most common Eurobond currencies are the U.S. dollar, Emu-zone euro, British pound sterling, and Japanese yen.

The Market for Euro-Denominated Eurobonds. The 12 gold stars on the European Union flag represent the 12 founding members of the European Economic Community, the predecessor of the European Union (EU). Although there are now 15 EU members, only 12 (Austria, Belgium, Finland, France, Germany, Greece, Ireland, Italy, Luxembourg, the Netherlands, Portugal, and Spain) are currently participating in European monetary union (Emu) and the conversion of their national currencies to the euro. Three EU members (Denmark, Sweden, and the United Kingdom) opted out of Emu, although they may join at a later date. Plans call for an eventual enlargement of the European Union and Emu to include Poland, Hungary and the Czech Republic, and possibly Bulgaria and Romania.

The economic and financial power of EU countries provides liquidity to the euro-denominated Eurobond market. According to the OECD, the 15 members of the European Union had a total population of 380 million people and gross domestic product (GDP) of $8.5 trillion in 2002. For comparison, the United States had a population of 281 million and GDP of $10.4 trillion. Japan's population of 127 million produced $3.9 trillion in 2002 GDP.

The bonds of Emu-zone governments and supranational agencies converted to the euro on January 1, 1999, according to each currency's value in the European exchange rate grid. Most corporate bonds denominated in Emu currencies also were converted around this time. Each nation determined the legal basis for conversion of bonds trading in its own internal market. The European Commission established rules for the conversion of external market Eurobonds.

> Emu bonds converted to the euro in 1999.

European corporations are finding that euro-denominated Eurobonds offer attractive interest rates relative to bank financing, without the bother of a commercial bank looking over one's shoulder. Liquidity in the euro market is attracting borrowers from many countries that are not part of Emu, particularly from countries that are associated with Emu. In fact, the first euro-denominated bond was a $2 billion domestic bond issue by the government of Sweden, which is not participating in Emu.

Since the introduction of the euro, the vast majority of all new bond issues within Emu-zone countries have been Eurobonds. Indeed, the domestic bond markets have largely been replaced by Eurobonds in Emu countries. Eurobonds are also displacing commercial bank loans, the traditional source of capital for European businesses. A study by the Bank for International Settlements estimates that one-third of European banks' corporate loan business is being diverted to public debt and equity issues by the introduction of the euro. Many European commercial banks are expanding their investment banking activities as public issues displace their commercial lending business.

> Within Emu, public issues are displacing bank loans.

The Association of International Bond Dealers. Eurobond dealers are members of the *Association of International Bond Dealers (AIBD)*, a self-regulated industry group based in Zurich. No commissions are charged in the Eurobond market; dealers make their profit through the bid-ask spread. Transactions in the secondary Eurobond market are conventionally settled within seven days. About 75 percent of all secondary market Eurobond transactions are cleared through *Euroclear*, which is operated out of Brussels and also provides settlement and clearing for most European equity transactions. The remaining Eurobond transactions are cleared through *Clearstream*, based in Luxembourg. Exchange listing is often required by the home governments of the firms issuing Eurobonds. Luxembourg is a convenient site for clearing operations because many Eurobonds are listed on the Luxembourg exchange to satisfy the listing requirement.

Application

An Example of a Eurodollar Bond

On April 23, 2003, Ford Motor Credit Corporation (Reuters' ticker symbol "FMCR") issued a $1.5 billion euro-denominated Eurobond maturing on May 2, 2006, with an annual coupon of 5.5 percent. FMCR paid the investment bankers (Credit Lyonnais of France, Deutsche Bank of Germany, and UBS Warburg of Switzerland) a 0.2 percent flotation fee worth about $30 million. The issue was noncallable and initially priced at 99.696 percent of par. This bond had a long first coupon, with slightly more than one year before it paid its first interest payment.

Yield to maturity is the interest rate i that is the solution to

$$Price = \sum_t CF_t/(1+i)^t$$

where CF_t represents the bond's promised payments, Price is the price of the bond, and i is the promised yield to maturity. With (365+9)/365 = 1.02468 of a year until the first coupon payment, the yield to maturity of FMCR's Eurobond at the time of issue is the solution to

$$99.696 = 5.5/(1+i)^{1.02468} + 5.5/(1+i)^{2.02468} + 105.5/(1+i)^{3.02468}$$

or i = 5.563 percent. This was a risk premium of 277 basis points (2.77 percent) over the yield on similar euro-denominated bonds issued by the German government.

On the morning of May 8, 2003, Reuters reported a quote of "100.460 bid and 100.790 ask" from ABN Amro Bank of the Netherlands. ABN Amro was willing to buy the bond at 100.49 percent or sell the bond at 100.76 percent of par value. On May 8, there remained (365–6)/365 = 0.98356 of a year before the first coupon payment. An investor buying this Eurobond from ABN Amro would pay the bank's ask price of 100.790. The promised yield to maturity based on this price is the solution to

$$100.790 = 5.5/(1+i)^{0.98356} + 5.5/(1+i)^{1.98356} + 105.5/(1+i)^{2.98356}$$

or i = 5.242 percent. Interest rates had fallen in the two weeks since the bond's issue, and the price of the bond had correspondingly risen.

Global Bonds

Global bonds trade in the Eurobond market and in one or more internal markets.

A global bond is a bond that trades in the Eurobond market as well as in one or more national bond markets. To appeal to a global investor base, borrowers must be large investment-grade borrowers (typically AAA-rated) and must borrow in actively traded currencies.

The World Bank established this market with a series of dollar-denominated issues in the late 1980s. Until recently, global bonds were denominated in dollars to take advantage of high liquidity in the dollar market. Since 1999, global bonds are increasingly being issued in euros.

Matsushita Electric Industrial Company was the first corporate borrower to tap the global bond market. In 1992, Matsushita issued $1 billion of 10-year fixed-rate bonds

Market Update

Brady Bonds

As oil prices rose in the 1970s, commercial banks accepted large deposits from oil-producing countries and companies. Much of this new-found wealth was loaned to the governments of less developed countries (LDCs). As oil and other commodity prices fell in the early 1980s, many of these LDCs were unable to service their loans. Banks responded with a variety of innovations to salvage some value from their troubled loan portfolios.

One solution was to exchange defaulted LDC loans for a new type of bond called a *Brady bond*, named after U.S. Treasury Secretary Nicholas Brady. Working with the IMF and the World Bank, Brady helped restructure defaulted LDC loans into publicly traded bonds collateralized by U.S. zero-coupon bonds (to ensure payment of the principal) and with maturities of 10 to 30 years. Issuing countries include Argentina, Brazil, Bulgaria, Columbia, Mexico, Morocco, Nigeria, the Philippines, Poland, and Venezuela.

Brady bonds are sometimes connected to raw materials in the LDCs through warrants or other options. For example, Brady bonds from Mexico, Venezuela, and Nigeria often have warrants linked to oil prices that provide for additional interest payments if oil prices are above a certain level. Brady bonds were effective in relieving the interest burden of many LDCs while preserving some value for the commercial banks.

at 7.25 percent (41 basis points higher than the rate on 10-year U.S. Treasuries). Matsushita's original allocation was 40 percent to the domestic U.S. bond market, 40 percent to Europe, and 20 percent to the Asia/Pacific region. This initial allocation did not constrain where these bonds were traded in the secondary market, so subsequent trades could occur in domestic bond markets or in the Eurobond market.

3.4 • Domestic and International Stock Markets

A Tour of the World's Major Stock Exchanges

Table 3.5 lists the world's largest stock markets, along with their primary market index, Web site, and market capitalization. Figure 3.7 displays national stock market capitalizations as a percentage of world stock market value. The United States has by far the largest equity market, with a total market cap of about $8.00 trillion at the end of 2002. Japan was second at $1.52 trillion, and the United Kingdom was third at $1.46 trillion.

Figure 3.8 displays stock returns to four geographic regions from 1970 through 2002. Returns to the developed economies of Europe and North America have been relatively stable compared to the volatile returns in the Pacific region. Although the Pacific region outpaced Europe and North America throughout most of the period, Europe and North America actually ended the period in the lead after the *Asian contagion* of 1997–1998 eroded equity values in these markets. Sometimes the markets move together, such as in the aftermath of the technology bubble in 2000 and 2001. At other times, there is less co-movement among the markets. For example, the European and North American markets were largely unaffected by the Asian contagion of 1997–1998.

TABLE 3.5
World's Largest Stock Markets

Rank	Equity market	Primary indices	website	Market cap ($ billions)
1	United States	NYSE Composite (1800), S&P Global 100	http://www.nyse.com	7,988
2	Japan	TSE 300 & 1000, Nikkei-Dow (225)	http://www.tse.or.jp	1,517
3	Great Britain	FTSE 100 & All Share (750), Euronext 100	http://www.londonstockexchange.com	1,456
4	France	CAC 40, Euronext 100	http://www.euronext.com	581
5	Germany	DAX 100	http://deutsche-boerse.com	443
6	Switzerland	Swiss Market Index (SMI 30)	http://www.swx.com	440
7	Canada	S&P/TSX Composite (300)	http://www.tse.com	415
8	Netherlands	AEX (25), Euronext 100	http://www.euronext.com	364
9	Italy	MIB 30, Banca Commerziale (200)	http://www.borsaitalia.it	309
10	Australia	All Ordinaries (500), S&P/ASX 100	http://www.asx.com.au	249
11	Hong Kong	Hang Seng (33), All Ordinaries (750)	http://www.hkex.com.hk	189
12	Spain	IBEX 35, BCN Global 100	http://www.bolsamadrid.es, http://www.borsabcn.es	176
13	Sweden	SX-16, OMX (30)	http://www.stockholmsborsen.se	157
14	Belgium	BEL-20, Euronext 100	http://www.euronext.com	99
15	Finland	HEX-20	http://www.hex.fi	106
16	Mexico	IPC (36)	http://www.bmv.com.mx	83
17	South Africa	All Share (523)	http://www.jse.co.za	94
18	Denmark	KFX (21)	http://www.xcse.dk	62
19	Malaysia	KLSE Composite (100)	http://www.klse.com.my	49
20	Brazil	IBOVESPA (550)	http://www.bovespa.com.br	62
21	Singapore	Straits Times (45)	http://www.ses.com.sg	38
22	Norway	OBX (25)	http://www.ose.no	28
23	Ireland	ISEQ (76)	http://www.dublinstockexchange.com	26
24	Austria	ATX (22)	http://www.wienerboerse.at	20
25	New Zealand	NZSE 30	http://www.nzse.co.nz	18

Source: Market capitalization estimated from FTSE and MSCI indexes (January 2003).

North American Stock Markets. The largest stock market in North America is the New York Stock Exchange (NYSE). In addition to nearly 2,000 domestic stocks, the NYSE lists more than 300 foreign stocks from over 40 countries. The NYSE executes trades out of a trading floor in New York using dedicated market makers to facilitate trade in individual stocks.

The National Association of Securities Dealers Automated Quotation System (Nasdaq) is an electronic trading system that trades even more foreign shares than the NYSE. The Nasdaq is split into two tiers: a relatively liquid National Market System (NMS) in large stocks and a less liquid non-NMS market in smaller companies. Although the Nasdaq has surpassed the NYSE in trading volume, the value of companies listed on the two Nasdaq systems is still smaller than the value of stocks traded on the NYSE. On a busy day, the Nasdaq processes over 2,000 transactions per second. There are several smaller regional exchanges, most notably the American Exchange (AMEX), the Pacific Exchange, and the Philadelphia Stock Exchange.

The most active stock exchange in Canada is the Toronto Stock Exchange. Stocks are also traded on regional exchanges in Montreal, Alberta, Vancouver, and Winnipeg,

FIGURE 3.7
The World's Major National Stock Markets by Issuer, $ Billions

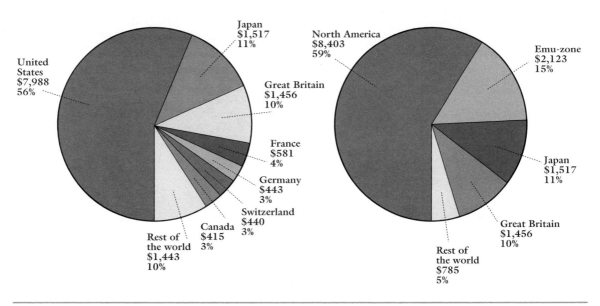

Source: Compiled from FTSE indices (December 2002)

and in the Canadian over-the-counter market. The total market capitalization in Canada was about $415 billion in December 2002.

Major European Stock Markets. Europe has more than 40 stock markets. The largest is the London Stock Exchange (LSE), which tracks U.K. equities with the FTSE (pronounced "foot-sie") 100 and FTSE

> London is an international money center.

All Shares 750 indices. The LSE also maintains a techMARK market for the shares of technology stocks and an AIM or Alternative Investment Market for the shares of smaller companies. The LSE plays a special role in international finance because of London's role as an international center for currency and Eurocurrency trading.

Euronext, an important new European exchange, was created in 2001 through an alliance of the Amsterdam, Brussels, and Paris exchanges. Euronext added the LSE to its alliance in 2001 and plans to add the exchanges from Helsinki (Finland), Lisbon (Portugal), Warsaw (Poland), and Luxembourg over the next few years. Euronext provides a common platform for trading stocks, bonds, derivatives, and commodities.

The next largest European stock market is the Frankfurt Stock Exchange in Germany, operated by Deutsche Börse AG. Other regional exchanges are in Switzerland at Zurich, Geneva, and Basle. There is also a Brussels-based counterpart of the Nasdaq called the Easdaq that trades the shares of small, growth-oriented firms.

The European stock exchanges actively compete for volume in both foreign and domestic stocks. Trading tends to gravitate toward the most liquid and operationally efficient market. Sometimes this is the LSE or Euronext, sometimes it is a national or local exchange, and sometimes shares are multiple-listed on several exchanges. European exchanges are actively establishing alliances with other exchanges around the world to harmonize trading rules and preserve market share. Such alliances are improving liquidity and efficiency and reshaping equity trading in Europe.

FIGURE 3.8
Returns to Regional Stock Market Indexes, Base = 100, in U.S. dollars

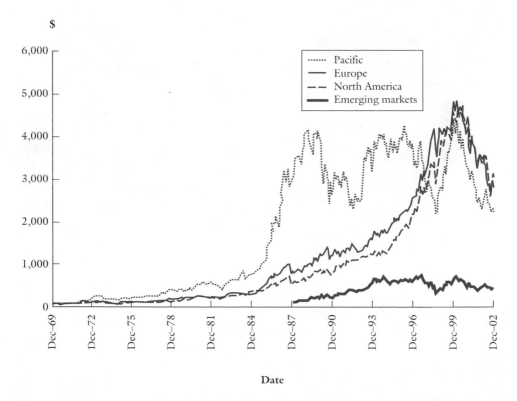

(Note: Most MSCI indices date back to December 31, 1969. The MSCI emerging market index was first quoted on December 31, 1987)

Source: MSCI indices.

Japanese Stock Markets. The largest stock exchange in Japan is the Tokyo Stock Exchange (TSE) in Tokyo, although the Osaka Stock Exchange near Kyoto is also one of the largest and most active exchanges in the world.[3] Smaller stock exchanges operate in Nagoya and Hiroshima. The value of stocks traded in Japan surpassed the value of stocks traded on the New York Stock Exchange in the late 1980s, but then fell behind the NYSE during a 1990–1991 crash in Japanese stock, bond, and real estate markets. The aftershocks of this collapse are still being felt in Japanese politics and consumer confidence, as well as in their markets and institutions.

The Japanese stock exchanges have had a difficult time attracting foreign companies because of controls on cross-border capital flows imposed by the Japanese government. Japan is deregulating its financial markets in a so-called "big bang" effort to make its financial markets competitive with other international markets. Changes are being implemented slowly and in stages, so Japan's big bang is really a series of "little pops" to introduce negotiated commissions, computerized trading, stock option trading, and off-exchange trading for large block and after-hours trade. The number of foreign com-

---

3 *Tokyo* and *Kyoto* translate literally as "Eastern capital" and "Western capital," respectively.

panies listed on the Tokyo Stock Exchange actually fell from 125 during Tokyo's hey-day in 1990 to fewer than 40 in 2002 as large multinational corporations delisted their shares from the exchange. The relative lack of competition from the Japanese exchanges has given smaller Asian stock markets room to grow.

Other Asian and Southeast Asian Stock Markets. Southeast Asia includes a num-ber of active stock markets in the "little dragons" or "tiger economies" of Hong Kong, Indonesia, Korea, Malaysia, Thailand, Taiwan, and Vietnam. Recently, China has witnessed rapid stock market growth in its evolution from a centrally planned to a mar-ket-driven economy. To stimulate this growth, the city of Shanghai built the world's largest trading floor and installed a computerized trading system.

Although many foreign companies delisted from the Hong Kong exchange prior to the 1997 transfer of power from the British to the Chinese, Hong Kong still trades the largest number of foreign stocks of any Asian market. Hong Kong is espe-cially renowned for trading the shares—called H-shares—of companies from the People's Republic of China. The performance of these shares has been highly volatile as investors respond to changes in the business climate within China. For example, Hong Kong's Hang Seng China Enterprises Index of H-shares fell from more than 2,000 in December 1994 to 685 on November 16, 1995, as the Chinese government removed several tax advantages available to shares listed in Hong Kong. Some Chinese companies have issued B-shares in Shenzhen and Shanghai that can be purchased by non-Chinese investors, as well as American depository receipts in the U.S. market.

Other Emerging Markets. The Bombay Stock Market in India trades a large number of shares, although foreign access to the market was restricted for many years by the Indian government. Around 7,000 companies are listed in India. About 3,000 of these are traded on a regular basis. The Bombay Stock Exchange trades over two-thirds of the value of India's stock market transactions. Foreign portfolio investment was prohibited until 1992, when up to 24 percent of the equity in individual companies was opened to registered foreign institutional investors. The largest companies from India were quick to take advantage of the relaxed limit on foreign ownership, and sold shares into inter-national markets in the form of global depository receipts. **Global depository receipts** are derivative securities representing ownership in the Indian company and are sold on stock exchanges outside India.

Stock markets in Africa, South America, Eastern and Central Europe, and the Asian continent are, with few exceptions, still in their infancy. The Johannesburg Stock Market in South Africa is by far the largest stock market on the African continent, with several globally competitive companies, including the diamond mining company, De Beers. The second largest African stock market is the Casablanca Stock Exchange in Morocco.

With the exception of the active stock market in Mexico City, Latin American stock markets are also relatively small, although there are large companies in Brazil (Telebras, Electrobras, Petrobras) and Argentina (YPF Energy, Telefonica de Argentina). The stock exchange in Mexico City is fairly large, with a December 2002 capitalization of about $83 billion.

Stock markets are gradually being established and nurtured in the former republics of the Soviet Union as these nations switch from centrally planned to market economies. Although Eastern and Central European stock markets have small capitalizations relative to developed markets and to local GDP, these local markets can be crucial to economic development.

Institutional Differences in Stock Exchange Operations

This section discusses institutional differences in the world's share trading systems.

Price Determination: Continuous Quotations Versus Periodic Call Auctions. The two most common methods for setting prices are a continuous quotation system and a periodic call auction. In a **continuous quotation system**, buy and sell orders are matched as they arrive. The market-making function might be provided by a *specialist* (a single individual with a monopoly on trading in particular shares) as on the NYSE, through *dealers* (called "jobbers" on the LSE) competing with each other and quoting bid and ask prices, or through automated rules as on electronic trading systems.

> Stock trading systems can be continuous or periodic.

A **periodic call auction** is sometimes used for less actively traded shares. For example, on the Paris Bourse active shares are traded continuously while less active shares are auctioned at intervals throughout the day. Call auctions are determined through a closed bid system in which all unfilled buy and sell orders are submitted to an exchange representative. The representative sets the price to accommodate the most orders and equate supply with demand. Trading is conducted after this price fixing as brokers attempt to match any remaining buy and sell orders. Other exchanges use an open outcry system. In Zurich, stocks are called for trading twice a day. On some exchanges (e.g., the NYSE), opening prices are determined through call auctions after which continuous trading takes place.

Spot and Forward Stock Market Transactions. The most common share-trading procedure is on a spot (or cash) basis, with transactions settled within a few days of trade. This is the procedure used on U.S., German, and Japanese exchanges. An alternative trading procedure is on a forward (or futures) basis, with transactions settled on a specified future date. London, Paris, and Zurich have some form of forward stock market.

> Stock trades are settled on a spot or forward basis.

Forward trades are settled biweekly in London and at the end of the month in Paris. Zurich allows more remote forward settlement dates. Stock exchanges that trade on a forward basis also trade on a spot basis or provide some mechanism for customers demanding cash transactions.

Like forward currency transactions, forward stock transactions are a form of credit instrument. Delivery is made either in cash (in a long stock trade) or in stock (in a short stock trade) on a specified future delivery date. The difference between the spot and forward price for a share of stock reflects the rate of interest (that is, the time value of money) in that currency. To ensure settlement, some form of deposit is usually required on forward stock transactions.

Some markets (including the United States) allow margin trading—buying stock on borrowed money—as another form of stock purchase on credit. The margin account is low risk to the broker because it is secured by stock, so interest rates on margin accounts can approach the level of short-term government interest rates.

International Differences in Regulations Governing Securities Issues

Securities Regulation in the United States. In the United States, the Securities Exchange Act of 1933 governs new securities issues, and the Securities Exchange Act of 1934 governs trade in outstanding securities. The Financial Services Modernization Act of 1999 deregulated the U.S. financial services industry, so that there is currently relatively open competition between commercial and investment banks, brokers, insurers, investment companies (pension and mutual funds), and other financial companies.

> The SEC regulates U.S. securities trading.

Market Update

The Growth of Online Brokers

Online brokers captured a large proportion of U.S. share trading during the 1990s. Online brokers offer discount brokerage services, sometimes charging less than $10 per trade. At the height of the dot.com bubble at the end of 1999, online trades accounted for nearly half of NYSE and Nasdaq transactions. The volume of online trading fell along with dot.com share prices. By 2002, online trading accounted for about one quarter of U.S. trades. The largest online brokers in the United States are Ameritrade, E-trade, and Charles Schwab.

In response to this fall in volume, online brokers are expanding their product lines with services such as bill payment, account management, tax preparation, mortgage lending, and trading in currencies and derivatives. They are also expanding the geographic scope of their operations through licensing agreements with foreign partners. Traditional brokers in many European and Asian countries are also beginning to offer online services.

http://www. ameritrade.com

http://www. etrade.com

The benefits of online trading include convenience and low service charges. Because of these attractions, online customers trade more frequently than the typical investor. The major risks of online trading include slow response during active markets and poor assurance that trades will be executed at market prices.

http://www. schwab.com

Companies issuing debt or equity securities to the public in amounts greater than $1.5 million are required to file a **registration statement** with the U.S. **Securities and Exchange Commission (SEC)** that discloses all relevant information and includes a financial history of the company, the state of existing businesses, and how the funds raised through the public offering are to be used. Once the registration statement is filed with the SEC, there is a waiting period of 20 days while the SEC reviews the accuracy and completeness of the registration statement. The issue is priced and sold after the waiting period.

The SEC's registration procedure applies to all securities issues with two exceptions:

- Loans maturing within nine months
- Private placements

The first exception to the SEC's registration requirement explicitly recognizes the difference between short-term money market and long-term capital market securities. This is why commercial paper in the United States is offered with maturities of nine months or less. Issues with maturities less than nine months must be accompanied by a brief **offering statement** rather than the full-fledged registration statement.

The second exception treats private placements differently from public securities issues. This has an enormous influence on the types of public disclosures that must be made and the type of control exerted by outside stakeholders in the firm. In the United States, **private placements** as defined by the Securities Act of 1933 conform to all five of the following conditions:

1. Shares are sold to large and sophisticated investors.
2. Shares are sold to only a few investors.
3. Investors must have access to information like that in a registration statement.

4. Investors are capable of sustaining losses.

5. Investors purchase the securities for their own portfolios and not for resale.

Securities issues satisfying these conditions are presumably placed with informed investors able to obtain accurate information on the issuer and to judge the merits of the investment for themselves.

If an offering does not conform to all five of these criteria, then it is a **public securities offering** and falls under the jurisdiction of the SEC. The U.S. securities laws require complete and accurate disclosure of all relevant information for public securities issues to ensure that investors are not fooled by exaggerated claims or outrageous promises. The securities laws do not ensure that an investment will meet its promised or expected return. Instead, the securities laws attempt to ensure that investors have enough information to judge the merits of a proposed investment for themselves.

Public debt and equity securities issues are organized by a **lead manager** (called a "book runner" in the United Kingdom) and perhaps one or more co-managers to share the risk of underwritten offerings. These securities issues are marketed by a **syndicate** (or selling group) familiar with the markets into which the placement will be made. The syndicate for securities issues placed into the U.S. dollar market typically includes a U.S. investment banker, such as Goldman Sachs or Merrill Lynch. Similarly, an issue sold to investors in the United Kingdom typically includes a U.K. investment banker, such as S.G. Warburg.

> Lead managers assume the risks of underwritten issues.

Securities Regulation in Japan. New public issues in Japan must be approved by the **Japanese Ministry of Finance (MoF)**. The waiting period in Japan is somewhat longer than in the United States, occasionally lasting several months. As in the United States, the issue is priced and sold after the waiting period. The Japanese government takes an active role in determining which companies are allowed to issue securities to the Japanese market and in regulating trade in these issues.

Commercial banks in Japan entered the investment banking and securities trading industries during 1995 as a part of Japan's "big bang" financial deregulation, although securities activities must be kept separate from banks' lending activities. Initially, five banks (Dai-Ichi Kangyo, Fuji, Sanwa, Sakura, and Mitsubishi) won approval to compete in the securities industry. Sumitomo Bank initially failed to win approval for its proposed investment banking subsidiary because the proposed name, Sumigin (a contraction of the characters for Sumitomo Bank), gave the appearance of linking Sumitomo's commercial and investment banking interests (the Japanese character for *gin* means "bank").

Securities Regulation in the European Union. The European Union is harmonizing securities regulations through the EU Capital Adequacy Directive and the EU Investment Securities Directive. Each of these directives came into force on January 1, 1996.

The **Capital Adequacy Directive (CAD)** specifies minimum standards governing the amount of market risk a bank or securities firm can take in relation to its capital base. The directive identifies specific methods for measuring the risk exposures of a financial institution or securities firm. The EU works with the Bank for International Settlements to ensure that EU capital adequacy regulations are consistent with the 1988 Basle Accord and its amendments. EU capital adequacy standards are likely to evolve as new methods for measuring risk exposures are developed and implemented by commercial and investment banks.

> The CAD sets capital adequacy requirements within the EU.

The **Investment Securities Directive (ISD)** allows investment services companies based in EU member states to operate in other EU countries so long as they have the approval of regulatory authorities in their home country. This so-called European "passport" has been available to EU financial institutions since 1993 through a series of EU banking directives. The ISD separately recognizes brokers/dealers and regulated securities exchanges as investment firms. Investment firms must satisfy a number of conditions to qualify:

1. The firm must meet the capital adequacy provisions of the CAD.
2. The firm's directors must be sufficiently experienced.
3. The firm must appropriately safeguard their clients' funds.

Regulated securities exchanges are similarly provided a European passport if they function regularly, have the regulatory approval of their home state, and satisfy the ISD's transparency provisions.

The individual states of the European Union are in various stages of implementation of these directives. Securities regulation is not yet fully harmonized in the European Union, and there remain differences in the regulations of individual EU states.

Global Equity Issues and Capital Market Integration

Stock Exchange Competition. Domestic stock markets often behave as though they have an obligation (if not a right) to conduct the bulk of trade in domestic stocks. When domestic companies have foreign owners, domestic residents feel they have less control over market forces, stock prices, local employment decisions, and ownership of their domestic industries. For this reason, many countries impose restrictions on foreign ownership of domestic assets.

With the increasing integration of the world's capital markets, national markets can no longer claim a monopoly on trade in their own national stocks. For example, company shares from all across the Middle East are traded in Riyadh, Saudi Arabia. Share trading in Europe has migrated toward the London Stock Exchange and Euronext because of the liquidity of these markets. Exchanges on the continent have fought back through innovation in trading rules and mechanisms. Trade in Germany is migrating away from the eight smaller exchanges toward the Frankfurt Stock Exchange, which accounts for more than 75 percent of German share trading. To remain viable, smaller German exchanges (e.g., Dusseldorf, Munich) are forming alliances with the Frankfurt exchange. Falling volume on the Tokyo Stock Exchange since the 1991 stock market crash in Japan has prompted an exodus of foreign listings from Tokyo to regional exchanges in other Southeast Asian countries, particularly to Hong Kong. This exodus, along with a growing demand for Japanese listings from companies based in mainland China, forced the Tokyo Stock Exchange to relax its rules governing foreign listings in 1994.

> Many MNCs list their shares on more than one stock exchange.

Stock exchanges in the United States are similarly under intense competition from foreign exchanges. Exchanges in the United States are disadvantaged by the SEC's disclosure and registration requirements, particularly the rule that foreign companies must prepare financial statements according to U.S. generally accepted accounting principles (GAAP). This requirement is intended to protect U.S. investors against false or misleading information. Foreign companies counter that the accounting conventions of their home countries provide enough information to investors and report it within the cultural context in which it occurs. The cost of translating financial statements into U.S. GAAP can be prohibitive. Largely because of this impediment, there has been little growth in the number of foreign shares traded on U.S. exchanges since the SEC's registration requirement was extended to the Nasdaq in 1983, despite the fact that the value of foreign shares held by U.S. residents has tripled since the mid-1980s. Competition between stock exchanges will continue to increase as barriers to cross-border portfolio investment erode.

The Benefits of Cross-Listing. Empirical studies confirm that global equity offerings can increase demand and benefit share prices. Studies of domestic equity issues generally document a slight decrease in share prices at the time of an issue. A domestic issue does not increase demand, and the price pressure effect of the increase in supply tends to depress the share price. Compounding this supply-demand effect is the information content of a new equity issue. In particular, managers are likely to issue equity rather than debt when they believe that their share prices are already overvalued.

In a study of U.S. firms cross-listing their shares in international markets, Chaplinsky and Ramchand document an increase in foreign shareholders and a 0.8 percent decrease in the adverse price reaction that typically accompanies equity issues.[4] Foerster and Karolyi find that foreign shares cross-listed in the United States actually increase in value by 1.2 percent at the time of the issue.[5] The benefits of global equity offerings are thus associated with the increase in the number international investors.

Capital Market Integration and Stock Exchange Convergence. Although each national market retains its unique character, markets are converging in a number of ways. The most visible change is in the way that trading information is processed and disseminated. Trades and prices in the major markets are now tracked by computer and relayed around the globe to other markets nearly instantaneously via satellite. Governments increasingly are relaxing barriers such as differential taxes and outright restrictions on cross-border financial transactions. Computer and telecommunications technologies have forged the segmented national markets of the early twentieth century into an increasingly integrated international network.

3.5 • DERIVATIVES MARKETS

Financial derivatives are traded on financial exchanges, as well as over the counter through commercial and investment banks. Derivatives are traded on a wide variety of financial prices including foreign exchange rates, interest rates, commodity prices, stock prices, and indices on these assets. The three main classes of derivatives are futures, options, and swaps.

- **Futures**—Like a forward contract, a futures contract is a commitment to exchange a specified amount of one asset for a specified amount of another asset at a specified time in the future.

Futures differ from forwards in that changes in the value of a futures contract are settled or *marked-to-market* periodically throughout the life of the contract. The gain or loss on a forward contract is settled at the maturity of the contract. Exchange-traded currency futures are marked-to-market on a daily basis, whereas OTC futures contracts can be tailored to fit the needs of the client.

- **Options**—A contract giving the option holder the right to buy or sell an underlying asset at a specified price and on a specified date.

The option writer (seller) holds the obligation to fulfill the other side of the contract.

---

4 Chaplinsky and Ramchand, "The Impact of Global Equity Offerings," *Journal of Finance* (2000).

5 Foerster and Karolyi, "The Effects of Market Segmentation and Investor Recognition on Asset Prices: Evidence from Foreign Stocks Listing in the United States," *Journal of Finance* (1999).

- **Swaps**—An agreement to exchange two liabilities (or assets) and, after a pre-arranged length of time, to re-exchange the liabilities (or assets).

Swaps bundle several forward contracts of various maturities into a single contract.

Derivatives are useful tools in managing exposures to financial price risks. They can be used to quickly and efficiently transform the nature of the firm's assets and liabilities; for example, from obligations in one currency to obligations in another. Because of their importance to multinational financial management, each of these derivative contracts is covered in depth in other chapters in the book.

> Derivatives are important risk management tools.

3.6 • SUMMARY

We began Chapter 3 with a description of the international activities of commercial banks in large financial centers. The trading rooms of these banks trade Eurocurrencies and spot and forward foreign exchange contracts in an active interbank market.

The Eurocurrency markets trade interest rate (deposit and loan) contracts denominated in a single currency but traded outside the borders of the country issuing that currency. The Eurocurrency markets are credit markets that operate outside of, or alongside, the national credit markets. These national and international interest rate markets are linked through the spot and forward foreign exchange markets. In the spot market, trades are made for immediate delivery. In the forward market, trades are made for future delivery at an agreed-upon date.

KEY TERMS

Basle Accord	internal and external markets
continuous quotation system versus periodic call auction	Japanese Ministry of Finance (MoF)
	lead manager and the syndicate
day count	liquidity
domestic and international bonds	offering statement
effective annual yield	options
EU Capital Adequacy Directive (CAD) and Investment Securities Directive (ISD)	private placements
	public securities offering
Eurobonds	registered and bearer bonds
Eurocurrency (e.g., Eurodollars and Euroyen)	registration statement
financial intermediaries	Securities and Exchange Commission (SEC)
financial (money and capital) markets	Society for Worldwide Interbank Financial Telecommunications (SWIFT)
foreign bonds	
futures	spot and forward markets
global bonds	swaps
global depository receipts	value-at-risk (VaR)
intermediated and nonintermediated (or direct) markets	

CONCEPTUAL QUESTIONS

3.1   What is the difference between a money market and a capital market?

3.2   Define liquidity.

3.3   What is the difference between intermediated and nonintermediated markets?

3.4   What is the difference between an internal and an external market?

3.5   What effect did the Basle Accord have on international banks?

3.6   What is the difference between spot and forward markets for foreign exchange?

3.7   What is the Eurocurrency market and what is its function?

3.8   What are the characteristics of a domestic bond? An international bond? A foreign bond? A Eurobond? A global bond?

3.9   What are the benefits and drawbacks of offering securities in bearer form relative to registered form?

3.10 What is the difference between a continuous quotation system and a periodic call auction?

3.11 What is the difference between a spot and a forward stock market?

3.12 Describe the characteristics of futures, options, and swaps.

PROBLEMS

3.1   In a bond market using a "30/360" price quotation convention, how many days' worth of accrued interest would fall on July 31?

3.2   In a bond market using an "actual/365" price quotation convention, how many days' worth of accrued interest would fall on July 31 if interest payments fall on June 30 and December 31?

3.3   In a bond market using a "30/360" price quotation convention, how many days' worth of accrued interest would fall on February 29 during a leap year?

3.4   It is the year 2004 and there are two years remaining until maturity on Matsushita Electric Industrial Company's 10-year global bonds issued with a coupon of 7.25 percent in 1996. The bonds pay a semiannual coupon of (7.25 percent)/2) = 3.625 percent. These bonds are nonamortizing, so they pay only interest until maturity, at which time they repay 100 percent of the principal amount. Matsushita's bonds are selling at par.
  a. What is the promised yield to maturity on this bond using the U.S. bond equivalent yield calculation?
  b. What is the promised yield to maturity on this bond using the German effective annual yield calculation?
  c. What is the promised yield to maturity on this bond using the Japanese bond yield calculation?

3.5   Refer to Matsushita's global bonds from problem 3.4. Suppose the bonds are selling at 101 percent of par value.
  a. What is the promised yield to maturity on this bond using the bond equivalent yield calculation of the United States?
  b. What is the promised yield to maturity on this bond using the German effective annual yield calculation?
  c. What is the promised yield to maturity on this bond using the Japanese bond yield calculation?

3.6 What is the relationship between the size of national stock markets in Table 3.6 and domestic bond markets in Table 3.3? Do nations with large stock markets also have large bond markets? Are there notable exceptions?

3.7 Access your library's electronic databases and search for announcements of recent alliances between stock exchanges. What new alliances have been announced since this book was printed?

SUGGESTED READINGS

The impacts of global equity offerings are examined in

Susan Chaplinsky and Latha Ramchand, "The Impact of Global Equity Offerings," *Journal of Finance* 55 (December 2000), pp. 2767–2789.

Stephen R. Foerster and G. Andrew Karolyi, "The Effects of Market Segmentation and Investor Recognition on Asset Prices: Evidence from Foreign Stocks Listing in the United States," *Journal of Finance* 54 (June 1999), pp. 981–1013.

Accounting disclosure of value-at-risk estimates is assessed in

Philippe Jorion, "How Informative Are Value-at-Risk Disclosures?" *Accounting Review* 77 (October 2002), pp. 911–931.

Foreign Exchange, Eurocurrencies, and Currency Risk Management

chapter 4

Overview

There was a story about the quantum theorist Werner Heisenberg on his deathbed, declaring that he will have two questions for God: why relativity, and why turbulence. Heisenberg says, "I really think He may have an answer to the first question."

James Gleick, *Chaos*

The **foreign exchange** (or **currency**) **market** allows one currency to be exchanged for another.[1] The spot foreign exchange market is a market for immediate exchange. The forward market is a market for future exchange on a prearranged date and at a prearranged price. This chapter introduces the following exchange-related topics:

- The Eurocurrency (interest rate) markets in bank deposits and loans
- The spot and forward foreign exchange markets
- The nature of currency risk and exposure to currency risk
- Hedging of currency risk exposures
- The empirical behaviour of exchange rates

An understanding of this material is essential for effective currency risk management by individuals, institutional investors, financial institutions, governments, or multinational corporations.

4.1 • THE EUROCURRENCY MARKET

The Eurocurrency market is an external credit market in bank deposits and loans. Eurocurrencies are variable rate contracts with short maturities, typically less than

---

1 Foreign exchange is often abbreviated as *forex* or *fx*.

one year. Eurocurrency markets allow savers and borrowers to transfer purchasing power within a currency over time.

Characteristics of the Eurocurrency Market

An Absence of Government Interference. Eurocurrency transactions in the external market fall outside the jurisdiction of any single nation. This results in the Eurocurrency market's most distinctive feature: a near-total absence of outside regulatory interference. In most countries, Eurocurrency transactions in the external market have these characteristics:

> Eurocurrencies have very little governmental interference.

- No reserve requirements
- No interest rate regulations or caps
- No withholding taxes
- No deposit insurance requirements[2]
- No regulations influencing credit allocation decisions
- Less stringent disclosure requirements

With market values in the hundreds of billions of dollars and little outside interference, the Eurocurrency market is the most competitive and efficient credit market in the world.

Banks making a market in Eurocurrencies quote **bid rates** at which they will take deposits and **offer** (or **ask**) **rates** at which they will make loans to other Eurocurrency banks. Dealer quotes are available online from services such as Quotronix and Reuters. About 50 percent of all spot and forward transactions occur through London banks.

> LIBOR and Euribor are benchmark offer rates for interbank deposits.

Consequently, the **London Interbank Bid Rate (LIBID)** and the **London Interbank Offer Rate (LIBOR)** are the most frequently quoted rates. LIBID is the bid rate that a Euromarket bank is willing to pay to attract a deposit from another Euromarket bank. LIBOR is the offer rate that a Euromarket bank demands in order to place a deposit at (or, equivalently, make a loan to) another Euromarket bank. LIBID and LIBOR are quoted for all major currencies, including U.S. dollars, yen, euros, and pounds sterling. The difference between a bank's offer and bid rates is called the **interbank spread** and is typically one-eighth percent for large interbank transactions in major currencies. Another popular benchmark is the **Euro Interbank Offered Rate (Euribor)**. Euribor is the interest rate on euro-denominated term deposits between major banks within the euro zone.

http://www.
euribor.org

The market is not entirely free from government interference. For example, the U.S. SEC Rule 144A, which governs private placements, imposes a reserve requirement on dollars deposited from a foreign bank to a U.S. bank. But for deposits and loans that are not linked to dollars, this external credit market remains essentially unregulated in the United States.

Floating-Rate Pricing. In most credit markets, lenders prefer short-term loans because they have lower interest rate risk and default risk than long-term loans. Borrowers with a preference for long-term loans must pay a premium to attract long-term funds. This supply and demand for loanable funds results in yield curves (the

---

2 In the United States, deposits at commercial banks are insured up to $100,000 through the Federal Deposit Insurance Corporation. Although deposit insurance in the European Union varies by country, a minimum level of protection is required by the Second Banking Directive of 1994, effective January 1999.

relation of fixed-rate bond yields to maturity) that are typically upward sloping. Eurocurrency deposits are no different. Lenders of Eurocurrencies prefer to make short-term, low-risk loans. Because of this preference, Eurocurrencies typically have maturities shorter than five years and interest rates tied to a variable-rate base. The short maturity keeps default risk to a minimum. The variable interest rate lowers interest rate risk relative to a fixed-rate contract of comparable maturity. The most common variable-rate base for interest rates in different currencies is LIBOR. Large, negotiable Eurocurrency certificates of deposit (CDs more than $100,000 in value) can be bought and sold just like large, negotiable CDs in the U.S. market. Fixed-rate Eurocurrency deposits and loans and Eurocurrencies with maturities longer than five years are also available, but the interbank market conducts most of its transactions in floating-rate Eurocurrency contracts with maturities shorter than five years.

> Eurocurrencies have short maturities and floating rates.

Interest Rates in the Domestic Credit and Eurocurrency Markets. The interbank wholesale Eurocurrency market is very competitive. The domestic lending rate is greater than LIBOR and the domestic deposit rate is less than LIBID, so the Eurocurrency market pays more interest on deposits and accepts less interest on loans than on comparable transactions in the domestic credit market. Figure 4.1 displays the relation between domestic interest rates and Eurocurrency bid and offer rates.

To make a profit, banks purchase funds at low rates and lend them out at higher rates. For example, a bank might pay 4 percent per year on the savings account of a depositor and lend these funds out to a small business at 6 percent per year. The 2 percent spread is the source of the bank's profit. For large loans to corporate customers in the external Eurocurrency market, the bank might charge 5.25 percent. For large deposits (greater than $1 million) in the external Eurocurrency market, the bank might be willing to pay 4.75 percent. In this case, the bank's spread falls to 0.5 percent (5.25 − 4.75). Corporate customers with large enough borrowing needs and good enough credit to be able to borrow in this market can improve on the rates they would face in the domestic market by 0.75 percent on both borrowing and lending.

Interest rate spreads are often quoted in **basis points**, where one basis point is 1/100 of 1 percent. The bank might quote borrowing and lending rates of 4.9375 percent and 5.0625 percent on large short-term transactions with other large international banks in

---

FIGURE 4.1
Spreads in Domestic and Eurocurrency Credit Markets

Domestic loan rate for commercial accounts

| 2% |

Domestic deposit rate for commercial accounts

Eurocurrency loan rate for commercial accounts

| $1/2$ % |

Eurocurrency deposit rate for commercial accounts

Eurocurrency loan rate in the interbank market

| $1/8$ % |

Eurocurrency deposit rate in the interbank market

LIBOR

| $1/8$ % |

LIBID

the Eurocurrency market. At these rates, the bank's bid-ask spread (ask price minus bid price) has fallen to 0.125 percent, or 12.5 basis points. The bank can afford to quote such a small bid-ask spread to large international banks with high credit quality because of the size of the transaction and the low default and interest rate risk. Larger bid-ask spreads would be quoted for smaller amounts, longer maturities, in volatile market conditions, or with banks of lower credit quality.

> One percent is equal to 100 basis points.

The interest rate extended to a corporate borrower depends on the borrower's creditworthiness. Interest rates on large loans to AAA-rated corporate borrowers are typically made at a minimum of 15 to 25 basis points (0.15 percent to 0.25 percent) over LIBOR. Larger spreads are charged on smaller loans and on loans to customers with lower credit quality.

The Fisher Equation

> Nominal interest rates are part real and part inflation.

When setting required returns, investors demand a return to compensate them for risk. They also try to anticipate future inflation. The Fisher equation relates nominal interests rates (i) to real interest rates (ι, pronounced "iota") and inflation rates (p).

$$(1+i) = (1+\iota)(1+p) \tag{4.1}$$

If investors care about real (or inflation-adjusted) returns, then they will set nominal required returns to compensate them for their real required return and expected inflation. For example, if inflation in a particular country is expected to be 5 percent and investors require a real return of 2 percent on a 1-year government security, then the nominal required return on the government security should be $i = (1+\iota)(1+p) - 1 = (1.02)(1.05) - 1 = 0.071$, or 7.1 percent.

Ex post, realized real return is determined by the realized nominal return and inflation. If a bond yields 7.1 percent in a particular year and realized inflation is 3 percent, then the realized real return is $\iota = [(1+i)/(1+p)] - 1 = (1.071/1.03) - 1 \approx 0.0398$, or 3.98 percent.

The Fisher equation can alternatively be written as $i = (1+\iota)(1+p) - 1 = \iota + p + \iota p$. If real interest rates and inflation rates are low, then the cross-product term ιp is small and $i \approx \iota + p$. In the example with $\iota = 0.02$ and $p = 0.05$, the nominal required return $i \approx 0.02 + 0.05 = 7$ percent, which is close to the exact answer of 7.1 percent.

When an expected real return or inflation is high, the exact form of Equation 4.1 should be used. For example, if expected inflation is 70 percent and real required return is 30 percent, then the approximation suggests a nominal return of 100 percent when the exact formula yields a nominal required return of $i = (1.30)(1.70) - 1 = 1.21$, or 121 percent.

4.2 • THE FOREIGN EXCHANGE MARKET

Functions of the Foreign Exchange Market

The foreign exchange market is essential for international trade, because it permits the transfer of purchasing power from one currency to another at a point in time. When used in combination with the Eurocurrency market, spot and forward currency markets allow investors to channel capital toward productive uses regardless of the timing of investment or currency of denomination.

> Currency markets allow the transfer of value across currencies.

The currency market also allows speculators to bet on the direction of changes in currency values. Currency speculation by international banks, hedge funds, and wealthy individuals ensures that foreign exchange rates represent a consensus of market participants and provides additional liquidity to the foreign exchange markets.

More important, foreign exchange markets provide a means to defend or hedge against currency risks. **Currency risk**, or **foreign exchange risk**, is the risk of unexpected changes in foreign currency exchange rates. Hedging can reduce the adverse consequences of unexpected changes in foreign exchange rates by taking offsetting positions in the currency markets.

> Currency risk is the risk of unexpected changes in currency values.

Finally, international portfolio diversification can greatly improve the return/risk performance of financial institutions, corporations, investment funds, and individuals. The growing demand for international portfolio diversification is accomplished through the international currency markets.

Foreign Exchange Transaction Volume

A recent survey by the Bank for International Settlements (BIS) found that forex transactions averaged more than $1.2 trillion per day in April 2001 (see Figure 4.2).[3] For comparison, gross domestic product in the United States was about $10 trillion during 2001. About 32 percent of forex transactions were in the spot market, 11 percent in forwards, and 55 percent in currency swaps. Currency swaps are similar in form and function to portfolios of currency forward contracts.

http://www.bis.org

Global forex volume fell from $1.49 trillion per day in the 1998 BIS survey to $1.21 trillion in 2001. Much of this decrease was attributable to the introduction of

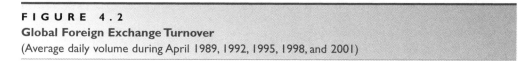

FIGURE 4.2
Global Foreign Exchange Turnover
(Average daily volume during April 1989, 1992, 1995, 1998, and 2001)

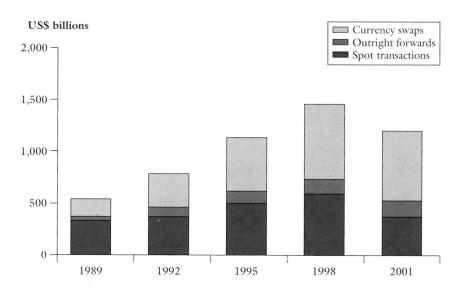

Source: Bank for International Settlements Triennial Central Bank Survey, March 2002.

3 The Bank for International Settlements surveys central banks every three years. In the 2001 survey, 48 central banks reported foreign exchange transactions from April 2001.

the euro (€) in 1999. As a part of European monetary union (Emu), the euro replaced the national currencies of Austria, Belgium, Finland, France, Germany, Greece, Ireland, Italy, Luxembourg, the Netherlands, Portugal, and Spain. With the elimination of cross-currency trading within these countries, average daily volume fell from $332 billion in 1998 to $234 billion in 2001 within the euro zone. Over 70 percent of the 2001 volume of $234 billion was from Germany ($88 billion), France ($48 billion), or the Netherlands ($30 billion).

As shown in Figure 4.3, the U.S. dollar was involved in more than 90 percent of all foreign exchange transactions, followed by the euro (38 percent), yen (23 percent), British pound sterling (13 percent), Swiss franc (6 percent), Canadian dollar (5 percent), Australian dollar (4 percent), Swedish krona (3 percent), and Hong Kong dollar (2 percent). Emerging market currencies accounted for another 5 percent of the total.[4]

The major currency trading centers are London, New York, and Tokyo (see Figure 4.4). London dominates the forex market with average daily volume of $504 billion. London is truly an international financial center; 85 percent of London's volume is conducted by foreign-owned financial institutions. Tokyo, which specializes in yen dealings, saw its trading volume curtailed during the 1990s by the Japanese recession. Tokyo's $147 billion average daily volume was only slightly more than the $101 billion average daily volume in Singapore, which actively trades a wider variety of currencies than Tokyo. Active foreign exchange markets are also conducted in Hong Kong, Zurich, Frankfurt, and Paris, as well as at other regional money centers.

FIGURE 4.3
Foreign Exchange Turnover by Currency

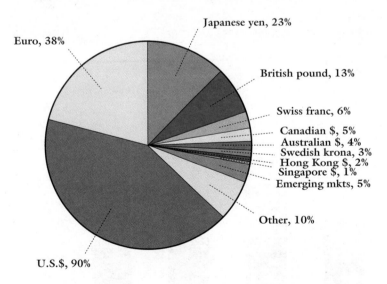

Note: These percentages sum to 200 percent rather 100 percent because two currencies are involved in each foreign exchange transaction.

Source: Bank for International Settlements Triennial Central Bank Survey, March 2002.

---

4 Because two currencies are involved in each foreign exchange transaction, these percentages sum to 200 percent rather 100 percent.

F I G U R E   4 . 4
Major Foreign Exchange Trading Centers (Average daily volume during April)

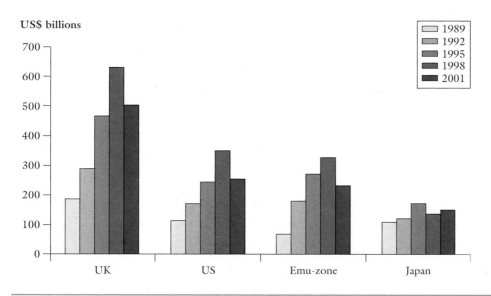

Source: Bank for International Settlements Triennial Central Bank Survey, March 2002.

Foreign Exchange Dealers and Brokers

Nearly half of all forex activity is conducted in an active interbank wholesale market, a network of large international banks and brokers (see Figure 4.5). These banks serve as **dealers** or **market makers**, buying and selling currencies at quoted exchange rates.[5] In the interbank market, spot transactions are conventionally settled within two business days. Forward transactions are settled on the prearranged contract date plus two days. Because their main function is to hedge currency risk, most customers prefer to settle only the gain or loss of a forward contract. Other customers contract with the bank to settle the full amount.

Dealers making a market in foreign exchange stand ready to quote **bid** and **offer** (**ask**) **prices** on major currencies, earning their profit by buying at their bid price and selling at a slightly higher offer price. **Bid-ask spreads** (ask price minus bid price) in this active global market depend on the size of the transaction, and the liquidity and volatility of the currencies being traded. Spreads are often as low as 10 basis points (0.0010, or 0.10 percent) for large currency transactions between major international banks.

> Banks serve as dealers in an active foreign exchange market.

Whenever a bank buys a currency in the foreign exchange market, it is simultaneously selling another currency. A bank has a **long position** in a particular currency when it has purchased that currency in the spot or forward market. Conversely, a bank is in a **short position** when it has sold that currency. By aggregating all of its expected future transactions, the bank can identify its **net position** in each currency at each forward date.

Foreign exchange **brokers** also operate in the international currency markets. Whereas dealers take a position in foreign exchange, brokers serve as matchmakers

5 Commercial bank profits from market-making generally exceed those from currency speculation. See Lyons, "Profits and Position Control: A Week of FX Dealing," *Journal of International Money and Finance* (1998).

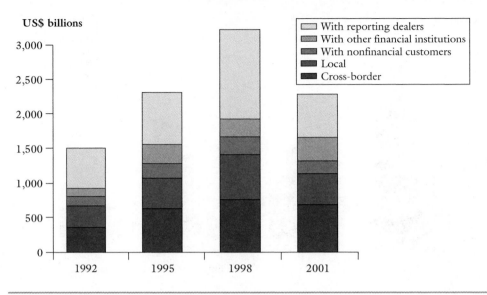

FIGURE 4.5
Foreign Exchange Market Turnover by Counterparty

US$ billions

Legend:
- With reporting dealers
- With other financial institutions
- With nonfinancial customers
- Local
- Cross-border

Source: Bank for International Settlements Triennial Central Bank Survey, March 2002.

and do not put their own money at risk. Brokers monitor the quotes of major international banks through computerized quotation systems such as Reuters, and they are able to quickly identify the banks offering the best rates. A major player, such as a central bank or a large commercial bank, can conceal its identity, and sometimes its intentions, through the use of a broker. For example, if the U.K. Chancellor of the Exchequer wants to dispose of an accumulated position in euros without signaling its activity to the market, it can use a broker to maintain anonymity. In a recent survey of foreign exchange transactions in London, about 30 percent of transactions were conducted through traditional brokers and about 5 percent were conducted through electronic brokers.

The interbank market makes up more than 80 percent of all forex transactions. The remaining business is with retail customers, including governments, businesses, and smaller customers such as domestic banks, investment funds, and individuals.

Retail Customers

Governments. Governments and their central banks can have a pronounced impact on exchange rates, especially in the short term, through their stated intentions and market activities. Suppose the central banks of the United States and Japan announce they are buying yen and selling dollars in an effort to stabilize the value of the yen. This activity should support the dollar value of the yen; that is, the spot exchange rate $S^{\$/¥}$.

> Central banks occasionally intervene in the currency markets.

Individual market participants could react in several ways to this announcement. If participants think the central banks will be successful in stabilizing the yen, the central banks may need to execute only token transactions to signal that they are indeed following through on their intentions. If participants expect the central banks to fail in their support of the yen, they may sell yen (to central banks or speculators betting on a stable rate) in anticipation of a yen depreciation. Hence, market response to the announcement depends on the credibility of the announcement and whether the market believes that government pressure can be sustained.

Businesses. Multinational corporations are the major nonbank participants in the forex market as they exchange cash flows associated with their multinational operations. MNCs often contract to pay or receive fixed amounts in foreign currencies at future dates, so they are exposed to currency risk. MNCs can hedge these future cash flows through the forward exchange market. Small businesses account for a small but growing forex volume as they interact with their customers and suppliers in other countries.

Other Retail Customers. Smaller financial institutions service individual and corporate clients in their domestic markets. For example, a European student attending American University in Washington, D.C., might ask that her local bank cash a euro-denominated check and exchange it for dollars. A local electronics retailer might ask the same bank to send a euro-denominated payment to Phillips N.V. in the Netherlands. The Washington bank will aggregate these and other euro transactions into a net transaction and then use the interbank forex market to execute and settle the net transaction. Even though they are not dealers in foreign exchange, smaller financial institutions can satisfy their clients' foreign exchange needs through the interbank market.

Other retail customers include individuals and internationally diversified funds. The forex needs of portfolios depend on their exposures to international markets and can be sizable for some funds. The forex needs of individuals are usually small and account for only a tiny fraction of all currency transactions. Foreign exchange is nevertheless very important to an individual planning a business trip or vacation getaway.

Efficiency of the Foreign Exchange Market

Liquidity is the ease with which one asset can be exchanged for another of equal value. Liquidity is related to transaction volume, as higher turnover supports greater liquidity. A market's volume and liquidity have a major impact on the allocational, operational, and informational efficiency of the market.

Allocational Efficiency. Allocational efficiency refers to how well a financial market channels capital toward its most productive uses. Allocational efficiency—the basic objective of any financial market—is greatest when there is high transaction volume and liquidity in freely floating currencies. Because of high liquidity, the interbank forex markets in dollars, yen, pounds, and euros are the most allocationally efficient markets in the world. Markets for less liquid currencies and for currencies with fixed or managed exchange rates are less efficient in their allocation of capital. Fixed exchange rate systems are less allocationally efficient, because governments intentionally disrupt the flow of capital in the pursuit of their policy objectives.

> Allocational efficiency refers to how well a market channels capital toward productive uses.

Operational Efficiency. Operational efficiency refers to how large an influence transactions costs and other market frictions have on the operation of a market. Large foreign exchange transactions between international banks have very low percentage transactions costs, making them the most operationally efficient markets on earth. High operational efficiency in the interbank forex market contributes to allocational efficiency, as low transactions costs facilitate the movement of capital to more productive uses.

> Operational efficiency refers to the influence of market frictions.

Market Update

Online Foreign Exchange Dealers

http://www.
forex-mg.com

http://www.
sonnetfinancial.
com

Commercial banks have been able to charge high prices on small transactions because their retail customers have had few alternatives, until recently, for currency exchange. The needs of individuals and small-to-midsize companies for quick and low-cost foreign exchange transfers have been largely unsatisfied.

To fill this market niche, a number of Internet-based foreign exchange dealers have begun to offer online trading in real time. Two of the more prominent dealers are Sonnet Financial Inc. and Money Garden Financial Group. Internet dealers keep costs down by pooling many small transactions and then settling only their net exposures. Although online volume is still less than 5 percent of total volume, forex dealers including large commercial banks are increasingly offering online services. Bid-ask spreads should shrink even further as volume grows and competition increases.

In contrast to the market for large interbank transfers, percentage fees on small transactions can be prohibitive. A 1994 European Commission study found that the average charge at EU commercial banks on an urgent transfer of Ecu100 was Ecu25.4, or 25.4 percent.[6] Despite this onerous fee, it took an average of 4.15 days to complete the transfers. Less than 1 percent of transfers were accomplished within one working day and more than 15 percent took longer than six working days.

Bid-ask spreads for travelers exchanging currencies at major international airports are between 2 and 6 percent. Transactions costs outside of airports can be higher still. For example, tourists visiting European resorts find that shopkeepers are more than happy to accept dollars. Unless tourists do a quick calculation, they won't notice the additional 20 percent charge hidden in the dollar prices. One way to avoid these charges is to use a major credit card, such as Visa or American Express. Credit card companies pay the foreign obligation in the local currency and bill the cardholder in his or her domestic currency at competitive exchange rates. By netting their transactions internally and only settling their net exposures in the foreign exchange market, credit card companies can afford to pass along competitive exchange rates to cardholders.[7]

> Informational efficiency refers to whether prices reflect "true" value.

Informational Efficiency. Informational efficiency refers to whether prices reflect "true" value. Through their dealing and trading activities, international commercial banks ensure that currency values represent a consensus of informed opinions and thus promote the informational efficiency of the currency market.

The international banks also provide a forum in which market participants can speculate on the direction of changes in currency values. Currency speculators take positions and seek to profit by anticipating the direction of future changes in currency values. Speculation is widely blamed by government officials for contributing to volatility and serving as a destabilizing influence in financial markets. Nevertheless, speculative activity by informed, profit-seeking participants promotes the informational efficiency of financial markets. Speculators bring new information

---

6 The European currency unit, or Ecu, was the predecessor to the euro.

7 This is not advisable when traveling in countries with high rates of credit card fraud, such as Nigeria.

to the market and ensure that prices reflect the consensus estimate of the value of the underlying instruments.

The notation used in *Multinational Finance*

Uppercase symbols are used for prices.
Lowercase symbols are used for changes in a price.

P_t^d or P_t^f = price of an asset in currency d or f at time t
p^d or p^f = inflation rate (change in the consumer price index) in currency d or f
i^d or i^f = nominal interest rate in currency d or f
ι^d (or ι^f) = real interest rate in currency d or f
$S_t^{d/f}$ = spot exchange rate between currencies d and f at time t
$s_t^{d/f}$ = change in the spot exchange rate between currencies d and f during period t
$F_t^{d/f}$ = forward exchange rate between currencies d and f for exchange at time t

---

Note: Time subscripts are dropped when it is unambiguous to do so.

4.3 • FOREIGN EXCHANGE RATES AND QUOTATIONS

Two Rules for Dealing with Foreign Exchange

In most markets, prices are stated as a currency value per unit of good or service. When you purchase a bottle of wine in Germany at a price of €20, the price is quoted as €20/bottle. The starting wage at McDonald's in the United States might be $5.15/hour. This is a natural way to state values, because a higher number in the numerator (euros or dollars) ascribes a higher value to the item being bought or sold in the denominator (a bottle of wine or an hour's wage).

Here's the rub. An exchange of currencies involves two currencies, either of which may be placed in the denominator. As an example, an exchange rate of €1.25/$ is equivalent to an exchange rate of 1/(€1.25/$) = $0.80/€. At this rate of exchange, $10 can be exchanged for ($10)(€1.25/$) = €12.50. If you buy dollars at €1.25/$, you are simultaneously selling euros at $0.80/€, and vice versa.

> Either currency can appear in the denominator of a foreign exchange quote.

Because two currencies are involved in every currency transaction, it is essential that you keep track of the currency units. If you don't, you'll end up multiplying when you should be dividing. This seems simple enough now, but as our discussion of foreign exchange instruments and contracts becomes more complex, it will become imperative to include the currency units wherever they appear in an equation. This is such an important point that it has its own rule.

RULE #1
Keep track of your currency units.

The next biggest source of confusion in currency trading is in keeping track of which currency is being bought and which currency is being sold. References to currency values invariably have the value of a single currency in mind. The statement "The dollar fell against the yen" refers to the dollar. Conversely, the statement "The yen rose against the dollar" refers to the yen. The currency that is being referred to in a foreign exchange bid or offer quote is called the **currency of reference** or **referent currency**.

> Keep track of your currency units.

Buying or selling a foreign currency is like buying or selling any other asset. It is easiest to think of the denominator as the currency that is being bought or sold. Foreign exchange prices are then just like the price of any other asset. For example, you could substitute unit for euro and think of the dollar price of the euro as $0.80/unit. You might just as well be buying bottles of wine. Rule #2 will remind of you of this point.

R U L E   # 2
**Think of buying or selling the currency in the *denominator*
of a foreign exchange quote.**

---

*Keep track of the currency
in the denominator.*

Figure 4.6 provides an example. Suppose you buy 1 million euros at a yen price of ¥115.4/€ and then sell 1 million euros at a price of ¥115.7/€. Remember, you are buying and selling euros—the currency in the denominator. The net result is that you spend (¥115.4/€)(€1,000,000) = ¥115,400,000 to buy 1 million euros and then sell them for (¥115.7/€)(€1,000,000) = ¥115,700,000, for a net profit of ¥300,000.

The bottom panel of Figure 4.6 illustrates what can go wrong. Suppose you are quoted euro-per-yen rates of 1/((¥115.7/€) ≈ €0.008643/¥ and 1/(¥115.4/€) ≈ €0.008666/¥. If you buy one million euros (the currency in the numerator!) at the "low" price of €0.008643/¥, your cost is in fact (€1,000,000)(¥115.7/€) = ¥115,700,000. If you then sell at the "high" price of €0.008666/¥, your payoff in yen is (€1,000,000)(¥115.4/€) = ¥115,400,000. This results in a net *loss* of ¥300,000. The simplest way to avoid this pitfall is to follow Rule #2 and think of the denominator as the currency of reference.

F I G U R E   4 . 6
Buying Low and Selling High

Rule #2
**Think of buying or selling the currency in the *denominator*
of a foreign exchange quote.**

An example following Rule #2

Exchange rates	$S^{¥/€}$ = ¥115.400/€	⇔	$S^{€/¥}$ = €0.008666/¥
	$S^{¥/€}$ = ¥115.700/€	⇔	$S^{€/¥}$ = €0.008643/¥

"Buy €1 at a price of ¥115.4/€ and sell it for ¥115.7/€"

Buy €1 at ¥115.400/€	≡	Sell ¥s at €0.008666/¥
Sell €1 at ¥115.700/€	≡	Buy ¥s at €0.008643/¥
⇒ ¥0.3/€ profit		⇒ €0.000023/¥ profit

An example of what can go wrong

"Buy ¥1 at a price of ¥115.4/€ and sell it for ¥115.7/€"

Buy ¥1 (sell euros) at ¥115.400/€	≡	Sell €s (buy yen) at €0.008666/¥
Sell ¥1 (buy euros) at ¥115.700/€	≡	Buy €s (sell yen) at €0.008643/¥
⇒ ¥0.3/€ loss!		⇒ €0.000023/¥ loss!

Foreign exchange quotations can be easy to understand if you follow these two simple rules. Make sure that you conscientiously apply them as you practice on the end-of-chapter problems. As our analysis becomes more and more complex in the chapters that follow, it will become increasingly important to be consistent in your use of these rules. Make your life easy and start now.

Foreign Exchange Quotation Conventions

In practice, foreign exchange quotations can follow a variety of conventions. Because the referent currency is not always placed in the denominator, some of these conventions can be difficult to interpret. The two most common conventions distinguish either between the U.S. dollar and another currency or between the domestic and a foreign currency. These two conventions are described here.

European and American Quotes for the U.S. Dollar. Interbank quotations that include the U.S. dollar are conventionally given in **European terms**, which state the foreign currency price of one U.S. dollar, such as a bid price of SFr1.7120/$ for the Swiss franc in Figure 4.7.[8] The U.S. dollar is the most frequently traded currency, and this convention is used for all interbank dollar quotes except those involving the British pound or the currencies of a few former colonies of the British Commonwealth.

> European quotes state the foreign currency price of one U.S. dollar.

The SFr1.7120/$ quote could be called "Swiss terms." It is convenient to the Swiss in that it treats the foreign currency (the U.S. dollar) just like any other asset. The "buy low and sell high" rule works for a resident of Switzerland because the dollar has a low Swiss franc value when it has a low franc price and has a high franc value when it has a high franc price.

When a bank is buying dollars, it is simultaneously selling francs. Consequently, the dollar bid price must equal the Swiss franc ask price. Following Rule #2, we could treat the Swiss franc as the currency of reference and place it in the denominator of the quote.

> American quotes state the dollar price of one unit of foreign currency.

$$S^{\$/SFr} = 1/S^{SFr/\$} = 1/(SFr1.7120/\$) \approx \$0.5841/SFr$$

FIGURE 4.7
Foreign Exchange Quotations for the Swiss Franc

	Outright quote SFr/$ (European terms)		Outright quote $/SFr (American terms)		Mid-rates[a] quoted in the financial press	
	Bid	Offer	Bid	Offer	SFr/$	$/SFr
Spot rate	1.7120	1.7130	0.5838	0.5841	1.7125	0.5839
1-month forward	1.7169	1.7179	0.5821	0.5824	1.7174	0.5823
3-month forward	1.7256	1.7267	0.5791	0.5795	1.7261	0.5793
6-month forward	1.7367	1.7379	0.5754	0.5758	1.7373	0.5756

[a] Mid-rates are averages of bid and ask rates.

---

8 Quotes such as "SFr1.7120/$ Bid and SFr1.7130/$ Ask" are called *outright* quotes. Traders often use an abbreviated *points* quote, such as "1.7120 to 30." Although they are a little less obvious than outright quotes, points quotes save time—and time is money in the fast-moving interbank currency markets.

A quote of the U.S. dollar price per foreign currency unit is called **American terms**. This is convenient to a U.S. resident in that it places the foreign currency in the denominator. Figure 4.7 maps dollar bid and ask prices into the corresponding Swiss franc prices.

European and American quotes are not possible for transactions that do not include the U.S. dollar. For these transactions, we need a quotation convention based on domestic and foreign (rather than U.S. and non-U.S.) currencies.

Direct and Indirect Quotes for Foreign Currency. Whenever a commercial bank is buying one currency, it is simultaneously selling another. For this reason, a bank's bid price for one currency is its offer price for another currency.

> Direct quotes state the domestic currency price of one unit of foreign currency.

The most straightforward way to quote bid and offer prices is with **direct quotes**, stating the price of a unit of foreign currency in domestic currency terms. This is a natural way to quote prices for a domestic resident because the foreign currency is in the denominator following Rule #2. For a U.S. resident, a direct quote for the Swiss franc might be

$0.5838/SFr Bid and $0.5841/SFr Ask

This means that the bank is willing to buy francs (and sell dollars) at $0.5838/SFr or sell francs (and buy dollars) at $0.5841/SFr. The bank's bid-ask spread is $0.0003/SFr.

> Indirect quotes state the foreign currency price of one unit of domestic currency.

The convention in many countries is to use **indirect quotes**, which state the price of a unit of domestic currency in foreign currency terms, such as SFr1.7120/$ for a U.S. resident. For example, an indirect Swiss franc quote to a U.S. resident might be

SFr1.7120/$ Bid and SFr1.7130/$ Ask

In this example, the bank is willing to buy dollars in the denominator (and sell francs in the numerator) at the SFr1.7120/$ price. It is also willing to sell dollars (and buy francs) at the SFr1.7130/$ price. The bank's spread is SFr.0010/$.

What If a Quote Doesn't Follow Rule #2? In the previous example, the bank could quote

SFr1.7130/$ Bid and SFr1.7120/$ Ask

In this case, the bid price is higher than the ask price. Does this mean that the bank is willing to lose money on every purchase and sale? Not at all. By quoting a higher bid price than ask price, the bank is indicating that it is willing to buy francs (in the *numerator!*) at SFr1.7130/$ or sell francs at the SFr1.7120/$ rate. This is, of course, equivalent to buying dollars at SFr1.7120/$ and selling dollars at SFr1.7130/$. The rule for determining the currency that is being quoted is as follows:

- When the bid quote is lower than the offer quote, the bank is buying and selling the currency in the denominator of the quote.
- When the bid quote is higher than the offer quote, the bank is buying and selling the currency in the numerator of the quote.

Note that these indirect quotes to a U.S. resident are equivalent to 1/(SFr1.7120/$) ≈ $0.5841/SFr and 1/(SFr1.7130/$) ≈ $0.5838/SFr. Swiss banks quoting these bid and offer prices to a Swiss resident with an indirect quote might quote

$0.5838/SFr Bid and $0.5841/SFr Ask

This bank is willing to buy francs (and sell dollars) at 58.38 cents per franc or sell francs (and buy dollars) at 58.41 cents per franc. Alternatively, the bank might quote

$0.5841/SFr Bid and $0.5838/SFr Ask

which means that the bank is willing to buy dollars (in the numerator) at the bid price and sell dollars (in the numerator) at the ask price. These quotes are equivalent.

Each of these examples makes sense if you follow Rule #2 and think of the denominator as the currency of reference.

The Special Case of the British Pound. Exchange rates for the British pound sterling are quoted in the interbank foreign exchange market as the foreign currency price per pound, such as $1.4960/£. The reason for this is historical. Prior to 1971, one British pound was worth 20 shillings and each shilling was worth 12 pence. The convention of keeping the pound in the denominator was convenient at that time because fractions of a pound were not easily translated into shillings and pence. Even though the British pound is now quoted in decimals, the convention of quoting exchange rates with the pound in the denominator has persisted.

Forward Premiums and Discounts

Forward premiums and discounts indicate a currency's value in the forward market relative to the spot market. Again, it is easiest to keep the currency of reference in the denominator of the foreign exchange quote.

- A currency is trading at a **forward premium** when the value of that currency in the forward market is *higher* than in the spot market.
- A currency is trading at a **forward discount** when the value of that currency in the forward market is *lower* than in the spot market.

Forward premiums and discounts can be expressed as a basis point spread. If the Swiss franc spot rate in terms of the dollar is $0.5839/SFr and the 6-month forward rate is $0.5756/SFr, then the franc is selling at a 6-month forward discount of $0.0083/SFr, or 83 basis points.[9] Common usage is to speak of the "forward premium" even when the forward rate is at a discount to the spot rate. This saves having to say "forward premium or discount" each time.

> A currency is at a forward premium when its value is higher in the forward than in the spot market.

Forward premiums are also quoted as an annualized percentage deviation from the current spot rate. The formula for this calculation is

Foreign Currency Premium

$$= (n)[(F_t^{d/f} - S_0^{d/f})] / (S_0^{d/f}) \qquad (4.2)$$

where n is the number of compounding periods per year. Multiplying by n translates the periodic forward premium into an annualized rate with n-period compounding. For example, a 6-month forward premium is annualized by multiplying the 6-month forward premium by n = 2. Similarly, a 1-month forward premium is multiplied by n = 12.

In the example with $S_0^{\$/SFr}$ = $0.5839/SFr and $F_1^{\$/SFr}$ = $0.5756/SFr, the annualized forward premium is calculated as

---

9 One basis point is 1/100th of 1 percent or, in this case, 1/100th of one Swiss cent.

$$(n)[(F_t^{d/f} - S_0^{d/f})] / (S_0^{d/f}) = (2) [(\$0.5756/SFr - \$0.5839/SFr)] / (\$0.5839/SFr)$$
$$\approx (-0.014215/\text{period}) (2 \text{ periods})$$
$$= -0.02843$$

or −2.843 percent on an annualized basis with semiannual compounding. Again, note that this formula only works for the currency (the franc) in the denominator.

Percentage Changes in Foreign Exchange Rates

In a floating exchange rate system, an increase in a currency value is called an *appreciation* and a decrease is called a *depreciation*.[10] Calculating percentage changes in exchange rates is similar to calculating a forward premium. As with any calculation involving foreign exchange, it is easiest to keep the referent currency in the denominator of the foreign exchange quote. The value of the foreign currency in the denominator of an exchange rate quote changes according to the formula

Percentage Change in Foreign Currency Value

= [(Ending rate − Beginning rate)] / (Beginning rate)   (4.3)

Suppose that the spot exchange rate between the dollar and the Swiss franc changes from \$0.5839/SFr to \$0.5725/SFr over a 6-month period. The percentage change in the dollar-per-franc spot rate is

$$[(\$0.5725/SFr - \$0.5839/SFr)] / (\$0.5839/SFr) \approx -0.0195$$

This is a fall in the value of the franc of 1.95 percent over the 6-month period, or −3.9 percent per year (2 times 1.95 percent) on an annualized basis with semiannual compounding.

If the franc falls, the dollar must rise. Rule #2 says that to find the percentage change in the value of the dollar, we should first place the dollar in the denominator of the foreign exchange quote. The beginning exchange rate is $1/(\$0.5839/SFr) \approx$ SFr1.7126/\$ and the ending rate is $1/(\$0.5725/SFr) \approx$ SFr1.7467/\$. The percentage rise in the value of the dollar (in the denominator) is then

$$[(SFr1.7467/\$ - SFr1.7126/\$)] / (SFr1.7126/\$) \approx +0.0199$$

This is a 1.99 percent rise in the value of the dollar over the 6-month period, or +3.98 percent (2 times 1.99 percent) on an annualized basis with semiannual compounding.

Percentage changes in direct and indirect foreign exchange rates are related, as an appreciation in one currency must be offset by a depreciation in the other currency.

$$S_1^{d/f}/S_0^{d/f} = (1/ S_1^{f/d})/(1/ S_0^{f/d}) = 1 / (S_1^{f/d}/S_0^{f/d})   (4.4)$$

where $S_t^{f/d} = 1/S_t^{d/f}$. Note that $(S_1^{d/f}/S_0^{d/f}) = (1+s^{d/f})$, where $s^{d/f}$ is the percentage change (stated in decimal form) in the spot exchange rate during the period. Equation 4.4 can then be rewritten as

$$(1 + s^{d/f}) = 1 / (1 + s^{f/d})   (4.5)$$

---

10 Under a fixed exchange rate system, changes are called *revaluations* or *devaluations*.

Application

Calculating Appreciations and Depreciations

Equation 4.5 provides a formula for calculating how much a currency appreciates when another depreciates, and vice versa. If you have trouble remembering formulas, here's an alternative method that might be easier to remember.

Suppose the yen-per-dollar exchange rate starts out at ¥100/$ and rises to ¥125/$. This situation can be graphically displayed as follows:

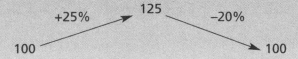

On the way up the hill, the dollar gains 25 percent. On the other side of the hill, the drop from 125 to 100 corresponds to a change of $(100-125)/125 = -0.20$, or -20 percent in the value of the yen. If the dollar in the denominator appreciates by 25 percent, then the yen must depreciate by 20 percent. This can be verified with Equation 4.5: $(1+s^{\$/¥}) = 1/(1+s^{¥/\$})$ ➡ $s^{\$/¥} = 1/(1.25)-1 = -0.20$, or -20 percent.

Let's try the example from the text in which the Swiss franc changes from $0.5839/SFr to $0.5725/SFr. The percentage change in the dollar-per-franc spot rate is

$$[(\$0.5725/SFr - \$0.5839/SFr)] / (\$0.5839/SFr) \approx -0.0195$$

or -1.95 percent. If the franc in the denominator falls to $(100.00-1.95) = 98.05$ percent of its beginning value, then the dollar in the numerator must go up accordingly.

An increase in the dollar from 98.05 to 100 results in $(100.00-98.05)/98.05 \approx +0.0199$, or a $+1.99$ percent appreciation of the dollar. Although this yields the same result as Equation 4.5, some students remember this graphical method more easily than the equation.

For a $+1.99$ percent change in the dollar that is offset by a -1.95 percent change in the franc, the algebra looks like this:

$$(1+s^{\$/SFr}) = (1-0.0195) \approx 1 / (1 + 0.0199) = 1 / (S_1^{\$/SFr}/S_0^{\$/SFr})$$

Note that an appreciation in one currency is offset by a depreciation of smaller magnitude in the other currency. This asymmetry is an unfortunate but essential part of the algebra of holding period returns.[11]

---

11 Percentage changes in currency values are symmetric when stated in continuously compounded returns. This convenient property is developed in Appendix 5-A.

A Reminder: Always Follow Rule #2

Just as the usual "buy low and sell high" rule appears reversed when dealing with the currency in the numerator of a foreign exchange quote, formulas for forward premiums or percentage changes are reversed when the referent currency is in the numerator. This can lead to some awkward and counterintuitive rules for the currency in the numerator of a foreign exchange quote. There is a simple remedy for keeping things straight—just follow Rule #2. If the currency that you would like to reference is in the numerator, simply move it to the denominator according to $1/(S^{f/d}) = S^{d/f}$. Following this convention will help you avoid needless confusion.

4.4 • EXPOSURE TO CURRENCY RISK

There is a difference between currency risk and currency risk exposure. **Risk** exists when the future is unknown; that is, whenever actual outcomes can deviate from expected outcomes. With regard to foreign exchange rates, an expected devaluation of a foreign currency by a foreign government does not constitute risk. Risk exists if and only if the actual devaluation can differ from the expectation. Similarly, risk does not exist simply because a promised foreign currency cash inflow is expected to be negatively affected by a depreciation of the foreign currency. Currency risk (or foreign exchange risk) exists if and only if the actual amount of a currency appreciation or depreciation is unknown.

The multinational corporation has an **exposure** to currency risk when the value of its assets or liabilities can change with unexpected changes in currency values. Exposure

> Currency risk exposure depends on how much is at risk in the foreign currency.

to currency risk depends on how much is at risk. If a U.S. corporation has €150,000 on deposit in a German bank, then this corporation's exposure to unexpected changes in the spot exchange rate between dollars and euros is €150,000. Note that it is natural to denominate foreign currency risk exposure in the foreign currency. If the €150,000 is converted into $150,000, then the dollar value of this amount is no longer exposed to unexpected changes in the dollar-per-euro exchange rate.

Monetary Versus Nonmonetary Assets and Liabilities

A useful way to categorize the firm's assets and liabilities is according to whether they are monetary (contractual) or nonmonetary (noncontractual) in nature. Consider the market value balance sheet at the top of Figure 4.8.

Monetary assets and liabilities are assets and liabilities with contractual payoffs, so that the size and timing of promised cash flows are known in advance. Monetary

> Monetary assets and liabilities have contractual payoffs.

contracts may be denominated in the domestic currency or a foreign currency. The firm's monetary assets include cash and money market securities, accounts receivable, domestic currency and Eurocurrency deposits, and the cash inflow side of forwards, futures, options, and swaps. Monetary liabilities include wages and accounts payable, domestic and Eurocurrency debt, and the cash outflow side of forwards, futures, options, and swaps.[12]

Real (nonmonetary) assets and liabilities are defined as all assets and liabilities that are not monetary in nature. Real assets include the firm's productive technologies

---

12 Futures, options, and swaps have contractual inflows and outflows much like a forward contract. These derivative instruments are discussed in detail in Part 3 of the book.

FIGURE 4.8
A Taxonomy of Exposures to Currency Risk

Market Value Balance Sheet

Monetary Assets	Monetary Liabilities
Real Assets	Owners' Equity

- **Economic exposure**   Potential change in the value of all future cash flows due to unexpected changes in exchange rates

  - Transaction exposure   Potential change in the value of *contractual* future cash flows (i.e., *monetary* assets and liabilities) due to unexpected changes in exchange rates

  - Operating exposure   Potential change in the value of *noncontractual* future cash flows (i.e., *nonmonetary* or *real* assets and liabilities) due to unexpected changes in exchange rates

- **Translation exposure**   Potential change in financial accounting statements due to changes in exchange rates (also called *accounting exposure*)

---

and capacities, whether these assets are tangible (such as a manufacturing plant) or intangible (such as a patent or copyright). Inventory is considered a real asset, unless payment has been contractually promised in some way. Returns on real assets are noncontractual and hence uncertain. Real assets can be exposed to currency risk regardless of where they are located. For example, a manufacturing plant can be exposed to currency risk if sales depend on foreign exchange values.

As the residual owner of the firm, common equity is a nonmonetary liability. The cash flows that accrue to equity depend on the noncontractual or operating cash flows of the firm's real assets and the contractual cash flows of the firm's monetary assets and liabilities. Although each of these asset and liability categories can be exposed to currency risk, the nature of the risk exposure varies depending on whether the asset or liability is contractual or noncontractual in nature.

Economic Exposure to Currency Risk

Economic exposure to currency risk refers to potential changes in all (monetary or nonmonetary) future cash flows due to unexpected changes in exchange rates. Managing the MNC's economic exposure to currency risk is an important long-term goal of the multinational financial manager. Economic exposure to currency risk can be divided into the **transaction exposure** of the firm's monetary assets and liabilities and the **operating exposure** of the firm's real assets.

Economic exposure to currency risk includes transaction and operating exposures.

Because the value of equity is the value of monetary and real assets minus the value of monetary liabilities, common equity is exposed to currency risk through the transaction exposure of monetary assets and liabilities and the operating exposure of real assets.

Transaction Exposure. Transaction exposure to currency risk refers to potential changes in the value of contractual (monetary) cash flows as a result of unexpected changes in currency values. Monetary contracts denominated in a foreign currency are fully exposed to changes in the value of that currency, so transaction exposure is an important short-term concern of the multinational financial manager. Domestic monetary contracts are not directly exposed to foreign currency risk, although they are exposed to domestic purchasing power risk.[13] The exposure of **net monetary assets** (monetary assets less monetary liabilities) depends on whether the exposures of monetary assets and monetary liabilities are offsetting. Because monetary assets and liabilities involve contractual cash flows, transaction exposure can be effectively hedged with financial market instruments that have contractual payoffs such as currency forwards, futures, options, or swaps.

> Transaction exposure refers to the exposure of monetary assets and liabilities to currency risk.

Operating Exposure. Operating exposure to currency risk refers to potential changes in the value of real (nonmonetary) assets or operating cash flows as a result of unexpected changes in currency values. Operating exposure is an important long-term concern of the multinational financial manager. Although the MNC can partially hedge against operating exposure with financial market instruments (forwards, futures, options, or swaps), the contractual cash flows of financial market hedges are not very effective at hedging the uncertain cash flows of the firm's real assets. Operating exposure is more effectively hedged through careful management of the firm's real assets, such as through the firm's location, production, sourcing, distribution, and marketing decisions. Whereas financial market hedges are easy to create and reverse, real asset hedges are more difficult to accomplish and can involve high entry and exit costs.

> Operating exposure refers to the exposure of nonmonetary assets to currency risk.

The Spectrum of Monetary/Nonmonetary Cash Flows. Figure 4.9 presents an example of the evolution of expected future cash flows from nonmonetary to monetary. Suppose U.S.-based GTE has invested in a cellular phone system in Delhi, India, through a 50 percent-owned subsidiary in India. The cellular phone system consists of a network of microwave relay stations and switching equipment in the greater Delhi area. At the time of investment, future proceeds from the investment can be estimated but are not known for certain. GTE's real assets—the microwave relay stations and switching equipment—have an operating exposure to currency risk because the dollar value of the proceeds from this investment depends on the dollar value of the rupee.

As GTE's advertising campaign begins to attract customers, some of these uncertain future proceeds become sales contracts with Delhi residents. This creates rupee-denominated receivables for GTE's Delhi subsidiary. Cash flows from these accounts receivable have transaction exposure for GTE because their dollar value depends on the rate of exchange between rupees and dollars.

GTE has economic exposure to currency risk even after the Delhi subsidiary contractually promises to repatriate dollars to GTE. If the dollar appreciates in value, GTE's promised cash flows will be unaffected because they are denominated in dol-

---

13 This is strictly true only if monetary cash flows are certain. If monetary cash flows are uncertain and payment depends in some way on exchange rates, then domestic monetary contracts are indirectly exposed to currency risk. For example, a receivable denominated in domestic currency might not be paid if an adverse exchange rate movement forces the domestic customer out of business.

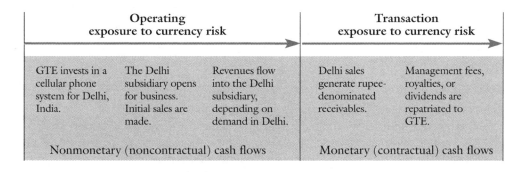

FIGURE 4.9
GTE's Exposure to Currency Risk in Delhi, India

lars. However, GTE's Delhi subsidiary must pay more in rupees to fulfill its dollar obligations. This hurts the value of the subsidiary and, hence, GTE's equity stake in that subsidiary. The subsidiary might also have trouble paying its obligations if its customers in Delhi are exposed to the dollar.

Once management fees, royalties, and dividends are repatriated in dollars to GTE, GTE has no more exposure to currency risk on these payments. Its economic exposure to currency risk remains, however, through the operating exposure of its Delhi subsidiary.

Accounting (Translation) Exposure to Currency Risk

Accounting (or **translation**) **exposure** refers to potential changes in financial accounting statements as a result of changes in currency values. Accounting exposure arises as the parent firm translates the financial accounting statements of its foreign subsidiaries back into its domestic currency using the generally accepted accounting principles of the parent country. The parent firm has accounting exposure to the extent that unexpected changes in exchange rates change the parent's financial accounting statements. Accounting exposure may or may not reflect changes in the value of the firm's assets or liabilities, and hence may or may not be related to the economic exposure of the firm.

> Accounting exposure may or may not be related to the economic exposure of cash flows and firm value.

Although accounting exposure may not be of direct concern to debt and equity stakeholders, it is vitally important to the managers of the firm. Performance evaluations and management compensation are often tied to accounting performance, so managers have a strong incentive to minimize their accounting exposure. To the extent that managers change their actions based on accounting exposure, debt and equity investors also should be concerned because it affects the value of the firm indirectly through the actions of the managers.

Corporate Views on Currency Risk Exposures

A survey by Jesswein, Kwok, and Folks polled corporate treasurers and chief financial officers concerning their views on the relative importance of these types of exposures to currency risk.[14] These individuals were asked whether they (1) strongly

---

14 Jesswein, Kwok, and Folks, "Adoption of Innovative Products in Currency Risk Management: Effects of Management Orientations and Product Characteristics," *Journal of Applied Corporate Finance* (1995).

agreed, (2) agreed, (3) were neutral, (4) disagreed, or (5) strongly disagreed with each of the following statements:

	Mean score of level of agreement
• Managing transaction exposure is important.	1.4
• Managing operating exposure is important.	1.8
• Managing translation exposure is important.	2.4

Mean responses are reported to the right of each question.

Corporate respondents felt that transaction exposure was the most important exposure. Operating exposure came in a close second, even though operating exposure is perhaps the more important long-term exposure. Many MNCs manage transaction exposure but not operating exposure. Transaction exposures to currency risk are one-for-one in that a percentage change in the value of a foreign currency causes the same percentage change in the value of exposed cash flows. The exposures of operating cash flows are more difficult to estimate and hedge.[15] Translation (accounting) exposure came in a distant third in importance to transaction and operating exposure in this U.S. survey.

Monetary assets and liabilities involve cash flows that are contractual in nominal terms, and so are directly exposed to changes in nominal exchange rates. Real assets, on the other hand, are primarily exposed to changes in real exchange rates. Real exchange rates measure changes in the relative purchasing power of two currencies by adjusting for inflation differences between the two currencies. Real exchange rates are an important concept in international finance and are introduced in Chapter 5.

4.5 • HEDGING TRANSACTION EXPOSURE WITH FORWARD CONTRACTS

Currency risk is a special case of a more general class of risk called financial price risk. **Financial price risk** arises from the possibility that a financial price—such as a currency value, an interest rate, or a commodity price—will differ from its expectation.

A survey of U.S. corporations by the Treasury Management Association found that 90 percent of respondent firms were exposed to interest rate risk, 75 percent faced currency risk, and 37 percent faced commodity price risk. Only 3 percent of respondents claimed no exposure to financial price risk, while 31 percent faced exposure to all three.[16]

Although interest rate, currency, and commodity price risks arise from different sources, the methods used to hedge exposures to these risks are similar. Here is an example of an exposure to currency risk that can be hedged with a forward contract.

An Example of Exposure to Currency Risk

Suppose you are a Canadian resident and have booked a vacation to Copenhagen, Denmark. When you booked the trip six months ago, you obligated yourself to pay a

---

15 This emphasis on managing the more visible of the two exposures reminds one of the story of the drunk who, upon losing his car keys while trying to open his car door one evening, starts looking for his keys under a nearby lamppost. His friend asks him why he isn't looking for the keys near the car. The drunk responds "It's too dark to see over there."

16 Phillips, "1995 Derivatives Practices and Instruments Survey," *Financial Management* (1995).

total of DKr25,000 in expenses including DKr20,000 for food and lodging and DKr5,000 for a quick side trip to visit a classmate that lives in Odense. The exchange rate was C$0.20/DKr when you booked the trip, so your expected Canadian dollar cost was (DKr25,000)(C$0.20/DKr) = C$5,000. At this point, you have a short (negative) position in Danish kroner.

As you pack for your trip, you discover to your dismay that the kroner has appreciated by 25 percent from C$0.20/DKr to C$0.25/DKr. The Canadian dollar cost of your kroner obligation has correspondingly increased from

$$(DKr25,000)(C\$0.20/DKr) = C\$5,000$$

to

$$(DKr25,000)(C\$0.25/DKr) = C\$6,250$$

The 25 percent appreciation of the kroner has increased the Canadian dollar value of your kroner obligation by 25 percent, or C$1,250. Perhaps you'll have to cancel your side trip.

A **risk profile** is a graph of the value of a particular position against an underlying source of risk. A risk profile for your underlying short kroner position is shown here:

Risk profile of a short DKr position

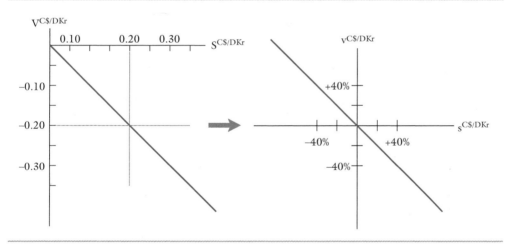

The risk profile on the left shows the Canadian dollar value of the kroner as a function of the C$-per-kroner exchange rate. The relationship between V$^{C\$/DKr}$ and S$^{C\$/DKr}$ is one-for-one, so the risk profile is a 45-degree line.

Recall that lowercase symbols refer to changes in value. The right-hand graph displays changes in the value of the underlying position, v$^{C\$/DKr}$, as a function of changes in the spot rate, s$^{C\$/DKr}$, after centering the graph on the expected spot rate C$0.20/DKr. You are short the kroner, so a 25 percent kroner appreciation results in a 25 percent increase in the Canadian dollar value of your kroner obligation.

The Exposure of a Forward Hedge

Six months ago, you could have hedged your short kroner position by buying the kroner and selling the Canadian dollar in the forward market. Suppose the 6-month forward rate at that time was F$^{C\$/DKr}$ =

Forward contracts can be used to reduce exposure to currency risk.

C$0.20/DKr. At this exchange rate, you could have purchased DKr25,000 (and sold C$5,000) six months forward. By purchasing the kroner forward, you could have ensured that your Canadian dollar obligation would have been C$5,000 irrespective of the spot exchange rate.

The following graph shows the risk profile of a long kroner forward contract. If the actual spot rate is equal to the forward rate of C$0.20/DKr, then there is no gain or loss on the forward (aside from the transaction cost built into the bid-ask spread). The DKr25,000 receipt equals the C$5,000 cost of the forward at the C$0.20/DKr spot rate. If the kroner appreciates to C$0.25/DKr, then the forward contract allows (indeed, requires) you to exchange C$5,000 for DKr25,000 at the C$0.20/DKr forward rate. This would have cost C$6,250 in the spot market, resulting in a C$1,250 gain over the market rate of exchange.

Risk profile of a long DKr position

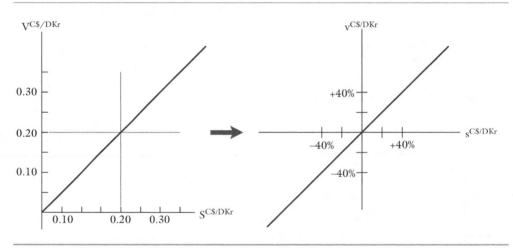

Of course, if the spot rate had fallen to C$0.15/DKr, you still would have had to pay C$5,000 for DKr25,000 according to the terms of the forward contract. Purchase of DKr25,000 in the spot market at C$0.15/DKr would have cost only C$3,750. Your opportunity cost on the long kroner forward contract would then have been C$1,250, or C$0.05/DKr.

The slope of a risk profile has the same sign as the underlying cash flow.

Here is a convenient way to relate the slope of the risk profile to the sign of the underlying long (+) or short (−) position.

T H E   S I G N   O F   A N   E X P O S U R E   T O   C U R R E N C Y   R I S K

If the currency of reference is in the denominator of the exchange rate, then the slope of the risk profile has the same sign as the underlying cash flow.

In this example, the underlying short kroner exposure loses from an appreciation and gains from a depreciation of the kroner. Conversely, a long kroner position as in the forward hedge gains from an appreciation and loses from a depreciation of the kroner. As long as the currency of reference is in the denominator of all foreign exchange quotes, the slope of the risk profile has the same sign as the underlying exposure.

Application

Foreign Exchange Losses at Japan Air Lines

In 1985, Japan Air Lines (JAL) entered into a 10-year forward agreement to buy $3.6 billion for ¥666 billion at a price of ¥666bn/$3.6bn ≈ ¥185/$. At the time of the forward agreement, the spot exchange rate was ¥240/$. By October 1994, the dollar had fallen to ¥100/$. If the contract had been settled in October 1994, Japan's largest airline would have had to pay ¥666 billion for dollars worth only ($3.6 billion)(¥100/$) = ¥360 billion. This would have been a foreign exchange loss of ¥306 billion, or $3.06 billion.

Since entering this agreement, JAL had charged some of the foreign exchange loss against operating profits. However, as of October 1994 the extent of the losses had not been fully reported. In late 1994, the Japanese Ministry of Finance required exchange-listed Japanese companies to disclose unrealized gains or losses from forward currency trading. JAL had a ¥45 billion ($450 million) unrealized loss at that time. JAL had been spending about ¥80 billion ($800 million) each year on new airplanes, so their total loss on the forward contract was about half their annual budget for new airplanes.

There is good news for JAL, however. Although the falling dollar resulted in losses on JAL's short dollar forward contracts, it also resulted in lower yen costs on JAL's new airplanes from U.S. manufacturers. News reports emphasized JAL's forex losses on the forward hedge and neglected to mention the gains on the underlying exposure.

Currency risk management can be a "damned if you do and damned if you don't" proposition for a financial manager. If exposures are left unhedged, exchange rates will move adversely about half the time and the manager will be open to criticism. If exposures are hedged, the financial manager can be criticized if exchange rates move in favor of the underlying exposure and against the hedge, as in the JAL case. The financial manager's best defense is to make sure that hedges are clearly associated with an underlying exposure and consistent with the MNC's overall financial policies.

The Exposure of the Hedged Position

The underlying short kroner position and the long kroner forward hedge have offsetting exposures to the spot exchange rate. This can be illustrated with time lines.

	Underlying short kroner exposure	
		−DKr25,000
+	Long kroner forward contract	+DKr25,000
		−C$5,000
=	**Hedged position**	
		−C$5,000

In the hedged position, the DKr25,000 underlying short position is offset by the DKr25,000 long position in the forward contract. The net result is an obligation of C$5,000 regardless of what happens to the kroner-per-C$ exchange rate.

Similarly, the two risk profiles can be combined to illustrate that the payoff to the hedged position is independent of the exchange rate.

The hedged position

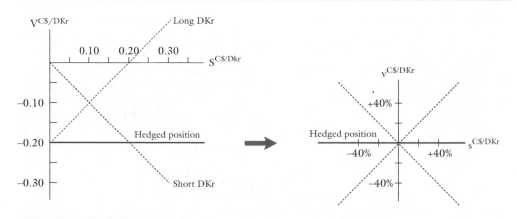

The hedged position is the sum of the two exposures. If the spot rate rises to C$0.25/DKr, then the C$0.05/DKr gain on the forward hedge exactly offsets the C$0.05/DKr loss on the underlying position. Conversely, if the exchange rate falls to C$0.15/DKr, then the C$0.05/DKr loss on the forward hedge exactly offsets the C$0.05/DKr gain on the underlying position. The net result is that you will be able to exchange your C$5,000 for DKr25,000 regardless of what happens to foreign exchange rates. If you'd hedged your kroner exposure, you could have been assured of an enjoyable side trip to Odense.

4.6 • THE EMPIRICAL BEHAVIOR OF EXCHANGE RATES

Daily Changes in Exchange Rates

It is useful to describe the empirical behavior of foreign exchange rates, because this behavior determines exchange rate risk. A convenient starting point is the process called a random walk. If exchange rates follow a **random walk**, then exchange rate changes at a particular point in time are independent of previous changes, have a zero mean, and are normally distributed. There is an equal probability of an appreciation or a depreciation in currency value. There is no memory in a random walk, so once a new exchange rate is established there is again an equal probability of further appreciation or depreciation.

For daily measurement intervals, nominal exchange rate changes are close to a random walk with a nearly equal probability of rising or falling. Because of this behavior, the best guess of tomorrow's exchange rate is simply today's exchange rate. The current spot rate outperforms most other exchange rate forecasts for forecasting horizons of up to one month.

> Exchange rate changes are close to a random walk.

Time-Varying Exchange Rate Volatility

> Exchange rate volatility is predictable.

Empirical investigations into the behavior of exchange rates reject the simplest form of the random walk model. In its place, researchers have modeled exchange rates as a process in which the following is true:

- Exchange rate changes are approximately normally distributed at each point in time.

- At each point in time, the variance of exchange rates depends on whether the most recent exchange rate changes have been large or small.

A time series exhibiting this behavior is frequently modeled as a **GARCH** process. GARCH stands for **generalized autoregressive conditional heteroskedasticity** and is a statistician's way of saying "Today's variance depends on the recent history of exchange rate changes." The literal translation is "variance (heteroskedasticity) depends on (is conditional on) previous (autoregressive) variances."

The variance of a GARCH(p,q) process at time t is described by[17]

$$\sigma_t^2 = a_0 + \Sigma_i \, a_i \, \sigma_{t-i}^2 + \Sigma_j \, b_j \, s_{t-j}^2 \qquad (4.6)$$

where a_0, a_i, and b_j are constants for $i = 1, ..., p$ and $j = 1, ..., q$, and

σ_{t-i}^2 = the exchange rate variance from period t–i for $i = 1, ..., p$

s_{t-j}^2 = the square of the percentage change in the spot exchange rate during period t-j for $j = 1, ..., q$

At each point in time, this GARCH process is normally distributed with conditional (time-varying) variance σ_t^2. The GARCH variance is called an *autoregressive conditional variance* because it depends on the recent history of variances σ_{t-i}^2 and squared spot rate changes s_{t-j}^2. The variables p and q identify the maximum number of lags that influence the variance through previous variances and squared spot rate changes. The summation over j forces the variance to respond to volatility during the most recent q periods, where volatility is measured by the square of the change in the spot exchange rate. The summation over i previous conditional variances smoothes the process so that it is not overly sensitive to recent squared spot rate changes.

A p p l i c a t i o n

J.P. Morgan's RiskMetrics System

J.P. Morgan has developed a system called *RiskMetrics* to assist clients in assessing and managing exposures to financial risks. The system provides users with daily data on more than 300 financial prices including interest rates, exchange rates, and national and regional stock market indices. RiskMetrics uses a restricted GARCH(1,1) version of Equation 4.6:

$$\sigma_t^2 = a \, \sigma_{t-1}^2 + (1-a) \, s_{t-1}^2$$

in which the intercept term is omitted and the parameter weights sum to one. For monthly intervals, the standard RiskMetrics model assigns a weight of a = 0.97 on the most recent conditional variance and a weight of (1–a) = 0.03 on the most recent squared spot rate change. For daily intervals, the model assigns weights of a = 0.95 and (1–a) = 0.05. RiskMetrics' model is an exponentially weighted moving average in which the impact of past spot rate changes on conditional variance decays at a rate of $(1-a)(a^t)$.

http://www. riskmetrics.com

---

17 Bollerslev, "Generalized Autoregressive Conditional Heteroskedasticity," *Journal of Econometrics* (1986).

The GARCH process includes the random walk model as a special case in which the mean spot rate change is zero and the parameters a_i and b_j are equal to zero at all lags. In this case, the variance σ_t^2 is a constant equal to a_0. Recent empirical studies of nominal exchange rates have rejected the random walk model in favor of GARCH specifications for yearly, monthly, weekly, daily, and intraday measurement intervals. The particular form of GARCH process is not as important as the recognition that volatility is autoregressive; that is, exchange rate volatility depends on recent market history.

4.7 • SUMMARY

The interbank market for foreign exchange is the most liquid and operationally efficient market in the world. Because of low transactions costs and high liquidity, the interbank market is also fairly efficient at allocating and pricing currencies. Even though the foreign exchange market is relatively efficient, exchange rates can be volatile.

We classified the MNC's exposure to currency risk as follows:

- Economic exposure: change in value due to unexpected changes in exchange rates
  - Transaction exposure: change in the value of contractual future cash flows (that is, cash flows from monetary assets and liabilities) due to unexpected changes in exchange rates
  - Operating exposure: change in the value of noncontractual future cash flows (that is, operating cash flows from nonmonetary assets and liabilities) due to unexpected changes in exchange rates
- Translation (accounting) exposure: change in financial accounting statements due to unexpected changes in currency exchange rates

Monetary contracts denominated in a foreign currency are fully exposed to foreign currency risk. Monetary contracts denominated in the domestic currency are not directly exposed to currency risk, although they are exposed to domestic purchasing power risk. Because the uncertain cash flows of the firm's real assets depend on foreign exchange rates, real assets are exposed to currency risk regardless of where they are located.

Nominal exchange rates changes are difficult to predict, being close to a random walk over daily intervals. However, exchange rate volatility is predictable in that it tends to come in waves. Despite the random nature of exchange rates, individuals and corporate financial managers will continue to demand exchange rate forecasts because of the potential for risk reduction and speculative gain. This is one forecast that you can trust.

Finally, remember these two important rules for dealing in foreign exchange:

Rule #1:   Keep track of your currency units.

Rule #2:   Think of buying or selling the currency in the denominator of a foreign exchange quote.

Conscientiously following these rules will help you avoid making careless mistakes when dealing with foreign exchange.

KEY TERMS

accounting (translation) exposure	informational efficiency
allocational efficiency	interbank spread
basis points	London Interbank Bid Rate (LIBID)
bid and offer (ask) rates	London Interbank Offer Rate (LIBOR)
bid-ask spread	long position
brokers	liquidity
currency of reference (referent currency)	monetary assets and liabilities
dealers (market makers)	net monetary assets
direct versus indirect quotes	net position
economic exposure	operating exposure
Euro Interbank Offered Rate (Euribor)	operational efficiency
European versus American terms	random walk
exposure	real (nonmonetary) assets and liabilities
financial price risk	risk
foreign exchange (currency) market	risk profile
foreign exchange (currency) risk	short position
forward premium or discount	transaction exposure
generalized autoregressive conditional heteroskedasticity (GARCH)	

CONCEPTUAL QUESTIONS

4.1   In what way is the Eurocurrency market different from an internal credit market?

4.2   What is the London Interbank Offer Rate (LIBOR)?

4.3   What is Rule #1 when dealing with foreign exchange? Why is it important?

4.4   What is Rule #2 when dealing with foreign exchange? Why is it important?

4.5   What are the functions of the foreign exchange market?

4.6   Define allocational, operational, and informational efficiency.

4.7   What is a forward premium? A forward discount? Why are forward prices for foreign currency seldom equal to current spot prices?

4.8   What is the difference between currency risk and currency risk exposure?

4.9   What are monetary assets and liabilities? What are real assets?

4.10   What are the two components of economic exposure to currency risk?

4.11   Under what conditions is accounting exposure to currency risk important to shareholders?

4.12   Will a foreign currency appreciation benefit a domestic exporter that has a receivable denominated in the foreign currency?

4.13   Describe the behavior of exchange rates.

PROBLEMS

4.1   Citigroup quotes Danish kroner on European terms as "DKr5.62/$ Bid and DKr5.87/$ Ask."

a. Which currency is Citigroup buying at the DKr5.62/$ bid rate, and which currency is Citigroup selling at the DKr5.87/$ offer rate?

b. What are the bid and ask prices in American terms? Which currency is Citigroup buying at these prices and which currency is Citigroup selling?

c. With the foreign currency in the numerator, the "DKr5.62/$ Bid and DKr5.87/$ Ask" quotes are indirect quotes for a U.S. resident. What are the bid and ask prices in direct terms for a U.S. resident? At these prices, which currency is Citigroup buying and which currency is Citigroup selling?

d. If you sell $1 million to Citigroup at their bid price of DKr5.62/$ and simultaneously buy $1 million at their offer price of DKr5.87/$, how many Danish krona ("krona" is the plural of kroner) will you make or lose? What is Citigroup's kroner profit or loss on the transaction?

4.2   You are interested in buying Swedish krona (SKr). Your bank quotes "SKr7.5050/$ Bid and SKr7.5150/$ Ask." What would you pay in dollars if you bought SKr10,000,000 at the current spot rate?

4.3   The following outright quotations are given for the Canadian dollar:

	Bid (C$/$)	Ask (C$/$)
Spot rate	1.2340	1.2350
1-month forward	1.2345	1.2365
3-month forward	1.2367	1.2382
6-month forward	1.2382	1.2397

Assume you reside in the United States. Calculate forward quotes for the Canadian dollar as an annual percentage premium or discount. Would a foreign exchange trader in Canada get a different answer if asked to calculate the annual percentage premium or discount on the U.S. dollar for each forward rate? Why?

4.4   Given the following spot and forward quotes, calculate forward premiums on Japanese yen as (a) a basis point premium, and (b) an annualized percentage premium.

Spot ($/¥)	Forward ($/¥)	Days Forward
0.009057355	0.008968408	30
0.009057355	0.008772945	90
0.009057355	0.008489101	180
0.009057355	0.007920290	360

4.5   In 1984, the number of German marks required to buy one U.S. dollar was 1.80. In 1987, the U.S. dollar was worth 2.00 marks. In 1992, the dollar was worth 1.50 marks. In 1997, the dollar was again worth 1.80 marks.

a. What was the percentage appreciation or depreciation of the dollar between 1984 and 1987? Between 1987 and 1992? Between 1992 and 1997?

b. What was the percentage appreciation or depreciation of the mark between 1984 and 1987? Between 1987 and 1992? Between 1992 and 1997? (*Hint*: Following Rule #2, convert the $S^{DM/\$}$ spot rates to $S^{\$/DM}$.)

4.6 A foreign exchange dealer in Warsaw provides quotes for spot and 1-month, 3-month, and 6-month forward rates for the Polish zloty against the dollar.

	Bid (PZ/$)	Ask (PZ/$)
Spot	4.0040	4.0200
1-month forward	3.9920	4.0090
3-month forward	3.9690	3.9888
6-month forward	3.9360	3.9580

a. What would you receive in dollars if you sold PZ 5 million at the spot rate?
b. What would it cost you in dollars to purchase PZ 20 million forward three months. When would you make payment?

4.7 You have sold ¥104 million (and purchased dollars) at a spot price of ¥104/$. One year later, you pay dollars to buy back the ¥104 million at the prevailing exchange rate of ¥100/$. How much have you gained or lost in dollars?

4.8 Euro bid and ask prices on the Japanese yen are quoted direct in Paris at €0.007634/¥ Bid and €0.007643/¥ Ask. What are the corresponding indirect quotes for euros?

4.9 Calculate appreciation or depreciation in each of the following:
a. If the dollar depreciates 10% against the yen, by what percentage does the yen appreciate against the dollar?
b. If the dollar appreciates 1000% against the ruble, by what percentage does the ruble depreciate against the dollar?

4.10 Dollars are trading at $S_0^{SFr/\$} = SFr0.7465/\$$ in the spot market. The 90-day forward rate is $F_1^{SFr/\$} = SFr0.7432/\$$. What is the forward premium on the dollar in basis point terms? What is the forward premium as an annualized percentage rate?

4.11 In what way are the following two quotes equivalent?
a. "$0.5841/SFr Bid and $0.5852/SFr Ask"
b. "$0.5852/SFr Bid and $0.5841/SFr Ask"

4.12 The Danish kroner is quoted in New York at $0.18536/DKr spot, $0.18519/DKr 30 days forward, $0.18500/DKr 90 days forward, and $0.18488/DKr 180 days forward. Calculate the forward discounts or premiums on the kroner.

4.13 Suppose that at time t=0 the dollar per yen spot rate $S_0^{\$/¥}$ is $0.0100/¥ and that the yen appreciates 25.86 percent during the next period.
a. What is the closing spot rate in dollars per yen $S_1^{\$/¥}$?
b. By what percentage does the dollar depreciate against the yen?

4.14 Hippity Hops is to deliver €1 million of hops to the Czech brewer Pilsner Urquel in one year. The spot and 1-year forward exchange rates between the Czech koruna and the euro are $S_0^{CZK/€} = F_1^{CZK/€} = Kor40/€$. The sale is invoiced in korunas. Pilsner Urquel promises to pay Hippity Hops CZK40 million in one year.

a. Identify Hippity Hops' expected cash flow in Czech korunas on a time line.

b. Draw a risk profile for Hippity Hops in terms of euros per koruna.

c. If the actual spot rate in one year is CZK25/€ (or €0.04/CZK), how much gain or loss will Hippity Hops have if it does not hedge its currency exposure? (Use the current spot exchange rate as the starting point in calculating the gain or loss.)

d. Form a forward market hedge based on the forward price $F_1^{CZK/€}$ = CZK40/€. Indicate how the hedge eliminates foreign exchange exposure by identifying the forward contract's cash inflows and outflows on a time line. Construct a payoff profile that combines the exposures of the underlying position and the forward contract.

4.15 Find a formula like Equation 4.2 for calculating a forward premium with currency d in the numerator. [*Hint*: Substitute $S_0^{d/f} = 1/(S_0^{f/d})$ and $F_t^{d/f} = 1/(F_t^{f/d})$ into Equation 4.2 to get currency d in the denominator, and then rearrange and simplify.]

4.16 Consider the balance sheet of a U.S. firm exporting to Europe. Euro-denominated accounts have been translated into U.S. dollars at the current exchange rate.

Cash (in $s)	$40,000	Wages payable (in $s)	$40,000
Accts receivable (in $s)	$30,000	Accts payable (in $s)	$70,000
Accts receivable (in €s)	$60,000	Bank note due (in €s)	$10,000
Inventory (in $s)	$20,000	**Current liabilities**	**$120,000**
Current assets	**$150,000**	Bank note (in €s)	$50,000
Plant and equipment	$50,000	Common equity	$30,000
Total assets	**$200,000**	**Total liabilities and equity**	**$200,000**

This firm considers inventory to be a real, rather than a monetary, asset.

a. What is the dollar value of the firm's monetary assets? What is the dollar value of the firm's monetary liabilities? What is the dollar value of net monetary assets?

b. What is the dollar value of the firm's monetary assets exposed to currency risk? Exposed monetary liabilities? Net exposed monetary assets (exposed monetary assets less exposed monetary liabilities)?

c. This firm has a bank note denominated in euros. Does this foreign currency liability increase or reduce the firm's net monetary exposure to currency risk? Explain.

d. Is the operating performance of a U.S. exporter such as this likely to be improved or worsened by a real appreciation of the euro? Explain.

4.17 Suppose you estimate a GARCH model (with p = q = 1) of monthly volatility in the value of the dollar and arrive at the following estimates:

$$\sigma_t^2 = 0.0034 + (0.40)\sigma_{t-1}^2 + (0.20)s_{t-1}^2$$

where the conditional variance (σ_{t-1}^2) and the square of the percentage change in the spot exchange rate (s_{t-1}^2) are from the previous period. If $\sigma_{t-1} = 0.05$ and $s_{t-1} = 0.10$, what is the GARCH estimate of conditional volatility?

SUGGESTED READINGS

The function and operation of foreign exchange dealers are examined in

Richard K. Lyons, "Profits and Position Control: A Week of FX Dealing," *Journal of International Money and Finance* 17 (February 1998), pp. 97–115.

Corporate exposures to financial price risk are surveyed in

Kurt Jesswein, Chuck C.Y. Kwok, and William R. Folks, Jr., "Adoption of Innovative Products in Currency Risk Management: Effects of Management Orientations and Product Characteristics," *Journal of Applied Corporate Finance* 8 (Fall 1995), pp. 115–124.

Aaron L. Phillips, "1995 Derivatives Practices and Instruments Survey," *Financial Management* 24 (Summer 1995), pp. 115–125.

The International Parity Conditions

chapter 5

Overview

Though this be madness, yet there is method in it.

William Shakespeare

This chapter describes how the currency and Eurocurrency markets are linked through a set of **international parity conditions** that relate the forward premium to the expected change in the spot rate and to cross-currency differences in nominal interest rates and inflation. These parity relations are then used to develop the real exchange rate (a measure of a currency's relative purchasing power) and exchange rate forecasts.

5.1 • THE LAW OF ONE PRICE

The law of one price, also known as **purchasing power parity** or **PPP**, is an important concept in international finance and economics:

THE LAW OF ONE PRICE (PPP)
Equivalent assets sell for the same price.

The implication is that an asset must have the same value regardless of the currency in which value is measured. For example, the law of one price implies that the spot exchange rate is determined by the price of an asset in the domestic currency relative to the price of that same asset in the foreign currency. If purchasing power parity does not hold, then there may be an opportunity to profit from the price difference.

> Arbitrage ensures that equivalent assets sell for the same price.

Arbitrage Profit

Although the popular press often uses the term **arbitrage** to refer to speculative positions, arbitrage is more strictly defined as a profitable position obtained with

- No net investment
- No risk

Arbitrage profit is a certain profit with no net investment or risk.

This type of "no money down and no risk" opportunity sounds too good to be true. In the high-stakes international currency markets, it usually is too good to be true once trading costs are included. Arbitrage opportunities are quickly exploited and, as market forces drive prices back toward equilibrium, just as quickly disappear.

Let P^d denote the price of an asset in the domestic currency and P^f denote the price of the same asset or an identical asset in the foreign currency. The law of one price requires that the value of an asset be the same whether value is measured in the foreign or domestic currency. This means that the spot exchange rate must equate the value of the asset in the foreign currency to the value in the domestic currency.

$$P^d / P^f = S^{d/f} \iff P^d = P^f S^{d/f} \tag{5.1}$$

If this equality does not hold within the bounds of transactions costs, then there is an opportunity for an arbitrage profit.[1]

As an example, suppose gold sells for $P^\$ = \$400/oz$ in New York and $P^£ = £250/oz$ in London. In the absence of market frictions, the no-arbitrage condition requires that the value of gold in dollars must equal the value of gold in pounds. So, $S^{\$/£} = P^\$/P^£ = (\$400/oz)/(£250/oz) = \$1.60/£$, or $£0.6250/\$$. If this relation does not hold, then there may be an opportunity to lock in a riskless arbitrage profit in cross-currency gold transactions.

For actively traded financial assets, such as major currencies in the interbank market, transactions costs are small in relation to trading volume. Purchasing power parity nearly always holds in these markets, because arbitrage ensures that prices are in equilibrium. Transactions costs are more prominent in markets for real assets, such as real estate. Real assets for which purchasing power parity is a fairly close approximation include actively traded commodities such as oil, silver, and gold.

The No-Arbitrage Condition

For there to be no arbitrage opportunities, PPP must hold (within the limits of transactions costs) for identical assets bought or sold simultaneously in two or more loca-

The no-arbitrage condition ensures that PPP holds within the bounds of transactions costs.

tions. This **no-arbitrage condition** is the foundation upon which the law of one price is built. Whether PPP holds depends on the extent to which market frictions restrain arbitrage from working its magic. Some barriers to the cross-border flow of real and financial assets are generated in the normal course of business as fees are charged for making a market, providing information, or transporting and delivering an asset.

Other barriers are imposed by governmental authorities, including trade barriers, taxes, and financial market controls.

Buying or selling real assets usually entails higher costs than trading a financial claim on the real asset. As an example, gold is costly to transport because of its weight, but a financial asset representing ownership of gold is easily transferred from one party to

---

1 Note that the currency units cancel one another in these equations. Keep track of your currency units to ensure that each variable always appears in its proper place.

Application

Arbitrage and the Yankee Farmer

Riskless arbitrage is a situation in which one can lock in a sure profit with no net investment or risk. Economist Hal Varian illustrates arbitrage with the following story:

> An economics professor and a Yankee farmer were waiting for a bus in New Hampshire. To pass the time, the farmer suggested that they play a game. "What kind of game would you like to play?" responded the professor. "Well," said the farmer, "how about this: I'll ask a question, and if you can't answer my question, you give me a dollar. Then you ask me a question and if I can't answer your question, I'll give you a dollar." "That sounds attractive," said the professor, "but I do have to warn you of something: I'm not just an ordinary person. I'm a professor of economics." "Oh," replied the farmer, "In that case we should change the rules. Tell you what: if you can't answer my question you still give me a dollar, but if I can't answer yours, I only have to give you 50 cents." "Yes," said the professor, "that sounds like a fair arrangement." "Okay," said the farmer. "Here's my question: what goes up the hill on seven legs and down the hill on three legs?" The professor pondered this riddle for awhile and finally replied. "Gosh, I don't know . . . what does go up the hill on seven legs and down the hill on three legs?" "Well," said the farmer, "I don't know, either. But if you give me your dollar, I'll give you my 50 cents!"

Source: Hal Varian, "The Arbitrage Principle in Financial Economics," *Economic Perspectives* (Fall 1987).

another and can be as simple as a piece of paper or a credit in an account. Although large amounts of gold are a nuisance to store (imagine a finance professor saying that!), foreign currency can be conveniently stored in the Eurocurrency market at competitive interest rates. Because of this difference between financial and real assets, actively traded financial assets are more likely to conform to the law of one price than similar real assets.

Transactions costs must be included in evaluating profit-making opportunities, whether the opportunities are arbitrage or speculative in nature. Suppose a London dealer quotes gold prices of £250/oz bid and £253/oz ask, a New York dealer quotes $401.60/oz bid and $406/oz ask, and the spot exchange rate is £0.6250/$. Stated in pounds, the New York dealer's prices are ($401.60/oz)(£0.6250/$) = £251/oz bid and ($406/oz)(£0.6250/$) = £253.75/oz ask, as shown here:

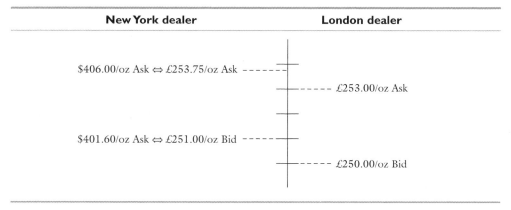

Gold bought at the New York dealer's ask price of $406/oz (or £253.75/oz) cannot be profitably sold at the London dealer's bid price of £250/oz. Conversely, gold purchased

in London at £253/oz cannot be profitably sold in New York at the $401.60/oz (or £251/oz) bid price. Including transactions costs in the exchange rate (e.g., £0.6250/$ bid and £0.6260/$ ask) would only make things worse. Arbitrage profit is not possible in this example, even though the New York and London dealers' prices are not identical.

The law of one price seldom holds for nontraded assets and cannot be used to compare assets that vary in quality. In such cases, either the asset is not standardized and PPP is not applicable (such as with housing costs in different locations), or the asset is not actively traded and there is no way to arbitrage price differences between two locations (such as between McDonald's hamburgers in London and New York).

5.2 • EXCHANGE RATE EQUILIBRIUM

Spot and forward currency and Eurocurrency contracts are traded in highly liquid financial markets. There are few governmental restrictions and transactions costs are very low for large transactions in these markets. Arbitrage between actively traded financial contracts ensures that the international parity conditions that follow hold within the bounds of transactions costs in these markets. These are international parity conditions that you can trust.

Locational Arbitrage and Bilateral Exchange Rate Equilibrium

In the absence of market frictions, the no-arbitrage condition for trade in spot exchange rates between two banks X and Y is

$$S_X^{d/f}/S_Y^{d/f} = 1 \qquad \Leftrightarrow \qquad S_X^{d/f} = S_Y^{d/f} \qquad (5.2)$$

This condition ensures that bilateral exchange rates are in equilibrium. If this relation does not hold within transactions costs, then there is an arbitrage opportunity.

An Example of Locational Arbitrage. Consider the example in Figure 5.1. Bank X is quoting "A$0.5838/€ Bid and A$0.5841/€ Ask," while Bank Y is quoting "A$0.5842/€ Bid and A$0.5845/€ Ask." If you buy €1 million from X at its A$0.5841/€ ask price and simultaneously sell €1 million to Y at its A$0.5842/€ bid price, you can lock in an arbitrage profit of A$100 (equal to 0.0001 of €1,000,000) with no net investment or risk. Transactions costs are built into the bid-ask spread, so this A$100 profit is free and clear. This transaction is called **locational arbitrage**.

Here's another way to view the exchange. You are buying from X at A$0.5841/€ and selling to Y at A$0.5842/€. The ratio from Equation 5.2 is $(S_Y^{A\$/€})/(S_X^{A\$/€}) \approx 1.0001712 > 1$, and your arbitrage profit is 0.01712 percent of the euro transaction amount. A €1 million transaction results in a profit of (€1,000,000)(0.0001712) = €171.2, or A$100 at X's A$ bid (or euro ask) price of €1.712/A$ = 1 / (A$0.5841/€).

Of course, if this is a good deal with a €1 million transaction, it is an even better deal with a €1 billion transaction. The larger the trade, the larger the profit. Trading €1 billion rather than €1 million would result in an A$100,000 arbitrage profit. If you can find such an opportunity, you've earned your salary for the day.

With exchange volume averaging more than $1 trillion per day, you can bet your bottom dollar (euro, or yen) that there are plenty of arbitrageurs looking for opportunities such as these. Dealers are just as vigilant in ensuring that their bid and offer quotes are within the bounds of other dealers. If a bank's bid or offer quotes drift outside of the

FIGURE 5.1
Arbitrage Profit in the Foreign Exchange Market

Bank X quotes "A\$0.5838/€ Bid and A\$0.5841/€ Offer"
Bank Y quotes "A\$0.5842/€ Bid and A\$0.5845/€ Offer"

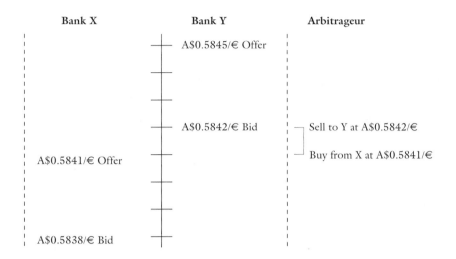

1. Arbitrageur buys €1 million from Bank X at its A\$0.5841/€ offer price.

2. Arbitrageur sells €1 million to Bank Y at its A\$0.5842/€ bid price.

Arbitrage Profit = (A\$0.0001/€) (€1,000,000) = A\$100
with **No Net Investment** and **No Risk**

narrow band defined by other dealers' quotes, they quickly find themselves inundated with buy (sell) orders for their low-priced (high-priced) currencies. Even if banks' quoted rates do not allow arbitrage, the banks offering the lowest offer (or highest bid) prices in a currency will attract the bulk of customer purchases (sales) in that currency.

The Long and the Short of It. A bank is in a long euro position and a short dollar position when, on balance, it has purchased euros and sold dollars. Conversely, a bank is in a short euro and long dollar position when it has sold euros and purchased dollars. Currency balances must be netted out; if a bank has bought €100 million and sold €120 million,

> A long (short) position in a currency refers to a purchase (sale) of that currency.

its net position is short €20 million. Dealers operating with a large foreign exchange imbalance risk big gains or losses if new information arrives and currency values change. For this reason, trading desks closely monitor their net positions and attempt to minimize their net exposures. This process further ensures that each bank's bid and offer rates are consistent with those of other banks.

Cross Rates and Triangular Arbitrage

An exchange rate that does not involve the domestic currency is called a **cross exchange rate**, or simply a **cross rate**. Financial newspapers such as *The Wall Street Journal* and the

London Financial Times publish bilateral exchange rates in a currency cross rate table like the one in Figure 5.2. Cross rate tables report bid-ask midpoints, so these rates do not represent prices that can actually be traded in the market.

Suppose you are given exchange rates for currencies d, e, and f. The no-arbitrage condition for **triangular arbitrage** in the currency markets is

$$S^{d/e}S^{e/f}S^{f/d} = 1 \qquad\qquad (5.3)$$

Again, remember to follow Rule #1 and keep track of the currencies in the numerators and denominators. The reciprocal $(S^{d/e}S^{e/f}S^{f/d})^{-1} = S^{e/d}S^{f/e}S^{d/f} = 1$ holds just as well as Equation 5.3. If this condition does not hold within the limits of transactions costs, then there is an opportunity for a riskless profit through triangular arbitrage.

An Example of Triangular Arbitrage. Suppose the following exchange rates hold between U.S. dollars, Swiss francs, and Japanese yen:

$$S^{\$/¥} = \$0.00960984/¥$$
$$S^{¥/SFr} = ¥60.750/SFr$$
$$S^{SFr/\$} = SFr1.7125/\$$$

The product of the spot rates is less than 1:

$$S^{\$/¥}S^{¥/SFr}S^{SFr/\$} = (\$0.00960984/¥)(¥60.750/SFr)(SFr1.7125/\$) = 0.999754 < 1$$

Thus, these rates are not in equilibrium and there is an arbitrage opportunity so long as transactions costs are not too high.

Suppose you start with $1 million and simultaneously make the following transactions in a *round turn* (that is, buying and then selling each currency in turn):

Buy ¥ with $	($1,000,000)/($0.00960984/¥)	= ¥104,060,000
Buy SFr with ¥	(¥104,060,000)/(¥60.750/SFr)	= SFr1,712,922
Buy $ with SFr	(SFr1,712,922)/(SFr1.7125/$)	= $1,000,246

There is no net investment if you execute these trades simultaneously. So long as your credit is good and your counterparties are trustworthy, each payment is covered by a receipt. With no net investment, you have no money at risk and you've captured a $246 arbitrage profit.

Suppose you go the wrong way on your round turn:

Buy SFr with $	($1,000,000)(SFr1.7125/$)	= SFr1,712,500
Buy ¥ with SFr	(SFr1,712,500)(¥60.750/SFr)	= ¥104,034,375
Buy $ with ¥	(¥104,034,375)($0.00960984/¥)	= $999,754

Oops! In this case, you've locked in an arbitrage *loss* of $246. How can you tell which direction to go on your round turn? If you start with dollars, do you buy yen or Swiss Francs?

Which Way Do You Go? The no-arbitrage condition is $S^{d/e}S^{e/f}S^{f/d} = 1$. If $S^{d/e}S^{e/f}S^{f/d} < 1$, then triangular arbitrage will force at least one of these exchange rates to go up. In this case, you want to buy the currency in the denominator of each spot rate with the currency in the numerator before arbitrage forces the spot rates to rise. Conversely, if $S^{d/e}S^{e/f}S^{f/d} > 1$ then at least one of the rates $S^{d/e}$, $S^{e/f}$, or $S^{f/d}$ must fall. In this case, you want to sell the

FIGURE 5.2
Currency Cross Rates, January 12, 2003

Currency	£	C$	€	HK$	¥	SFr	US$	Peso	A$	Real	Ren	DKr	Rupee	Rouble	Rand	SKr
U.K. pound	1.000	0.402	0.659	0.080	0.005	0.451	0.622	0.187	0.363	0.193	0.075	0.088	0.013	0.020	0.073	0.072
Canadian dollar	2.488	1.000	1.634	0.198	0.013	1.120	1.546	0.466	0.903	0.480	0.187	0.220	0.032	0.049	0.182	0.179
Euro	1.518	0.612	1.000	0.121	0.008	0.685	0.947	0.285	0.553	0.294	0.114	0.135	0.020	0.030	0.111	0.109
Hong Kong dollar	12.55	5.047	8.248	1.000	0.065	5.651	7.799	2.349	4.558	2.423	0.943	1.110	0.163	0.245	0.918	0.902
Japanese yen	191.5	77.24	126.1	15.30	1.000	86.48	119.4	35.95	69.63	37.09	14.44	16.99	2.493	3.751	14.04	13.80
Swiss franc	2.221	0.893	1.460	0.177	0.012	1.000	1.381	0.416	0.807	0.429	0.167	0.196	0.029	0.043	0.162	0.160
U.S. dollar	1.609	0.647	1.057	0.128	0.008	0.724	1.000	0.301	0.584	0.311	0.121	0.142	0.021	0.031	0.118	0.116
Argentine peso	5.374	2.161	3.530	0.428	0.028	2.420	3.340	1.000	1.952	1.038	0.404	0.475	0.070	0.105	0.393	0.386
Australian dollar	2.756	1.108	1.810	0.220	0.014	1.241	1.713	0.516	1.000	0.532	0.207	0.244	0.036	0.054	0.201	0.198
Brazilian real	5.423	2.181	3.563	0.432	0.028	2.442	3.371	1.015	1.970	1.000	0.408	0.480	0.070	0.106	0.397	0.390
Chinese renminbi	13.33	5.362	8.759	1.063	0.069	6.004	8.287	2.496	4.843	2.575	1.000	1.179	0.173	0.260	0.975	0.958
Danish krone	11.31	4.548	7.430	0.901	0.059	5.093	7.029	2.117	4.108	2.184	0.850	1.000	0.147	0.221	0.827	0.813
Indian rupee	77.31	31.09	50.79	6.161	0.403	34.81	48.05	14.47	28.08	14.93	5.812	6.839	1.000	1.510	5.653	5.555
Russian ruble	51.26	20.62	33.68	4.085	0.267	23.08	31.86	9.596	18.62	9.899	3.854	4.534	0.665	1.000	3.748	3.683
S. African rand	13.71	5.513	8.987	1.092	0.071	6.173	8.520	2.566	4.979	2.647	1.031	1.213	0.178	0.268	1.000	0.985
Swedish krona	13.93	5.601	9.169	1.110	0.073	6.272	8.656	2.607	5.059	2.689	1.047	1.232	0.181	0.272	1.018	1.000

Source: http://www.oanda.com.

currency in the denominator of each spot rate for the currency in the numerator before the spot rates fall.

Here is a rule for determining which currencies to buy and sell in triangular arbitrage:

- **If $S^{d/e}S^{e/f}S^{f/d} < 1$, then $S^{d/e}$, $S^{e/f}$, or $S^{f/d}$ must rise.**
  - ⟺ **Buy the currencies in the denominators with the currencies in the numerators.**
- **If $S^{d/e}S^{e/f}S^{f/d} > 1$, then $S^{d/e}$, $S^{e/f}$, or $S^{f/d}$ must fall.**
  - ⟺ **Sell the currencies in the denominators for the currencies in the numerators.**

In our example, $S^{\$/¥}S^{¥/SFr}S^{SFr/\$} = 0.999754 < 1$. One or more of these rates must rise, so you should buy the currency in the denominator of each spot rate with the currency in the numerator. You should (1) buy yen with dollars at $S^{\$/¥}$, (2) buy francs with yen at $S^{¥/SFr}$, and (3) buy dollars with francs at $S^{SFr/\$}$. In this example, triangular arbitrage is worth doing so long as transactions costs on the round turn are less than $(1-S^{\$/¥}S^{¥/SFr}S^{SFr/\$}) = 0.0246$ percent of the transaction amount (that is, \$246 on a \$1 million round turn).

Here's a complementary way of viewing the example. The inequality

$$S^{\$/¥}S^{¥/SFr}S^{SFr/\$} = 0.999754 < 1$$

can be restated as

$$(S^{\$/¥}S^{¥/SFr}S^{SFr/\$})^{-1} = S^{¥/\$}S^{SFr/¥}S^{\$/SFr} = 1.000246 > 1$$

This satisfies the second bulleted condition, so we should (1) sell dollars for yen, (2) sell yen for francs, and (3) sell francs for dollars. Of course, whenever you sell the currency in the denominator you are simultaneously buying the currency in the numerator. Viewed in this way, the second bullet is the same prescription as the first; (1) buy yen with dollars (or sell dollars for yen), (2) buy francs with yen (or sell yen for francs), and (3) buy dollars with francs (or sell francs for dollars).

In actuality, all three spot rates (as well as any related bilateral exchange rates) will probably change as arbitrage forces markets into equilibrium. Cross rate tables must be internally consistent within the bounds of transactions costs to preclude arbitrage opportunities. Currency markets are highly competitive, and arbitrage opportunities are difficult to find and fleeting at best.

5.3 • INTEREST RATE PARITY

Interest rate parity, or **IRP**, states that the forward premium between two currencies is determined by the nominal interest rate differential between those currencies. $F_t^{d/f}$ is the t–period forward exchange rate initiated at time 0 for exchange at time t. $S_0^{d/f}$ is the spot rate at time 0. Nominal interest rates in the two currencies are denoted i^f and i^d. Interest rate parity relates the currency and Eurocurrency markets as follows:[2]

$$F_t^{d/f}/S_0^{d/f} = [(1+i^d)/(1+i^f)]^t \qquad (5.4)$$

According to interest rate parity, the forward premium in Equation 5.4 reflects the interest rate differential on the right-hand side. For major currencies, nominal interest rate

---

2 The nominal interest rates i^f and i^d in Equation 5.4 are geometric mean interest rates satisfying $(1+i)^t = (1+i_1)(1+i_2)\dots(1+i_t)$, where each term represents an interest rate over a single period.

contracts are actively traded in the Eurocurrency markets. Likewise, there are active spot and forward markets for major currencies. Because each price in Equation 5.4 is actively traded, interest rate parity always holds within the bounds of transactions costs in the interbank markets.

Locational arbitrage takes advantage of price discrepancies between two locations, and triangular arbitrage takes advantage of price disequilibriums across three bilateral cross rates. Through a similar mechanism, **covered interest arbitrage** ensures that currency and Eurocurrency markets are in equilibrium. Covered interest arbitrage takes advantage of an interest rate differential that is not fully reflected in the forward premium. Disequilibrium in the interest rate parity relation induces arbitrageurs to borrow in one currency, lend in another, and cover the difference in the foreign exchange market.

> Covered interest arbitrage forces currency and Eurocurrency markets into equilibrium.

Covered Interest Arbitrage

An Example. Figure 5.3 presents an example of covered interest arbitrage. Although this example ignores bid-ask spreads, it is easy to include transactions costs by using the appropriate bid or offer prices when trading each contract. Suppose the following rates hold:

$$S_0^{\$/£} = \$1.25/£ \qquad i^\$ = 8.1500\%$$
$$F_1^{\$/£} = \$1.20/£ \qquad i^£ = 11.5625\%$$

FIGURE 5.3
Covered Interest Arbitrage and Interest Rate Parity

$$F_t^{d/f}/S_0^{d/f} = [(1 + i^d)/(1 + i^f)]^t$$

Given the following
$i^\$ = 8.15\%$
$i^£ = 11.5625\%$
$S_0^{\$/£} = \$1.25/£$
$F_t^{\$/£} = \$1.20/£$

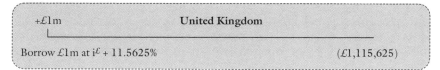

United Kingdom +£1m
Borrow £1m at $i^£$ + 11.5625% (£1,115,625)

Spot Market Sell £1m for $1.25m at $S_0^{\$/£}=\$1.25/£$

Forward Market Buy £1,115,625 forward and sell $1,338,750 forward at $F_1^{\$/£}=\$1.20/£$

Invest $1.25m at $i^\$=8.15\%$ $1,351,875
($1,250,000) **United States**

Today   One Year Later

Interest rate parity does not hold, because $F_1^{\$/\pounds}/S_0^{\$/\pounds} = 0.96 < 0.969412 = (1+i^\$)/(1+i^\pounds)$. Covered interest arbitrage proceeds as follows:

1. Borrow £1 million in the Eurocurrency market at the prevailing market interest rate of $i^\pounds = 11.5625$ percent for one year. Your obligation will be £1,115,625 in one year.

2. Exchange the £1 million for \$1.25 million at the spot exchange rate. This leaves you with a net dollar inflow today and a pound obligation in one year.

3. Invest the \$1.25 million in Eurodollars at the market rate of $i^\$ = 8.15$ percent. Your payoff will be \$1,250,000(1.0815) = \$1,351,875 in one year. The \$1.25 million outflow leaves you with a zero net position at time zero. You now have a cash inflow of \$1,351,875 and a cash outflow of £1,115,625 in one year.

4. You owe £1,115,625 in one year, based on your Europound loan in step 1. To cover this obligation, sign a 1-year forward contract in which you agree to sell \$1,338,750 = (\$1.2/£)(£1,115,625) and buy £1,115,625 at the forward rate of $F_1^{\$/\pounds} = \$1.2/\pounds$.

This transaction offsets your pound liability and leaves you with a profit of \$13,125.

Which Way Do You Go? We face the same problem here as in triangular arbitrage. Which currency do we borrow and which currency do we lend in order to take advantage of a market disequilibrium? Suppose $F_t^{d/f}/S_0^{d/f} > (1+i^d)^t/(1+i^f)^t$, so that domestic interest rates are too low and foreign interest rates are too high to justify the forward premium. If the markets are to get back into equilibrium, at least one of these rates must change.

- If the ratio $F_t^{d/f}/S_0^{d/f}$ is too high, then either $F_t^{d/f}$ must fall or $S_0^{d/f}$ must rise.
- If the ratio $(1+i^d)^t/(1+i^f)^t$ is too low, then either i^d must rise or i^f must fall.

In the previous example in which $F_t^{d/f}/S_0^{d/f} > (1+i^d)^t/(1+i^f)^t$, you should borrow at the domestic rate i^d and lend at the foreign rate i^f while covering your cash flows at the forward rate $F_t^{d/f}$. This will lock in an arbitrage profit based on the difference between the two ratios. Conversely, if $F_t^{d/f}/S_0^{d/f} < (1+i^d)^t/(1+i^f)^t$, then domestic interest rates are too high or foreign interest rates are too low to justify the forward premium. In this case, you want to borrow in the foreign currency and lend in the domestic currency. This suggests the following rules:

- If $F_t^{d/f}/S_0^{d/f} > (1+i^d)^t/(1+i^f)^t$, then borrow at i^d, buy $S_0^{d/f}$, lend at i^f, and sell $F_t^{d/f}$.
- If $F_t^{d/f}/S_0^{d/f} < (1+i^d)^t/(1+i^f)^t$, then borrow at i^f, buy $F_t^{d/f}$, lend at i^d, and sell $S_0^{d/f}$.

As with triangular arbitrage, using indirect quotes leads to an equivalent set of rules.

Foreign exchange traders will tell you that interest rate differentials determine the forward premium and not vice versa. Forward rates are almost entirely an interest rate play. If there is a disequilibrium, exchange rates are much more likely to change than Eurocurrency interest rates. Nevertheless, these rules send you in the right direction in your search for an arbitrage profit.

Changes in Spot and Forward Exchange Rates

Over daily measurement intervals, the empirical behavior of spot and forward exchange rates is nearly random, with an equal probability of rising or falling. Although there are periods of high and low volatility, your best guess for tomorrow's spot or forward exchange rate is usually today's spot or forward rate.

> Forward premiums are determined by interest rate differentials.

Even though day-to-day changes are random, covered interest arbitrage ensures that the ratio of forward to spot exchange rates is determined by the differential between foreign and domestic interest rates. Because interest rates are far less volatile than exchange rates, spot and forward exchange rates move up or down in tandem with daily changes in exchange rates. The forward premium only changes when a foreign or domestic interest rate changes.

5.4 • LESS RELIABLE INTERNATIONAL PARITY CONDITIONS

Covered interest arbitrage is possible because each of the contracts in the interest rate parity relation is actively traded in the interbank market. Disequilibria involving contractual cash flows in these markets are quickly forced back into equilibrium. Disequilibria in non-traded prices cannot be so easily arbitraged, and can persist for long periods of time. Nevertheless, speculative activity suggests that the parity relations in this section should hold in the long run.

Relative Purchasing Power Parity

In our discussion of the law of one price, P^d and P^f represented the domestic and foreign prices of a single asset or of two identical assets. Suppose the asset is a standardized basket of consumer goods and services, such as a consumer price index. Let P_t^d and P_t^f represent the prices of domestic and foreign consumer price indexes at time t.[3] Percentage changes in consumer price levels are

$$p_t^d = (P_t^d - P_{t-1}^d) / P_{t-1}^d \qquad \text{and} \qquad p_t^f = (P_t^f - P_{t-1}^f) / P_{t-1}^f$$

Relative to an arbitrarily defined base period at t=0, consumer prices at time t depend on inflation during the intervening periods according to

$$P_t^d = P_0^d(1+p_1^d)(1+p_2^d) \ldots (1+p_t^d) \qquad \text{and} \qquad P_t^f = P_0^f(1+p_1^f)(1+p_2^f) \ldots (1+p_t^f)$$

The spot rate should change according to expectations of domestic and foreign inflation.[4]

$$E[S_t^{d/f}] / S_0^{d/f} = [(1+E[p^d]) / (1+E[p^f])]^t \tag{5.5}$$

This form of the law of one price is known as **relative purchasing power parity**, or **RPPP**. RPPP states that the expected appreciation or depreciation of the spot rate is determined by the expected inflation differential. As a special case, if inflation is a known constant in each currency, then RPPP can be stated as $E[S_t^{d/f}]/S_0^{d/f} = [(1+p^d)/(1+p^f)]^t$.

> Expected spot rate changes are determined by expectations of future inflation.

---

[3] In reality, people in different countries consume different goods and services so that these prices reflect different consumption baskets. Because PPP does not allow us to compare two different consumption baskets, we need to interpret the following equations with a dose of literary license.

[4] Equation 5.5 is derived as $E[S_t^{d/f}]/S_0^{d/f} = E[(P_t^d/P_t^f)]/(P_0^d/P_0^f) = (E[P_t^d]/E[P_t^f])/(P_0^d/P_0^f) = (E[P_t^d]/P_0^d)/(E[P_t^f]/P_0^f) = (1+E[p^d])^t/(1+E[p^f])^t$, where the ratio $(E[P_t]/P_0) = (1+E[p])^t$ is one plus the expected geometric mean inflation rate over the next t periods satisfying $(1+E[p])^t = (1+E[p_1])(1+E[p_2])...(1+E[p_t])$.

Because neither expected inflation nor expected future spot rates of exchange are traded contracts, this relationship only holds on average. Over measurement intervals of a few days or even months, spot exchange rates move in nearly a random fashion and Equation 5.5 has low predictive power. In the long run, inflation differences eventually prevail and exchange rate changes are more highly correlated with inflation differentials.

Figure 5.4 graphs mean annual changes in spot exchange rates against inflation differentials relative to the U.S. dollar for major currencies in the period since 1960. As predicted by RPPP, the dollar tended to rise against currencies with higher inflation, such as the South African rand, the Spanish peseta, and the Italian lira. Conversely, the dollar tended to fall against currencies with lower inflation, such as the Swiss franc, the German mark, and the Singapore dollar. Although it is comforting to know that inflation differentials are eventually reflected in exchange rates, there is quite a bit of variability around the theoretical 45-degree line even over this 40-year period. RPPP holds only over the long run and is of no use in predicting day-to-day changes in spot exchange rates.

Forward Rates as Predictors of Future Spot Rates

Forward rates predict future spot rates.

Forward parity asserts that forward exchange rates are unbiased predictors of future spot rates; that is, $F_t^{d/f} = E[S_t^{d/f}]$. If forward parity holds, then forward premiums reflect the expected change in the spot exchange rate according to

$$F_t^{d/f} / S_0^{d/f} = E[S_t^{d/f}] / S_0^{d/f} \qquad (5.6)$$

FIGURE 5.4
Relative Purchasing Power Parity

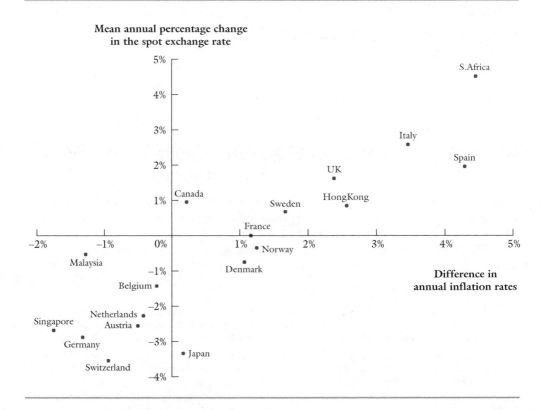

Although there is no way to arbitrage a price difference, speculative activity ensures that the forward rate does not diverge too far from the market's consensus expectation.

Forward rates are not good predictors of future spot rates over short forecasting horizons. Figure 5.5 plots $s^{¥/\$}$ against the forward premium $FP^{¥/\$} = (F_t^{d/f}/S_{t-1}^{d/f})-1$ for 1-month forward rates for the U.S. dollar against the Japanese yen over a recent 10-year period. Forward parity predicts the differences between actual and predicted spot rates should lie along a 45-degree line according to

$$s_t^{¥/\$} = \alpha + \beta\, FP_t^{¥/\$} + e_t \qquad (5.7)$$

with $\alpha = 0$ and $\beta = 1$. Contrary to theory, there is almost no relation between exchange rate changes and forward premiums over 1-month horizons in Figure 5.5. Apparently, 1-month forward rates are not good predictors of next month's spot rates.

Froot and Thaler review 75 empirical studies of this relation over short forecasting periods and find that the slope coefficient in Equation 5.7 is always less than unity and often negative.[5] The mean slope coefficient across the studies they reviewed was –0.88. This empirical finding is referred to as the **forward premium anomaly** and is often interpreted as evidence of a bias in forward exchange rates. However, this bias (if it exists) is small in magnitude and unreliable as an exchange rate predictor. Moreover, some of the persistence in the forward premium appears to be a consequence of persistence in other factors, such as in exchange rate volatility, rather than in the forward premium per se.[6]

FIGURE 5.5
One-Month Forward Rates as Predictors of Spot Rates: Yen per Dollar Exchange Rates

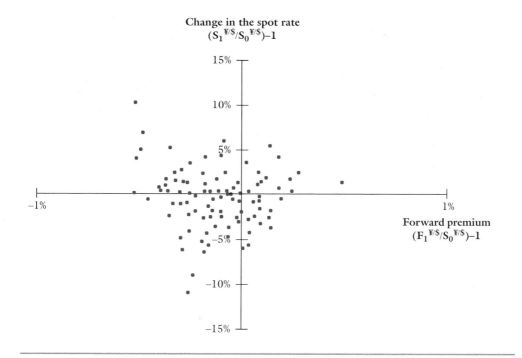

---

5 Froot and Thaler, "Anomalies: Foreign Exchange," *Journal of Economic Perspectives* (1990).

6 See Baillie and Bollerslev, "The Forward Premium Anomaly Is Not as Bad as You Think," *Journal of International Money and Finance* (2000) and Moore and Roche, "Less of a Puzzle: A New Look at the Forward Forex Market," *Journal of International Economics* (2003).

In this book, we'll often use forward exchange rates as predictors of future spot rates. At the very least, the forward premium reflects the relative opportunity cost of capital in the two currencies through interest rate parity. The forecasting performance of forward rates improves considerably over longer forecasting horizons. The long-run performance of forward rates as predictors of future spot rates is similar to the long-run performance of inflation rate differentials displayed in Figure 5.4.

The International Fisher Relation

> The international Fisher relation relates interest rates to inflation differentials.

Interest rate parity in Equation 5.4 includes the ratio $(1+i^d)/(1+i^f)$. From the Fisher equation, each of the nominal interest rate compensates for a required real return ι and expected inflation $E[p]$. Substituting the Fisher equation in the numerator and denominator leads to

$$(1+i^d) / (1+i^f) = [(1+\iota^d)(1+E[p^d])] / [(1+\iota^f)(1+E[p^f])]$$

Real interest parity asserts that real required returns on comparable assets are equal across currencies, so that $\iota^d = \iota^f$. This is a consequence of the law of one price applied to real rates of return in different currencies. If real interest parity holds, then $(1+\iota^d)$ and $(1+\iota^f)$ cancel and the nominal interest rate differential reflects the expected inflation differential according to $(1+i^d)/(1+i^f) = (1+E[p^d])/(1+E[p^f])$. Measured over t periods, the relation is

$$[(1+i^d) / (1+i^f)]^t = [(1+E[p^d]) / (1+E[p^f])]^t \qquad (5.8)$$

This relation is called the **international Fisher relation**.

Figure 5.6 compares yield differentials on 3-month government securities to realized inflation differentials over the corresponding 3-month periods using the U.K. and the U.S. for illustration. As you can see from the figure, there is almost no relation between realized inflation and nominal interest rate differentials for quarterly intervals.

FIGURE 5.6
International Fisher Relation (pound sterling versus U.S. dollar on an annualized basis)

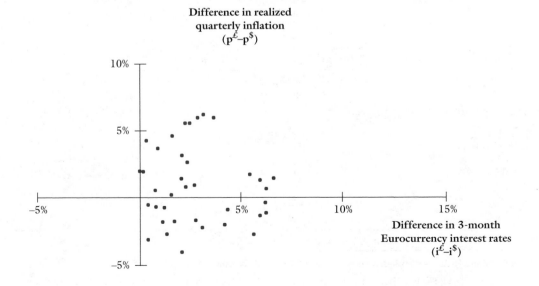

There are two reasons the international Fisher relation is not visible in Figure 5.6. First, expected real returns are not always equal across currencies.[7] Figure 5.7 plots realized real returns, $\iota = (1+i)/(1+p)-1$, to 3-month Euroyen, Europound, and Eurodollar contracts over 1983–2002. In the early 1990s, real Eurodollar returns were persistently lower than real returns in most other eurocurrencies. At other times, real returns appear to be approximately equal across currencies. Second, volatility in realized inflation makes it difficult to test real interest parity and further obscures the international Fisher relation.

Investors attracted to high real interest rates eventually drive prices upward in currencies with high promised real returns. This, in turn, drives promised yields downward and pushes real rates back toward equilibrium. Still, at any given point in time, there can be fairly substantial cross-currency differences in real interest rates. Variations in real interest rates across currencies and over time mean that inflation differentials have little power to

> Real interest rates are not equal across currencies and fluctuate over time as well.

FIGURE 5.7
Real Interest Rates

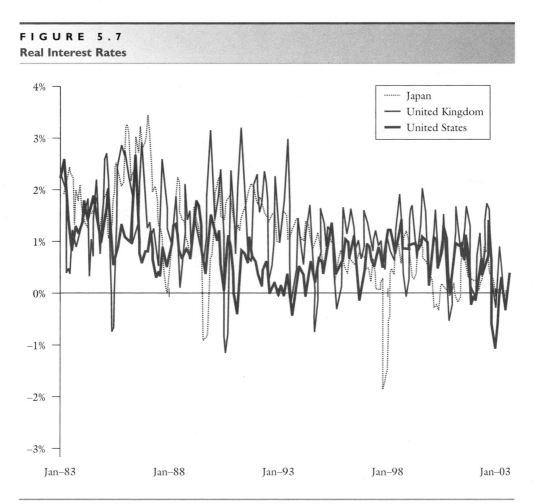

Sources: Three-month Eurocurrency interest rates and quarterly inflation from the Bank of Japan, the Bank of England, and the U.S. Federal Reserve System.

---

7 See Mishkin, "Are Real Interest Rates Equal Across Countries? An Empirical Investigation of International Parity Conditions," *Journal of Finance* (1984).

explain interest rate differentials. As with other international parity conditions that involve nontraded prices, Equation 5.8 holds only over the long run.

Uncovered Interest Parity

Uncovered interest parity equates nominal interest rate differences to expected changes in exchange rates.

The international parity conditions are summarized in Figure 5.8. Note that the ratios that lie diagonally across the figure must also be equal in equilibrium. For example, because interest rates are tied to the forward premium and the forward premium is a predictor of change in the spot rate, then

$$[(1+i^d) / (1+i^f)]^t = E[S_t^{d/f}] / S_0^{d/f} \qquad (5.9)$$

This relation is called **uncovered interest parity** (or *Fisher Open*) and states that nominal interest rates reflect expected changes in exchange rates, and vice versa. Similarly, the other diagonal equality in Figure 5.8 should hold in equilibrium:

$$F_t^{d/f} / S_0^{d/f} = [(1+E[p^d]) / (1+E[p^f])]^t \qquad (5.10)$$

This completes the circuit of international parity conditions relating exchange rates, real and nominal interest rates, and inflation in the currency and Eurocurrency markets.

FIGURE 5.8
International Parity Conditions (implications of the law of one price)

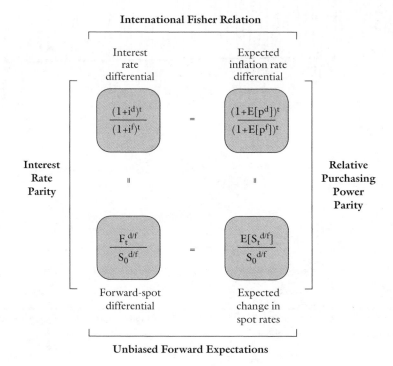

International Fisher Relation

Interest rate differential — Expected inflation rate differential

$$\frac{(1+i^d)^t}{(1+i^f)^t} = \frac{(1+E[p^d])^t}{(1+E[p^f])^t}$$

Interest Rate Parity   Relative Purchasing Power Parity

‖   ‖

$$\frac{F_t^{d/f}}{S_0^{d/f}} = \frac{E[S_t^{d/f}]}{S_0^{d/f}}$$

Forward-spot differential — Expected change in spot rates

Unbiased Forward Expectations

5.5 • THE REAL EXCHANGE RATE

Suppose you invest $100,000 in a 1-year certificate of deposit earning 10 percent. At the end of the year, you'll have $110,000 in the bank. This sounds great. But what if inflation was also 10 percent during the year? Solving the Fisher equation, your real rate of return during the period was $\iota^\$ = (1+i^\$)/(1+p^\$) - 1 = (1.10/1.10) - 1 = 0\%$. This is not so great. In real or purchasing power terms, you are no better off than at the start of the year. And you are a year older, if not wiser.

A similar phenomenon occurs with changes in exchange rates. If you look only at changes in nominal exchange rates, you'll miss real changes in purchasing power across currencies. In order to identify real, as opposed to nominal, changes in spot rates of exchange, we need to adjust nominal exchange rates for the effects of inflation.

Real Changes in Purchasing Power

Suppose today's spot exchange rate is $S_0^{¥/\$} = ¥100/\$$, as in Figure 5.9. Expected inflation is $E[p^¥] = 0$ in Japan and $E[p^\$] = 10$ percent in the United States. If change in the nominal exchange rate merely reflects changes in the relative purchasing power of the yen and the dollar, the expected future spot rate in one period should be

$$E[S_1^{¥/\$}] = S_0^{¥/\$} [(1+E[p^¥])/(1+E[p^\$])] = (¥100/\$)(1.00/1.10) = ¥90.91/\$$$

according to RPPP in Equation 5.5. Suppose that one year later the inflation estimates turn out to be accurate but the dollar has appreciated to $S_1^{¥/\$} = ¥110/\$$. In nominal terms, this is a 10 percent appreciation of the dollar. But, relative to the expected spot rate of ¥90.91/$, this is a 21 percent real (inflation-adjusted) appreciation of the dollar:

$$\frac{(\text{Actual}) - (\text{Expected})}{(\text{Expected})} = (¥110/\$ - ¥90.91/\$)/(¥90.91/\$) = 21\%$$

This 21 percent real surprise in the level of the exchange rate is shown in the top panel of Figure 5.9. In this example, the dollar has experienced a 21 percent appreciation in purchasing power relative to the yen. The real exchange rate captures changes in the purchasing power of a currency relative to other currencies by backing out the effects of inflation from changes in nominal exchange rates.

The Real Exchange Rate

In deriving the international parity conditions, we used the law of one price as our guiding principle. This faith is well founded for actively traded financial contracts, such as currencies and Eurocurrencies traded in the interbank markets. For these assets, arbitrage is quick to eliminate deviations from PPP. For less actively traded assets, especially those with many barriers to trade such as land or labor, deviations from PPP can persist for several years.

The **real exchange rate** $X_t^{d/f}$ is the nominal exchange rate $S_t^{d/f}$ adjusted for relative changes in domestic and foreign price levels (that is, adjusted for differential inflation) since an arbitrarily defined base period at time t=0:

$$X_t^{d/f} = (S_t^{d/f}/S_0^{d/f}) ((1+p_1^f)/(1+p_1^d)) ((1+p_2^f)/(1+p_2^d)) \ldots ((1+p_t^f)/(1+p_t^d))$$

$$= (S_t^{d/f}/S_0^{d/f}) \prod_{\tau=1}^{t} [(1+p_\tau^f)/(1+p_\tau^d)] \tag{5.11}$$

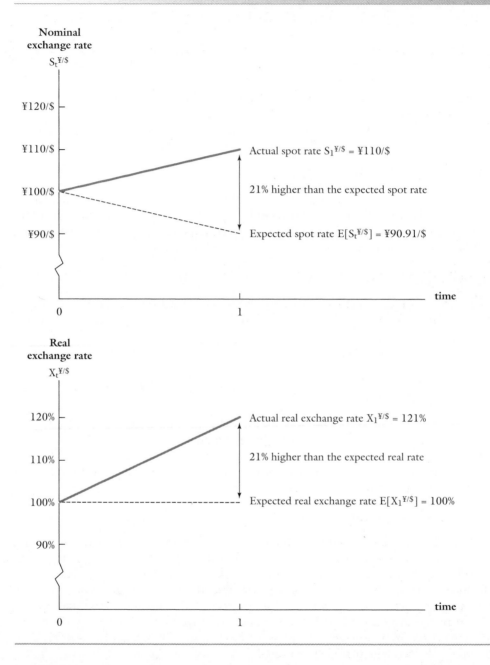

FIGURE 5.9
Deviations from Expected Future Spot Rates: Changes in the Real Exchange Rate

Changes in a real exchange rate indicate changes in relative purchasing power.

Dividing the nominal spot rate $S_t^{d/f}$ at time t by the base period spot rate $S_0^{d/f}$ states the real exchange rate as a percentage of the beginning spot rate. The inflation adjustment indicates whether this change in the nominal exchange rate reflects the inflation differential between the two currencies. If change in the nominal spot rate of exchange exactly offsets the mean inflation differential, then the real exchange rate will remain at 100 percent of its base level.

Real exchange rates provide a measure of change in the purchasing power of two currencies relative to a base period. The formula for calculating the percentage change in the real exchange rate during a single period is

$$1 + x_t^{d/f} = (X_t^{d/f} / X_{t-1}^{d/f}) = (S_t^{d/f} / S_{t-1}^{d/f})\,[(1 + p_t^f)/(1 + p_t^d)] \tag{5.12}$$

The percentage change in the real exchange rate depends only on change in the nominal exchange rate and the inflation differential during the period.

It is somewhat misleading to retain the currency units on the symbols for the real exchange rate. The currency units cancel from the ratio $S_t^{d/f}/S_0^{d/f}$ in Equations 5.11 and 5.12. The inflation rates are also unit-less. The resulting measure $X_t^{d/f}$ is a number, such as 1.21, representing a 21 percent increase in the real value of the currency in the denominator relative to the base period. The currency units are retained as a reminder that the real exchange rate measures the purchasing power of the currency in the denominator in terms of the currency in the numerator.

Let's return to Figure 5.9. The ratio $(S_1^{¥/\$})/(S_0^{¥/\$}) = (¥110/\$)/(¥100/\$) = 1.10$ indicates that the dollar increased 10 percent in nominal terms during the period. This was despite the fact that dollar inflation was 10 percent higher than yen inflation. By definition, the beginning level of the real exchange rate is $X_0^{¥/\$} = 1.00$. Equations 5.11 and 5.12 yield

$$1 + x_1^{¥/\$} = X_1^{¥/\$}/X_0^{¥/\$} = [(¥110/\$)/(¥100/\$)][(1.10)/(1.00)] = 1.21$$

or a real exchange rate that is 21 percent higher than at the start of the period. The dollar rose in purchasing power by 21 percent in this example.

It is convenient to pick a base period in which the relative purchasing power of the two currencies is close to equilibrium. In this case, PPP holds and $S_0^{d/f} = P_0^d/P_0^f$. Because any base period can be chosen, the level of the real exchange rate is not necessarily informative. In particular, it is inappropriate to claim that a currency is overvalued simply because the level of the real exchange rate is greater than 1. It may be that the currency was even more overvalued (that is, had greater purchasing power than other currencies) in the base period and is only slightly less overvalued now. Further, there are cross-currency differences in prices, so that a currency can have more purchasing power in some assets than others. Because choice of the base period is arbitrary, a change in the real exchange rate merely indicates change in the purchasing power of one currency relative to another.

Figure 5.10 plots the real value of the U.S. dollar against the British pound and Japanese yen from 1971 through 2002. The mean level is set to 100 for each series. Because the dollar is of interest in this figure, the dollar is placed in the denominator of each real exchange rate series. If RPPP held at all times, the real value of the dollar would remain at 100 percent of its base value.

As Figure 5.10 shows, there are large and persistent deviations from real purchasing power parity. The dollar rose in purchasing power in the early 1980s, reaching its peak in March 1985. In September 1985, the Group of Ten (in the Plaza Accord) agreed to cooperate in an attempt to bring down the real value of the dollar. It is difficult to tell whether this coalition was successful. The subsequent fall in the value of the dollar may have been caused by monetary or political factors. In fact, the dollar had already begun to fall in real terms by the spring of 1985. In any case, by 1987 the dollar had fallen in real terms back to its 1980 value.

> Real exchange rates deviate from PPP.

Academic studies have reached similar conclusions:

- Deviations from real exchange rate parity can be substantial in the short run.

> Deviations from real PPP can last several years.

- Deviations from real exchange rate parity can last several years.

Although real exchange rates tend to revert to their long-run average, in the short run there can be substantial deviations from the long-run average. In a study of real exchange

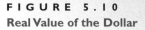

FIGURE 5.10
Real Value of the Dollar

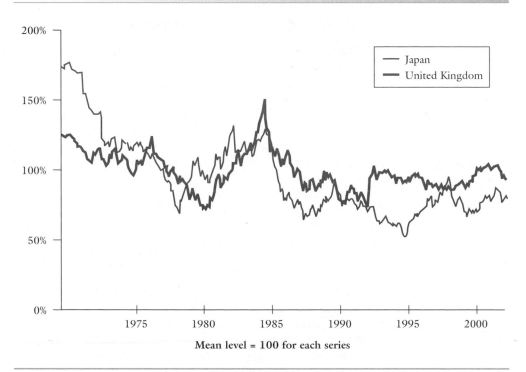

Mean level = 100 for each series

rates over a 200-year sample period, Lothian and Taylor estimate that it takes 3 to 6 years for a real exchange rate disequilibrium to be reduced by half.[8]

Deviations from parity in real exchange rates appear to be a consequence of differential frictions in the markets for real and financial assets, with goods prices adjusting more slowly than financial prices.[9] PPP holds for actively traded financial assets, but seldom holds for inactively traded goods such as land or labor. Hence, PPP typically does not hold for general price levels, either. It can take markets a long time to bring prices back into equilibrium.

The Effect of a Change in the Real Exchange Rate

If relative purchasing power parity holds, then changes in nominal exchange rates should reflect the difference between foreign and domestic inflation. This implies that nominal exchange rate changes should have little economic significance of their own. Real changes in exchange rates, on the other hand, have a profound impact on MNCs' operating exposures to currency risk and a country's international trade. In particular,

- A **real appreciation** of the domestic currency raises the price of domestic goods relative to foreign goods.

- A **real depreciation** of the domestic currency lowers the price of domestic goods relative to foreign goods.

---

8 Lothian and Taylor, "Real Exchange Rate Behavior: The Recent Float from the Perspective of the Past Two Centuries," *Journal of Political Economy* (1996). Similar estimates are found in Abuaf and Jorion, "Purchasing Power Parity in the Long Run," *Journal of Finance* (1990).

9 Dornbusch, "Expectations and Exchange Rate Dynamics," *Journal of Political Economy* (1976).

Market Update

The International Cost of Living

The cost of living is an example of a price that varies around the world. Even if you could transport your lifestyle to another location, the cost of maintaining that lifestyle would vary depending on the cost and availability of local goods and services. Here are 2000 international cost of living indices using Zurich (Switzerland) as the base.

Location	Cost of living index	$S_0^{f/\$}$	Location	Cost of living index	$S_0^{f/\$}$
Tokyo	140.1	112.21	Amsterdam	74.2	1.1132
Oslo	105.0	9.0616	Dublin	72.6	1.1132
New York	103.8	1.0000	Luxembourg	71.3	1.1132
Chicago	100.0	1.0000	Sydney	70.9	1.8295
Zurich	100.0	1.6855	Berlin	70.4	1.1132
Stockholm	99.3	9.6604	Brussels	69.5	1.1132
Singapore	98.1	1.7361	Milan	66.8	1.1132
Seoul	97.3	1216.9	Athens	63.4	325.20
Caracas	96.4	698.85	Mexico City	62.2	9.4670
London	94.8	0.6836	Rio de Janeiro	62.0	1.8050
Geneva	94.4	1.6855	Kuala Lumpur	59.6	3.8000
Copenhagen	92.7	8.3059	Sao Paulo	59.2	1.9632
Taipei	91.1	33.123	Moscow	59.1	31.337
Los Angeles	89.1	1.0000	Barcelona	57.0	1.1132
Hong Kong	88.6	7.7991	Lisbon	56.3	1.1132
Shanghai	86.3	8.2771	Madrid	55.5	1.1132
Helsinki	83.4	1.1132	Bangkok	55.0	43.952
Paris	81.6	1.1132	Johannesburg	50.9	7.6439
Vienna	80.7	1.1132	Manila	48.5	50.429
Montreal	74.4	1.5219	Bombay	37.4	46.780

To estimate the current cost of living, adjust the index as if it were a real exchange rate:

$$\text{Current cost of living} \approx (2000 \text{ cost}) \ (S_t^{f/\$}/S_0^{f/\$}) \ [(1+p^\$) / (1+p^f)]^t$$

Use today's exchange rate $S_t^{f/\$}$ and realized inflation rates since 2000. December 2000 exchange rates against the U.S. dollar are provided in the table as a base rate, $S_0^{f/\$}$.

Source: Cost of living indices from "Prices and Earnings Around the Globe," Union Bank of Switzerland, 2000. Indices reflect 111 goods and services weighted by consumer habits. Exchange rates are from the U.S. Federal Reserve Board of St. Louis.

http://www.ubs.com

http://www.stls.frb.org

A real appreciation of the domestic currency is both good and bad news for the domestic economy. A real appreciation helps domestic importers and consumers because raw materials and imported goods cost less. This also helps to hold down inflation. On the other hand, it hurts domestic exporters and their workers as goods and services produced by domestic companies are relatively expensive in international markets. The effect on domestic producers is asymmetric, in that goods and services competing on the world market are hurt more than those competing solely on the domestic market. This shifts resources

> A real appreciation of a currency indicates an increase in purchasing power.

Application

Keeping Track of Your Currency Units

In each of the international parity conditions, the currency in the numerator (denominator) stays in the numerator (denominator) of the interest rates and exchange rates. For example, in relative purchasing power parity

$$E[S_t^{d/f}]/S_0^{d/f} = [(1+E[p^d])/(1+E[p^f])]^t \qquad (5.5)$$

the domestic currency in the numerator of each spot rate also appears in the numerator of the ratio of inflation rates on the right-hand side. The foreign currency appears in the denominator.

Real exchange rates are the only exception to this rule. With a real exchange rate, we want to *reverse* the effects of inflation on nominal exchange rates:

$$1+x_t^{d/f} = (X_t^{d/f}/X_{t-1}^{d/f}) = (S_t^{d/f}/S_{t-1}^{d/f}) [(1+p_t^f)/(1+p_t^d)] \qquad (5.12)$$

The currency in the numerator of the spot rates moves to the denominator of the ratio of inflation rates, and vice versa. Real exchange rates provide the only exception to the "numerator to numerator and denominator to denominator" rule.

---

within the domestic economy from export-oriented firms toward firms that import goods or services from other countries or that compete primarily in the domestic market.

Consider the labor expense of a Japanese firm that manufactures goods in Japan and sells these goods in Japanese and foreign markets. Two countervailing forces are at work when the yen appreciates in real terms. A real appreciation of the yen increases the costs of Japanese manufacturers relative to foreign competitors. Conversely, the labor costs of non-Japanese competitors remain constant in their local currencies but decrease in terms of yen. Under these conditions, Japanese factories face a real cost disadvantage.

Consider instead a Japanese bank looking for investment opportunities overseas. A real appreciation of the yen means that foreign assets become less expensive for the Japanese bank. If the bank is in the market for a real estate purchase, a real appreciation of the yen makes California real estate relatively less expensive than Japanese real estate. As capital flows out of costly Japanese assets and into relatively less expensive assets in the United States, the value of the yen will tend to fall. Market equilibrium will eventually be restored, if only in passing.

A real depreciation of the domestic currency is the flip side of a real appreciation. A real depreciation of the domestic currency results in lower prices for domestic goods in both foreign and domestic markets. This promotes domestic employment. On the downside, a real depreciation results in higher prices for imported goods and an increase in domestic inflation. Which of these countervailing forces eventually triumphs determines whether a real depreciation is, in aggregate, good or bad for the domestic economy.

5.6 • EXCHANGE RATE FORECASTING

Managers can deal with exposure to currency risk in several ways. First, they can ignore it in the belief that currency exposure is diversifiable and does not change investors' required returns. Although this may be true, managers are seldom as diversified as equity and care about the firm's total (rather than just systematic) risk. Second, managers can hedge cur-

Application

rency risk, perhaps through the financial markets. This is consistent with managers' preferences, and often the preferred alternative. A third alternative is to actively manage the firm's currency risk exposures, hedging when exchange rates are expected to turn against the MNC and accepting exposure to currency risk when they are expected to favor the MNC. This is an effective strategy if, and only if, the MNC can successfully anticipate exchange rate changes.

The concept of informational efficiency is particularly important for answering this question. In an informationally efficient market, currencies are correctly priced based on available information. In an efficient market, it is not possible to consistently "beat the market" and earn returns beyond those obtainable by chance in positions of similar risk. The premise that markets are informationally efficient is called the **efficient market hypothesis**.

Attempts to forecast short-term changes in exchange rates in the floating-rate era since Bretton Woods have had difficulty beating a naive guess of today's spot exchange rate. Long-run forecasts of nominal exchange rates have difficulty beating the forward rate as a predictor. It is difficult to beat these naive guesses because of the highly random nature of day-to-day changes in exchange rates.

> Changes in currency values are difficult to predict.

Market-Based Exchange Rate Forecasts

Exchange rate forecasts are provided by several of the international parity conditions.

- $E[S_t^{d/f}] = F_t^{d/f}$ forward parity
- $E[S_t^{d/f}] = S_0^{d/f} [(1+i^d)/(1+i^f)]^t$ a combination of forward and interest rate parity
- $E[S_t^{d/f}] = S_0^{d/f} [(1+p^d)/(1+p^f)]^t$ relative purchasing power parity

The first two are equivalent if interest rate parity is enforced through covered interest arbitrage.

The beauty of market-based forecasts is that anyone with access to a financial newspaper can make them. Unfortunately, these forecasts do not work well in the short term. The international parity conditions provide a signal as to which direction a currency should change in equilibrium. Over daily intervals, this signal is weak relative to exchange rate volatility. As the forecasting horizon lengthens, the signal-to-noise ratio improves.[10] Beyond one year, cross-currency inflation and interest rate differentials begin to impose themselves and forecasts based on the parity conditions begin to dominate the current spot rate as predictors of nominal exchange rates.

---

10 As shown in Appendix 5-A, the strength of the signals from the international parity conditions increases with time. If exchange rates are a random walk, then exchange rate volatility increases with the square root of time and the signal-to-noise ratio increases at the rate $T/\sqrt{T} = \sqrt{T}$.

International parity conditions can be used to forecast exchange rates.

Although the international parity conditions are useful for forecasting long-term trends in nominal exchange rates, they are less helpful in forecasting real exchange rates because real exchange rates are assumed to be constant in the international parity relations. Real exchange rate forecasts are important for managing operating exposures to currency risk. The best that can be said from the international parity conditions is that real exchange rates will eventually return to their long-run average.

Model-Based Exchange Rate Forecasts

To add value for their clients, forecasters supplement market-based forecasts with technical or fundamental analysis. **Technical analysis** looks for recurring patterns that predict future exchange rates, and can be effective for short-term forecasts. **Fundamental analysis** tries to link exchange rate behavior to economic fundamentals, and is useful for long-term forecasts. Some forecasters faithfully use only one approach and forswear the other. Others combine what they consider to be the best features of each approach.

Technical analysis uses past price patterns to forecast exchange rates.

Technical Analysis. Technical analysts believe that there are patterns in exchange rates and that these patterns allow them to predict future exchange rates. This would not be possible in a **weak form efficient market**, in which prices fully reflect the information in past prices. Some technical forecasters use statistical measures such as autocorrelations or filter rules to identify patterns in the data. Others use heuristic rules of thumb or intuition. Some of these patterns are only in the eye of the beholder, but others can be useful predictors.

Technical analysis has often been dismissed by an academic literature that presumes exchange rate movements are random. Nevertheless, technical analysis has always been popular among practitioners. A survey of foreign exchange dealers in London found that more than 90 percent of respondents placed some weight on technical analysis.[11]

A popular technical trading rule is to borrow in a currency with a low nominal interest rate and invest in a currency with a higher nominal interest rate. Exchange rates are close to a random walk, so this should yield a positive return. Froot and Thaler estimated that borrowing for one year in one currency and investing these funds in another currency at a 1 percent higher interest rate yields an expected payoff of 2 percent per year.[12] For example, based on a $1,000 initial amount, this trading strategy has an expected payoff of $20. Unfortunately, Froot and Thaler find that the standard deviation of this strategy is 36 percent. Because 68 percent of the normal distribution is within one standard deviation of the mean, there is a 32 percent chance of actual return being more than $380 ($20 + $360) or less than –$340 ($20 – $360). Positive expected returns to this strategy come with a great deal of risk. Although most investors prefer more conventional investments, nominal interest rate differences can help improve exchange rate forecasts.[13]

Fundamental analysis uses economic data to forecast long-term exchange rate trends.

Fundamental Analysis. Fundamental analysis typically employs an econometric model to discern the causes of changes in currency values from economic data, such as the balance of payments, money supply, industrial production, or consumer confidence.

---

11 Taylor and Allen, "The Use of Technical Analysis in the Foreign Exchange Market," *Journal of International Money and Finance* (June 1992).

12 Froot and Thaler, "Anomalies." See also Baz, Breedon, Naik, and Peress, "Optimal Portfolios of Foreign Currencies," *Journal of Portfolio Management* (Fall 2001).

13 Neely and Weller, "Technical Trading Rules in the European Monetary System," *Journal of International Money and Finance* 8 (June 1999).

Fundamental analysts believe that the foreign exchange market is not semistrong form efficient. Prices in a **semistrong form efficient market** reflect all publicly available information, including past price and volume histories, balance-of-payments data, and other publicly available economic information. Fundamental analysts believe that publicly available information can lead to superior exchange rate forecasts.

The link between currency values and fundamental information can be difficult to establish. A part of the reason is that exchange rates react only to new information. For example, if the market has already incorporated its expectations regarding inflation into exchange rates, then only that part of a government inflation report that is unexpected will cause a further change in exchange rates. Without a precise estimate of expected inflation, it is difficult to demonstrate a link between unexpected inflation and exchange rate changes. Further, exchange rates may respond to fundamental variables with a lag, or only in the long run. For these reasons, exchange rates do not respond to fundamental information in an easy-to-decipher way. Nevertheless, fundamental analysis can have good predictive power for long-term forecasts.[14]

5.7 • SUMMARY

This chapter develops the implications of the law of one price (also known as purchasing power parity, or PPP) for international currency and Eurocurrency markets. The law of one price states that

---

Equivalent assets sell for the same price.

The law of one price is enforced by the profit-making activities of market participants. Riskless arbitrage ensures that the following international parity conditions hold within the bounds of transactions costs in the interbank currency and Eurocurrency markets.

Purchasing power parity	$P_t^d/P_t^f = S_t^{d/f}$	(5.1)
Bilateral equilibrium	$S_Y^{d/f}/S_X^{d/f} = 1$	(5.2)
Triangular equilibrium	$S^{d/e}S^{e/f}S^{f/d} = 1$	(5.3)
Interest rate parity	$F_t^{d/f}/S_0^{d/f} = [(1+i^d)/(1+i^f)]^t$	(5.4)

The law of one price has implications for noncontractual prices as well, but only in the long run. International parity conditions that include expectations of future price and exchange rate levels include

Relative PPP	$E[S_t^{d/f}]/S_0^{d/f} = [(1+E[p^d])/(1+E[p^f])]^t$	(5.5)
Unbiased forward expectations	$F_t^{d/f}/S_0^{d/f} = E[S_t^{d/f}]/S_0^{d/f}$	(5.6)
International Fisher relation	$[(1+i^d)/(1+i^f)]^t = [(1+E[p^d])/(1+E[p^f])]^t$	(5.8)

Because they are at least partially based on nontraded contracts, these relations are less reliable than those in Equations 5.1 through 5.4.

Real exchange rates measure the purchasing power of a currency relative to another currency or currencies. Change in the real exchange rate during period t is calculated as

$$1+x_t^{d/f} = (X_t^{d/f}/X_{t-1}^{d/f}) = (S_t^{d/f}/S_{t-1}^{d/f})[(1+p_t^f)/(1+p_t^d)] \qquad (5.12)$$

---

14 See Mark and Sul, "Nominal Exchange Rates and Monetary Fundamentals: Evidence from a Small Post–Bretton Woods Panel," *Journal of International Economics* (February 2001).

Changes in real exchange rates have the following effects:

- A real appreciation of the domestic currency raises the price of domestic goods relative to foreign goods.
- A real depreciation of the domestic currency lowers the price of domestic goods relative to foreign goods.

Empirical evidence indicates that deviations from PPP can be substantial in the short run and are typically returned to equilibrium only after a period of several years.

KEY TERMS

arbitrage and the no-arbitrage condition
cross exchange rates (cross rates)
efficient market hypothesis
  (weak form, semistrong form)
forward parity and the unbiased forward
  expectations hypothesis
forward premium anomaly
fundamental analysis
interest rate parity (IRP) and covered
  interest arbitrage
international Fisher relation

international parity conditions
locational arbitrage
purchasing power parity (PPP)
real appreciation or depreciation
real exchange rate
real interest parity
relative purchasing power parity (RPPP)
technical analysis
triangular arbitrage
uncovered interest parity (Fisher Open)

CONCEPTUAL QUESTIONS

5.1   What is the law of one price?

5.2   What is an arbitrage profit?

5.3   What is the difference between locational, triangular, and covered interest arbitrage?

5.4   What is relative purchasing power parity?

5.5   What does the international Fisher relation say about interest rate and inflation differentials?

5.6   What are real changes in exchange rates?

5.7   Are real exchange rates in equilibrium at all times?

5.8   What is the effect of a real appreciation of the domestic currency on the purchasing power of domestic residents?

5.9   Will an appreciation of the domestic currency help or hurt a domestic exporter?

5.10   Describe the behavior of real exchange rates.

5.11   What methods can be used to forecast future spot rates of exchange?

5.12   How can the international parity conditions allow you to forecast next year's spot rate?

PROBLEMS

5.1   Calculate the following cross exchange rates:
    a. If exchange rates are 200 yen per dollar and 50 U.S. cents per Swiss franc, what is the exchange rate of yen per franc?
    b. The dollar is trading at ¥100/$ and at SFr1.60/$. What is the yen per franc rate?

5.2 As a percentage of an arbitrary starting amount, about how large would transactions costs have to be to make arbitrage between the exchange rates $S^{SFr/\$} = SFr1.7223/\$$, $S^{\$/¥} = \$0.009711/¥$, and $S^{¥/SFr} = ¥61.740/SFr$ unprofitable?

5.3 Given $S_0^{£/\$} = £0.6361/\$$ and the 180-day forward rate $F_1^{£/\$} = £0.6352/\$$, what is the dollar forward premium? Based on the unbiased forward expectations hypothesis, by how much is the dollar expected to appreciate or depreciate over the next 180 days? Provide a forecast of the spot rate of exchange in 180 days.

5.4 Mexico's new peso is quoted in direct terms at $¥28.7356/NP$ BID and $¥28.7715/NP$ ASK in Tokyo. The yen is quoted in direct terms at $NP0.03416/¥$ BID and $NP0.03420/¥$ ASK in Mexico City.
   a. Calculate the bid-ask spread as a percentage of the bid price from the Japanese and from the Mexican perspective.
   b. Is there an opportunity for profitable arbitrage? If so, describe the necessary transactions using a ¥1 million starting amount.

5.5 The real rate of interest on bank loans and deposits is 2 percent in both the United Kingdom and the United States. Inflation in the United States is 6 percent. In equilibrium, what is the U.K.'s inflation rate?

5.6 The current spot exchange rate is $S_0^{¥/\$} = ¥190/\$$ and the 1-year forward rate is $F_1^{¥/\$} = ¥210/\$$. The prime rate in the United States is 15 percent.
   a. What should the Japanese prime rate be?
   b. According to forward parity, by how much should the dollar change in value during the next year?

5.7 Suppose $S_0^{\$/£} = \$1.25/£$ and the 1-year forward rate is $F_1^{\$/£} = \$1.20/£$. The real interest rate on a riskless government security is 2 percent in both England and the United States. The U.S. inflation rate is 5 percent.
   a. What is England's inflation rate if the equilibrium relationships hold?
   b. What is England's nominal required rate of return on riskless government securities?

5.8 Suppose that for the same basket of goods the time zero price indices in countries D and F are $P_0^D = D100$ and $P_0^F = F1$, so that $S_0^{D/F} = P_0^D/P_0^F = D100/F$. Inflation rates in countries D and F are expected to be 10 percent and 21 percent per period, respectively, over the foreseeable future.
   a. What are the expected price levels $E[P_1^D]$ and $E[P_1^F]$ and the expected nominal spot rate of exchange $E[S_1^{D/F}]$ in one period?
   b. Looking two years into the future, what are the expected price levels in each country ($E[P_2^D]$ and $E[P_2^F]$)?

5.9 A foreign exchange dealer in Tokyo provides the following quotes for spot exchange and 1-month, 3-month, and 6-month forward exchange between the U.S. dollar and the Malaysian ringgit:

	Bid (MR/$)	Ask (MR/$)
Spot	4.0040	4.0200
1-month forward	3.9920	4.0090
3-months forward	3.9690	3.9888
6-months forward	3.9360	3.9580

   a. In New York, 3-month U.S. Treasury bills yield 7 percent per annum. What should be the annualized yield on 3-month Malaysian government bills? Use the U.S. dollar ask quotes for simplicity.

b. Verify your answer to part a with a hypothetical investment of $10 million for three months in each country. Use only ask quotes for simplicity and ignore other fees, charges, and taxes.

5.10 Quotes for the U.S. dollar and Thai baht (Bt) are as follows:

Spot contract midpoint	$S_0^{Bt/\$} = Bt24.96/\$$
1-year forward contract midpoint	$F_1^{Bt/\$} = Bt25.64/\$$
1-year Eurodollar interest rate	$i^\$ = 6.125\%$ per year

a. Your newspaper does not quote 1-year Eurocurrency interest rates on Thai baht. Make your own estimate of i^{Bt}.
b. Suppose that you can trade at the prices for $S^{Bt/\$}$, $F^{Bt/\$}$ and $i^\$$ just given and that you can also either borrow or lend at a Thai Eurocurrency interest rate of $i^{Bt} = 10$ percent per year. Based on a $1 million initial amount, how much profit can you generate through covered interest arbitrage?

5.11 You have $1 million that you are free to invest in any currency. You can trade at the following prices:

Spot rate, Mexican new pesos per dollar	NP10/$
6-month forward rate for Mexican new pesos	NP11/$
6-month Mexican interest rate	18%
6-month U.S. interest rate	6%

Is covered interest arbitrage worthwhile? If so, explain the steps and compute the profit based on your initial $1 million. Calculate your profit in dollars at time zero.

5.12 Currency exchange rates and Eurocurrency interest rates are as follows:

Current Singapore dollar (S$) spot rate	$0.50/S$
1-year Singapore dollar (S$) forward rate	$0.51/S$
1-year Singapore dollar (S$) interest rate	4.0%
1-year U.S. interest rate	6.0%

In what direction will covered interest arbitrage force the quoted rates to change? Explain the steps and compute the profit based on a $1 million initial position.

5.13 Suppose $P_0^D = 100$, $P_0^F = 1$, and $S_0^{D/F} = D100/F$. Inflation in countries D and F is expected to be $p^D = 10$ percent and $p^F = 21$ percent, respectively, over the foreseeable future.
a. What are the expected price levels $E[P_1^F]$ and $E[P_1^D]$ and the expected nominal exchange rate $E[S_1^{D/F}]$ in one period?
b. What is the expected real exchange rate $X_1^{D/F}$ in one period using time zero as a base?
c. Looking two years into the future, what are the expected price levels in each country ($E[P_2^F]$ and $E[P_2^D]$) and the expected real exchange rate $E[X_2^{D/F}]$?

5.14 One year ago, the spot exchange rate between Japanese yen and Swiss franc was $S_1^{¥/SFr} = ¥160/SFr$. Today, the spot rate is $S_0^{¥/SFr} = ¥155/SFr$. Inflation during the year was $p^¥ = 2$ percent and $p^{SFr} = 3$ percent in Japan and Switzerland, respectively.

a. What was the percentage change in the nominal value of the Swiss franc?

b. One year ago, what nominal exchange rate would you have predicted for today based on the difference in inflation rates?

c. What was the percentage change in the real exchange rate, $x_0^{¥/SFr}$, during the year?

d. What was the percentage change in the relative purchasing power of the franc?

e. What was the percentage change in the relative purchasing power of the yen?

5.15 Indicate whether each of the following individuals uses technical or fundamental analysis in forecasting currency values.

a. An investor uses charts of historical exchange rate movements to predict future exchange rate movements.

b. A hedger uses a computer program called a neural network to identify patterns in exchange rates. The neural network uses past price information to generate a signal indicating whether a particular currency exposure should be hedged.

c. A speculator gathers the most recent balance-of-payments data from countries participating in European monetary union. She uses this data to make long-term forecasts of the value of the euro against the U.S. dollar.

d. A currency has been trading in a narrow range during the last several months. The currency falls in value days after the government announces it has suspended payments on dollar-denominated loans. A hedge fund manager sells the currency after comparing the size of the dollar-denominated loans to the country's foreign exchange reserves.

e. A currency has been trading in a narrow range during the last several months. The currency falls in value after the government announces it has suspended payments on dollar-denominated loans. A hedge fund manager sells the currency after noticing that the currency has fallen in value for three successive days.

SUGGESTED READINGS

The international parity conditions are investigated in

Niso Abuaf and Philippe Jorion, "Purchasing Power Parity in the Long Run," *Journal of Finance* 47 (March 1990), pp. 157–174.

Richard T. Baillie and Tim Bollerslev, "The Forward Premium Anomaly Is Not as Bad as You Think," *Journal of International Money and Finance* 19 (August 2000) pp. 471–488.

Rudiger Dornbusch, "Expectations and Exchange Rate Dynamics," *Journal of Political Economy* 84 (December 1976), pp. 1161–1176.

James R. Lothian and Mark P. Taylor, "Real Exchange Rate Behavior: The Recent Float from the Perspective of the Past Two Centuries," *Journal of Political Economy* 104 (June 1996), pp. 488–509.

Frederic S. Mishkin, "Are Real Interest Rates Equal Across Countries? An Empirical Investigation of International Parity Conditions," *Journal of Finance* 39 (December 1984), pp. 1345–1357.

Michael J. Moore and Maurice J. Roche, "Less of a Puzzle: A New Look at the Forward Forex Market," *Journal of International Economics* 58 (December 2002), pp. 387–411.

The performance of exchange rate forecasts and exchange rate forecasters is discussed in

Jamil Baz, Francis Breedon, Vasant Naik, and Joel Peress, "Optimal Portfolios of Foreign Currencies," *Journal of Portfolio Management* 28 (Fall 2001), pp. 102–111.

Bradford Cornell, "Spot Rates, Forward Rates, and Exchange Market Efficiency," *Journal of Financial Economics* 5, No.1 (1976), pp. 55–65.

Kenneth Froot and Richard Thaler, "Anomalies: Foreign Exchange," *Journal of Economic Perspectives* 4 (1990), pp. 179–192.

Blake LeBaron, "Technical Trading Rule Profitability and Foreign Exchange Intervention," *Journal of International Economics* 49 (October 1999), pp. 125–143.

Nelson C. Mark and Donggyu Sul, "Nominal Exchange Rates and Monetary Fundamentals: Evidence from a Small Post–Bretton Woods Panel," *Journal of International Economics* 53 (February 2001), pp. 29–52.

Christopher J. Neely and Paul A. Weller, "Technical Trading Rules in the European Monetary System," *Journal of International Money and Finance* 18 (June 1999), pp. 429–458.

Mark P. Taylor and Helen Allen, "The Use of Technical Analysis in the Foreign Exchange Market," *Journal of International Money and Finance* 11 (June 1992), pp. 304–314.

ontinuous Time Finance

Legend has it that many years ago the bankers of the world employed nearsighted men in green accountants' visors and armbands to compound interest continuously in the smoky back rooms of commercial banks. But no matter how fast they worked, it proved impossible for these unfortunate lackeys to compound interest on a continuous basis. One day, a particularly clever worker discovered that holding period rates of return can be transformed into continuously compounded rates of return with a simple formula. Here's what he discovered.

Continuously Compounded Rates of Return

As the number of compounding intervals within a period approaches infinity, returns are said to be compounded continuously. At any instant, the rate of return is then called the instantaneous rate of return. Henceforth, let's denote continuously compounded rates of return with *italics*, so that i will represent the continuously compounded version of a holding period interest rate i.

Suppose you have an amount V_0 today and you want to know how large this value will be after T periods if it earns a continuously compounded rate of interest i. With continuous compounding, the value of V_0 at time T is given by

$$V_T = V_0 \, e^{iT} \tag{5A.1}$$

where the number e is a constant approximately equal to 2.718. Conversely, the present value of a cash flow to be received at time T with continuous compounding is given by

$$V_0 = V_T/e^{iT} = V_T \, e^{-iT} \tag{5A.2}$$

The formula for converting a rate of return i with periodic (for example, annual) compounding into a continuously compounded rate is $i = \ln(1+i)$ where ln is the natural logarithm function with base e. The equation follows from

$$(1+i) = e^i \quad \Leftrightarrow \quad \ln(1+i) = \ln(e^i) = i \tag{5A.3}$$

For example, the continuously compounded annual rate of return i that is equivalent to an annual rate i = 12.64 percent with annual compounding is $i = \ln(1 + 0.1264) = 11.90$ percent per year. That is, $e^{0.1190} = 1.1264$ and $\ln(1.1264) = 0.1190$. A 12.64 percent rate of return with annual compounding is equivalent to an 11.90 percent annual return with continuous compounding.

Because the algebra of continuously compounded returns requires a knowledge of natural logarithms, let's review the properties of the natural logarithm and its inverse, the exponential function e.

$$\begin{aligned}
e^{\ln(x)} &= \ln(e^x) = x & \text{(5A.4)} \\
\ln(AB) &= \ln(A) + \ln(B) & \text{(5A.5)} \\
\ln(A/B) &= \ln(A) - \ln(B) & \text{(5A.6)} \\
\ln(A^C) &= C \ln(A) & \text{(5A.7)}
\end{aligned}$$

Continuously compounded rates are additive over time. These properties make calculating the compound rate of return over a series of continuously compounded rates of return easy, because *continuously compounded rates are additive* rather than multiplicative over time.

$$\ln[(1+i_1)(1+i_2)...(1+i_T)] = \ln[e^{i1}\,e^{i2}...\,e^{iT}] = \ln[e^{(i1+i2+...+iT)}]$$

$$= i_1 + i_2 + ... + i_T \qquad (5A.8)$$

Let's try an example. The average rate of return over three periods with annual holding period returns (that is, without compounding) of 10 percent, 16 percent, and 12 percent is found with a geometric average as follows:

Geometric mean return with periodic compounding:

$$(1+i_{avg}) = [(1.10)(1.16)(1.12)]^{1/3}$$

$$= 1.1264, \text{ or } 12.64\% \text{ per year (compounded annually)}$$

An equivalent answer can be found with continuously compounded rates of return:

Arithmetic mean return with continuous compounding:

$$i_{avg} = [\ln(1.10) + \ln(1.12) + \ln(1.16)]/3 = [0.0953 + 0.1133 + 0.1484]/3$$

$$= 0.1190, \text{ or } 11.9\% \text{ per year (compounded continuously)}$$

This is equivalent to the $e^{0.1190} = 12.64$ percent average rate of return with annual compounding.

International Parity Conditions in Continuous Time

The international parity conditions in continuous time are a straightforward application of logarithms. Over a single period, the parity conditions are

$$F_1^{d/f}/S_0^{d/f} = E[S_1^{d/f}]/S_0^{d/f} = (1+i^d)/(1+i^f) = (1+E[p^d])/(1+E[p^f]) \qquad (5A.9)$$

Using i to indicate a continuously compounded interest rate and p to indicate a continuously compounded inflation rate, the parity conditions over a single period can be restated as

$$\ln(F_1^{d/f}/S_0^{d/f}) = \ln(E[S_1^{d/f}]/S_0^{d/f}) = i^d - i^f = E[p^d] - E[p^f] \qquad (5A.10)$$

Over t periods, we can apply the rule $\ln(A^C) = C \ln(A)$ to solve for the t-period international parity conditions in continuously compounded returns:

$$\ln(F_t^{d/f}/S_0^{d/f}) = \ln(E[S_t^{d/f}]/S_0^{d/f}) = t(i^d - i^f) = t(E[p^d] - E[p^f]) \qquad (5A.11)$$

where the interest and inflation rates are continuously compounded mean rates of return over the t periods.

Empirical tests of the international parity conditions are generally conducted in continuously compounded returns because they are additive and are more likely to satisfy an assumption of linearity. We'll return to continuously compounded returns in the next chapter and in the chapters on currency options and options on real assets.

Real Exchange Rates in Continuous Time

Translating Equation 5.12 into continuously compounded returns, the continuously compounded change in the real exchange rate $x_t^{d/f}$ is

$$x_t^{d/f} = \ln(1+x_t^{d/f})$$
$$= \ln[(S_t^{d/f}/S_{t-1}^{d/f})(1+p_t^f)/(1+p_t^d)]$$
$$= \ln(S_t^{d/f}) - \ln(S_{t-1}^{d/f}) + \ln(1+p_t^f) - \ln(1+p_t^d)$$
$$= \ln(S_t^{d/f}/S_{t-1}^{d/f}) + p_t^f - p_t^d \qquad (5A.12)$$

In continuously compounded returns, change in the real exchange rate is equal to the change in the nominal exchange rate adjusted for the difference in inflation. This formulation is commonly used in empirical tests of purchasing power parity.

Consider the real exchange rate example from Chapter 5 in which $p_t^{¥} = 0$ percent, $p_t^{\$} = 10$ percent, $S_{t-1}^{¥/\$} = ¥100/\$$, and $S_t^{¥/\$} = ¥110/\$$. The continuously compounded change in the real rate of exchange during period t is

$$x_t^{¥/\$} = \ln(S_t^{¥/\$}/S_{t-1}^{¥/\$}) + \ln(1+p_t^{\$}) - \ln(1+p_t^{¥})$$
$$= \ln((¥110/\$)/(¥100/\$)) + \ln(1.10) - \ln(1.00)$$
$$= \ln(1.10) + (0.09531 - 0.00000)$$
$$= 0.09531 + 0.09531$$
$$= 0.19062$$

As in the original example, the real appreciation of the dollar is $e^{0.19062} - 1 = 21$ percent in holding period rate of return.

SUMMARY

Continuously compounded returns are convenient because they are additive rather than multiplicative. Continuously compounded returns i are related to holding period returns i according to

$$(1+i) = e^i \quad \Leftrightarrow \quad \ln(1+i) = \ln(e^i) = i \qquad (5A.3)$$

Over a single period, the international parity conditions can be stated in continuously compounded returns as

$$\ln(F_1^{d/f}/S_0^{d/f}) = \ln(E[S_1^{d/f}]/S_0^{d/f}) = i^d - i^f = E[p^d] - E[p^f] \qquad (5A.13)$$

where i and p represent continuously compounded interest and inflation rates, respectively. In words, the forward premium/discount to the currency spot rate and the expected change in the spot rate are determined by interest rate differentials between the two currencies. If real interest rates are constant across the two currencies, then interest rate differentials are, in turn, determined by inflation differentials. Finally, continuously compounded change in the real exchange rate during period t, $x_t^{d/f}$, is given by

$$x_t^{d/f} = \ln(S_t^{d/f}/S_{t-1}^{d/f}) + p_t^f - p_t^d \qquad (5A.12)$$

where $p_t^d = \ln(1+p_t^d)$ and $p_t^f = \ln(1+p_t^f)$ are the continuously compounded inflation rates observed during the period.

PROBLEMS

5A.1 Suppose you earn a 100 percent return in one period and then lose 50 percent of your value in the next period. Compute your average periodic rate of return over the two periods using geometric holding period returns. Now, compute your average periodic rate of return using continuously compounded returns. Are these equivalent?

5A.2 Suppose $P_0^D = D100$, $P_0^F = F1$, and $S_0^{D/F} = D100/F$. Inflation rates are $p^D = 10$ percent and $p^F = 21$ percent in holding period returns. Transform these inflation rates to continuously compounded returns and find $E[P_1^D]$, $E[P_1^F]$, $E[S_1^{D/F}]$, $E[P_2^D]$, $E[P_2^F]$ and $E[S_1^{D/F}]$ according to the international parity conditions. (Note that this is a repeat of problem 5.8 in continuously compounded returns.)

Derivative Securities for Currency Risk Management

part three

Currency Futures and Futures Markets

chapter 6

Overview

The best thing about the future is that it comes only one day at a time.

Abraham Lincoln

Currency futures contracts are similar to currency forward contracts in that each represents a commitment to exchange one currency for another at a specified price and on a specified future date. Whereas forward contracts are traded in an interbank market and are customized to fit the needs of each client, futures contracts are standardized contracts that trade on organized futures exchanges. Standardization means that futures contracts come in only a limited number of currencies, expiration dates, and transaction amounts. Although this promotes liquidity, it comes at the price of flexibility. For a corporate treasurer, the choice of a forward or futures contract depends on the trade-off between costs, flexibility, and liquidity.

Currency futures have become a major force in international markets in recent years. The major users are large banks and multinational corporations that are increasingly integrating their risk management operations and using the financial futures markets to hedge their currency risk exposures. If an exposure can be approximately matched by a standardized futures contract traded on a futures exchange, the futures contract can be a low-cost substitute for the customized forward contracts traded in the interbank market.

6.1 • FINANCIAL FUTURES EXCHANGES

Spot and forward markets for agricultural products and commodities, such as gold and silver, have been around as long as recorded history. Futures contracts are a relative newcomer, first appearing in Europe as the *lettre de faire* in medieval times. Organized commodity futures exchanges grew up somewhat later. One of the first known futures exchanges serviced the rice market at Osaka, Japan, in the early 1700s. This market bore many similarities to present-day futures markets. Rice futures contracts were standardized according to weight and quality, traded through a futures exchange clearinghouse, and had a specified contract life.

As shown in Figure 6.1, derivatives volume has exploded in the last ten years. According to the Futures Industry Association, a trade group serving futures exchanges, there were more than seven times as many derivatives contracts traded in 2002 (5,994 million) as in 1992 (848 million). Much of this growth has occurred outside the developed markets of North America and Western Europe.

http://www.
futuresindustry.
org

In the United States, the Chicago Board of Trade (CBOT) began trading spot and forward contracts on agricultural produce in 1848. Agricultural futures contracts were introduced on the CBOT during the 1860s. Another Chicago futures exchange, the Chicago Mercantile Exchange (CME), began trading currency futures contracts in 1972 in response to the dramatic increase in currency risk following the 1971 collapse of the Bretton Woods exchange rate agreement.

Currency futures began trading on the CME in 1972.

Financial futures exchanges today trade both currency and interest rate futures and are often, but not always, associated with a commodity futures exchange. Financial futures are nearly identical in operation to commodity futures. The only substantive

http://www.
cme.com

http://www.
cbot.com

FIGURE 6.1
The Growth of Exchange-Traded Derivatives

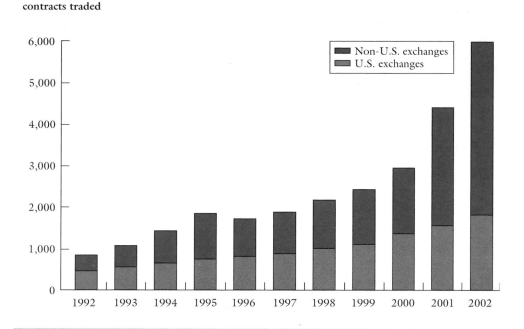

Millions of
contracts traded

Source: Futures Industry Association (http://www.futuresindustry.org).

difference is the deliverable asset. Many financial futures exchanges also trade option contracts on interest rates and currencies, and sometimes on individual stocks, bonds, or indices as well. Currency futures accounted for about 10 percent (61 million contracts) of global derivatives volume in 2002.

Table 6.1 ranks the world's top derivatives exchanges by contract volume. Currency futures are traded in lesser volumes at other national and regional exchanges, such as the

TABLE 6.1
Top 30 Futures Exchanges

| Exchange | Contract volume (millions) | | |
	2002	2001	Growth
1 Eurex, Germany and Switzerland *	536.0	435.1	23%
2 Chicago Mercantile Exchange, United States	444.5	316.0	41%
3 Chicago Board of Trade, United States	276.3	210.0	32%
4 Euronext, France (Paris) **	221.3	210.4	5%
5 New York Mercantile Exchange, United States	107.4	85.0	26%
6 Brazilian Mercantile & Futures Exchange (BM&F), (São Paulo)	95.9	94.2	2%
7 The Tokyo Commodity Exchange, Japan	75.4	56.5	33%
8 London Metal Exchange, United Kingdom	56.3	56.2	0%
9 Korea Stock Exchange (Seoul)	42.9	31.5	36%
10 Sydney Futures Exchange, Australia	34.0	34.1	0%
11 Singapore Exchanges	32.6	30.6	7%
12 International Petroleum Exchange, United Kingdom (London)	30.2	26.1	16%
13 Central Japan Commodity Exchange, Japan (Nagoya)	30.0	27.8	8%
14 Stockholmbörsen (OM), Sweden (Stockholm)	20.2	23.4	−14%
15 Tokyo Grain Exchange, Japan	18.7	22.7	−18%
16 MEFF Renta Variable, Spain (Madrid)	17.3	13.4	29%
17 New York Board of Trade, United States	16.3	14.0	16%
18 Korea Futures Exchange (Seoul)	14.6	11.5	27%
19 Tokyo Stock Exchange, Japan	13.6	12.5	9%
20 Shanghai Futures Exchange, People's Republic of China	12.2	5.6	117%
21 South African Futures Exchange (Sandton/Johannesburg)	11.2	11.9	−5%
22 Osaka Securities Exchange, Japan	11.1	10.5	6%
23 National Stock Exchange of India (Mumbai/Bombay)	10.2	1.2	767%
24 Bourse de Montréal, Canada	8.1	7.3	11%
25 Italian Derivatives Market	7.1	6.0	17%
26 Taiwan Futures Exchange	6.4	4.3	47%
27 Hong Kong Exchanges & Clearing	6.2	5.8	7%
28 Osaka Mercantile Exchange, Japan	5.2	3.4	54%
29 Kansai Commodities Exchange, Japan	3.9	2.9	33%
30 Tokyo International Financial Futures Exchange, Japan	4.5	7.6	−41%

* Eurex was created in 1998 through a merger of Deutsche Terminborse (DTB) of Frankfurt and the Switzerland Options and Financial Futures Exchange (Soffex) of Zurich. Eurex trades futures and options on financial price indices including stocks, bonds, and currencies.

** Euronext was created in 2001 through a merger of exchanges from Amsterdam, Brussels, Lisbon, London, and Paris. Euronext trades a variety of assets including stocks, bonds, derivatives, and commodities.

Source: Derived from Futures Industry Association statistics. Volume figures are not directly comparable as contract sizes vary by exchange. See http://www.futuresindustry.org.

Market Update

Competition Between International Exchanges

One of the most active futures exchanges in Table 6.1 is the Eurex, which trades futures and options on indices and individual stocks, bonds, and currencies. Eurex was created in 1998 through a merger of DTB (Deutsche Terminbörse) and Zurich's SOFFEX (Swiss Options and Financial Futures Exchange). Eurex has subsequently formed alliances with derivatives exchanges in Vienna (Austria), Dublin (Ireland), and the CBOT (United States).

The other large European futures exchange, Euronext, was created in 2001 through a merger of the Amsterdam, Brussels, and Paris exchanges. Euronext trades stocks, bonds, commodities, and derivatives. In fall 2001, Euronext acquired the London International Financial Futures Exchange for €907 million in cash, a 100 percent premium to LIFFE's pre-acquisition share price. Euronext subsequently signed deals with exchanges in Helsinki (Finland), Lisbon (Portugal), Warsaw (Poland), and Luxembourg.

Eurex clears and settles its trades through Clearstream, a wholly-owned subsidiary. Euronext settles through Euroclear, an independent clearinghouse. Settling a transaction within either house costs about one-half euro, about the same as in the United States. However, if one client is on Euroclear and the other on Clearstream, the cost of settlement can be as high as €30. The different standards and communication systems used by the clearinghouses can further increase the back-office costs of trade.

Exchanges are actively forming alliances in a battle over market share. For example, the Globex trading system links derivatives trading from the Chicago Mercantile Exchange (CME), Euronext, Singapore (SGX), Spain (MEFF), Montreal, and Brazilian (BM&F) exchanges. Created in 1992 from an alliance between the Singapore and Chicago exchanges, Globex provides a 24-hour electronic trading platform for a variety of global derivatives contracts.

MidAmerica Commodities Exchange in the United States and the New Zealand Futures Exchange. These exchanges trade a variety of currency futures contracts based on price quotations in the local currency. For example, the Chicago Mercantile Exchange (CME) quotes dollar prices on a variety of currency futures contracts, including on pounds (£62,500 contract size), euros (€125,000), and yen (¥12,500,000). Many exchanges also offer cross-rate futures contracts. The CME offers a wide variety, including €125,000 euro futures contracts priced in pounds, yen, and Swiss francs.

On U.S. exchanges, futures contracts expire on the Monday before the third Wednesday of each contract month. The previous Friday is the last day of trade. Contract sizes vary by exchange. Japanese yen futures have a contract size of ¥12,500,000 on the CME and a contract size of ¥6,250,000 on the Philadelphia Stock Exchange (PHLX). As of spring 2003, CME yen futures expired in March, June, September, and December.

Standardized contracts promote liquidity, but reduce the flexibility of futures contracts relative to forward contracts. If the amount of a futures contract does not evenly divide into an underlying exposure or if futures contracts do not expire on the same day as an underlying exposure, then futures will not permit a perfect hedge of currency risk.

6.2 • THE OPERATION OF FUTURES MARKETS

Looking Good, Billy Ray! Feeling Good, Louis!

An interesting scene involving the futures market for frozen concentrated orange juice is in the movie *Trading Places*. Eddie Murphy plays a down-and-out con artist named Billy Ray. Dan Akroyd plays a rich, privileged Ivy-Leaguer named Louis, who trades commodity futures on behalf of a pair of brothers named Duke. The Duke brothers make a one-dollar bet over which of these men—Louis (Dan Akroyd) or Billy Ray (Eddie Murphy)—would prosper if their fortunes were reversed. To wit: Is it heredity or environment that makes the man? In an amusing social experiment, the Dukes hire Billy Ray and fire Louis. Louis and Billy Ray eventually discover the Dukes' ruse and join forces to seek their revenge.

In the movie, the futures market is concerned over the effect of the winter weather on the orange harvest. A U.S. Department of Agriculture (USDA) report on the status of the orange juice crop finds that the winter was not as bad as expected. The Dukes conspire to steal the report before it becomes public. Louis and Billy Ray intercept the report and send the Duke brothers a false report stating that the winter's toll was worse than expected. On the exchange floor the morning of the report, Louis and Billy Ray play out the following scene:

9 A.M.   Frozen Concentrated Orange Juice (FCOJ) futures open at $102. The Dukes, thinking the orange harvest will be small, buy FCOJ futures in anticipation of a price rise. Observing the Dukes' behavior, other traders follow their lead and buy futures contracts. Louis and Billy Ray are only too happy to oblige and sell as many contracts as they can. By 10 a.m., the price has risen to $142.

10 A.M.   The USDA report is read over the television: "The cold winter has apparently not affected the orange harvest."

While Louis and Billy Ray are short the orange juice futures contract, most traders (especially the Dukes) are long. Panic selling sets in, and the price starts to fall. Louis and Billy Ray have closed out their position by the time the price hits $29. With an initial margin of 2 percent, Louis and Billy Ray have earned up to ($142–$29)/(0.02)($29) = 19,483% on their investments in FCOJ futures. When the Duke brothers' margin call comes in at $394 million, the Dukes are bankrupt.

"Looking good, Billy Ray! Feeling good, Louis!"

Forces Moving the Futures Markets

This amusing scene faithfully represents two powerful forces moving the market:

- *Public information.* Information is only valuable when it differs from expectations. "The winter was bad" conveys no information to the market if the market already knew the winter was bad. "The winter was worse than expected" conveys much information that is relevant to the value of oranges and frozen orange juice futures contracts.

- *Private information.* The value of private information is clearly portrayed. Private information (if it is accurate!) can let investors buy before the price rises and sell before the price falls.

Although entertaining, this fanciful scene is unrealistic as the price movements of the FCOJ futures contract are greatly exaggerated. Price movement from $102 to $142 and then back to $29 is highly unlikely, and trading would be halted in any case if the exchange has daily price limits. Many commodities trade within a ±1 percent band of opening price. Based on an opening price of $102, a 1 percent daily price limit would limit movement up or down by $1.02. This trading delay would have given the Duke brothers and the rest of the market a chance to incorporate information on the orange juice harvest in a more reasoned manner.

6.3 • FUTURES CONTRACTS

Forward Contracts and Default Risk

The major problem with forward contracts is that forwards are pure credit instruments. Whichever way the price of the spot rate of exchange moves, one party has an incentive to default. Consider a forward contract on pounds sterling at a rate of $1.4754/£. If the pound appreciates to $1.5000/£ on the expiration date, then whoever has agreed to sell pounds at the forward rate of $1.4754/£ has an incentive to default. If the pound depreciates to $1.4500/£, then the party obliged to buy pounds at the forward rate of $1.4754/£ has an incentive to default.

> The problem with forward contracts is that one side always has an incentive to default.

The Futures Contract Solution

Futures contracts provide a remedy for the default risk inherent in forward contracts through the following conventions (see Figure 6.2):

- An exchange clearinghouse takes one side of every transaction.
- Futures contracts are marked to market on a daily basis.
- An initial margin and a maintenance margin are required.

> Futures contracts reduce default risk relative to forward contracts.

The slogan of the Chicago Board of Trade Clearing Corporation is "A Party to Every Trade." With the exchange clearinghouse on the other side of every transaction, players in the futures market are assured daily settlement of their contract by the clearinghouse. The exchange insures itself against loss through a performance bond called a **margin requirement** and by settling any changes in the value of a contract on a daily basis, or **marking-to-market**. This means that at any given time both the trader and the clearinghouse face at most one day's risk in the futures contract. The clearinghouse further reduces its risk by requiring that for every futures contract bought, another one is sold. This leaves the clearinghouse with a zero net position.

Margin accounts serve to protect the interests of the broker, although margin accounts on futures perform this function in a different way than margin accounts on stock. A margin account on a share of stock allows an equity investor to borrow from the broker in order to buy additional stock. A maintenance margin serves as a down payment on the price of the stock, with the difference between the price of the stock and the maintenance margin being borrowed from the broker. The borrower must pay back the broker when the stock position is liquidated. On a futures contract, the maintenance margin is not a down payment on a loan; rather, it is a performance bond ensuring that the customer will make required payments as the contract is marked to market each day.

Suppose a €125,000 futures contract is purchased at a price of $1.1754/€ on the Chicago Mercantile Exchange. The purchaser must deposit an initial margin, although no dollars or euros are exchanged upon purchase of the contract. If the futures price rises by $0.0010/€ to $1.1764/€ at the close of trading on the following day, then the

---

FIGURE 6.2
Forwards Versus CME Futures Contracts*

	Forwards	Exchange-traded futures
1. Location	Interbank	Exchange floor (or electronic trading system)
2. Maturity	Negotiated; typically from one week to 10 years	CME contracts expire on the Monday before the third Wednesday of the month; last trading day is the previous Friday; seller chooses when to make delivery during the delivery month
3. Amount	Negotiated; usually more than $5 million	In increments of a contract amount, such as €125,000 for euros on the CME; "open interest" = number of contracts
4. Fees	Bid-ask spread	Commissions charged per "round turn" (usually about $30 per contract on the CME)
5. Counterparty	Bank	Exchange clearinghouse
6. Collateral	Negotiated; depending on the customer's credit risk	Purchaser must deposit an initial margin (bank letter of credit, T-bills, cash, etc.); contract is then "marked to market" daily; an initial margin and a maintenance margin ensure daily payment
7. Settlement	Nearly all	Less than 5% settled by physical delivery; most positions are closed early by buying the opposite futures position; open interest is then netted out
8. Trading hours	24 hours	During exchange hours; Singapore's SIMEX and the CME share their contracts through the Globex2 trading system during off-exchange hours

* CME stands for Chicago Mercantile Exchange.

---

clearinghouse adds ($0.0010/€)(€125,000) = $125 to the purchaser's margin account. If the contract price subsequently falls back to $1.4754/€, $125 is transferred from the customer's margin account to the clearinghouse. This daily marking to market ensures that the clearinghouse's exposure to currency price risk is at most one day.

Maintenance margins and price limits for futures contracts are determined by the exchanges and vary by contract and by exchange. The CME has no price limits during the first 15 minutes of trade. A schedule of expanding price limits follows the 15-minute opening period. Limits are also waived during the last 15 minutes of trade for expiring contracts. Margin requirements and daily price limits are periodically revised by the exchanges according to volatility in the underlying asset.

Suppose the maintenance margin is $2,000 for a €125,000 futures contract on the CME. The minimum dollar price tick of one basis point (0.01 percent) on the CME euro futures contract is worth ($0.0001/€)(€125,000/contract) = $12.50 per contract. If the maximum price move before a limit is reached is 100 basis points (1 percent), then the value of the contract can move up or down by $1,250. Since the $2,000 maintenance margin is greater than the daily price limit of $1,250, the clearinghouse can recoup one-day variations (up to the price limit) in the futures contract. Maintenance margins are set large enough to cover all but the most extreme price movements. If an investor cannot meet a margin call, the exchange clearinghouse cancels the contract and offsets its position in the futures market on the following day.

Don't be fooled by price limits. Just because prices are artificially limited to a band around the current price does not mean that true prices can't exceed these bounds. If

Application

Price Limits

There was a story of a farmer who, tired of the fluctuations in temperature that occur from one day to the next and the effects on his crops, decided to eliminate the problem by having his thermometer altered so that it could move no more than five degrees in either direction from the previous day's reading.

From *Investments* by William F. Sharpe, (Englewood Cliffs, NJ: Prentice-Hall, Inc., 3d edition).

true price moves more than the price limit in a single day, default risk exists on the difference. Fortunately, since the exchange clearinghouse is on the other side of every transaction, the holder of a futures contract can rest assured that payment will be received. The futures exchange clearinghouse further reduces its credit risk by requiring that futures be traded through a brokerage house called a **futures commission merchant** rather than an end customer. If an end customer cannot meet its margin call, it is the broker rather than the clearinghouse that bears the consequences.

A Futures Contract as a Portfolio of One-Day Forward Contracts

Because futures are marked to market each day, a futures contract can be viewed as a bundle of consecutive one-day forward contracts. Each day, the previous day's forward contract is replaced by a new one-day forward contract with a delivery price equal to the closing (or settlement) price from the previous day's contract. At the end of each day, the previous forward contract is settled and a new 1-day forward contract is created. The purchaser of a futures contract buys the entire package. A 3-month futures contract, for instance, contains 90 renewable 1-day forward contracts. The futures exchange clearinghouse renews the contract daily until expiration, so long as the maintenance margin is satisfied. On the investor's side of the futures contract, an offsetting transaction can be made at any time to cancel the position.

> A futures contract is a package of renewable one-day forward contracts.

Forward and futures contracts are equivalent once they are adjusted for differences in contract terms and liquidity. Indeed, the difference between a futures and a forward contract is operational rather than valuational, in that it depends on the contracts themselves (the deliverable asset, settlement procedures, maturity dates, and amounts) and not directly on prices.[1] As with forward contracts, the expected return on a futures contract is determined by relative interest rates according to interest rate parity:

$$F_t^{d/f} = S_0^{d/f} [(1+i^d) / (1+i^f)]^t \qquad (6.1)$$

As with forward contracts, futures contracts allow you to hedge against nominal, but not real, changes in currency values. If inflation in the foreign currency is more than expected, for example, the forward rate won't buy as much purchasing power as you expected. In general, currency forward and futures contracts can eliminate currency risk but not inflation or interest rate risk within any single currency.

---

1 See French, "A Comparison of Futures and Forward Prices," *Journal of Financial Economics* (1983).

6.4 • FORWARD VERSUS FUTURES MARKET HEDGES

Both futures and forward prices are determined according to interest rate parity. Suppose we denote futures and forward prices for a foreign currency f in terms of the domestic currency d at time t for exchange at time T as $\text{Fut}_{t,T}^{d/f}$ and $F_{t,T}^{d/f}$, respectively. At expiration, both futures and forward prices converge to spot prices because

$$\text{Fut}_{t,T}^{d/f} = F_{t,T}^{d/f} = S_t^{d/f} \, [(1+i^d)/(1+i^f)]^{T-t} = S_T^{d/f} \text{ as } t \to T$$

The rest of this section compares futures and forward market hedges of currency risk.

Exposure to Currency Risk and Currency Risk Profiles

Minton Distributing is a U.S. firm that buys Japanese VCRs and distributes them to a chain of retail stores in Germany. It is now the third Friday in December. Minton has promised to pay its Japanese supplier ¥37,500,000 on the third Friday in March (which happens to be the expiration date of a CME futures contract). The German retailer has promised to pay Minton €250,000 on the same date. Minton's expected cash flows are shown here:

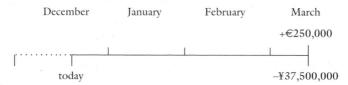

Minton is short yen and long euros three months forward. Minton's yen and euro cash flow exposures and risk profiles are as follows:

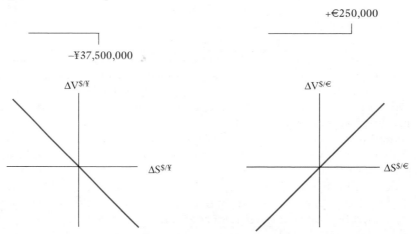

Depending on the exchange rates $S^{\$/¥}$ and $S^{\$/€}$, Minton might be spending some sleepless nights between now and March.

Forward Market Hedges

Minton can hedge these risk exposures in the forward market by buying ¥37,500,000 forward and selling €250,000 forward. Suppose forward rates are equal to current spot rates such that $S_0^{\$/¥} = F_{0,T}^{\$/¥} = \$0.00800/¥$ and $S_0^{\$/€} = F_{0,T}^{\$/€} = \$1.2000/€$. Buying yen forward is equivalent to selling (¥37,500,000)($0.00800/¥) = $300,000. Selling euros forward is equivalent to buying (€250,000)($1.2000/€) = $300,000. These forward contracts lock in the following cash flows and payoff profiles:

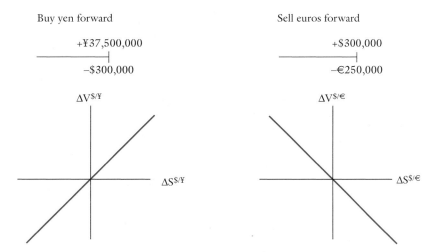

In this example, the $300,000 cash outflow of the long yen position exactly offsets the $300,000 cash inflow of the short euro position. When combined with Minton's underlying short yen and long euro positions, these transactions exactly neutralize Minton's exposures to yen and euro currency risks.

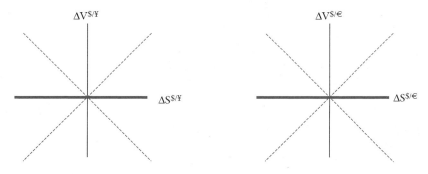

Minton can now sleep soundly at night.

Futures Market Hedges

Because these cash flows are an integer multiple of the standard CME futures contracts and occur on a CME futures contract expiration date, they can be hedged exactly in the futures market. To hedge against currency risk, Minton needs to go long yen and short euros. For Minton's risk exposures, this means buying three CME 3-month yen futures contracts (and simultaneously selling dollars) worth ¥37,500,000 and selling two CME 3-month euro futures contracts (and simultaneously buying dollars) worth €250,000. Once this is done, cash inflows (outflows) in each currency are exactly offset by outflows (inflows) and Minton has no net exposure to currency risk.

Forwards Versus Futures: Vivé la Différence

The biggest operational difference between futures contracts and forward contracts is that changes in the underlying spot rate of exchange are settled daily in the futures contract, whereas they are settled at maturity in the forward contract. Suppose the current yen spot rate is $S_0^{\$/¥} = \$0.010000/¥$ and that 180-day Eurocurrency interest rates are $i^\$ = 4.03$ percent and $i^¥ = 1.00$ percent. Today's futures and forward prices for exchange in one 6-month period are given by interest rate parity:

> The biggest difference between forward and futures contracts is in the daily marking-to-market.

$$\begin{aligned}
\mathrm{Fut}_{0,1}^{\$/\yen} &= F_{0,1}^{\$/\yen} = S_0^{\$/\yen}\,[(1+i\$)/(1+i\yen)]^{1-0} \\
&= (\$0.010000/\yen)[(1.0403)/(1.0100)]^1 \\
&= \$0.010300/\yen
\end{aligned} \qquad (6.2)$$

The yen must sell at a forward premium because Eurodollar interest rates are greater than Euroyen interest rates.

Suppose actual spot rates rise by $0.000005/\yen$ per day over each of the next 180 days to $S_1^{\$/\yen} = (\$0.010000/\yen) + (\$0.000005/\yen)(180) = \$0.010900/\yen$. This is a 9 percent increase over the current spot rate of $0.010000/\yen$. The purchaser of a yen forward contract would pay $F_1^{\$/\yen} = \$0.010300/\yen$ at expiration for yen worth $0.010900/\yen$ in the spot market for a net gain of $0.000600/\yen$ at expiration.

Settlement of a forward contract at expiration

$$\begin{array}{r}+\$.010900/\yen \\ -\$.010300/\yen = \$.000600/\yen\end{array}$$

| day 1 | . . . | day 178 | day 179 | day 180 |

This is a 6 percent profit on each yen purchased.

In contrast, the futures contract is settled one day at a time. According to interest rate parity, the spot price is expected to rise by $(\$0.0003/\yen)/(180\text{ days}) = \$.0000016/\yen$ per day. If in fact the yen rises by $(\$0.0009/\yen)/(180\text{ days}) = \$0.000005/\yen$ per day, there is a net gain at each daily settlement of $(\$0.0006/\yen)/(180\text{ days}) = \$.000003\overline{3}/\yen$. Accumulated over 180 days, this equals a 6 percent gain. At expiration, the accumulated gain on the futures contract is the same as the gain on the forward contract. The difference is that the gain is received one day at a time.

Daily settlement of a futures contract

$+\$.000003\overline{3}/\yen$ $\quad\quad +\$.000003\overline{3}/\yen$ $\quad +\$.000003\overline{3}/\yen$ $\quad +\$.000003\overline{3}/\yen = \$\$.000600/\yen$

| day 1 | . . . | day 178 | day 179 | day 180 |

In the more general case in which exchange rates fluctuate randomly over time, the net gain at the expiration of the forward contract still equals the sum of the daily settlements on a comparable futures contract. Figure 6.3 shows spot and futures prices that begin at $S_0^{\$/\yen} = \$0.010000/\yen$ and $\mathrm{Fut}_{0,1}^{\$/\yen} = \$0.0103000/\yen$ and then fluctuate randomly toward a spot price at expiration of $S_T^{\$/\yen} = \$0.010900/\yen$. As in the previous example, day-to-day changes in the futures price are settled daily through the margin account as the contract is marked to market. At the end of the contract, the futures price will have converged to the spot price. Since the beginning and ending points are the same as in the previous example, the sum of the payments to or from each customer's margin account over the life of the futures contract must equal the gain or loss at expiration on a comparable forward contract. The size and timing of the cash flows from the futures contract depend on the time path of the futures price, but the net gain or loss is the same as the forward contract. This is the reason futures and forwards are near substitutes and share the same risk profiles.

> The gain or loss at expiration of a forward contract equals the accumulated gain or loss on a comparable futures contract.

Standardized or Customized: Which Do You Choose?

The size, timing, and currency underlying a forward contract are negotiated between a commercial bank and its client. This means that the transaction exposure of a for-

FIGURE 6.3
Futures and Spot Price Convergence

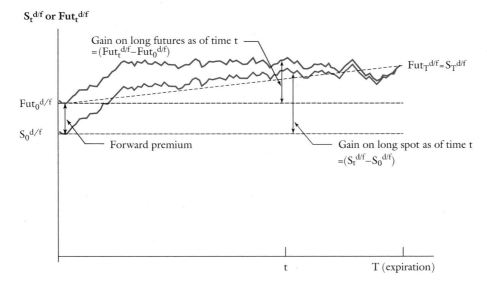

$S_t^{d/f}$ or $Fut_t^{d/f}$

Gain on long futures as of time t
= $(Fut_t^{d/f} - Fut_0^{d/f})$

$Fut_T^{d/f} = S_T^{d/f}$

$Fut_0^{d/f}$

$S_0^{d/f}$

Forward premium

Gain on long spot as of time t
= $(S_t^{d/f} - S_0^{d/f})$

t   T (expiration)

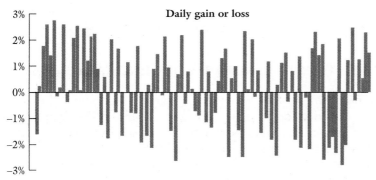

Daily gain or loss

eign currency cash inflow or outflow can be matched exactly with a forward contract. If the size and timing of the foreign currency cash flow are exactly offset by a forward contract, the forward contract provides a **perfect hedge** against currency risk.

Futures contracts can provide a perfect hedge against currency risk only when the underlying transaction falls on the same day and is in an integer multiple of a futures contract. To the extent that the amount or timing of expected future cash flows do not match standardized exchange-traded futures contracts, futures contracts can provide only an imperfect hedge. The size mismatch is a problem only for small transactions. The maturity mismatch can be important, because exchange-traded futures contracts cannot be tailored to the maturity date of the underlying exposure. For the same reason, forward and futures contracts cannot be compared on cost alone unless the size and maturity of the forward and futures positions are identical.

> A perfect hedge exactly offsets the underlying exposure.

Market Update

The Price of a Seat on the CME

The Chicago Mercantile Exchange trades commodity and financial futures and options on trading floors in downtown Chicago. Several types of memberships, or seats, are available.

* The highest price paid for one of the 625 seats on the CME's commodity trading floor was $925,000 on August 18, 1994.

* The highest price paid for one of the 813 seats on the International Monetary Market (IMM) was $850,000 on August 17, 1994. Each seat trades in currency, interest rate, and stock index futures on the IMM and options on the Index and Option Market.

* The highest price paid for an Index and Option Market (IOM) seat was $345,000 on March 27, 2000. The 1,287 seats trade in index futures and options on futures.

* The 413 seats on the new Growth and Emerging Markets (GEM) division of the exchange have recently sold for around $30,000.

Full CME memberships, including 17,999 restricted Class A shares of CME Holdings and the right to trade all CME products, have recently sold for more than $1 million.

6.5 • FUTURES HEDGES USING CROSS EXCHANGE RATES

Multinational enterprises with cash flows in multiple currencies should determine their net exposure in each currency and at each future date. If Minton Distributing hedges using CME futures contracts denominated in dollars as in this example, then the dollar cash flow on the yen contract exactly offsets the dollar cash flow on the euro contract. Total hedging costs might be reduced if Minton buys yen and sells euros directly using a cross-rate futures contract, rather than going through dollars as in the CME futures contracts.

Minton can trade a ¥/€ futures contract on the CME. Triangular arbitrage ensures that cross exchange rates are in equilibrium, so the ¥/€ spot exchange rate must be $S^{¥/€}$ = $(S^{¥/\$})(S^{\$/€})$ = ($1.2000/€)/($0.00800/¥) = ¥150/€. At this spot rate, each contract is worth (¥150/€)(€125,000) = ¥18,750,000. If Minton sells two ¥/€ futures contracts, then Minton's exposure in euros is 2(€125,000) = €250,000 short. The offsetting exposure in yen is 2(¥18,750,000) = ¥37,500,000 long. Minton's exposure to currency risk is completely hedged with this position. The commission charged on two ¥/€ CME futures contracts will be less than the commission charged on three CME futures contracts (one $/¥ and two $/€ contracts) when going through dollars.

Minton should shop around in order to hedge currency exposure most effectively and at the least cost. For example, Minton could consider trading ¥/€ futures contracts on the Tokyo International Financial Futures Exchange (TIFFE). Minton faces several obstacles to trading this contract in Japan. Minton would need to have established a relation with a brokerage house that is authorized to trade futures contracts on the TIFFE. Foreign customers are often charged a higher commission than domestic customers are charged, especially if the foreign customer does not have an established relation with a Japanese futures commission merchant. If Minton has a Japanese subsidiary, a cross-rate hedge on the Tokyo exchange might be less expensive than multiple contracts on the CME. Finally, for this particular transaction, the size of the ¥/€ futures contract traded in Tokyo might not match the size and timing of Minton's underlying exposures.

6.6 • Hedging with Currency Futures

Forward contracts hedge foreign currency cash flows one to one when the forward contract matches the size, timing, and currency of the underlying exposure. Futures hedges also provide a perfect hedge against currency risk when the amount of a transaction that is exposed to currency risk is an even multiple of a futures contract and matures on the same date as a futures contract in the same currency. Exchange-traded futures contracts cannot be tailored to meet the unique needs of each hedger because they come in only a limited number of contract sizes, maturities, and currencies. A classification of futures hedges as a function of the maturity and currency of the underlying currency exposure is presented in Figure 6.4.

Maturity Mismatches and Delta Hedges

A futures hedge is called a **delta hedge** when there is a mismatch between the maturity (but not the currency) of a futures contract and the underlying exposure. When there is a maturity mismatch, a futures hedge cannot provide a perfect hedge against currency risk.

FIGURE 6.4
A Classification of Futures Hedges

Hedge (hedge ratio estimation)		Currency	
		Exact match	Mismatch
Maturity	Exact match	Perfect hedge $(s_t^{d/f} = \alpha + \beta s_t^{d/f} + e_t)$ (such that $\alpha = 0$ and $\beta = 1$)	Cross hedge $(s_t^{d/f_1} = \alpha + \beta s_t^{d/f_2} + e_t)$
	Mismatch	Delta hedge $(s_t^{d/f} = \alpha + \beta fut_t^{d/f} + e_t)$	Delta-cross hedge $(s_t^{d/f_1} = \alpha + \beta fut_t^{d/f_2} + e_t)$

Key: $s_t^{d/f} = (S_t^{d/f} - S_{t-1}^{d/f})/S_{t-1}^{d/f}$
$fut_t^{d/f} = (Fut_t^{d/f} - Fut_{t-1}^{d/f})/Fut_{t-1}^{d/f}$
d = domestic currency
f_1 = foreign currency in which the underlying exposure is denominated
f_2 = foreign currency used to hedge against the underlying exposure
f = foreign currency when $f_1 = f_2$

Suppose that today is Friday, March 13, (time 0) and that Chen Machinery Company has a S$10 million (Singapore dollar) obligation coming due on Friday, October 26. There are 227 days between March 13 and October 26, so with annual compounding this is t = (227/365) of one year. The nearest CME Singapore dollar futures contracts mature on Friday, September 11, and on Friday, December 16. This maturity mismatch is shown here:

> When there is a maturity mismatch, a futures hedge is called a delta hedge.

A hedge with the futures contract that expires on September 11 only hedges against currency risk through that date. Chen remains exposed to changes in currency values from the end of the contract through October 26. The December futures contract is a better choice because it can hedge currency risk through October 26 and can then be sold. December 16 is 278 days after March 13, so the time until expiration of the December contract is T = (278/365) of one year.

Suppose the spot exchange rate is $S_0^{\$/S\$}$ = $0.6010/S$ on March 13. Annual interest rates in the United States and Singapore are $i^\$$ = 6.24% and $i^{S\$}$ = 4.04%, respectively. According to interest rate parity, the forward price for exchange on October 26 is

$$F_{0,t}^{\$/S\$} = S_0^{\$/S\$} [(1+i^\$)/(1+i^{S\$})]^t$$
$$= (\$0.6010/S\$)[(1.0624)/(1.0404)]^{(227/365)} \cong \$0.6089/S\$ \qquad (6.3)$$

Chen can form a perfect hedge with a long forward contract for delivery of S$10 million on October 26 in exchange for ($0.6089/S$)(S$10,000,000) = $6,089,000. As we shall see, the futures hedge using the December 16 futures contract is not quite as precise.

The Basis Risk of a Delta Hedge

> Basis is the difference between nominal interest rates in two currencies.

In a futures hedge, the underlying position is settled in the spot market and the futures position is settled at the futures price. Although futures prices converge to spot prices at expiration, prior to expiration there is a risk that nominal interest rates will change in one or both currencies. If interest rates change unexpectedly, the forward premium or discount will also change unexpectedly through interest rate parity.

The relative interest rate differential is often approximated by the simple difference in nominal interest rates ($i^d - i^f$). This difference is called the **basis**. The basis changes as interest rate levels in the two currencies rise and fall unexpectedly. The risk of unexpected change in the relationship between the futures prices and spot prices is called **basis risk**. When there is a maturity mismatch between the futures contract and the underlying currency exposure, basis risk makes a futures hedge slightly riskier than a forward hedge.

Using the Chen Machinery Company example, here is how basis is determined and how it can change prior to expiration. As with a forward contract, the price of the March 13 S$ futures contract for December delivery (i.e., at time T in 278 days) is determined by interest rate parity.

$$Fut_{0,T}^{\$/S\$} = S_0^{\$/S\$} [(1+i^\$)/(1+i^{S\$})]^T$$
$$= (\$0.6010/S\$)[(1.0624)/(1.0404)]^{(278/365)} \cong \$0.6107/S\$ \qquad (6.4)$$

When this price is set on March 13, the expectation is that on October 26 the spot price will not have risen by the full amount. The expectation of the October 26 spot price is the same as the price for forward delivery on that date.

$$F_{0,t}^{\$/S\$} = E[S_{0,t}^{\$/S\$}] = S_0^{\$/S\$} [(1+i^\$)/(1+i^{S\$})]^t \qquad (6.5)$$
$$= (\$0.6010/S\$)[(1.0624)/(1.0404)]^{(227/365)} \cong \$0.6089/S\$$$

This expectation will hold only if the ratio of interest rates, $(1+i^\$)/(1+i^{S\$})$ = (1.0624)/(1.0404) = 1.02115, remains constant. This ratio is the "basis" for changes in futures prices over time.

The convergence of futures prices to the spot price at expiration is almost linear over time, so the basis $i^\$ - i^{S\$}$ = 6.24% − 4.04% = 2.20% is often used in lieu of the ratio of interest rates in Equation 6.5. Using this approximation, the spot price on October 26 is predicted to be (0.0220)(227/365) = 0.0137, or 1.37 percent above the March spot price. This suggests an October spot price of ($0.6010/S$)(1.0137) = $0.6092/S$, which is fairly close to the forward price of $0.6089/S$ from Equation 6.5.

As of October 26, there are still 51 days remaining on the December futures contract. The December futures contract provides a perfect hedge of Chen's October 26 exposure so long as the basis of 2.20 percent does not change. If the basis changes, then the futures hedge is imperfect and there will be some variability in the hedged payoffs. Figure 6.5 provides an example of basis risk using three scenarios.

Scenario #1. Scenario #1 reflects the market expectation. In this scenario, the basis $i^\$-i^{S\$}$ does not change and the spot rate on October 26 turns out to be the $0.6089/S$ rate predicted by Equation 6.5. On October 26, the futures price for December delivery is based on the prevailing spot exchange rate of $0.6089/S$, the basis of 2.20 percent

> Basis risk is the risk of unexpected change in the relationship between spot prices and futures prices.

per year, and the (T − t) = (278 − 227) = 51 days remaining on the futures contract:

$$Fut_{t,T}^{\$/S\$} = S_t^{\$/S\$} [(1+i^\$)/(1+i^{S\$})]^{T-t}$$
$$= (\$0.6089/S\$)[(1.0624)/(1.0404)]^{(51/365)} \cong \$0.6107/S\$$$

This is the same price as in Equation 6.4. In this scenario, the gains (losses) on the long futures position and on the short underlying spot position are as follows:

Profit on futures: $(Fut_{t,T}^{\$/S\$}-Fut_{0,T}^{\$/S\$})$ = ($0.6107/S$−$0.6107/S$) = $0.00/S$

Profit (loss) on underlying short position in the spot currency:
$$-(S_t^{\$/S\$}-E[S_t^{\$/S\$}]) = -(\$0.6089/S\$-\$0.6089/S\$) = \$0.00/S\$$$

In this scenario, there is no net gain or loss on the combined position.

Scenario #2. In Scenario #2 the Singapore dollar rises in value to $S_t^{\$/S\$}$ = $0.6255/S$ on October 26 in response to a rise in the short-term S$ interest rate to $i^{S\$}$ = 4.54%. At this higher S$ interest rate, the October futures price for December delivery is

$$Fut_{t,T}^{\$/S\$} = S_t^{\$/S\$} [(1+i^\$)/(1+i^{S\$})]^{T-t}$$
$$= (\$0.6255/S\$)[(1.0624)/(1.0454)]^{(51/365)} \cong \$0.6269/S\$$$

The gains (losses) on the futures and spot positions are now as follows:

Profit on futures: $(Fut_{t,T}^{\$/S\$}-Fut_{0,T}^{\$/S\$})$
$$= (\$0.6269/S\$-\$0.6107/S\$) = +\$0.0162/S\$$$

FIGURE 6.5
An Example of a Futures Hedge

time 0	time t	time T
Mar 13	Oct 26	Dec 16

Profit on long S\$ futures position: $(\text{Fut}_{t,T}^{\$/S\$} - \text{Fut}_{0,T}^{\$/S\$})$

Unexpected profit on short S\$ spot position: $-(S_t^{\$/S\$} - E[S_t^{\$/S\$}])$

Time zero: $S_0^{\$/S\$} = \$0.6010/S\$$ $\qquad i\$ = 6.24\%$ $\qquad i^{S\$} = 4.04\%$

$\Rightarrow \text{Fut}_{0,T}^{\$/S\$}$ $= S_0^{\$/S\$}[(1+i\$)/(1+i^{S\$})]^T$

$= (\$0.6010/S\$)\ [(1.0624)/(1.0404)]^{(278/365)} \cong \$0.6107/S\$$

Scenario #1: $S_t^{\$/S\$} = \$0.6089/S\$$ $\qquad i\$ = 6.24\%$ $\qquad i^{S\$} = 4.04\%$

$\text{Fut}_{t,T}^{\$/S\$} = (\$0.6089/S\$)\ [(1.0624)/(1.0404)]^{(51/365)} \cong \$0.6107/S\$$

Profit on futures:	$+(\$0.6107/S\$ - \$0.6107/S\$)$	$+\$0.0000/S\$$
Profit on spot:	$-(\$0.6089/S\$ - \$0.6089/S\$)$	$-\$0.0000/S\$$
Net gain		$\$0.0000/S\$$

Scenario #2: $S_t^{\$/S\$} = \$0.6255/S\$$ $\qquad i\$ = 6.24\%$ $\qquad i^{S\$} = 4.54\%$

$\text{Fut}_{t,T}^{\$/S\$} = (\$0.6255/S\$)\ [(1.0624)/(1.0454)]^{(51/365)} \cong \$0.6269/S\$$

Profit on futures:	$+(\$0.6269/S\$ - \$0.6107/S\$)$	$+\$0.0162/S\$$
Profit on spot:	$-(\$0.6255/S\$ - \$0.6089/S\$)$	$-\$0.0166/S\$$
Net gain		$-\$0.0004/S\$$

Scenario #3: $S_t^{\$/S\$} = \$0.5774/S\$$ $\qquad i\$ = 6.74\%$ $\qquad i^{S\$} = 4.04\%$

$\text{Fut}_{t,T}^{\$/S\$} = (\$0.5774/S\$)\ [(1.0674)/(1.0404)]^{(51/365)} \cong \$0.5795/S\$$

Profit on futures:	$+(\$0.5795/S\$ - \$0.6107/S\$)$	$-\$0.0312/S\$$
Profit on spot:	$-(\$0.5774/S\$ - \$0.6089/S\$)$	$+\$0.0315/S\$$
Net gain		$+\$0.0003/S\$$

Profit (loss) on the underlying short position in the spot currency:

$-(S_t^{\$/S\$} - E[S_t^{\$/S\$}])$

$= -(\$0.6255/S\$ - \$0.6089/S\$) = -\$0.0166/S\$$

The net position is then $+(\$0.0162/S\$) - (\$0.0166/S\$) = -\$0.0004/S\$$, or $-\$4,000$ based on the S\$10 million underlying positions. This loss arises because of a change in the Singapore dollar interest rate and not because of change in the spot exchange rate.[2]

Scenario #3. In Scenario #3, the spot rate falls to $S_t^{\$/S\$} = \$0.5774/S\$$ in response to a rise in dollar interest rates to $i\$ = 6.74$ percent. Singaporean interest rates remain unchanged at $i^{S\$} = 4.04$ percent. The October futures price for December delivery is

---

2 Try problem 6.6 at the end of the chapter if you are still unconvinced that it is basis risk and not the spot rate change that is the source of risk in a futures hedge.

Market Update

Metallgesellschaft's Oil Futures Hedge

Metallgesellschaft A.G. is a large multinational corporation based in Germany with interests in engineering, metals, and mining. In 1991, Metallgesellschaft's U.S. subsidiary MG Refining and Marketing (MGRM) nearly drove Metallgesellschaft into bankruptcy through an ill-fated hedging strategy in crude oil futures. MGRM had arranged long-term contracts to supply U.S. retailers with gasoline, heating oil, and jet fuel. Many of these were fixed-rate contracts that guaranteed a set price over the life of the contract.

To hedge the risk of these delivery obligations, MGRM formed a "rolling hedge" of long positions in crude oil futures contracts of the nearest maturity. Each quarter, the long position was rolled over into the next quarter's contract. MGRM used a one-to-one hedging strategy in which long-term obligations were hedged dollar-for-dollar with positions in near-term crude oil futures contracts.

Although the intent of this hedging strategy was well-intentioned, the mismatch between the long-term delivery obligations and the short-term long positions in oil futures created havoc for MGRM. Fluctuations in the price of near-term futures contracts resulted in wildly fluctuating short-term cash flow needs that did not match the maturity of MGRM's long-term delivery contracts. Metallgesellschaft nearly went bankrupt in 1991 as a result of the cash flow drain on the parent from the maturity mismatch in this hedge. Metallgesellschaft's experience is a reminder that the timing of a financial hedge must match the exposure of the underlying transaction.

Metallgesellschaft's difficulties are described in the *Journal of Applied Corporate Finance* (Spring 1995).

$$\text{Fut}_{t,T}^{\$/S\$} = S_t^{\$/S\$}\,[(1+i^{\$})/(1+i^{S\$})]^{T-t}$$
$$= (\$0.5774/S\$)[(1.0674)/(1.0404)]^{(51/365)} \cong \$0.5795/S\$$$

In this instance, the profit (loss) on the two positions are

Profit on futures: $(\text{Fut}_{t,T}^{\$/S\$} - \text{Fut}_{0,T}^{\$/S\$}) = (\$0.5795/S\$ - \$0.6107/S\$) = -\$0.0312/S\$$
Profit (loss) on the underlying short position in the spot currency:
$-(S_t^{\$/S\$} - E[S_t^{\$/S\$}]) = -(\$0.5774/S\$ - \$0.6089/S\$) = +\$0.0315/S\$$

The net gain is $(-\$0.0312/S\$ + \$0.0315/S\$) = +\$0.0003/S\$$, or $3,000 based on the S\$10 million short and long positions. Again, it is basis risk that spoils the futures hedge.

Chen's unhedged short position in Singapore dollars is exposed to considerable currency risk. If the range of spot rates is from $0.5774/S\$ to $0.6255/S\$, as in Scenarios #2 and #3, then the range of dollar obligations is $481,000 (from –$5,774,000 to –$6,255,000) on the S\$10 million underlying exposure in the spot market. This risk arises from *variability in the level of the exchange rate*. A forward contract can reduce the variability of the hedged position to zero. The futures hedge does almost as well, producing a $7,000 range of outcomes (from –$4,000 to +$3,000). The remaining risk in the futures hedge arises from *variability in the basis*—the risk that interest rates in one or both currencies will change unexpectedly. The futures hedge transforms the nature of Chen's currency risk exposure from a bet on exchange rate levels to a bet on the difference between domestic and foreign interest rates.

Futures Hedging Using the Hedge Ratio

The Forward Hedge. The hedge ratio N_F^* of a futures position is defined as

$$N_F^* = \text{Amount in forward position / Amount exposed to currency risk}   \text{(6.6)}$$

In a perfect forward hedge, the forward contract is the same size as the underlying exposure. A forward contract provides a perfect hedge because gains (losses) on the underlying position are exactly offset by losses (gains) on the forward position. The optimal hedge ratio is thus $N_F^* = -1$, where the minus sign indicates that the forward position is opposite (short) the underlying exposure.

The Futures Delta Hedge. As with forward contracts, most of the change in the value of a futures contract is derived from change in the underlying spot rate of exchange. However, because futures contracts are exposed to basis risk, there is not a one-to-one relation between spot prices and futures prices. For this reason, futures contracts do not generally provide perfect hedges against currency exposure. However, futures contracts can provide very good hedges, because basis risk is small relative to currency risk.

The relation between changes in spot and futures prices can be viewed as a regression equation:

$$s_t^{\$/S\$} = \alpha + \beta \; fut_t^{\$/S\$} + e_t \tag{6.7}$$

where $s_t^{\$/S\$} = (S_t^{\$/S\$} - S_{t-1}^{\$/S\$})/S_{t-1}^{\$/S\$}$ and $fut_t^{\$/S\$} = (Fut_t^{\$/S\$} - Fut_{t-1}^{\$/S\$})/Fut_{t-1}^{\$/S\$}$ are percentage changes in spot and futures prices during period t. In the Chen example, this regression should be estimated using futures contracts that mature in $7\frac{1}{2}$ months (for example, from March through October). The regression then provides an estimate of how well changes in futures prices predict changes in spot prices over $7\frac{1}{2}$-month maturities.

The regression in Equation 6.7 is shown graphically in Figure 6.6. Since both spot and futures prices are close to a random walk, the expectation of both $fut_t^{\$/S\$}$ and $s_t^{\$/S\$}$ is zero, and the intercept term α in this regression is usually ignored. As in any regression, the slope β in Equation 6.7 is equal to

$$\beta = (\sigma_{s,fut})/(\sigma_{fut}^2) = \rho_{s,fut} \, (\sigma_s / \sigma_{fut}) \tag{6.8}$$

This slope (β) measures changes in futures prices relative to changes in spot prices. The error term e_t captures any variation in spot rate changes $s_t^{\$/S\$}$ that is unrelated to futures price changes $fut_t^{\$/S\$}$.

If the historical relation between spot prices and futures prices is a reasonable approximation of the expected future relation, then this regression can be used to estimate the number of futures contracts that will minimize the variance of the hedged position. Let N_S be the size of the underlying exposure to currency risk and N_{Fut} the amount of currency to be bought or sold in the futures market to offset the underlying exposure. The optimal amount in futures to minimize the risk of the futures hedge is

$$N_{Fut}^* = \text{Amount in futures contracts/Amount exposed to currency risk}   \text{(6.9)}$$
$$= -\beta$$

In this context, the hedge ratio provides the optimal amount in the futures hedge per unit of value exposed to currency risk. A futures hedge formed in this fashion is called a delta hedge because it minimizes the variance (the Δ, or delta) of the hedged position.[3]

---

[3] Ederington develops the properties of the delta hedge ratio in "The Hedging Performance of the New Futures Markets," *Journal of Finance* (1979).

FIGURE 6.6
Linear Regression and the Hedge Ratio

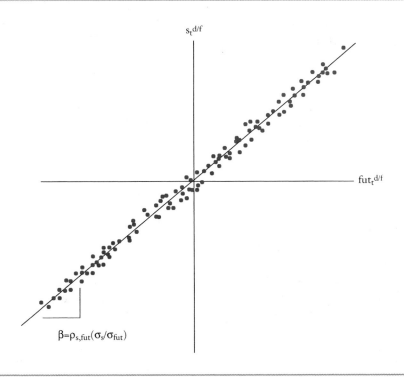

Hedge quality is measured by the r-square of the regression in Equation 6.7. The r-square (or *coefficient of determination*) is bounded by zero and one, and measures the percentage of the variation in $s_t^{\$/S\$}$ that is explained by variation in $fut_t^{\$/S\$}$. A high r-square indicates low basis risk and a high-quality delta hedge. A low r-square means that basis risk is high relative to the underlying currency risk.

> Hedge quality is measured by r-square.

The regression in Equation 6.7 is designed to estimate basis risk over the maturity of a proposed hedge. Unfortunately, it is difficult to construct a sample of futures prices of constant maturity t because exchanged-traded futures come in only a limited assortment of maturities. In the Chen example, this would be a $7\frac{1}{2}$-month maturity. Exchange-traded futures expire only every three months, and the futures prices on any single contract converge to the spot rate at maturity. Fortunately, interest rate parity determines both the forward price and the futures price for a given maturity. It is much easier to construct a sample of forward prices of constant maturity than a sample of futures prices of constant maturity, so the hedge ratio is conventionally estimated from the relation of forward price changes to spot rate changes over the desired maturity.

An Example of a Delta Hedge. Suppose the regression in Equation 6.7 yields a regression coefficient of $\beta = 1.025$. The futures hedge should then consist of

$$N_{Fut}{}^* = \text{(Amount in futures contracts)/(Amount exposed)} = -\beta$$
$$\Rightarrow \text{(Amount in futures contracts)} = (-\beta)\,\text{(Amount exposed)}$$

For Chen's underlying S\$10 million short exposure, this requires a long position of

$$\text{Amount in futures contract} = (-1.025)(-S\$10,000,000)$$
$$= S\$10,250,000$$

The variability in the hedged position can be minimized with S\$10,250,000 of December futures. On the CME, this would be worth (S\$10,250,000)/(S\$125,000/ contract) = 82 futures contracts.

Cross Hedges and Delta-Cross Hedges

A **delta-cross hedge** is used when there are both maturity and currency mismatches between the underlying exposure and the futures hedge. The regression in Equation 6.7 must be modified for a delta-cross hedge to include both basis risk from the maturity mismatch as well as currency cross-rate risk from the currency mismatch. The general form of the regression equation for estimating the optimal hedge ratio of a delta-cross hedge is

> Delta-cross hedges have both maturity and currency mismatches.

$$s_t^{d/f_1} = \alpha + \beta \; fut_t^{d/f_2} + e_t \tag{6.10}$$

for an underlying transaction exposure in currency f_1 and a futures hedge in currency f_2. The interpretation of the slope coefficient as the optimal hedge ratio is the same as in Equation 6.9; that is, buy futures contracts according to the ratio $N_{fut}{}^* = -\beta$.

A **cross hedge** is a special case of the delta-cross hedge. As discussed earlier, in a cross hedge there is a currency mismatch but not a maturity mismatch. The optimal hedge ratio of a cross hedge is estimated from

> Cross hedges have only a currency mismatch.

$$s_t^{d/f_1} = \alpha + \beta \; s_t^{d/f_2} + e_t \tag{6.11}$$

This is identical to Equation 6.10 except that fut_t^{d/f_2} is replaced by s_t^{d/f_2}. Spot rate changes s_t^{d/f_2} can be substituted for fut_t^{d/f_2} because futures prices converge to spot prices at maturity, and the maturity of the futures contract is the same as that of the underlying transaction exposure in the spot market.

If futures are not available in the currency that you wish to hedge, a cross hedge using a futures contract on a currency that is closely related to the desired currency can at least partially hedge against currency risk. As an example, a U.K.-based corporation can hedge a Canadian dollar (C\$) obligation with a long U.S. dollar futures contract because the U.S. and Canadian dollars are highly correlated. For a U.S. dollar hedge of a Canadian dollar obligation, the spot exposure is in Canadian dollars and the futures exposure is in U.S. dollars as in the following regression:

$$s_t^{£/C\$} = \alpha + \beta \; fut_t^{£/\$} + e_t \tag{6.12}$$

The quality of this cross-rate futures hedge is only as good as the correlation between the pound sterling values of the Canadian and U.S. dollars.

When both the maturity and the currency match that of the underlying obligation, Equation 6.10 reduces to

$$s_t^{d/f} = \alpha + \beta \; s_t^{d/f} + e_t \tag{6.13}$$

Since the correlation of $s_t^{d/f}$ with itself is +1, this is a perfect hedge ($r^2 = 1$) and the optimal hedge ratio is $N_{Fut}{}^* = -\beta = -1$. In this circumstance, the futures hedge is equivalent to a forward market hedge, and currency risk can be completely eliminated.

6.7 • SUMMARY

Forward contracts are pure credit instruments and are therefore subject to default risk. Futures contracts reduce the risk of default relative to forward contracts through the following conventions:

- An exchange clearinghouse takes one side of every transaction.
- An initial and a maintenance margin are required.
- Futures contracts are marked to market on a daily basis.

Because they are marked to market daily, futures contracts are essentially a bundle of consecutive one-day forward contracts. This means that they are functionally equivalent to forward contracts and, aside from contractual differences, are priced in the same way. Whereas forward contracts can form perfect hedges against transaction exposure, futures hedges are imperfect when there is a mismatch between the size, maturity, or currency of the underlying exposure and of the futures contract used to hedge the exposure. The choice between a forward or futures contract depends on the cost of each contract and on how closely the underlying risk profile is to that of a standardized futures contract.

A delta hedge is used when the timing of the transaction exposed to currency risk is not the same as the maturity of available futures contracts. While a delta hedge can eliminate currency risk, it typically cannot eliminate basis risk; that is, the risk that the relation of futures prices to spot prices will change. This is because spot and futures prices do not move in unison when there are changes in the basis—the difference in nominal interest rates between the foreign and domestic currencies. The hedge ratio of a delta hedge can be estimated from

$$s_t^{d/f} = \alpha + \beta \, fut_t^{d/f} + e_t \tag{6.7}$$

where $s_t^{d/f}$ and $fut_t^{d/f}$ are percentage changes in spot and futures prices, respectively. The hedge ratio

$$N_{Fut}^* = \text{Amount in futures contracts/Amount exposed} = -\beta \tag{6.9}$$

minimizes the risk of the hedged position.

Similarly, futures do not provide a perfect hedge when there is a currency mismatch even if there is a maturity match. A futures hedge with a maturity match but using a currency that is closely related to the exposed currency is called a cross hedge. For an underlying exposure in foreign currency f_1 and a futures hedge using currency f_2, the hedge ratio is estimated from the regression

$$s_t^{d/f_1} = \alpha + \beta \, s_t^{d/f_2} + e_t \tag{6.11}$$

where d is the hedger's domestic currency of reference.

A futures hedge for which there are both currency and maturity mismatches is called a delta-cross hedge. This is the most general form of futures hedge:

$$s_t^{d/f_1} = \alpha + \beta \, fut_t^{d/f_2} + e_t \tag{6.10}$$

If the underlying exposure and the futures contracts are in the same currency, then $f_1 = f_2 = f$, and the hedge is a delta hedge. If there is a maturity match but a currency mismatch, then $fut_t^{d/f_2} = s_t^{d/f_2}$ and the hedge is a cross hedge. If there is a match on both maturity and currency, then a futures hedge is equivalent to a forward market hedge and the futures hedge can completely eliminate currency risk so long as the underlying transaction exposure is an even increment of the futures contract size.

KEY TERMS

basis	futures commission merchant
basis risk	hedge quality
cross hedge	hedge ratio
currency futures contact	margin requirement
delta-cross hedge	marking-to-market
delta hedge	perfect hedge

CONCEPTUAL QUESTIONS

6.1 How do currency forward and futures contracts differ with respect to maturity, settlement, and the size and timing of cash flows?

6.2 What is the primary role of the exchange clearinghouse?

6.3 Draw and explain the payoff profile associated with a currency futures contract.

6.4 What is a delta hedge? A cross hedge? A delta-cross hedge?

6.5 What is the basis? What is basis risk?

6.6 How do you measure the quality of a futures hedge?

PROBLEMS

6.1 On September 11, a U.S.-based MNC with a customer in Singapore expects to receive S$3,000,000. The current spot exchange rate is $0.5950/S$. The transfer will occur on December 10. The current S$ futures price for December delivery is $0.6075/S$. The size of the CME futures contract is S$125,000. How many futures contracts should the U.S. multinational buy or sell in order to hedge this forward obligation? What is the MNC's net profit (or loss) on December 10 if the spot rate on that date is $0.5900/S$?

6.2 Snow White Manufacturing makes snowmobiles, some of which it sells to Japan for recreation in the wilderness of the northern islands. Snow White is expecting a payment of ¥9 million in six months.
  a. Draw a time line illustrating the transaction.
  b. Draw a payoff profile with $/¥ on the axes.
  c. Suppose Snow White takes out a forward contract to hedge this transaction. Describe this contract.
  d. If Snow White takes out a futures contract instead of a forward contract, describe the advantages/disadvantages to Snow White.

6.3 Suppose that at time zero the spot rate equals the 90-day forward rate at $S^{\$/S\$} = F^{\$/S\$} = \$0.65/S\$$. Assume that the spot rate increases by $0.0002/S$ each day over the ensuing 90 days. You buy Singapore dollars in both the forward and futures markets. Draw a time line for each contract showing the cash inflows/outflows arising from the daily change in the spot rate.

6.4 Suppose Cotton Bolls, Inc. does business with companies in Israel (shekel) and Singapore. Cotton Bolls expects to pay 500,000 shekels and receive 125,000 Singapore dollars on the Friday before the third Wednesday of April. Forward rates for that date are $F^{\$/shekel} = \$0.1625/shekel$ and $F^{\$/S\$} = \$0.65/S\$$.

a. Show time lines illustrating each transaction.

b. How would Cotton Bolls hedge these transactions with $/shekel and $/S$ futures contracts?

c. Suppose the forward rate is S$0.2500/shekel. Describe a cross hedge that would accomplish the same objective as the two hedges in part b.

6.5 You work for Texas Instruments in the United States and are considering ways to hedge a 10 billion Danish kroner (DKr) obligation due in six months. Your currency of reference is the U.S. dollar. The current spot exchange rate is $S_0^{\$/DKr} = \$0.80/DKr$ (or $S_0^{DKr/\$} = DKr1.25/\$$).

a. A futures exchange in Copenhagen trades futures contracts on the U.S. dollar that expire in seven months with a contract size of $50,000. You estimate $\beta = 1.025$ based on the regression $s_t^{\$/DKr} = \alpha + \beta\ fut_t^{\$/DKr} + e_t$. The r-square of the regression is 0.98. How many futures contracts should you buy to minimize the risk of your hedged position?

b. A merchant bank in Chicago is willing to sell a euro (€) futures contract in any amount with a maturity on the date that your obligation is due in six months. Based on the regression $s_t^{\$/DKr} = \alpha + \beta\ s_t^{\$/€} + e_t$, you estimate $\beta = 1.04$. The r-square of the regression is 0.89. How large of a position in this euro futures contract should you take to minimize the risk of your hedged position?

c. Euronext in Frankfurt trades €/$ futures contracts that expire in seven months and have a contract size of $50,000. Based on the regression $s_t^{\$/DKr} = \alpha + \beta\ fut_t^{\$/€} + e_t$, you estimate $\beta = 1.05$. The r-square of this regression is 0.86. How many futures contracts should you buy to minimize the risk of your hedged position?

d. Which of these futures market hedges provides the best quality?

6.6 Refer to Figure 6.5. It is now March 13 and the current spot exchange rate between U.S. dollars ($) and Singapore dollars (S$) is $0.6010/S$. You have a S$10 million obligation due on October 26. The nearest S$ futures contract expires on December 16. Interest rates are 6.24 percent in the United States and 4.04 percent in Singapore.

a. Suppose the spot exchange rate on October 26 is $0.6089/S$. Fill in the three scenarios in Figure 6.5 assuming (1) $i^\$ = 6.24\%$ and $i^{S\$} = 4.04\%$, (2) $i^\$ = 6.24\%$ and $i^{S\$} = 4.54\%$, and (3) $i^\$ = 6.74\%$ and $i^{S\$} = 4.04\%$.

b. Suppose interest rates do not change (so that $i^\$ = 6.24\%$ and $i^{S\$} = 4.04\%$) but that the spot exchange rate does change. Fill in the three scenarios in Figure 6.5 assuming (1) $S_t^{\$/S\$} = \$0.6089/S\$$, (2) $S_t^{\$/S\$} = \$0.6255/S\$$, and (3) $S_t^{\$/S\$} = \$0.5774/S\$$.

SUGGESTED READINGS

Comparisons of futures and forwards contracts appear in

Kenneth R. French, "A Comparison of Futures and Forward Prices," *Journal of Financial Economics* 12, No. 3 (November 1983), pp. 311–342.

A thorough coverage of currency and interest rate futures contracts appears in

Edward W. Schwarz, Joanne M. Hill, and Thomas Schneeweis, *Financial Futures: Fundamentals, Strategies, and Applications* (Homewood, Illinois: Irwin Publishing, 1986).

An easy-to-read introduction to forwards, futures, swaps, and options appears in

Charles W. Smithson, "A LEGO Approach to Financial Engineering: An Introduction to Forwards, Futures, Swaps, and Options," *Midland Corporate Finance Journal* 4, No. 4 (Winter 1987), pp. 16–28.

The properties of the delta hedge ratio are developed in

Louis Ederington, "The Hedging Performance of the New Futures Markets," *Journal of Finance* 34, No. 1 (1979), pp. 157–170.

A discussion of appropriate and inappropriate hedging strategies surrounding Metallgesellschaft's crude oil futures hedges appears in the following articles from the *Journal of Applied Corporate Finance* 8, No. 1 (Spring 1995):

Franklin R. Edwards and Michael S. Canter, "The Collapse of Metallgesellschaft: Unhedgeable Risks, Poor Hedging Strategy, or Just Bad Luck?"

Antonio S. Mello and John E. Parsons, "Maturity Structure of a Hedge Matters: Lessons from the Metallgesellschaft Debacle."

Christopher L. Culp and Merton H. Miller, "Hedging in the Theory of Corporate Finance: A Reply to Our Critics."

along with

Christopher L. Culp and Merton H. Miller, "Metallgesellschaft and the Economics of Synthetic Storage," *Journal of Applied Corporate Finance* 7, No. 4 (Winter 1994), pp. 62–76.

Currency Options and Options Markets

chapter 7

Overview

There are two times in a man's life when he should not speculate: when he can't afford it and when he can.

Mark Twain

Currency forward and futures contracts share a common characteristic; what is gained on one side of the contract price is lost on the other. There are times when investors, hedgers, or speculators would rather have a one-sided payoff on a currency transaction. Currency options provide such an instrument.

The multinational corporation encounters many different types of options through its investment and financing activities. Some are attached to corporate securities, such as call options that allow the firm to repurchase its bonds at a prearranged price, convertibility options that allow investors to convert bonds into common stock at a prearranged conversion price, and interest rate *caps* or *floors* attached to floating rate Eurocurrencies. Other options are embedded in the firm's real investments, such as options to expand, contract, suspend, or abandon an investment project.

Financial options are derivative securities, in that their value is derived from the value of some underlying asset. For currency options, the underlying asset is the spot rate of exchange between two currencies. As exchange rates change, so do option values written on the exchange rate. This chapter employs a few simple graphs to develop the intuition behind option valuation and its use in hedging currency risks. The technical details of option valuation are presented in the appendix to this chapter.

7.1 • WHAT IS AN OPTION?

An option refers to a choice. If your instructor offers you the option of taking the final examination a week late, it is your choice whether to exercise this option. Once the option

> In an option, one side has the option and the other an obligation to perform.

is offered, it is the instructor's obligation to fulfill the contract. If one side of the agreement has the option, the other side has an obligation.

The difference between an option and a forward or futures contract comes down to choice. Foreign currency options are like foreign currency forward contracts in that they allow two parties to exchange currencies according to a prearranged date, amount, and rate of exchange. In a forward contract, both sides have an obligation to perform. In an option contract, one side has the option of forcing the exchange while the other side has an obligation to perform if the option holder exercises the option. This is the fundamental difference between option and forward contracts.

Types of Currency Options

There are two types of options—calls and puts:

- A currency **call option** is the right to buy the underlying currency at a specified price and on a specified date.
- A currency **put option** is the right to sell the underlying currency at a specified price and on a specified date.

If you sell or *write* a currency call option, the buyer of the option has the right to buy one currency with another currency at the contract's **exercise price**, or **strike price**. The option writer has the obligation to sell the stated amount of currency to the option holder. A currency put option holder has the right to sell a specified amount of currency at the exercise price. A currency put option writer has the obligation to buy the currency from the put option holder, should the option be exercised.

Markets in Currency Options

Exchange-Traded Currency Options. Currency options were first traded on an organized exchange in 1983 at the Philadelphia Stock Exchange (PSE). Today, standardized currency options on major currencies trade at a large number of exchanges around the world including the Chicago Mercantile Exchange (CME), the Korea Stock Exchange (KSE), and the Euronext and Eurex exchanges in Europe. A seat on the CME's Index Option Market (IOM) recently sold for $400,000. Table 7.1 lists the top 20 options exchanges based on contract volume.

Figure 7.1 shows how to read PSE and CME options quotations in *The Wall Street Journal*. The underlying asset or deliverable instrument of the option is the currency being bought or sold.[1] PSE contracts are settled in spot currency. The deliverable instrument of the CME contract is the CME currency futures contract expiring one week after the expiration of the option contract. Options on spot and futures prices are nearly identical in their ability to hedge currency risk because (1) spot and futures prices move in unison and (2) spot and futures price volatilities are nearly the same.

A currency option quote, such as a "British pound Dec 145 call" option traded on the Philadelphia exchange or a "British pound Oct 1450 put" option from the Chicago Mercantile Exchange, identifies several terms and conditions, as shown in Figure 7.2. Consider the PSE call option. Each PSE pound sterling option contract is worth £31,250. The holder of this option has the right to buy £31,250 British pounds sterling at an exercise price of $K^{\$/£} = \$1.45/£$ on the expiration date of the contract. We'll use $K^{d/f}$ to indicate the exercise price in domestic currency per foreign currency unit. PSE currency options expire on the Saturday before the third Wednesday of the month,

---

[1] This is the *currency of reference*. Following Rule #2 of Chapter 4, it is best to keep this currency in the *denominator* of a currency option quotation.

TABLE 7.1
Top 20 Options Exchanges

	Exchange	Contract volume (millions)		
		2001	2000	Growth
1	Korea Stock Exchange (Seoul)	1,889.8	823.3	130%
2	Euronext, France (Paris) *	475.0	404.0	18%
3	Eurex, Germany and Switzerland **	265.2	239.0	11%
4	Chicago Mercantile Exchange, United States	113.9	95.7	19%
5	Chicago Board of Trade, United States	67.6	50.3	34%
6	Stockholmbörsen (OM), Sweden (Stockholm)	40.7	39.3	4%
7	New York Mercantile Exchange, United States	26.4	18.0	47%
8	MEFF Renta Variable, Spain (Madrid)	24.1	23.6	2%
9	South African Futures Exchange (Sandton/Johannesburg)	19.7	24.3	−19%
10	Italian Derivatives Market	10.2	11.0	-8%
11	Osaka Securities Exchange, Japan	9.5	7.0	35%
12	Bourse de Montréal, Canada	6.4	5.4	20%
13	Brazilian Mercantile & Futures Exchange (BM&F), (São Paulo)	5.7	3.7	54%
14	Hong Kong Exchanges & Clearing	4.8	4.7	1.7%
15	New York Board of Trade, United States	4.7	3.9	21%
16	National Stock Exchange of India (Mumbai/Bombay)	3.1	0.7	354%
17	London Metal Exchange, United Kingdom	2.3	3.2	−27%
18	Sydney Futures Exchange, Australia	2.3	1.8	27%
19	Taiwan Futures Exchange	1.6	0.0	–
20	Tokyo Stock Exchange, Japan	1.1	1.1	6%

* Euronext was created in 2001 through a merger of exchanges from Amsterdam, Brussels, Lisbon, London, and Paris. Euronext trades a variety of assets including stocks, bonds, derivatives, and commodities.

** Eurex was created in 1998 through a merger of Deutsche Terminborse (DTB) of Frankfurt and the Switzerland Options and Financial Futures Exchange (Soffex) of Zurich. Eurex trades futures and options on financial price indices including stocks, bonds, and currencies.

Source: Futures Industry Association statistics. Volume figures include options on individual equities. Figures are not directly comparable as contract sizes and the methods for counting option volumes vary by exchange. See http://www.futuresindustry.org.

so the last day on which they can be traded is the previous Friday. The third Wednesday of the month is the settlement date on which currencies are exchanged.

The PSE contract is a **European option**, exercisable only at expiration. A single contract on the PSE is worth £31,250, so the holder of this option pays £31,250($1.45/£) = $45,312.50 and receives £31,250

European options are exercisable only at expiration.

upon exercise. Options that are exercisable anytime until expiration are called **American options.** Holders of American options are usually better off if they leave the options unexercised rather than exercise early.[2] Because early exercise options are seldom exercised, European and American currency call options are nearly equivalent in a freely floating exchange rate system.

2 The option to exercise an American put option early is valuable when the future value of exercising early and investing the exercise price at the riskfree rate of interest is greater than the expected value of the put option at expiration. Under conditions encountered in practice, the early exercise option is usually not valuable. We'll leave this complicated topic to a specialized course in option pricing.

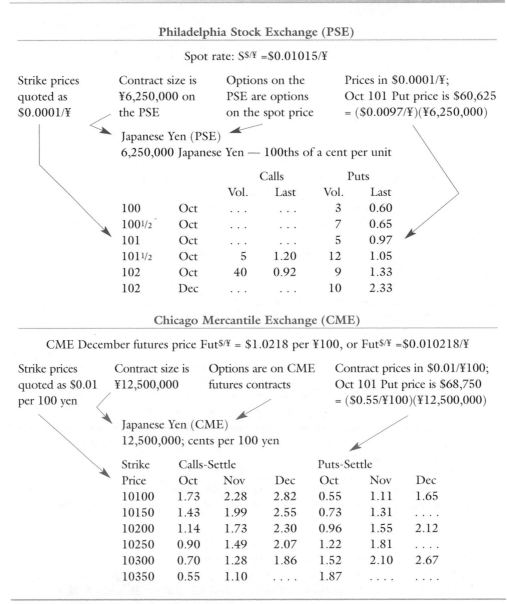

FIGURE 7.1
Explanation of Currency Option Prices Reported in *The Wall Street Journal*

Philadelphia Stock Exchange (PSE)

Spot rate: $S^{\$/¥} = \$0.01015/¥$

Strike prices quoted as $0.0001/¥	Contract size is ¥6,250,000 on the PSE	Options on the PSE are options on the spot price	Prices in $0.0001/¥; Oct 101 Put price is $60,625 = ($0.0097/¥)(¥6,250,000)

Japanese Yen (PSE)
6,250,000 Japanese Yen — 100ths of a cent per unit

		Calls		Puts	
		Vol.	Last	Vol.	Last
100	Oct	. . .	. . .	3	0.60
100½	Oct	. . .	. . .	7	0.65
101	Oct	. . .	. . .	5	0.97
101½	Oct	5	1.20	12	1.05
102	Oct	40	0.92	9	1.33
102	Dec	. . .	. . .	10	2.33

Chicago Mercantile Exchange (CME)

CME December futures price $\text{Fut}^{\$/¥} = \$1.0218$ per ¥100, or $\text{Fut}^{\$/¥} = \$0.010218/¥$

Strike prices quoted as $0.01 per 100 yen	Contract size is ¥12,500,000	Options are on CME futures contracts	Contract prices in $0.01/¥100; Oct 101 Put price is $68,750 = ($0.55/¥100)(¥12,500,000)

Japanese Yen (CME)
12,500,000; cents per 100 yen

Strike Price	Calls-Settle			Puts-Settle		
	Oct	Nov	Dec	Oct	Nov	Dec
10100	1.73	2.28	2.82	0.55	1.11	1.65
10150	1.43	1.99	2.55	0.73	1.31	. . . .
10200	1.14	1.73	2.30	0.96	1.55	2.12
10250	0.90	1.49	2.07	1.22	1.81	. . . .
10300	0.70	1.28	1.86	1.52	2.10	2.67
10350	0.55	1.10	. . . .	1.87	. . . .	. . . .

Over-the-Counter Currency Options. Commercial and investment banks conduct an active over-the-counter (OTC) market in currency options. Whereas exchange-traded options are standardized contracts, OTC options are customized to fit the needs of the banks' wholesale or retail customers. Expiration dates and contract amounts are specified by the customer in the OTC market, and prices and fees are then quoted by the bank.

Retail clients include corporations and financial institutions exposed to currency risk. These clients value the right to exercise a currency option and typically do not want the obligation from writing option contracts. International commercial and investment banks are the principal writers (sellers) of currency options. This asymmetry between buyers and sellers

OTC options are customized to the needs of individual customers.

FIGURE 7.2
Currency Option Quotations

British pound Dec 145 call (European-style) on the PSE
or
British pound Dec 1450 put (American style) on the CME

• The type of option	Call option on the Philadelphia Stock Exchange (PSE)
	Put option on the Chicago Mercantile Exchange (CME)
• The underlying asset	British pound sterling on each exchange
• The expiration date	Third Wednesday in December on each exchange
• The exercise price	$1.45/£ spot rate on the PSE
	$1.45/£ futures price on the CME
• Rule for exercise	European options are exercisable only at expiration
	American options are exercisable anytime until expiration
• Pounds/contract	£31,250 on the PSE
	£62,500 on the CME
• Other	Margin requirements, taxes, etc.

is not seen in currency forward and futures markets. International banks also maintain an active wholesale market in which they hedge, or reinsure, the net currency risk exposures in their asset/liability portfolios.

7.2 • Option Payoff Profiles

A Zero-Sum Game

Currency Call Options. The following left-hand graph plots the dollar value of a purchased (or long) pound sterling call option as a function of the spot rate of exchange between dollars and pounds at expiration. The time subscript T on the call option value and on the spot exchange rate are reminders that these are values at expiration.

Payoff profile of a long pound call at expiration

Payoff profile of a short pound call at expiration

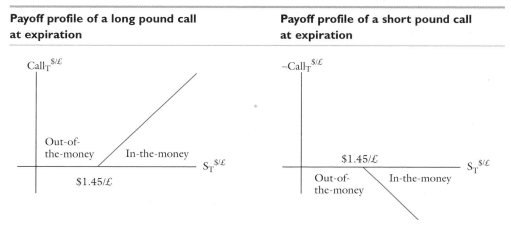

The deliverable instrument is the pound. A call option for which the spot rate of exchange is below the exercise price is called **out-of-the-money**. In this case, it is cheaper to buy pounds in the spot market than at the exercise price of $1.45/£. If the spot rate closes above the exercise price, the call option is **in-the-money**. Suppose the spot rate at expiration is $1.50/£ on a £125,000 CME option. The option holder has the right to call the option and buy pounds sterling at a price of $1.45/£ from the option writer. The option holder can then sell this £125,000 in the spot market at $1.50/£ for a five-cents-per-pound profit, or (£125,000)($0.05/£) = $6,250.

The right-hand graph plots the call option value from the perspective of the option writer. This contract is a zero-sum game, in that any value gained by the option holder is a loss to the option writer. Consequently, the risk profile—*or payoff profile*—of the short call is the mirror image of the long call.

Currency Put Options. The dollar values of long and short pounds sterling put options at expiration are graphed here:

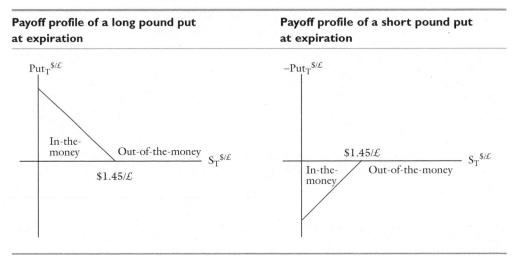

| Payoff profile of a long pound put at expiration | Payoff profile of a short pound put at expiration |

Currency put options are options to sell the underlying currency (in this case, the pound), so these options are in-the-money when the exercise price is greater than the underlying exchange rate. If the exercise price on a £125,000 CME currency put option is $1.45/£, then the option holder will exercise the option at expiration when the underlying exchange rate is below $1.45/£. For example, if the spot rate at expiration is $1.40/£, then the option holder can buy £125,000 in the spot market for $1.40/£ and simultaneously exercise the option to sell £125,000 to the option writer for $1.45/£, for a net profit of (£125,000)($0.05/£) = $6,250. As shown in the right-hand graph, any gain in value to the option holder is a loss to the option writer.

Hedging with Options

Suppose a U.S. firm anticipates a £31,250 cash inflow on December 13, which happens to be a Friday on which PSE currency options expire. If left unhedged, the dollar value of this cash flow will depend on the spot rate of exchange prevailing on the expiration date. The firm can cancel this exposure by selling £31,250 pounds and buying dollars at the forward exchange rate with an expiration date on Friday, December 13.

In contrast to forward contracts, option payoffs are asymmetric. An option expiring out-of-the-money has no value regardless of how little or far it is out-of-the-money. In contrast, an option expiring in-the-money has more value the more in-the-money it is. A financial manager hedging a £31,250 cash inflow with a long pound put option is compensated for any fall in the value of the pound below the exercise price $K^{\$/£}$. If the spot exchange rate rises above $K^{\$/£}$, however, the corporation captures the full benefit of the higher value of the pound on its underlying exposure without any further gain or loss from the put option contract. Because of the characteristic shape of an option's payoff profile, currency options are used as a form of insurance or "disaster hedge" against unfavorable changes in the value of a currency. When used to hedge currency risk, currency options allow the option holder to participate in gains on one side of the exercise price while limiting losses on the other side.

7.3 • PROFIT AND LOSS ON CURRENCY OPTIONS

Options to buy or sell currencies are not free; option sellers demand a premium for writing an option. The premium depends on the writer's expected losses should the option expire in-the-money. The effect of this option premium on the profit or loss of an option can be obtained by superimposing the premium on the option's payoff profile.

Profit and Loss on a Currency Call Option at Expiration

Figure 7.3 displays profit or loss at the expiration of a currency call option as a function of the underlying exchange rate. Consider an Australian dollar call option quoted as "A$ Dec 6400 call" and selling on the CME at a price of $0.0120/A$. This has an exercise price of $0.6400/A$ and expires on the third Wednesday in December. The deliverable instrument of a CME currency option is the corresponding CME futures contract. Each

---

FIGURE 7.3
Profit/Loss on a Call Option at Expiration

$K^{\$/A\$} = \$0.6400/A\$$
Contract size = A$100,000
Current call option price = $0.0120/A$

Premium cost = ($0.0120/A$)(A$100,000) = $1,200
Exercise price = ($0.6400/A$)(A$100,000) = $64,000

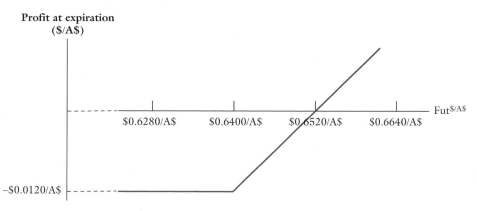

Exchange rate	$0.6280/A$	$0.6400/A$	$0.6520/A$	$0.6640/A$	$0.7720/A$
Payments					
Premium cost	−$1,200	−$1,200	−$1,200	−$1,200	−$1,200
Exercise price	$0	$0	−$64,000	−$64,000	−$64,000
Receipts					
A$ sale	$0	$0	$65,200	$66,400	$77,200
Net profit or loss	−$1,200	−$1,200	$0	$1,200	$12,000

Australian dollar option contract on the CME is worth A\$100,000. At an exercise price of \$0.6400/A\$, this option costs (\$0.6400/A\$)(A\$100,000) = \$64,000 to exercise. At a price or option premium of \$0.0120/A\$, the option costs (\$0.0120/A\$)(A\$100,000) = \$1,200 to purchase.

The value of this option at expiration depends on the difference between the futures price and the exercise price. Profit or loss at expiration is shown in Figure 7.3 at several possible exchange rates. This graph combines the option value at expiration with the initial cost of the option. For example, if the actual futures price is \$0.6520/A\$ at expiration, then selling A\$100,000 in the futures market yields \$65,200, which just covers the \$64,000 exercise price and the original \$1,200 option premium.

This is a zero-sum game between the option writer and the option holder, as the option writer's payoff profile is a mirror image of the seller's. The option holder gains (and the writer loses) whenever the futures price closes above \$0.6520/A\$. The option holder loses (and the writer gains) whenever the futures price closes below \$0.6520/A\$.

Profit and Loss on a Currency Put Option at Expiration

Profit and loss positions as a function of closing futures prices are shown in Figure 7.4 for a currency put option. Consider a CME "A\$ Dec 6400 put" selling at \$0.0160/A\$. At this price, one A\$100,000 contract costs (\$0.0160/A\$)(A\$100,000) = \$1,600. The cost of exercise is again \$64,000 at the \$0.6400/A\$ exercise price.

The payoff to the writer of this put option is the mirror image of the option holder's payoff. The option holder gains at expiration when the exchange rate closes at any price below \$0.6240/A\$. The option writer gains at expiration whenever the exchange rate closes above \$0.6240/A\$. Again, currency options are a zero-sum game; the payoff to the option holder is equal in magnitude and opposite in sign to that of the option writer.

7.4 • AT-THE-MONEY OPTIONS

Suppose a currency option is **at-the-money**, with an exercise price equal to the current exchange rate. If exchange rates are a random walk, then the exercise price also equals the expected exchange rate on the expiration date. Centering the origin of a payoff profile on an exercise price provides a graph of changes in option values against changes in exchange rates, as shown here for long and short call options on U.K. pounds sterling:

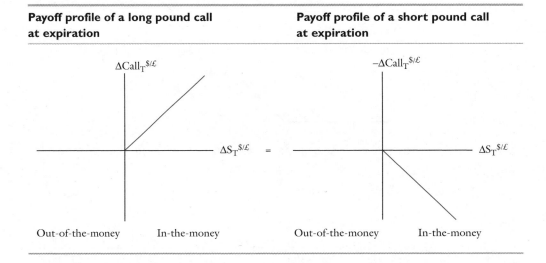

Payoff profile of a long pound call at expiration	**Payoff profile of a short pound call at expiration**

$\Delta Call_T^{\$/\pounds}$ $\quad\quad\quad\quad\quad$ $-\Delta Call_T^{\$/\pounds}$

$\Delta S_T^{\$/\pounds}$ $\quad = \quad$ $\Delta S_T^{\$/\pounds}$

Out-of-the-money $\quad$ In-the-money $\quad\quad\quad$ Out-of-the-money $\quad$ In-the-money

FIGURE 7.4
Profit/Loss on a Put Option at Expiration

$K^{\$/A\$} = \$0.6400/A\$$
Contract size = A\$100,000
Current put option price = \$0.0160/A\$

Premium cost = (\$0.0160/A\$)(A\$100,000) = \$1,600
Exercise price = (\$0.6400/A\$)(A\$100,000) = \$64,000

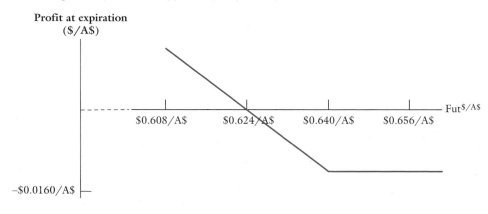

Exchange rate	$0.0000/A$	$0.6080/A$	$0.6240/A$	$0.6400/A$	$0.6560/A$
Payments					
Premium cost	−$1,600	−$1,600	−$1,600	−$1,600	−$1,600
Spot A$ purchase	$0	−$60,800	−$62,400	$0	$0
Receipts					
Exercise price	$64,000	$64,000	$64,000	$0	$0
Net profit or loss	$62,400	$1,600	$0	−$1,600	−$1,600

The deliverable instrument is the pound, so the pound is kept in the denominator and prices are stated in dollars.

A Call by Any Other Name

Buying pounds at the spot rate $S^{\$/\pounds}$ means that you are simultaneously selling dollars at the spot rate $S^{\pounds/\$}$. For this reason, an option to buy pounds at a price of $K^{\$/\pounds}$ is the same contract as an option to sell dollars at $K^{\pounds/\$}$. That is, *a call option to buy pounds sterling is equivalent to a put option to sell dollars.* The payoff profiles of a pound call and its counterpart, the dollar put, are shown here:

> A call option to buy one currency is a put option to sell another.

Payoff profile of a long pound call at expiration

Payoff profile of a long dollar put at expiration

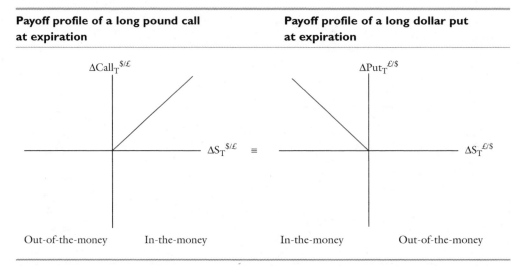

Prices in these figures are related according to $P^{\$/£} = (P^{£/\$})^{-1}$. This option is in-the-money when the spot rate $S^{\$/£}$ is above the exercise price $K^{\$/£}$ or, equivalently, when the spot rate $S^{£/\$}$ is below the exercise price $K^{£/\$}$. Since a call option to buy pounds with dollars is equivalent to a put option to sell dollars for pounds, these payoff profiles are equivalent. In this sense, a currency option is simultaneously both a put and a call.

On the other side of the contract, the option writer has an obligation to sell pounds and buy dollars. From the option writer's perspective, an obligation to sell pounds for dollars is equivalent to an obligation to buy dollars with pounds. These equivalent payoffs are shown next:

Payoff profile of a short pound call at expiration

Payoff profile of a short dollar put at expiration

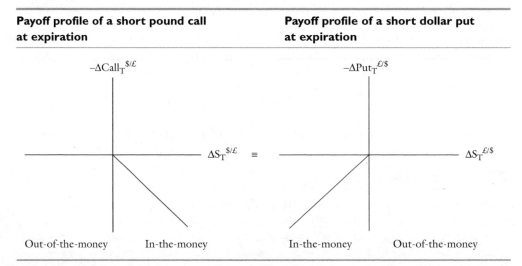

Shakespeare wrote, "A rose by any other name would smell as sweet." This is true for currency options as well. An in-the-money pound call is just as sweet to the option holder as the corresponding in-the-money dollar put.

A Forward by Any Other Name

A long forward is equivalent to a long call and a short put.

Suppose you purchase an at-the-money pound call and simultaneously sell an at-the-money pound put with the same expiration date. The payoff profiles of these positions at expiration can be combined into a single payoff profile, as shown here:

Long pound call	+	Short pound put	=	Long pound forward

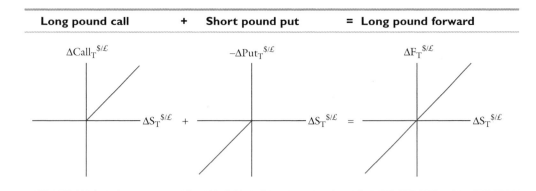

Does the graph on the right look familiar? It should. A combination of a long pound call and a short pound put with the same exercise price and expiration date creates a long forward position on pounds sterling.

Conversely, a short pound call and a long pound put with the same exercise price and expiration date is equivalent to a short forward position in pounds sterling:

Short pound call	+	Long pound put	=	Short pound forward

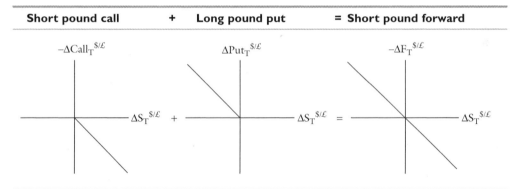

If the value of the pound is below the exercise price at expiration, the long put allows you to sell pounds at the above-market exercise price. If the value of the pound is above the exercise price at expiration, the short call forces you to buy pounds at the below-market exercise price. The resulting payoff profile exactly matches that of a short pound forward position with the same contract price and expiration date.

A Forward by Any Other Name: The Case of Put-Call Parity

The previous discussion showed that the risk profile of a forward contract is exactly replicated in the payoff profile of a combination of a long at-the-money call and a short at-the-money put. **Put-call parity** relates the value of a long call, a short put, the exercise price, and the forward price at expiration as follows:

> Put-call parity relates call and put values to the value of a forward contract.

$$\text{Call}_T^{d/f} - \text{Put}_T^{d/f} + K^{d/f} = F_T^{d/f} \qquad (7.1)$$

The put-call relation at expiration of the option can be shown graphically.

Note that an option holder pays the exercise price on a currency call option and receives the exercise price on a currency put option:

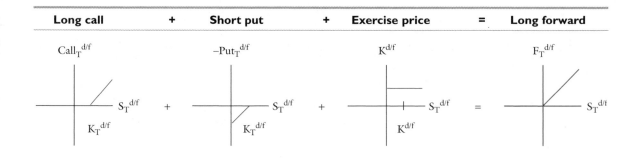

7.5 • THE DETERMINANTS OF CURRENCY OPTION VALUES

Option payoff profiles can make even the most complex option positions seem transparent. Yet these graphs only give option values at expiration. This section discusses the values of American currency options *prior* to expiration.

Currency option values are a function of the six variables shown in the following chart. When each of these determinants is increased (while holding the other determinants constant), the price of an American currency call or put option will respond as indicated.[3]

	Option value determinant	Call$^{d/f}$	Put$^{d/f}$
1.	Underlying exchange rate ($S^{d/f}$ or Fut$^{d/f}$)	Call price ↑	Put price ↓
2.	Exercise price ($K^{d/f}$)	Call price ↓	Put price ↑
3.	Riskless rate of interest in currency d (i^d)	Call price ↑	Put price ↓
4.	Riskless rate of interest in currency f (i^f)	Call price ↓	Put price ↑
5.	Volatility in the underlying exchange rate (σ)	Call price ↑	Put price ↑
6.	Time to expiration (T)	Call price ↑	Put price ↑

Volatility is measured by the standard deviation of continuously compounded returns to the underlying asset. With the exception of volatility, each of these determinants is readily observable for currency options quoted on major exchanges. The exercise price and expiration date are stated in the option contract. The underlying exchange rate and the foreign and domestic interest rates are quoted in the financial press. The volatility of the underlying exchange rate is not directly observable, which makes it an extremely important ingredient in option valuation.

> With the exception of volatility, the determinants of currency option values are easily observed.

Options have two sources of value: the *intrinsic value* of immediate exercise and the *time value* reflecting the value of waiting until expiration before exercise. These two components of option value are illustrated for a call option in Figure 7.5.

The Intrinsic Value of an Option

> The intrinsic value of an option is the value if it is exercised immediately.

The **intrinsic value** of an option is the value of the option if it is exercised today. Consider the currency call and put options presented here:

---

[3] This table is true for American options priced according to the models developed in Appendix 7-A.

FIGURE 7.5
The Components of Currency Call Option Value

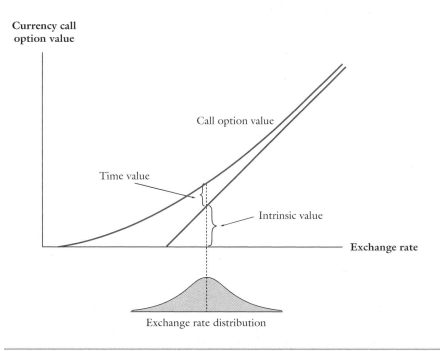

Call and put option values at exercise diagram with normal exchange rate distribution

Call option value when exercised

$\text{Call}_T^{d/f}$

$K^{d/f}$ $S_T^{d/f}$

Put option value when exercised

$\text{Put}_T^{d/f}$

$K^{d/f}$ $S_T^{d/f}$

If a call or put option is out-of-the-money, its intrinsic value is zero. If an option is in-the-money, its intrinsic value is equal to the difference between the exercise price and the value of the underlying asset. Call and put option values at exercise on the spot exchange rate are determined as follows:

$$\text{Call option value when exercised} = \text{Max } [(S_t^{d/f} - K^{d/f}), 0]$$
$$\text{Put option value when exercised} = \text{Max } [(K^{d/f} - S_t^{d/f}), 0]$$

These are the intrinsic values of the call and put options, respectively. Every graph that has appeared up to this point in the chapter has been a graph of intrinsic value.

As the underlying asset value moves away from the exercise price, option values follow a one-way path. Currency call option holders gain when the underlying exchange rate rises above the exercise price, but cannot lose more than the option premium as the underlying exchange rate falls below the exercise price. Put option holders gain as the underlying exchange rate falls below the exercise price, but lose, at most, the option premium as the exchange rate rises. It is this asymmetry that gives options their unique role as a disaster hedge.

The Time Value of an Option

Time value is the difference between market value and intrinsic value.

The **time value** of an option is the option's market value minus its intrinsic value. Although time value depends on all six variables, the two most critical variables are volatility in the underlying exchange rate and the time to expiration. Variability in the underlying (spot or futures) exchange rate determines how far in- or out-of-the-money an option is likely to expire. Time to expiration has an effect that is similar to volatility. For a given volatility, having more time until expiration results in more variable outcomes at expiration. The general rules for American options are as follows:

> **As exchange rate volatility increases, the values of American call and put options increase.**

> **As the time to expiration increases, the values of American call and put options increase.**

That is, American option values are greater if volatility in the underlying asset (the exchange rate for currency options) increases or if the time to expiration is longer.

Consider the payoffs to a dollar call and a dollar put option, each with an exercise price of $K^{¥/\$} = ¥100/\$$. Suppose the spot rate at expiration will be either ¥90.484/$ or ¥110.517/$.[4] Payoffs to these options are as follows:

	Closing spot exchange rate $S_T{}^{¥/\$}$	
	¥90.484/$	**¥110.517/$**
Value of a call	¥0/$	¥10.517/$
Value of a put	¥9.516/$	¥0/$

Suppose the volatility of the spot rate increases such that the spot rate at expiration can be as low as ¥81.873/$ or as high as ¥122.140/$.[5] The values of a dollar call and a dollar put at these spot rates and with an exercise price of ¥100/$ are as follows:

	Closing spot exchange rate $S_T{}^{¥/\$}$	
	¥81.873/$	**¥122.140/$**
Value of a call	¥0/$	¥22.140/$
Value of a put	¥18.127/$	¥0/$

Because option holders continue to gain on one side of the exercise price but do not suffer continued losses on the other side, options become more valuable as the end-of-

---

4 These spot prices correspond to ±10 percent in continuously compounded returns from the current spot rate of $S^{¥/\$} = ¥100/\$$; $(¥100/\$)e^{-0.10} = ¥90.484/\$$ and $(¥100/\$)e^{+0.10} = ¥110.517/\$$. See section 7.8.

5 These closing spot rates correspond to ±20 percent in continuously compounded returns; $(¥100/\$)e^{-0.20} = ¥81.873/\$$ and $(¥100/\$)e^{+0.20} = ¥122.140/\$$.

period exchange rate distribution becomes more dispersed. For this reason, prior to expiration more good things than bad can happen to option value.

Let's do this same exercise graphically using the out-of-the-money call options shown next. At expiration, only that portion of the exchange rate distribution that expires in-the-money has value. The out-of-the-money call option in the left graph has little value because there is little likelihood of the spot rate climbing above the exercise price. As the variability of end-of-period exchange rates increases in the graph on the right, there is an increasing probability that the spot rate will close above the exercise price.

Exchange rate volatility and out-of-the-money call option value

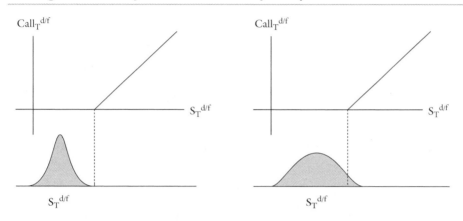

The next two graphs show that an at-the-money call option gains from an increase in volatility. An at-the-money call option gains if the spot rate closes farther above the exercise price but does not lose if the spot rate closes farther below the exercise price. As the variability of end-of-period exchange rates increases (the right graph), an area of the distribution falls farther in-the-money and the option is more valuable.

Exchange rate volatility and at-the-money call option value

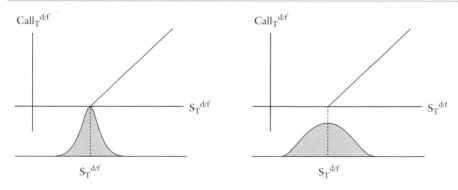

The same general principle holds for the in-the-money call options shown as follows. If an underlying exchange rate is below the exercise price at expiration, the option has zero value regardless of how far the closing price falls below the exercise price. On the other hand, as the spot rate increases the call option continues to increase in value. Thus, in-the-money call options benefit from higher volatility.

Options gain in value from volatility in the underlying asset.

Exchange rate volatility and in-the-money call option value

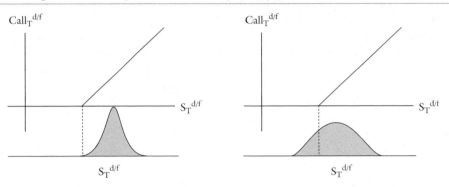

Similarly, currency put options gain more in value from exchange rate decreases than they lose in value from increases of the same magnitude. The general rule is that currency options gain from increasing variability in the distribution of end-of-period exchange rates regardless of whether the option is out-of-the-money, at-the-money, or in-the-money. In turn, variability in the distribution of end-of-period exchange rates depends on exchange rate volatility and on the time to expiration of the option.

7.6 • COMBINATIONS OF OPTIONS

Two or more option positions can be combined by snapping together the corresponding option payoff profiles. This is a simple yet powerful technique for understanding the risks and potential payoffs of even the most arcane option positions.

Here's an example. In early 1995, a rogue trader named Nick Leeson drove the United Kingdom's Barings Bank into bankruptcy through unauthorized speculation in Nikkei stock index futures on the Singapore and Osaka stock exchanges. Leeson sold *option straddles* on the Nikkei index at a time when volatility on the index was low. A long option straddle is a combination of a long call and a long put on the same underlying asset and with the same exercise price. Leeson formed a short straddle by simultaneously selling calls and puts on the Nikkei index. The payoff profiles on a long and a short straddle on the Nikkei index look like this:

Long straddle   **Short straddle**

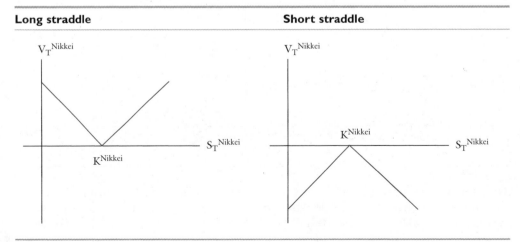

Including the proceeds from the sale of the call and the put, the profit/loss diagram on the short straddle position at expiration looks like this:

Profit/loss on a short straddle

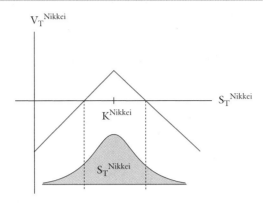

A probability distribution for the Nikkei index at expiration appears below the diagram.

Leeson placed a bet on the volatility of the Nikkei index. In option parlance, Leeson "sold volatility." As long as the Nikkei index did not vary too much, Leeson would have won his bet. As seen in the diagram, Leeson wins if the end-of-period Nikkei index falls between the two points at which the profit/loss pyramid crosses the x-axis. Leeson loses if the Nikkei index rises too high or falls too low. Volatility on the Nikkei index was low at the time Leeson sold his position, so the proceeds from the sale were small (and Leeson's gamble was large) relative to what would have been received on this position in a high volatility market. As it turned out, the Nikkei index fell below the profitable range. Leeson incurred further losses by buying futures on the Nikkei index in the hopes of a recovery that, to Barings' regret, never occurred.

7.7 • HEDGING WITH CURRENCY OPTIONS

Individual transactions can be hedged against currency risk. However, it is more cost-effective to first offset transactions within the firm and then hedge the firm's net exposures to currency risks. Exposures evolve over time, and hedging strategies need to adapt to these changing circumstances. This section presents several measures that are useful in managing the firm's evolving exposure to currency risk.

Delta Hedges

The sensitivity of option value to change in the value of the underlying asset is called the **option delta**. Call option deltas are positive, as shown in Figure 7.5. The delta of a call option increases as the underlying asset increases in price. For deep-in-the-money call options, the slope of option value approaches a delta of one (that is, a 45-degree line). The delta of a put option is negative and increases toward zero as the price of the underlying asset increases, as shown in Figure 7.6.

Option delta is also called the **hedge ratio** because it indicates the number of options required to offset one unit of the underlying asset.[6] This measure is useful when hedging an underlying spot, forward, or futures position. Suppose the delta of a currency call option on the yen/dollar futures price is +0.50. For a given (small) change in the futures price, option value increases by exactly 50 percent of that amount.

---

6 This hedge ratio is similar to the delta-hedge of Chapter 6. Each hedge ratio identifies the ratio that minimizes variability in the hedged position.

FIGURE 7.6
The Components of Currency Put Option Value

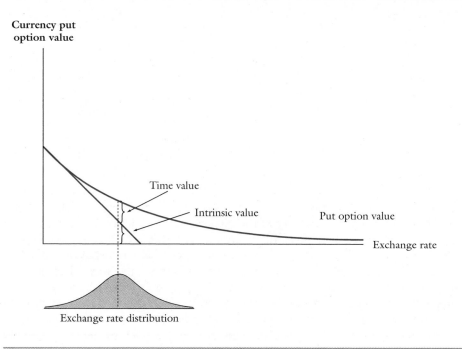

To form a *delta-neutral hedge* of a forward position with an option position, an off-setting position is taken according to the hedge ratio. For example, a Japanese firm can hedge a future dollar obligation of $1 million with a long dollar call option. For a long call with a delta of +0.50, the firm should take a $2 million option position to offset the underlying $1 million obligation. A small increase in the yen value of the dollar results in a loss in value on the underlying forward obligation. This loss is offset by a gain in value on the long call position. Note that the expiration date of this option does not need to match that of the underlying forward obligation.

The $1 million forward obligation also could be offset by writing a $4 million put option with a delta of −0.25. An increase in the value of the dollar futures price then increases the yen value of the forward obligation at the same time that it decreases the yen obligation on the short put option.

Conversely, a future cash inflow of $1 million can be delta-hedged with (1) a short position of $1.25 million on a dollar call option with a delta of +0.80, or (2) a long position of $3 million on a dollar put option with a delta of −0.33.

More Funny Greek Letters

Delta is a measure of the rate of change or sensitivity of option value to change in the underlying asset value. A delta-hedge uses this measure to offset an underlying exchange rate exposure with a currency option position that has the same sensitivity to an exchange rate change. However, as can be seen by the option values in Figures 7.5 and 7.6, delta changes as the underlying price changes. As delta changes, so does the hedge ratio that matches the sensitivities of the option and underlying positions.

When the delta of an option hedge changes at a different rate than that of the under-lying position, even small changes in an underlying exchange rate can quickly throw a delta-hedge out of balance. The option pricing methods in Appendix 7-A assume con-tinuous rebalancing. In practice, option hedges must be monitored to make sure they do not become too unbalanced.

The rate of change of delta with a change in the underlying asset price is called the **option gamma**.[7] Gamma measures the *curvature* of option value in Figures 7.5 and 7.6. Many option hedges are designed to be gamma-neutral as well as delta-neutral. Matching on gamma usually means forming a hedge with payoffs that match those of the underlying position. Hedges that are both delta-neutral and gamma-neutral are far less likely to become unbalanced with changes in underlying asset values.

Another useful measure of option sensitivity is **vega**, which is the sensitivity of option value to changes in the volatility (i.e. standard deviation) of the underlying asset. All else constant, vega is greatest for long-term options. As time to expiration decreases, so too does option vega. Vega is also greatest for near-the-money options and least for options that are deep in- or out-of-the-money.

Finally, **theta** is the sensitivity of option value to change in the time to expiration. All else constant, theta increases in absolute value as the time to expiration decreases, so that currency options lose most of their value just prior to expiration. Theta is also greater in absolute value for near-the-money than for deep in- or out-of-the-money options.

7.8 • EXCHANGE RATE VOLATILITY REVISITED (ADVANCED)

The behavior of exchange rates is best examined in continuously compounded returns, so let's start this section with a brief review. If you find the algebra to be unfamiliar, try to follow the intuition behind the algebra. If necessary, skip the numeric examples alto-gether. You don't really need the algebra of continuous compounding to follow the dis-cussion of exchange rate volatility.[8]

Continuously Compounded Returns and the Normal Distribution

Continuously compounded returns r (in italics) are related to holding period returns r according to

$$r = \ln(1+r) \text{ or } r = e^r - 1 \qquad (7.2)$$

For example, if the yen/dollar spot rate appreciates from ¥100/$ to ¥110.517/$, then the holding period rate of change of r = 10.517% is equivalent to a continuously com-pounded change of $r = \ln(1+r) = \ln(1.10517) = 0.10 = 10\%$. Conversely, if the spot rate depreciates by a continuously compounded 10 percent from an initial price of ¥100/$, then the holding period rate of change of $e^{-0.10} - 1 = -0.09516 = -9.516\%$ will result in an end-of-period spot rate of ¥90.484/$.

Because the normal distribution has convenient statistical properties, continuously compounded returns are often assumed to be independently and identically distributed (iid) as normal with mean μ and variance σ^2, or $N(\mu, \sigma^2)$. The parameter σ^2 is the **instantaneous variance** and is usually assumed to be a constant. Whether returns are

---

7 In calculus terminology, delta is the first derivative of option value with respect to the underlying asset price. Gamma is the second derivative.

8 Continuous compounding is also discussed in Appendix 5-A.

iid normal is an empirical question that we shall examine shortly. For now, let's develop the statistical properties of iid normal distributions.

The term *identically* in the phrase "independently and identically distributed" means that returns are drawn from the same distribution at every instant of time. The term *independently* means that the return realized at each instant of time does not depend on previous returns nor influence future returns. The assumption of iid returns implies that the return series is **stationary**, in that the process generating returns is identical at every instant of time. A snapshot of the return distribution at one instant yields the same snapshot as at every other instant.

In an iid normal return series, return variance increases linearly with time. That is, the end-of-period variance after T periods is T times the instantaneous variance:

$$\sigma_T^2 = T\,\sigma^2 \tag{7.3}$$

where σ^2 is the instantaneous (or continuously compounded) variance measured over a single period and σ_T^2 is variance measured over T periods. This implies $\sigma_T = (\sqrt{T})\sigma$, so the standard deviation increases with the square root of time. Equation 7.3 identifies the manner in which volatility σ and time to expiration T interact to increase the variability of the end-of-period return distribution σ_T.

Volatility can be estimated in several ways. The two most prominent methods are called historical volatility and implied volatility. Historical volatility is a backward-looking measure that captures observed variations over the recent past in the hope that history will repeat itself. Implied volatility is a forward-looking measure that uses current option prices to estimate volatility in the underlying asset. Because it is based on current prices, implied volatility reflects the expectations of participants in the options markets.

Historical Volatility

Historical volatility is the actual volatility realized over some historical period.

Historical volatility is the actual volatility of an exchange rate realized over some historical period. Historical volatility can be estimated by calculating the observed standard deviation of continuously compounded returns r_t sampled over T periods:

$$\sigma = \sqrt{[(1/T) \Sigma_t\,(r_t - \mu)^2]} \tag{7.4}$$

As an example, suppose the standard deviation of continuously compounded daily changes in the yen/dollar spot rate is estimated from Equation 7.4 to be $\sigma = 0.00645 = 0.645\%$ per trading day over the 252 trading (or business) days in a particular calendar year. Assuming zero volatility on nontrading days, such as weekends and holidays, the annual standard deviation of continuously compounded changes in the exchange rate is $\sigma = (\sqrt{T})\sigma_T = (\sqrt{252})(0.00645) = 0.1024$, or 10.24% per year. If exchange rates are normally distributed, plus or minus one standard deviation results in plus or minus 10.24 percent per year in normally distributed, continuously compounded returns.

Suppose the spot rate of exchange is currently $S^{¥/\$} = ¥130/\$$, as shown in Figure 7.7. Plus two standard deviations of 10.24 percent in continuously compounded returns is $(2)(0.1024) = 0.2048$, or 20.48 percent in continuously compounded returns. As a periodic rate of change over t periods, the rate of change is $r = e^{(2\sigma\sqrt{t})} - 1 = e^{+0.2048} - 1 = 22.73\%$. Two standard deviations above the ¥130/\$ spot rate is thus $(¥130/\$)(1.2273) = ¥159.55/\$$. In periodic returns, this is a 22.73 percent increase in the spot rate. Similarly, two standard deviations below the spot rate is $S^{¥/\$}e^{(-0.2048)} = (¥130/\$)(0.8148) = ¥105.93/\$$. This is equivalent to a $(1 - 0.8148) = 18.52\%$ decrease in the spot rate. About 95 percent of the normal distribution falls within two standard deviations of the mean, so

FIGURE 7.7
Exchange Rate Volatility

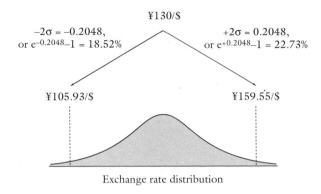

¥130/$

$-2\sigma = -0.2048$,
or $e^{-0.2048}-1 = 18.52\%$

$+2\sigma = 0.2048$,
or $e^{+0.2048}-1 = 22.73\%$

¥105.93/$ ¥159.55/$

Exchange rate distribution

there is a 95 percent chance that the actual spot rate of exchange in one year will fall between ¥105.93/$ and ¥159.55/$.

As a check, let's back out continuously compounded changes implied by a change in the spot rate from ¥130/$ to either ¥105.93/$ or ¥159.55/$. If the spot rate moves from ¥130/$ to ¥159.55/$, the percentage change is (¥159.55/$)/(¥130/$) − 1 = 0.2273 = 22.73%. In continuously compounded returns, this is equal to ln(1.2273) = 0.2048, or 20.48 percent. Conversely, a move from ¥130/$ to ¥105.93/$ results in a continuously compounded return of ln((¥105.93/$)/(¥130/$)) = −0.2048, or −20.48 percent.

Here's another useful fact about exchange rate volatility. Exchange rate volatility measured in continuously compounded returns does not depend on the currency of reference. To verify this, let's perform the same calculations using dollar/yen quotes. The yen/dollar exchange rates convert into dollar/yen spot rates according to $S^{\$/¥} = 1/S^{¥/\$}$:

$$1/(¥159.55/\$) = \$0.0062676/¥$$
$$1/(¥130.00/\$) = \$0.0076923/¥$$
$$1/(¥105.93/\$) = \$0.0094402/¥$$

A 22.73 percent dollar appreciation from ¥130/$ to ¥159.55/$ is equivalent to a 19.52 percent yen depreciation from $0.0076923/¥ to $0.0062676/¥. A 19.52 percent dollar depreciation from ¥130.00/$ to ¥105.93/$ is the same as a 22.73 percent yen appreciation from $0.0076923/¥ to $0.0094402/¥. Alternatively,

$$\ln[(\$0.0062676/¥)/(\$0.0076923/¥)] = \ln(0.8148) = -0.2048$$

and

$$\ln[(\$0.0094402/¥)/(\$0.0076923/¥)] = \ln(1.2273) = 0.2048$$

Sure enough, these represent ±20.48 percent changes in continuously compounded returns.

Implied Volatility

There are six determinants of a currency option value: (1) the spot rate of exchange $S^{d/f}$, (2) the exercise price $K^{d/f}$, (3) the riskfree rate i^d in the domestic currency, (4) the riskfree

Implied volatility is the volatility that is implied by the option price.

rate i^f in the foreign currency, (5) time to expiration T, and (6) the volatility of the underlying asset σ. For publicly traded options, the values of five of the six determinants, as well as the option value itself, are published in the financial press. The only unobservable determinant is the volatility of the underlying asset.

Suppose you know the equation specifying how option values are related to these six variables. Then, given five of the six inputs and the option price, the value of the single unknown determinant (that is, exchange rate volatility) can be found by trial and error.[9] Volatility estimated in this way is called **implied volatility**, because it is implied by the option price and the other option value determinants.

As an example, consider a "December A\$ 73 call" trading on the Philadelphia exchange. Suppose the following values are known:

Value of call option	**Call$/A$**	**=**	**$0.0102/A$**
Price of underlying asset	S$/A$	=	$0.7020/A$
Exercise price	K$/A$	=	$0.7300/A$
Domestic riskless rate	i$	=	4%
Foreign riskless rate	iA$	=	0%
Time to expiration	T	=	2$1/2$ months
Volatility of the spot rate	σ	=	?

Solving the currency option pricing model from Appendix 7-A for the standard deviation of the spot rate yields an implied volatility of 0.148, or 14.8 percent per year. This is the only standard deviation that (when combined with the five other inputs) results in an option value of $0.0102/A$.

A Cautionary Note on Implied Volatilities

Let's look at another quote, a "December A\$ 63 call" on the Philadelphia exchange. Suppose the following prices can be found in *The Wall Street Journal*:

Value of call option	**Call$/A$**	**=**	**$0.0710/A$**
Price of underlying asset	S$/A$	=	$0.7020/A$
Exercise price	K$/A$	=	$0.6300/A$
Domestic riskless rate	i$	=	4%
Foreign riskless rate	iA$	=	0%
Time to expiration	T	=	2$1/2$ months
Volatility of the spot rate	σ	=	?

Both options are based on the December spot rate, so the implied volatility of this option should be the same as that of the previous option. However, trying to find an implied volatility for the $0.63/A$ call based on these prices is futile. There is no value for volatility that yields a call price of $0.0710/A$. What's wrong?

The Wall Street Journal reports prices from the last trade of the previous day. The call option's time of last trade may or may not correspond to the time of last trade of the exchange rate underlying the option. Suppose the last time this option traded on the

---

9 Several authors have developed closed-form solutions that provide approximations to implied volatility. See Bharadia, Christofides, and Salkin, "A Quadratic Method for the Calculation of Implied Volatility Using the Garman-Kohlhagen Model," *Financial Analysts Journal* (1996).

Philadelphia exchange was at noon, at which time the spot rate was $0.6900/A$. The implied volatility at that instant is determined from the following:

Value of call option	Call$/A$	=	$0.0710/A$
Price of underlying asset	S$/A$	=	$0.6900/A$
Exercise price	K$/A$	=	$0.6300/A$
Domestic riskless rate	i$	=	4%
Foreign riskless rate	iA$	=	0%
Time to expiration	T	=	2$1/2$ months
Volatility of the spot rate	σ	=	?

The implied volatility in this example is 22.4 percent per year. There was no solution to the previous example because the end-of-day exchange rate was used to price an option that last traded at noon. This example suggests a general result: *Beware of prices in thinly traded markets.* In this example, we were comparing apples and oranges. Or, more precisely, we were comparing the size of apples (or options) at two different times of the growing season.

> Beware of prices in thinly traded markets.

Volatility and Probability of Exercise

Let's go back to the example of a December A$ 73 call on the PSE:

Value of call option	Call$/A$	=	$0.0102/A$
Price of underlying asset	S$/A$	=	$0.7020/A$
Exercise price	K$/A$	=	$0.7300/A$
Domestic riskless rate	i$	=	4%
Foreign riskless rate	iA$	=	0%
Time to expiration	T	=	2$1/2$ months
Volatility of the spot rate	σ	=	14.8%

What is the probability of this option being in-the-money on the expiration date in December? The spot rate would have to go from $S_0^{\$/A\$} = \$0.7020/A\$$ to $S_T^{\$/A\$} = \$0.73/A\$$ for a continuously compounded change of $\ln(1+r) = \ln[(\$0.73/A\$)/(\$0.7020/A\$)] = 0.039$, or 3.9 percent. The standard deviation over 2.5 months is $\sigma_T = (\sqrt{T})\sigma = (2.5/12)^{1/2}(0.148) = 0.0676$, or 6.76 percent per 2.5 months. The change in the underlying exchange rate must be $(0.039)/0.067 = 0.58$, or 58 percent of one standard deviation above the current spot rate. The probability mass of the normal distribution above 0.58σ is about 0.40. Thus, there is about a 40 percent chance of this option expiring in-the-money.

Time-Varying Volatility

Recall that empirical investigations of exchange rate behavior reject the simple random walk model. Instead, researchers have found that exchange rates can be described as having **generalized autoregressive conditional heteroskedasticity (GARCH)**:[10]

- At each point in time, instantaneous returns are normally distributed.
- The instantaneous variance at each point in time depends on whether exchange rate changes in the recent past have been large or small.

---

10 A more complete discussion of the GARCH model appears in Chapter 4.

The fact that foreign exchange volatility is not a constant means that option pricing models that assume stationary price changes (such as the binomial and the Black-Scholes models of Appendix 7-A) are misspecified for currency options. An implied volatility is actually a time-weighted average of the instantaneous variances prevailing over the life of the option. For this reason, implied volatilities obtained from traded option values may not represent the instantaneous volatility at any point in time during the life of the option.

As an example, implied volatilities can be as large as 20 percent per year during turbulent periods in the foreign exchange markets. A 20 percent implied volatility on a 5-month currency option might represent a 40 percent standard deviation over the first month and a 10 percent standard deviation over the remaining four months.[11] Because of time-varying volatility, foreign exchange volatilities estimated from option pricing models are at best imprecise estimates of current and expected future exchange rate volatility.

7.9 • SUMMARY

An option represents a choice. Holders of options can exercise options at their discretion. Sellers (or writers) of options have an obligation to perform at the option of the option holders.

Currency options are useful for hedging or speculating because, in contrast to forward and futures contracts, their payoffs are asymmetric. This asymmetry allows currency options to serve as a disaster hedge against unfavorable changes in the value of a currency or as a bet on the direction or volatility of foreign exchange rates.

Options can be categorized along several dimensions. The most important is whether the option is a call or a put.

- A call option is the right to buy the underlying asset.
- A put option is the right to sell the underlying asset.

Whenever you buy one currency you simultaneously sell another, so a call option on one currency is simultaneously a put option on another currency.

There are six determinants of a currency option value: (1) the value of the underlying exchange rate, (2) the exercise price of the option, (3) the riskless rate in the domestic currency, (4) the riskless rate in the foreign currency, (5) the time to expiration on the option, and (6) the volatility of the underlying exchange rate. With the exception of volatility, each of these determinants is readily observable for currency options quoted on major exchanges. The most important determinant—and the only one that cannot be found in the financial section of a newspaper—is the volatility of the underlying exchange rate.

Option values can be decomposed as follows:

$$\text{Option value} = \text{Intrinsic value} + \text{Time value}$$

The intrinsic value of a currency option is its value if it is exercised immediately. Intrinsic value depends on the difference between the underlying exchange rate and the exercise price. The time value of a currency option comes from the possibility that currency values will move further in-the-money and the intrinsic value of the option will increase prior to expiration of the option.

---

11 Recall that continuously compounded returns are additive. The average of a $(0.4)^2 = 0.16$ variance over the first month with a $(0.10)^2 = 0.01$ variance over the subsequent four months is $[0.16+4(0.01)]/5 = 0.04$. This is equivalent to a standard deviation of $(0.04)^{1/2} = 0.20$, or 20 percent with continuous compounding.

There are two ways to estimate the volatility of exchange rates. Historical volatility is calculated from the time series of exchange rate changes. Implied volatility is the exchange rate volatility that is implied by the value of an option, given the other determinants of option value.

KEY TERMS

American option
at-the-money
call option
European option
exercise price (or strike price)
generalized autoregressive conditional
   heteroskedasticity (GARCH)
hedge ratio
historical volatility
implied volatility
in-the-money
instantaneous variance

intrinsic value
option delta
option gamma
option theta
option vega
out-of-the-money
put option
put-call parity
stationary series
time value
volatility

CONCEPTUAL QUESTIONS

7.1   What is the difference between a call option and a put option?

7.2   What are the differences between exchange-traded and over-the-counter currency options?

7.3   In what sense is a currency call option also a currency put option?

7.4   In what sense is a currency forward contract a combination of a put and a call?

7.5   What are the six determinants of a currency option value?

7.6   What determines the intrinsic value of an option? What determines the time value of an option?

7.7   In what ways can you estimate currency volatility?

PROBLEMS

7.1   Suppose the yen value of a dollar is ¥100/$ and that it has an equal probability of moving to either ¥90.484/$ or ¥110.517/$ in one period. To what continuously compounded rates of return do these changes correspond?

7.2   Suppose the spot rate is ¥105/$ and there is an equal chance that it will fall to ¥70.38/$ or rise to ¥156.64/$. To what continuously compounded rates of return do these changes correspond?

7.3   Using one year (252 trading days) of historical data, you have estimated a daily standard deviation of $0.00742 = 0.742\%$ for the $S^{\$/A\$}$ exchange rate.
   a. What is the annual standard deviation of the $S^{\$/A\$}$ exchange rate if exchange rate changes are independently and identically distributed as normal?
   b. Suppose the current spot rate of exchange is A$1.40/$. Find the exchange rates that are plus or minus two standard deviations from this rate after one year based on the annual volatility in part a.

c. Verify that $S^{\$/A\$}$ volatility is equal to $S^{A\$/\$}$ volatility by (1) translating your $\pm 2\sigma$ $S^{\$/A\$}$ rates into $S^{A\$/\$}$ rates and (2) finding the annual standard deviation implied by these rates from $r = \ln(S_1^{A\$/\$}/S_0^{A\$/\$})$.

7.4 Section 7.5 used graphs to show how volatility affects the time value of out-of-the-money, at-the-money, and in-the-money call options. Use similar graphs to show how volatility affects the time value of out-of-the-money, at-the-money, and in-the-money put options.

7.5 Construct an option position (i.e., some combination of calls and/or puts) with the same risk profile ($\Delta Call^{\$/A\$}$ versus $\Delta S^{\$/A\$}$) as a forward contract to buy A$ at a forward price of $F_1^{\$/A\$} = \$0.75/A\$$. Use both words and graphs.
a. Label the axes.
b. Identify the asset underlying the option(s).
c. Indicate whether each option is a put or a call.
d. Indicate whether you are buying or selling the option.
e. Indicate the exercise price.

7.6 Suppose you believe that the market has underestimated the volatility of the yen/dollar exchange rate. You are not sure whether the dollar will rise or fall in value, only that it will probably rise or fall by a larger amount than expected by other market participants. Consider forming a "purchased straddle" by combining a purchased dollar call and a purchased dollar put with the same exercise price $K^{\yen/\$}$ and expiration date. Diagram the payoff profile of this position at expiration.

7.7 You head the currency trading desk at Bearings Bank in London. As the middleman in a deal between the U.K. and Danish governments, you have just paid £1,000,000 to the U.K. government and have been promised DKr8,438,000 from the Danish government in three months. All else constant, you wouldn't mind leaving this long krone position open. However, next month's referendum in Denmark may close the possibility of Denmark joining the European Union. If this happens, you expect the krone to drop on world markets. As a hedge, you are considering purchasing a call option on pounds sterling with an exercise price of DKr8.4500/£ that sells for DKr0.1464/£. Fill in the call option values at expiration in the following table. Refer to the long call in Figure 7.3 for reference.

Spot rate at expiration (DKr/£):   8.00   8.40   8.42   8.44   8.46   8.48
Call value at expiration (DKr/£):

7.8 Based on the information in problem 7.7, draw the payoff profile for a long krone put option at expiration. Note that these exchange rates are reciprocals of those in problem 7.7.

Spot rate at expiration (£/DKr) .12500 .11905 .11876 .11848 .11820 .11792
Put value at expiration (£/DKr):

Label your axes and plot each of the points. Draw a profit/loss graph for this long krone put at expiration. Refer to the long put in Figure 7.4 for reference.

7.9 Based on the prices and exchange rates in problems 7.7 and 7.8, use graphs to show how a short pound call is equivalent to a short krone put.

Suggested Readings

The Black-Scholes option pricing model (see Appendix 7-A) was introduced in

Fischer Black and Myron Scholes, "The Pricing of Options and Corporate Liabilities," *Journal of Political Economy* 81 (May–June 1973), pp. 637–659.

Fischer Black modified the original model to value options on futures in

Fischer Black, "The Pricing of Commodity Options," *Journal of Financial Economics* 3, No. 1/2 (1976), pp. 167–179.

The option pricing model was adapted to currency options in

Nahum Biger and John Hull, "The Valuation of Currency Options," *Financial Management* 12 (Spring 1983), pp. 24–28.

Mark Garman and Steve W. Kohlhagen, "Foreign Currency Option Values," *Journal of International Money and Finance* 2, No. 3 (1983), pp. 231–237.

Jimmy E. Hilliard, Jeff Madura, and Alan L. Tucker, "Currency Options Pricing with Stochastic Domestic and Foreign Interest Rates," *Journal of Financial and Quantitative Analysis* 26, No. 2 (June 1991), pp. 139–151.

The practical aspects of option use are discussed in

M.A.J. Bharadia, N. Christofides, and G.R. Salkin, "A Quadratic Method for the Calculation of Implied Volatility Using the Garman-Kohlhagen Model," *Financial Analysts Journal* 52 (March/April 1996), pp. 61–64.

Fischer Black, "How to Use the Holes in Black-Scholes," *Journal of Applied Corporate Finance* 1, No. 4 (1989), pp. 67–73.

Currency Option Valuation

Option valuation involves the mathematics of stochastic processes. The term **stochastic** means *random*, and stochastic processes model randomness. Study of stochastic processes has revolutionized asset valuation since its introduction in the early 1970s. Although the mathematics of stochastic processes can be intimidating, the good news is that it doesn't take a rocket scientist to use options to hedge financial price risks, such as currency risk, using the option payoff profiles in the body of this chapter.

The option pricing models in this appendix will help those with an interest in options to develop a deeper understanding of how option prices move with changes in the option value determinants.

7A.1 • THE BINOMIAL OPTION PRICING MODEL

Binomial Option Payoffs

In the body of the chapter, we concentrated on option values at expiration. To value options prior to expiration, we need to develop an option pricing model. The simplest way to do this is with the binomial pricing model.

The **binomial option pricing model** begins with the simplest possible (nontrivial) circumstance in which there are only two possible outcomes in the underlying exchange rate. To illustrate, let's take the perspective of a Japanese resident purchasing a European call option to buy U.S. dollars in one period on the Tokyo Stock Exchange. The currency of reference is the U.S. dollar, so we'll keep dollars in the denominator. For convenience, the option contract size is assumed to be one dollar. The option is exercisable in one period with an exercise price equal to the expected future spot exchange rate of $E[S_1^{¥/\$}] = K^{¥/\$}$ = ¥100/\$. The current spot rate is also ¥100/\$.

Suppose that the exchange rate at expiration of the option in one period will be either ¥90.484/\$ or ¥110.517/\$ with equal probability. The payoff on this foreign currency call option will be zero if the exchange rate closes out-of-the-money at ¥90.484/\$. An option holder would be better off buying dollars in the spot market at ¥90.484/\$ than at the exercise price of ¥100/\$, so the option will remain unexercised at expiration. If the spot rate closes in-the-money at ¥110.517/\$, a call option holder can exercise the option to buy dollars from the option writer at the ¥100/\$ exercise price and then sell dollars in the foreign exchange market at the market rate of ¥110.517/\$. The payoff at expiration on this call option position is $(S_1^{¥/\$} - K^{¥/\$})$ = $(¥110.517/\$ - ¥100/\$)$ = ¥10.517/\$. These alternatives are depicted graphically:

Payoff profile of a long dollar call

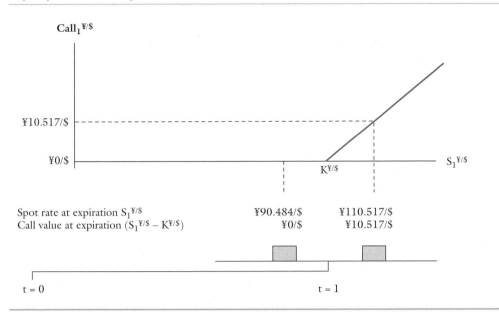

Spot rate at expiration $S_1^{¥/\$}$	¥90.484/$	¥110.517/$
Call value at expiration $(S_1^{¥/\$} - K^{¥/\$})$	¥0/$	¥10.517/$

To value this option prior to expiration, let's replicate the call option payoffs with money market instruments and then find the value of this position in the money market.

"Buy a Dollar and Borrow Yen"

Compare this payoff profile with that of buying one dollar today at the current spot rate of ¥100/$ and borrowing (¥90.484)/1.05 = ¥86.175 from a bank at the 5 percent Japanese rate of interest. The yen value of the dollar will fluctuate, depending on the spot exchange rate $S^{¥/\$}$. In contrast, the yen value of the loan repayment is –¥90.484, regardless of the spot rate of exchange. In sum, the "buy a dollar and borrow yen" strategy replicates the call option payoff. This is represented graphically here:

Buy $1	**+**	**Borrow ¥86.175**	**= Buy a dollar and borrow yen**
			= A call option on dollars

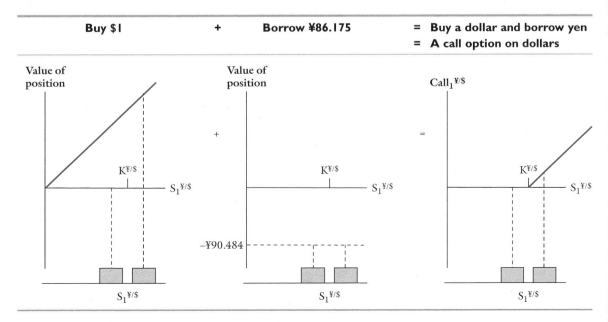

Algebraically, the payoffs on these strategies as a function of the end-of-period spot exchange rate are as follows:

Closing spot rate $S_1^{¥/\$}$	¥90.484/$	¥110.517/$
Yen value of $1	¥90.484	¥110.517
Loan repayment	−¥90.484	−¥90.484
Net payoff	¥0	¥20.033

These values represent the spread of possible values in the "buy a dollar and borrow yen" strategy, given the two possible outcomes in the spot exchange rate. The value of this position at today's ¥100/$ spot exchange rate is as follows:

> Value of "buy a dollar and borrow yen"
> = present value of the "buy $1 and borrow ¥86.175" strategy
> = ¥100 − ¥86.175 bank loan
> = ¥13.825

This money market strategy is a multiple of the call option strategy. The next section values the call option prior to expiration by scaling down the "buy a dollar and borrow yen" strategy until the payoffs on the two strategies are equal.

Using the Hedge Ratio to Value Currency Options

The **option delta** or **hedge ratio** indicates the number of call options required to replicate the payoff from buying one unit (in this case, one dollar) of the underlying asset:

> Option delta = $\dfrac{\text{(Spread of possible option prices)}}{\text{(Spread of possible underlying asset values)}}$
>
>   = number of call options required to replicate one unit of the underlying asset

For our example, this is equal to (¥10.517)/(¥20.033) = 0.52498 call options per dollar. The payoff on the dollar call option is 52.498 percent of the value of the "buy a dollar and borrow yen" strategy, regardless of the future spot rate of exchange, so the value of the call must be 52.498 percent of the value of the "buy a dollar and borrow yen" strategy.

Instead of buying $1, suppose you buy $0.52498 and borrow (¥86.175)(0.52498) = ¥45.240 at the 5 percent yen interest rate.[12] In one period, you'll owe ¥45.240(1.05) = ¥47.502 on the loan. Your payoff on the "buy $0.52498" strategy will be 52.498 percent of the "buy a dollar" strategy; that is, either ¥47.502 or ¥58.019 with equal probability. Your net payoff on this money market position will be as follows:

Closing spot rate $S_1^{¥/\$}$	¥90.484/$	¥110.517/$
Yen value of $0.52498	¥47.502	¥58.019
Loan repayment	−¥47.502	−¥47.502
Net payoff	¥0	¥10.517

---

12 Since we're making up the rules as we go, let's assume that call options are infinitely divisible, so that you can split them up into as many pieces as desired. If you don't like this assumption, you can multiply all contracts and prices by 10,000 and achieve a similar result.

The payoff to the call option strategy is now identical to the payoff from buying $0.52498 and borrowing ¥45.240 at 5 percent and paying off ¥47.502 in one period. Since the payoffs are identical, arbitrage will ensure that the value of this "buy $0.52498 and borrow yen" strategy is equal to the "buy a dollar call option" strategy:[13]

> Value of a one-dollar call option
> = 52.498 percent of the value of a "buy $1 and borrow ¥86.175" strategy
> = Value of "buy $0.52498 and borrow ¥45.240"
> = ¥52.498 − ¥45.240
> = ¥7.2578

Voilà! You've valued your first call option. If payoffs are binomially distributed, the payoffs to a foreign currency call option can be replicated by borrowing the domestic currency and buying the foreign currency according to the proportion in the hedge ratio.

A General Case of the Binomial Model

In the previous example, there are only two possible outcomes for the end-of-period spot exchange rate. The *binomial option pricing model* is easily extended to an arbitrary number of outcomes by allowing the exchange rate to bifurcate (or split) several times in succession. Suppose the underlying exchange rate diverges from ¥100/$ by ±1 percent twice in succession. After the first split, the exchange rate is $(¥100/\$)e^{\pm.01} = ¥99.005$ or ¥101.005/$ with equal probability:

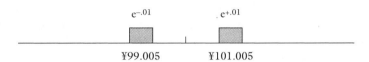

As these outcomes diverge by an additional ±1 percent, there are three possible outcomes: ¥98.020/$ with 25 percent probability, ¥100/$ with 50 percent probability, and ¥102.020/$ with a 25 percent probability:

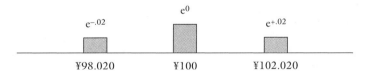

These outcomes correspond to −2 percent, 0 percent, and +2 percent in continuously compounded returns. Another round of ±1 percent changes results in ±3 percent (each with 1/8 probability) and ±1 percent (each with 3/8 probability) as follows:

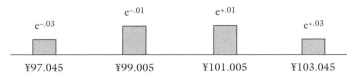

The next bifurcation results in five possible outcomes, and so on. This type of repetitive bifurcation can be summarized in a tree diagram:

---

13 If you are still uncomfortable with the assumption of infinite divisibility, compare the payoffs to buying a call option on $10,000 versus buying $5,249.80 and borrowing ¥452,400 at 5 percent. The larger the transaction, the less we have to worry about an asset's divisibility.

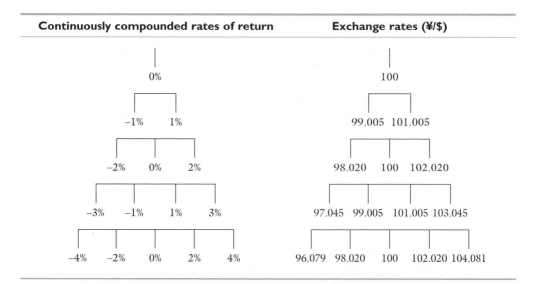

Continuously compounded rates of return	Exchange rates (¥/$)

If the probabilities and distances of up and down movements are equal at each bifurcation, then the continuously compounded end-of-period rate of return approaches the normal distribution as the number of bifurcations increases.

The binomial model can be generalized by allowing the process generating up and down movements to bifurcate over shorter and shorter intervals. The binomially distributed up-and-down movements are halved each time the interval is halved. As an example, the standard deviation created by eight yen/dollar exchange rate bifurcations of ±1 percent each is 3.75 percent, or ¥3.75/$.[14] In the limit, the distribution of continuously compounded exchange rates approaches the normal distribution. The binomial model is then equivalent to the currency option pricing model presented in the next section.

7A.2 • CURRENCY OPTION PRICING

A Starting Point: The Black-Scholes Option Pricing Model

In 1973, Fischer Black and Myron Scholes borrowed a model from fluid dynamics (a branch of engineering) to create a formula for the value of a European option on a share of nondividend-paying stock. A key assumption in the **Black-Scholes option pricing model (OPM)** was that continuously compounded returns are normally distributed with constant mean μ and standard deviation σ.[15] The Black-Scholes formula for the value of a European call option on a share of nondividend-paying stock is

$$\text{Call} = P \times N(d_1) - e^{-iT} \times K \times N(d_2) \qquad (7A.1)$$

where Call = the value of a call option on a share of nondividend-paying stock
    P   = the current share price

---

14 You can verify this standard deviation on a spreadsheet. Allow the ¥100/$ exchange rate to vary by ±1% successively over eight periods and calculate the standard deviation of the resulting exchange rate distribution.

15 The instantaneous change in the exchange rate is $dS/S = \mu\,dt + \sigma\,dz$, where μ and σ are the instantaneous mean and standard deviation of the exchange rate, dt is an instant of time, and $dz \sim N(0,1)$ is iid over time.

K   = the exercise price of the call option
i = a constant riskless rate of interest in continuously compounded returns
σ   = the instantaneous standard deviation of return on the stock
T   = the time to expiration of the option expressed as a fraction of one period
d_1 = [ln(P/K) + (i + (σ²/2))T] / (σ√T)
d_2 = (d₁ – σ√T)
N(·) = the standard normal cumulative distribution function

The value of a put option on a share of stock can be found from put-call parity:

$$\text{Call} - \text{Put} + e^{-iT} \times K = P \qquad \Leftrightarrow \qquad \text{Put} = \text{Call} - P + e^{-iT} \times K \qquad (7A.2)$$

The term $e^{-iT} = 1 / (1+i)^T$ discounts the exercise price back to the present at the riskless rate of interest. As in the binomial model, this equation is enforced through riskless arbitrage with a replicating portfolio. Riskless arbitrage ensures that the appropriate discount rate is the riskless rate of interest.

Here is the intuition behind the Black-Scholes formula. At expiration, time value is equal to zero and call option value is composed entirely of intrinsic value:

$$\text{Call}_T = \text{Max} [0, P_T - K]$$

Prior to expiration, the actual closing price is a random variable that will not be known until expiration. To value a call option prior to expiration, we need to find the expected value of $[P_T - K]$ given the option expires in-the-money (that is, given $P_T > K$). In

Application

The Holes in Black-Scholes

Although the option pricing formulas presented in this appendix work well in most circumstances, you should be aware of their limitations.

1. The most important input in any option pricing formula is volatility. For exchange-traded options, volatility is also the only input that cannot be read directly out of a financial newspaper. Regardless of how sophisticated the option pricing model, option values are only as reliable as the estimate of volatility.

2. The formulas assume that continuously compounded returns are normally distributed and stationary over time. Empirical studies have found that returns to most assets (including currencies) are **leptokurtic**, with more probability mass around the mean and in the tails and less probability mass in the shoulders relative to the normal distribution. Assets also have volatilities that vary over time. These differences between the Black-Scholes assumptions and actual asset returns biases option values calculated with the Black-Scholes formulas.

3. Although these formulas are for European options, many exchange-traded and OTC options are American options. The early-exercise feature of American currency options makes them worth slightly more than European currency options at the same exercise price.

See Black, "How to Use the Holes in Black-Scholes," *Journal of Applied Corporate Finance* (1989).

the Black-Scholes formula, $N(d_1)$ is the probability that the call option will expire in-the-money. This probability is shown in the following graph:

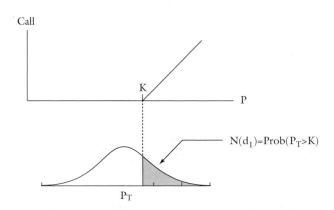

The term $P \times N(d_1)$ in Equation 7A.1 is the expected value of share price at expiration, given $P_T > K$. Similarly, $K \times N(d_2)$ is the expected value of the exercise price at expiration, given $P_T > K$. The e^{-iT} term in Equation 7A.1 discounts the exercise price to the present at the riskless rate of interest. Option value is thus the present value of the option's expected value at expiration.

An Extension of the Black-Scholes OPM to Currency Options

Biger and Hull applied the Black-Scholes framework to European currency options by replacing stock prices with exchange rates and assuming constant interest rates in the foreign and domestic currencies.[16] Biger and Hull's European currency option pricing formula can be stated either in terms of spot exchange rates or in terms of forward exchange rates:

$$\text{Call}^{d/f} = e^{-i^d T} [\, F_T^{d/f} \times N(d_1) - K^{d/f} \times N(d_2) \,] \qquad (7A.3)$$

$$\Leftrightarrow \quad \text{Call}^{d/f} = e^{-i^f T} [\, S^{d/f} \times N(d_1) \,] - e^{-i^d T} [\, K^{d/f} \times N(d_2) \,] \qquad (7A.4)$$

where
$\text{Call}^{d/f}$ = the value of a call option on one unit of foreign currency
$S^{d/f}$ = today's spot exchange rate
$F_T^{d/f}$ = today's forward exchange rate for delivery at time T
$K^{d/f}$ = the exercise price on one unit of foreign currency
i^d = the riskless domestic interest rate in continuously compounded returns
i^f = the riskless foreign interest rate in continuously compounded returns
σ = the instantaneous standard deviation of the exchange rate
T = the time to expiration of the option expressed as a fraction of one period
d_1 = $[\, \ln (S^{d/f} / K^{d/f}) + (i^d - i^f + (\sigma^2/2))T \,] / (\sigma \sqrt{T})$

---

16 Biger and Hull, "The Valuation of Currency Options," *Financial Management* (1983). See also Garman and Kohlhagen, "Foreign Currency Option Values," *Journal of International Money and Finance* (1983); Hilliard, Madura, and Tucker, "Currency Options Pricing with Stochastic Domestic and Foreign Interest Rates," *Journal of Financial and Quantitative Analysis* (1991).

$$d_2 \quad = (d_1 - \sigma\sqrt{T})$$
$$N(\cdot) \quad = \text{the standard normal cumulative distribution function}$$

Equations 7A.3 and 7A.4 are related through interest rate parity, which states (in continuously compounded returns) that $F_T^{d/f} = S_0^{d/f} e^{+i^d T} e^{-i^f T}$. The value of a put option on foreign currency is found from put-call parity:

$$\text{Put}^{d/f} = \text{Call}^{d/f} + (K^{d/f} - FT^{d/f}) \cdot e^{-i^d T} \qquad (7A.5)$$

$$\Leftrightarrow \quad \text{Put}^{d/f} = \text{Call}^{d/f} - e^{-i^f T} \cdot S^{d/f} + e^{-i^d T} \cdot K^{d/f} \qquad (7A.6)$$

where interest rate parity again ensures that $F_T^{d/f} = S_0^{d/f} e^{+i^d T} e^{-i^f T}$.

As in the Black-Scholes OPM, $N(d_1)$ is the probability of a call option expiring in-the-money. Because a put option with the same exercise price is in-the-money whenever a call is out-of-the-money and vice versa, the probability of a put option expiring in-the-money is $1 - N(d_1)$. $N(d_1)$ is also equal to the hedge ratio—the number of call options required to replicate the payoff from buying one unit of foreign currency. Because the probability of a put being exercised is 1 minus the probability of a call being exercised, the hedge ratio for a put option is equal to $1 - N(d_1)$.

The International Monetary Market of the Chicago Mercantile Exchange, as well as many other options exchanges around the world, trades options on futures rather than options on spot exchange rates. The volatilities of futures and spot prices are nearly identical and futures prices converge to spot prices at expiration, so the differences between options on futures and options on spot exchange rates are minor.[17] Equations 7A.3 and 7.5 work with forward exchange rates as well as with futures prices.

Solution of the option pricing problem proved to be a turning point in the evolution of finance. The OPM set the stage for the subsequent introduction and growth of options trading on a variety of assets, including stocks, bonds, commodities, interest rates, and exchange rates. Unfortunately for practitioners, the OPM also made a course in stochastic processes a required part of doctoral programs in finance.

KEY TERMS

binomial option pricing model   leptokurtic
Black-Scholes option pricing model   stochastic
hedge ratio (option delta)

PROBLEMS

7A.1 What is the value of a European call option on U.S. dollars with an exercise price of ¥100/$ and a maturity date six months from now if the current spot rate of exchange is ¥80/$ and the continuously compounded riskfree rate in both Japan and the United States is 5 percent? You have estimated the instantaneous standard deviation of the yen/dollar exchange rate as 10 percent per year based on the variability of past currency movements.

7A.2 Suppose that in problem 7A.1 the currency markets are undergoing a period of unusually high volatility. If the true standard deviation of the yen/dollar spot rate

---

17 For an adaptation of the Black-Scholes model to options on futures, see Black, "The Pricing of Commodity Options," *Journal of Financial Economics* (1976).

is 20 percent, by how much have you under- or overestimated the value of the dollar call option?

7A.3 Consider the following "December Yen 84 call" on the Philadelphia exchange:

Current call price	$0.000118/¥
Price of underlying asset	$0.008345/¥
Exercise price	$0.008400/¥
Riskless rate in dollars	4% (continuously compounded)
Riskless rate in yen	4% (continuously compounded)
Time to expiration	2 ½ months

What is the volatility of the dollar-per-yen exchange rate implied by the currency option pricing model?

7A.4 As head of currency trading at Ball Bearings Bank in London, you need to price a series of options of various maturity on Danish kroner. The current spot rate is DKr8.4528/£. Riskless interest rates in the United Kingdom and in Denmark are 1.74 percent and 1.30 percent per three months, respectively. Instantaneous volatility on the pound/krone spot rate is 5 percent per three months. The international parity conditions hold.

a. Assume an exercise price of $K^{DKr/\pounds} = $ DKr8.5000/£. Fill in the following table based on the international parity conditions and the currency option pricing formulas in Equations 7A.4 and 7A.6:

	Maturities			
	1 month	3 months	6 months	1 year
Forward rate (DKr/£)				
Call option value				
Put option value				

b. Repeat part a using the currency option pricing formula in Equation 7A.3 and 7A.5.

c. Draw a payoff profile that includes all four call options on the same graph.

d. Draw a payoff profile that includes all four put options on the same graph.

7A.5 Rather than varying the maturity of the options as in problem 7A.4, let's vary the exercise price. Fill in the following table, assuming a 3-month time to expiration and the information from problem 7A.4:

	Exercise prices (DKr/£)			
	8.200	8.400	8.600	8.800
Call option value				
Put option value				

Currency Swaps and Swaps Markets

chapter 8

Overview

Never take a job for which you have to change clothes.

Henry David Thoreau

A **currency swap** is a contractual agreement to exchange a principal amount of two currencies and, after a prearranged length of time, to give back the original principal. Interest payments in each currency also typically are swapped during the life of the agreement. As an example, suppose British Petroleum issues pound sterling debt to finance an oil refinery in the United States at the same time that Ford Motor Corporation issues dollar debt to finance a manufacturing plant in the United Kingdom. The operating cash flows of each foreign subsidiary are in the foreign currency, but interest expenses on each parent's debt are in the parents' domestic currencies. The financial performance of each foreign subsidiary depends on foreign exchange rates, so each firm is exposed to currency risk. If the two parent corporations agree to exchange their domestic-currency debt for foreign-currency debt, then each firm's exposure to currency risk can be reduced. This exchange of debt is an example of a currency swap.

The swap is called an **interest rate swap** if the principal amounts are in the same currency. In an interest rate swap, the principal amount is called **notional principal** because it is used only to calculate interest payments and is not exchanged. Only the **difference check** between the two interest payments is exchanged. As an example, suppose that both IBM and Boeing Corporation have 5-year $100 million bond issues outstanding and that IBM's debt bears a fixed rate of 9 percent while Boeing's carries a floating rate pegged to the 90-day Treasury bill rate. IBM is concerned over the shortening life cycle of its product line and does not want to be locked into fixed interest payments. Meanwhile, Boeing has secured long-term contracts for a certain number of planes at fixed prices, so it prefers to exchange its existing floating rate for fixed rate debt. If IBM and Boeing agree to pay each other's interest payments, they can effectively swap their debt obligations without having to incur the costs of repurchasing their old debt and issuing new debt. This is an example of a fixed-for-floating interest rate swap.

Swaps differ from other forms of derivative securities in that they often involve long-term, rather than short-term, exposures to financial price risks. For example, many currency risks can be cost-effectively hedged for maturities of up to one year on currency futures or options exchanges, or for up to five years in the forward markets. But beyond a few years, forward contracts are either nonexistent or have relatively large bid-ask spreads for even actively traded currencies. Swaps provide a cost-effective vehicle for quickly changing the exposure of a corporation, institution, investment fund, or government agency to long-term financial price risk.

8.1 • PARALLEL LOANS: NECESSITY IS THE MOTHER OF INVENTION

Swap contracts evolved out of a financial arrangement called a parallel loan that was developed in London during the 1970s.[1] Throughout the 1970s, the United Kingdom imposed a tax on cross-border currency transactions involving pounds sterling as a way of slowing the flow of pounds out of the country. This made it expensive for both British-based and foreign-based MNCs to transfer funds to or from their foreign subsidiaries. These firms had a need for a legal funding method that circumvented the pound sterling tax. In the pursuit of this objective, a new funding instrument was created that possesses several benefits over borrowing directly in foreign markets.

One alternative for MNCs to fund foreign operations is to borrow funds directly in the foreign country. This is especially attractive when the foreign country has a well-developed capital market and the MNC is well known in the foreign country. Debt raised in a foreign country to finance foreign operations is a "natural hedge" in that interest payments are deducted from revenues in the functional currency of the subsidiary. Keeping as many cash inflows and outflows as possible in the local currency shields the subsidiary from currency risk. The livelihood of the foreign subsidiary then depends on its operating performance and not on changes in exchange rates over which it has no control.

Consider the U.S. branch (BP^{US}) of British Petroleum (BP). Suppose BP^{US} is financed with pound sterling debt and equity capital but operates domestically in the U.S. market. The functional currency of BP is pounds sterling, so it is convenient to keep the dollar in the denominator of the exchange rate and consider changes in the pound sterling value of BP^{US}. The currencies in the operating cash flow of BP^{US} and the risk profile shared by BP^{US} and its parent are shown as follows:

1 Early swap markets are described in Smith, Smithson and Wakeman, "The Market for Interest Rate Swaps," *Financial Management* (1988).

Risk profile for BP^{US}

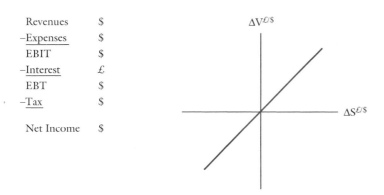

Revenues	$
−Expenses	$
EBIT	$
−Interest	£
EBT	$
−Tax	$
Net Income	$

With operating cash inflows in dollars and interest payments in pounds sterling, both the parent and the subsidiary face currency risk. As the value of the dollar appreciates relative to the pound, debt denominated in pounds becomes less of a burden on the U.S. subsidiary. If the dollar depreciates, however, U.S. dollar cash inflows may be unable to cover the pound-denominated interest payments.[2]

A U.S. multinational with a U.K. subsidiary faces a similar exposure in the opposite direction. For example, Ford Motor Company (Ford) operates a manufacturing and assembly plant in Coventry, England (Ford^{UK}). Both BP and Ford have an incentive to fund their foreign operations with debt denominated in the foreign currency because that is the currency in which their other local revenues and costs are denominated. In the presence of a U.K. tax on cross-border pound sterling transactions, both multinationals also have an incentive to fund their foreign subsidiaries without running afoul of the U.K. tax. This means ensuring that no pounds sterling cross the United Kingdom's borders. But how can these MNCs fund their foreign operations without sending funds across the United Kingdom's borders?

Alternative #1: Borrow Foreign Currency in the Foreign Market

One alternative is for each multinational to fund its foreign operations with debt raised directly in the foreign country. In this alternative, BP^{US} borrows dollars in the U.S. debt market and Ford^{UK} borrows pounds in the U.K. market. Suppose borrowing costs for fixed rate debt in the United States and in the United Kingdom are as follows:

	Borrower	
Country	BP	Ford
United Kingdom	5%	7%
United States	8%	6%

In this example, each MNC has a relative advantage borrowing in its domestic market, where the firms have established reputations and the information costs faced by lenders are low.

> MNCs can fund foreign operations by borrowing in foreign markets.

2 For simplicity, this example ignores economic exposure to currency risk. In particular, if the pound falls in value, the prices of products manufactured in the United Kingdom are likely to become more competitive on world markets. Whether this long-term impact overcomes the short-term impact of the more expensive dollar interest costs depends in part on the price elasticity of demand for U.K. products.

Suppose the foreign subsidiary of each multinational borrows multiyear fixed rate debt in the foreign market. BP^{US} borrows an amount X$^\$$ from Citigroup in the United States to fund its U.S. operations. Ford^{UK} borrows an amount X$^£$ from Hong Kong and Shanghai Banking Corporation (HSBC) in the United Kingdom to fund its U.K. operations. This situation is shown here:

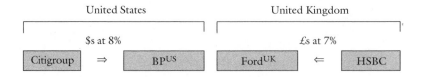

The resulting expected future cash flows can be shown on a time line as follows:

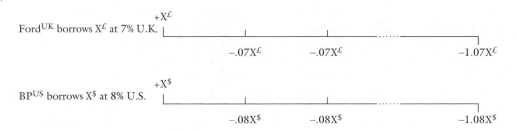

Foreign firms face a disadvantage relative to comparable domestic firms when borrowing in the domestic market. Of course, each parent could borrow in its domestic credit market and then lend the funds to its subsidiary. But each firm would then have to pay the U.K. tax on cross-border pound transactions.

Alternative #2: A Parallel Loan

In a **parallel loan**, the MNC borrows in its own currency where it enjoys a relative advantage in borrowing costs and then trades this debt for a counterparty's foreign currency debt. This combines the low domestic borrowing rates with foreign-source financing of the foreign subsidiaries. One possible parallel loan arrangement is presented here:

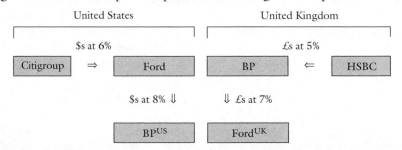

In this example, each parent borrows domestic currency at its domestic borrowing cost. These funds are then loaned to the subsidiary of the foreign parent at the rate that the subsidiary would have had to pay in the domestic market.

The U.S. Perspective. From Ford's perspective, expected cash flows over the next several years look like this:

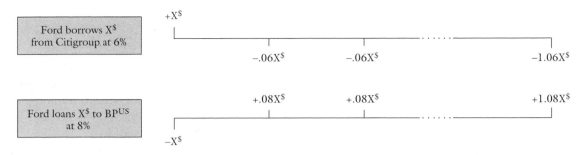

The timing of these cash flows can be contractually set so that they precisely overlap. Similarly, the counterparties could set the principal amounts equal in value so that $X^\$ = X^\pounds S^{\$/\pounds}$. This arrangement provides the following net cash flows to Ford Motor Company in the United States:

Ford earns 2 percent of the face amount $X^\$$ in annual interest. If both loans are riskless, then this is a pure arbitrage profit with no net investment and no risk. It is important to note that BP^{US} is not averse to this loan because the 8 percent cost is the same rate that it would have paid had it borrowed dollars directly in the U.S. market.

> Parallel loans can provide a cost savings to each counterparty.

The U.K. Perspective. The situation of British Petroleum in the United Kingdom is the flip side of Ford in the United States. British Petroleum borrows a face amount $X^\pounds = X^\$ S^{\pounds/\$}$ at 5 percent in the United Kingdom and then loans this to $Ford^{UK}$ at 7 percent, earning 2 percent of $X^\pounds$ per year on the deal.

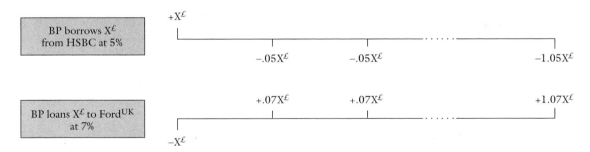

As before, the 2 percent difference in annual interest accrues to the parent firm.

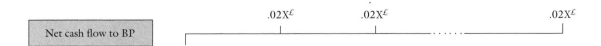

Again, this does not hurt the foreign subsidiary of the counterparty because the 7 percent cost of debt is the same as $Ford^{UK}$ would have paid without the parallel loan agreement. Both foreign subsidiaries are no worse off, and the parent firms BP and Ford earn 2 percent per year on the face value of the loans.

8.2 • Pros and Cons of Parallel Loans

Benefits of Parallel Loans

This parallel loan arrangement has several advantages. First, it legally circumvents the U.K. tax on cross-border pound transactions. Neither the original principal nor the interest checks need to cross a border. The pounds raised by BP can be sent directly to Ford^{UK} within the United Kingdom, just as dollars raised by Ford can be sent directly to BP^{US} within the United States. Second, the parallel loans allow each multinational to borrow in its home market where it enjoys low relative borrowing costs. Third, parallel loans reduce exposure to currency risk by allowing each foreign subsidiary to be financed with low-cost foreign-source debt. Fourth, parallel loans allow the parent firms to access new capital markets, which can further reduce their overall cost of capital. These benefits are especially valuable for MNCs with exposures in multiple currencies.

> Parallel loans allow MNCs to acquire low-cost financing in foreign countries.

Problems with Parallel Loans

Despite these advantages, parallel loans were difficult and costly to arrange in the early days. Drawbacks of the parallel loan arrangement include (1) default risk, (2) an adverse balance sheet impact, and (3) search costs.

Default Risk. Each loan in a parallel loan arrangement is a separate agreement, so if one party defaults it does not release the other party from its obligation. One remedy for this problem is to link the loans in a separate agreement defining the **rights of set-off** should one party default on its obligation. Because these rights of set-off are not linked in a single document to the parallel loans, settlement of disputes arising from one party's default is not foolproof. Often, the issue is jurisdiction. Because the two sides of the parallel loan are executed in different countries, the agreement defining the rights of set-off must be binding in each country. In this way, recourse is available in either country.

> Parallel loans suffer from default risk.

Balance Sheet Impact. Because the parallel loans are two separate contracts (actually, three contracts if you count the rights of set-off agreement), parallel loans must appear on both sides of the consolidated balance sheet for accounting, tax, and regulatory purposes. On the liability side of the balance sheet, this raises the corporation's book value debt-to-equity ratio. For example, if a firm's debt and equity are each worth $5 million, then the debt-to-equity ratio is one to one. If an additional asset and an offsetting liability worth $5 million are added through a parallel loan, then the apparent debt-to-equity ratio rises to two to one. Even though this additional debt is effectively canceled by the parallel loan on the asset side of the balance sheet, the higher perceived level of financial leverage can impair the ability of the parent firm to raise additional debt.

Search Costs. When parallel loans were first introduced, there was not an active market for them. Investment banks served as brokers rather than dealers, acting as matchmakers but putting none of their own money at risk. The absence of dealers able to make a market in parallel loans resulted in high search costs and slow growth.

8.3 • Swaps to the Rescue

> Currency swaps remedy the problems of parallel loans.

The remedy to these problems was to package the parallel loans in a single legal agreement called a **swap contract**. A swap contract identifies the currencies of denomination and the amount and timing of all future cash inflows and outflows. The swap contract releases each party from its obligation should the other party default on its obligation. By binding the rights of set-off into a single contract along with the two loans, the swap contract neatly avoids many of the vexing legal issues surrounding default in parallel loans. Because the entire package is covered by a single legal agreement, in the event of default the aggrieved party can simply stop making interest payments on its side of the contract and, if necessary, seek compensation in court.

Accounting and regulatory conventions in most countries treat swaps as off-balance-sheet transactions that appear in the footnotes to financial statements. The swap contract includes both loans in a single contract, so neither loan needs to be capitalized on the balance sheet. The swap's impact is felt through interest expense on the income statement and, in the case of currency swaps, through foreign currency transactions. Because neither side of the swap is capitalized on the balance sheet, swaps do not create the appearance of high levels of debt on the firm's consolidated balance sheet.

Volume in the swaps market grew by leaps and bounds after their introduction in the 1970s. In 1981, Salomon Brothers (now Salomon Smith Barney) engineered a currency swap between the World Bank and International Business Machines (IBM) that, because of the stature of the participants, served to legitimize the swap market. By the early to middle 1980s, investment bankers such as Salomon Brothers were nurturing an increasingly active market in currency and interest rate swaps. These early swaps were customized, low-volume, high-margin deals. As volume and liquidity grew, international investment and commercial banks began serving as swap dealers and the market turned into a high-volume, low-margin business. As swap dealers began making a market in swaps, search costs were greatly reduced, thus eliminating the last of the three problems with parallel loans. Today, commercial banks have the lead over investment banks as the major dealers in the market using standardized swap contracts that follow conventions set forth by the *International Swaps and Derivatives Association (ISDA)*.

http://www.isda.org

Figure 8.1 shows the phenomenal growth in over-the-counter (OTC) derivatives trading during the last two decades. This figure shows the outstanding notional principal in interest rate swaps and options and currency swaps held by ISDA members. The bulk of this amount was in interest rate swaps, followed by interest rate options and currency swaps. Notional principal outstanding was $99.8 trillion in 2002.

8.4 • SWAPS AS PORTFOLIOS OF FORWARD CONTRACTS

You've taken a fast-track job as a junior analyst with Merck & Co. It's your first day on the job and Judy Lewent, Merck's CFO, brings you into her office to discuss the currency exposure of Merck's operations. You only get one chance to make a first impression, and you are eager to demonstrate that your time at school was well spent.

Lewent: Please step into my office. I want to get your opinion on a persistent problem that we face here at Merck. We have sales in more than 140 countries worldwide. Yet 70 percent of our research and development expenses, the bulk of our production expenses, and most of our interest expenses are in dollars. Our dividends are also paid in dollars. I'm particularly concerned about our exposure to the countries of the European Union. A high percentage of our sales come from these countries, yet our operating expenses are largely in dollars. What do you suggest?

(Okay . . . now what was it that you studied in school? Think fast! Ah, yes. A currency swap might be just the thing. Stepping into the breach, you suggest a dollar-for-euro currency swap.)

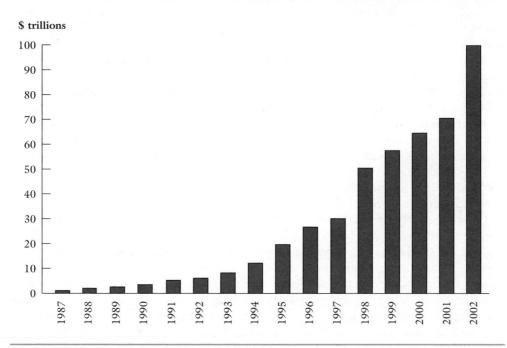

FIGURE 8.1
Notional Amounts Outstanding in OTC Derivatives Markets ($ trillions)

Source: International Swaps Dealers Association (http://www.isda.org). Statistics include interest rate and currency derivatives.

> *You:*   Well, we might consider a currency swap for euros. We could swap our dollar debt for euro debt on the same amount of principal and thereby convert some of our dollar expenses to euro expenses. Our counterparty would pay the dollar interest payments on our debt and we would pay the euro interest payment on a comparable amount of euro debt. This would form a natural hedge against revenues from countries in the European Union.
>
> *Lewent:* Who do you propose as a counterparty?
>
> *You:*   This should be a fairly standard financial transaction, so I'd suggest an international bank making a market in currency swaps. I have a classmate in the swap department at UBS Warburg. I'm sure she could give us a quote.
>
> *Lewent:* What if they default on their side of the deal?
>
> *You:*   We'd stop paying them as soon as they stopped paying us. At most, we'd be out six months' interest on the notional principal.
>
> *Lewent:* If Merck is out six months' interest, we'll also be out one junior analyst.

How do you respond? What is the default risk of a swap contract?

> A swap is a portfolio of forward contracts, each with a different maturity date.

Ms. Lewent's question is most easily answered by comparing the swap contract to a futures contract. Futures contracts are nothing more than a bundle of consecutive one-day forward contracts in which changes in wealth due to changes in exchange rates are marked to market daily. Swaps are also a bundle of forward contracts. But instead of being laid end-to-end as consecutive one-day forward contracts, a swap is a bundle of *simultaneous* (rather than consecutive) forward contracts, each with a different maturity date.

Suppose a domestic firm borrows an amount X^d in a T-period nonamortizing loan with periodic (fixed or floating rate) interest payments $C_t^d = i_t^d X^d$ throughout the life of the loan:

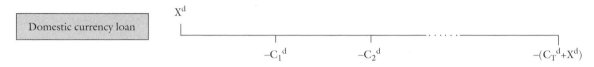

If the company has a need to hedge revenues from a foreign subsidiary, it can swap this domestic currency loan for a foreign currency loan of equal value ($X^d = X^f S^{d/f}$) paying interest payments $C_t^f = i_t^f X^f$. If the principal being received is set equal to the principal being paid, there is no reason to exchange the principal amounts, and the principal is called notional principal. Rather than exchange the full amount of the interest payments, only the difference check need be exchanged. This difference check is equal to ($C_t^d - C_t^f S_t^{d/f}$) after translating the foreign currency interest payment into domestic currency. From the perspective of the domestic firm, the net cash flows look like this:

This is equivalent to a portfolio of T forward contracts each with successively longer maturities.

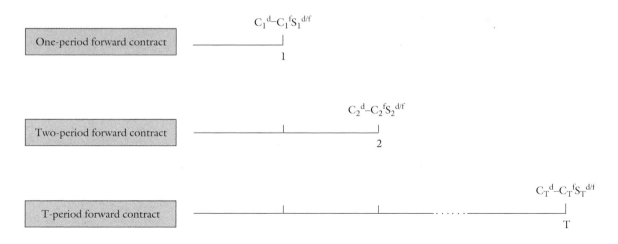

Swaps are essentially bundles of forward contracts of different maturities. Ms. Lewent's concern is at least partially justified because swap contracts, like forward contracts, are subject to default risk. Although the risk and consequences of default are somewhat more than in a comparable futures contract, they are far less than for straight debt because of the rights of set-off built into the swap contract.

A futures contract reduces default risk relative to a forward contract by (1) requiring a margin, (2) having an exchange clearinghouse as the counterparty, and (3) marking to market daily. Swaps can be evaluated along these same three dimensions. First, swaps do not generally require a performance bond, such as a margin requirement, and this tends to give swaps slightly more default risk than comparable futures contracts. Second, a commercial or investment bank making a market in swaps will generally be the counterparty. To the extent that the bank is more prone to default than a clearinghouse, this tends to slightly increase default risk. Third, whereas futures are marked to market daily, swaps are essentially marked to market each time an interest payment is due. Because the performance period between payments is longer (typically six months) than the daily performance period of a comparable futures contract, swaps are more risky than futures contracts. The default risk of a swap contract falls somewhere between the risk of a comparable futures contract (which is negligible) and the risk of the forward contract with the longest maturity in the bundle of forward contracts that make up the swap.

Swaps are far less risky than straight debt, because if one side defaults the other side is released from its obligations as well. Further, the entire principal is not at risk as it is in a loan, because of the exchange of actual or notional principals at the beginning and at the end of the contract. The interest payments are less at risk than in straight debt, because the difference check depends on the difference between the interest rates rather than on the level of one of the interest rates. For these reasons, swaps are far less risky than comparable straight debt.[3]

8.5 • CURRENCY SWAPS

Financial engineering is a buzzword on Wall Street that aptly describes the "name of the game" in investment banking. The rapid pace of financial innovation in the creation or engineering of new financial products to meet both old and new financing needs is truly extraordinary. This high rate of technological innovation is both a blessing and a curse for multinational financial managers. The blessing is that access to capital markets is far greater today than at any time in history. The curse is that it is difficult to keep abreast of innovations in new financial products. Without a thorough understanding of the benefits and risks of financial contracting, value can easily be destroyed rather than created. Fortunately, financial products that at first appear to be new and curious contracts are in most cases new versions of established contracts. This section shows how currency swaps can be used to transform the nature of the firm's liabilities.

> Currency coupon swaps trade fixed for floating rate payments in different currencies.

The most common form of currency swap is the **currency coupon swap**, a fixed-for-floating rate nonamortizing currency swap, traded primarily through international commercial banks. In a nonamortizing loan, the entire principal is repaid at maturity and only interest is paid during the life of the loan. Currency swaps also come with amortizing loans in which periodic payments spread the principal repayment throughout the life of the loans. Currency swaps can be structured as fixed-for-fixed, fixed-for-floating, or floating-for-floating swaps of either the non-amortizing or amortizing variety.

Dealers quote **swap pricing schedules** for actively traded swaps. A dealer such as Citigroup might quote the following schedule for nonamortizing fixed-for-floating curren-

---

3 Litzenberger discusses the default risk of swaps along with applicable portions of the U.S. bankruptcy code in "Swaps: Plain and Fanciful," *Journal of Finance* (1992).

cy coupon swaps between Australian (A$) and U.S. dollars with semiannual ("sa") interest payments on maturities of two to five years.

Currency Coupon Swaps (A$/$)

Maturity	Bid (in A$)	Ask (in A$)
2 years	6.07% sa	6.17% sa
3 years	6.33% sa	6.43% sa
4 years	6.47% sa	6.57% sa
5 years	6.63% sa	6.73% sa

All quotes against 6-month dollar LIBOR flat.

Citigroup pays its bid rate and receives its ask rate on the fixed rate side of the swap. For example, if Citigroup receives the fixed rate payments on a 5-year swap, it receives two semiannual payments of $(6.73\%)/2 = 3.365$ percent of the notional principal. The annualized yield on this amount is calculated from

$$\text{Annualized yield} = [1 + (i/N)]^N - 1$$

where $N = 2$ is the number of compounding periods per year and i is the total interest paid per year. With semiannual payments of 3.365 percent, the annualized yield to Citigroup on the fixed rate payments is $(1.03365)^2 - 1 = 0.06842$, or 6.842 percent. In receiving 10 more basis points than it pays on the fixed rate side, Citigroup earns a bid-ask spread of 10 basis points by buying funds low (at the bid rate) and selling funds high (at the ask rate).

The floating rate side of this swap has semiannual interest payments at the 6-month LIBOR rate. By setting the floating rate side of each swap at LIBOR flat, the swap bank has zero net exposure to LIBOR as long as the bank's swap book is in balance—that is, the bank's net exposure in each currency is zero.

A Note on Day Count Conventions

Before using this swap pricing schedule, we need to introduce one technical detail. Floating-rate Eurocurrency interest rates such as LIBOR are conventionally quoted on a "Actual/360" or **money market yield** basis, assuming 360 days in a year and interest that accrues over the actual number of calendar days between two payment dates. In contrast, many fixed-rate instruments including U.S. Treasury bonds are quoted as a **bond equivalent yield** (either "Actual/365" or "Actual/Actual") based on 365 days in a year. This **day count** convention defines the way in which interest accrues over time.[4]

This difference means that a 10 percent money market yield (MMY) on the floating-rate side of a swap is not equivalent to a 10 percent bond equivalent yield (BEY) on the fixed-rate side. The approximate relation between the two is

$$MMY = BEY(360/365)$$

or, equivalently,

$$BEY = MMY(365/360)$$

---

4 Day count conventions are discussed in section 3.3.

For example, a 10 percent BEY on a U.S. Treasury bond is approximately the same as a (10%)(360/365) = 9.863 percent MMY on a Eurodollar deposit pegged to LIBOR. This transformation allows you to compare floating-rate yields based on a 360-day year with fixed-rate yields based on a 365-day year. No adjustment is necessary when the fixed- and floating-rate sides of the swap have the same day count convention.

An Example of a Currency Swap

The Swap Bank Receives the Fixed Rate. America, Inc. (AI) has $50 million of 5-year debt at a floating rate of 6-month ($) LIBOR + 125 bps. AI wants fixed-rate Australian dollar debt to fund its operations in Australia. Citigroup agrees to pay AI's floating-rate dollar debt in exchange for a fixed-rate Australian dollar payment from AI. Suppose the spot exchange rate is $S^{\$/A\$}$ = $0.6667/A$. At this spot rate, $50 million is equal in value to A$75 million.

Citigroup receives fixed-rate Australian dollar interest payments at a rate of 6.68% + 5 bps = 6.73% (quoted as a bond equivalent yield) on the principal amount. Citigroup pays the floating 6-month LIBOR Eurodollar rate (quoted as a money market yield). Cash transactions proceed as follows:

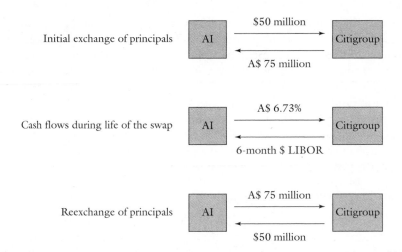

AI's original cost of debt was 125 basis points over the LIBOR Eurodollar rate. Citigroup only pays LIBOR flat, so AI still must pay this premium. After converting the 125 floating rate basis points to a bond equivalent yield, AI's net cost of fixed rate Australian dollar funds is 0.0673 + 0.0125(365/360) = 0.0800, or 8.00 percent.

The Swap Bank Pays the Fixed Rate. Expert Systems (ES), a software developer based in Australia, has A$75 million of 5-year fixed-rate debt with a 7.68 percent bond equivalent yield. ES wants floating-rate dollar debt to fund its operations in the United States. Citigroup agrees to pay ES's fixed-rate Australian dollar debt in exchange for floating-rate dollar payments. At the spot rate of $S^{\$/A\$}$ = $0.6667/A$, the A$75 million debt is equivalent to $50 million.

Citigroup pays the fixed-rate Australian dollar debt at 6.68% − 5 bps = 6.63%. Citigroup receives the floating-rate dollar debt at 6-month LIBOR flat. Transactions during the life of the swap proceed as follows:

Application

Currency Risk Management at Ford Motor Company

Divisional managers have an incentive to hedge against currency risk in order to reduce the variability of their divisional performance. But hedges are not costless, and one division's risk exposures may be offset by risk exposures elsewhere in the company. By "netting" risk exposures across the entire company, corporate headquarters can take an integrated approach to the management of currency risk. Duplicate or offsetting hedges can then be avoided and financing costs minimized.

Ford Motor Company is exposed to many different currency risks through its sales and production around the world. Ford instituted a program called "Ford 2000" to integrate its regional operations into Ford Automotive Operations. This division is responsible for coordinating Ford's manufacturing operations in North America, Europe, Asia-Pacific, and Latin America.

One of the advantages of being a multinational corporation is that operating exposure to currency risk is lower than that of a purely domestic company. At Ford, operating exposure is managed by establishing manufacturing operations in each of the regions in which Ford does business. Manufacturing operations in each region are then used to support sales in that same region. This provides a natural hedge as both revenues and expenses are drawn from the same region.

Nevertheless, the individual regions can and do face currency risks. With its regional operations consolidated under one roof, Ford can more easily match these regional currency exposures internally. After matching exposures, Corporate Treasury then manages Ford's net transaction exposure in the financial markets. By offsetting exposures internally before going to the financial markets, Ford minimizes its external hedging costs and maximizes the effectiveness of its hedging strategies.

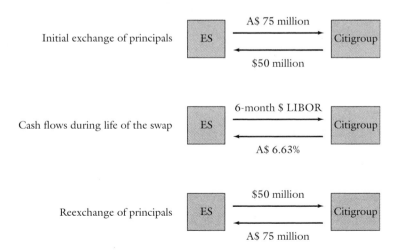

On the floating-rate side, Citigroup's cost of funds is the 6-month LIBOR Eurodollar rate. The difference between ES's fixed-rate U.S. dollar outflows and inflows is 0.0768 − 0.0663 = 0.0105, or 105 basis points. After converting this to a money market yield,

ES's net cost of floating-rate Eurodollar funds is LIBOR + (105 bps)(360/365) = LIBOR + 104 bps.

The Swap Bank's Gains. From Citigroup's perspective, the AI and ES swaps offset one another. On the floating-rate side, Citigroup is paying the 6-month LIBOR dollar interest rate to AI on $50 million principal and receiving the 6-month LIBOR dollar rate from ES on $50 million principal. These transactions net out to zero over the life of the swap. On the fixed-rate side, Citigroup is paying 6.63 percent semiannually in Australian dollars and receiving 6.73 percent semiannually on the same principal amount. This leaves a bid-ask profit of 10 basis points on every Australian dollar of notional principal, or $50,000 annually on a $50 million transaction.

8.6 • INTEREST RATE SWAPS

An interest rate swap is a variant of the currency swap in which both sides of the swap are denominated in the same currency. Since the principal amounts are in the same currency, the principal is notional and needn't be exchanged. Notional principal is used only to calculate interest payments. Only the difference check between the interest payments is exchanged when interest payments are due.

> Coupon swaps trade fixed for floating rate interest payments.

The most common interest rate swap is a fixed-for-floating **coupon swap** that offsets fixed-rate debt with floating-rate debt pegged to an interest rate index, such as 6-month LIBOR. Coupon swaps come in maturities of one to fifteen years.[5] Citigroup might quote prices on a U.S. dollar coupon swap as follows:

Coupon Swaps ($s)

Maturity	Bank Pays Fixed Rate	Bank Receives Fixed Rate	Current TN Rate
2 years	2 yr TN sa + 19bps	2 yr TN sa + 40bps	7.05%
3 years	3 yr TN sa + 24bps	3 yr TN sa + 47bps	7.42%
4 years	4 yr TN sa + 28bps	4 yr TN sa + 53bps	7.85%
5 years	5 yr TN sa + 33bps	5 yr TN sa + 60bps	7.92%

This schedule assumes nonamortizing debt and semiannual rates (sa).

All quotes are against 6-month dollar LIBOR flat.

TN = U.S. Treasury note rate.

An Example of an Interest Rate Swap

The Swap Bank Pays the Fixed Rate. Skittish Co. has $50 million of 5-year debt with a bond equivalent yield of 9 percent compounded semiannually. This is 1.08 percent over the current 5-year T-note yield of 7.92 percent. Skittish prefers floating-rate debt because its operating cash flows are sensitive to interest rates. Skittish's investment banker, Salomon Smith Barney, quotes a rate of LIBOR + 100 bps on a new debt issue. This is higher than Skittish believes is appropriate, given Skittish's credit rating. Skittish is looking for a less costly source of floating-rate debt.

---

5 The payoffs on interest rate swaps can be replicated by a portfolio of Eurodollar futures contracts. See Minton, "An Empirical Examination of Basic Valuation Models for Plain Vanilla U.S. Interest Rate Swaps," *Journal of Financial Economics* (1997).

Application

Risk Management at Altria Group, Inc.

Altria Group, Inc. is a U.S.-based holding company with 2002 revenues of $80.4 billion. Altria's portfolio includes Philip Morris, Kraft Foods, and a majority stake in the world's second largest brewer, SABMiller plc (formed in 2002 through a merger of Miller Brewing and South African Brewing). Forty-six percent of 2002 revenues were from international operations.

Altria's globally diversified operations expose the company to a wide variety of interest rate, currency, and commodity price risks. Altria uses a method called *value-at-risk* to estimate its potential losses from unexpected changes in financial prices. Based on normal market conditions and a 95 percent confidence interval, Altria estimates its maximum one-day losses from fluctuations in financial prices as follows:

Financial price risk	Maximum one-day loss
Instruments sensitive to interest rates	$95 million
Instruments sensitive to exchange rates	$47 million
Instruments sensitive to commodity prices	$6 million

In 2002, Altria managed its currency risk exposures with the following instruments:

Instruments sensitive to exchange rates	Notional principal outstanding
Currency forwards	$3.7 billion
Currency options	$10.1 billion
Currency swaps	$2.5 billion

Altria designates many of these positions as hedges, according to SFAS No. 133 "Accounting for Derivative Instruments and Hedging Activities" (see Chapter 13).

Altria Group's annual report can be accessed through their Web site at http://www.altria.com.

Citigroup agrees to a fixed-for-floating swap with Skittish. According to the swap pricing schedule, Citigroup will pay Skittish a fixed-rate 5-year note with semiannual compounding at 33 basis points over the 5-year T-note rate. With the T-note at 7.92 percent, this means a bond equivalent yield of $0.0792 + 0.0033 = 0.0825$, or 8.25 percent with semiannual compounding, for an annualized yield of $[1+(0.0825/2)]^2 - 1 = 0.0842$, or 8.42 percent. On the other side of the coupon swap, Skittish pays Citigroup a floating-rate 5-year note at LIBOR with semiannual payments.

On the original loan, Skittish was paying 9 percent fixed. After the swap, Skittish receives 8.25 percent fixed from Citigroup and pays LIBOR floating to Citigroup. The difference between Skittish's 9 percent fixed-rate payments and 8.25 percent fixed-rate receipts leaves a net cost of 75 basis points on the fixed-rate side. Stating this as a money market yield, Skittish's net cost on the fixed-rate side is (75 bps) (360/365) = 74 basis points. Skittish's net cost of floating rate funds is then LIBOR + 74 bps in money market yield. This is 26 basis points below the LIBOR + 100 bps rate quoted by Salomon Smith Barney on new debt.

The Swap Bank Receives the Fixed Rate. Trendy Co. has $50 million of 5-year debt with a cost of 6-month LIBOR + 125 bps in money market yield. Trendy prefers fixed-rate debt, but issues of similar risk are yielding 9.90 percent in bond equivalent yield. Citigroup comes to the rescue again with an agreement to pay Trendy a floating rate in exchange for a fixed-rate payment from Trendy. According to the swap pricing schedule, Citigroup pays Trendy the 6-month LIBOR rate and Trendy pays Citigroup the 5-year T-note rate plus 60 bps for a semiannually compounded bond equivalent yield of 0.0792 + 0.0060 = 0.0852, or 8.52 percent. Trendy's cost of fixed rate funds is 0.0852 + (0.0125)(365/360) = 0.0979, or 9.79 percent in bond equivalent yield. This is a savings of 11 bps over the 9.90 percent funding available in the market.

The Swap Bank's Gains. From Citigroup's perspective, the interest rate swap with Trendy offsets the interest rate swap with Skittish. On the fixed-rate side, Citigroup receives 60 bps while paying only 33 bps over the Treasury note rate, for a spread of 27 basis points. Citigroup earns ($50 million)(60bps–33bps) = $135,000 per year in semiannually compounded bond equivalent yield on the notional principal of $50 million. Because each of the fixed-rate contracts pays semiannual interest payments over five years, Citigroup is fully hedged on the fixed-rate side. The floating-rate side of each swap is against 6-month LIBOR flat, so Citigroup is also fully hedged on the floating-rate side.

Combinations of Currency and Interest Rate Swaps

Interest rate and currency swaps can be combined to form new financial products. For example, a currency coupon swap in which the domestic rate is fixed and the foreign rate is floating can be combined with an interest rate swap in the foreign currency to create a *fixed-for-fixed currency swap*. If the fixed-rate side of a currency coupon swap is combined with the fixed-rate side of a fixed-for-floating interest rate swap in the domestic currency, the net result is a *floating-for-floating currency swap*. Floating-for-floating swaps that pair two different interest rate indexes in the same currency, such as 6-month Eurodollar rates with the U.S. 30-day T-bill rate, are called *basis swaps*. Interest rate and currency swaps can be combined in this way to transform the nature of the firm's currency and interest rate exposures quickly and at low cost.

8.7 • OTHER TYPES OF SWAPS

Financial price risk refers to the risk of unexpected changes in a financial price, such as currency values, interest rates, or commodity prices. Not surprisingly, swap contracts are traded on each of these financial prices. Swap contracts can be traded, in principal, on any asset or liability. Although there is some standardization of contracts in the most liquid segments of the currency and interest rate swap markets, customized swap contracts are written on a wide variety of other assets and in a wide variety of combinations.

Figure 8.2 displays the notional amount outstanding in the over-the-counter (OTC) swaps market conducted through commercial and investment banks. Interest rate swaps were by far the most commonly traded swaps, with $89,995 billion in notional principal outstanding at the end of June 2002. Currency swaps were second in notional outstanding with $18,075 billion. Equity swaps are a rapidly growing segment of the market and accounted for $2,214 billion in notional principal. Commodity swaps are less frequently traded, but still accounted for $777 billion. Swaps on commodities and equities are described next.

FIGURE 8.2
Notional Amounts Outstanding in OTC Derivatives Markets

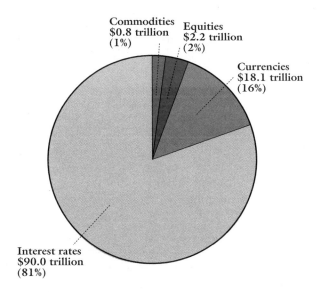

Source: Bank for International Settlements (http://www.bis.org), *BIS Quarterly Review*, December 2002.

Commodity Swaps

Just as swaps are traded on currencies and interest rates, **commodity swaps** are traded against a variety of commodity prices including oil, gold, and pork belly prices. The first commodity swap was a fixed-for-floating oil price swap engineered by Chase Manhattan Bank in 1986.

Commodity swaps can be based either on two different commodities or on the same commodity. Indeed, the currency swap can be thought of as a subset of the commodity swap in which the commodities underlying each contract are currencies. When the commodities are the same, commodity swaps typically take the form of a floating-for-fixed swap in which one party makes periodic payments at a fixed per-unit price for a given quantity of some commodity while the other party makes periodic payments at a floating rate pegged to the spot commodity price. In this case, the principal is notional and there is typically no exchange of principal. Commodity swaps across two different commodities can be structured as fixed-for-fixed, fixed-for-floating, or floating-for-floating swaps. In this case, the commodities could be exchanged but the difference in spot prices is usually settled in cash. This minimizes the transactions costs associated with the swap.

Equity Swaps

Swap contracts can also be written on asset portfolios. Consider portfolio managers Mrs. Bear and Mr. Bull. Mrs. Bear has $100 million invested in a well-diversified portfolio of stocks that is highly correlated with the S&P 500 and wants to get into 10-year T-bonds for one year. Mr. Bull has a $100 million portfolio of 10-year T-bonds and wishes to get into stocks for one year. Unfortunately for Mr. Bull and Mrs. Bear, it is expensive to sell an entire portfolio and then reinvest the proceeds in a new asset class.

In this circumstance, opposites attract. Mr. Bull and Mrs. Bear could form a **debt-for-equity swap** in which Mrs. Bear pays Mr. Bull the S&P 500 return on a $100 million notional principal and Mr. Bull pays Mrs. Bear the returns from his $100 million portfolio of 10-year T-bonds.[6] This swap could be engineered with a 1-year term. With a single swap transaction, Mr. Bull and Mrs. Bear can replicate the payoffs of their desired positions and avoid the transactions costs of buying and selling (and, after one year, selling and then buying) individual assets. Bankers Trust introduced this type of debt-for-equity swap in 1989.[7]

A number of combinations and variations of this debt-for-equity swap are possible. The plain-vanilla fixed-for-S&P 500 equity swap could be combined with a fixed-for-floating interest rate swap to create a floating-for-S&P 500 swap. The T-bond position could be swapped against the Nikkei 225 on the Japanese market rather than the S&P 500. An S&P 500 position could be swapped for another equity portfolio, such as the Nikkei 225 or a small-capitalization index on the U.S. market. These swaps allow large investors such as mutual funds and pension funds the luxury of changing their asset allocation decisions without suffering the transactions costs of buying and selling individual assets.

Swaptions

A **swaption** is a derivative contract granting the right to enter into a swap. The fixed-rate side of a swaption usually has the option and the floating-rate side the obligation because the floating-rate side (for example, LIBOR) adjusts to changing market conditions and has less need for an option. The most common forms of swaptions include mirror-image swaptions (the fixed-rate receiver has the option to cancel), right-to-terminate swaptions (the fixed-rate payer has the option to cancel), and extendible swaptions (the fixed-rate side has the right to extend the contract life). The option component of each of these swaps is like an option on the underlying fixed-rate bond and is priced accordingly.

8.8 • HEDGING THE SWAP BANK'S FINANCIAL RISK EXPOSURE

Swap pricing schedules are regularly updated to reflect changes in market pricing and to correct imbalances in the bank's swap portfolio, or **swap book**. Swap banks hedge their net swap positions in their swap books either internally within the bank or externally in the spot, forward, futures, options, swaps, or bond markets. Once the swap bank finds an offsetting position, as Citigroup was able to do in the currency and interest rate swap examples, it can offset its positions on the two swaps. The swap bank is then hedged against the financial price risk underlying the swap.

Mismatches in the bank's swap book can arise across a number of dimensions including mismatches in currencies, maturities, or money market instruments. For example, if the bank is paying funds on swaps pegged to 6-month LIBOR and receiving funds on swaps pegged to 1-month T-bills, the swap bank has a maturity mismatch as well as basis risk between LIBOR and T-Bill rates. By continually monitoring and then balanc-

---

6 Hill and Naviwala, "Synthetic and Enhanced Index Strategies Using Futures on U.S. Indexes," *Journal of Portfolio Management* (1999).

7 Another type of swap, the *LDC debt-equity swap* or *debt swap*, allows investors to trade the external debt obligations of less-developed countries (LDCs) for equity positions in government-owned companies based in the issuing country. Don't confuse these LDC debt swaps with the debt-for-equity swap of Mr. Bull and Mrs. Bear.

ing the swap bank's net position across currencies, fixed-versus-floating interest rates, and floating interest rate exposures at all forward dates, management can ensure that the bank is not caught by surprise by large changes in these financial prices.

8.9 • THE BENEFITS OF SWAPS TO THE MULTINATIONAL CORPORATION

Swaps provide corporations with a great deal of flexibility in their financing choices. In particular, swaps allow corporations to transform the nature of their obligations at very low cost and without having to repurchase and then reissue those obligations. They also allow the corporation to separate the form of debt offered to the market from the form of debt preferred by the corporation and ultimately paid to the market.

> Swaps provide the MNC with financial flexibility.

Consider the example of the parallel loans in section 8.2. Each parent wanted to issue foreign-currency debt but was deterred by the high interest rate demanded by foreign suppliers of debt capital. Swap contracts allow firms to separate the currency of denomination on their original debt offering from the currency of denomination on their ultimate obligation. If the domestic market is willing to pay a higher price for the debt of domestic corporations than for the debt of foreign corporations, then domestic firms can issue domestic currency debt where its comparative borrowing advantage is greatest and then swap into foreign currency debt through a swap contract. This allows corporations to seek funds from their lowest-cost sources and then swap back into the form of debt desired.

If there were no barriers to issuing debt in whatever market offered the highest price, price differences between markets would disappear and swaps would be no better than other financing alternatives. In fact, there remain barriers to the free flow of capital between markets including transaction and information costs, differential taxes and regulations across markets, and legal restrictions on currency transactions. Swaps are valuable financing vehicles because they allow corporations to access the lowest cost sources of funds and thereby reduce their cost of capital. They also provide firms with flexibility in transforming the nature of their debt obligations.

8.10 • SUMMARY

Currency swaps are patterned after parallel loan agreements in which two firms borrow in their home markets and then loan the funds to each other's foreign subsidiaries. Parallel loans allow parent firms with foreign subsidiaries to indirectly obtain foreign-currency debt financing for their foreign subsidiaries at low-cost foreign-currency rates despite facing higher borrowing costs in foreign debt markets.

These shortcomings make parallel loans poor vehicles for cross-border financing:

- There can be difficulties in adjudicating disputes between parties to the parallel loan.
- Parallel loans must be capitalized and placed on the balance sheet as an asset and an offsetting liability, thus inflating debt-to-equity ratios.
- There are high search costs in finding firms with parallel funding needs.

Packaging the parallel loans into a single swap contract remedies these problems:

- Because one party can cancel the agreement if the other party does not fulfill its obligation, default risk is greatly reduced.
- Swaps are foreign currency transactions that are reported in the financial statements only in footnotes.
- Search costs are reduced as volume expands.

Currency swaps are in essence a bundle of forward contracts of different maturities, so they are subject to default risk. Although the consequences of default are somewhat more than in a comparable portfolio of futures, they are far less than for a straight debt instrument. The reason for this lower default risk is because the rights of set-off specify that if one side defaults on its payments the other side is released from its obligations as well. The exchange of principals further reduces the counterparties' risk exposures.

Swaps are valuable financing vehicles for multinational corporations because they allow corporations to arbitrage across domestic and international credit markets and to reduce their cost of capital by financing in the lowest-cost market. Swaps are especially useful for transforming long-maturity debt obligations that are not easily refinanced directly in the long-term debt markets.

KEY TERMS

bond equivalent yield (BEY)	interest rate swap
commodity swap	money market yield (MMY)
coupon swap	notional principal
currency coupon swap	parallel loan
currency swap	rights of set-off
day count	swap book
debt-for-equity swap	swap contract
difference check	swap pricing schedule
financial engineering	swaption
financial price risk	

CONCEPTUAL QUESTIONS

8.1   What is a parallel loan arrangement? What are its advantages and disadvantages?

8.2   How can a currency swap remedy the problems of parallel loans?

8.3   How are swaps related to forward contracts?

8.4   What is a currency coupon swap?

8.5   What is a coupon swap?

8.6   What is the difference between a bond equivalent yield and a money market yield?

PROBLEMS

8.1   Sunflower International can borrow in the United States at 5 percent and in Italy at 8 percent. Rosa Internationale can borrow in Italy at 7 percent and in the United States at 9 percent.

a. Suppose Sunflower and Rosa borrow 3-year, nonamortizing debt in the foreign currency (dollar or lire). Draw time lines for Sunflower and Rosa showing percentages for interest payments (e.g., 8 percent) and principal (e.g., 100 percent). Assume annual interest payments.

b. Suppose the two companies arrange a parallel loan in which Sunflower charges Rosa 9 percent on dollars and Rosa charges Sunflower 8 percent interest on lire. Draw time lines illustrating the parallel loans.

c. What are Sunflower's net borrowing costs in lire?

d. What are Rosa's net borrowing costs in dollars?

8.2 The Little Prince Co. (LP) has $100 million of 2-year fixed-rate debt with a bond equivalent yield of 8.25 percent compounded semiannually. Given the nature of LP's assets and, hence, its financing needs, LP would prefer to have floating-rate debt. The market is asking LIBOR + 100 bps. How could an investment banker help LP achieve its objective with a swap contract?

8.3 Consider the following swap pricing schedule for currency coupon swaps of yen and pounds sterling:

Currency Coupon Swap Pricing Schedule (¥/£)

Maturity	Midrate (in £)
2 years	5.93% sa
3 years	6.18% sa
4 years	6.30% sa
5 years	6.41% sa

Deduct 5 bps if the bank is paying a fixed rate.

Add 5 bps if the bank is receiving a fixed rate.

All quotes are against 6-month yen LIBOR flat.

Like U.S. Treasury securities, bonds in Japan and the United Kingdom are quoted as a bond equivalent yield.

a. Japan, Inc. (JI) has 3-year yen debt at a floating-rate money market yield of 6-month (¥) LIBOR + 105 bps. JI wants fixed-rate pound sterling debt to fund its U.K. operations. Describe JI's yen-for-pound currency coupon swap.

b. British Dog, Ltd. (BD) has 3-year fixed-rate pound debt at a bond equivalent yield of 7.45 percent. BD wants floating-rate yen debt to fund its expansion into Japan. Describe BD's pound-for-yen currency coupon swap.

c. What does the swap bank gain from these transactions?

8.4 As VP Finance (Europe) at GE Capital, you manage GE's European exposures to currency risk. GE's lightbulb plant in Poland generates Polish zloty (Zl) cash inflows of about Zl 40 million per year, or about $10 million at the current exchange rate of $0.25/Zl, although this amount is expected to fluctuate with Polish interest rates. GE's policy is to hedge one-half of expected cash flows from operations for up to five years. Banks are unwilling to quote forward exchange rates beyond one year because of illiquidity in the zloty forward market. Salomon Smith Barney quotes the following pricing schedule for currency coupon swaps of zlotys and dollars:

Currency Coupon Swap Pricing Schedule (Zl/$)

Maturity	Midrate (in Zl)
2 years	8.28% sa
3 years	8.06% sa
4 years	7.98% sa
5 years	7.94% sa

Deduct 50 bps if the bank is paying a fixed rate.

Add 50 bps if the bank is receiving a fixed rate.

All quotes are against 6-month dollar LIBOR flat.

a. How can you hedge your zloty cash inflows in the absence of a zloty forward market?

b. Suppose GE has 5-year dollar debt at a bond equivalent yield of 8.34 percent. GE wants floating-rate zloty debt to fund its Polish operations. Describe GE's dollar-for-zloty currency coupon swap.

c. Solidarity Partners (SP) has 5-year debt at a floating-rate money market yield of 6-month ($) LIBOR + 265 bps. SP wants fixed-rate dollar debt to fund its U.S. operations. Describe SP's zloty-for-dollar currency coupon swap.

d. What does the swap bank gain from these transactions?

8.5 In problem 8.4, GE swapped fixed-rate dollar debt for floating-rate zloty debt with a 5-year maturity. Suppose that after one year GE decides it wants to swap its floating-rate zloty debt for fixed-rate zloty debt. A swap bank quotes the following pricing schedule for Polish zloty coupon swaps.

Coupon Swap Pricing Schedule

Maturity	Bank Pays Fixed Rate	Bank Receives Fixed Rate	Current TN Rate
2 years	2 yr TN sa + 16bps	2 yr TN sa + 62bps	8.28%
3 years	3 yr TN sa + 20bps	3 yr TN sa + 70bps	8.06%
4 years	4 yr TN sa + 24bps	4 yr TN sa + 78bps	7.98%
5 years	5 yr TN sa + 28bps	5 yr TN sa + 86bps	7.92%

This schedule assumes nonamortizing debt and semiannual rates (sa).

All quotes are against 6-month (zloty) LIBOR flat.

TN = Polish Treasury note rate.

a. Ford Motor Company (FMC) has 4-year floating-rate zloty debt at 6-month LIBOR plus 45 basis points. FMC wants to swap into fixed-rate zloty debt. Describe FMC's floating-for-fixed zloty coupon swap.

b. Polish Motors (PM) has 4-year fixed-rate zloty debt at a bond equivalent yield of 9.83 percent. PM wants to swap into floating-rate zloty debt. Describe PM's fixed-for-floating zloty coupon swap.

c. What does the swap bank gain from these transactions?

Suggested Readings

Swaps are discussed in

Joanne M. Hill and Humza Naviwala, "Synthetic and Enhanced Index Strategies Using Futures on U.S. Indexes," *Journal of Portfolio Management* (May 1999), pp. 61–74.

Robert H. Litzenberger, "Swaps: Plain and Fanciful," *Journal of Finance* 47 (July 1992) pp. 831–850.

Bernadette A. Minton, "An Empirical Examination of Basic Valuation Models for Plain Vanilla U.S. Interest Rate Swaps," *Journal of Financial Economics* 44 (May 1997) pp. 251–277.

Clifford W. Smith, Jr., Charles W. Smithson, and Lee M. Wakeman, "The Market for Interest Rate Swaps," *Financial Management* 17 (Winter 1988) pp. 34–44.

Managing the Risks of Multinational Operations

part four

The Rationale for Hedging Currency Risks

chapter 9

Overview

Human history more and more becomes a race between education and catastrophe.

H. G. Wells

Why should the corporation engaged in international operations bother to hedge its exposures to currency risk? On the surface, the answer seems obvious. Hedging creates value by reducing the risk of assets exposed to currency fluctuations. However, the conditions under which hedging adds value are not as obvious as one might think. What if currency risk is entirely diversifiable and does not matter to investors? In this case, hedging can reduce the variability of operating cash flows, but cannot change investors' required returns or the corporation's cost of capital. Where, then, is the value in hedging?

Consider the discounted cash flow approach in which firm value is equal to the present value of expected future cash flows discounted at a rate that reflects the systematic risk of those cash flows. Let $E[CF_t]$ represent the firm's expected cash flow at time t and i the appropriate risk-adjusted discount rate. Firm value is determined by

$$V = \Sigma_t \, [\, E[CF_t] \, / \, (1+i)^t \,] \tag{9.1}$$

To add value, hedging must either increase the firm's expected future cash flows or reduce the risk of these cash flows in a way that cannot be replicated by individual investors. If hedges have no impact on the firm's expected future cash flows or discount rate, then hedging has no impact on firm value. Conversely, if hedging is to add value to the firm, then it must affect either expected future cash flows or the cost of capital.

The issue of whether exposure to currency risk affects the discount rate in the *denominator* of Equation 9.1 is discussed in Chapters 20 and 21 on international port-folio diversification and asset pricing. The net result of that discussion is that hedging exposure to currency risk is unlikely to reduce the required return of U.S. investors who are already diversified across a broad set of international assets. Hedging currency risk exposure probably can reduce the required return of investors who are not internation-ally diversified, such as those in emerging markets.

This chapter shows how hedging exposures to currency risk (or financial price risks in general) can increase expected cash flows in the *numerator* of Equation 9.1. The existence of financial market imperfections is a necessary condition for corporate risk hedging to have value.[1] By taking advantage of financial market imperfections, the corporation can create value for investors through their risk-hedging activities.

9.1 • A PERFECT MODEL FOR AN IMPERFECT WORLD

It helps to have a starting point for discussing the conditions under which corporate risk hedging can add value to the firm. A convenient point of entry is the work of Franco Modigliani and Merton Miller (referred to as MM).[2] Their landmark article on corporate financial policy set the stage for the development of corporate finance as we know it today. Modigliani and Miller each have won the Nobel Prize in Economics, largely for their work in this area. Their contribution was in identifying conditions under which financial policy, including hedging strategy, does not matter. At the heart of MM's work are the perfect financial market assumptions:

- *Frictionless markets*—no transactions costs, government intervention, taxes, costs of financial distress, or agency costs
- *Equal access to market prices*—everyone is a price taker in a barrier-free market
- *Rational investors*—return is good and risk is bad
- *Equal access to costless information*—everyone has instantaneous and costless access to all public information

In this stylized world, the law of one price holds. Rational investors operating in a perfect financial market will not allow different prices for equivalent assets to exist simultaneously. Arbitrage activity will quickly force asset prices to equality on comparable-risk assets.

> The law of one price always holds in a perfect financial market.

These assumptions are quite powerful and are invoked at several points in this text. For example, whether everyone has equal access to frictionless markets is discussed in the context of the corporation's cost of capital in Chapter 16 and investors' required returns in Part 6. Differences in national tax rates play a key role in the multinational corporation's cross-border investment decisions in Part 5. Capital flow barriers affect the multinational corporation's financing decisions in Chapter 16 and provide the motivation for the discussion of currency swaps in Chapter 8.

In this chapter, we develop the implications of frictionless markets for financial pol-icy, including hedging policy. We'll then investigate what happens as, one by one, we

---

1 Using data from New Zealand, where firms are required to disclose derivatives usage, Berkman and Bradbury find empirical support for many of this chapter's hedging rationale in "Empirical Evidence on the Corporate Use of Derivatives," *Financial Management* (1996).

2 Modigliani and Miller, "The Cost of Capital, Corporation Finance, and the Theory of Investment," *American Economic Review* (1958). The assumptions listed here are similar to those of MM.

relax the assumptions of frictionless markets. It will turn out that corporations have an incentive to hedge foreign exchange risk when faced with differential taxes or tax rates, costs of financial distress, or agency costs between the stakeholders of the firm.

9.2 • When Hedging Adds Value

The Multinational Corporation's Financial Policy

Equal access to perfect financial markets has an important consequence: *Individual investors can replicate any financial action that the firm can take.* For example, if additional financial leverage is desirable, investors can create "homemade leverage" by borrowing in the financial markets and investing the proceeds in common stock. Similarly, if investors want to hedge a particular financial price risk such as currency risk, then costless "homemade hedging" through the financial markets is possible.

> In perfect markets, investors can replicate the corporation's financial actions.

Because of equal access to perfect financial markets, the firm's financial policies and strategies become irrelevant. Investors can create "homemade" financial transactions that are equivalent to anything the firm can create. Firm value is then solely determined by the value of expected future investment cash flows. This is Miller and Modigliani's famous **irrelevance proposition**.

If financial markets are perfect, then corporate financial policy is irrelevant.

MM's assumptions are obviously a poor description of the real world. They intentionally assume away much that is interesting in the real world. Yet, by starting from this point, we can identify conditions that are necessary for financial policy to have value. By establishing the case in which financial policy does not matter, MM allow the discussion of real-world financial policy to focus on how real-world market imperfections influence firm value and, hence, corporate financial policy.

Let's restate MM's irrelevance proposition in its converse form.

If financial policy is to increase firm value, then it must increase the firm's expected future cash flows or decrease the discount rate in a way that cannot be replicated by individual investors.

If corporate financial policy is to have value, then at least one of the perfect market assumptions cannot hold. A firm's financial policies are important to firm valuation only if they affect cash flows or the discount rate through a change in taxes, transaction costs, bankruptcy costs, agency costs, information costs, or greater access to capital markets. Miller and Modigliani's irrelevance proposition is summarized in Figure 9.1.

The Multinational Corporation's Hedging Policy

Corporate risk hedging is a part of the firm's overall financial policy, so MM's basic argument applies to multinational corporation's hedging policy as well. With regard to corporate risk hedging, Miller and Modigliani's proposition can be restated as follows:

If financial markets are perfect, then corporate hedging policy has no value.

The rationale is as follows. If individual investors can already costlessly recreate corporate hedges through homemade hedging in the financial marketplace, then corporate

FIGURE 9.1
The Perfect Market Assumptions and Their Implications

Assume perfect financial markets

1. Frictionless markets	No transactions costs
	No government intervention
	No taxes
	No costs of financial distress
	No agency costs
2. Equal access to market prices	Perfect competition
	No barriers to entry
3. Rational investors	More return is good and more risk is bad
4. Equal access to costless information	Instantaneous and costless access to all public information

Modigliani and Miller's (MM) Irrelevance Proposition

- If financial markets are perfect, then corporate financial policy is irrelevant.

- If financial policy is to increase firm value, then it must either increase the firm's expected future cash flows or decrease the discount rate in a way that cannot be replicated by individual investors.

MM's Irrelevance Proposition for Corporate Risk Hedging

- If financial markets are perfect, then corporate hedging policy has no value.

- If corporate hedging policy is to increase firm value, then it must either increase the firm's expected future cash flows or decrease the discount rate in a way that cannot be replicated by individual investors.

hedging cannot add value to the firm or its investors. That is, corporations are unable to engage in hedging activities that investors cannot already construct for themselves.

If risk hedging has no value in a perfect financial market, then a necessary condition for hedging to have value is that financial markets be imperfect. Let's restate the hedging irrelevance proposition in its converse form.

> **If corporate hedging policy is to increase firm value, then it must increase the firm's expected future cash flows or decrease the discount rate in a way that cannot be replicated by individual investors.**

This means that if corporate hedging policy is to have value, then at least one of the MM assumptions cannot hold.

Market imperfections are greater across national boundaries than within those boundaries. Because of this, MNCs are well positioned to take advantage of cross-border differences in prices and costs. The impact of financial market imperfections on the value of the MNC's asset and liabilities is correspondingly greater than for domestic firms.

> Market imperfections are greater across national boundaries than within national boundaries.

The remainder of this chapter discusses three market imperfections that affect the corporation's hedging policy and risk management strategies:

- Tax schedule convexity
- Costs of financial distress
- Stakeholder game-playing

Imperfections in these areas create incentives to hedge on the part of one or more of the firm's principal stakeholders: stockholders, bondholders, or management. The value that can be added by hedging financial price risk depends on the extent of the imperfections.[3]

9.3 • CONVEXITY IN THE TAX SCHEDULE

Tax schedules are said to be **convex** when the effective tax rate is greater at high levels than at low levels of taxable income. In the presence of a convex tax schedule, MNCs can reduce their expected tax payment by reducing the variability of investment outcomes. Two factors contribute to tax schedule convexity: (1) progressive taxation and (2) tax preference items.

> Convex tax schedules have higher tax rates at higher levels of income.

Progressive Taxation

Progressive taxation is a tax system in which larger taxable incomes receive a higher tax rate. Most nations have progressive taxes on individual income. National taxes on corporate income are usually progressive only over a narrow range of taxable incomes. Tax rates of more than 100 percent on individual income have, at times, been imposed on very high incomes in socialist countries, such as Sweden.

Suppose the taxable income of Cricket International, a U.K.-based multinational corporation, will be either £0 or £500,000, with equal probability (that is, a 50 percent probability of each). The variability of Cricket's taxable income arises entirely from variability in the pound value of the U.S. dollar, so this exposure can be hedged in the forward market. Income up to £250,000 is taxed at a rate of 15 percent. Income in excess of £250,000 is taxed at 35 percent.

If Cricket does not hedge its currency risk, its situation is as in the dashed lines in Figure 9.2. If Cricket's taxable income is zero, then its tax bill is also zero. If Cricket's taxable income is £500,000, then it pays $(0.15)(£250,000) = £37,500$ on the first £250,000 of income and an additional $(0.35)(£250,000) = £87,500$ on the next £250,000 of income. Total taxes on £500,000 of taxable income are then £37,500 + £87,500 = £125,000. The expected tax payment is $(1/2)(£0) + (1/2)(£125,000) = £62,500$.

If Cricket can hedge its currency risk and lock in taxable income of $(1/2)(£0) + (1/2)(£500,000) = £250,000$ for certain, then it will also lock in a tax payment of $(0.15)(£250,000) = £37,500$ for certain. This is £25,000 less than the expected tax payment of £62,500 on unhedged taxable income. In essence, Cricket is avoiding the 50 percent probability of having to pay an additional 20 percent tax rate (35 percent versus 15 percent) on the second £250,000 of taxable income; that is, $(1/2)(0.20)(£250,000) = £25,000$. This £25,000 reduction in the expected tax liability is a 10 percent savings in taxes based on the £250,000 level of expected income.

Tax Preference Items

Tax preference items are items such as tax-loss carryforwards and carrybacks and investment tax credits that are used to shield corporate taxable income from taxes. To

---

3 Nance, Smith, and Smithson, "On the Determinants of Corporate Hedging," *Journal of Finance* (1993).

FIGURE 9.2
A Progressive Corporate Tax Schedule

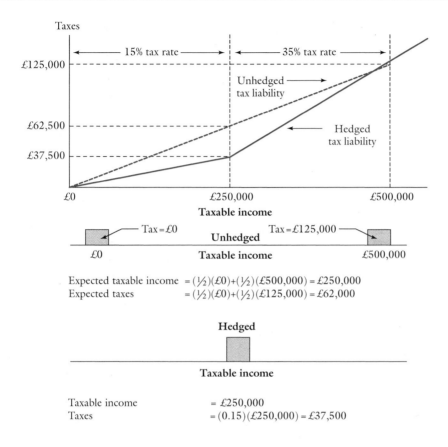

The corporate tax rate is 15 percent on the first £250,000 of taxable income and 35 percent thereafter. In the absence of hedging, taxable income is either £0 or £500,000 with equal probability. Hedging results in taxable income of £250,000 with certainty.

maximize the present value of tax shields from operating losses, deductions generally should be taken as soon as possible. Unfortunately, the firm cannot use operating losses to reduce its tax liability until it earns operating profits. This delay reduces the present value of tax-loss carryforwards and carrybacks.

Investment tax credits are credits against taxes that are designed to stimulate investment in real assets. Investment tax credits can only be used if the firm shows an operating profit. If there is some chance that the firm will show a loss if it is unhedged, then hedging can sometimes lock in a profit and ensure that the corporation can use the investment tax credit.

Figure 9.3 shows an example of how tax-loss carryforwards result in a convex tax schedule. In Figure 9.3, the U.S.-based corporation Exports-R-Us is exporting its goods to consumers in Finland. The components of taxable income are shown in the exporter's income statement at the top of the figure. Expenses ($1 million per year) are in dollars while revenues (FM5 million) are in Finnish markkas, so the U.S. exporter is exposed to currency risk. Suppose the spot rate will be either $0.15/FM

FIGURE 9.3

A Tax Preference Item: Tax-Loss Carryforwards

A U.S. Exporter's Income Statement		
FM revenues	FM5,000,000	FM5,000,000
Spot rate $S^{\$/FM}$	$.1500/FM	$.2500/FM
$ revenues	$750,000	$1,250,000
Operating expense	$1,000,000	$1,000,000
Taxable income	–$250,000	+$250,000

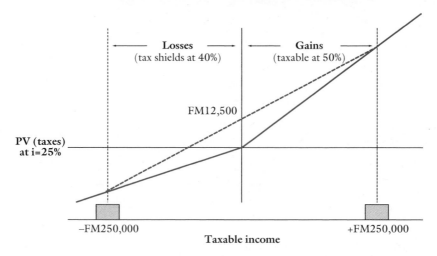

Unhedged

Expected taxable income = $(\frac{1}{2})$ (–FM250,000) + $(\frac{1}{2})$(+FM250,000) = FM0
Expected PV (taxes)　　= $(\frac{1}{2})$ (–FM100,000) + $(\frac{1}{2})$(+FM125,000) = FM12,500

Hedged

Taxable income　　　　　　　　　　　　　　　　　　　= FM0
Taxes　　　　　　　　　　　　　　　　　　　　　　　= FM0

Revenues are FM5 million. Operating expenses are $1 million. The spot rate will be $0.15/FM or $0.25/FM with equal probability. A forward rate of $0.20/FM can be locked in with certainty. Gains are taxed immediately at a rate of 50 percent. Losses are carried forward one period. The discount rate for carryforwards is 25 percent, so losses generate a present value tax shield of $(50\%)/(1.25) = 40\%$ of the loss.

---

or $0.25/FM with equal probability. Expected taxable income is $(\frac{1}{2})(\$250,000) + (\frac{1}{2})(-\$250,000) = \$0$.

Tax schedule convexity arises because gains are taxed immediately at a rate of $T_C = 50$ percent, while losses are carried forward until a gain is realized. Refer to the diagram at the bottom of Figure 9.3. Tax on an operating profit of $250,000 is $125,000 payable immediately. In the event of a $250,000 operating loss, the most favorable outcome is for the tax shield on the loss to be recaptured in the year following the loss. If 1-year discount bonds yield $i_B\$ = 6.2$ percent in the United States, then the present value of the tax shield received in one year on an operating loss of $250,000 is only $(\$250,000)(0.50)/(1.062) \approx \$117,702$. The net result is that while gains are taxed at 50 percent, losses recouped in the following year yield a tax shield of only $(0.50)/(1.062) \approx 0.47081$, or about 47 percent, in present value terms. The expected tax payment on a present value basis is then $E[PV(taxes)] = (1/2)(\$125,000–\$117,702) = \$3,649$.

In general, losses that are offset by gains t periods into the future generate tax shields at a rate of $T_C/(1+i_B)^t$, where i_B is the firm's cost of debt. If losses are not expected to be recouped until four years later in the previous example, then the present value of the $125,000 tax shield is only $T_C/(1+i_B)^t = \$125,000/(1.062)^4 = \$98,268$. The expected tax payment on a present value basis is $E[PV(taxes)] = (1/2)(\$125,000–\$98,268) = \$13,366$. Tax schedule convexity is greatest when interest rates are high and several years pass before tax-loss carryforwards can be captured. If the MNC is able to reduce the currency-induced variability of taxable income through hedging, then it can increase the value of the firm by reducing expected tax payments.

The Value of U.S. Tax Incentives to Hedge

Graham and Smith have quantified the value of tax incentives to hedge for firms in the United States.[4] They model the major provisions of the U.S. tax code and then simulate the tax savings achieved through hedging. These authors estimate that a 5 percent reduction in the variability of taxable income results in a 3 percent reduction in taxes for U.S. firms. This is a savings of $142,360 for the typical NYSE/AMEX firm. In some cases, tax savings from a 5 percent reduction in the variability of taxable income approach 8 percent. The tax codes of most nations create tax schedule convexity through progressive taxation and tax preference items, so tax savings through hedging are likely to be achieved in other countries as well. Of course, these potential gains from hedging must be compared to the costs of hedging.

There is one other factor to consider. In order for hedging to have value, risk exposures must be systematically related to some underlying financial price such as a foreign currency value. Consider the transaction exposure of a corporation's contractual cash flow denominated in foreign currency. The amount and timing of contractual cash flows are known in advance, and their value depends one-for-one on the value of the foreign currency. In this situation, an offsetting position can be taken with a currency forward contract and the exposure to currency risk can be perfectly hedged.

Operating exposures are more difficult to hedge. Real asset values do not move one-for-one with currency values, so hedges using derivative instruments such as currency forward contracts cannot perfectly offset the underlying risk exposures. Financial market hedges can only provide an approximate hedge of operating exposures to currency risk.

9.4 • COSTS OF FINANCIAL DISTRESS

Costs of financial distress can be direct or indirect. **Direct costs of financial distress** can be directly observed during bankruptcy, liquidation, or reorganization. They include attorney and court fees for settling the various claims on the firm's remaining assets. More

> Costs of financial distress can be direct or indirect.

---

difficult to classify and measure are the various **indirect costs**, such as the costs of lost credibility in the marketplace and various forms of stakeholder gamesmanship that accompany financial distress.

Equity as a Call Option on Firm Value

The effect of direct costs of financial distress on corporate financial policy is easiest to illustrate by viewing the equity claim as a form of call option on firm value. A **call option** is an option to buy an underlying asset at a predetermined price and on a predetermined expiration date. Suppose debt is given a claim (called the exercise price of the option) on the assets of the firm. Equity holds a claim on any residual value after the debt has been paid its promised amount. In the event of bankruptcy, the firm's assets go first to the bondholders. Any remaining value goes to equity. The positions of debt and equity are shown in Figure 9.4 in the absence of costs of financial distress.

> Equity can be viewed as a call option on firm value.

Viewed in this way, equity holds a call option on the value of the firm's assets. If assets are worth more than the promised payment to debtholders, then equity will exercise its option to buy the assets of the firm from the debtholders at the exercise

FIGURE 9.4
The Equity Call Option on Firm Value

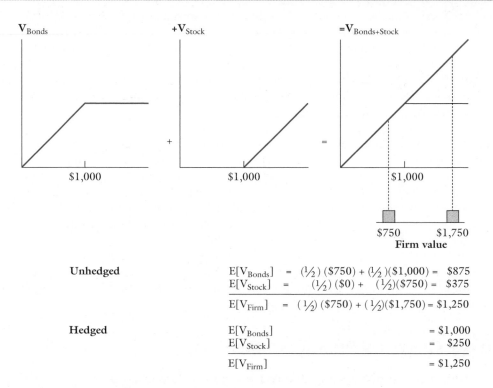

Unhedged

$E[V_{Bonds}] = (\frac{1}{2})(\$750) + (\frac{1}{2})(\$1,000) = \$875$
$E[V_{Stock}] = (\frac{1}{2})(\$0) + (\frac{1}{2})(\$750) = \$375$

$E[V_{Firm}] = (\frac{1}{2})(\$750) + (\frac{1}{2})(\$1,750) = \$1,250$

Hedged

$E[V_{Bonds}] = \$1,000$
$E[V_{Stock}] = \$250$

$E[V_{Firm}] = \$1,250$

Debtholders have been promised a payment of $1,000 in one period. Equity has the option of repurchasing the firm from debtholders for $1,000 at that time. In the absence of hedging, firm value is either $750 or $1,750 with equal probability. Hedging results in firm value of $1,250 with certainty. There are no costs of financial distress in this example.

price. If assets are worth less than the promised claim, equity will not exercise its option and debt receives 100 percent of the value of the firm. In this case, debt would receive less than its promised claim.

Suppose that the firm has promised to pay bondholders $1,000 one period and that the assets of the firm will be worth either $750 or $1,750 at that time, depending on the value of the firm's foreign currency cash flows. If these events are equally likely, then the expected value of the firm is

$$E[V_{Firm}] = (1/2)(\$750) + (1/2)(\$1,750) = \$1,250$$

Suppose, further, that there are no costs of financial distress and that in one year the assets of the firm will be split between debt and equity according to their claims on the firm. The two possible outcomes are shown in Figure 9.4. If the firm is worth $750, then equity will not exercise its option to buy the firm back from the bond-holders at a price of $1,000. In this case, equity receives nothing and debt receives the $750 value of the firm (rather than its promised claim of $1,000). If the firm is worth $1,750, then equity will exercise its call option and pay bondholders their promised claim of $1,000. In this case, equity retains the residual $750 value after paying the bondholders their $1,000 claim. The $1,250 expected value of the firm is split between debt and equity according to

$$E[V_{Bonds}] = (1/2)(\$750) + (1/2)(\$1,000) = \$875$$

and

$$E[V_{Stock}] = (1/2)(\$0) + (1/2)(\$750) = \$375$$

Thus, $E[V_{Firm}] = E[V_{Bonds}] + E[V_{Stock}] = \$875 + \$375 = \$1,250$.

Suppose hedging can completely eliminate foreign exchange risk and lock in a firm value of $(1/2)(\$750) + (1/2)(\$1,750) = \$1,250$ with certainty (see Figure 9.4). The total cash flow generated by the assets of the firm has not changed. There is still $1,250 to share between debt and equity. However, the distribution of this cash flow between debt and equity does change; debt is certain to receive its promised payment of $1,000 and equity is certain to receive the residual value of $250. In this example, equity is worth $125 more when the firm's cash flows are left unhedged than when they are hedged ($375 versus $250). The value of debt increases by a corresponding amount—from $875 to $1,000—when currency risk is hedged.

This example illustrates an important property of options.[5]

Option values increase as the volatility of the underlying asset increases.

A decrease in the variability of firm value through hedging is good news for debt and bad news for the equity call option, other things held constant. What debt gains, equity must give up. In this example, the net effect of hedging was a $125 increase in the value of debt and a corresponding $125 decrease in the value of the equity call option. Equity has a disincentive to hedge unless hedging can create value for the firm in some other way, such as through a reduction in expected costs of financial distress. Viewing equity as a call option on the value of the firm will prove useful as we add direct and indirect costs of financial distress in the next two sections.

---

5 Volatility and option valuation are discussed in Chapters 7 and 18.

Direct Costs of Financial Distress

Direct costs of financial distress are incurred during bankruptcy, liquidation, or reorganization. Figure 9.5 extends the equity call option example to include direct costs.

An Example with Direct Costs of Financial Distress. Suppose direct bankruptcy costs of $500 are incurred if the company defaults on its debt obligation. If firm assets are worth $750 at the end of the period, then direct bankruptcy costs absorb $500 and debtholders receive the remaining $250. If the firm is worth $1,750, then no direct bankruptcy costs are incurred. In this case, debt receives its promised payment of $1,000 and equity receives the remaining $750. The expected value of the firm net of bankruptcy costs is

> Direct financial distress costs are incurred during bankruptcy.

$$E[V_{Firm}] = (^{1}/_{2})(\$250) + (^{1}/_{2})(\$1,750) = \$1,000$$

This is split between debt and equity according to

$$E[V_{Bonds}] = (^{1}/_{2})(\$250) + (^{1}/_{2})(\$1,000) = \$625$$

FIGURE 9.5
The Equity Call Option with Direct Costs of Financial Distress

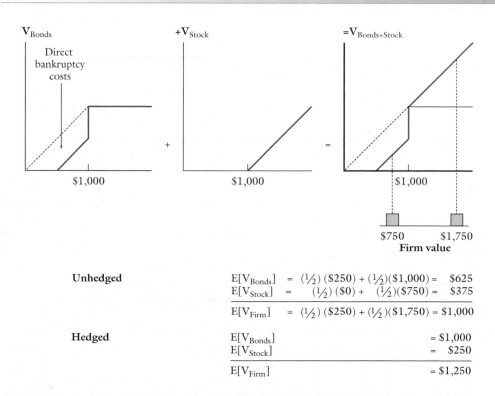

Unhedged		
$E[V_{Bonds}]$	=	$(\tfrac{1}{2})\,(\$250) + (\tfrac{1}{2})(\$1,000) = \ \ \$625$
$E[V_{Stock}]$	=	$(\tfrac{1}{2})\,(\$0) + \ \ (\tfrac{1}{2})(\$750) = \ \ \$375$
$E[V_{Firm}]$	=	$(\tfrac{1}{2})\,(\$250) + (\tfrac{1}{2}\,)(\$1,750) = \$1,000$

Hedged	
$E[V_{Bonds}]$	$= \$1,000$
$E[V_{Stock}]$	$= \ \ \$250$
$E[V_{Firm}]$	$= \$1,250$

Debtholders have been promised a payment of $1,000 in one period. If end-of-period firm value is less than this promised payment, direct bankruptcy costs of $500 are incurred. Equity has the option of repurchasing the firm from debtholders for $1,000 in one period. In the absence of hedging, firm value is either $750 or $1,750 with equal probability. Hedging results in firm value of $1,250 with certainty.

and

$$E[V_{Stock}] = (1/2)(\$0) + (1/2)(\$750) = \$375$$

Thus, $E[V_{Firm}] = E[V_{Bonds}] + E[V_{Stock}] = \$625 + \$375 = \$1,000$.

The firm can reduce its expected bankruptcy costs by hedging its exposure to currency risk. As before, if hedging can eliminate currency risk and lock in a firm value of \$1,250 with certainty, then bonds always receive their promised payment of \$1,000 and stock receives the \$250 residual value. The \$500 direct bankruptcy cost can be avoided entirely. By hedging its currency risk, this firm can avoid the direct costs of financial distress.

Who benefits from this reduction in expected bankruptcy costs through hedging? Because debtholders have first claim on corporate assets, corporate hedging of business risk helps debtholders first and may or may not add value to equityholders. In our example, the value of corporate debt increased by \$375 (from \$625 to \$1,000). In contrast, the \$250 value of the equity in the hedged alternative is \$125 less than the \$375 value of the equity in the unhedged alternative. The \$375 increase in debt value comes from two sources: the $(1/2)(\$0) + (1/2)(\$500) = \$250$ reduction in expected bankruptcy costs and a \$125 transfer in value from the equity to the debt.

The reason that equity lost value in this example is best understood by viewing equity as a call option on the assets of the firm. Option values are positively related to both the level and the variability of the asset returns underlying the option. The \$250 increase in the value of firm assets net of bankruptcy costs is good news for both debt and equity. The decrease in the variability of firm assets is good news for debt but bad news for equity. In this example, the net effect is a \$375 increase in the value of debt and a \$125 decrease in the value of the equity call option.

Does this mean that it is not in the best interests of equity to hedge against currency risk? Not necessarily. It is useful to look at the costs and benefits of hedging in two ways: (1) after debt has been issued (we'll call this the *endgame*) and (2) at the time debt is issued (that is, during the *opening moves*).

Opening Moves: Reducing the Cost of Debt Through a Hedging Policy. Hedging can benefit equity in its initial negotiations with debt. Both debt and equity stakeholders can observe the behavior of other firms in bankruptcy and can formulate expectations of the probability of bankruptcy and the direct and indirect costs associated with bankruptcy. Debtholders and equityholders price their claims on the firm based on these expectations. As the expected costs of financial distress rise, debtholders require higher interest rates to compensate for these additional risks. If the variability of firm value can be reduced through hedging, then debt can be raised at lower cost and with fewer binding restrictions in the debt covenants. With lower and less restrictive financial costs, more value can be left over for equity. Whether equity ultimately wins or loses through corporate hedging depends on whether the debt goes up more or less in value than the savings in expected bankruptcy costs. In this way, a properly conceived and executed hedging policy can increase the value of both debt and equity by avoiding the costs of financial distress.

> Equity may or may not gain by hedging currency risk.

The Endgame: Reducing Bankruptcy Costs with a Prepackaged Bankruptcy. There are other circumstances in which both debt and equity can gain through hedging, even when the firm has already issued debt and then fallen into financial distress. In the example of direct bankruptcy costs, there is a 50 percent probability of bankruptcy if the firm does not hedge. Equityholders want to avoid hedging, because hedging reduces the value of the equity call option. Debtholders, on the other hand, prefer that the firm hedge.

In order to avoid the direct costs of formal bankruptcy, the firm's stakeholders may be able to negotiate a "prepackaged bankruptcy" prior to formal bankruptcy proceedings. If debt is willing to accept less than its promised $1,000 payment in exchange for equity's promise to hedge the firm's exposure to currency risk, direct bankruptcy costs can be avoided entirely in this example. Debtholders gain if they can capture more than their $625 expected payoff when the firm does not hedge. Equityholders gain if they can capture more than their $375 expected payoff in the unhedged case.

Suppose debt and equity agree to split the $250 reduction in expected bankruptcy costs that is achieved through hedging. In exchange for equity's promise to hedge, debtholders could accept a certain payoff of $750. This is a $125 increase from their expected unhedged payoff of $625. If debt is paid $750, there is $450 of firm value left over for equity. This is a $125 increase over equity's expected unhedged payoff of $325. By negotiating prior to formal bankruptcy, both debt and equity stand to gain.[6]

Indirect Costs of Financial Distress

Indirect costs of financial distress are far more important to corporate hedging decisions than are direct costs. The effects of indirect costs are also more subtle. In particular, financial distress affects the firm's customers, suppliers, and employees, as well as debtholders, equityholders, and management. This means that indirect costs of financial distress influence the activities of the firm not just in bankruptcy but prior to bankruptcy as well. Financial distress can affect the firm's operations in several ways:

- Lost credibility
  - Lower revenues
  - Higher operating costs
  - Higher financial costs
- Stakeholder gamesmanship

The net result of lost credibility in the marketplace is lower expected future cash flows and a lower firm value. Stakeholder gamesmanship arising from conflicts of interest among the firm's stakeholders also detracts from firm value.

The Costs of Lost Credibility. Firms often find it more difficult to sell their products once rumors of an impending collapse hit the newspapers. This is especially true of products for which quality and after-sale service are important marketing tools. Customers shopping for quality items will be reluctant to purchase from a vendor in the midst of a bankruptcy sale. The customer knows that the remaining products will be those that were not already purchased by other customers. The quality of the remaining goods is questionable, and there will be no recourse for unsatisfied customers once the firm is out of business.

Foreign customers can be in an even worse position than local customers when it comes to getting an exporter's quality merchandise or service. A multinational corporation in financial distress takes care of its home market first. Foreign markets are more likely to get lower quality goods. Consequently, foreign consumers can be even more sensitive to rumors of financial distress than domestic customers. Offsetting this natural tendency is the fact that foreign customers may not be as informed as domestic customers about the company's financial situation.

---

6 See Gilson, "Managing Default: Some Evidence on How Firms Choose Between Workouts and Chapter 11," *Journal of Applied Corporate Finance* (1991); or McConnell and Servaes, "The Economics of Pre-Packaged Bankruptcy," *Journal of Applied Corporate Finance* (1991).

Firms in financial distress also find it more difficult to purchase materials and labor to run their operations. Suppliers tend to put more effort into providing quality parts and prompt service to repeat customers, so a firm in financial distress can find itself receiving other firms' rejected goods or inferior services.

Suppliers are especially sensitive to the financial situation of foreign partners, because of poor recourse in foreign courts. Suppliers that ordinarily sell on credit terms such as "30 days, same as cash" or "2/10, net 60" (that is, a 2 percent discount if paid in 10 days, otherwise due in 60 days) demand that firms in financial distress pay their bills COD (cash on delivery) or finance their sales through bank letters of credit that guarantee payment to the supplier. Employees also demand their compensation in cash and may be unwilling to work toward the long-term betterment of the firm.

Conflicts of Interest Between Debt and Equity. It is during difficult times that the struggle for the firm's assets is most contentious. During financial distress, debt and equity stakeholders shift their focus from firm value maximization to endgame strategies that maximize their claim over the firm's diminishing resources. Debt wants to preserve the value of its claim, whereas equity wants to increase the value of its call option, even if this is at the expense of debtholders. In particular, equity has the following incentives during financial distress:

- An incentive to underinvest in new projects
- An incentive to take large risks

Underinvestment occurs when equity refuses to supply additional capital for positive-NPV investments during financial distress. Why should equity invest more funds (even in positive-NPV investments) if debt gets the first claim on any value generated by the project? On the contrary, equity has an incentive to pull out any funds that it can before liquidation, perhaps as an extra cash dividend. This is when the protective covenants on bonds (in particular, a limitation on liquidating dividends) can be important to the bondholders. Through bond covenants, debt can reduce the ability of other stakeholders playing games with the funds that they have loaned to the firm.

In financial distress, equity has an incentive to promote risky ventures. By taking on risky projects, equity can increase the variability of investment outcomes. This increases the value of equity's call option on firm value. In some cases, equity may even want to take on negative-NPV projects if equity value increases because of more variable outcomes, despite the decrease in firm value from the negative-NPV investment. In this case, debtholders bear the brunt of both the negative-NPV project and the value transfer to the equity call option from increased volatility in the value of the firm. Protective bond covenants are specifically written to prevent this sort of gamesmanship.

An Example with Direct and Indirect Costs of Financial Distress. Suppose that indirect costs of financial distress cause a $250 decrease in the distribution of firm value in the previous example. This means that the value of firm assets will be either $500 or $1,500 with equal probability one year later. If direct bankruptcy costs still total $500, then the positions of debt and equity are as shown in Figure 9.6. Without hedging, the expected value of the firm is

$$E[V_{Firm}] = (\$0) + (^1/_2)(\$1,500) = \$750$$

This is split between debt and equity according to

$$E[V_{Bonds}] = (^1/_2)(\$0) + (^1/_2)(\$1,000) = \$500$$

$$E[V_{Stock}] = (^1/_2)(\$0) + (^1/_2)(\$500) = \$250$$

FIGURE 9.6

The Equity Call Option with Direct and Indirect Costs of Financial Distress

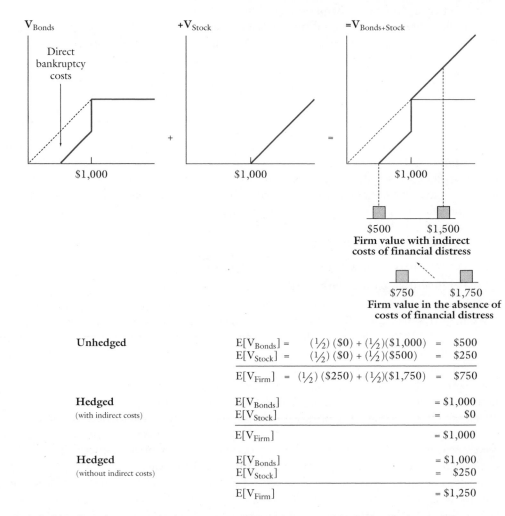

Debtholders have been promised a payment of $1,000 in one period. If end-of-period firm value is less than this promised payment, direct bankruptcy costs of $500 are incurred. Equity has the option of repurchasing the firm from debtholders for $1,000 in one period. In the absence of hedging, firm value is either $750 or $1,750 with equal probability before indirect costs of financial distress. If the firm does not hedge, indirect costs of financial distress drain $250 from firm value. Hedging is assumed to eliminate the indirect costs (and avoid the direct costs) of financial distress and results in firm value of $1,250 with certainty.

In this example, both debt and equity suffer from the costs of financial distress.

If the firm hedges its currency risk and locks in a firm value of $1,000, direct costs of financial distress can be avoided and bondholders receive their promised payment of $1,000 with certainty. Unfortunately, stockholders receive nothing. This is similar to the situation with direct costs, except that firm value has been shifted to the left by the $250 indirect cost of financial distress.

Suppose the firm can avoid the indirect costs of financial distress through its risk management policies, perhaps because hedging reduces the perceived risk of the firm and improves its credibility in the marketplace. If indirect costs can be eliminated entirely, then the distribution of firm value reverts to its original position of either $750 or $1,750 with equal probability. Hedged, this results in firm value of $1,250 with certainty, as in the original example. Debt receives its promised payment of $1,000 and equity receives $250 with certainty. Comparing the unhedged situation with both direct and indirect costs to the hedged situation with no costs of financial distress in Figure 9.4, debtholders are unambiguously better off while the expected value of equity is unchanged.

As in the situation with direct costs alone, this reduction in expected costs of financial distress through hedging can create value for both debt and equity stakeholders. First, firms in financial distress can find that hedging allows negotiation of a prepackaged bankruptcy that benefits both debt and equity stakeholders. Second, as debtholders negotiate their initial contract, they should be willing to accept a smaller promised return in the hedged firm than in the unhedged firm. As debtholders' required return decreases in the hedged firm, more of the value is left for equityholders.

The Value of Distress-Related Incentives to Hedge

In summary, viewing equity as a call option on firm value in the presence of financial distress costs yields the following conclusions:

- Hedging can increase firm value and the expected cash flows available to debt and equity by reducing the direct and indirect costs of financial distress.
- Hedging generally increases the value of debtholders by reducing the variability of operating cash flows and ensuring that debtholders receive their promised payments.
- Equity may or may not benefit from risk hedging, depending on whether the increase in firm value is more or less than the value transfer to the debt from the reduction in risk.

In addition to a reduction in the deadweight costs of financial distress, hedging can further benefit the firm if it results in additional debt capacity. Hedging results in more predictable cash flows to debt. This allows the hedged firm to issue more debt than the unhedged firm at the same cost of debt. Additional debt then results in additional tax shields for the firm. Graham and Rogers estimate the tax benefits associated with increased debt capacity average 1.1 percent of firm value for U.S. firms.[7]

In practice, equity may or may not prefer to hedge currency risk, depending on whether the benefit from avoiding the costs of financial distress is more or less than the transfer in value to the debt from reduction in the variability of operating cash flows.

9.5 • AGENCY COSTS

In MM's perfect world, the firm's optimal investment criterion is simple: Accept all positive-NPV projects. This decision rule maximizes the value of both debt and equity stakeholders in the firm. The previous section discussed conflicts of interest

---

7 Graham and Rogers, "Do Firms Hedge in Response to Tax Incentives," *Journal of Finance* (2002). In contrast to Graham and Smith's "Tax Incentives to Hedge," Graham and Rogers find no evidence that firms hedge in response to tax convexity.

that arise between debt and equity in financial distress. In this section, we'll turn to conflicts of interest between managers and other stakeholders.

As in the conflict between debt and equity, conflicts between managers and other stakeholders are especially prevalent when financial distress threatens the corporation. In financial distress, the "accept all positive-NPV projects" rule can act against the interests of debt, equity, or management, as each of these stakeholders acts in its own self-interest.

Conflicts of Interest Between Managers and Other Stakeholders

Although managers are hired to run the firm, their objectives are naturally different from those of other stakeholders. This leads to agency conflicts as managers act nominally as agents for the firm's stakeholders, but in actuality, in their own interests. These interests can be in conflict with those of other stakeholders. Agency conflicts give rise to **agency costs** as other stakeholders try to ensure that managers do not act against their interests.

> Agency costs are the costs of ensuring that managers act in the interests of other stakeholders.

Managers are seldom as diversified as other stakeholders. Managers' livelihoods are intimately tied to the health of the company. In contrast, debt and equity stakeholders typically hold diversified portfolios of assets. This means that managers are concerned with the total risk of the company, whereas debt and equityholders are more concerned with the contribution of the company to the risk of their portfolios. Managers thus have an incentive to hedge against currency risk even if these risks are diversifiable to other stakeholders. Hedging reduces the variability of the MNC's total cash flow and thus reduces the managers' exposure to currency risk.

Even if managers wanted to act in the best interests of equity, most countries have laws that ensure managers consider the concerns of a broader set of stakeholders, particularly labor. For example, German law requires that workers in publicly traded German firms hold a proportion of seats on the supervisory board. The firm's bankers are also represented on the board. Indeed, the German supervisory board was established during the 1800s to give banks a voice in the governance of the firm.[8]

Management's Incentive to Hedge

Because their performance is usually based on unit performance, unit managers have an incentive to hedge their unit's transaction exposure to currency risk. This is true even if the corporation as a whole is hedged against exposure to currency risk.

Management of Transaction Exposure. Consider a firm based in the United States with an export and an import division. The export division buys jewelry in Santa Fe, New Mexico, and sells it in Paris, France. Contracts are denominated in euros and payable in six months. A typical transaction in this division is as follows:

The import division of the company buys Parisian fashions in France and sells these items to tourists in Santa Fe. Again, sales are invoiced in euros and payable in six months. A typical transaction in this division is as follows:

---

8 Cornell and Shapiro make a similar point with regard to U.S. corporation law in "Corporate Stakeholders and Corporate Finance," *Financial Management* (1987).

t=6 months

t=0   – 1 million euros

These two transactions net to zero, so the firm and its investors have no need to pay the costs of hedging each division's exposure to the euro-per-dollar spot rate.

Divisional managers have an incentive to hedge and reduce the variability of divisional performance. If managers from both divisions hedge their exposures, there is neither a gain in expected cash flows nor a reduction in risk on the firm's zero net position in euros. The cost of the offsetting hedges is a deadweight loss to the firm's debt and equity stakeholders. If only one manager hedges, there is a loss from the cost of the hedge, as well as a new and, from the firm's point of view, undesirable exposure to currency risk from the hedge.

Management of Translation Exposure. Because management is usually judged on accounting performance rather than on financial (cash flow) performance, managers have an incentive to hedge their accounting (translation) exposure to currency risk. This is so even if the exposure is purely an accounting artifact and is unrelated to operating cash flow or firm value. By reducing the variability of accounting income, managers can reduce the variability of their performance evaluations and personal wealth. Hedging translation exposure may or may not cause collateral damage to other stakeholders.

Avoiding the Discipline of External Financial Markets. Managers are often more concerned with maximizing the total corporate wealth over which they have control, rather than with maximizing the wealth of shareholders. This means that they sometimes promote negative-NPV projects that nevertheless provide some private benefit to management. Capital markets discipline management against accepting negative-NPV projects by valuing the expected returns and risks of the firm's investments and pronouncing a verdict in the form of a share price. Managers have an incentive to hedge if, by reducing cash flow variability, they can finance projects internally and avoid the discipline of external financial markets. Risk management strategies that allow managers to avoid external financial markets can increase the agency conflicts between managers and shareholders.[9]

Aligning the Incentives of Managers and Shareholders

If a contract could be designed that aligned the objectives of managers and equityholders, managers would have no need to hedge against transaction or translation exposure. In the absence of such an optimal contract, management has an incentive to hedge. If hedging also reduces the costs of agency conflicts between managers and shareholders, then it can actually increase the value of the firm to shareholders by aligning management's incentives with those of shareholders.[10] Managers' actions will then be consistent with shareholders' preferences. Whether this is the lowest-cost or most effective way to align the incentives of managers with those of other stakeholders is an open question.

---

9 This argument is developed by Tufano in "Agency Costs of Corporate Risk Management," *Financial Management* (1998).

10 Aggarwal makes this argument in "Management of Accounting Exposure to Currency Changes: Role and Evidence of Agency Costs," *Managerial Finance* (1991).

9.6 • THE HEDGING DECISION

The decision of whether and how much to hedge must be made on a case-by-case basis. Although the need to hedge is greater for smaller, less-diversified, and riskier firms, the costs of hedging are also greater for these firms. For example, there are large economies of scale in direct bankruptcy costs, so small firms experience larger direct costs as a percent of assets than large firms do.[11] Unfortunately for small firms, there are also large economies of scale in the cost of most financial hedges. Bid-ask spreads on forward, option, and swap contracts traded through commercial or investment banks are much narrower for larger transactions, so firms attempting to hedge small amounts can face relatively large percentage transaction costs. In contrast to the large economies of scale on these contracts, exchange-traded options and futures contracts have a fixed cost per contract, so that costs are proportional to the number of contracts traded.

9.7 • SUMMARY

This chapter provides the rationale for hedging currency risk. The perfect market assumptions were introduced as a way of identifying conditions under which hedging policy matters. Perfect financial markets have the following properties:

- Frictionless markets
- Equal access to market prices
- Rational investors
- Equal access to costless information

If hedging policy (indeed, any financial policy) is to have value, then one or more of these perfect market assumptions cannot hold. This leads to the following rule:

If corporate hedging policy is to increase firm value, then it must increase the firm's expected future cash flows or decrease the discount rate in a way that cannot be replicated by individual investors.

The importance of currency risk exposure depends on the presence of one or more market imperfections. Particularly important imperfections with respect to the firm's hedging policies are

- Convex tax schedules with different tax rates at different levels of taxable income
- Costs of financial distress (both direct and indirect)
- Agency costs

Hedging can create value for shareholders (indeed, for all stakeholders) by reducing taxes, costs of financial distress, or agency costs.

KEY TERMS

agency costs	indirect costs of financial distress
call option	irrelevance proposition
convex tax schedule	progressive taxation
direct costs of financial distress	tax preference items

---

11 See Warner, "Bankruptcy Costs: Some Evidence," *Journal of Finance* (1977).

CONCEPTUAL QUESTIONS

9.1 Describe the conditions that can lead to tax schedule convexity.

9.2 Define financial distress. Give examples of direct and indirect costs of financial distress.

9.3 What is an agency conflict? How can agency costs be reduced?

PROBLEMS

Tax schedule convexity: progressive taxation

9.1 Suppose corporate income up to one million rand is taxed at a 20 percent rate in South Africa. Income over one million rand is taxed at 40 percent. The taxable income of Widget International (a multinational corporation based in South Africa) will be either R500,000 or R1,500,000 with equal probability. This variability arises entirely from variation in the value of the rand against the Dutch guilder.

    a. Draw a graph similar to Figure 9.2 depicting tax schedule convexity in South Africa.

    b. What is Widget's expected tax liability if it does not hedge its currency risk?

    c. Draw a line in your graph between R500,000 and R1,500,000. What is Widget's expected tax liability (and hence its after-tax income) if it is able to completely hedge its currency risk exposure and lock in taxable income of R1,000,000 with certainty?

    d. In what way does hedging have value for Widget International?

Tax schedule convexity: tax-loss carryforwards

9.2 Suppose taxable income will be either $250,000 or –$250,000 depending on the value of the dollar against the euro. If taxable income is positive, taxes are paid immediately at the rate of 50 percent. If taxable income is negative, tax shields from the resulting tax-loss carryforward are not recovered until a future date. Variability in taxable income can be completely eliminated by hedging against currency risk. In each of the following scenarios, find the present value of expected taxes when taxable income is unhedged and when it is hedged.

    a. Use a discount rate of 25 percent. Assume tax-loss carryforwards can be recovered in one year.

    b. Use a discount rate of 0 percent. Assume tax-loss carryforwards can be recovered in one year.

    c. Use a discount rate of 25 percent. Assume tax-loss carryforwards cannot be recovered until two years have passed.

Direct and indirect costs of financial distress: debt gains at equity's expense

9.3 Gidget International is domiciled in the Land of Make Believe. The local currency is called the Goodwill (abbreviated G). Gidget will own assets worth either G6,000 or G16,000 this year (with equal probability), depending on the value of the local currency on world currency markets. Gidget has a promised payment to debt of G10,000 due in one year. Although there are no taxes in the Land of Make Believe, there are lawyers (this isn't a perfect world, after all). If Gidget cannot meet its debt obligations, legal fees will impose direct bankruptcy costs of G2,000 as the firm is divided amongst its creditors.

a. How much will the debt and equity owners receive at asset values of G16,000 and of G6,000?
b. Draw the value of debt and of equity as a function of the value of firm assets as in Figure 9.5.
c. How can hedging increase the value of Gidget International in the presence of direct bankruptcy costs? Who wins—debt, equity, or both?

Direct and indirect costs of financial distress

9.4   Refer to problem 9.3. Suppose that, in the absence of risk hedging, the indirect costs of financial distress shift sales downward and result in an asset value of either G14,000 or G4,000 with equal probability. How much will each stakeholder receive at each of these values?
a. Draw the value of debt and of equity as a function of firm value, as in Figure 9.6.
b. Can hedging increase the value of Gidget International in the presence of both direct and indirect costs of financial distress? Who wins—debt? equity? or both?

Direct and indirect costs of financial distress

9.5   Suppose that a firm has promised to pay bondholders £10,000 in one period and that, depending on the value of the dollar, the firm will be worth either £9,000 or £19,000 with equal probability at that time. The assets of the firm will be worth £14,000 if it hedges against currency risk.
a. Identify the value of debt and of equity under both unhedged and hedged scenarios, assuming there are no costs of financial distress.
b. Suppose the firm will incur direct costs of £1,000 in bankruptcy. Identify the value of debt and of equity under both unhedged and hedged scenarios.
c. In addition to the £1,000 direct bankruptcy cost, suppose indirect costs reduce the asset value of the firm to either £6,000 or £18,000 (before the £1,000 direct bankruptcy cost) with equal probability. Hedging can eliminate both direct and indirect bankruptcy costs, resulting in firm value of £14,000 with certainty. Identify the value of debt and of equity under both unhedged and hedged scenarios.

SUGGESTED READINGS

A thorough and readable survey of financial risk management, including the rationale for hedging financial price risks, appears in

Clifford W. Smith, Jr., Charles W. Smithson, and D. Sykes Wilford, *Managing Financial Risk* (Burr Ridge, Ill.: Ballinger Publishing Company, 1990).

Imperfections that contribute to the incentive of corporate stakeholders to hedge currency risk are discussed in the following articles

Raj Aggarwal, "Management of Accounting Exposure to Currency Changes: Role and Evidence of Agency Costs," *Managerial Finance* 17, No. 4 (1991), pp. 10–22.

Henk Berkman and Michael L. Bradbury, "Empirical Evidence on the Corporate Use of Derivatives," *Financial Management* 25 (Summer 1996), pp. 5–13.

Bradford Cornell and Alan Shapiro, "Corporate Stakeholders and Corporate Finance," *Financial Management* 16, No. 1 (1987), pp. 5–14.

John R. Graham and Clifford W. Smith, Jr., "Tax Incentives to Hedge," *Journal of Finance* 54 (December 1999), pp. 2241–2262.

John R. Graham and Daniel A. Rogers, "Do Firms Hedge in Response to Tax Incentives," *Journal of Finance* 57 (April 2002).

Franco Modigliani and Merton Miller, "The Cost of Capital, Corporation Finance, and the Theory of Investment," *American Economic Review* 48 (June 1958), pp. 261–297.

Deanna R. Nance, Clifford W. Smith, Jr., and Charles W. Smithson, "On the Determinants of Corporate Hedging," *Journal of Finance* 48 (March 1993), pp. 267–284.

Peter Tufano, "Agency Costs of Corporate Risk Management," *Financial Management* 27, No. 1 (Spring 1998), pp. 67–77.

Jerold B. Warner, "Bankruptcy Costs: Some Evidence," *Journal of Finance* 32, No. 2 (May 1977), pp. 337–347.

Prepackaged bankruptcies are discussed in

Stuart C. Gilson, "Managing Default: Some Evidence on How Firms Choose Between Workouts and Chapter 11," *Journal of Applied Corporate Finance* 4 (Summer 1991), pp. 62–70.

John J. McConnell and Henri Servaes, "The Economics of Pre-Packaged Bankruptcy," *Journal of Applied Corporate Finance* 4 (Summer 1991), pp. 93–97.

Multinational Treasury Management

chapter 10

Overview

When I look back on all these worries I remember the story of the old man who said on his deathbed that he had had a lot of trouble in his life, most of which never happened.

Winston Churchill

As corporations grow beyond their traditional domestic markets and become multinational in scope, they must develop a financial system capable of managing the transactions and risks of the individual operating divisions and the corporation as a whole. The treasury of the MNC fulfills this role, serving as a *corporate bank* that manages cash flows within the corporation and between the corporation and its external partners. The modern corporate treasury performs several functions:

- Determining the MNC's overall financial goals and strategies
- Managing domestic and international trade
- Financing domestic and international trade
- Consolidating and managing the financial flows of the firm
- Identifying, measuring, and managing the firm's risk exposures

Treasury management has both an internal and an external dimension. Internally, treasury must set policies and establish procedures for how the operating divisions of the firm are to interact with each other. Externally, treasury must coordinate the firm's interaction with its customers, suppliers, investors, and host governments.

This chapter covers the multinational dimensions of the first four functions of the modern corporate treasury. The last function—currency risk management—is covered in the next three chapters.

10.1 • Determining the Firm's Financial Goals and Strategies

The Multinational Corporation's Strategic Business Plan

The highly competitive and fast-changing global marketplace demands that corporations continually reassess their business and financial strategies. The process of creating a strategic business plan includes the following steps:

1. Identify the firm's core competencies and potential growth opportunities.
2. Evaluate the business environment within which the firm operates.
3. Formulate a strategic plan for turning the firm's core competencies into sustainable competitive advantages.
4. Develop robust processes for implementing the strategic business plan.

Financial strategy should complement the overall business plan.

The strategic plan should incorporate all of the corporation's existing businesses. It should promote the refinement of existing core competencies and the development of new ones. It should be flexible enough to adapt to the exigencies of the global marketplace. Finally, the plan should be continuously updated and revised so that it is a dynamic, living guide rather than a static anchor for the firm.[1]

Financial Strategies as Complements to the Overall Business Plan

Financial strategy should not stand as an island apart from other operations. Instead, financial strategy should complement the overall strategic business plan. A properly conceived strategic financial plan integrates and promotes the core operations of the corporation and furthers the goals and objectives of the corporation's individual business units. The financial plan should be formulated at the highest levels of management and faithfully implemented on an ongoing basis to meet the firm's changing needs.

The way that the firm deals with currency risk is a key element of financial policy. Failure to set risk management guidelines and then monitor the corporation's risk management activities can expose the firm to financial loss or even ruin. Management must decide whether currency risk exposures will be managed, how actively they will be managed, and the extent to which the firm is willing to take speculative positions in the pursuit of its business and financial objectives. Failure to take action in hedging currency risk is a de facto decision to take a speculative position in foreign exchange. Yet the firm may choose to go well beyond a passive posture toward currency risk as it attempts to extract as much value as possible from the firm's operating cash flows.

Some commercial and investment banks include currency speculation among their core competencies. For manufacturing and service firms, a better use of the corporate

Risk management should complement the firm's overall business plan.

treasury is as a complement to other business activities. Speculative profits from the treasury's financial market operations are more often due to chance than to any enduring expertise in anticipating market movements. Even more important, other business units are unlikely to operate at peak effectiveness if speculative activity in the treasury is distracting top management from operating the firm's core businesses. A financial strategy of taking speculative positions that are independent of the firm's operating cash flows is, in the long run, likely to destroy rather than enhance shareholder wealth.

---

1 A mathematics teacher would point out that *continuous* updating is unattainable in the real world. Let us say that updates to the strategic plan must be made discretely, but very often.

This is not to say that the treasury should avoid speculative positions. Treasury may choose to leave a forward exposure unhedged if it believes that a forward price will not yield as much value as accepting the future spot price. But choosing to leave an existing operating cash flow unhedged is vastly different from taking outright speculative positions for speculation's sake. Taking informed but unhedged positions on forward transactions is also a far cry from ignoring currency risks entirely. In any case, treasury's activity should complement and not compete with the firm's other business operations.

10.2 • MANAGING THE CORPORATION'S INTERNATIONAL TRADE

International trade can be riskier than domestic trade because of the greater geographic and cultural distances between buyer and seller. Exporters must take extra precautions to ensure payment from faraway customers. Importers must protect themselves against late shipments, or goods or services of inferior quality. When disputes arise, claimants often must pursue their grievances through foreign legal systems and on the home turf of their trading partners. This section describes how the MNC can manage the costs and risks of cross-border trade and protect itself against trade and legal disputes.

The Legal Environment

A major barrier to international trade is that each nation has jurisdiction over business transactions within its national borders and imposes its own laws on these transactions. Disagreements between parties are difficult to settle because the legal issues span two or more legal jurisdictions. Moreover, there is no single doctrine that defines international commercial law. It is not surprising that cross-border shipments are more difficult to execute than domestic shipments.

> International trade is handicapped by the wide divergence in national legal systems.

Most of the nations in Europe and Latin America use a *civil law* system in which laws are codified as a set of rules. The United Kingdom and most of its former colonies (including the United States) use a *common law* system that relies heavily on the decisions of judges in previous court cases. Civil and common law systems are offshoots of ancient Roman law, differing in their emphasis on legal rules or specific case examples. Many Muslim nations follow a form of Islamic law based on the Koran and other holy scriptures that combines elements of civil law and common law. Communist and socialist countries, such as China and Russia, have historically relied on centrally planned economies that did not recognize private property rights. Laws in these countries are rapidly evolving as their legal systems are adapted to market-based rather than state-based economies. International trade is handicapped by this wide divergence in national legal systems.

More than one-half of international trade is conducted under the terms of the *United Nations Convention on Contracts for the International Sale of Goods (CISG)*. The CISG was created in 1988 to standardize and codify the legal rules for international sales. Nearly 60 countries have ratified the CISG, including Canada, China, Mexico, Russia, the United States, and nearly all the EU countries. Countries that had not ratified the CISG as of June 2002 included the United Kingdom, Japan, Ireland, Brazil, Indonesia, and India.

Managing the Costs and Risks of International Shipping

Cross-border trade can be time-consuming and cumbersome due to the logistics involved in shipping goods from one country to another. The costs and risks of

If something can go
wrong, it will.

international shipments can be reduced through the use of specialists to coordinate the transfer of goods. In many cases, a **freight shipper** (or **freight forwarder**) is used to coordinate the logistics of transportation. These agents select the best mode of transportation and arrange for a particular carrier to handle the physical shipment of goods.

International sales conform to Murphy's Law: "If something can go wrong, it will." For this reason, it is advisable to clearly specify the terms of trade in writing, including who is responsible for insurance coverage, who bears the risk of loss during shipping, who pays for transportation and loading/unloading of the goods, and who is responsible for export/import clearance. Because each of these is customarily specified in writing, cross-border shipments are accompanied by a bewildering array of documentation:

- *Commercial invoice*—a document that describes the merchandise, identifies the buyer and seller, and specifies delivery and payment terms
- *Packing list*—An itemization of the number of packages and contents of a shipment
- *Certificate of origin*—a document certifying the country of origin of the goods, required by some nations
- *Shipper's export declaration*—a document required by some government agencies (e.g., the U.S. Department of Commerce on export shipments valued over $500)
- *Export license*—permission that is required before some goods can be exported
- *Bill of lading*—a contract between the owner of goods (usually an exporter) and a commercial carrier, issued by the carrier when it receives goods for shipment
- *Dock receipt*—a document indicating that the goods have been delivered to a dock for transportation by a carrier
- *Warehouse receipt*—a document indicating that the goods have been delivered from a carrier to a warehouse
- *Inspection certificate*—third-party certification that goods meet certain specifications, sometimes required by the buyer, a bank, or a governmental agency
- *Insurance certificate*—proof of insurance for goods in transit, often required by sales contracts to insure against loss or damage

Arranging physical transportation can be quite time-consuming. Many commercial banks have a shipping subsidiary or affiliate that arranges the carriage of goods for their banking clients. This arrangement reduces shipping and financing costs by facilitating communication between importers, exporters, banks, insurers, and carriers.

Managing the Costs and Risks of International Payments

International trade requires
assurance of timely payment and delivery of goods
or services.

Exporters must have assurance that they will receive payment on the goods that they deliver. Importers must have assurance that they will receive the goods that they have purchased. There are four ways that exporters can arrange for payment:

- Open account
- Cash in advance
- Documentary collections
- Documentary credits

These payment methods have financial implications, as we shall see in a later section.

These payment mechanisms differ in the protection provided to the buyer and seller, as shown in Table 10.1 and Figure 10.1. Which payment terms are adopted in any particular sale depends on industry conventions, the bargaining positions of the buyer and the seller, and the probability and consequences of default.

Open Account. Most domestic sales are made on **open account.** Under an open account arrangement, the seller delivers the goods directly to the buyer. The seller then bills the buyer for the goods under agreed-upon payment terms such as "net 30" (payment is due in 30 days) or "1/10, net 60" (1 percent discount if paid in 10 days, otherwise the net amount is due in 60 days). This arrangement is most convenient for the buyer.

Although sales on open account might attract business, they are otherwise an unattractive payment mechanism for exporters. First, the exporter must pay for the inputs to produce its goods well before it ships the goods and receives final payment. Second, the exporter is exposed to credit risk because the buyer may default on payment. An open account is appropriate only when the buyer and seller have established a long-term relationship and the buyer's credit record is good.

TABLE 10.1
Methods of Payment in International Trade

	Time of payment	Goods available to buyer	Risk to seller	Risk to buyer
Cash in advance	Before shipment	After payment	None (unless legal action is taken by buyer)	Relies on seller to ship goods as agreed
Open account	After buyer receives shipment as agreed	Before payment	Relies on buyer to pay account as agreed	None (unless legal action is taken by seller)
Documentary collections				
Sight draft	Payable on presentation of draft to buyer	After payment	Buyer may refuse to pay when documents are presented—goods must be shipped home or sold under duress in the foreign country	Same as letter of credit
Time draft	On maturity of draft	Before payment	Relies on buyer to pay draft; otherwise same as sight draft	Legal consequences if an accepted draft is not honored by buyer
Documentary credits				
Letter of credit (L/C)	Payable when shipment is made	After payment	Low risk if seller meets terms of L/C that has been issued or confirmed by a creditworthy bank; risk of nonpayment due to currency unavailability	Relies on seller to ship goods described in trade documents; L/Cs are more time-consuming to arrange than other payment methods

FIGURE 10.1
The Risks of International Payment Methods

Seller's Perspective	Payment Mechanism	Buyer's Perspective
Highest risk trade terms		Most advantageous trade terms
⇑	Open account Draft Letter of credit Cash in advance	⇓
Lowest risk trade terms		Least advantageous trade terms

Cash in Advance. **Cash in advance** requires the buyer to pay for the goods prior to shipment. This protects the seller, although the cost of this protection may be a reduced sales price. Cash in advance is least convenient for the buyer, because the buyer must trust the seller to deliver the goods in a timely manner and in good condition. Cash in advance is used when the buyer has a poor credit history or where demand far outstrips supply. It is seldom used when the buyer and seller have a long and satisfactory (dispute-free) relationship.

Documentary Collections. Commercial banks are in the business of assuming credit and collection risks. Commercial banks are also in the business of facilitating trade, especially for buyers and sellers from different countries. By bringing one or more commercial banks into the transaction to assist in shipment and collections, the total costs of international transactions can be reduced.

The documentary collection is the instrument most frequently used as an international payment mechanism. In a documentary collection, the seller draws a **draft** (also called a **trade bill** or **bill of exchange**) that instructs the *drawee* (the buyer or its bank) to pay the seller according to the terms of the draft. A **sight draft** is payable on demand, whereas a **time draft** is payable at a specified future time. The drawee is liable to the seller if it accepts the draft by signing it. A time draft that is drawn on and accepted by the buyer is called a **trade acceptance**. A time draft that is drawn on and accepted by a commercial bank is called a **banker's acceptance**.

> Most international trade is conducted using drafts.

The draft and the trade documents are then presented to a commercial bank. If the buyer and seller cannot agree on a single bank to serve as a go-between, they can each retain a bank to represent their own individual interests. The trade documents giving control over the goods are released to the buyer only when the buyer or its commercial bank pays the draft or accepts the draft for payment.

> Bankers' acceptances are time drafts drawn on and accepted by commercial banks.

Bankers' acceptances are especially useful in international trade, because they substitute the credit risk of the accepting bank for that of the buyer. An exporter holding a banker's acceptance can sell it at a discount to reduce its accounts receivable balance and accelerate payment on the sale. The discount from the face value of the acceptance depends on the time value of money and the reputation of the accepting bank.

Selling a banker's acceptance is only possible if the banker's acceptance is **negotiable**. To be negotiable, a banker's acceptance must meet five requirements: (1) It must be in writing, (2) a representative of the bank must sign it, (3) it must contain an unconditional payment guarantee upon receipt of the trade documents, (4) it must be payable on demand (a sight draft) or at a specified time (a time draft), and (5) it must be payable either to order or bearer.

Figure 10.2 illustrates how trade can be accomplished through a banker's acceptance. After negotiating the terms of trade (A), the exporter sends an invoice to the importer (B). The importer writes a time draft drawn on its bank (C). The bank accepts the draft by signing it and forwards it to the exporter (D). The exporter then initiates shipment of the goods (E). Upon receipt of the goods, the warehouse signs the trade documents indicating that the shipment meets the specified terms of trade and is in good condition (F). The trade documents are then sent to the importer's bank by the exporter (G). Upon receipt of the trade documents, the bank either

FIGURE 10.2
Payment Through a Bankers' Acceptance

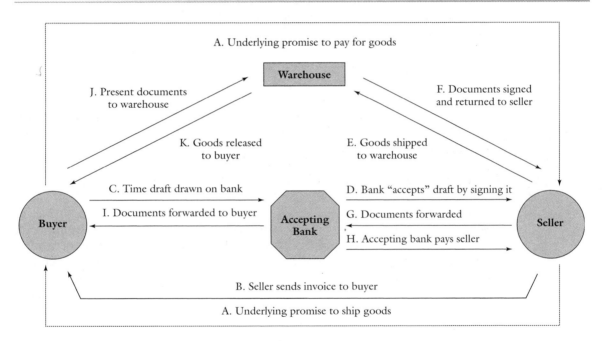

A. Buyer and seller negotiate trade terms.
B. Seller sends an invoice to the buyer with the agreed-upon trade terms.
C. Buyer writes a time draft written on a creditworthy bank agreeable to both parties.
D. Bank "accepts" the draft by signing it and thereby guarantees payment upon receipt of the trade documents.
E. Goods are shipped to a warehouse in the buyer's country.
F. Shipping documents are signed by the warehouse and returned to the seller.
G. Completed trade documents are sent to the accepting bank.
H. Bank honors its acceptance and pays seller.
I. Issuing bank forwards trade documents to the buyer.
J. Buyer presents documents to the warehouse.
K. Buyer collects goods from warehouse.

sends payment to the exporter or stands by its promise to pay at the specified future date (H). The trade documents are forwarded to the importer (I). Finally, the importer presents the trade documents to the warehouse (J) and collects the goods (K). The timing of the payment from the importer to the bank depends on the importer's cash flow needs, its credit standing, and its relationship with the bank.

Documentary Credits. The biggest risks faced by an exporter are that the buyer will default on payment, pay too little in an attempt to renegotiate the terms of trade, or pay too late. These risks can be greatly reduced by having the importer's bank issue a **letter of credit** that guarantees payment upon presentation of the trade documents specified in the letter of credit. Like a banker's acceptance, the letter of credit protects the exporter because payment is guaranteed by a commercial bank rather than the importer.

> A letter of credit guarantees payment upon presentation of the trade documents.

The *Uniform Rules and Usances of the International Chamber of Commerce* describes two legal principles surrounding the international letter of credit:

- *Independence principle*—the letter of credit is independent of the sales transaction
- *Strict compliance principle*—the issuing bank must honor the letter of credit upon receipt of the documents specified in the letter of credit

The independence and strict compliance principles protect the right of the exporter to receive payment under the terms of the letter of credit. This substitutes the credit standing of the issuing bank for that of the buyer.[2]

A letter of credit is termed *irrevocable* if payment is conditional upon receipt of the trade documents identified in the letter of credit. If the letter of credit stipulates additional conditions under which the buyer or the issuing bank can declare the letter of credit invalid, the letter of credit is called *revocable*. Nearly all letters of credit are irrevocable. In fact, if the letter of credit says nothing about revocability, it is assumed to be irrevocable under international law. With the exception of cash in advance, the irrevocable letter of credit provides exporters with the highest level of assurance that payment will be made.

Under an *unconfirmed letter of credit*, the buyer instructs its bank to issue a letter of credit that promises the exporter that payment will be made by the issuing bank upon receipt of the documents specified in the letter of credit. Whether the issuing bank requires the buyer to pay for the letter of credit in advance or at some later date depends on the buyer's creditworthiness and banking relationship. In an unconfirmed letter of credit, the exporter is still exposed to the risk that the issuing bank will default or delay payment. This risk can be substantial in some developing countries.

One way to mitigate the default risk of the issuing bank is for the letter of credit to be confirmed by an advisory bank selected by the exporter. The advisory bank confirms that the terms of trade, required documents, and letter of credit are in good order and that the issuing bank is in good financial health. Upon confirming that this is the case, the advisory bank promises payment to the exporter regardless of whether the issuing bank honors its obligation. The letter of credit is then called a *confirmed letter of credit*. Payment terms on a confirmed letter of credit primarily depend on the default risk of the bank originally issuing the letter of credit. The sequence of events in international trade under a confirmed letter of credit is similar to that of a banker's acceptance. An illustration appears in Figure 10.3.

---

2 Under U.S. law, the buyer can prevent the issuing bank from honoring the letter of credit if the buyer can demonstrate fraud in the transaction (for example, shipment of substitute or inferior goods). This is the only exception to the independence and strict compliance principles. Consequently, commercial banks have a stake in ensuring that the terms of trade are met by both parties.

FIGURE 10.3
Payment Through a Bank Letter of Credit (L/C)

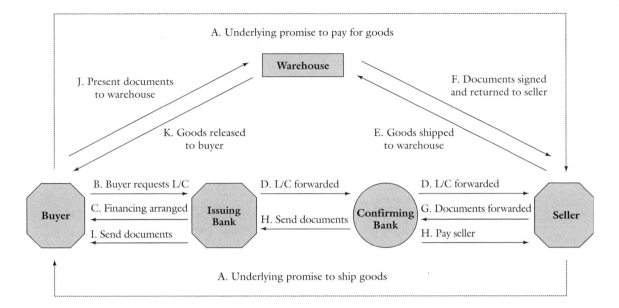

A. Buyer and seller negotiate trade terms.
B. Importer applies for a *letter of credit* (L/C) from an *issuing bank*.
C. Issuing bank arranges payment with buyer, usually through a line of credit.
D. Letter of credit is sent to *confirming bank* in the seller's country and then to seller.
E. Goods are shipped to a warehouse in the buyer's country.
F. Shipping documents are signed by the warehouse and returned to the seller.
G. Completed documents are sent to the confirming bank.
H. Confirming bank pays seller and sends documents to issuing bank.
I. Issuing bank forwards documents to the buyer.
J. Buyer presents documents to the warehouse.
K. Buyer collects goods from warehouse.

Countertrade (Barter)

Countertrade refers to a variety of barter-like techniques used to exchange goods or services without the use of cash. Barter is easiest to arrange when the values of the goods being exchanged are the same and the shipments take place at the same time.

> Countertrade involves an exchange of goods or services without the use of cash.

Countries with limited currency reserves often use countertrade to promote foreign trade or attract key industries. Companies from industrialized countries participate in countertrade to gain a foothold in developing markets and to diversify their operations. Countertrade is difficult to negotiate and execute, but it is sometimes the only way for countries without hard currency to pay for manufactured goods or MNCs to gain access to developing markets. The two most common forms of countertrade are

- *Counterpurchase.* Counterpurchase is a barter arrangement in which one contract is conditional upon fulfillment of another. Counterpurchase arrangements account for nearly half of all countertrade activity.

Market Update

The Large Print Giveth and the Small Print Taketh Away

Letters of credit have facilitated cross-border trade for many centuries. Yet, they are not without risk. In 1995, many Chinese importers postponed payments on letters of credit or insisted on renegotiating contracts over such apparently innocuous problems as misspellings, imprecise wordings, or even the color of the official stamps.* If a country's banks fail to honor letters of credit, it raises the costs of doing business for local companies and their foreign partners.

*"Exporters Angry as Chinese Postpone Payments," *London Financial Times* (September 1, 1995), p. 10.

- *Offset.* An offset is countertrade required as a condition of trade. Offsets are estimated to account for about 25 percent of countertrade activity.

Less commonly used countertrade arrangements include

- *Buy-back.* A buy-back is an agreement to build a turnkey plant in exchange for specific amounts of the plant's output over a period of time. For example, DaimlerChrysler could build an automobile plant in China and provide training to local employees in exchange for a certain number of vehicles over several years.
- *Switch trade.* Switch trade is a counterpurchase agreement in which a seller of goods has the right to sell its claim to another party.
- *Compensation trade.* Compensation trade is a form of barter in which one of the flows is partly in goods and partly in hard currency.

Note that these arrangements are not mutually exclusive. For example, a counterpurchase agreement could be in the form of compensation trade.

It is difficult to determine the magnitude of countertrade activity because countertrade is not reported as business income in many countries. Estimates of the importance of countertrade to international commerce vary widely, typically falling in a range from 10 to 40 percent of all cross-border trade. Some MNCs with a high proportion of business in developing countries rely heavily on countertrade. For example, PepsiCo has traded soft drinks for Stolichnaya vodka, and Coca-Cola has traded syrup for Lada automobiles from Russia. Countertrade is most suited to large firms with diversified markets and products and experience in international markets. These companies are better able to assume and manage the costs and risks of countertrade.

http://www.
irta.com

The *International Reciprocal Trade Association*, a trade group representing barter exchange companies that facilitate trade in bartered goods and services, estimates that $8.8 billion was bartered during 2001. Barter is likely to continue to be useful to companies and countries operating in markets that lack hard currencies.

10.3 • FINANCING THE CORPORATION'S INTERNATIONAL TRADE

Money does not grow on trees, so someone must finance a sale of goods between the time an order is made and the time the goods are received by the buyer. When a sale is paid for in advance, the buyer is providing financing for the seller. When a sale is made on open account, the seller is providing the financing to the buyer. Some international payment methods, such as bankers' acceptances and letters of credit, allow someone other than the buyer or seller to provide financing for international trade. These financing alternatives are described here and summarized in Table 10.2.

The Exporter's Perspective

The corporation's sources and uses of cash can be categorized as follows:

- Sources of cash
  - A decrease in an asset account
  - An increase in a liability account
- Uses of cash
  - An increase in an asset account
  - A decrease in a liability account

As an exporter manufactures goods, work-in-process inventory increases. An increase in inventory is an increase in an asset account and therefore a use of cash. When a sale is booked on open account, the asset is transferred out of inventory and into accounts receivable. If sale is made through a trade or banker's acceptance, the acceptance is a negotiable instrument and therefore marketable. Whether the sale resides in accounts receivable or in marketable securities, the exporter is now in a position to recoup its investment in working capital and capture a gain on the sale.

TABLE 10.2
Methods of Payment and the Financing of International Trade

	Seller's Perspective	**Buyer's Perspective**
Cash in advance	Financing provided by buyer	Because the transaction is not secured, financing usually must come from some other source
Open account	Accounts receivable can be discounted to the bank or sold to a factor; long-term receivables can be sold to a forfaiter	Financing provided by seller
Documentary collections		
Trade acceptance	Trade acceptances can be discounted, or sold to a bank at a discount to face value, either with or without recourse	In an accepted time draft, the seller extends credit to the buyer
Bankers' acceptance	Bankers' acceptances are negotiable and can be sold at a discount to face value	The buyer's bank charges a fee in the form of a compensating balance, a required line of credit, or an outright transaction fee
Documentary credits		
Letter of credit (L/C)	In the United States, exporters do not borrow against or discount L/Cs; in some other countries, L/Cs can be discounted or used as collateral	L/Cs tie up the buyer's borrowing capacity; bank fees for unconfirmed L/Cs range from 0.125% to 0.5% of the face amount; confirmed L/Cs add another 0.05% to 0.5%

International payment methods create financing sources in one of the following ways:

- A decrease in a current asset account
  - Sell short-term accounts receivable at a discount to face value
  - Sell medium-term or long-term accounts receivable at a discount to face value
  - Sell a marketable security, such as a trade or banker's acceptance, at a discount to face value
- An increase in a current liability account
  - Borrow against an asset, such as accounts receivable or inventory

Each of these sources of financing has an opportunity cost. As with other financial transactions, the exporter must shop around for the best value. The least-cost financing method in any particular circumstance depends on competitive conditions in the exporter's goods and financial markets, and the exporter's borrowing capacity and banking relationships.

Sell a Current Asset. Credit risks are high on export sales, and collections can be costly. For this reason, many exporters are unwilling or unable to support an in-house credit and collections department. One alternative is for the exporter to **factor** or sell receivables at a discount to face value to a third party that is better able to bear the costs and risks of credit assessments and collections. These third parties are called *factors*, and include commercial banks and other financial institutions. Most factoring is done on a nonrecourse basis, although the factor may insist on recourse when credit risks are high.

> Factoring is the sale of a receivable at a discount to face value.

Factors can have an advantage over in-house credit departments in bearing international credit and collection risks. Because of the volume of trade that they service, factors can maintain greater access to credit information on foreign customers and can diversify credit and collection risks over a broader customer base. Factors' comparative advantage in credit assessments and collections is greatest over small firms with a high proportion of export sales and geographically dispersed customers.

Forfaiting resembles factoring but involves medium- to long-term receivables with maturities of one year or longer. In a typical forfaiting arrangement, a commercial bank purchases a medium-term receivable with a 1- to 5-year maturity from an exporter at a discount and without recourse. The bank provides the financing and assumes the credit and collection risks for the exporter. The receivable is typically denominated in an actively traded currency, such as the U.S. dollar, British pound, or euro.

Forfaiting is commonly used by European Union banks to finance export sales to eastern and central Europe. Many financial markets in these markets are still developing, and importers can find it difficult to obtain financing from local sources. EU manufacturers can increase sales by arranging financing for their eastern European customers. Political risks are high in some of these countries, and importers can be poor commercial risks as well. In these circumstances, neither importers nor exporters are well positioned to assume the risks of international trade. Through long years of experience in these markets, EU banks have developed expertise in estimating and managing commercial and political risks in eastern and central Europe.

> Discounting is the sale of a trade acceptance at a discount to face value.

A trade acceptance is a time draft that a buyer draws on itself. Commercial banks are willing to purchase trade acceptances at a discount to face value. This factoring process, known as **discounting**, allows exporters to sell their trade acceptances and hence accelerate receipt of this source of cash. Discounting may be done with or without recourse. Trade acceptances discounted with recourse require the seller to pay the bank the face value of the draft should the buyer fail to pay the bill when due. Trade acceptances discounted without recourse release the seller from this responsibility. The bank assumes the credit risk on trade acceptances discounted without recourse, so bank fees and interest rates on discounts without recourse are higher than on acceptances discounted with recourse.

A banker's acceptance is a time draft drawn on a commercial bank. When the bank accepts the draft, it promises to pay the holder a stated amount on a specified future date. For this service, banks charge a fee that is taken out of the face value of the acceptance at maturity. Maturities range up to 180 days on bankers' acceptances. The outstanding balance of bankers' acceptances is greater than $100 billion and finances around one quarter of U.S. international trade.

Like trade acceptances, bankers' acceptances are negotiable instruments that can be sold at a discount to face value. The size of the discount reflects the time value of money and the credit risk of the accepting bank. Discount rates on prime bankers' acceptances are near the discount rates on prime commercial paper. For large firms with access to the commercial paper market, the cost of commercial paper (including placement fees and back-up lines of credit) is frequently lower than the cost of a banker's acceptance. Small and medium-sized firms without access to the commercial paper market are more likely to use bankers' acceptances to finance their international trade.

The costs and risks of a trade or banker's acceptance can be reduced by insuring it against commercial and political risks through national or international trade insurance agencies, such as the World Bank's *Multilateral Investment Guarantee Agency* or the U.S. government's *Export-Import Bank (Eximbank)*. These agencies provide guarantees and insurance against credit and political risks for companies engaged in international trade.

http://www.
miga.org

http://www.
eximbank.info

Borrow Against a Current Asset. An exporter can lower its financing costs by using current assets as collateral. Accounts receivable and inventory balances are often used as collateral to reduce the interest cost on bank lines of credit and short-term loans. Similarly, marketable securities and bank demand deposits can be used as compensating balances to reduce the risk of nonpayment to the bank on short-term borrowings. The use of compensating balances or collateral provides insurance to the bank and thereby reduces the costs charged by the bank.

In some countries, such as Hong Kong, letters of credit can be discounted or used as collateral for bank borrowings. In the United States, letters of credit are not typically discounted or used as collateral.

The Importer's Perspective

The most convenient method of payment for the importer is for the exporter to extend credit by allowing purchase on open account. The least convenient method of payment for the importer is cash in advance. This requires that the buyer obtain a source of cash prior to purchase, either by reducing an asset account or increasing a liability account. Payment of cash in advance may be undesirable or even impossible for some importers, in which case other sources of financing are needed.

In an accepted trade draft, the seller extends credit to the buyer. This credit does not come free of charge; the seller will try to cover shipping, credit, and collection costs in the payment terms offered to the buyer. The terms agreed to in a banker's acceptance include these costs, as well as any bank fees, lines of credit, or compensating balance requirements that the bank demands for accepting the draft.

Letters of credit also tie up the importer's borrowing capacity. Bank fees on unconfirmed letters of credit range from 0.125 to 0.5 percent of the face amount of the credit. Another 0.05 to 0.5 percent is charged if the letter of credit is confirmed by a bank in the seller's country. Whether the buyer or seller ultimately bears the shipping and financing costs is determined by their respective bargaining positions and abilities.

The All-In Cost of Export Financing

All-in cost includes all cash flows associated with a transaction.

The **all-in cost** of export financing, such as a discounted draft, includes the discount rate on the draft along with any bank fees and insurance premiums. To identify the all-in cost, simply identify all cash flows associated with the transaction on a time line.

As an example, suppose a 1 percent acceptance fee is charged on a 6-month banker's acceptance with a face value of $1 million. The fee, equal to $(0.01)(\$1,000,000) = \$10,000$, is taken out of the face value at maturity. This acceptance fee may well be worth paying, because it greatly reduces the credit risk of the receivable to the exporter. The holder of the acceptance receives $990,000 at maturity.

An exporter can convert this banker's acceptance into cash by selling it on a discount basis, much like a U.S. Treasury bill. If the current discount rate on prime banker's acceptances is 8 percent compounded semiannually (or 4 percent per six months), then the exporter will receive $(\$990,000)/(1.04) = \$951,923$ immediately.

If the exporter's opportunity cost on accounts receivable financing is 10 percent compounded semiannually (or 5 percent per six months), then the exporter is better off selling the acceptance to the bank at the lower 8 percent rate. At the 10 percent discount rate, the receivable is only worth $(\$990,000)/(1.05) = \$942,857$. Selling the acceptance to the bank for $951,923 results in a gain of $9,066 in net present value to the exporter.

The all-in cost of trade financing includes the acceptance fee on the banker's acceptance. Without the acceptance fee, the exporter would have received the $1 million face value of the receivable (assuming the buyer has no credit risk). If the exporter insists on a banker's acceptance (and incurs the 1 percent acceptance fee) and then sells the acceptance for $951,923 (incurring a 4 percent semiannual opportunity cost), it forgoes the $1 million face value of the receivable. The resulting cash flows look like this:

$951,923

−$1,000,000

The all-in cost of this acceptance to the exporter is

$$(\$1,000,000/\$951,923) - 1 = 0.0505$$

or 5.05 percent per six months. This is equivalent to a 10.10 percent annual cost compounded semiannually. The effective annual cost is $(1.0505)^2 - 1 = 0.1036$, or 10.36 percent. This includes the 1 percent semiannual cost of obtaining the acceptance from the bank and the 4 percent semiannual cost of discounting the acceptance with the bank. The all-in cost of other financing methods can be found in a similar manner.

10.4 • MANAGING THE MULTINATIONAL CORPORATION'S CASH FLOWS

Treasury's management of the multinational corporation's cash flows has both an internal and an external dimension. Activities in this area include

- Cash management

- Multinational netting
- Forecasting funds needs
- Managing relations between the operating divisions of the firm and with external investors, partners, suppliers, and customers
  - Setting or negotiating transfer prices between the firm's operating divisions
  - Determining the required return (or hurdle rate) on new investments
  - Credit assessment and approval

Individual business units transact with other business units within the firm as products are moved through the corporate value chain. Treasury serves as a central clearinghouse for the transfer payments associated with these transactions, and treasury is sometimes involved in setting or negotiating internal transfer prices on these intrafirm transactions. Consolidating all of these operations in a central clearinghouse allows the treasury to monitor and forecast the company's funds needs, minimize transactions costs, manage exposures to operating and financial risks, and take advantage of market opportunities as they arise.

Cash Management

Multinational Netting. To effectively manage the corporation's financial resources, the MNC's treasury department must implement a cash management system that tracks cash receipts and disbursements within the company and with the company's external partners. The MNC's treasury has several cash management tools at its disposal. Chief among these tools is a process called **multinational netting** in which intrafirm transfers are minimized by "netting" offsetting cash flows in various currencies.[3]

> Multinational netting of transactions eliminates offsetting cash flows.

Forecasting Funds Needs. By tracking cash flows to and from the firm's external suppliers and customers and serving as a central clearinghouse for intrafirm transactions, the MNC's treasury is in an excellent position to forecast the funds needs of the corporation. With accurate forecasts of funds needs, the treasury can ensure that each operating division has sufficient funds to run its operations. When cash is in short supply, the treasury can use its banking relationships to draw upon its lines of credit. When there is temporarily excess cash in the system, the treasury can pay down obligations or invest in money market instruments in the currencies of its choice. By forecasting funds needs, the treasury can use multinational netting both across operating divisions and over time to minimize the number and size of transactions in the external financial markets. By consolidating intrafirm transactions and serving as a single source of funds, the treasury can obtain funds from the source that minimizes the firm's cost of capital.

Managing Internal and External Relations

Credit Management. Managing international credit relations is a good deal harder than managing domestic relations because of cross-border differences in laws, business and accounting conventions, banking relations, and political systems. The risks of multinational credits can be managed through the payment mechanisms and trade finance vehicles described earlier in this chapter.

Transfer Pricing. In most countries, **transfer prices** on intrafirm transactions are required to be set at market value.[4] When market prices are not available—such as on

---

3 Multinational netting is discussed in more detail in the next chapter.

4 National tax codes (e.g., Section 486 of the U.S. Internal Revenue Code) require transfer prices be set as if they were arms-length transactions between unrelated parties.

transfers of intermediate goods or services—the corporate treasury has some latitude in setting transfer prices. All else constant, the MNC has a tax incentive to shift revenues toward low-tax jurisdictions and shift expenses toward high-tax jurisdictions.

Transfer pricing decisions should be made to benefit the corporation as a whole. Nevertheless, individual units are subject to performance standards and have incentives to maximize sales prices and minimize costs on transfers of goods or services. This can create disputes within the MNC if headquarters determines transfer prices purely for tax reasons and not according to the value added at each stage of the production process. Treasury must ensure that the managers of the individual business units are not unjustly rewarded or penalized by transfer prices that diverge from market prices.

Identifying Divisional Costs of Capital. Disputes also arise among operating divisions over hurdle rates on new investments. Finance theory states that managers should use a discount rate that reflects the opportunity cost of capital in order to maximize shareholder wealth. However, managers are often more interested in maximizing the corporate resources over which they have control. This can result in artificially low divisional hurdle rates as managers try to justify new investments in their divisions. The chief financial officer must insist that market-based hurdle rates are used within the company in the evaluation of new investment proposals. Treasury is in contact with capital markets on a continuing basis, and so is in a good position to identify required returns on new investments. Treasury can also be an independent arbiter as it is relatively detached from the managerial fiefdoms of the operating divisions.

10.5 • RISK MANAGEMENT IN THE MULTINATIONAL CORPORATION

Risk management is a central responsibility of the multinational treasury. Some risks are faced by any corporation—domestic or multinational. These include loss of income due to natural or manmade disasters, labor strikes, or occupational health or safety hazards. Businesses protect themselves from these risks with a variety of strategies and products, including fire and property/casualty insurance.

Other risks are unique to corporations with multinational operations, particularly currency and foreign political risks. Whereas political risk affects all of the major disciplines of business (marketing, human and operational resource management, and logistics), currency risk is distinctly financial in nature.

The Five Steps of a Currency Risk Management Program

Currency risk management begins with a forecast of future exchange rates and volatilities. Given these forecasts, the impact of potential exchange rate changes on operating cash flows is estimated from past and expected future exchange rate sensitivities. The procedure is as follows:

1. Identify those currencies to which the firm is exposed, as well as the distribution of future exchange rates for each of these currencies.
2. Estimate the firm's sensitivity to changes in these currency values.
3. Determine the desirability of hedging, given the firm's estimated risk exposures and risk management policy.
4. Evaluate the cost/benefit performance of each hedging alternative, given the forecasted exchange rate distributions. Select and implement the hedging instrument or strategy.

5. Monitor the firm's evolving exposures and revisit these steps as necessary.

Management of currency risk should not be a one-time affair. Exposure to currency risk changes over time with changes in exchange rates and the geographic and product mix of the firm. Managers should monitor and periodically reassess the firm's risk management policies, strategies, and positions in light of changing market and company conditions.

Estimates of exposure can be based on the income statement or the balance sheet. Estimates of the operating exposures of revenues and operating expenses can help the financial manager understand the components of the firm's overall exposure to currency risk. In combination with the net exposure of monetary assets and liabilities, cash flow-based estimates of exposure can assist the financial manager in formulating a plan that manages exposures and can react to changing conditions.

> Managers should proact rather than just react.

Estimates of exposure based on the past relationship between operating cash flows and exchange rates are appropriate only if the historical relationship is expected to persist into the future. Estimates based on past outcomes will not work for evolving businesses or newly acquired business units. These situations call for a heavier-than-usual dose of managerial judgment.

To be proactive rather than reactive, managers should try to answer these questions:

- What is likely to happen to exchange rates and to our business in the future?
- How has the relationship between exchange rates and operating cash flows changed?
- How might our competitors respond to a change in exchange rates?

Several *decision support tools* are useful in answering these questions, including scenario analysis, Monte Carlo simulation, and decision trees.

- *Scenario analysis.* Scenario analysis is a process of asking "What if?" In the context of exposure to currency risk, scenario analysis consists of asking "What if exchange rates change?" Scenario analysis answers this question by evaluating the impact of a few representative exchange rate scenarios on the firm.
- *Monte Carlo simulation.* Monte Carlo simulation is similar to scenario analysis, but uses the entire distribution of exchange rates rather than just a few representative scenarios.[5]
- *Decision trees.* Decision trees can be used in conjunction with scenario analysis or simulation to assess possible competitive responses to new business conditions, perhaps arising from currency fluctuations. Decision trees are graphical representations of sequential decisions that allow managers to ask questions such as "What if exchange rates appreciate and we follow this course of action?" or "What if exchange rates appreciate and our competitors respond in this way?"

These decision support tools encourage the manager to try to anticipate possible future events, rather than simply reacting to unfortunate circumstances after the fact. They can help in establishing proactive strategies for dealing with an uncertain future.

To Hedge or Not to Hedge: Formulating a Risk Management Policy

To ensure that the corporate treasury's hedging and risk management strategies are consistent with the overall goals of the corporation, top management must be actively

---

5 The use of simulation in currency risk management is described in Lewent and Kearney, "Identifying, Measuring, and Hedging Currency Risk at Merck," *Journal of Applied Corporate Finance* (1990).

involved in formulating risk management policy and monitoring its implementation. This sounds obvious, but most derivative-related losses result from a failure to follow this simple rule. A framework for characterizing the corporation's risk management policy appears in Figure 10.4.

The MNC must first decide whether it will take a passive or an active approach to hedging its exposures to currency risk. *Passive management* does not try to anticipate currency movements, assuming instead that financial markets are informationally efficient. Passive policies often apply the same hedging rule to each exposure. For example, if corporate policy is to hedge 50 percent of net yen exposures at each maturity, then this rule can be uniformly applied regardless of market or company conditions or the value of the yen.

Passive hedging strategies can be applied in either a static or a dynamic manner. A *static approach* hedges exposures as they are incurred and then leaves these hedges in place until maturity. A static approach is appropriate only for companies with infrequent and easily identifiable transaction exposures. More effective but time-consuming is a *dynamic approach* that periodically reviews underlying exposures and hedges and revises these positions as appropriate. Dynamic strategies can adapt to changing market or company conditions, but are nevertheless applied with little managerial discretion following risk management policy.

Active management selectively hedges currency risk exposures depending on the financial manager's market view, so that actual positions can diverge from the MNC's average or benchmark position.[6] Active positions give rise to the risk that hedged return will differ from the benchmark return. For example, overall policy might call for a benchmark position in a forward contract for 50 percent of the net yen exposure. Active management might diverge from this benchmark when the yen is expected to appreciate or depreciate, in which case the returns and risks are likely to differ from the benchmark as well. The performance of active currency risk management should be measured against the benchmark position.

FIGURE 10.4
Risk Management Policy

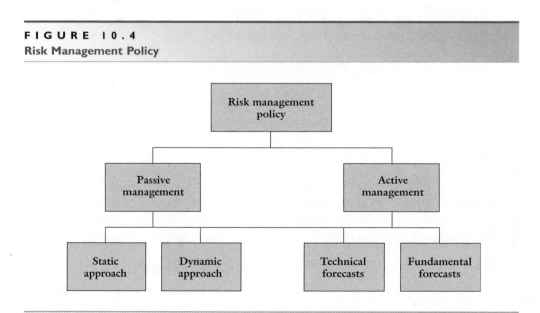

6 See Thomas, "Active Management," *Journal of Portfolio Management* (Winter 2000).

Two forecasting approaches are available to managers who think they possess the expertise and risk tolerance to actively manage foreign exchange exposures. **Technical analysis** uses recent exchange rate movements to predict the direction of future exchange rate movements. Technical models have achieved some success in forecasting near-term exchange rates. **Fundamental analysis** uses macroeconomic data (such as money supply or GNP growth) to forecast long-term exchange rates. Although technical and fundamental forecasts sometimes have difficulty beating spot (forward) exchange rates as predictors of short-term (long-term) spot exchange rates, they are nevertheless popular with practitioners.

Derivatives Usage by U.S. Corporations

Bodnar, Hayt, and Marston surveyed risk management practices at U.S. firms.[7] About half of the respondents in manufacturing and service industries used derivatives for risk management purposes. Derivatives usage was strongly related to firm size, with the following usage rates:

> Large firms are more likely to use derivatives.

Market Update

Recommendations of the G-30 Global Derivatives Study Group*

The Group of 30 established a Global Derivatives Study Group to study the use of derivatives and recommend risk management guidelines. The Group recommends that each dealer or end-user of derivatives does the following:

- Determine at the highest level of policy and decision making the scope of its involvement in derivatives activities.
- Value derivatives positions at market, at least for risk management purposes.
- Quantify market risk under adverse market conditions against limits, perform stress simulations, and forecast cash investing and funding needs.
- Assess the credit risk arising from derivatives activities based on frequent measures of current and potential exposure against credit limits.
- Work with other participants to ensure legal enforceability of derivatives transactions within and across jurisdictions.
- Establish market and credit-risk management functions with clear authority, independent of the dealing function.
- Voluntarily adopt accounting and disclosure practices for international harmonization and greater transparency, pending the arrival of international standards.

Although most of these points are common sense, the consequences of not following these recommendations can be severe. Derivatives-related failures, such as the Barings Bank, can be directly traced to a failure to enforce one or more of these guidelines.

*The Group of 30 (G30) Global Derivatives Study Group, *Derivatives: Practices and Principles* (1993).

---

7 Bodnar, Hayt, and Marston, "1998 Wharton Survey of Financial Risk Management by U.S. Non-Financial Firms," *Financial Management* (1998).

- Large firms (83 percent)
- Medium-sized firms (45 percent)
- Small firms (12 percent)

Among those firms using derivatives, usage rates depended on the type of risk exposure. Currency risk was the most commonly hedged risk, closely followed by interest rate risk:

- Currency risk (83 percent)
- Interest rate risk (76 percent)
- Commodity price risk (56 percent)

Firms hedged transaction exposures to currency risk before operating or translation exposures, probably because transaction exposures are easier to identify and to hedge

---

 ## Market Update

Barings Bank (In for a Penny—In for a Pound)

As one of the world's more venerable merchant banks, London's Barings Bank had frequently been involved in affairs of state during its distinguished 233-year history. It had bankrolled kings, wars, business magnates, and the Louisiana Purchase for the U.S. government. Its owners and top management boasted five hereditary peerages and nearly half a billion dollars in owners' equity.

Despite this long and distinguished history, Barings Bank unexpectedly collapsed over the weekend of February 23–24, 1995. Nick Leeson, a 28-year-old Barings trader based in Singapore, had accumulated massive positions in Nikkei stock index futures trading on the Singapore International Monetary Exchange (SIMEX) and the Osaka futures exchange. When the market moved against him, Leeson doubled his bets in the futures markets and added index options to his position in the hopes of a market turnaround. On February 25, 1995, Barings announced that it had lost $1.4 billion on these contracts—more than three times Barings' book equity. The Bank of England then placed Barings into bankruptcy proceedings.

Industry practice is to closely monitor market exposures and isolate the trading and bookkeeping functions. Contrary to industry practice, Barings had placed Leeson in charge of both trading and bookkeeping in the Singapore office and had then failed to monitor Leeson's trading activities. This recipe for disaster allowed Leeson to hide the size of Barings' Nikkei exposures from top management in London, even though the size of Barings' exposure was common knowledge on the Osaka and Singapore exchanges.

Had Leeson acted properly as an agent of Barings Bank, he would have promptly disclosed his initial losses to headquarters. He probably would have lost his job in the process, but Barings could have recognized the initial losses and then continued in business. Instead, Leeson gambled everything on an unlikely market turnaround. If Leeson's gamble had paid off, he might have been lauded by his colleagues and the press as a financial genius. Instead, he received a 6½ year sentence from a Singapore court of justice.

The principal/agent relationship is prone to trouble during financial distress. The fact that Leeson was speculating rather than hedging served to reinforce the chasm between the incentives of the agent (Leeson) and the principal (Barings' owners). Without proper monitoring, Leeson was free to run amok and, ultimately, lead Barings to ruin.

with derivatives. Firms tended not to hedge the full amount of their exposures. The average amount hedged was less than 50 percent for all types of currency risk exposures, including transaction exposure (40 to 49 percent), operating exposure (7 percent), and translation exposure (12 percent). A large majority of derivatives users (89 percent) centralized or coordinated their currency risk management activities.

> Most firms centralize their risk management activities.

10.6 • SUMMARY

The goal of treasury management is to allow the core business activities of the corporation to attain their potentials. To add to corporate value, the officers of the multinational treasury must do the following:

- Determine the firm's overall financial goals.
- Manage the corporation's international transactions.
- Arrange financing for the corporation's international transactions.
- Consolidate and manage the financial flows of the firm.
- Identify, measure, and manage the firm's risk exposures.

The first four of these functions are discussed in this chapter. The last function—risk management—is important enough to warrant separate treatment and is covered in the next several chapters.

KEY TERMS

all-in cost
banker's or trade acceptance
cash in advance
countertrade
discounting
draft (trade bill, bill of exchange)
factoring
forfaiting

freight shippers (freight forwarders)
fundamental or technical analysis
letter of credit
multinational netting
negotiable acceptance
open account
sight or time draft
transfer prices

CONCEPTUAL QUESTIONS

10.1 What is multinational treasury management?
10.2 What function does a firm's strategic business plan perform?
10.3 Why is international trade more difficult than domestic trade?
10.4 Why use a freight forwarder?
10.5 Describe four methods of payment on international sales.
10.6 What is a bankers' acceptance, and how is it used in international trade?
10.7 What is discounting, and how is it used in international trade?
10.8 How is factoring different from forfaiting?
10.9 What is countertrade? When is it most likely to be used?
10.10 What is multinational netting?

10.11 How can the treasury division assist in managing relations among the operating units of the multinational corporation?

10.12 What are the five steps in a currency risk management program?

10.13 What is the difference between passive and active currency risk management?

10.14 What is the difference between technical and fundamental analysis?

10.15 Are small, medium, or large firms most likely to use derivatives to hedge currency risk? How do firms benchmark their hedges?

PROBLEMS

10.1 Fruit of the Loom, Inc., has a bankers' acceptance drawn on Banque Paribas with a face value of $10 million due in 90 days. Paribas will take out an acceptance fee of $10,000 at maturity. Fruit of the Loom's U.S. bank is willing to buy the acceptance at a discount rate of 6 percent compounded quarterly.
a. How much will Fruit of the Loom receive if it sells the bankers' acceptance?
b. What is the all-in cost of the acceptance?

10.2 Suppose Fruit of the Loom, Inc., sells $10 million in accounts receivables to a factor. The receivables are due in 90 days. The factor charges a 2 percent per month factoring fee, as well as the face amount, for purchasing the accounts receivable from Fruit of the Loom on a nonrecourse basis.
a. How much will Fruit of the Loom receive for its receivables?
b. What is the all-in cost of the acceptance?

10.3 Savvy Fare has a bankers' acceptance drawn on Credit Lyonnais with a face value of $1 million due in six months. Credit Lyonnais receives an acceptance fee of $2,000 at maturity. A U.S. bank is willing to buy the acceptance at a discount rate of 5 percent compounded quarterly.
a. How much will Savvy Fare receive if it sells the bankers' acceptance?
b. What is the all-in cost of the acceptance, including the acceptance fee?

10.4 Suppose Savvy Fare sells $1 million in accounts receivable to a factor. The receivables are due in six months. The factor charges an upfront fee of 4 percent for purchasing the receivables on a nonrecourse basis. The factor also charges a factoring fee of 1 percent per month for every month outstanding on the receivables. The 1 percent per month factoring fee is paid at the time the receivables are sold to the factor.
a. How much will Savvy Fare receive for its receivables?
b. What is the all-in cost of the acceptance to Savvy Fare?

SUGGESTED READINGS

Currency risk hedging policies and practices are described in

Gordon M. Bodnar, Gregory S. Hayt, and Richard C. Marston, "1998 Wharton Survey of Financial Risk Management by U.S. Non-Financial Firms," *Financial Management* 27 (Winter 1998), pp. 70–91.

Judy C. Lewent and A. John Kearney, "Identifying, Measuring, and Hedging Currency Risk at Merck," *Journal of Applied Corporate Finance* 2, No. 4 (1990), pp. 19–28.

Lee R. Thomas, III, "Active Management," *Journal of Portfolio Management* 26 (Winter 2000), pp. 25–32.

Managing Transaction Exposure to Currency Risk

chapter 11

Overview

He who multiplies riches multiplies cares.

Benjamin Franklin

Transaction exposure to currency risk is defined as change in the value of monetary (or contractual) cash flows due to an unexpected change in exchange rates. Nearly every foreign currency transaction is exposed to this risk at some time. The good news is that transaction exposures are relatively easy to identify and manage, either by offsetting transactions within the firm or through external financial market hedges.

11.1 • AN EXAMPLE OF TRANSACTION EXPOSURE TO CURRENCY RISK

An Imaginary Tale

Rupert Taylor hadn't always been a successful business tycoon. Growing up in Australia, his early passion was for Australian-rules football. Rupert was born with size and speed, and through athletic competition he developed daring and an indomitable will to succeed. He was particularly adept at running from A to B and picking up a ball or knocking someone down (preferably both). After a coach from the University of Florida witnessed his domination of a regional all-star game, he was offered a scholarship to play American-rules football in the United States.

Rupert attacked this new sport with his customary enthusiasm. Perhaps too enthusiastically, for within days of his arrival he had antagonized most of his teammates with his aggressive play. Frustrated with his inability to play within rules, he became belligerent with teammates and coaches alike. He was thrown off the team when he attacked and seriously injured a teammate during an intrasquad scrimmage.

Rupert returned to Australia to work in his father's beer distributorship in Melbourne. Although his athletic career was at an end, the lessons learned from a life of competition remained. He set about expanding his father's business through a series of bold business deals, ruthlessly forcing out his competitors. In the coup d'grace, Rupert obtained the exclusive right to import and distribute Anheuser-Busch products in Melbourne.

A Real-World Example

Rupert's problems are now the problems of success. He has an accounts payable balance of $10 million with Anheuser-Busch that is invoiced in U.S. dollars and due in three months. The cash flows associated with this transaction are shown here:

Rupert's underlying exposure

$$-\$10,000,000$$

The value of Rupert's obligation in Australian dollars (A$) rises and falls with the value of the U.S. dollar. If the spot exchange rate stays at the current level of $S_0^{A\$/\$} =$ A$1.60/$, Rupert will owe ($10 million)(A$1.60/$) = A$16 million. If the U.S. dollar rises to A$1.70/$, he will owe A$17 million. If the U.S. dollar falls to A$1.50/$, he will owe A$15 million. Rupert doesn't mind a bit of calculated risk, but this transaction exposure to the U.S. dollar is one that he would just as soon avoid.

Rupert's exposure can be represented as a **risk profile** showing the Australian dollar value of his U.S. dollar obligation ($V^{A\$/\$}$) as a function of the value of the U.S. dollar ($S^{A\$/\$}$).

Rupert's risk profile (in levels)

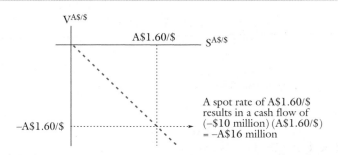

A spot rate of A$1.60/$ results in a cash flow of (−$10 million) (A$1.60/$) = −A$16 million

---

Alternatively, Rupert's risk profile can be shown as the percentage change in the Australian dollar value of his obligation ($v^{A\$/\$} = \Delta V^{A\$/\$}/V^{A\$/\$}$) as a function of the percentage change in the value of the dollar ($s^{A\$/\$} = \Delta S^{A\$/\$}/S^{A\$/\$}$).

Rupert's risk profile (in percentage changes)

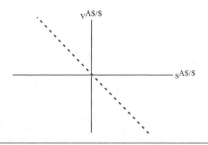

This is the same as the risk profile in levels, except that the origin is centered on the point $(S^{A\$/\$}, V^{A\$/\$}) = (A\$1.60/\$, -A\$1.60/\$)$, rather than $(0,0)$. In either representation, the value of Rupert's obligation rises and falls inversely to the value of the U.S. dollar.

11.2 • MANAGING TRANSACTION EXPOSURE INTERNALLY

Geographically diversified operations can provide a natural hedge of currency risk. Consider General Electric (GE), a U.S.-based multinational corporation. GE's exposure to any single currency is reduced because of the diversity of currencies in which it operates. Moreover, inflows and outflows within GE often offset one another. The multinational treasury can manage currency risk exposures internally through multinational netting or leading and lagging.

Multinational Netting

In the MNC, one business unit's exposure to currency risk is often offset by the exposure of another unit within the firm. Currency risk management begins with a process of **multinational netting** that identifies offsetting currency transactions within the firm. The multinational treasury can identify the exposure of the corporation as a whole by consolidating and netting the exposures of the firm's operating units.

> Intrafirm currency risk exposures sometimes cancel out.

An Example. Consider the intracompany transactions of the U.S.-based multinational corporation depicted in Figure 11.1. Intrafirm transactions for this company are denominated in U.S. and H.K. dollars, yen, and pounds. The values of these intrafirm transactions are restated in the parent's currency of reference (U.S. dollars) in Figure 11.2. After this translation to the U.S. dollar, intrafirm transfers include the following:

- Value of $140,000 due the U.S. parent
- Value of $100,000 due the U.K. affiliate
- Value of $80,000 due the Hong Kong affiliate
- Value of $100,000 due the Japanese affiliate

Total payments among the units are $420,000 without any netting of cash flows.

Treasury can minimize the MNC's overall transactions costs by coordinating the cash flows of its operating units. In Figure 11.3, funds transfers are reduced from $420,000 to $160,000 by eliminating redundant transfers. In this way, intrafirm transactions are periodically (daily, weekly, or monthly) reconciled and internal debits and credits allocated across the operating units according to the net amount due each unit. Actual payments can be transferred in whatever currencies the operating units prefer.

In contrast to diversified MNCs, importers and exporters usually cannot offset their exposures internally. For example, to hedge internally Rupert Taylor would need a U.S. dollar cash inflow to offset his U.S. dollar obligation. Rupert could begin exporting Foster's beer to the United States to create a U.S. dollar receivable. But creating an export business merely to hedge an import business is putting the cart before the horse. Rupert can hedge his U.S. dollar exposure much more easily through the financial markets without the considerable risks of starting up a new business venture.

Internal Hedges of Transaction Exposure. Hedging decisions are centralized in the corporate treasury to minimize the firm's overall risk exposures and hedging costs. Nevertheless, managers of individual operating units often wish to stabilize their accounting income or cash flow through hedging. In these cases, treasury can write internal hedging contracts (such as currency forwards or options) for the individual

FIGURE 11.1
The Internal Cash Flows of a Multinational Corporation

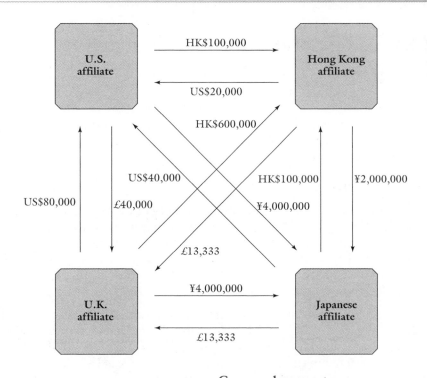

Cross exchange rates

	H.K.	Japan	U.K.	U.S.
H.K. dollar		10.000	0.0667	0.1000
Japanese yen	0.1000		0.0067	0.0100
U.K. pound sterling	15.000	150.00		1.5000
U.S. dollar	10.000	100.00	0.6667	

operating units. By writing contracts internally and netting offsetting exposures whenever possible, treasury can minimize its external financial market transactions. Consolidating and netting exposures rather than hedging each individual exposure allows managers of individual units to hedge as needed while avoiding the costs (commissions and bid-ask spreads) of hedging in external financial markets.

Treasury should charge *market prices* to the individual operating units for hedging exposures within the firm. For example, a request from an operating unit for a long 3-month forward contract on the U.S. dollar should be quoted the market's bid rate for a transaction of comparable size. The dollar bid rate is used because the treasury is buying and the operating division is selling the dollar forward, just like in a transaction with a commercial bank. Treasury can quote these prices through its commercial and investment banking relations. Market prices reflect the true cost of hedging and allow the treasury to benchmark internal hedges to transactions that could be realized in the financial market.

Charge market prices for internal hedges of currency risk.

FIGURE 11.2
The Internal Cash Flows of a Multinational Corporation

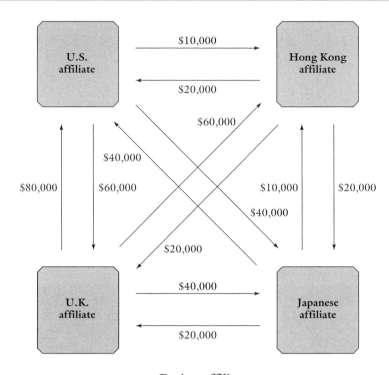

	Paying affiliate				
Receiving affiliate	U.S.	U.K.	H.K.	Japan	Total receipts
United States	$0	$80,000	$20,000	$40,000	$140,000
United Kingdom	$60,000	$0	$20,000	$20,000	$100,000
Hong Kong	$10,000	$60,000	$0	$10,000	$80,000
Japan	$40,000	$40,000	$20,000	$0	$100,000
Total payments	$110,000	$180,000	$60,000	$70,000	$420,000

This places the corporate treasury at the center of the firm's cash flow and risk management activities. Centralized treasury management promotes efficiency and reduces the risk that a divisional manager will put the entire company at risk with an ill-advised financial market hedge that could go awry.

Leading and Lagging

In some cases, altering the timing of cash flows can reduce transaction exposure. This process is known as **leading and lagging**. For example, if a U.S. parent is short euros, euro repatriations from foreign subsidiaries to the parent can be accelerated. This is known as *leading*. Similarly, the U.S. parent can delay or *lag* euro payments to its foreign subsidiaries. Of course, the euro balances and risk exposures of the parent's subsidiaries will change accordingly. Like multinational netting, leading and lagging works best when the currency needs of the individual units within the MNC offset one another.

FIGURE 11.3
Cash Flows After Multinational Netting

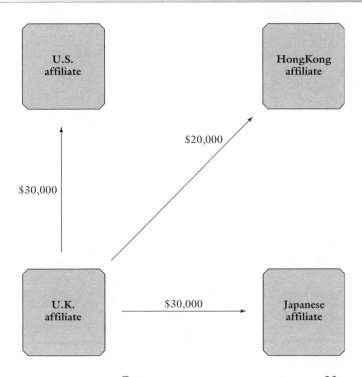

Receiving affiliate	Gross		Net	
	receipts	payments	receipts	payments
United States	$140,000	$110,000	$30,000	$0
United Kingdom	$100,000	$180,000	$0	$80,000
Hong Kong	$80,000	$60,000	$20,000	$0
Japan	$100,000	$70,000	$30,000	$0
Total payments	$420,000	$420,000	$80,000	$80,000

An External Market Example. In principle, altering the timing of internal cash flows is no different than altering the timing of external cash flows. External financial market transactions provide a performance benchmark for internal treasury transactions that is both reliable and relevant.

Suppose Rupert pays Anheuser-Busch $10 million every January, April, July, and October. Rupert also has cash inflows of $7.5 million every February, May, August, and November from an export sales contract with a partner in New Zealand. Rupert's position is shown in Figure 11.4. Although he has denominated this contract in U.S. dollars to offset his dollar payables, Rupert has a mismatch in the timing of his dollar cash inflows and outflows.

Rupert can synchronize his inflows and outflows if he can accelerate or *lead* his receivables by one month. This can be done in several ways:

- Factoring: sell receivables to the bank at a discount to the $7.5 million face value

FIGURE 11.4
Leading and Lagging

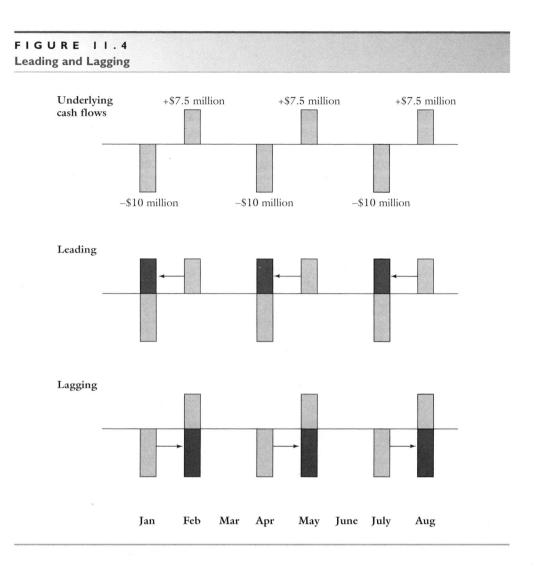

- Borrowing: borrow $7.5 million for one month using receivables as collateral
- Renegotiating: negotiate with his customer to receive payment one month earlier

If Rupert uses any of these alternatives, he'll be giving up $7.5 million in one month for a lesser amount today. Rupert needs to calculate the **all-in cost** of each alternative, including any bank fees or placement fees. All-in cost is the interest rate implied by today's inflow and next month's outflow (or foregone inflow), as shown here:

> All-in cost is based on all cash flows associated with a transaction.

All-in cost

Suppose the cost of each alternative is as follows:

- Factoring: the bank will buy the receivables for $7.48 million

- Borrowing: the bank charges a monthly rate of 0.25 percent on a line of credit
- Renegotiating: the New Zealand customer is willing to pay $7.46 one month early

The all-in cost of each alternative is then:

- Factoring: ($7.5/$7.48)–1 = 0.002674, or 0.2674 percent per month
- Borrowing: ($7.5/7.481297)–1 = 0.002500, or 0.25 percent per month
- Renegotiating: ($7.5/$7.46)–1 = 0.005362, or 0.5362 percent per month

Rupert's lowest cost alternative is to borrow from the bank at a monthly cost of 0.25 percent using accounts receivable as collateral. Note that Rupert is exposed to the credit risk of his New Zealand customer in this alternative. If the customer is not creditworthy, Rupert might prefer to sell his receivables to the bank without recourse for $7.48 million.

Alternatively, Rupert can negotiate with Anheuser-Busch to delay or *lag* his $10 million payable by one month. He'd then owe $2.5 million plus one month's interest on the lagged payable of $7.5 million every February, May, August, and November. Rupert will prefer this alternative if Anheuser-Busch charges less than his borrowing cost of 0.25 percent per month on delayed payables.

This is an example of cash management with external partners. Treasury usually has even more control over the timing of internal transactions. With control over the timing of transfer payments within the MNC, treasury can smooth its cash flow streams in each currency and ensure that funds are available for each operating unit as needed.

Internal Cash Management Systems. Although leading and lagging can be beneficial to the corporation as a whole, it can distort the rates of return earned by the various operating units. In essence, leading or lagging creates a loan from one unit of the firm to another. This calls for an internal recognition of the distortion caused by leading or lagging. The best alternative for solving the incentive problems created by leading or lagging is for treasury to recognize the cash flows of the operating units as they occur. Once the cash flows are paid or received, the onus of managing the timing of the cash flows can then be on the treasury and not on the operating units.

Treasury should apply *market interest rates* whenever it alters the timing of intracompany cash flows. The market rate of interest depends on the time value of money and the riskiness of the cash flow. Selling a receivable to treasury is similar

> Apply market interest rates when leading or lagging.

to factoring, in that the interest rate should reflect the credit risk of the cash flow. If a bank is willing to purchase 1-month receivables at an effective rate of 0.2674 percent per month as in the previous example, then the same rate should be applied to an operating unit when accelerating this cash flow internally. The unit that is selling its receivable to treasury (or to another unit) should be credited with $7.48 million today for a $7.5 million foregone receivable in one month. This benchmarks the cash flows to interest rates actually charged in the market on similar transactions.

Many national governments place limits on corporate leading and lagging. Japan places a 360-day limit. Most Latin American countries and many Asian countries place even more restrictive limits on leading and lagging and, in some cases, on multinational netting as well. There are no limits on leading and lagging activities in the United States, the United Kingdom, Canada, or Mexico. Managers should check local regulations before getting too aggressive with this cash management tool.

Corporate Treasuries and Commercial Banks. Corporate treasuries manage cash flows in much the same way that commercial banks manage cash flows. Although commercial banks have much higher transaction volumes, particularly with external customers, treasury's cash management process is necessarily much the same as a bank's. Each tries to balance the size and timing of their cash flows so that they are nearly always hedged. Banks earn a profit on their bid-ask spreads. Corporate treasuries try to minimize the cost of funds, while ensuring that cash is available for operations.

Consider the U.S. bank's exposure to the Australian dollar in Figure 11.5. As shown in the top figure, this bank faces inflows of A$12 million and outflows of A$6 million

FIGURE 11.5
A U.S. Bank's Exposures to the Australian Dollar

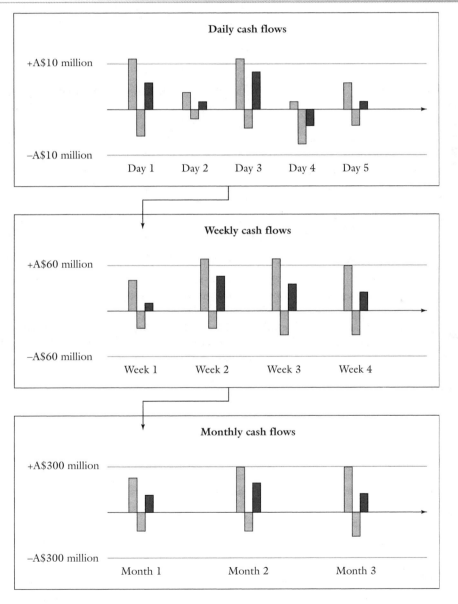

Cash inflows (outflows) are positive (negative) values.
Net cash flows are in green.

on day 1 for a net cash inflow of +A\$6 million. On day 2, inflows and outflows net to +A\$2 million. During the first week, the bank expects to receive a total of A\$36 million and pay A\$24 million for a net inflow of A\$12 million. The aggregate of the first week's cash flows are shown as week 1 in the middle figure. During the first month, the bank expects to receive a total of A\$240 million and pay A\$120 million for a net inflow of A\$120 million, as shown in the bottom figure. Although this bank is negatively exposed to the A\$ over some periods (such as day 4), on balance this bank is positively exposed to the Australian dollar during the next several months.

Commercial banks make markets in interest rates and currencies, buying low and selling high and making a profit on the difference. To minimize currency risk, they try to keep their net exposures to a minimum in each currency and at each forward date. To this end, banks keep track of their exposures on a daily basis out several months. Beyond that time, they report their exposures on a less frequent (e.g., weekly or monthly) basis. If the bank begins to accumulate an unbalanced position in a foreign currency, it will hedge or lay off this exposure through the financial markets. For example, the U.S. bank in Figure 11.5 might sell Australian dollars forward in weekly maturities for up to one month ahead and monthly maturities beyond one month to reduce its exposure to currency risk. The task facing the corporate treasury is in many ways the same as the task facing a commercial bank, just on a smaller scale.

There are other alternatives for hedging currency risk exposures through the financial markets. The most common methods are described in the next section.

11.3 • MANAGING TRANSACTION EXPOSURE IN THE FINANCIAL MARKETS

When the corporation's transaction exposures to currency risk are not internally offsetting, the treasury must consider hedging its exposures in the financial markets. Financial

> Financial hedges work well for transaction exposures.

market hedges are appropriate for hedging transaction exposures because their contractual payoffs can be matched to the underlying foreign currency transactions. The exposure of an asset denominated in a foreign currency to an unexpected change in that foreign currency value is one-to-one, so identification and management of transaction exposure is relatively straightforward.

Financial market hedging instruments include

- Currency forwards
- Currency futures
- Money market hedges
- Currency swaps
- Currency options

Table 11.1 summarizes the characteristics of each of these financial market hedges. More detailed treatments of currency futures, options, and swaps appear in the chapters on derivative securities.

Hedging with Currency Forwards

Consider Rupert Taylor's U.S. dollar forward obligation. Rupert can hedge 100 percent of his forward obligation with a long **currency forward** contract of \$10 million.

Rupert's forward hedge

+$10,000,000

—A$16,000,000

A long forward position of $10 million is equivalent to a short forward position of A$16 million at $F_1^{A\$/\$} = A\$1.60/\$$, where $F_1^{A\$/\$}$ is the forward rate for exchange in three months. The combination of Rupert's underlying exposure with the forward market hedge results in no net U.S. dollar exposure.

Rupert's forward hedged position

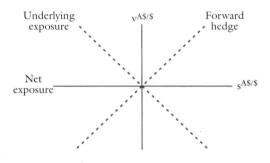

TABLE 11.1
Financial Market Hedges of Transaction Exposures

Vehicles	Advantages	Disadvantages
Currency forwards	Provides an exact hedge of transactions of known date and amount (near-term or long-term)	Bid-ask spreads can be large, especially on long-dated forwards and forwards in infrequently traded currencies
Currency futures	Low-cost hedge if the amount and maturity match the underlying exposure; low-risk hedge because of marking-to-market	Exchange-traded futures come in only a limited number of currencies and maturities; daily marking-to-market can cause a cash flow mismatch
Money market hedges	Forward positions can be built in currencies for which there are no forward markets	Relatively expensive hedge; may not be possible if there are constraints on borrowing or lending in the foreign currency
Currency swaps	Low-cost switch into other currencies or payoff structures (e.g., fixed versus floating)	Innovative swaps are costly; may not the best choice for near-term exposures
Currency options	"Disaster hedge" insures against unfavorable currency movements	Option premiums reflect option values, so this hedging instrument can be expensive

Regardless of the exchange rate, Rupert will have locked in an obligation of A$16 million for his shipment of beer. He will make an operating profit if he can sell the beer in Australia for more than A$16 million.

Partial Hedges. Many MNCs use forwards to reduce rather than eliminate exposures to currency risk. For example, if Rupert anticipates a depreciation of the U.S. dollar, he might choose to hedge only a portion of his exposure. A forward hedge of 50 cents on every dollar of underlying exposure results in the following net exposure. This partial hedge can be accomplished with a $5 million long forward position. The resulting net exposure is as shown.

Rupert's forward hedged position (50 percent cover)

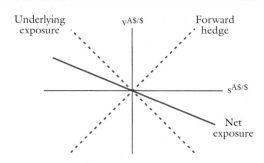

Partial hedges such as this are quite common. A survey by Bodnar, Hayt, and Marston found that U.S. firms typically hedge about 50 percent of near-term transaction exposures such as Rupert's 3-month dollar obligation.[1] Only a third of U.S. firms hedged more than 75 percent of their total near-term transaction exposures to currency risk.

Currency Speculation. If Rupert anticipates an appreciation of the U.S. dollar, he might be tempted to buy more than $10 million forward. However, this would tilt the nature of his business away from beer distribution toward currency speculation. The value of this particular transaction would then begin to depend more on the exchange rate and less on his beer sales. Unless Rupert has some special skill in forecasting exchange rates (which he almost surely does not), he is better off sticking to what he knows best.

Hedging with Currency Futures

Hedging with a currency futures contract is similar to a forward market hedge. Exchange-traded **currency futures** contracts come in standard currencies, amounts, and settlement dates. Over-the-counter futures contracts offered by commercial and investment banks can be tailored to the size, timing, and currency needs of the customer. Whereas gains or losses on forward contracts are settled at maturity, futures contracts are settled or *marked-to-market* based on daily changes in exchange rates. Aside from this difference, a currency futures position can be used to hedge foreign exchange exposure in the same way as a currency forward contract.

Futures are like forwards with periodic marking-to-market.

If a forward or futures market hedge is expensive or simply unavailable in a particular currency, a **currency cross-hedge** can be formed using a related currency. Suppose

---

1 Bodnar, Hayt, and Marston, "1998 Wharton Survey of Derivatives Usage by U.S. Non-Financial Firms," *Financial Management* (1998).

Rupert is importing Labatt beer from Canada and wants to hedge his Canadian dollar (C$) obligation due in three months. Bid-ask spreads on Canadian dollar forwards are much wider than on U.S. dollar forwards because of lower trading volume in Canadian dollars, especially on small transactions such as Rupert's. If Canadian dollar futures are unavailable, then Rupert needs an alternative way to hedge his obligation.

The value of the Canadian dollar is highly correlated with the U.S. dollar, so a cross-hedge using actively traded U.S. dollar forward or futures contracts can eliminate most of Rupert's exposure to the Canadian dollar. A cross-hedge using a related currency can sometimes cost less than a hedge in a thinly traded currency and can be nearly as effective, depending on the correlation between the exposed and the cross-hedged currencies.

Money Market Hedges

Forward or futures contracts are sometimes unavailable or prohibitively expensive for distant expiration dates in thinly traded currencies. In these circumstances, it is sometimes possible to form a **money market hedge** that replicates the forward exchange rate through the spot currency and Eurocurrency markets. A money market hedge is a form of *synthetic* or *homemade forward contract* constructed from other financial instruments.

> Money market hedges can replicate forward hedges.

In particular, Rupert can replicate a long dollar forward contract and hedge his dollar obligation due in three months by (1) borrowing Australian dollars from his local bank for three months, (2) converting Australian dollars to U.S. dollars in the spot market, and (3) investing the resulting U.S. dollars in a 3-month Eurodollar interest rate contract.

Rupert's money market hedge

Borrow an amount such that A$16 million is due in one period at an interest rate of $i^{A\$}$

$+$A$16 million$/(1+i^{A\$})$

$-$A$16 million

Convert to U.S. $s at today's spot rate

$+$$10 million$/(1+i^{\$})$

$-$A$16 million$/(1+i^{A\$})$

Invest this amount at $i^{\$}$

$+$$10 million

$-$$10 million$/(1+i^{\$})$

Net position

$\Rightarrow$

$+$$10 million

$-$A$16 million

Each of the time lines on the left represents a 3-month contract in the interest rate parity relation, $S_0^{A\$/\$}[(1+i^{A\$})/(1+i^{\$})] = F_1^{A\$/\$}$. In combination, the three contracts replicate the payoff on a long U.S. dollar forward contract, as shown on the right-hand side of the chart.

In practice, the last two legs of this hedge are sufficient to eliminate the foreign exchange risk of Rupert's underlying dollar obligation. Omitting the first transaction results in an *uncovered money market hedge*.

Rupert's uncovered money market hedge

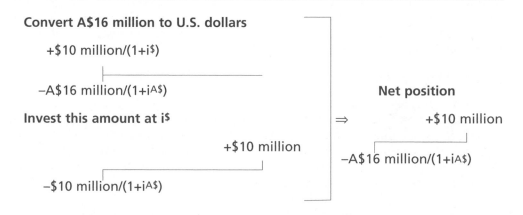

Leaving the first leg of the money market hedge uncovered reduces Rupert's transactions costs on the hedge, while ensuring him of a $10 million cash inflow in three months. This forward cash inflow exactly offsets his underlying U.S. dollar exposure. The uncovered position differs from the money market hedge in that, rather than paying A$16 million in three months, Rupert pays the present value of A$16 million today. Although this hedge eliminates Rupert's exposure to the U.S. dollar, it leaves him exposed to interest rate risk in the Australian dollar.

Hedging with Currency Swaps

Forwards, futures, and money market hedges can be used to hedge a single foreign currency cash flow. The exposure of a long-term contract that calls for periodic cash flows in a foreign currency can be hedged with a portfolio of forwards or futures of varying maturities. Alternatively, long-term contracts with periodic foreign currency cash flows can be hedged with a single contract, a **currency swap**, in which two counterparties agree to make payments on each other's foreign currency debt for a fixed period of time.

> A currency swap is an agreement to exchange interest payments in two currencies.

Suppose Anheuser-Busch holds a contract with a distributor in Taiwan calling for quarterly payments of 340 million in new Taiwan dollars (T$) over the next five years. These promised cash inflows are denominated in new Taiwan dollars, rather than U.S. dollars as in Anheuser-Busch's Australian contract. The promised cash flows from this contract expose Anheuser-Busch to the $S^{\$/T\$}$ exchange rate.

Anheuser-Busch's underlying Taiwan dollar exposures

If Anheuser-Busch has outstanding debt denominated in U.S. dollars, it can swap some of this U.S. dollar debt for a counterparty's Taiwan dollar debt and lock in Taiwan dollar cash outflows. For example, Anheuser-Busch could agree to make quarterly payments of T$340 million over five years on a counterparty's Taiwan dollar debt in exchange for the counterparty making quarterly payments of $10 million on Anheuser-Busch's U.S. dollar debt. Anheuser-Busch's net cash flows would look like this:

Anheuser-Busch's currency swap

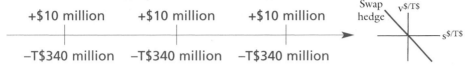

+$10 million   +$10 million   +$10 million

−T$340 million   −T$340 million   −T$340 million

When combined with Anheuser-Busch's underlying exposure to the Taiwan dollar, the net result is a stream of $10 million payments every three months for the next five years.

Anheuser-Busch's hedged position

+$10 million   +$10 million   +$10 million

Currency swaps such as this can quickly and inexpensively change a foreign currency liability into a domestic currency liability, or vice versa. Commercial and investment banks maintain an active market in interest rate and currency swaps.

Hedging with Currency Options

Payoffs on currency forwards, futures, money market hedges, and swaps are symmetric. These financial market hedges are used to minimize the variability of a hedged position. **Currency options** have a somewhat different role to play. A **currency call option** gives the buyer (or holder) of the option the right but not the obligation to buy an underlying currency at a contractually determined **exercise price** or exchange rate on (or perhaps before) a contractually determined **expiration date**. The seller (or writer) of the option has the obligation to deliver the specified currency at the exercise price. Conversely, a **currency put option** gives the buyer the right to sell an underlying currency at the exercise price. The option writer then has the obligation to buy the currency at the exercise price.

   This asymmetry between the buyer's option and the seller's obligation results in the following payoff profile at the expiration of a dollar call with an exercise price of A$1.60/$.

A long call option on the U.S. dollar

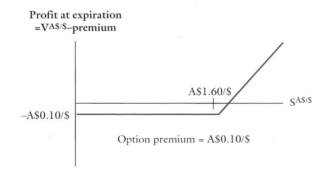

Profit at expiration
=V$^{A\$/\$}$−premium

A$1.60/$

$S^{A\$/\$}$

−A$0.10/$

Option premium = A$0.10/$

The option premium of A$0.10/$ is the price of the option and is paid by the buyer to the seller at the time the option is purchased. The option premium compensates the seller for the expected loss should the option be exercised by the buyer. The y-axis is the profit of the position at expiration, equal to the value of the option minus the option premium.

Because of their asymmetric payoffs, currency options can be used as an insurance pol-

> Currency options can insure against adverse currency movements.

icy against an adverse movement in a foreign currency value. For example, Rupert can hedge his exposure to the U.S. dollar with a 3-month call option on the U.S. dollar. If the exercise price at which currencies are exchanged is set equal to the expected future spot rate of $F_1^{A\$/\$} = E[S_1^{A\$/\$}] = A\$1.60/\$$, the resulting hedged position looks like this:

A long call option on the U.S. dollar

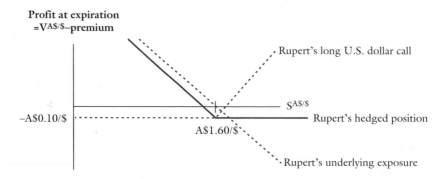

If the U.S. dollar rises above A$1.60/$ in three months, Rupert has an option to buy $10 million at the below-market exercise price of A$1.60/$. Any loss on the underlying position is then offset by a gain on the call option position. At an option premium of A$0.10/$, this call option will cost Rupert (A$0.10/$)($10 million) = A$1 million. For this price, Rupert can cap the Australian dollar value of his obligation at A$17 million (= A$16 million for the underlying obligation at A$1.60/$, plus A$1 million for the U.S. dollar call option).

If the U.S. dollar spot rate falls below A$1.60/$, Rupert can pay off his U.S. dollar obligation at the prevailing exchange rate. In this case, Rupert's option to buy U.S. dollars at A$1.60/$ has no value and he simply loses the option premium. His net position is his underlying obligation at the prevailing spot rate less the A$1 million that he paid for the dollar call option.

Just as currency forward contracts are an *obligation* to buy one currency for another, currency options are an option to buy one currency and simultaneously sell another currency. For this reason, currency options can protect against currency appreciations or depreciations.

For example, if Rupert wants to protect against an appreciation of the U.S. dollar, he can buy a call option on the U.S. dollar. This protects Rupert against an appreciation of the A$/$ exchange rate or, equivalently, a depreciation of the $/A$ exchange rate. The A$/$ option to buy U.S. dollars is simultaneously an option to sell Australian dollars.

Conversely, Rupert can protect against an appreciation of the $/A$ exchange rate with an option to buy Australian dollars at a fixed $/A$ exchange rate. This option to buy Australian dollars is simultaneously an option to sell U.S. dollars, so the option can protect against an appreciation (depreciation) of the Australian (U.S.) dollar.

Market Update

J.P. Morgan and RiskMetrics*

Growth in derivatives trading during the 1980s and 1990s was truly phenomenal. Unfortunately, as derivatives became a part of the financial manager's toolkit, losses related to derivatives trading correspondingly increased. The early 1990s saw a rising call by industry watchdogs and policy makers for standards, transparency, and consistency in measuring and reporting risks related to derivative products.

U.S. investment banker J.P. Morgan provides free access to a central component of its internal system for measuring financial risks. The system—*RiskMetrics*—provides users with daily data on more than 300 financial prices, including interest rates, exchange rates, and equity indices markets. The system estimates volatilities and correlations between indices, and is designed to assist users in assessing their exposures to financial price risks. J. P. Morgan's stated objective in providing access to the system is to promote greater transparency so that financial managers can concentrate on developing informed risk management strategies. For a fee, J.P. Morgan will fine-tune the system to a particular user's needs.

http://www. riskmetrics.com

Computers and statistical analysis are central to measurement, management, and control of the risks that come with derivative use. Yet statistical analysis cannot replace good judgment. As J.P. Morgan's publication *Introduction to RiskMetrics* states in bold print on page 1: "We remind our readers that no amount of sophisticated analytics will replace experience and professional judgment in managing risks."

* *RiskMetrics* is a registered trademark of J. P. Morgan and Company.

In either case, if the currency moves against your underlying position, you can recoup your losses through the corresponding currency call option.

11.4 • TREASURY MANAGEMENT IN PRACTICE

Derivatives Usage

Table 11.2 presents the results of a survey by Jesswein, Kwok, and Folks of financial officers at large U.S. corporations regarding their use of financial derivatives in currency risk hedging.[2] This survey indicates that the forward contract is the instrument of choice when the size and timing of a contractual cash flow is known in advance. Over 90 percent of these financial managers have used forward contracts. Approximately 50 percent of these financial managers have used over-the-counter (OTC) currency options or swaps. Exchange-traded currency futures, options, and futures options tend to be used for smaller positions, and hence by smaller firms than the firms in this sample.[3]

> Forwards are the most popular currency hedge.

Many exotic positions involve combinations of derivative positions. For example, a *cylinder option* is a combination of two options that places a cap and a floor on gains

---

2 Jesswein, Kwok, and Folks, "What New Currency Risk Products Are Companies Using, and Why?" *Journal of Applied Corporate Finance* (Fall 1995).

3 Exchange-traded futures options are options on an exchange-traded futures contract.

TABLE 11.2
Corporate Use of Currency Risk Management Products

Type of product	Used often (A)	Used occasionally (B)	Used once or twice (C)	Percentage of adoption (A+B+C)
Forward contracts	72.3%	17.9%	2.9%	93.0%
Foreign currency swaps	16.4	17.0	19.3	52.6
Over-the-counter currency options	18.8	19.4	10.6	48.8
Cylinder options	7.0	9.9	11.7	28.7
Synthetic (homemade) forwards	3.0	8.9	10.1	22.0
Foreign currency futures contracts	4.1	10.7	5.3	20.1
Exchange-traded currency options	3.6	6.5	7.1	17.3
Exchange-traded futures options	1.8	3.0	4.2	8.9

Source: Adapted from Jesswein, Kwok, and Folks, "What New Currency Risk Products Are Companies Using, and Why?" *Journal of Applied Corporate Finance* (Fall 1995).

or losses from exchange rate changes. Synthetic or homemade forwards can be constructed in a number of ways, such as with a money market hedge or through a combination of a put and a call option (see Chapter 7).

Active Management of Currency Risk

It is very difficult to outperform the market's exchange rate expectations. Nevertheless, most financial managers incorporate their view of the market into their risk management decisions. Figure 11.6 presents the results of a survey by Bodnar, Hayt, and Marston on derivatives usage at U.S. firms.[4]

As shown in Figure 11.6, about 10 percent of U.S. derivatives users "frequently" alter the size or timing of their hedges based on their exchange rate expectations. Many more firms "sometimes" alter the size (51 percent) or timing (49 percent) of their hedges based on their market view. Nearly a third of respondents stated they "actively take positions" in foreign exchange, although the survey did not ask whether these positions were risk-reducing or speculative in nature. A large proportion of U.S. firms actively manage their foreign exchange exposures. Active foreign exchange risk management is the norm in other countries as well.[5]

> A majority of firms actively manage forex exposures.

Benchmarking the Performance of an Actively Managed Hedge. Firms that actively manage their currency risk exposures need to evaluate their performance against a benchmark. As shown in Figure 11.7, 42 percent of firms that benchmarked used forward rates for comparison. Forward rates are a simple and appropriate benchmark, as they reflect the market's view of future spot rates through forward parity and the opportunity costs of capital in the foreign and domestic currencies through interest rate parity. Another 17 percent of firms benchmarked their perform-

---

4 Bodnar, Hayt and Marston, "1998 Wharton Survey."

5 See, for example, Bodnar and Gebhardt, "Derivatives Usage in Risk Management by U.S. and German Non-Financial Firms: A Comparative Survey," *Journal of International Financial Management & Accounting* (Autumn 1999).

FIGURE 11.6
Active Currency Risk Management

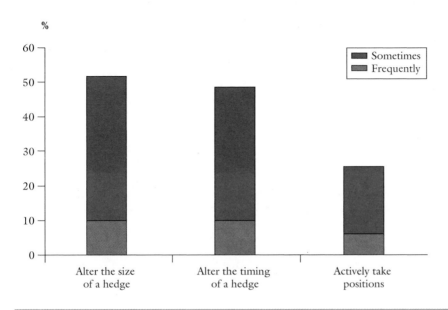

Source: Bodnar, Hayt, and Marston, "1998 Wharton Survey of Financial Risk Management by U.S. Non-Financial Firms," *Financial Management* (Winter 1998).

FIGURE 11.7
Risk Management Benchmarks

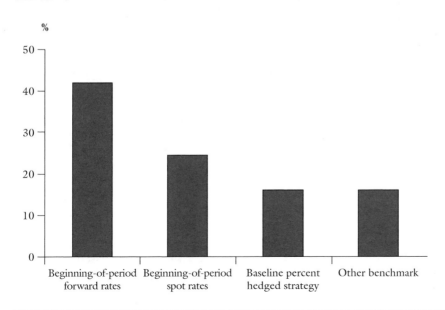

Source: Bodnar, Hayt, and Marston, "1998 Wharton Survey of Financial Risk Management by U.S. Non-Financial Firms," *Financial Management* (Winter 1998).

Market Update

J.P. Morgan's Event Risk Indicator*

A key input into the financial manager's hedging decision is the probability of a cata-strophic event. To assist its clients in determining when to hedge against currency risk, J.P. Morgan has developed an *Event Risk Indicator (ERI)* for assessing the likelihood of a currency crash based on past crashes. The index ranges from 0.0 to 1.0. The value of the index is not a probability, although higher values do indicate a higher probability of a crash. According to J.P. Morgan's estimates, hedging when the index rises above 0.4 allows a hedger to avoid 90 percent of currency crashes. The index is above 0.4 about 30 percent of the time.

* J.P. Morgan's Event Risk Indicator can be accessed through their Web site at http://www.jpmorgan.com.

http://www.
jpmorgan.com

ance against a baseline that was less than 100 percent of the amount exposed. Another 17 percent used some other form of benchmark, such as an unhedged posi-tion or an option hedge.

Curiously, 24 percent of firms that benchmarked used the spot exchange rate from the beginning of the period to evaluate the performance of their hedges. The ran-dom nature of exchange rate movements makes this appropriate only for short-term exposures. Forward rates are generally preferable as benchmarks, because they reflect market prices for future currency exchange. Spot rates do not reflect the market's expectations of future spot rates, the relative opportunity costs of capital, or inflation differences.

About 40 percent of respondents in the survey manage their currency risk expo-sures in a passive manner. Correspondingly, about 44 percent of firms in the survey indicated that they did not benchmark their hedging performance. Hopefully, these firms do not benchmark because they have decided, after a thorough review by top management, that a passive hedging approach to currency risk management is suffi-cient for their risk-management needs.

Evaluating the Performance of Active Risk Management. Once a benchmark is selected, the performance of a hedge or hedged program must be evaluated accord-ing to some criterion. Bodnar, Hayt, and Marston asked derivatives users how they evaluate the risk management function. The results are reported in Figure 11.8.

"Risk reduction relative to a benchmark" was the performance criterion in 40 per-cent of the firms. These firms believe that risk reduction was the overriding objective in their risk management operations. However, a majority of firms included some measure of profit or loss in their performance criteria. The objective "risk-adjusted performance" (i.e. profits or savings adjusted for volatility), "absolute profit or loss," or "increased profits (or reduced costs) relative to a benchmark" was used in more than 60 percent of firms. The latter two criteria are strictly profit-based and were used in 40 percent of firms. This is a surprising result, as a profit-based performance criterion encourages the financial manager to actively take positions in the currency markets rather than using the markets to reduce risk. Evaluating managers based on the profitability of their positions relative to a benchmark can encourage them to seek, rather than avoid, risk.

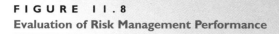

FIGURE 11.8
Evaluation of Risk Management Performance

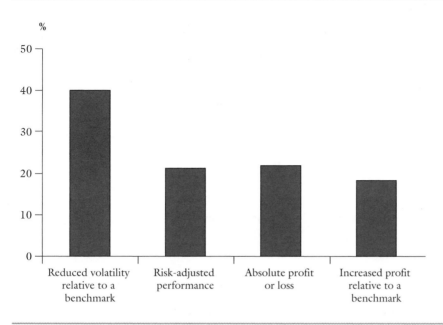

Source: Bodnar, Hayt, and Marston, "1998 Wharton Survey of Financial Risk Management by U.S. Non-Financial Firms," *Financial Management* (Winter 1998).

11.5 • SUMMARY

Transaction exposure to currency risk is defined as change in the value of a contractual cash flow due to an unexpected change in an exchange rate. Transaction exposure is hard to ignore because the value of a monetary asset denominated in a foreign currency moves one-to-one with a change in the foreign exchange rate. For this reason, financial managers rank transaction exposure as the most important exposure to currency risk.

Transaction exposures should first be offset within the firm. Once this is done, the financial manager must choose which of the firm's net transaction exposures to hedge and how much of each net exposure to hedge in the external financial markets. Financial market hedges include

- Currency forwards (the basic building block of derivative instruments)
- Currency futures (like forwards, but marked-to-market daily)
- Money market hedges (synthetic forwards)
- Currency options (insurance against extreme currency movements)
- Currency swaps (used for long-term hedges)

It is imperative that top management be involved in establishing and administering the firm's risk management policies. Managerial oversight is necessary to ensure that risk management is implemented in a way that supports, rather than competes with, the firm's core businesses.

KEY TERMS

all-in cost	exercise price
currency call option	expiration date
currency cross-hedge	leading and lagging
currency forwards	money market hedge
currency futures	multinational netting
currency options	risk profile
currency put option	transaction exposure
currency swaps	

CONCEPTUAL QUESTIONS

11.1 What is transaction exposure to currency risk?

11.2 What is a risk profile?

11.3 In what ways can diversified multinational operations provide a natural hedge of transaction exposure to currency risk?

11.4 What is multinational netting? Why is it used by multinational corporations?

11.5 What is leading and lagging? Why is it used by multinational corporations?

11.6 Define each of the following: (a) currency forwards, (b) currency futures, (c) currency options, (d) currency swaps, and (e) money market hedges.

11.7 What is a currency cross-hedge? Why might it be used?

11.8 Do many firms actively manage their currency risk exposures?

PROBLEMS

11.1 Refer to the following set of transactions. Identify cash flows after netting of internal transactions.

Receiving affiliate	U.S.	Can.	Mex.	P.R.	Total receipts	Net receipts	Net payments
		Paying affiliate					
United States	0	$300	$500	$600	_____	_____	_____
Canada	$500	0	$400	$200	_____	_____	_____
Mexico	$400	$700	0	$200	_____	_____	_____
Puerto Rico	$400	$900	$400	0	_____	_____	_____
Total payments	_____				_____	_____	_____

11.2 Refer to the set of transactions in the graph that follows. Identify the net transactions within this system by filling in the following table. Draw a new set of transactions to identify which division pays funds and which division receives funds after multinational netting of transactions.

Receiving affiliate	Paying affiliate				Total receipts	Net receipts	Net payments
	U.S.	**Can.**	**Mex.**	**P.R.**			
United States							
Canada							
Mexico							
Puerto Rico							
Total payments							

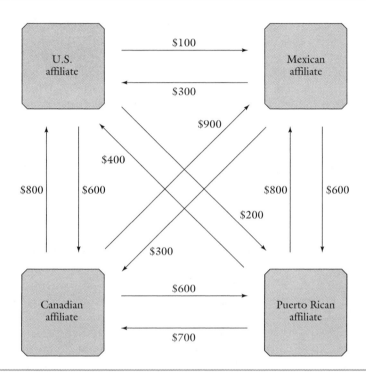

11.3 You have recently graduated from college and accepted a position in the receivables division of Ex-Im-Age Corporation, a software company located in California and specializing in language-independent, icon-based software. Ex-Im-Age has just made a large sale to Germany, and has a euro-denominated accounts receivable balance of €1,000,000 that is expected to be received in six months.

a. Represent Ex-Im-Age's euro exposure as a risk profile showing (i) the dollar value of the euro receivable ($V^{\$/€}$) as a function of the dollar value of the euro ($S^{\$/€}$), and (ii) change in the dollar value of the euro receivable ($\Delta V^{\$/€}$) as a function of change in the dollar value of the euro ($\Delta S^{\$/€}$).

b. Using risk profiles, show how Ex-Im-Age's euro exposure can be hedged with each of the following: (i) a currency forward contract, (ii) currency futures contracts, (iii) a money market hedge, and (iv) a currency option contract.

11.4 It is February 14, and Rupert Taylor has an obligation to pay Anheuser-Busch $5 million on May 13. Rupert's bank quotes "A$1.6010/$ BID and A$1.6020/$ ASK" in the spot market and "A$1.6025/$ BID and A$1.6035/$ ASK" for exchange on May 13. Rupert must pay the bank's asking price if he wants to buy dollars from the bank. Evaluate each of the following statements:

   a. The dollar is selling at a forward premium, so Rupert is better off buying dollars in the spot market rather than in the forward market.

   b. If Rupert expects the dollar to close below the forward ask price of A$1.6035/$, he should hedge his entire $5 million exposure by purchasing dollars forward.

   c. If Rupert expects the dollar to close above A$1.6035/$, he should hedge his entire $5 million exposure by purchasing dollars forward.

   d. If Rupert expects the dollar to close above the forward ask price of A$1.6035/$, he should buy even more than $5 million in the forward market in the expectation of making a profit on the difference between the actual spot exchange rate in three months and his forward exchange rate from the bank.

   e. Within the next month, Rupert anticipates incurring an additional $5 million obligation that will also be payable on May 13. Rupert should not hedge more than his original $5 million exposure even if he expects the dollar to close above the bank's forward asking price of A$1.6035/$.

11.5 Given the same information as in problem 11.4, answer the following questions.

   a. How can Rupert hedge his dollar exposure with a currency futures contract? What is the difference between a futures contract and a forward contract? Does the currency futures contract need to be traded on an Australian exchange?

   b. How can Rupert replicate a long forward position with a money market hedge? What is the likely cost of such a hedge compared to a currency forward hedge?

   c. How can Rupert hedge his dollar exposure with a currency option?

   d. Suppose Rupert expects a dollar exposure of about $5 million every three months until his distribution contract with Anheuser-Busch expires in five years. How can Rupert hedge his dollar exposure with a currency swap?

11.6 Suppose $S_0^{\$/£} = \$1.25/£$, $F_1^{\$/£} = \$1.2/£$, $i^£ = 11.56\%$, and $i^\$ = 9.82\%$. You are to receive £100,000 on a shipment of Madonna albums in one year. You want to fix the amount you must pay in dollars to avoid foreign exchange risk.

   a. Form a forward market hedge. Identify which currency you are buying and which currency you are selling forward. When will currency actually change hands—today or in one year?

   b. Form a money market hedge that replicates the payoff on the forward contract by using the spot currency and Eurocurrency markets. Identify each contract in the hedge. Does this hedge eliminate the foreign exchange risk?

   c. Are these currency and Eurocurrency markets in equilibrium? How would you arbitrage the difference from the parity condition? (Refer to interest rate parity in Chapter 5.)

SUGGESTED READINGS

Studies of firms' hedging policies and practices appear in

Gordon M. Bodnar and Gunther Gebhardt, "Derivatives Usage in Risk Management by U.S. and German Non-Financial Firms: A Comparative Survey," *Journal of International Financial Management & Accounting* 10 (Autumn 1999), pp. 153–187.

Gordon M. Bodnar, Gregory S. Hayt, and Richard C. Marston, "1998 Wharton Survey of Derivatives Usage by U.S. Non-Financial Firms," *Financial Management* 27 (Winter 1998), pp. 70–91.

Kurt Jesswein, Chuck C.Y. Kwok, and William R. Folks, Jr., "What New Currency Risk Products Are Companies Using, and Why?" *Journal of Applied Corporate Finance* 8 (Fall 1995), pp. 115–124.

Managing Operating Exposure to Currency Risk

chapter 12

Overview

To get anywhere, or even to live a long time, a man has to guess, and guess right, over and over again, without enough data for a logical answer.

Robert Heinlein, *Time Enough for Love*

Chapter 11 discussed **transaction exposure**—the exposure of monetary (contractual) cash flows to currency risk. Transaction exposure is the most visible exposure to currency risk and commands the most attention from multinational financial managers.

Less visible, but perhaps even more important, is the firm's operating exposure to currency risk. **Operating exposure** to currency risk is defined as change in the value of nonmonetary cash flows (that is, the noncontractual cash flows of the firm's real assets) due to unexpected changes in foreign currency values. Although operating exposure is more difficult to measure and manage than transaction exposure, it is usually the more important long-term exposure because it involves the firm's core business activities.

12.1 • MANAGING OPERATING EXPOSURES TO CURRENCY RISK

Operating exposure refers to changes in the value of operating cash flows generated by the firm's real assets due to unexpected changes in one or more foreign currency values. Real assets include physical assets, such as plant and equipment. Real assets also include human assets, such as key technical or managerial personnel and the organizational structure that binds them together. Operating exposures to currency risk depend on the firm's operating environment, and on that of its competitors.

> Operating exposure is the sensitivity of operating cash flows to exchange rates.

Operating Exposure and the Competitive Environment

Market Segmentation Versus Market Integration. Operating exposure to currency risk depends on the extent of market segmentation or integration for the firm's inputs and outputs. In an **integrated market**, purchasing power parity holds so that equivalent assets trade for the same price regardless of where they are traded. If purchasing power parity does not hold, then the market is at least partially **segmented** from other markets. This integration/segmentation dichotomy holds for markets in goods, services, factors of production (labor and materials), and financial assets and liabilities. Common causes of market segmentation include transactions costs, transportation costs, information costs or barriers, legal or institutional barriers, and government intervention in the form of taxes, tariffs, or other barriers to trade.

When markets are completely segmented from other markets, prices are determined entirely in the local market. In contrast, prices in globally integrated markets are determined by worldwide supply and demand. The domestic currency prices fluctuate one for one with exchange rates in an integrated market, so that purchasing power parity is maintained. Real-world prices typically fall somewhere between these two extremes. For example, labor costs tend to be determined by local supply and demand, whereas the prices of actively traded financial assets (currencies, interest rates, or financial claims on oil or gold) are set in globally competitive markets.

> Segmented markets are at least partially insulated from currency risk exposure.

Market Segmentation/Integration and Price Determination. Figure 12.1 classifies firms according to whether input costs and output prices are determined locally or in a competitive global marketplace. The degree of market integration determines the extent to which the values of the firm's assets move with foreign exchange rates. The foreign currency exposures that characterize local firms, importers, exporters, or global firms are indicated by plus or minus signs in the quadrants of Figure 12.1.

Domestic firms with revenues and expenses that are locally determined (shown in the upper-left quadrant of Figure 12.1) are the least sensitive to currency movements. This is the case when local factor and product markets are segmented from foreign markets. For example, service industries that rely heavily on local labor are relatively insensitive to currency fluctuations. Labor is relatively immobile, and wages typically move with domestic inflation rather than with foreign currency values. Consequently,

FIGURE 12.1
A Taxonomy of Exposures to Foreign Currency Risk (exposures in parentheses)

		Revenues	
		Local	Global
Operating expenses	Local	Domestic firms (0)	Exporters (+)
	Global	Importers (−)	Global MNCs and importers or exporters of globally priced goods (+, −, or 0)

local labor costs tend to be less dependent on foreign currency values than are most other factor inputs. Local service companies also tend to compete with other local companies and not with global companies, so both revenues and operating expenses depend more on the local economy than on foreign currency values.

The classic importer is a MNC with international involvement through its operating expenses, buying goods in competitive world markets and selling them in local markets. If the local market is segmented from other markets (shown in the lower-left quadrant of Figure 12.1), the importer has a negative exposure to foreign currency values. If the importer competes in goods such as oil or electronics for which there is a competitive global market (lower-right quadrant), then local prices move with foreign currency values. In this case, both revenues and costs are exposed to foreign currency risk.

Exporters face the opposite exposure. The classic exporter is a MNC with international involvement through its revenue stream. The exporter manufactures goods in a local economy and sells into competitive global markets. If the local market is segmented from other markets (upper-right quadrant), the exporter is positively exposed to foreign currency values. If the exporter's goods are sold in competitive global markets (lower-right quadrant), then both costs and revenues move with foreign currency values.

The nature of the MNC's exposures to currency risk depends on the particular products and markets in which it competes. For the truly global corporation operating in integrated global markets, both revenues and operating expenses are likely to be sensitive to exchange rates. Seldom are revenues matched one for one with operating expenses, so currency risk management becomes an important function of the multinational financial manager.

> Operating exposure depends on the firm's products and markets.

Measuring the Exposure of Operating Cash Flows

Exposure to foreign currency risk is defined as the percentage change in the domestic currency value of an asset or liability, $v^d = \Delta V^d / V^d$, resulting from a percentage change in the spot exchange rate, $s^{d/f} = \Delta S^{d/f} / S^{d/f}$.

$$\text{Exposure}^f = v^d / s^{d/f} \qquad (12.1)$$

This measure of exposure, which captures the sensitivity of an asset or liability to changes in foreign currency values, is graphically displayed in Figure 12.2 for monetary assets and liabilities denominated in a foreign currency. Monetary cash flows that are denominated in a foreign currency have a fixed or contractual value in that currency. The domestic currency value of monetary cash flows denominated in a foreign currency changes one for one with a change in the value of the foreign currency. This one-for-one relation is reflected in the lines of slope +1 (for assets denominated in a foreign currency) and −1 (for liabilities denominated in a foreign currency) in Figure 12.2.

In contrast to monetary assets and liabilities, the value of a real asset can change more or less than one for one with changes in currency values. Real assets seldom move one for one with exchange rates because the operating cash flows generated by the firm's real assets are uncertain. Even if a 1 percent increase in a foreign currency value is accompanied, *on average*, by a 1 percent increase in firm value, the actual change is likely to be more or less than 1 percent because of uncertainty over future revenues and operating costs.

> Real assets are exposed to changes in real exchange rates.

Another difference between transaction and operating exposure is that the operating exposure of real assets is to real, rather than nominal, exchange rate changes. For example, a real foreign currency appreciation raises the prices of foreign goods relative to domestic goods. This improves the competitive position of

FIGURE 12.2
The Exposures of Monetary Assets and Liabilities

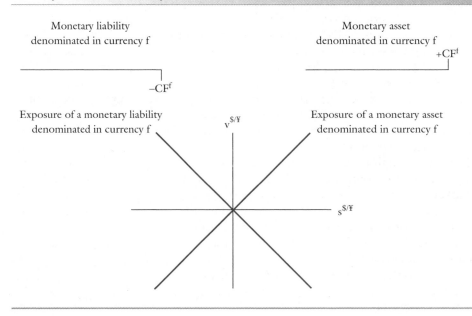

exporters and undermines that of importers. In contrast, nominal exchange rate changes that merely pass inflation differences through to prices have no impact on the competitive positions of real assets.

12.2 • The Exposure of Shareholders' Equity

Shareholders' equity has a residual claim on the assets of the firm after all the financial obligations of the firm have been satisfied. As such, equity absorbs the transaction exposure of **net monetary assets** (monetary assets less monetary liabilities) as well as the operating exposure of real assets. Shareholders' exposure to currency risk is thus the sum of the transaction exposure of net monetary assets and the operating exposure of the firm's real assets.

> Equity faces the net exposure of all other assets and liabilities.

An Illustration of an Exporter's Operating Exposure

Consider the common size balance sheet of the domestic exporter shown in Figure 12.3. For simplicity, this exporter's balance sheet is presented in cents (rather than percents) based on a 1-dollar unit of the firm. Forty cents of every dollar in this firm are invested in monetary assets denominated in a foreign currency. Twenty cents of every dollar are in monetary liabilities denominated in the foreign currency. This leaves net monetary assets of 20 cents with a transaction exposure to currency risk.

Suppose the foreign currency unexpectedly appreciates by 10 percent, resulting in a 10 percent appreciation in both nominal and real terms. As the nominal value of the foreign currency appreciates, foreign monetary assets rise by 4 cents and foreign monetary liabilities rise by 2 cents in value. This results in a $(20¢)(0.10) = 2¢$ increase in the value of the firm in the domestic currency. As the residual owner of the firm, equity gains the net 2 cents in value from the 10 percent appreciation in the foreign currency.

FIGURE 12.3
The Exposure of Shareholders' Equity

Foreign currency monetary assets (40¢)	Foreign currency monetary liabilities (20¢)
	Domestic currency monetary liabilities (40¢)
Domestic currency monetary assets (25¢)	
Real assets (35¢)	Equity (40¢)

Net monetary assets exposed to currency risk (20¢)

Operating exposure of real assets (35¢)

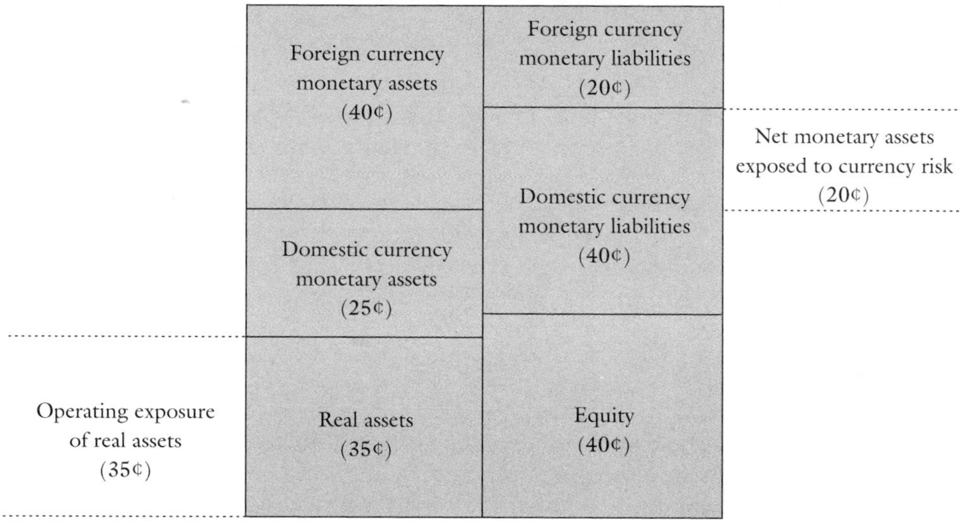

This exporter has invested 35 cents of every dollar in real assets. The real assets of a classic exporter are positively exposed to foreign currency values. The magnitude of this operating exposure may be more or less than one for one. As the foreign currency appreciates in real (purchasing power) terms, the purchasing power of foreign customers increases. If the exporter retains its sales price in the foreign currency, then (assuming other exporters do not change their price) its contribution margin will increase on the same sales volume. If the exporter retains its existing sales price and contribution margin in the domestic currency, then a foreign currency appreciation results in a drop in the foreign currency sales price and export volume will rise.

Suppose this exporter's real assets are exposed one for one to the foreign currency. In this case, a 10 percent appreciation of the foreign currency results, on average, in a 10 percent increase in the value of real assets. This is an increase of 3.5 cents per dollar, based on real assets of 35 cents. When combined with the increase in firm value of 2 cents from the exposure of net monetary assets, a 10 percent appreciation of the foreign currency is likely to increase the value of shareholders' equity by 5.5 cents. The actual change in value is likely to be more or less than this amount because the change in the value of real assets is uncertain.

Two perspectives can be taken in estimating the exposure of shareholders' equity to currency risk. The first perspective views the firm from outside and measures the impact of exchange rate changes on the value of the firm's equity in the financial marketplace. The second approach attempts to separately identify the exposures of revenues and operating expenses generated by the firm's real assets. These elements of operating exposure are then combined with the transaction exposures of the firm's monetary assets and liabilities. This internal or managerial view of currency risk exposure is useful for anticipating the impact of, and formulating competitive response to, changes in currency values. Estimates of these exposures are more easily done by management than by external analysts, because management has greater access to information on the firm's operating cash flows, business strategies, and risk exposures.

Market-Based Measures of the Exposure of Shareholders' Equity

Exposure as a Regression Coefficient. Viewed from outside the firm, the exposure of equity to currency risk can be estimated by the slope coefficient in a regression of stock returns on change in the spot exchange rate:

$$r_t^d = \alpha^d + \beta^f s_t^{d/f} + \varepsilon_t^d \tag{12.2}$$

where r_t^d = equity return in the domestic currency d in period t

$s_t^{d/f}$ = percentage change in the spot exchange rate during period t

Equation 12.2 decomposes the change in firm value into two parts: a part that is exposed to currency risk ($\beta^f s_t^{d/f}$) and a part that is independent of currency risk ($\alpha^d + \varepsilon_t^d$). The regression coefficient β^f captures the sensitivity of equity value to changes in the value of the foreign currency f. The regression coefficient is equal to

$$\beta^f = \rho_{r,s}(\sigma_r/\sigma_s) \tag{12.3}$$

where σ_r is the standard deviation of equity returns, σ_s is the standard deviation of spot rate changes, and $\rho_{r,s}$ is the correlation between equity returns and spot rate changes. The intercept term α^d is the expected equity return in the domestic currency when the spot rate equals its expectation, $E[s^{d/f}] = 0$. The error term ε_t^d is conventionally assumed to be normally distributed with an expected value of zero.

If a particular firm is not exposed to changes in the value of a foreign currency, the regression in Equation 12.2 yields a slope coefficient of $\beta^f = 0$. Changes in the exchange rate then have no power to explain changes in domestic equity value. The slope coefficient in Equation 12.2 is nonzero if there is a (positive or negative) relation between domestic equity values and foreign exchange rates. The greater the equity exposure, the greater the magnitude of β^f. This conceptualization of currency risk exposure as a regression coefficient is illustrated in Figure 12.4.

> Exposure to currency risk can be measured as a regression coefficient.

Variability around the regression line is measured by **r-square** (also called the coefficient of determination). R-square is equal to the square of the correlation coefficient, $(\rho_{r,s})^2$, and measures the percent of the variation in r_t^d that is explained (in a statistical sense) by variation in $s_t^{d/f}$. If the correlation between r^d and $s^{d/f}$ is zero, then r-square is zero and firm value is not exposed to the exchange rate. If the correlation between r^d and $s^{d/f}$ is 0.2, then r-square is $(0.2)^2 = 0.04$ and 4 percent of the variation in equity value comes from variability in the exchange rate. If the correlation between r^d and $s^{d/f}$ is +1, then r-square is $(1.0)^2 = 1.0$. In this case, the variance of the error term ε_t^d is zero in Equation 12.2, and variability in $s^{d/f}$ explains 100 percent of the variability in value $v^{d/f}$ or, equivalently, in the return r^d.

An Example. Consider Phillips NV, one of the world's largest electronics companies with 2001 sales of €32.3 billion (about $30 billion) and more than 250,000 employees. Phillips is incorporated in the Netherlands and has its principal listing in Amsterdam. Its manufacturing base is primarily in Europe, from where it exports to more than 60 countries around the world. For a European exporter such as Phillips, a real appreciation of the euro raises operating costs relative to Phillips's non-euro competitors. Conversely, a real depreciation lowers Phillips's operating costs relative to its non-euro competitors.

Suppose the sensitivity of Phillips's euro share price to changes in the value of the dollar is estimated as $\beta^\$ = 0.1$ in the following regression:

FIGURE 12.4
The Operating Exposures of Real Assets

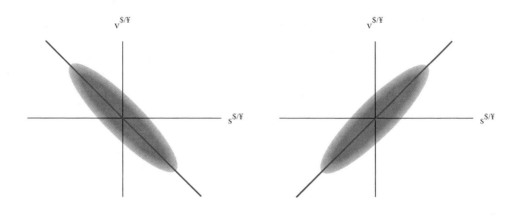

A U.S. importer's yen exposure   A U.S. exporter's yen exposure

$$r_t^{\text{€}} = \alpha^{\text{€}} + \beta^{\$} s_t^{\text{€}/\$} + \varepsilon_t^{\text{€}} \qquad\qquad (12.4)$$

According to this measure of exposure, a 10 percent dollar appreciation is associated with a 1 percent increase in the euro value of Phillips shares, on average. Conversely, a 10 percent depreciation of the dollar is associated with a 1 percent decrease in Phillips's euro share price. Because there is not a perfect correlation between Phillips's share price and the spot exchange rate, actual changes in share prices are likely to vary more or less than expected with changes in exchange rates.

Phillips is exposed to a variety of currencies besides the dollar. Phillips is exposed to changes in the value of the pound sterling through its sales and operations in the United Kingdom. Phillips is directly exposed to the yen through its sales to Asia and indirectly through the exposures of its Japanese competitors, such as Sony and Toshiba. Even if the euro doesn't change against the dollar or the pound, the company's competitive position in the United Kingdom and the United States is diminished if its Asian competitors benefit from an appreciation of these currencies against the yen.

> MNCs can be exposed to more than one foreign currency.

A more inclusive measure of Phillips's currency exposures can be estimated with a multiple regression such as the following:

$$r_t^{\text{€}} = \alpha^{\text{€}} + \beta^{\pounds} s_t^{\text{€}/\pounds} + \beta^{\$} s_t^{\text{€}/\$} + \beta^{\yen} s_t^{\text{€}/\yen} + \dots + \varepsilon_t^{\text{€}} \qquad\qquad (12.5)$$

where the coefficients $\beta^{\pounds}$, $\beta^{\$}$, and $\beta^{\yen}$ represent the sensitivity of Phillips's euro share price to changes in the value of each currency. This multiple regression approach reminds us that a MNC such as Phillips has exposure not just to a single currency but to any number of currencies, depending on the nature and geographic scope of its operations and on those of its competitors.

A word of caution is in order. Multiple regressions such as Equation 12.5 suffer from multicollinearity when the independent variables are correlated. Multicollinearity results in slope coefficients that are imprecise (that is, have large standard errors).

Multicollinearity is a concern in Equation 12.5 because the spot rates are related through their common dependence on the euro. Using either Equation 12.4 or Equation 12.5, the firm is considered to be exposed to a particular currency if and only if the slope coefficient is statistically significant at a given (e.g., 5 percent) level of significance. Multicollinearity won't make an insignificant coefficient appear significant in Equation 12.5. However, it can make one or more important exposures appear statistically insignificant through its effect on the standard errors of the slope coefficients. Equation 12.5 can be used in conjunction with a set of single regressions as in Equation 12.4 to identify and estimate the firm's principal exposures to currency risk.

Regressions based on historical relationships can be unsatisfactory indicators of current and expected future exposure to currency risk. Regressions are necessarily backward looking. Because the competitive environment and the firm's mix of international sales and expenses change over time, regressions based on historical data can provide inaccurate measures of the firm's current exposures. Regression coefficients based on historical performance also do not allow the financial manager to perform "what-if" analyses of proposed changes to the firm's operations. This creates a need for a more flexible, forward-looking measure of operating exposure to currency risk. This is the topic of the next section.

An Insider's View of Operating Exposure

Managers can develop a better sense of the sensitivity of the firm's operating cash flows to currency risk by unbundling the revenues and expenses of the firm and examining the sensitivity of each to changes in foreign exchange rates. Using data from internal operations, managers can estimate the following for each major business unit:

$$rev_t^d = \alpha_{rev}^d + \beta_{rev}^f s_t^{d/f} + \varepsilon_t^d \qquad (12.6)$$

$$exp_t^d = \alpha_{exp}^d + \beta_{exp}^f s_t^{d/f} + \varepsilon_t^d \qquad (12.7)$$

where rev_t^d and exp_t^d represent percentage changes in revenues and expenses, respectively. Separating these two components of operating cash flow allows managers to determine to what extent revenues and expenses from different business units are exposed to currency risk. Armed with estimates of the past sensitivities of revenues and expenses, managers are in a better position to assess the exposure of future operating cash flows to currency risk as well as competitors' responses to exchange rate changes. The operating exposure of the firm's real assets can then be combined with the net transaction exposure of the firm's monetary assets and liabilities to estimate the exposure of shareholders' equity. As a final reality check, this insider's estimate of equity's currency risk exposure can be compared to a market-based estimate from Equation 12.2.

> Unbundling revenues and costs can help in identifying currency risk exposures.

12.3 • MANAGING OPERATING EXPOSURE IN THE FINANCIAL MARKETS

Financial Market Hedging Alternatives

> Operating exposures are usually long term.

Transaction exposures to currency risk are mostly short term in nature. In contrast, operating exposures typically have a very long time horizon. Hedges of operating exposures need to be long-lived to match the cash flows of these underlying exposures.

An Exporter's Financial Market Hedging Alternatives. Exporters typically have operating cash inflows denominated in one or more foreign currencies. These foreign currency inflows can be at least partially hedged by locking in foreign currency cash outflows through the financial markets. Here are some alternatives for hedging in the financial markets:

- Sell the foreign currency with long-dated forward contracts.
- Finance a foreign project with foreign debt capital.
- Use currency swaps to acquire financial liabilities in the foreign currency, such as with a swap of existing domestic currency debt for foreign currency debt.
- Use a rolling hedge (a series of consecutive short-term forward or futures contracts) to repeatedly sell the foreign currency.

Each of these financial alternatives locks in contractual cash outflows that are in the same currency as the firm's operating cash inflows. This reduces the exposure of both the foreign subsidiary and the parent corporation to foreign currency fluctuations.

An Importer's Financial Market Hedging Alternatives. Conversely, importers buy their goods from foreign suppliers and have operating cash outflows in foreign currencies. An importer has the following alternatives for hedging foreign currency outflows through the financial markets:

- Buy the foreign currency with long-dated forward contracts.
- Invest in long-dated foreign bonds.
- Use currency swaps to acquire financial assets in the foreign currency, such as with a swap of existing foreign currency debt for domestic currency debt.
- Use a rolling hedge to repeatedly buy the foreign currency with a series of consecutive short-term forward or futures contracts.

These financial alternatives lock in contractual cash inflows in the foreign currency that hopefully offset the importer's noncontractual foreign currency cash outflows.

Advantages and Disadvantages of Financial Market Hedges

The main advantage of a financial market hedge is that the costs of buying or selling financial instruments are low compared to the costs of investing or disinvesting in real assets. In isolation, financial market transactions are also more likely to be zero-NPV transactions than are changes in the firm's operations.

The main disadvantage of a financial market hedge is that the contractual cash flows of a financial instrument cannot fully hedge the uncertain operating cash flows of the firm's real assets. Hedging operating exposure with a financial market hedge does not reduce the operating exposure itself. Rather, it offsets this operating exposure with a financial hedge that has a roughly opposite exposure to currency risk. Thus, it changes the transaction exposure of the firm in a way that hopefully offsets the operating exposure of the firm. Because the contractual cash flows of a financial market hedge do not match the uncertain cash flows of an operating exposure to currency risk, a financial market hedge is almost certain to over- or underhedge the underlying exposure.

> Financial market hedges cannot completely hedge operating exposures.

Consider Duracell International's exports of batteries from the United States to Japan. There are two sources of variability to dollar cash flows from Duracell's Japanese sales: (1) variability in yen revenues, and (2) variability in the dollar value of the yen. Suppose Duracell expects revenues of ¥100 million next year from Japan, but actual revenues can be as little as ¥50 million or as much as ¥150 million according to the following distribution:

Duracell's revenues from Japanese sales

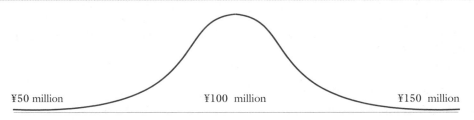

¥50 million   ¥100 million   ¥150 million

Given the level of yen revenues, the dollar value of Duracell's sales depends on the spot rate of exchange. At a forward and expected future spot rate of $F_1^{\$/¥} = E[S_1^{\$/¥}] = \$0.01/¥$, the resulting expected dollar inflow is $(¥100 \text{ million})(\$0.01/¥) = \$1$ million. As a classic exporter, Duracell is positively exposed to the value of the yen. Change in the dollar value of Duracell's yen cash flow $(v^{\$/¥})$ with respect to a change in the spot rate $(s^{\$/¥})$ is shown as a positively sloped 45-degree line:

Underlying yen exposure   +¥100 million

Risk profile of the underlying yen exposure

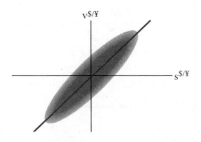

Uncertainty about the magnitude of Duracell's yen cash inflow is represented in the risk profile as a fuzzy area around the 45-degree line.

Duracell can hedge the expected cash flow of ¥100 million by selling ¥100 million forward, thus securing an expected cash inflow of $1 million:

Sell yen forward   +$1 million

                                            −¥100 million

Risk profile of the forward hedge

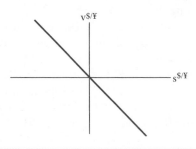

There is no uncertainty about the terms of this forward contract, so the risk profile is represented by a negatively sloped 45-degree line. The resulting combination of the underlying yen exposure and the forward market hedge looks like this:

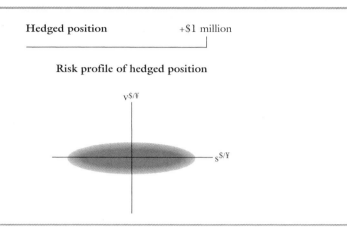

Hedged position   +$1 million

Risk profile of hedged position

The *expected* payoff of the yen side of this hedged position is zero, but the actual dollar payoff will depend on yen revenues and the value of the yen.

To focus on the variability of yen revenues, suppose the actual spot rate equals its expectation of $0.01/¥. In the top panel of Figure 12.5, variability in the hedged cash flows is shown as a function of the level of revenues in yen. In general, the net exposure of the hedged position depends on sales as well as the exchange rate. Duracell is perfectly hedged only when yen revenues are exactly ¥100 million. If yen revenues are any other amount, Duracell has a mismatch between its underlying exposure and the size of its forward hedge.

If yen revenues are only ¥50 million, the forward contract overhedges by ¥50 million. Duracell receives $1 million on the long dollar forward position, but must pay ¥100 million on the short side of the forward contract against only ¥50 million in sales. The net result is a $1 million cash inflow and a ¥50 million cash outflow. The ¥50 million cash outflow costs $500,000 at the $0.01/¥ spot rate, for net revenues in dollars of $500,000. Conversely, the forward contract underhedges by ¥50 million when Japanese sales are ¥150 million. In this case, Duracell receives $1 million on the long dollar forward position but must pay ¥100 million on short yen side of the forward contract against ¥150 million in revenues. This results in cash flows of $1 million and ¥50 million, or a total of $1.5 million at a spot rate of $0.01/¥.

Duracell's "hedged" position remains exposed to currency risk because of uncertainty in the magnitude of yen revenues. Consider the case when Japanese sales are ¥50 million, as shown in the middle panel of Figure 12.5. The $1 million forward hedge results in a short position of ¥50 million plus the $1 million from the forward contract. If the yen appreciates to $0.015/¥, this short position costs $750,000. The net cash flow in dollars falls to $1,000,000 – $750,000 = $250,000. If the yen depreciates to $0.005/¥, the ¥50 million short position costs $250,000 and dollar revenues are $1,000,000 – $250,000 = $750,000. In this way, exchange rate variability causes the value of the net position to vary from $250,000 to $750,000.

Conversely, if Japanese sales are ¥150 million, then the $1 million forward hedge results in a long position of ¥50 million plus the $1 million from the forward contract, as shown in the bottom panel of Figure 12.5. At an exchange rate of $0.015/¥, Duracell's net cash flow is $1,000,000 + $750,000 = $1,750,000. If the yen depreciates to $0.005/¥, the net cash flow is $1,000,000 + $250,000 = $1,250,000. With

FIGURE 12.5
Duracell's Operating Exposure

	Uncertain yen revenues		
Underlying revenues in yen	+¥50 million	+¥100 million	+¥150 million
Cash flows of the forward hedge			
long dollars	+$1 million	+$1 million	+$1 million
short yen	−¥100 million	−¥100 million	−¥100 million
Net position			
in dollars	+$1 million	+$1 million	+$1 million
in yen	−¥50 million	¥0 million	+¥50 million
	Exchange rate uncertainty at revenues of ¥50 million		
Underlying revenues in yen	+¥50 million	+¥50 million	+¥50 million
Cash flows of the forward hedge			
long dollars	+$1 million	+$1 million	+$1 million
short yen	−¥100 million	−¥100 million	−¥100 million
Net position			
in dollars	+$1 million	+$1 million	+$1 million
in yen	−¥50 million	−¥50 million	−¥50 million
Actual exchange rate	$0.005/¥	$0.010/¥	$0.015/¥
Actual revenues in dollars	+$750,000	+$500,000	+$250,000
	Exchange rate uncertainty at revenues of ¥150 million		
Underlying revenues in yen	+¥150 million	+¥150 million	+¥150 million
Cash flows of the forward hedge			
long dollars	+$1 million	+$1 million	+$1 million
short yen	−¥100 million	−¥100 million	−¥100 million
Net position			
in dollars	+$1 million	+$1 million	+$1 million
in yen	+¥50 million	+¥50 million	+¥50 million
Actual exchange rate	$0.005/¥	$0.010/¥	$0.015/¥
Actual revenues in dollars	+$1,250,000	+$1,500,000	+$1,750,000

underlying revenues of ¥150 million, exchange rate variability causes the value of the net position to vary between $1,250,000 and $1,750,000.

Assessing the Effectiveness of a Financial Market Hedge

Because of the mismatch between the certain cash flows of a financial market hedge and the uncertain cash flows of the underlying operating exposure, it is important for managers to undertake an analysis of the likely performance of financial market hedges.[1] Managers should assess the performance of financial market hedges of operating exposures in the following ways:

- Vary pro forma operating performance within reasonable limits.
- Vary the exchange rate and assess the resulting competitive position of the firm.

---

[1] The r-square of the regression $r_t^d = \alpha^d + \beta^f s_t^{d/f} + \varepsilon_t^d$ can be used as a measure of the quality of the hedge. Chapter 6 discusses this measure of hedge quality in the context of foreign currency futures contracts.

- Assess the interaction of operating performance with exchange rate changes.

The effectiveness of various financial market hedges can then be investigated in the following ways:[2]

- Vary the type of hedge (e.g., forwards, futures, options, or swaps).
- Vary the amount of the hedge.
- Vary the term or maturity of the hedge.

In many cases, management will choose to hedge less than the expected cash flow. For example, Duracell may choose to sell only ¥50 million forward rather than the full ¥100 million expected operating cash flow. This partially reduces the sensitivity of operating performance to the exchange rate while avoiding the risk of overhedging.

12.4 • MANAGING OPERATING EXPOSURE THROUGH OPERATIONS

Trying to hedge an operating exposure with a financial market hedge is like trying to cure a general malaise such as the common cold with a precise surgical instrument, such as a scalpel. Financial market hedges can reduce the discomfort of an operating exposure to currency risk, but cannot cure the underlying cause.

This section discusses how the MNC can reduce operating exposure to currency risk and possibly increase operating cash flow by adjusting operations in response to, or in anticipation of, changes in exchange rates. Because they treat the underlying cause, operating hedges are potentially more effective than financial hedges in reducing operating exposure to currency risk. However, they also fundamentally change the MNC's operations and should be undertaken only after due consideration.

> Operational hedges are seldom zero-NPV.

By themselves, financial market hedges are zero-NPV transactions. Financial hedges create value by combining with an underlying risk exposure to reduce the firm's expected taxes, financial distress costs, or agency costs. A firm that is contemplating an operational hedge cannot assume that proposed changes in operations are zero-NPV. Although some operational changes might be good for stakeholders, others are likely to destroy value. A capital budgeting analysis should be performed (as in Chapter 15) to fully evaluate any proposed change in operations.

Flexibility and the MNC's Competitive Advantage over Domestic Firms

MNCs have a natural advantage over domestic firms in responding to changes in real exchange rates. A real exchange rate change results in a change in one currency's purchasing power relative to another. This, in turn, can lead to a currency appearing overvalued or undervalued relative to another. Prices of goods and services are slow to react to changes in real exchange rates, and purchasing power parity can take several years to be restored. In the meantime, MNCs can take advantage of cross-border price differences in labor and materials.

> The MNC has flexibility in responding to changes in real exchange rates.

Although the world's markets for goods and services are becoming increasingly integrated, it is nevertheless difficult to establish reliable cross-border relations. Compared to domestic trade, the costs and risks of international shipments and of international

---

2 These variations are described in Lewent and Kearney, "Identifying, Measuring, and Hedging Currency Risk at Merck," *Journal of Applied Corporate Finance* (1990).

payments are high. Domestic firms without an established network of foreign suppliers or customers must overcome these trade barriers if they hope to take advantage of differential prices in foreign markets. International diversification provides the MNC with greater flexibility in its plant location, production and sourcing, marketing, and general management decisions.

Types of Operational Hedges

Whether any of the operational hedges that follow are viable in a particular circumstance depends on competitive conditions in the corporation's host countries and markets. Each relies on geographic dispersion to reduce the MNC's operating exposure to currency risk.

Plant Location. The MNC can gain an advantage over domestic rivals by securing low-cost labor, capital, or resources through its plant location decisions. These decisions must consider a number of factors, including labor costs, labor and capital productivities, taxes and tariffs, and legal, institutional, and social infrastructures.

Product Sourcing. Importers and MNCs with a global manufacturing base or established networks of foreign suppliers can respond more quickly than domestic competitors to real changes in currency values. As local real costs or exchange rates change, MNCs can shift production toward the lowest real costs. Diversifying production across countries also hedges against exposures to political risks, such as expropriation or changes in tariffs.

Market Selection and Promotion. When local markets are segmented from global competition, local prices and costs are slow to adjust to real changes in foreign exchange rates. In these circumstances, a real appreciation of the foreign currency benefits exporters by increasing the purchasing power of foreign customers. In the presence of real exchange rate changes, globally diversified MNCs can shift their marketing efforts toward countries with overvalued currencies and thus create a spectrum of favorable pricing alternatives. These alternatives are developed in the next section.

Combining Operational and Financial Hedges

Allayannis, Ihrig, and Weston investigate the impact of financial and operating hedges on risk management and firm value.[3] These authors find that geographic dispersion of a MNC's subsidiaries across countries does not, by itself, reduce the MNC's exposure to currency risk. In contrast, these authors found that financial hedging strategies are related to lower currency risk exposures. Moreover, firms that used operational hedges in conjunction with financial hedges tended to have higher market values than other firms. These results suggest that a combination of operating and financial hedges can help maximize the value of the firm.

12.5 • Pricing Strategy and the Firm's Competitive Environment

An Example of an Exporter's Operating Exposure to Currency Risk

The MNC's pricing decisions are an important component of overall business and financial strategy. Pricing decisions also affect the firm's operating exposure to currency risk. An example of an exporter's exposure will illustrate the main effects.

---

3 Allayannis, Ihrig, and Weston, "Exchange-Rate Hedging: Financial Versus Operational Strategies," *American Economic Review* (2001).

Imagine a hair growth product that is so strong it can grow hair on a bowling ball. Now, imagine how much bald men and women around the world would be willing to pay for such a product. Let's call our imaginary product GroMane, manufactured by Tao Corporation of Singapore for sale in the United States. Tao's income statement is shown in U.S. and Singapore dollars as the "base case" in the leftmost columns of Figure 12.6.

Tao Corporation manufactures GroMane in Singapore for sale in the United States at a price of $10 per bottle. The $10 price is equivalent to S$20 at the current exchange rate of $S_0^{S\$/\$} = S\$2.00/\$$. Inflation is the same in Singapore and the United States, and expected future exchange rates are expected to remain constant at $E[S_t^{S\$/\$}] = S\$2.00/\$$. Labor expense is Tao's only cost of goods sold (COGS) and is S$10 per bottle. Tao's labor force is local, and labor costs are contractually fixed in Singapore dollars. The production costs of Tao's international competitors are similarly fixed in their own local currencies. Corporate income taxes in Singapore are assumed to be 50 percent.

Tao expects to sell 2,000 bottles per year in perpetuity for an annual after-tax cash flow of $E[CF^\$] = \$5,000$, or $E[CF^{S\$}] = S\$10,000$ at the current exchange rate. The hurdle rate on investments of this type is $i^\$ = i^{S\$} = 10$ percent in both countries. With perpetual cash flows, the value of Tao Corporation is $V^\$ = (\$5,000)/(0.1) = \$50,000$.[4] This is equivalent to $V^{S\$} = (S\$10,000)/(0.1) = S\$100,000$ at the $\$0.50/S\$$ exchange rate.

FIGURE 12.6
Tao Corporation's Operating Exposure

					Twenty-five percent appreciation of the U.S. dollar to S$2.50/$					
			Maintain $10 price		Maintain S$20 price					
	Base case S$2.00/$		Sales volume remains constant		Elastic demand Sell 50% more		Inelastic demand Sell 10% more			
Income statement	U.S. dollar	Singapore dollar	U.S. dollar	Singapore dollar	U.S. dollar	Singapore dollar	U.S. dollar	Singapore dollar		
Price per bottle	$10	S$20	$10	S$25	$8	S$20	$8	S$20		
Cost per bottle	$5	S$10	$4	S$10	$4	S$10	$4	S$10		
Bottles sold	2,000	2,000	2,000	2,000	3,000	3,000	2,200	2,200		
Revenues	20,000	40,000	20,000	50,000	24,000	60,000	17,600	44,000		
– Cost of goods sold	–10,000	–20,000	–8,000	–20,000	–12,000	–30,000	–8,800	–22,000		
Before-tax profit	10,000	20,000	12,000	30,000	12,000	30,000	8,800	22,000		
– Tax (at 50%)	–5,000	–10,000	–6,000	–15,000	-6,000	–15,000	–4,400	–11,000		
Net cash flow	5,000	10,000	6,000	15,000	6,000	15,000	4,400	11,000		
Value of Tao at $i^\$ = i^{S\$} = 10\%$	$50,000	S$100,000	$60,000	S$150,000	$60,000	S$150,000	$44,000	S$110,000		
Percentage change in value			20%	50%	20%	50%	–12%	+10%		

---

4 The assumption of perpetual cash flows simplifies our algebra. Recall that the value V of a perpetual cash flow CF discounted at a rate i is simply $V = CF/i$.

Alternative Pricing Strategies

Suppose the U.S. dollar unexpectedly appreciates by 25 percent, from S$2.00/$ to S$2.50/$, and is expected to remain at this new level indefinitely. This is a 20 percent depreciation of the Singapore dollar. Suppose further that the U.S. dollar retains its value against other currencies, so that the Singapore dollar depreciates by 20 percent against all other currencies. What is the value of Tao Corporation after this Singapore dollar depreciation?

Tao's situation with respect to the exchange rate is that of the classic exporter. Tao's cost of goods sold is fixed in Singapore dollars and is unlikely to change as the Singapore dollar changes in value against other currencies. In contrast, the price that Tao receives for GroMane is determined in the U.S. market. In this situation, a depreciation of the Singapore dollar enhances Tao's competitive position relative to its non-Singaporean competition.

Pricing strategies that Tao can pursue in response to a depreciation of the Singapore dollar include the following:

- *Constant foreign currency price.* Hold the U.S. dollar price constant at $10 per bottle (or S$25 per bottle at $0.40/S$) and try to sell the same quantity in the United States.

- *Constant domestic currency price.* Hold the Singapore dollar price constant at S$20 per bottle ($8/btl at $0.40/S$) and try to increase sales volume in the United States.

Constant Foreign Currency Price. If Tao holds its dollar price constant at $10 per bottle, it receives S$25 per bottle at the $0.40/S$ spot rate as shown in Figure 12.6. Because the dollar price is unchanged, Tao's annual sales of 2,000 bottles should remain unchanged, assuming no change in the position of Tao's competitors in the U.S. market. The S$25 per bottle price increases Tao's contribution margin to S$15 per bottle, or S$7.50 per bottle after corporate income taxes. After-tax cash flow is (S$7.50/bottle)(2,000 bottles) = S$15,000 per year, which is worth S$150,000 at the 10 percent discount rate. The value of Tao in Singapore dollars should increase if it does nothing more than maintain its U.S. dollar price for GroMane.

The dollar value of Tao may or may not increase depending on which effect dominates: the increase in contribution margin at the higher Singapore dollar sales price or the decrease in the value of the Singapore dollar. In this example, the increase in contribution margin dominates, and Tao's U.S. dollar value increases to $60,000 at the $0.40/S$ exchange rate.

Constant Domestic Currency Price. What will happen to Tao's value if it follows the second pricing strategy and holds the Singapore dollar price constant at S$20? Tao's contribution margin remains S$10 per bottle, but the lower U.S. dollar price of $8 per bottle should increase sales volume in the United States. All else equal, the value of Tao in Singapore dollars should go up. As before, the U.S. dollar value may go up or down, depending on whether the increase in sales volume is enough to overcome the 20 percent depreciation in the Singapore dollar. This depends on the price elasticity of demand.

Optimal Pricing and the Price Elasticity of Demand

The exporter's optimal pricing strategy depends on the price elasticity of demand that it faces in its markets. **Price elasticity of demand** is defined as minus the percentage change in quantity demanded (Q) for a given percentage change in price (P).

$$\text{Price elasticity of demand} = -(\Delta Q/Q)/(\Delta P/P) \qquad (12.8)$$

If percentage changes in quantity sold are equal to percentage changes in price, then the product has unit elasticity. This is a useful starting point, because goods with unit elasticity will see no change in total revenue (Rev = PQ) with a change in price. What is lost (or gained) in price is exactly offset by a gain (or loss) in quantity sold. Elasticities greater than one are said to be *elastic* and result in a decrease in revenue with an increase in price. Elasticities less than one are said to be *inelastic* and result in an increase in revenue with an increase in price. The firm's price elasticity of demand is an important component of operating exposure to currency risk.

Strictly speaking, elasticity holds only for infinitesimally small changes in price and quantity. Larger changes are multiplicative rather than additive. For example, if price decreases by 20 percent, then quantity sold must increase by 25 percent to leave revenue unchanged. Algebraically, this is given by $\text{Rev}_1{}^\$ = P_1{}^\$ Q_1 = [(0.80)P_0{}^\$][(1.25)Q_0] = P_0{}^\$ Q_0 = \text{Rev}_0{}^\$$. For this reason, price elasticity measures the sensitivity of sales volume to infinitesimally small changes in price.

Suppose the beneficial effects of GroMane on hair retention are quickly lost and difficult to recover once treatment is suspended. Whether GroMane is price elastic or inelastic will depend on whether GroMane customers have other sources of supply in the U.S. market. In the absence of substitutes, customers are likely to do almost anything to replenish their supply. If Tao owns a patent on GroMane and can control supply, demand is likely to be price inelastic. On the other hand, demand is likely to be price elastic if customers have access to other sources of GroMane or there are generic substitutes in a competitive U.S. market.

The Consequences of Alternative Pricing Strategies

The possible consequences of Tao's export pricing choices are shown for constant S$20 prices in the right half of Figure 12.6.

Price Elastic Demand. Suppose Tao keeps the Singapore dollar price of GroMane unchanged at S$20 per bottle. This reduces the U.S. dollar price of GroMane to $8 per bottle at the $0.40/S$ spot exchange rate. This reduction in the U.S. dollar price of GroMane should increase Tao's sales in the United States. The amount of the sales increase depends on the price elasticity of demand.

Suppose the 20 percent decrease in the U.S. dollar price of GroMane increases sales volume by 50 percent, to 3,000 bottles. This increases revenues to (3,000 bottles)(S$20/bottle) = S$60,000, but also increases costs to (3,000 bottles)(S$10/bottle) = S$30,000. The net result is a S$15,000 annual after-tax cash flow and a S$150,000 value for Tao. Tao is (again) worth $60,000 at the $0.40/S$ spot exchange rate. The dollar value of Tao increases to $60,000 (from $50,000 in the base case) because the additional cash flow on a 50 percent increase in sales volume more than offsets the 20 percent depreciation of the Singapore dollar.

Price Inelastic Demand. The columns at the right of Figure 12.6 show what can happen when demand is price inelastic. If Tao holds its Singapore dollar price fixed at S$20 per bottle (or $8 per bottle) in this example, the increase in sales volume is not sufficient to offset the decrease in contribution margin. Sales volume increases by only 10 percent on a 20 percent fall in price. If price is set at S$20 per bottle rather than the S$25 price from the "maintain dollar price" strategy, revenues fall by 12 percent according to $\text{Rev}_1{}^\$ = P_1{}^\$ Q_1 = [(0.80)P_0{}^\$][(1.10)Q_0] = (0.88)\text{Rev}_0{}^\$$. Faced with inelastic demand, Tao is better off holding its dollar price fixed at $10 per bottle (or S$25 per bottle) and reaping the benefits of the higher S$ contribution margin.

Reprise

Section 12.5 illustrates how currency risk exposure interacts with the firm's pricing strategies through the price elasticity of demand for the firm's goods or services. The history of price changes can be used to estimate a product's price elasticity of demand. History also provides a record of how the firm's competitors have responded to price changes and other competitive pressures. The MNC must combine this experience with current market conditions in formulating its pricing strategies.

12.6 • SUMMARY

This chapter deals with the operating exposure of real assets to currency risk and with the exposure of shareholders' equity to currency risk. Operating exposure is more difficult to measure and manage than transaction exposure because it involves *uncertain* rather than contractual cash flows.

As the residual owner of the firm, the exposure of shareholders' equity is determined by the net transaction exposures of monetary assets and liabilities and the operating exposure of the firm's real assets. Whereas monetary assets and liabilities are exposed to changes in nominal exchange rates, operating cash flows are exposed to changes in real exchange rates. Thus, equity is exposed to both real and nominal changes in currency values.

The classic importer buys its goods in foreign markets at prices that are determined in the foreign markets and sells these goods to domestic customers at prices that are determined in the domestic market. Thus, importers tend to gain (lose) from a real appreciation (depreciation) of the domestic currency. Conversely, the classic exporter tends to gain (lose) from a real depreciation (appreciation) of the domestic currency. How much the firm wins or loses in value depends on the firm's pricing policies and the price elasticity of demand for its products.

Operating strategies for reducing the firm's sensitivity to unexpected changes in real exchange rates include marketing and production strategies that allow the multinational corporation to enhance revenues and reduce operating and financial costs while taking advantage of the benefits of international portfolio diversification. The key difference between financial and operating hedges of currency risk is that changes in operations directly affect the value of the corporation.

KEY TERMS

integrated versus segmented markets
net monetary assets
operating exposure

price elasticity of demand
r-square
transaction exposure

CONCEPTUAL QUESTIONS

12.1   What is operating exposure to currency risk, and why is it important?

12.2   In a discounted cash flow framework, in what ways can operating risk affect the value of the multinational corporation?

12.3   What is an integrated market? A segmented market? Why is this distinction important in multinational financial management?

12.4 How is an importer affected by a real depreciation of the domestic currency? An exporter? A diversified multinational corporation competing in globally competitive goods and financial markets?

12.5 What is meant by the statement "Exposure is a regression coefficient"?

12.6 Suppose the correlation of a share of stock with a foreign currency value is +0.10. Calculate r-square. What does it tell you?

12.7 Define net monetary assets. Define the net exposure of monetary assets and liabilities to currency risk. Why are these measures important?

12.8 List several financial market alternatives for hedging operating exposure to currency risk. How effective are these in hedging the nonmonetary cash flows of real assets? Why might firms hedge through the financial markets rather than through changes in operations?

12.9 List several operating strategies for hedging operating risk. What are the advantages and disadvantages of these hedges compared to financial market hedges?

12.10 What is the price elasticity of demand, and why is it important?

12.11 What five steps are involved in estimating the impact of exchange rate changes on the value of the firm's real assets or on the value of equity?

PROBLEMS

12.1 Sterling & Company is a world renowned manufacturer of silverware. Their factory is in Sevenoaks in the United Kingdom. Although Sterling exports to companies around the world, its biggest customers are in the United States. Accounts that are denominated in dollars are indicated in the following balance sheet. The exchange rate is currently $1.50/£.

	Value in local currency	Value in pounds		Value in local currency	Value in pounds
Cash ($)	$30,000	£20,000	Payables ($)	$45,000	£30,000
Cash (£)		£20,000	Payables (£)		£10,000
Receivables(£)		£30,000			
Inventory (£)	_____	£10,000		_____	
Current assets		£80,000	Current liabilities		£40,000
			Long-term debt ($)	$90,000	£60,000
			Long-term debt (£)		£20,000
Real assets	_____	£80,000	Net worth	_____	£40,000
Total assets		£160,000	Total liabilities		£160,000

a. What is the value of monetary assets and of monetary liabilities that are exposed to the dollar? What is the value of net monetary assets with a dollar exposure?

b. If the dollar appreciates by 10 percent, by how much will monetary assets change in value? By how much will monetary liabilities change in value? What are the r-squares of these relations?

c. Suppose inventory is not exposed to the dollar and that the exposure of real assets to the value of the dollar is $\beta^\$ = \rho_{r,s}(\sigma_r/\sigma_s)$, where $\rho_{r,s} = 0.10$, $\sigma_R =$

0.20, and $\sigma_s = 0.10$. If the dollar rises in value by 10 percent, by how much are Sterling & Company's real assets likely to change in value? What is the r-square of this relation? Do you have much confidence in this estimate of the change in value? Why or why not.

d. Given your results in parts b and c, by how much is Sterling & Company's equity likely to change in value with a 10 percent appreciation of the dollar?

e. Sterling has a relatively large amount of debt denominated in dollars. Is this amount of dollar debt reasonable given their operating exposure from part c? Relate your answer to the r-square of the exposure coefficient in part c.

f. Sterling is considering opening a manufacturing plant in the United States to hedge their exposure to the dollar. Discuss the advantages and disadvantages of this operating hedge of Sterling's dollar exposure.

12.2 Why is operating exposure to currency risk more difficult to manage than transaction exposure?

12.3 Studies have found that corporations based in the United States typically have low exposures to other currencies. In contrast, studies have found that a much higher percentage of firms in other countries (including Canada, Germany, and Japan) are exposed to the dollar. Why might this be? What does it suggest about currency risk management in these countries relative to currency risk management in the United States?

12.4 Dow of the United States makes bungee cords for sale in the United Kingdom. Dow charges $6 per cord, or £4 at the $1.50/£ spot rate. At this price, Dow expects annual sales of 20,000 cords in perpetuity. Variable costs are $3 per cord in the United States. The discount rate is 10 percent in each currency. Dow is considering its price response to a 20 percent pound depreciation from $1.50/£ to $1.20/£ (corresponding to a 25 percent dollar appreciation from £0.6667/$ to £0.8333/$. Reconstruct Figure 12.6 as follows:

a. Estimate Dow's value (in pounds and dollars) assuming it maintains the £4 U.K. price and sales volume in the United Kingdom does not change.

b. Estimate Dow's value (in pounds and dollars) assuming Dow maintains the $6 U.S. price (or, a £5 price) and U.K. sales volume falls by 50 percent. What is Dow's optimal pricing strategy if demand is price elastic in this way?

c. Estimate Dow's value (in pounds and dollars) assuming Dow maintains the $6 U.S. price (or, a £5 price) and U.K. sales volume falls by 10 percent. What is Dow's optimal pricing strategy if demand is price inelastic in this way?

SUGGESTED READINGS

Merck's use of computed modeling of the corporate hedging decision is found in

Judy C. Lewent and A. John Kearney, "Identifying, Measuring, and Hedging Currency Risk at Merck," *Journal of Applied Corporate Finance* 2, No. 4 (1990), pp. 19–28.

The effect of financial and operating hedges on firm value is investigated in

George Allayannis, Jane Ihrig, and James P. Weston, "Exchange-Rate Hedging: Financial Versus Operational Strategies," *American Economic Review* 91 (May 2001), pp. 391–395.

Managing Translation Exposure to Currency Risk

chapter 13

Overview

Evolution has her own accounting system and that's the only one that matters.

R. Buckminster Fuller

In consolidating its financial statements, a parent company with foreign operations must translate the assets and liabilities of its foreign affiliates into its reporting currency. **Translation exposure** (also called **accounting exposure**) refers to the impact of exchange rate changes on the parent firm's consolidated financial statements.

This chapter begins with a review of the most common foreign currency translation methods using the history of accounting standards in the United States for illustration. The advantages and disadvantages of these translation methods are compared. Reasons for and against hedging the firm's translation exposure to currency risk are then discussed. Hedge accounting for derivative transactions concludes the chapter.

> Translation exposure refers to the impact of exchange rate changes on consolidated financial statements.

13.1 • MEASURING TRANSLATION EXPOSURE

Translation accounting methods typically fall into one of three categories:

* The current/noncurrent method
* The temporal or monetary/nonmonetary method
* The current rate method

These accounting translation methods are summarized in Figure 13.1. Differences between these translation methods arise when some accounts are translated at current exchange rates and other accounts are translated at historical rates.

All three methods have been used at various times in the United States. Prior to 1976, most companies used the current/noncurrent method. A temporal (monetary/nonmonetary) method was introduced in 1976 with Statement of Financial Accounting Standards No. 8 (FAS #8), "Accounting for the Translation of Foreign Currency Transactions and Foreign Currency Financial Statements." In 1982, this method was replaced by the current rate method of FAS #52, "Foreign Currency Translation." We'll use U.S. history to illustrate each of these accounting translation methods.

The Current/Noncurrent Method in Use Prior to 1976

Current/noncurrent methods classify short- and long-term accounts differently.

The **current/noncurrent method** translates current (short-term) and noncurrent (long-term) assets and liabilities differently. The following rules are typical of the current/noncurrent method used in the United States prior to the introduction of FAS #8 in 1976:

1. Current assets and liabilities are translated at the current exchange rate.
2. Noncurrent assets and liabilities are translated at historical exchange rates.
3. Most income statement items are related to current assets or liabilities and are translated at the average exchange rate over the reporting period.
4. Depreciation is related to noncurrent assets and translated at the historical exchange rate.

The current exchange rate is the one prevailing on the date of the financial statement. Historical exchange rates are those that prevailed when items were first entered into the accounts.

From a financial perspective, the current/noncurrent method correctly values current assets and liabilities that are monetary in nature. However, it typically misvalues long-term debt. Like short-term debt, long-term debt is a monetary liability that

FIGURE 13.1
A Summary of Accounting Translation Methods

	Current/ noncurrent method	Monetary/ nonmonetary method	Current rate method
Assets			
Short-term financial assets	current	current	current
Long-term financial assets	historical	current	historical
Real assets	historical	historical	historical
Liabilities and owner's equity			
Short-term financial liabilities	current	current	current
Long-term financial liabilities	historical	current	historical
Net worth (common equity)	historical	historical	historical
Translation gains or losses	flowed through the income statement	flowed through the income statement	reported as a cumulative translation adjustment in net worth

Note: Table entries indicate whether current or historical exchange rates are used for translating the assets and liabilities of foreign subsidiaries into the parent's consolidated financial statements.

should be translated at the current exchange rate and not at the historical rate. Real assets are valued at their historical exchange rates, assuming they have no operating exposure to currency risk.

Suppose a U.S. parent using the current/noncurrent method establishes a French affiliate in the year 2003. Each of the foreign subsidiary's accounts is denominated in euros (€), so the parent's translation exposure is to the euro. Figure 13.2 shows the end-of-year balance sheet translated at the prevailing exchange rate of $1.00/€. Figure 13.2 also shows the balance sheet effect of a change in the exchange rate from $1.00/€ to $0.80/€ during 2003. If inflation is equal in the euro and the U.S. dollar, then this also reflects a 20 percent real depreciation of the euro against the dollar.

A key measure of accounting exposure under any translation method is net exposed assets. **Net exposed assets** is equal to the book value of assets that are exposed to currency risk less the book value of liabilities that are exposed to currency risk. The MNC's translation exposure under the current/noncurrent method is equal to the exposure of net working capital; that is, the exposure of current assets net of exposed current liabilities. As the euro falls to $0.80/€ in Figure 13.2, the dollar value of exposed assets falls by $1,500 (from $7,500 to $6,000). The dollar value of exposed liabilities falls by $1,000 (from $5,000 to $4,000). The change in net exposed assets is [−$1,500−(−$1,000)] = −$500.

> Net exposed assets equals exposed assets less exposed liabilities.

Gains or losses from translation exposure to currency risk are not reflected in net income under the current/noncurrent method. Instead, they are absorbed into net worth (common equity) in the balance sheet. In Figure 13.2, translation exposure results in a loss of $500. This translation loss results in a $500 decrease in net worth.

Because only current assets and liabilities have a translation exposure under this method, translation exposure can be calculated directly from net working capital. In our example, the French affiliate's net working capital is NWC€ = (€7,500−€5,000) = €2,500 in Figure 13.2. A 20 percent depreciation of the euro

FIGURE 13.2
An Example of the Current/Noncurrent Method

Assets	Value in euros	Dec. '03 value at $1.00/€	Dec. '04 value at $0.80/€		Translation gains or losses
Cash and marketable securities	€2,500	$2,500	$2,000	Exposed assets	−$500
Accounts receivable	€2,500	$2,500	$2,000		−$500
Inventory	€2,500	$2,500	$2,000		−$500
Plant and equipment	€7,500	$7,500	$7,500		$0
Total assets	€15,000	$15,000	$13,500		−$1,500
Liabilities					
Accounts payable	€2,500	$2,500	$2,000	Exposed liabilities	−$500
Short-term debt	€2,500	$2,500	$2,000		−$500
Long-term debt	€5,000	$5,000	$5,000		$0
Net worth*	€5,000	$5,000	$4,500		−$500 Net exposure
Total liabilities and net worth	€15,000	$15,000	$13,500		−$1,500

* Net worth of $4,500 includes $5,000 in common equity valued at historical cost and a translation loss of $500.

results in a 20 percent ($500) translation loss for the U.S. parent: $(1+s^{\$/\mathsf{C}})(\text{NWC}^{\mathsf{C}})$ = ($0.80/\mathsf{C}–$1.00/\mathsf{C})(C2,500) = –$500.

Because most businesses maintain positive net working capital, a foreign currency appreciation (depreciation) is typically associated with a translation gain (loss) under the current/noncurrent method.

The Temporal Method of FAS #8 (1976–1982)

> The temporal method classifies accounts as monetary or nonmonetary.

The **temporal** or **monetary/nonmonetary method** of foreign currency translation was introduced by FAS #8 in the United States and was used from 1976 through most of 1982. FAS #8 applied the following rules:[1]

1. Monetary assets and liabilities are translated at the current exchange rate.

2. All other assets and liabilities are translated at historical exchange rates.

3. Most income statement items are related to current items and are translated at the average exchange rate over the reporting period.

4. Depreciation and COGS are related to real (nonmonetary) assets and are translated at historical exchange rates.

As under other translation accounting methods, net exposed assets are equal to exposed monetary assets less exposed monetary liabilities.

Consider the financial statements of the French affiliate shown in Figure 13.3. Including long-term debt as an exposed liability under the FAS #8 rules, net exposed assets are (C7,500–C10,000) = –C2,500 in Figure 13.3. As the euro falls to $0.80/$\mathsf{C}$, the dollar value of exposed assets falls by $1,500 (from $7,500 to $6,000). The dollar value of exposed liabilities falls by $2,000 (from $10,000 to $8,000). Exposed liabilities fall by more than exposed assets, so the net effect is a translation gain of $500. For most firms, the value of monetary assets is less than that of monetary liabilities, so an appreciation (depreciation) of a foreign currency results in a translation loss (gain) under the temporal and monetary/nonmonetary methods.

In many ways, FAS #8 was an improvement over the current/noncurrent method that it replaced. In particular, the temporal method correctly valued monetary assets and liabilities at the current exchange rate. Nonmonetary assets and liabilities were valued at historical exchange rates, as in the current/noncurrent method.

Unfortunately, FAS #8 had a fatal flaw. Translation gains or losses were reflected in earnings on the income statement and then flowed into retained earnings on the balance sheet. Under FAS #8, translation restatements of balance sheet accounts could overwhelm operating performance and negatively affect reported earnings. Consequently, a profitable year could be obscured by currency translation adjustments over which the manager had no control. This caused more than a few sleepless nights for the accountants and managers of publicly traded firms, and made the temporal method unpopular.

> FAS #8 reports translation gains (losses) in net income.

The Current Rate Method of FAS #52 (1982–present)

In December 1982, the FASB proposed the **current rate method** of FAS #52 to replace the temporal method of FAS #8. FAS #52 applies the following rules:

---

1 The monetary/nonmonetary method treats inventory as a nonmonetary (real) asset that is translated at historical exchange rates. The temporal method of FAS #8 allowed inventory to be translated at the current exchange rate if domestic inventories were valued at market on the parent's balance sheet.

FIGURE 13.3
An Example of the Temporal Method of FAS #8

Assets	Value in euros	Dec. '03 value at $1.00/€	Dec. '04 value at $0.80/€	Translation gains or losses
Cash and marketable securities	€2,500	$2,500	$2,000 ⎤	−$500
Accounts receivable	€2,500	$2,500	$2,000 ⎥ Exposed assets	−$500
Inventory* (at current exchange rates)	€2,500	$2,500	$2,000 ⎦	−$500
Plant and equipment	€7,500	$7,500	$7,500	$0
Total assets	€15,000	$15,000	$13,500	−$1,500
Liabilities				
Accounts payable	€2,500	$2,500	$2,000 ⎤	−$500
Short-term debt	€2,500	$2,500	$2,000 ⎥ Exposed liabilities	−$500
Long-term debt	€5,000	$5,000	$4,000 ⎦	−$1,000
Net worth**	€5,000	$5,000	$5,500	+$500 ⎤ Net exposure
Total liabilities & net worth	€15,000	$15,000	$13,500	−$1,500

* FAS #8 translated inventory at the current exchange rate if the parent valued domestic inventories at market. (The monetary/nonmonetary method translates inventory at historical exchange rates.)

** Net worth of $5,500 includes $5,000 in common equity valued at historical cost and a translation gain of $500 that flows through the income statement.

1. All assets and liabilities except common equity are translated at the current exchange rate.
2. Common equity is translated at historical exchange rates.
3. Income statement items are translated at a current exchange rate.[2]
4. Any imbalance between the book value of assets and liabilities is recorded as a separate equity account called the **cumulative translation adjustment (CTA)**.

> The current rate method translates most accounts at the current exchange rate.

Gains or losses caused by translation adjustments are not included in the calculation of net income under FAS #52. Rather, they are placed into the cumulative translation adjustment account in the equity section of the balance sheet.

Accountants and financial managers preferred FAS #52 to FAS #8 for two reasons. From a financial perspective, valuing real assets at current exchange rates (rather than at historical exchange rates as in FAS #8) better reflects the exposure of most real assets. From a practical perspective, the cumulative translation adjustment account allows balance sheet gains or losses to be isolated from reported income, rather than flowed through income into retained earnings, as in FAS #8. Even though this change is cosmetic in that it affects only accounting performance and not cash flows, it relieves managers of the burden of explaining poor earnings outcomes arising from balance-sheet translation effects.

---

2 Under FAS #52, firms are given a choice of translating income statement items at the average exchange rate for the reporting period, the exchange rates prevailing on the dates that the various income statement items were entered on the company's books, or a weighted average exchange rate for the period.

Figure 13.4 presents an example of translation exposure under the current rate method. Under this method, net exposed assets equal the net worth of the firm (total assets minus monetary liabilities). In the example, net exposed assets equal the net worth of the foreign affiliate: (€15,000–€10,000) = €5,000. A 20 percent depreciation in the value of the euro results in a 20 percent ($1,000) decrease in the book value of the foreign affiliate. This translation loss of $1,000 is absorbed by the cumulative translation adjustment account in the equity section of the balance sheet.

> In FAS #52, translation gains or losses flow into a CTA account.

13.2 • WHICH TRANSLATION METHOD IS THE MOST REALISTIC?

Which translation method is the most relevant in the sense of reflecting market value? The current/noncurrent method is clearly the least relevant, because it values long-term debt (a monetary liability) at historical cost. The other translation accounting methods correctly value monetary assets and liabilities at the current exchange rate.

The key issue is whether the real assets of a foreign subsidiary should be translated at historical exchange rates as in FAS #8 or at the current exchange rate as in FAS #52. The answer depends on the firm's operating exposure to currency risk. The temporal method of FAS #8 assumes the real assets of a foreign subsidiary are unaffected by exchange rates. The current rate method of FAS #52 assumes real assets have a one-to-one exposure to exchange rates. For most firms, the truth is somewhere between these two positions.

The most obvious effect of a foreign currency depreciation is a decrease in the domestic currency value of foreign assets (P^d) according to $P^d = P^f S^{d/f}$. However, a foreign currency depreciation also tends to increase the competitiveness and value of foreign assets in the foreign currency. This increase ($\Delta P^f > 0$) in the foreign currency value of foreign

---

FIGURE 13.4
An Example of the Current Rate Method of FAS #52

Assets	Value in euros	Dec. '03 value at $1.00/€	Dec. '04 value at $0.80/€		Translation gains or losses
Cash and marketable securities	€2,500	$2,500	$2,000		–$500
Accounts receivable	€2,500	$2,500	$2,000	Exposed assets	–$500
Inventory	€2,500	$2,500	$2,000		–$500
Plant and equipment	€7,500	$7,500	$6,000		–$1,500
Total assets	€15,000	$15,000	$12,000		–$3,000
Liabilities					
Accounts payable	€2,500	$2,500	$2,000		–$500
Short-term debt	€2,500	$2,500	$2,000	Exposed liabilities	–$500
Long-term debt	€5,000	$5,000	$4,000		–$1,000
Net worth					
Common equity	€5,000	$5,000	$5,000		$0 Net exposure
Cumulative translation adj	——	$0	–$1,000		–$1,000
Total liabilities and net worth	€15,000	$15,000	$12,000		–$3,000

assets may or may not be enough to offset the decrease ($\Delta S^{d/f} < 0$) in the value of the foreign currency. Consequently, each of these translation accounting methods is a simplified view of the true operating exposure of the foreign subsidiary's real assets. No simple accounting convention can hope to accommodate the variety of operating exposures observed in practice.

A number of empirical studies have compared the temporal method of FAS #8 to the current rate method of FAS #52. These studies typically estimate an **earnings response coefficient** that captures the relation of stock returns to earnings surprises (actual minus expected earnings) around the time of corporate earnings announcements. If earnings provide value-relevant information to investors, then earnings that are above expectations (positive earnings surprises) will be associated with positive stock returns. Conversely, earnings that are below expectations (negative surprises) will be associated with negative returns. By examining the strength of this relation, the information content of earnings announcements and the quality of reported earnings can be appraised.

The quality of accounting earnings appears to have improved under FAS #52. Collins and Salatka found that the earnings response coefficients of U.S. multinationals improved when FAS #52 was adopted.[3] Bartov found that this improvement in earnings quality appears only in those firms that designate a foreign currency as their functional currency.[4] The source of improvement in the quality of reported earnings may not have been in the switch from the temporal to the current rate method, but in the isolation of reported earnings from changes in translated balance sheet accounts through the cumulative translation adjustment account. Regardless of the source of improvement, FAS #52 seems to have improved the relevance of accounting earnings for U.S. multinationals.

> FAS #52 improved the quality of earnings.

13.3 • CORPORATE HEDGING OF TRANSLATION EXPOSURE

Finance theory states that the firm should only consider hedging risk exposures that are related to firm value. Hedging has value when it can reduce the variability of firm value and thereby reduce expected taxes, costs of financial distress, or agency costs.[5] There is no value in hedging noncash transactions that do not cost or risk cash.

Translation exposure involves income statement and balance sheet accounts. It may or may not involve cash flows. Consider an inventory of crude oil held by a foreign subsidiary of a U.S. parent. Oil prices rise and fall with the dollar, so an appreciation (depreciation) of a currency against the dollar typically decreases (increases) the price of oil in that currency. If oil inventory is carried at historical cost on the foreign subsidiary's balance sheet and translated back to the parent's financial statements at the current exchange rate, then the U.S. parent has a translation exposure to currency risk without a corresponding economic (transaction or operating) exposure. Hedging this foreign currency translation exposure with a financial market transaction is unlikely to increase shareholder value. To the extent that hedging a noncash translation exposure increases risk or costs cash, hedging can actually decrease the value of the firm.

> Only risk exposures that are related to firm value should be hedged.

---

3 Collins and Salatka, "Noisy Accounting Earnings Signals and Earnings Response Coefficients: The Case of Foreign Currency Accounting," *Contemporary Accounting Research* (1994).

4 Bartov, "Foreign Currency Exposure of Multinational Firms: Accounting Measures and Market Valuation," *Contemporary Accounting Research* (1997).

5 See the discussion of market imperfections and hedging motives in Chapter 9.

Conversely, suppose the U.S. subsidiary of a foreign-based parent has an inventory of oil. The price of oil is associated with the dollar, so the foreign parent has an economic exposure to the dollar. If inventory is translated back to the parent at historical exchange rates, then the parent corporation has an economic but not a translation exposure to currency risk. Even though it has no translation exposure to the value of the dollar, the parent's economic exposure might be worth hedging.

Information-Based Reasons for Hedging Translation Exposure

In a perfect financial market, the firm's borrowing capacity and required return on investment are determined in the marketplace by rational, informed investors. Managing translation exposures that do not involve cash flows will not add to the value of the firm.

> Hedging translation exposure can create value if it improves the quality of earnings.

In the real world of imperfect markets, there are situations in which translation exposure to currency risk can have valuation-relevant consequences above and beyond the firm's economic exposure. Management of translation exposure may be justifiable in these circumstances. In particular, hedging may improve the informativeness of earnings by reducing extraneous noise. Higher quality accounting earnings allow investors to more accurately assess the ability of management and the value of the firm's investments.[6]

Here are three practical reasons for hedging translation exposure to currency risk:

- *Satisfying loan covenants.* Loan covenants require that a firm maintain certain levels of performance, such as in operating profit or interest coverage. Violation of a loan covenant can lead to a reduction in borrowing capacity. In these circumstances, a hedge of translation exposure can ensure that the corporation retains access to funds. The perfect market view is that the firm's borrowing capacity is determined in the marketplace and not through artifices such as loan covenants. Nevertheless, accounting constraints can have an indirect effect on borrowing capacity, cash flow, and firm value.

- *Meeting profit forecasts.* The perfect market view is that investors see through accounting profits to cash flows and the firm's intrinsic value. In a less-than-efficient market, a firm that has announced a profit forecast might wish to retain its credibility with analysts and investors by hedging against a translation loss. Management's credibility might be worth protecting, even if it means hedging a noncash translation exposure with a financial market hedge that costs and risks cash.

- *Retaining a credit rating.* Managers have an incentive to hedge translation exposure if the firm's credit rating depends on accounting profits and not just on its underlying cash flows. Although investors would see through to the firm's underlying cash flows and intrinsic value in a perfect market, information is imperfect and costly to acquire in the real world. To the extent that hedging translation exposure can avoid a downgrade in a credit rating, hedging can preserve value by maintaining the firm's access to funds.

Note that each justification relies on costly or restricted access to information on the part of investors or information providers.

Cross-Country Differences in Hedging of Translation Exposure

Several studies have documented higher derivatives usage in non-U.S. than in U.S. companies and a greater willingness to hedge translation exposure to currency risk.

---

6 See DeMarzo and Duffie, "Corporate Incentives for Hedging and Hedge Accounting," *Review of Financial Studies* (1995).

- Belk and Glaum reported that companies in the United Kingdom are more likely to hedge translation exposure than their counterparts in the United States.[7]

- Hakkarainen, et al., found that industrial companies in Finland are more likely than U.S. firms to hedge translation exposure, perhaps because of the foreign currency translation rules specified in the Finnish Accounting Act of 1993.[8]

- In a sample of U.S. and German nonfinancial firms matched on size and industry, Bodnar and Gebhardt found derivatives usage by 78 percent of German firms and only 57 percent of comparable U.S. firms.[9] Bodnar and Gebhardt also documented national differences in (1) the goal of hedging, (2) the choice of hedging instruments, and (3) the influence of managers' market view when taking derivatives positions.

> Non-U.S. firms are more willing than U.S. firms to hedge translation exposure.

Reasons for these cross-country differences in hedging policies appear to be related to differences in national financial reporting standards, the relative importance of financial accounting statements, or corporate policies controlling derivatives usage.

There is evidence that multinational corporations adapt their translation hedging activities to the prevailing generally accepted accounting principles (GAAP) regarding foreign currency translation. For example, Houston and Mueller found that U.S. MNCs were less inclined to hedge translation exposure after FAS #52 isolated balance sheet translation gains or losses from reported income.[10] Godfrey and Yee found that Australian mining companies increased their hedging activities after changes in Australian GAAP increased their translation exposures.[11] These results suggest that managers are sensitive to their translation exposure to currency risk.

Aligning Managerial Incentives with Shareholder Objectives

Managerial performance evaluations should be tied to financial performance—to underlying cash flows and values—and not merely to accounting profits. Nevertheless, managers are often evaluated based on accounting performance simply because it is easier to measure accounting flows than financial performance. If risk-averse managers are not allowed to hedge, they may forgo value-creating investments that would expose them to too much currency risk. Allowing managers to hedge against translation exposure can reduce **agency costs** (i.e., the costs of ensuring that managers act in the best interests of shareholders) by aligning managerial incentives with shareholder objectives.[12]

> Hedging translation exposure can align managerial incentives with shareholder objectives.

The multinational treasury can facilitate this process by providing internal hedges to managers of individual operating units. For example, if a division manager wants to

7 Belk and Glaum, "The Management of Foreign Exchange Risk in U.K. Multinationals: An Empirical Investigation," *Accounting and Business Research* (1990).

8 See Hakkarainen, et al., "The Foreign Exchange Exposure Management Practices of Finnish Industrial Firms," *Journal of International Financial Management & Accounting* (1998).

9 Bodnar and Gebhardt, "Derivatives Usage in Risk Management by U.S. and German Non-Financial Firms: A Comparative Survey," *Journal of International Financial Management & Accounting* (1999).

10 Houston and Mueller, "Foreign Exchange Rate Hedging and SFAS No. 52—Relatives or Strangers?" *Accounting Horizons* (1988).

11 Godfrey and Yee, "Mining Sector Currency Risk Management Strategies: Responses to Foreign Currency Accounting Regulation," *The Accounting Review* (1996).

12 Aggarwal, "Management of Accounting Exposure to Currency Changes: Role and Evidence of Agency Costs," *Managerial Finance* (1991).

hedge divisional accounting performance against a drop in the local currency, treasury can quote prices on currency forward or option contracts that allow the manager to lock in an accounting profit for performance evaluation purposes. The internal cost of this hedge to the operating division should be based on market prices, such as forward rates or option premiums. Benchmarking divisional performance to a hedged position reduces the dependence of divisional performance measures on exchange rates and can help align managers' incentives with shareholder preferences.

Even though it has provided a hedge to an internal operating division of the firm, treasury does not have to actually execute this hedge in the external financial markets. Instead, treasury should make its own assessment of the desirability of hedging based on cash flow (rather than accounting profit) considerations after netting exposures across the individual operating divisions.

Value-based incentive plans based on economic value added are another way to align managerial incentives with shareholder objectives. **Economic value added (EVA)** is a method of financial performance evaluation that adjusts accounting performance for a charge reflecting investors' required return on investment.[13] Alternatively, divisional performance can be benchmarked to the performance of other divisions or to firms with similar exposures to currency risk. Each of these methods of performance evaluation is an attempt to align managerial incentives with shareholder objectives.

To Hedge or Not to Hedge: Policy Recommendations

> Only hedge exposures that cost or risk cash.

The decision of whether to hedge translation exposure to currency risk depends on the company, its owners and managers, and the markets in which it is traded. It must therefore be made on a case-by-case basis. Nevertheless, here are some general recommendations.

1. As a general rule, do not hedge translation exposures in the financial markets unless the purpose of the hedge is to reduce transaction or operating exposure to currency risk. Exceptions can occur in the following circumstances:

   a. Investors have restricted access to information about the firm.

   b. Corporate access to funds depends on accounting measures.

2. Foreign affiliates should use local sources of debt or equity capital to the extent permitted by the corporation's overall financial plan. This minimizes the translation and, more importantly, the economic exposure of foreign affiliates.

3. Managerial performance evaluation and compensation should be structured so that managers are insulated from unexpected changes in exchange rates. This can be done in the following ways:

   a. Benchmark divisional performance to the performance of other divisions or firms with similar exposures to currency risk.

   b. Allow managers to hedge their exposures through the corporate treasury.

4. If hedging of an individual unit's translation exposure is deemed necessary to align managerial incentives with shareholder objectives, the corporate treasury should quote market prices to the individual units.

   a. If individual units have noncash exposures, treasury should hedge internally.

   b. External financial market hedges should be used only for hedging the firm's net transaction or operating exposures to currency risk.

---

13 Jacque and Vaaler, "The International Control Conundrum with Exchange Risk: An EVA Framwork," *Journal of International Business Studies* (2001).

With regard to items 3 and 4, accounting performance can impact real costs in the real world of imperfect financial markets. Providing a way for managers to reduce this source of uncertainty will ultimately benefit shareholders and other corporate stakeholders.

13.4 • ACCOUNTING FOR FINANCIAL MARKET TRANSACTIONS

The growth in derivatives usage during the 1980s and 1990s created a need for accounting standards to recognize and report on derivative usage. Derivatives-related failures in the early 1990s (see box) lent urgency to this need. In response, the merits of alternative accounting standards for financial market transactions (including derivative instruments) are being actively debated in academic, political, and business circles around the world.

Standard-setters in the United States were the first to take formal action. After several years of contentious debate, the *Financial Accounting Standards Board (FASB)* adopted Financial Accounting Standards No. 133 (FAS #133), "Accounting for Derivative Instruments and Hedging Activities," in June 1998. This accounting standard has four key elements:

1. Derivatives are assets and liabilities that should be reported in financial statements.

2. Fair (market) value is the most relevant measure of value.

3. Only assets and liabilities should be reported as such. Income and expenses should be reported on the income statement.

4. Special accounting rules should be limited to qualifying hedge transactions.

Under FAS #133, derivatives are included on the balance sheet at fair (market) value and derivative gains or losses are immediately recognized in earnings. If certain conditions are met, derivative instruments can be designated as a hedge to offset the risk of another asset, liability, or anticipated transaction. Special accounting rules apply to qualifying hedge transactions. FAS #133 was effective for fiscal years beginning after June 15, 1999.

> FAS #133 values derivatives at market.

FAS #133 was widely hailed by investors, regulators, and academicians as promoting transparency in financial accounts. It was not well received by investment bankers and securities traders, who felt that the complexity of the new standard would deter users from trading in derivatives. The standard requires substantially more effort on the part of financial managers and their accountants to comply with the new and complex rules, especially on qualifying hedge transactions. Commercial banks also objected to the standard, because it does not apply market value accounting consistently across the balance sheet. In particular, long-term assets and liabilities are accounted for differently depending on whether they are a part of a qualified hedge. The rest of this section describes the four key elements of the FAS #133 standard.

Derivatives Should Be Reported

Standard-setters around the world were nearly unanimous in their response to the derivatives-related failures of the 1990s. The universally proposed short-term fix was to increase disclosure of off-balance-sheet derivative transactions, particularly currency and interest rate futures, options, and swaps. Off-balance-sheet transactions can be effective risk management tools. They also expose companies to financial price risks that might not be apparent to investors.

Market Update

Some (In)Famous Derivatives-Related Losses

Derivatives-related losses have appeared in the financial and popular press with increasing frequency in recent years. This is not a coincidence. With the increasing use of derivative instruments for corporate risk-hedging purposes, mistakes are bound to occur. Here are some of the biggest derivatives-related losses.

Loss	Firm	Derivative product	Year
$3.5 billion	Long-Term Capital Management (LTCM)*	Currency, interest rate, and equity derivatives	1998
$1.6 billion	Orange County, California	Interest rate derivatives	1994
$1.5 billion	Kashima Oil	Currency derivatives	1994
$1.3 billion	MG Corp (Metallgesellschaft)	Crude oil futures	1993
$1.3 billion	Barings Bank	Equity futures and options	1995
$1.0 billion	Showa Shell Sekiyu	Currency forwards	1993

* In September 1998, the U.S. Federal Reserve Board organized a bailout of LTCM by 16 commercial and investment banks. LTCM was privately held and did not disclose its losses. The value of the bailout was estimated to be about $3.5 billion.

Financial contracts are two-sided bets; for every loser, there is a winner on the other side of the contract. The winners are less likely to make the headlines.

U.S.— http://www.fasb.org

U.K.— http://www.icaew.co.uk

Canada— http://www.cica.ca

IASB— http://www.iasc.org.uk

In the United States, the Financial Accounting Standards Board adopted FAS #119, "Disclosures about Derivative Financial Instruments," requiring detailed disclosures of derivative activities in annual reports beginning in 1994. The U.K.'s Accounting Standards Board (ASB) published an exposure draft (FRED #13) that proposed disclosure of derivatives for fiscal years after 1997. Canada's Accounting Standards Board (AcSB) published a discussion paper in 1997 that similarly proposed derivatives disclosure. Increased disclosure of derivatives transactions has also been recommended by the International Accounting Standards Board, the Group of 30's Global Derivatives Study Group, and other standard-setting bodies around the world. The intent of each of these standards is to promote transparency in reported financial statements.

Use of Fair (Market) Value

An ideal accounting standard would be both *reliable* and *relevant*. The Financial Accounting Standards Board (FASB) in the United States provides the following definitions in "Statement of Financial Accounting Concepts No. 2."[14]

- *Reliability.* "The quality of information that assures that information is reasonably free from error and bias and faithfully represents what it purports to represent"

- *Relevance.* "The capacity of information to make a difference in a decision by helping users to form predictions about outcomes of past, present, and future events or to confirm or correct prior expectations"

---

14 See Kirschenheiter, "Information Quality and Correlated Signals," *Journal of Accounting Research* (1997), for a model of the reliability/relevance trade-off in the context of fair (market) value accounting.

Market Update

International Accounting Standards

The *International Accounting Standards Committee (IASC)* was formed in 1973 with the goal of promoting the harmonization or convergence of accounting standards around the world. To this end, the IASC developed a series of International Accounting Standards (IAS) that could apply to both emerging and developed economies.

In 2001, the *International Accounting Standards Board (IASB)* replaced the International Accounting Standards Committee (IASC) and focused on harmonizing the accounting standards of developed economies. The IASB board includes representatives from Australia, Canada, France, Germany, Japan, Scotland, South Africa, Switzerland, the United Kingdom, and the United States. The board has a number of nonvoting participants from the European Commission, FASB, the International Organization of Securities Commissioners, the People's Republic of China, and other national and international groups. The pronouncements of the IASB are called International Financial Reporting Standards (IFRS) and are a significant force in global accounting and financial reporting.

The IASB promotes the harmonization of accounting standards.

Harmonized standards are important to international investors, because they make it easier to compare companies from different countries. Many multinational corporations use the IASB's standards to report their financial performance to international investors. Several national securities regulators, including the European Commission and the U.S. Securities and Exchange Commission, are discussing allowing foreign issuers to use the IASB standards rather than forcing foreign companies to adopt national standards. Indeed, exchange-listed companies in the European Union are scheduled to adopt IASB standards in 2005. International accounting standards will ease the reporting requirements of MNCs and facilitate the international flow of capital.

Reliability is a function of the estimation process, whereas relevance is a function of the economic environment. An ideal accounting standard would be *reliable* in that two different accountants examining the same situation would reach the same accounting valuation. An ideal standard also would be *relevant* to decision makers in that the assigned valuation would be timely and accurate, reflect the economic reality of the situation, and have predictive value for decision makers. Unfortunately, it can be difficult to achieve both of these objectives concurrently.

The international trend in financial accounting has been toward fair (or market) value accounting. Market values have high relevance to the extent that market prices reflect economic reality. Unfortunately, many assets and liabilities do not have readily observable market values. Examples include inventory, plant and equipment, and privately placed debt or equity. In these situations, market value accounting lacks reliability. Historical costs are reliable, in that everyone can agree on the book value of an asset or liability that is entered into financial statements at historical cost. But historical costs seldom reflect economic reality, and so lack relevance.

Market values are more relevant but sometimes less reliable than historical costs.

Market value accounting standards have been proposed by accounting standard-setters in the United States, the United Kingdom, Canada, Australia, and the European Union, as well as by the *International Accounting Standards Committee*. In the United States, FAS #133 requires market value accounting for short-term financial assets and liabilities and derivative securities that are held for trading or hedging purposes. Investment or financing positions intended to be held for the long term or to maturity are valued on a historical cost basis. Critics of FAS #133 argue that the distinction between short-term trading and long-term financial instruments allows management too much flexibility in their accounting choices.

A draft proposal by the United Kingdom's *Accounting Standards Board* goes even further than FASB's standard. Under the proposed U.K. standard, market value accounting would be extended to all long-term financial instruments, including long-term debt. The ASB proposes that gains and losses on long-term financial instruments be shown in a separate statement of total recognized gains and losses, rather than flowed through the income statement. This treatment would be much like the use of the cumulative translation adjustment (CTA) account in the FAS #52 translation accounting standard. The IASB's proposed standard is similar to the U.K. standard in that it would value all long-term financial instruments at market value.

Assets and Liabilities Should Appear on the Balance Sheet

As the values of financial assets and liabilities change, so too does the value of the firm. Hence, it is important for the firm to realize gains and losses on financial assets and liabilities as they occur. According to FAS #133, financial assets and liabilities such as derivative transactions are measured on the balance sheet at market value, even if they have offsetting cash flows that result in no net cost, as in a currency forward or swap contract. Changes in value from marking-to-market are reported in earnings. Under this rule, gains or losses from currency speculation are recognized immediately.

> Derivatives appear on the balance sheet, unless they are a hedge.

The only exception to this rule is for derivatives transactions used to hedge an underlying risk exposure. Rather than recognizing gains or losses immediately as financial assets and liabilities are marked to market, gains or losses from hedges are recognized as the hedge and its underlying exposure mature. In this case, special hedge accounting rules apply.

Accounting for Hedge Transactions

According to FAS #133 and other national and international accounting standards, accounting for gains or losses associated with derivatives transactions depends on the *use* of the derivative. The reason for these special *hedge accounting rules* is that financial market transactions distort the balance sheet when they are used as hedges. Hedge accounting rules recognize hedges that reduce risk by offsetting a gain or loss on an underlying exposure.

Derivatives and the Balance Sheet. To illustrate the impact of including derivative hedges on the balance sheet, consider the balance sheet of U.S.-based Brothers and Sons, Inc.

Brothers and Sons, Inc.

Assets		Liabilities and Owner's Equity	
Accounts receivable (£1,500)	$2,500	Accounts payable	$1,000
Plant and equipment	$2,500	Owner's equity	$4,000
Total assets	$5,000	Liabilities and owner's equity	$5,000

Brothers has a market value debt ratio of ($1,000/$5,000) = 0.20, or 20 percent. Brothers' accounts receivable balance is a £1,500 receivable denominated in pounds sterling, due in three months, and carried on Brothers' books at the current spot rate of £0.60/$.

To hedge this balance, suppose Brothers sells £1,500 at the forward exchange rate of £0.60/$. This transaction creates an asset ($2,500) and an offsetting liability (£1,500), each with a maturity of three months. If Brothers places the forward contract on the balance sheet by recognizing a dollar receivable of $2,500 with an offsetting pound payable worth $2,500 at the forward rate of £0.60/$, the balance sheet will look like this:

Brothers and Sons, Inc.

Assets		Liabilities and Owner's Equity	
Accounts receivable	$2,500	Accounts payable	$1,000
Forward asset (long dollar)	$2,500	Forward liability (short pound)	$2,500
Plant and equipment	$2,500	Owner's equity	$4,000
Total assets	$7,500	Liabilities and owner's equity	$7,500

These offsetting entries inflate Brothers' apparent debt ratio to ($3,500/$7,500) ≈ 0.48, or 48 percent. Yet, Brothers is no more highly levered after the hedge transaction than before. If anything, Brothers is less risky after the hedge than before.

Currency forwards, futures, options, and swaps inflate reported debt ratios when they are capitalized on the balance sheet because they increase both assets and liabilities by the same amount. This is despite the fact that they are usually used to reduce risk, such as in Brothers' hedge of its pound sterling exposure. To avoid capitalizing hedges on the balance sheet, FAS #133 allows special accounting rules for qualifying hedge transactions.

Hedging Versus Speculation. In a survey on derivatives usage, financial managers at large U.S. corporations were asked, "Do you speculate?" Respondents were nearly unanimous in answering "No!"[15] In a follow-up survey the following year, executives were asked, "Does your view of the markets cause you to alter the timing of your hedge? The size of your hedge? To actively take positions?"[16] This question elicited quite a different response. With regard to foreign exchange transactions, 72 percent said they sometimes altered the timing of their hedges, 60 percent said they altered the sizes of their hedges, and 39 percent said they actively took positions in foreign currency without any underlying exposure. These were the same executives who, just one year earlier, claimed they did not speculate. Apparently, these executives believe there is a difference between outright speculation and active foreign exchange management.[17]

Accounting for derivatives is troublesome because it is difficult to distinguish between a hedge and a speculative position. Suppose you are a U.S.-based MNC with

---

15 Bodnar, Hayt, Marston, and Smithson, "Wharton Survey of Derivatives Usage by U.S. Non-Financial Firms," *Financial Management* (1995).

16 Bodnar, Hayt, and Marston, "1995 Wharton Survey of Derivatives Usage by U.S. Non-Financial Firms," *Financial Management* (1996).

17 The difference between hedging and speculating is something like pornography. Although it's difficult to define, you'll usually know it when you see it.

Hedging and speculation
are points on a continuum.

a receivable of ¥1 billion, which is worth $10 million at the forward
exchange rate of $F_1^{¥/\$} = ¥100/\$$.

+ $¥1 billion

This position gains (loses) in value with a yen appreciation (depreciation). To hedge your
position, you can sell yen at the forward exchange rate. How many yen should you sell?

+ $???

+ $???

Your preferred hedging strategy will depend on your hedging policy and your exchange
rate expectations. A conservative position might hedge 100 percent of the forward
exposure. Alternatively, if you expect the yen to appreciation, you might leave the bal-
ance uncovered and gamble on the value of the yen.

A continuum of hedges is possible depending on the amount of yen sold (or pur-
chased) forward. Here are some alternatives along this slippery slope:

1. Sell ¥1,000 million forward to eliminate your exposure to the yen.

2. Sell ¥500 million forward to cut your exposure to the yen in half.

3. Do not hedge and accept the future spot exchange rate.

4. Sell ¥1,500 million forward to take advantage of an expected depreciation of
   the yen.

5. Buy ¥500 million forward to take advantage of an expected appreciation of the
   yen.

Most people would say that strategies 1 and 2 are conservative and that 4 and 5 are
speculative. Yet, these are really just points along a continuum. If leaving a forward
position uncovered as in strategy 3 is a form of currency speculation, then is selling a
single yen forward a hedge? Speculation? Neither? Both? Is a position taken in antici-
pation of a possible future transaction a hedge or speculation? Accounting standards
for hedge transactions must deal with these difficult issues.

Qualifying a Hedge. To qualify for hedge accounting treatment under the FASB stan-
dard (and under the proposed standards of Australia, Canada, the United Kingdom, and
the IASB), a hedge must be clearly defined, measurable, and effective.

Derivatives used for hedg-
ing qualify for special rules.

This requires that financial managers document their reasons for enter-
ing, modifying, or canceling a hedge. This documentation process can
be time-consuming and complex.

FAS #133 allows hedge accounting where there is a clearly identifiable exposure
that is offset with a clearly identifiable hedge transaction. This makes it not too diffi-
cult to qualify a hedge of a transaction exposure to currency risk. An example is a for-
eign currency receivable due in 90 days that is hedged with a 90-day forward contract.
Another example would be a rolling hedge in which a long-term transaction exposure
is hedged with successive short-term forward contracts or a currency swap contract. It
is more difficult, but still possible, to qualify a hedge when there is not a clearly defined
underlying exposure. This is the case for most operating exposures, as well as for *net*
transaction exposures.

FAS #133 recognizes derivative gains or losses immediately in earnings, along with the offsetting losses or gains on the underlying exposure. For hedges of anticipated foreign currency transactions, FAS #133 calls for gains or losses to be recognized in a balance sheet reserve account and then flowed into earnings when the underlying exposure is recognized and capitalized on the balance sheet. This allows both sides of the hedged position to be recognized at the same time.

13.5 • ACCOUNTING, DISCLOSURE, AND CORPORATE HEDGING ACTIVITIES

The Market Effects of Increased Accounting Disclosure

When there is inadequate accounting disclosure, informational asymmetries among investors can create **adverse selection costs** as uninformed investors attempt to protect themselves against trading with informed investors. Adverse selection costs inflate the bid-ask spread and impair liquidity in the firm's shares. To overcome investors' reluctance to buy shares in illiquid markets, firms must issue capital at lower prices, resulting in a higher cost of capital. Increased accounting disclosure can reduce information asymmetries and adverse selection costs, resulting in smaller bid-ask spreads, greater liquidity, and a lower cost of capital.

> Information asymmetries impair liquidity and result in higher bid-ask spreads and capital costs.

The diversity of accounting conventions around the world creates even more asymmetry between informed and uninformed investors, despite the efforts of the IASB to internationalize accounting standards. Without detailed information about future prospects, investor uncertainty and diversity of opinion can lead to higher share price volatility and lower trading volume. If the costs of becoming an expert on national and international accounting standards could be overcome, increased accounting disclosure should increase the quality of earnings, trading volume, and share price sensitivity to underlying risk exposures, and decrease share price volatility, bid-ask spreads, and the equity cost of capital. Several recent studies have investigated these issues.

Accounting Disclosure in the United States. When U.S. firms issue securities to the public, they are required to file a 10-K statement with the Securities and Exchange Commission (SEC) that discloses information about the firms' securities. Since 1997, the SEC has required that 10-K statements include information about corporate exposures to interest rate, exchange rate, or commodity price risks. These forward-looking, quantitative risk assessments must be disclosed as (1) tables of fair values and contract terms sufficient to identify the expected maturity dates and cash flows

> U.S. publicly traded firms disclose their financial price risk exposures in their 10-Ks.

of financial price risks, (2) sensitivity analyses of the likely effect on earnings, cash flows, and market values of possible changes in financial prices, or (3) value-at-risk measures expressing estimates of potential loss with a certain level of confidence and over a certain horizon due to adverse movements in financial prices. Studies have found that increased disclosures about financial price risks have the following share price effects:

- Increased share price sensitivity to underlying financial prices[18]

---

[18] Rajgopal, "Early Evidence on the Informativeness of the SEC's Market Risk Disclosures: The Case of Commodity Price Risk Exposure of Oil and Gas Producers," *Accounting Review* (2002).

- Lower trading volume sensitivity to changes in underlying financial prices[19]

These results are consistent with increased accounting disclosure increasing the consensus of opinion, reducing investor uncertainty, and increasing the quality of information.

Accounting Disclosure in Germany. Additional evidence on the value of accounting disclosure to international investors comes from Germany. Disclosure requirements under German accounting standards are relatively low. To attract international investors, several German firms have adopted U.S. FASB or international IASB standards that substantially increase the firm's disclosure requirements. Increased disclosure should lower adverse selection costs and result in lower bid-ask spreads and higher trading volume. Consistent with theory, Leuz and Verrecchia found that this commitment to increased disclosure results in lower bid-ask spreads and higher trading volume, ceteris paribus.[20] In a related study, Leuz found that improvement in the information quality of German financial statements is not related to the choice of U.S. FASB or international IASB standards.[21]

The Impact of FAS #133 on Corporate Hedging Activities

Bodnar, Hayt, and Marston surveyed U.S. firms on the impact of FAS #133 on corporate hedging activities and derivatives usage.[22] As shown in Figure 13.5, 37 percent of derivatives users expressed high concern over the accounting treatment of derivatives. This survey was conducted at the time of the June 1998 release of FAS #133, so this concern may be more or less important today. High concern over the derivatives' market risk (i.e., unexpected changes in market values) was expressed by 31 percent of derivatives users. Monitoring and evaluating hedge performance was of high concern to 29 percent of users. Respondents thought the remaining four issues were of relatively low concern. It should be noted that credit risk caused the most concern among derivatives users in the 1995 Wharton survey.[23]

Given the concern regarding the accounting treatment of derivatives, the authors asked derivatives users about the potential impact of FAS #133. Most respondents (73 percent) stated FAS #133 would have no effect on their derivatives use. Responses of the 27 percent of respondents that believed FAS #133 would have an effect on their use of derivatives are shown in Figure 13.6. Of this group, 38 percent anticipated a reduction and 9 percent anticipated an increase in derivatives use. Many firms thought that FAS #133 would change the types of hedging instruments used (58 percent) or the timing of their hedge transactions (38 percent). Only 13 percent, or 3.5 percent of all respondents, felt FAS #133 would cause a significant change in the firm's overall hedging strategy or approach to risk management.

19 Linsmeier, et. al., "The Effect of Mandated Market Risk Disclosures on Trading Volume Sensitivity to Interest Rate, Exchange Rate, and Commodity Price Movements," *Accounting Review* (2002).

20 Leuz and Verrecchia, "The Economic Consequences of Increased Disclosure," *Journal of Accounting Research* (2000).

21 Leuz, "IAS Versus U.S. GAAP: Information Asymmetry-Based Evidence from Germany's New Market." *Journal of Accounting Research* (2003).

22 Bodnar, Hayt, and Marston, "1998 Wharton Survey of Financial Risk Management by U.S. Non-Financial Firms," *Financial Management* (1998).

23 Bodnar, Hayt, and Marston, "1995 Wharton Survey."

FIGURE 13.5
Concerns Regarding Derivatives

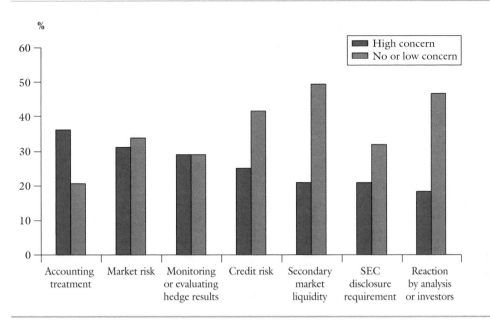

Source: Bodnar, Hayt, and Marston, "1998 Wharton Survey of Financial Risk Management by U.S. Non-Financial Firms," *Financial Management* 27 (Winter 1998).

FIGURE 13.6
What Will Be the Most Likely Impact of FAS #133?
(Accounting for Derivative Instruments and Hedging Activities, effective June 1998)

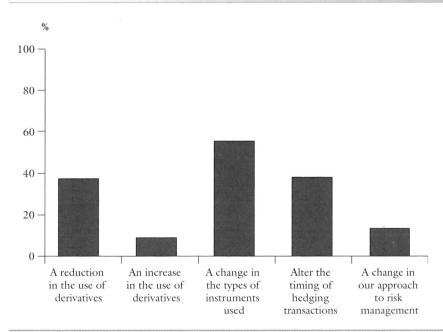

Source: Bodnar, Hayt, and Marston, "1998 Wharton Survey of Financial Risk Management by U.S. Non-Financial Firms," *Financial Management* 27 (Winter 1998).

13.6 • SUMMARY

Translation (or accounting) exposure refers to the impact of changes in currency values on a firm's consolidated financial statements. Differences between accounting translation methods arise when some accounts are translated at current exchange rates and other accounts are translated at historical rates.

The current/noncurrent method translates current assets and liabilities at current exchange rates and other balance sheet accounts at historical exchange rates. This method correctly values short-term (current) monetary assets and liabilities, but misvalues long-term (noncurrent) monetary accounts. Translating real assets at historical exchange rates implicitly assumes they have no exposure to currency risk. The current/noncurrent method was used in the United States prior to 1976.

The temporal or monetary/nonmonetary translation method applies current exchange rates to monetary (contractual) assets and liabilities and historical rates to nonmonetary (real) assets and shareholders' equity. This method correctly values monetary assets and liabilities at the current exchange rate. Nonmonetary (real) assets and liabilities are valued at historical exchange rates, as if they have no exposure to currency risk. The temporal method (FAS #8) used in the United States during 1976–1981 was widely criticized because gains or losses on balance sheet accounts were reported in net income.

The current rate method translates all assets and liabilities except common equity at the current exchange rate. Common equity is translated at historical exchange rates. This method correctly values monetary assets and liabilities, and implicitly assumes that real assets are exposed one for one to exchange rate changes. The United States has used a current rate method (FAS #52) since 1981 in which translation gains or losses from changes in balance sheet accounts do not appear in reported earnings. Instead, they are recorded as a cumulative translation adjustment in the equity portion of the balance sheet.

According to finance theory, only exposures that are directly related to cash flow should be hedged. Chapter 9 reviewed circumstances in which hedging can *directly* increase expected cash flows through reductions in expected taxes, agency costs, or costs of financial distress. Translation exposure can also have *indirect* cash flow consequences above and beyond the firm's transaction and operating exposures when these conditions hold:

- Loan covenants are tied to accounting income.
- Meeting profit forecasts retains management's credibility in the marketplace.
- Credit ratings are tied to accounting performance rather than cash flow.

Whether for legitimate or for self-serving reasons, many managers prefer to hedge translation exposure to currency risk. Allowing managers to hedge against currency risk can be valuable when it helps to align managerial incentives with shareholder objectives.

Finally, we discussed accounting for financial market transactions, including derivative instruments such as forwards, futures, options, and swaps. This is a difficult area of accounting because the affect of a financial market transaction depends on how it is used—as an investment, to fund operations, as a hedge, or for speculative purposes. In the United States, FAS #133 applies the following rules to derivatives transactions:

- Derivatives are assets and liabilities that should be reported in financial statements.

- Fair (market) value is the most relevant measure of value.
- Changes in the values of assets and liabilities should be reported on the balance sheet rather than on the income statement.
- Special rules for hedge accounting are limited to qualifying hedge transactions.

Financial managers must document and justify their hedges in order to qualify for the hedge accounting rules and keep derivatives off the balance sheet.

KEY TERMS

adverse selection costs
agency costs
cumulative translation adjustment (CTA)
current rate translation method
 (FAS #52 in the United States)
current/noncurrent translation method

earnings response coefficient
economic value added (EVA)
net exposed assets
temporal (monetary/nonmonetary) translation method (FAS #8 in the United States)
translation (accounting) exposure

CONCEPTUAL QUESTIONS

13.1 What are the advantages and disadvantages of valuing assets and liabilities at historical cost? At market value?

13.2 List the rules of the current/noncurrent translation method.

13.3 List the rules of the monetary/nonmonetary translation method.

13.4 List the rules of the current rate translation method.

13.5 Which translation method is the most realistic from the perspective of finance theory?

13.6 Did the switch from FAS #8 to FAS #52 in the United States improve the quality or informativeness of corporate earnings? How can we tell?

13.7 According to finance theory, what determines whether an exposure to currency risk should be hedged?

13.8 List three information-based reasons for hedging a translation exposure to currency risk.

13.9 How can corporate hedging of translation exposure reduce the agency conflict between managers and other stakeholders? In what other ways can agency conflicts be reduced?

13.10 Identify several cross-border differences in corporate hedging of translation exposure. What might account for these differences?

13.11 Recommend some general policies for deciding whether to hedge a translation exposure to currency risk.

13.12 How did accounting standard-setters react to the prominent derivatives-related failures of the 1990s?

13.13 Describe the four key elements of FAS #133, "Accounting for Derivative Instruments and Hedging Activities."

13.14 What is the International Accounting Standards Board? Over which national accounting organizations does it have jurisdiction?

13.15 What is a hedge? Why is it difficult to distinguish a hedge from a speculative position. How does FAS #133 qualify a hedge?

PROBLEMS

13.1 Finlandiva, a furniture manufacturer based in Finland, is owned by Couch Potato, Inc., of the United States. Finlandiva's balance sheet at the current exchange rate of $1.00/€ is shown in the following table:

Assets	Value in euros	Value at $1.00/€	Value at $0.80/€	Translation gains or losses
Cash and marketable securities	€50,000	$50,000		
Accounts receivable	€30,000	$30,000		
Inventory	€20,000	$20,000		
Plant and equipment	€900,000	$900,000		
Total assets	€1,000,000	$1,000,000		

Liabilities	Value in euros	Value at $1.00/€	Value at $0.80/€	Translation gains or losses
Accounts payable	€125,000	$125,000		
Short-term debt	€75,000	$75,000		
Long-term debt	€750,000	$750,000		
Net worth	€50,000	$50,000		
Total liabilities and net worth	€1,000,000	$1,000,000		

Answer each of the following questions under the current/noncurrent rate method, the temporal method of FAS #8, and the current rate method of FAS #52. (Use current exchange rates for inventory in the temporal method.)
a. Identify Couch Potato's exposed assets, exposed liabilities, and net exposed assets under each accounting translation method.
b. Identify the impact of a 20 percent depreciation of the euro on Couch Potato's consolidated balance sheets under each accounting translation method.

13.2 Vincent's Folly, a yo-yo manufacturer based in Canada, is owned by YoBeta, Inc., of the United States. Vincent's balance sheet at the current exchange rate of C$1.60/$ is shown as follows:

Assets	Value in C$	Value at C$1.60/$	Value at C$1.50/$	Translation gains or losses
Cash and marketable securities	C$320,000	$200,000		
Accounts receivable	C$160,000	$100,000		
Inventory	C$640,000	$400,000		
Plant and equipment	C$480,000	$300,000		
Total assets	C$1,600,000	$1,000,000		
Liabilities				
Accounts payable	C$320,000	$200,000		
Wages payable	C$160,000	$100,000		
Net worth	C$1,120,000	$700,000		
Total liabilities and net worth	C$1,600,000	$1,000,000		

Answer each of the following questions under the current/noncurrent rate method, the temporal method of FAS #8, and the current rate method of FAS #52. (Use current exchange rates for inventory in the temporal method.)

a. Identify YoBeta's exposed assets, exposed liabilities, and net exposed assets under each accounting translation method.

b. Identify the impact of a depreciation of the U.S. dollar from C$1.60/$ to C$1.50/$ on YoBeta's consolidated balance sheets under each accounting translation method.

13.3 Silver Saddle Motel of Sante Fe, New Mexico, has the following balance sheet:

Assets		Liabilities and Owner's Equity	
Current assets		Current liabilities	
Cash and marketable securities	$15,000	Accounts payable	$30,000
Accounts receivable	$10,000	Wages payable	$10,000
Fixed assets		Short-term debt	$50,000
Furnishings (beds and blankets)	$25,000	Long-term liabilities	
Property and buildings	$950,000	Long-term debt	$500,000
		Owner's equity	$410,000
Total assets	$1,000,000	Liabilities and owner's equity	$1,000,000

Silver Saddle's accounts payable balance is a Peso300,000 purchase of authentic Mexican rugs and blankets for use in the motel. The purchase was placed on the books at an exchange rate of $0.10/peso. The balance is due in six months and is payable in Mexican pesos. To hedge this peso exposure, Silver Saddle buys Peso300,000 six months forward at a forward rate of $0.10/peso.

a. What will Silver Saddle's accounts look like if this forward transaction is capitalized on the balance sheet?

b. Calculate Silver Saddle's ratio of long-term debt to total assets and current ratio (current assets to current liabilities) before and after the forward contract is capitalized on the balance sheet. Is Silver Saddle's financial risk higher or lower after the Mexican peso liability is hedged? How do you reconcile this conclusion with the apparent deterioration in Silver Saddle's leverage and current ratios? Explain.

c. Can Silver Saddle qualify this hedge under the FAS #133 rules? What will Silver Saddle's balance sheet look like if the forward currency transaction is accounted for as a hedge?

13.4 Consider Silver Saddle Motel's balance sheet from problem 13.3. Silver Saddle anticipates a payment of €10,000 in six months from a German tourist agency. The payment will reserve a block of rooms for a group of German tourists. The tourist agency insists on paying in euros so that they would not be exposed to any currency risk. Silver Saddle can hedge its euro exposure at a forward rate of $1.00/€, which also happens to be the current spot rate of exchange.

a. Repeat parts a through c of problem 13.3 for this forward hedge.

b. In what ways is this hedge different from the forward hedge in problem 13.3?

SUGGESTED READINGS

Translation exposure to currency risk is discussed in

Raj Aggarwal, "Management of Accounting Exposure to Currency Changes: Role and Evidence of Agency Costs," *Managerial Finance* 17, No. 4 (1991), pp. 10–22.

Eli Bartov, "Foreign Currency Exposure of Multinational Firms: Accounting Measures and Market Valuation," *Contemporary Accounting Research* 14 (Winter 1997), pp. 623–652.

P.A. Belk and M. Glaum, "The Management of Foreign Exchange Risk in U.K. Multinationals: An Empirical Investigation," *Accounting and Business Research* 21 (Winter 1990), pp. 3–14.

Gordon M. Bodnar and Gunther Gebhardt, "Derivatives Usage in Risk Management by U.S. and German Non-Financial Firms: A Comparative Survey," *Journal of International Financial Management & Accounting* 10 (Autumn 1999), pp. 153–187.

Gordon M. Bodnar, Gregory S. Hayt, and Richard C. Marston, "1995 Wharton Survey of Derivatives Usage by U.S. Non-Financial Firms," *Financial Management* 25 (Winter 1996), pp. 113–133.

Gordon M. Bodnar, Gregory S. Hayt, and Richard C. Marston, "1998 Wharton Survey of Financial Risk Management by U.S. Non-Financial Firms," *Financial Management* 27 (Winter 1998), pp. 70–91.

Gordon M. Bodnar, Gregory S. Hayt, Richard C. Marston, and Charles W. Smithson, "Wharton Survey of Derivatives Usage by U.S. Non-Financial Firms," *Financial Management* 24 (Summer 1995), pp. 104–114.

Dan W. Collins and W.K. Salatka, "Noisy Accounting Earnings Signals and Earnings Response Coefficients: The Case of Foreign Currency Accounting," *Contemporary Accounting Research* 10 (Spring 1994), pp. 119–160.

Peter M. DeMarzo and Darrell Duffie, "Corporate Incentives for Hedging and Hedge Accounting," *Review of Financial Studies* (Fall 1995), pp. 743–771.

Jayne M. Godfrey and Benita Yee, "Mining Sector Currency Risk Management Strategies: Responses to Foreign Currency Accounting Regulation," *The Accounting Review* 26 (Summer 1996), pp. 200–214.

Antti Hakkarainen, Nathan Joseph, Eero Kasanen, and Vesa Puttonen, "The Foreign Exchange Exposure Management Practices of Finnish Industrial Firms," *Journal of International Financial Management & Accounting* 9, No. 1 (1998), pp. 34–57.

Carol Olson Houston and Gerhard G. Mueller, "Foreign Exchange Rate Hedging and SFAS No. 52—Relatives or Strangers?" *Accounting Horizons* 2 (December 1988), pp. 50–57.

Laurent L. Jacque and Paul M. Vaaler, "The International Control Conundrum with Exchange Risk: An EVA Framwork," *Journal of International Business Studies* 32, No. 4 (2001), pp. 813–832.

Thomas J. Linsmeier, Daniel B. Thornton, Mohan Venkatachalam, and Michael Welker, "The Effect of Mandated Market Risk Disclosures on Trading Volume Sensitivity to Interest Rate, Exchange Rate, and Commodity Price Movements," *Accounting Review* (April 2002), pp. 343–377.

Michael Kirschenheiter, "Information Quality and Correlated Signals," *Journal of Accounting Research* 35 (Spring 1997), pp. 43–59.

Christian Leuz and Robert E. Verrecchia, "The Economic Consequences of Increased Disclosure," *Journal of Accounting Research* 38 (Supplement 2000) pp. 91–124.

Shivaram Rajgopal, "Early Evidence on the Informativeness of the SEC's Market Risk Disclosures: The Case of Commodity Price Risk Exposure of Oil and Gas Producers," *Accounting Review* 74 (July 2002), pp. 251–280.

Country
Risk Management
chapter 14

Overview

Listen up, my Cossack brethren. We'll ride into the valley like the wind, the thunder of our horses and the lightning of our steel striking fear in the hearts of our enemies!
. . . And remember—stay out of Mrs. Caldwell's garden.

Gary Larsen, *The Far Side*

Country risk is the risk that the business environment in a host country will change unexpectedly. A corporation is exposed to country risk to the extent that its value changes with unexpected events in that country. Exposure to country risk results in more uncertain investment outcomes for the multinational corporation.

> Country risk is the risk that the business environment in a host country will unexpectedly change.

Two important sources of country risk are political risk and financial risk. **Political risk** is the risk that a sovereign host government will unexpectedly change the rules of the game under which businesses operate. Political risks arise because of unexpected changes in the political environment within a host country or in the relationship of a host country to another country. **Financial risk** refers more generally to unexpected events in a country's financial or economic condition. Financial risk is determined by a host of financial and economic factors, many of which are interrelated with political risk.

Indices of country risk usually have political and financial components. International lenders use country risk indices to judge the risks of lending to a particular country. As any loan officer knows, a creditworthy borrower has both the *ability* and the *willingness* to repay a loan. In a sense, financial risk indices reflect a country's ability to repay its loans, whereas political risk indices reflect a country's willingness to repay its loans. Country risk indices are used by MNCs in much the same way that they are used by international

> Country risk indices are used to judge the risks of investing in a particular country.

lenders; that is, to judge the risks of investing in a particular country. Country risk can affect the value of a MNC through changes in or investors' required returns.

This chapter begins with a description of country risk and its cash flow consequences for international investors and the multinational corporation. Strategies for reducing the MNC's exposure to country risk, preferably while maximizing the expected return on investment, are then examined. The chapter concludes with a section on the impact of country risk on investors' required return and the MNC's cost of capital.

14.1 • COUNTRY RISK ASSESSMENT

Like other sources of risk, country risk is based on *unexpected* change in the business environment of a host country. If a multinational corporation knows with certainty that a foreign income tax rate is to be increased from 10 percent to 30 percent, then this is not a source of risk. The higher tax rate will reduce future profitability, but by knowing the new tax rules in advance the firm can incorporate these rules into its investment, financial, and tax-planning decisions. The MNC faces country risk from the possibility that an *unexpected* change in that country's business environment will affect the value of the firm.

An entire industry is devoted to providing assessments of country risk (see Figure 14.1). Many of these services combine political risk assessment with an overall assessment of the business or financial climate in a country. For example, the Coface Group (see Figure 14.2) assigns an overall ranking similar to a Moody's or S&P bond rating to summarize a country's average credit risk. Predictably, the lowest risks are found in developed countries in Europe, North America, Asia, and the Middle East. The highest risks are in developing countries, mostly in Africa and Central Europe.

In similar fashion, Political Risk Services' *International Country Risk Guide (ICRG)* produces a composite index that is a weighted average of political (50 percent), financial (25 percent), and economic (25 percent) risk factors. The ICRG political risk index is based on qualitative elements that encompass a country's political leadership, the extent of government corruption, and internal and external political tensions. The ICRG economic risk index is based on quantitative elements, including a country's inflation rate, current account balance, and foreign trade collection experience. The ICRG financial risk index has both qualitative and quantitative components, including recent losses from currency controls, asset expropriations, contract renegotiations, payment delays, and loan restructurings or cancellations.

Country risk rankings from various sources are positively correlated. Erb, Harvey, and Viskanta calculated a cross-country correlation of 0.35 between the ICRG composite risk index and Institutional Investor's credit risk index and concluded that these indices reflect the same underlying economic phenomena.[1]

Companies that rate country risk typically provide macro assessments of country credit risk. **Macro risks** affect all firms in a host country. Examples of macro country risks include unexpected changes in a host country's monetary or fiscal policies, banking system, tax rates, capital controls, exchange rates, or bankruptcy and ownership laws. Changes in any of these policy variables affect MNCs doing business in the country. Companies that rate country risk supplement their ratings with written analyses of the factors that contribute to country risk.

> Macro risks affect all firms in a host country.

---

1 Erb, Harvey, and Viskanta, "Political Risk, Financial Risk and Economic Risk," *Financial Analysts Journal* (1996).

FIGURE 14.1
Political and Country Risk Rating Services

Bank of America   http://www.bankamerica.com

Country data forecasts/country risk monitor/country outlooks
Ability to pay foreign debt, trade performance, government fiscal responsibility,
foreign indebtedness, income per capita, involvement in international trade

Business Environment Risk Intelligence (BERI) S.A.   http://www.beri.com

Political, operational, remittance/repatriation, and composite risk indices

Coface Group   http://www.coface-usa.com

Country risk ratings, ala corporate bond ratings, of political and financial risks

Dun and Bradstreet   http://www.dnb.com

International Risk and Payment Review

Economist Intelligence Unit (EIU)   http://www.eiu.com

Political, policy, medium-term lending, short-term trade, composite risk indices

Euromoney   http://www.euromoney.com

Risk Assessment Index
Political, financial, economic, and composite risk indices

Institutional Investor   http://www.iimagazine.com

Country credit rating index

Moody's Investor Services   http://www.moodys.com

Sovereign debt ratings

Organization for Economic Co-Operation and Development   http://www.oecd.org

Annual economic surveys of leading industrial countries

Political Risk Services   http://www.prsgroup.com

International Country Risk Guide
 • Political, financial, economic, and composite risk measures
Coplin-O'Leary Rating System
 • Financial transfer, direct investment, export market, and composite risk indices

Standard and Poor's Ratings Group   http://www.standardpoor.com

Sovereign debt ratings

For an extra fee, these companies provide assessments of **micro risks** that are specific to an industry, company, or project. Unexpected changes in immigration laws are an example of a political risk that differentially impacts some assets within a country. Most governments keep tight controls on foreign labor working within their borders. Employers attempting to bring foreign labor into a host country must demonstrate that imported laborers

> Micro risks are specific to an industry, company, or project.

FIGURE 14.2
Country Risk Rankings

Rank	Africa	Asia	Europe	Middle East	Americas
A1		Australia, New Zealand	Austria, Belgium, Denmark, Finland, France, Iceland, Ireland, Luxembourg, Netherlands, Norway, Spain, Sweden, Switzerland, United Kingdom		Canada
A2	Botswana	Hong Kong, Japan, Malaysia, Singapore, S. Korea, Taiwan	Germany, Greece, Hungary, Italy, Portugal, Slovenia	Bahrain, Kuwait, Oman, Qatar, United Arab Emirates	United States
A3	Mauritius, Namibia	China, Thailand	Cyprus, Czech Rep., Estonia		Chile, Trinidad
A4	Egypt, Morocco, S. Africa, Swaziland, Tunisia	India, Philippines	Latvia, Lithuania, Poland, Slovakia	Saudi Arabia, Israel	Dominican Rep., Mexico, Panama
B	Algeria, Benin, Burkina Faso, Cameroon, Gabon, Lesotho, Mali, Senegal, Uganda	Bangladesh, Sri Lanka, Papua West Guinea	Bulgaria, Croatia, Russia,	Egypt, Jordan	Bolivia, Brazil, Colombia, Costa Rica, El Salvador, Guatemala, Honduras, Paraguay, Peru, Uruguay, Venezuela
C	Angola, Chad, Congo, Central African Rep., Djibouti, Ethiopia, Ghana, Guinea, Ivory Coast, Kenya, Libya, Mauritania, Mozambique, Niger, Seychelles, Tanzania, Togo	Indonesia, Myanmar (Laos), Nepal, Vietnam	Azerbaijan, Kazakhstan, Romania	Iran, Lebanon, Syria, Turkey, Yemen	Haiti, Jamaica
D	Comoros, Equatorial Guinea, Gambia, Guinea Bissau, Liberia, Madagascar, Malawi, Nigeria, Sao Tome, Sierra Leone, Somalia, Sudan, Zambia, Zimbabwe	Afghanistan, Cambodia, Mongolia, N. Korea, Pakistan	Albania, Armenia, Belarus, Bosnia-Herzegovina, Georgia, Kyrgyzstan, Macedonia, Moldova, Tajikistan, Turkmenistan, Ukraine, Uzbekistan, Yugoslavia	Iraq	Argentina, Cuba, Ecuador, Guyana, Nicaragua

Source: The Coface Group (http://www.coface-usa.com), as of April 2003. Ratings measure average default risk on corporate payments, and reflect local business, financial, and political outlooks. See the website for current ratings. See the Web site for current ratings.

are not displacing domestic workers. Changes in immigration policies can adversely affect the competitive position of a MNC relative to local and global competitors if the MNC uses imported labor, such as expatriate managers from the home office.

Political Risk

Political risk is the risk of an unexpected change in the political, legal, or regulatory environment. Political risks arise because of unexpected changes in the political environment within a host country or the relationship of a host country to other countries.

> Political risk refers to unexpected changes in the political environment.

Political risk is related to instability in a government or its policies. Stable governments tend to follow stable policies. Unstable governments are more likely to change policies and create political risks for the MNC. Policy instability is most pronounced when there is a factional change in government; that is, when a government changes hands. The bigger the factional change, the more likely is a change in governmental policies. In addition to the stability of government policies, the MNC also must consider whether a change in policy is likely to be to its benefit or detriment. It is the adverse consequences of political risk that detract from firm value and most concern managers and other stakeholders.

Policy stability is greatest when power resides in a single political party. In democratic countries, governmental policies change through elections, referendums, and the normal legislative process. Changes tend to be small when the incumbent party retains power. Similarly, the policies of communist and socialist countries are likely to change only incrementally when the ruling party retains control. Political stability is somewhat less when control of the government passes from one group to another, such as between Democrats and Republicans in the United States, factions of the Liberal Democratic Party (LDP) in Japan, or factions of the Communist Party in Russia.

Policy stability is least when factional change is the result of an armed conflict, such as a war, revolution, insurrection, or coup. For example, after the Shah of Iran was deposed during the Iranian revolution of 1979, Iran expropriated (that is, seized) several billion dollars worth of Iranian assets from U.S.-based multinational corporations. The biggest losers were U.S. oil companies with investments in Iran. In response, the United States froze Iranian assets in the United States. It took the U.S.-Iran Claims Tribunal (an international tribunal based in the Netherlands) more than ten years to settle the resulting disputes. The largest settlement went to Amoco Corporation for $600 million. This settlement was only a fraction of Amoco's losses during the revolution and its aftermath.

MNCs are exposed to political risk, at least in part because their objectives differ from those of sovereign host governments. A government's primary responsibility is to its citizens, and then to its society as a whole. Corporations are responsible to stockholders, bondholders and other creditors, employees, suppliers, and customers. Quite often, these stakeholders are concentrated in the MNC's home country and not in the host countries in which the corporation conducts its foreign operations. Even if corporate and governmental constituencies were one and the same, political leaders are responsible for the public good, and corporate leaders are responsible for the private welfare of their stakeholders. It is not surprising that governments and MNCs come into conflict.

Companies that specialize in political risk analysis base their analyses on an intimate knowledge of the local political environment, experience, and guesswork. Although these companies summarize their analyses into quantifiable measures of political risk, these political risk ratings largely depend on qualitative factors. The written analyses that accompany a political risk rating are at least as important as the rating itself.

Market Update

Political Risk in the United States: California's Unitary Tax

In 1977, the state of California adopted an unusual unitary tax system for companies operating within the state. Under the unitary method, tax was calculated as a percentage of a company's worldwide income instead of only on income earned in the state. At the time California adopted the unitary tax, several MNCs either postponed or canceled planned investments in the state because of the additional financial disclosure required to document worldwide income.

This peculiar tax posed a political risk for both foreign and domestic U.S. firms. Barclays Bank of the United Kingdom and Colgate-Palmolive of the United States challenged the unitary tax in U.S. courts on the grounds that it discriminated against foreign (Barclays) and out-of-state (Colgate-Palmolive) companies. The U.S. Supreme Court upheld the constitutionality of California's unitary tax in June 1994, declaring that the tax did not infringe on the U.S. Congress' right to "regulate commerce with foreign nations, and among the several states." By the time the suit was settled in the courts, the issue was moot. In response to plant closings and canceled investments, California had already allowed foreign multinationals to choose to be taxed according to the unitary method or on income earned within the United States. This example is a reminder that political risk exists in even the most stable countries.

Financial Risk

> Financial risk refers to unexpected changes in the financial environment.

In addition to political risk, country risk assessments usually include an assessment of a country's financial or economic risk. Financial risk factors include quantitative macroeconomic factors as well as qualitative factors that reflect a nation's financial or economic health. Quantitative macroeconomic factors include the following:

- Currency risk
- Interest rate risk
- Inflation risk
- The current account balance
- The balance of trade

A government's monetary, fiscal, and trade policies influence these macroeconomic factors. These factors are also influenced by many domestic and international events that are outside governmental control.

Many qualitative factors influence the financial environment. Like the quantitative factors, many of these qualitative factors have a political dimension. Political Risk Services' *International Country Risk Guide* includes assessments of the following factors in their financial risk index:

- Loan defaults or loan restructurings
- Payment delays
- Cancellations of contracts by a host government
- Losses from exchange controls
- Expropriation of private investments

Other companies include assessments of the extent of restrictive trade practices, tariffs, or trade regulations and the state of private ownership and bankruptcy laws. Political risk itself is sometimes included as a separate qualitative factor in determining a country's financial risk. Risk rating agencies summarize these factors into one or a few indices that reflect the local financial environment.

Specific Types of Country Risk

This section describes several specific sources of political risk that can affect the MNC's value and hence concern the MNC's financial manager. These political risks are summarized in Figure 14.3.

Expropriation. Mao Zedong wrote: "political power grows out of the barrel of a gun." Indeed, the most extreme form of political risk is **expropriation**, in which a company's physical or financial assets are seized or confiscated by a foreign government. This most often occurs

> Expropriation can occur after wars or revolutions.

following insurrections or revolutions, such as Iran's 1979 revolution, as the new regime attempts to throw out the foreign infidels and make a fresh start. Some form of expropriation is a possibility whenever extraordinary events take place. For example, the United States

---

FIGURE 14.3
An Overview of Country Risks

Political Risks

Business environment factors
- Taxes and tariffs
- Local content and labor regulations
- Protection of intellectual property rights
- Protectionism
- Tradition of law and order

Political environment factors
- Civil war
- Corruption
- Military or religion in politics
- Racial or ethnic tensions
- Terrorism

Financial Risks

Macro (economic) factors
- Currency risk
- Inflation risk
- Interest rate risk
- The current account
- The balance of trade

Micro factors
- Cancellation of contracts by a host government
- Capital controls on investment, repatriation, or foreign exchange
- Expropriation
- Involuntary loan defaults or restructurings
- Payment delays

Market Update

Political Risk in Indonesia

President Suharto assumed power in Indonesia in 1967 and ruled for more than 30 years. During this time, Indonesian law prohibited foreign investors from holding majority stakes in Indonesian firms. MNCs doing business in Indonesia routinely formed alliances with members of the Suharto family. When President Suharto was deposed during the currency and stock market crisis of 1998, there were massive public demonstrations and riots against the government amidst charges of nepotism and corruption.

Although the transfer of power to Suharto's successor, B.J. Habibie, went fairly smoothly, companies doing business with the Suharto family were exposed to significant new political risks. For example, the Indonesian Attorney General's Office reviewed nearly $100 billion worth of deals that had been personally approved by former President Suharto. Many contracts with foreign MNCs were canceled or renegotiated on less favorable terms. These renegotiated contracts were a form of expropriation by the Indonesian government.

---

froze Osama bin Laden's U.S. assets (at least those that could be identified) after the Saudi millionaire and terrorist was implicated in the 1998 bombings of U.S. embassies in Nairobi (Kenya) and Tanzania. This is a common governmental response to real or perceived injuries by foreign parties.

From a conceptual standpoint, expropriation risk is relatively easy to handle. Nobody appreciates having assets confiscated, but you can plan ahead if you know that this is a possibility. Chapter 15 incorporates expropriation risk into a capital budgeting analysis by (1) assuming that expropriation is a diversifiable risk and hence does not affect the required return on investment, and (2) adjusting expected future cash flows for the probability of expropriation. In practice, expropriation is a messy affair that involves disruptions in operations in the short term, negotiations with the host government and affiliated parties in the intermediate term, and litigation through international courts in the long term.

Disruptions in Operations. Expropriation is the most extreme form of political risk. However, political risk comes in many more subtle forms that can disrupt the local and even worldwide operations of the MNC. Although the consequences for the MNC are not as catastrophic as outright expropriation, disruptions in operations are far more prevalent than disruptions in ownership.

Political risks often disrupt operations.

Governments impose burdens on MNCs through tariffs, local content regulations that require a certain percentage of the final product to be manufactured locally, foreign exchange controls, limitations on the use of expatriate workers, and taxes and regulations within the host country. In the absence of change in the business environment, each of these burdens is merely a cost of foreign operations. Host governments also occasionally provide incentives for foreign direct investment in the form of subsidized financing, import subsidies, or privileged access to restricted markets. If the magnitude of costs or incentives can change unexpectedly for political reasons, then this uncertainty creates a political source of risk in the host country.

Although political risk is relatively low in the United States, both foreign and domestic companies doing business in the United States are exposed to a variety of political risks. For example, the U.S. Congress periodically tinkers with the U.S. tax code. Both foreign and domestic firms are subjected to periodic changes in the U.S. regulatory environment as well. Firms face political risk as these regulations evolve. Disruptions in the MNC's operations are bound to occur as governments implement their fiscal, monetary, and social agendas.

Protectionism. Foreign firms often must overcome distrust and resentment in host countries. Although some products (such as Parisian fashions and U.S. cigarettes) command a certain romantic cachet among select foreign clienteles, local residents usually have a strong preference for homegrown products and services. Foreign firms exporting to the United States face "buy American" sentiment from individuals, government officials, labor unions, and special interest groups. Similarly, Germans prefer German beer, French prefer French wine, and Japanese prefer Japanese rice. This economic manifestation of nationalism is called **protectionism** when it is codified in a nation's business laws, regulations, or tax code.

> Protectionism is found in most countries.

Governments routinely impose regulations to protect some segments of the domestic economy from foreign competition. For example, many governments impose *local content rules* that specify the percentage of goods that must be manufactured locally. Protectionism is particularly prevalent in manufacturing and agriculture.

It can be difficult to gain entry to foreign markets, even when the local government does not expressly restrict competition. For example, investment securities have historically been sold to individuals in Japan through networks of local agents visiting investors in their homes. This institutional structure began to change during the Japanese financial difficulties of the 1990s, as Japan began liberalizing its financial markets to allow greater access by foreign brokers, investors, and investment bankers. Nevertheless, a non-Japanese securities firm trying to establish a distribution network in Japan still faces formidable entry costs. The considerable uncertainty over the course and pace of reform are a significant political source of risk in Japanese financial markets.

Blocked Funds. Funds generated by foreign investment that cannot be immediately remitted to the parent company are called **blocked funds**. Blocked funds arise from repatriation restrictions placed by a host government on remittances to the parent company. An extreme form of restriction occurs when a host government does not allow its currency to be freely converted or exchanged into other currencies. Currency inconvertibility effectively locks cash flows from foreign sources in the foreign economy.

> Repatriation restrictions can create blocked funds.

Blocked funds may or may not earn a rate of return in the foreign market that exceeds their cost of capital. If the host government has imposed both capital inflow and outflow restrictions, local rates of return can exceed comparable rates of return elsewhere in the world. More commonly, the host government places restrictions only on capital outflows to prevent capital flight and retain currency in a struggling local economy. In this circumstance, local rates of return are likely to be below rates of return available elsewhere.

In the absence of unexpected change in repatriation restrictions or currency convertibility, blocked funds are simply a cost of foreign operations.[2] Blocked funds become a political source of risk only when unexpected changes arising from political events affect the MNC's ability to remit funds from its foreign operations.

---

2 A procedure for valuing blocked funds is presented in Chapter 15.

Loss of Intellectual Property Rights. Another example of a political source of risk lies in the MNC's potential loss of intellectual property rights to competitors or former business partners through a government's actions or inactions. **Intellectual property rights** are patents, copyrights, trademarks, or proprietary technologies or processes (that is, trade secrets) that are the basis of the MNC's competitive advantage in local and global markets. Corporations protect their intellectual property by restricting access to products, technologies, or processes. To the extent that a host government allows one or more local firms to steal or otherwise misappropriate the intellectual property rights of another company, that company is exposed to a political source of risk.

> Intellectual property rights include patents, copyrights, trademarks, and trade secrets.

MNCs must be especially careful to minimize their exposure to this political source of risk in developing countries. Developing countries are usually more interested in obtaining technology to promote economic growth than in protecting the intellectual property rights of foreign individuals or companies. If the MNC does not exercise vigilance in the management, control, and transfer of its intellectual property rights, it can find itself competing against former partners in foreign markets or even in its own domestic market.

14.2 • STRATEGIES FOR MANAGING COUNTRY RISK

The magazine *Sports Illustrated* asked the following question during the 1992 Olympic Games in Barcelona: "How do you avoid being an ugly American in Barcelona?" The answer was "Don't go." Staying home—that is, not investing—is always an option for the MNC. According to discounted cash flow methodology, the MNC should forgo any project with a negative net present value. It is especially important that the MNC consider all of the real options that come with foreign investment, as well as any opportunity costs of investing.[3]

With a little forethought, the MNC can take steps to maximize the expected return and minimize the damage of any negative political or financial events that might take place in a foreign country. Once an investment decision has been made, the MNC has four options for increasing the returns and decreasing the risks of foreign investment:

- Negotiate the environment with the host country.
- Obtain political risk insurance.
- Structure operations to minimize the MNC's risk exposure and maximize return.
- Plan for disaster recovery.

Each of these strategies is discussed in the following sections.

Negotiating the Environment

When a multinational corporation invests in a foreign asset, it enters a relationship with a foreign host government. Some elements of this relationship are explicit, such as the laws of the host country that govern the corporation's behavior. Other elements are implicit, such as an expectation on the part of the MNC that the host government will not impose punitive tariffs or regulations after the firm has invested. As in any relationship, foreign direct investment involves give-and-take between the MNC and the host government.

---

3 Investment decisions in the presence of real options are discussed in Chapter 18.

Before investment, the MNC must negotiate with the host government to create an environment that maximizes its expected return on investment while minimizing exposure to political and financial risks. This negotiation often culminates in an **investment agreement** that spells out the rights and responsibilities of the MNC and the host government. In colonial times, these agreements were called *concessions* because they gave the multinational firm privileged or monopoly access to the resources of the host country, sometimes with little compensation to the host country. In today's more competitive international business environment, investment agreements are less likely to be concessions and more likely to benefit both the MNC and the local economy.

> An investment agreement specifies each party's rights and responsibilities.

The investment agreement should specify the rights and responsibilities of each party with regard to the investment and financial environments. The investment agreement also should specify remedies in case the relationship turns sour. In particular, it should specify a venue and identify jurisdiction for the international arbitration of disputes. The beauty of a well-conceived and carefully written investment agreement is that it allows both parties to act like gentlemen.

The Investment Environment. These items in the investment environment should be negotiated:

- Tax rates, taxable bases, tariffs, and tax holidays
- Concessions that grant the MNC privileged access to restricted markets (e.g., an agreement that restricts the entry of competing firms)
- Obligations to undertake tie-in projects (e.g., negative-NPV infrastructure projects such as airports, ship yards, rail yards, schools, or hospitals)
- Rights or restrictions on imports from, or exports to, other markets (e.g., requirements on local sourcing of labor or materials or host-country quotas on local production)
- Provisions for planned divestiture of the investment (e.g., build-operate-transfer project financing transfers ownership to the host government after a prespecified period of time)
- Allowable uses of expatriate managers or technicians to run local operations
- Assurances of performance on the part of the MNC and the host government
  - Remedies against expropriation, renegotiation, or delay
  - Provisions and venues for international arbitration of disputes

Each of these items in the investment environment affects cash flows from the project.

The Financial Environment. These financial items should be negotiated:

- Rules governing remittance of cash flows from affiliates to the parent corporation
  - Transfer prices
  - Management fees
  - Royalties
  - Loan repayments
  - Dividends
- Access to capital markets in the host country
- The possibility of subsidized financing from the host government
- The corporate governance environment
  - Host-country restrictions on ownership of the local subsidiary
  - Remedies in the case of nonperformance or default by either party
  - Provisions for international arbitration of disputes

By negotiating with the host government prior to investment, the MNC can avoid adverse outcomes and more easily manage its affairs.

Political Risk Insurance

Insurance contracts, such as insurance against political risk, are a form of put option. A put option is an option to sell an underlying asset at a specified exercise price on or before a specified date. Put options are used to protect against a drop in the value of the underlying asset. Insurance contracts are out-of-the-money put options in that they insure against negative outcomes but are left unexercised if the outcome is neutral or positive.

Many political risks can be mitigated through political risk insurance. A corporation's need for insurance depends on the extent of its geographic diversification and its exposure to political risk. MNCs that have geographically diversified operations and cash flows in a large number of countries and currencies are, in essence, self-insuring. Less-diversified companies, especially those with a major proportion of their operations located in a single foreign country, have a much greater need for political risk insurance.

Insurable Risks. An insurable political risk would ideally possess the following conditions:

1. The loss is identifiable in time, place, cause, and amount.
2. A large number of individuals or businesses are exposed to the risk, ideally in an independently and identically distributed manner.
3. The expected loss over the life of the contract is estimable, so that the insurer can set reasonable premiums.
4. The loss is outside the influence of the insured.

The first condition is necessary to write an enforceable insurance contract based on a specific risk and on a specific insured amount.

The second condition allows an insurer to spread losses across a large pool of insured parties. The relevant risk to the insurer is then the risk of the portfolio, rather than that of any single insurance contract in isolation. In this respect, micro political risks are better candidates for insurance than macro political risks because the insured events are more likely to be independent within any single country. Insurers must spread their macro political risks across a number of countries, ideally with independent political risk outcomes.

The third condition allows the insurer to set reasonable premiums based on the insurer's exposures to political risks. Private insurers will insist that premiums cover expected losses from political risk insurance. Governmental agencies sometimes set premiums below those of private insurance to promote trade with particular countries. Although governments are able to capture some societal benefits that private insurers cannot (such as increased or more stable employment in the domestic economy), in most instances the costs of below-market political risk insurance premiums are borne by the taxpayers of the sponsoring country.

The last condition rules out moral hazard. **Moral hazard** is the risk that the existence of a contract will change the behaviors of parties to the contract. In the present context, the last condition precludes the insured parties from influencing the outcome or consequences of a political source of risk. This is a necessary condition, as insurance coverage reduces the incentives of insured parties to avoid losses or reduce the amounts lost in the event of adverse outcomes. For example, automobile owners are less concerned with protecting their vehicles when they are insured than when they are not insured.

Insurable Political Risks. Exposed assets can be insured against the following political sources of risk:

- Expropriation due to any of the following:
  - War
  - Revolution
  - Insurrection
  - Civil disturbance
  - Terrorism
- Repatriation restrictions
- Currency inconvertibility

As with any insurance policy, premiums rise as coverage is expanded to include more risks, as the insured amount increases, or as the likelihood of an adverse outcome increases.

Political Risk Insurers. Political risk insurance is available from international agencies, governmental export credit agencies, and private insurers. Here are the major players:

- International agencies
  - The World Bank—Multilateral Investment Guarantee Agency
- Government export credit agencies
  - Canada—Export Development Corporation
  - France—Compagnie Francaise d'Assurances pour le Commerce Exterieur
  - Germany—Hermes Kreditversicherung
  - Hong Kong—Export Credit Insurance Corporation
  - Italy—Sezione Speciale per l'Assicurazione del Credito all'Esportazione
  - Japan—Ministry of International Trade and Industry
  - Netherlands—Nederlandsche Credietverzekering Maatschappij NV
  - United Kingdom—Export Credits Guarantee Department
  - United States—Overseas Private Investment Corporation (OPIC)
- Private insurers
  - Lloyd's of London
  - London-based Nelson Hurst PLC
  - U.S.-based American International Group (AIG)
  - U.S.-based Chubb Corporation
  - U.S.-based Reliance National Insurance Company
  - Bermuda-based Exporters Insurance Company
  - Bermuda-based Sovereign Risk Insurance Ltd.

By diversifying across countries and industries, these insurers spread political sources of risk from individual countries across their entire portfolio.

The World Bank created the Multilateral Investment Guarantee Agency (MIGA) in 1990 to promote international trade. MIGA now has an insured portfolio of several billion dollars. Companies based in the United States can obtain political risk insurance through a U.S. government agency called the Overseas Private Investment Corporation (OPIC), as well as through private insurers such as Lloyd's of London and the American International Group. OPIC is the largest national political risk insurer, with annual guarantees of more than $10 billion dollars. Many other countries offer political risk insurance through government agencies.

Prior to the 1990s, government agencies such as OPIC were the primary underwriters of political risk insurance. Private insurers were not as active in insuring trade or investment risks. Political risk cover typically was available only up to about $10 million and for

Private insurers provide liquidity and have increased insurable terms and amounts.

terms of only about three years. During the 1990s, private insurers emerged as significant players in the market for political risk insurance. These insurers have provided much-needed liquidity, increased insurable amounts to over $100 million, and extended terms to as long as ten years. There is also an emerging reinsurance market that allows insurers to lay off their political risks onto other insurers or private investors.

Growth in the private market for political risk insurance was driven by the increase in project finance during the 1990s. Project finance is a way to raise nonrecourse financing for a specific project. The project is established as a separate legal entity in the host country and relies heavily on debt financing with payments contractually linked to the cash flow generated by the project. Project finance has become a popular way to fund infrastructure projects in developing economies, especially power generation capacity and transportation (roads, rail, or airport) projects. Investors such as financial institutions rely on political risk insurance to mitigate the political risks of investment in these economies.

The costs of political risk insurance depend on the risks. Annual insurance premiums through private insurers can be as high as 10 percent of the amount of the investment in high-risk countries. OPIC insurance premiums are generally less than those of private insurers. The premiums of private insurers vary widely, so it makes sense to shop around.

Political Risk and the Structure of Foreign Operations

The MNC's investment decisions are made through its capital budgeting process. Although this process culminates in a "go/no go" choice, it should consider alternatives that determine how the investment is structured. These choices influence the project's marketing, production, distribution, human resource, and financial leverage decisions. Careful choices in these areas can reduce the MNC's exposure to the consequences of harmful actions on the part of hostile or opportunistic host governments.

The MNC can limit its political risk exposures.

Limit the Scope of Technology Transfer to Foreign Affiliates. Assets that reside in a foreign country are at risk of expropriation. This is as true for intellectual property rights, such as proprietary technologies or production processes, as it is for physical assets such as a manufacturing plant. The MNC can reduce its exposure to expropriation by limiting the scope of any technology transfer to include only nonessential steps of the production process.

Limit Dependence on Any Single Partner. A host government has more to gain through expropriation when an entire production process is housed in a single location. By maintaining relationships with more than one host government, the MNC can reduce its exposure to any single government and thereby reduce the risk of expropriation. For example, an automaker can source its engines from one country, the drivetrain from another country, and the chassis from a third country.

Similarly, maintaining more than one source for each component limits the corporation's exposure to political risk. A loss of capacity in one location can then be filled by other international sources. This also reduces the MNC's exposure to other sources of business risk, such as a labor strike. Of course, the benefits of diversification must be balanced against the costs of maintaining relations with more than one partner.

Enlist Local Partners. Local partners can reduce the MNC's exposure to political risk. For example, raising local debt and equity funds reduces the amount of money that the MNC has at risk in the local economy. Enlisting local employees or managers to run the business also helps insulate the MNC from adverse changes in the political environment. The likelihood and magnitude of adverse outcomes are reduced when local stakeholders are present to represent the MNC in local affairs.

Use More Stringent Investment Criteria. The most commonly used capital budgeting criteria are net present value and internal rate of return. According to this methodology, expected cash flows from investment are discounted at a rate that reflects investors' opportunity cost of capital. All incremental cash flows are to be included, and the discount rate should depend on the systematic risk of the asset.

MNCs sometimes modify this methodology when investing in uncertain environments. The two most common modifications to capital budgeting theory on investment in locations with high country risk are use of a short-term investment horizon and use of an inflated hurdle rate. The motivation for using a short-term horizon for investments in risky countries is to capture a return on investment before the situation in the host country can change. The **discounted payback period**—the length of time needed to recoup the present value of an investment—can be used to favor projects with a rapid return on investment.

Another common variation of net present value is to use an inflated or above-market hurdle rate on investments exposed to high country risk. Use of an inflated hurdle rate can be justified when it is difficult to value managerial flexibility in the face of uncertain investment environments. In particular, it can be difficult to value managerial options to expand, contract, or abandon a project with discounted cash flow methods. An inflated hurdle rate builds in a margin of safety for managers, and perhaps also for debt and equity stakeholders.

Truncated investment horizons and inflated hurdle rates are, at best, ad hoc adjustments for high country risk. A better approach for capital-intensive projects is to try to identify possible future states of the world and anticipate how the MNC might respond to each state. In this way, the MNC can proact to an uncertain world and proceed with its investment decision in the most informed way.

Planning for Disaster Recovery

Once invested, the firm must work with its foreign partners in business and government to minimize the adverse consequences of political or financial events. If a worst-case scenario occurs, the corporation must take action to minimize its losses with an eye toward leveraging its experiences into new growth opportunities. Ideally, disaster recovery strategies are planned in advance. Advance planning can greatly increase the speed and effectiveness of the MNC's response to adverse outcomes.

> Disaster recovery strategies should be planned in advance.

Consider the Iraqi invasion of Kuwait in August 1990. Iraqi troops took just 12 hours to occupy the tiny, oil-rich country. In addition to threatening world peace, this invasion created a number of new risks for oil companies with operations in the Middle East. Assets were jeopardized, personnel were endangered, shipments and procurement became riskier and more difficult, and oil price volatility increased. Even before the U.N.-led counterattack against Iraq in January 1991, Kuwait officials had hired U.S.-based Bechtel Corporation as project manager to restore Kuwait's damaged oil capacity. Bechtel engineers entered Kuwait in March 1991, just days after Iraqi troops were ousted from the desert kingdom. Bechtel mobilized an international workforce of more than 16,000 specialists from more than 40 countries to put out about 650 wellhead fires, assess the economic and environmental damage, and coordinate operations, procurement, logistics, and reconstruction of Kuwait's oil production capacity. After the last fires were extinguished in November 1991, Bechtel sent more than 200 engineers to rebuild

Kuwait's infrastructure to its prewar production capacity of two million barrels per day. Although Bechtel's operations were by far the most extensive, other oil companies with assets in the region mounted similar disaster recovery operations. By being prepared with a disaster recovery plan, the MNC can minimize its losses and retain its foothold in foreign markets.

14.3 • PROTECTING THE MULTINATIONAL'S COMPETITIVE ADVANTAGES

Intellectual Property Rights

At the root of the multinational corporation's competitive advantages are its ownership-specific intellectual property rights including patents, copyrights, trademarks, and trade secrets. In order to encourage innovation, most governments allow protection of specific intellectual property rights for a fixed length of time after their creation. These protections provide a temporary monopoly to the inventor or creator.

A **patent** is a government-approved right to make, use, or sell an invention for a period of time. In the United States, patents can be obtained on processes, products, machines, new chemical compounds, improvements on the processes, machines, or compounds, ornamental designs for products, and plants produced by asexual reproduction. Patent protection in the U.S. lasts 20 years, with the exception of design patents lasting 14 years. Patent protection lasts for shorter periods in most other countries. The United States follows a *first-to-invent* doctrine, whereas many other countries follow a *first-to-file* doctrine in which patent privileges go to the first individual or corporation to file a patent application. In Japan, patents can be filed on the idea of a *patentable creation*; that is, before a process, machine, or compound is invented and refined. This makes patent law an important competitive weapon in Japan. Most countries grant patent protection to pharmaceuticals used in the treatment of disease, but many countries also regulate this industry and set prices on prescription drugs.

A **copyright** prohibits the unauthorized reproduction of creative works, including books, magazines, drawings, paintings, musical compositions, and sound and video recordings. Copyright protection in the United States lasts for the life of the creator plus an additional 50 years. Computer software is an example of a creative work for which copyright laws vary greatly from country to country. Although the United States and most other developed countries extend copyright protection to computer software, many developing countries do not.

A **trademark** is a distinctive name, word, symbol, or device used to distinguish a company's goods or services from those of its competitors. Trademark protection varies from country to country. Trademark protection in the United States is for 10-year terms. As it does with patents, the United States follows a first-to-invent policy by granting trademark protection to the first company to commercially establish a trademark in the marketplace. Most other countries follow a first-to-file policy, whether or not that individual or corporation has established the trademark in the marketplace. For this reason, MNCs can find their trademarks legally copied and used by competitors in foreign markets. If a local company already has trademark protection, the multinational can find itself competing against its own trademark. Registering a trademark in all possible future markets is a good idea for the MNC with a distinctive trademark or trade name.

Trade secrets are ideas, processes, formulas, techniques, devices, or information that a company uses to its competitive advantage. In the United States, protection of trade secrets is extended as long as the owner takes reasonable steps to maintain secrecy. This category includes a wide range of ideas and processes that may or may not be patentable. The decision of whether or not to patent a trade secret is an important decision. Had Coca-Cola patented its formula for Coke when it was created in 1914, it would have lost its patent protection just prior to World War I. By keeping it a trade secret, Coca-Cola has squeezed an extra 85 years of life out of the formula.

Loss of Competitive Advantage

The MNC's intellectual property rights can be lost in any of three ways. First, these competitive advantages naturally dissipate as new products and technologies erode the value of old innovations. Managers must continually strive to leverage their core competencies into new products and new markets. Second, competitors can steal intellectual property rights. Third, the company's intellectual property rights can be transferred, either intentionally or unintentionally, to licensees and joint venture partners. This transfer can come with or without the knowledge and consent of the MNC. The rest of this section discusses the last two of these threats.

Theft of Intellectual Property Rights. Theft of intellectual property rights is a growing problem, especially for MNCs based in the developed countries of North America, Southeast Asia, and Western Europe. Developing countries are desperate for technologies that will improve their standards of living, and they often pay less attention to intellectual property rights than more developed countries do. The governments of less-developed countries often allow their local companies to acquire "by hook or by crook" any technology they can in fields such as pharmaceuticals, electronics, computer software, and publishing. Mechanisms for the protection of intellectual property rights are lax or nonexistent in many of these countries. Licensees sometimes steal technology with the implicit or even explicit cooperation of the host government. Intellectual property rights are vulnerable even in some developed and developing countries, including Hong Kong, Italy, South Korea, and Taiwan. To make matters worse, patent and trademark rights are conferred by individual nations, so contractual restrictions on where and when the licensee can sell a product may not have force in other countries. When patent protection is suspect, the risk of losing production technology makes cross-border collaboration less attractive.

Sleeping with the Enemy. The MNC can extend its expertise into new areas, markets, or technologies by participating in strategic alliances and joint ventures. As Prahalad and Hamel observed, "Unlike physical assets, [core] competencies do not deteriorate as they are applied and shared. They grow."[4] However, in the dynamic give-and-take of a strategic alliance lies the MNC's biggest threat; i.e., the threat of an ally looting the company of its competitive advantages and then competing head-to-head with its former partner. How does the MNC allow its core competencies to grow through a strategic alliance without losing its competitive edge? Critical elements in a successful partnership include finding the right partner and appropriately structuring the deal.

Finding the Right Partner and Managing the Relationship

The first and most important element in a successful partnership is in choosing the right partner.[5] In a successful partnership, neither party gains at the other party's expense.

---

[4] Prahalad and Hamel, "The Core Competence of the Corporation," *Harvard Business Review* (1990).

[5] American author Jean Kerr wrote: "Marrying a man is like buying something you've been admiring for a long time in a shop window. You may love it when you get it home, but it doesn't always go with everything else."

Market Update

The Modern Pirates of the High Seas

Developed countries such as the United States are fighting a fierce cross-border battle with developing countries over protection of intellectual property rights. The conflict basically comes down to the "haves" against the "have-nots." To a company in the United States, the unauthorized use of another's intellectual property rights is called piracy. In China, pirated versions of software programs such as Microsoft's *Windows* are called "patriotic software" because of their ability to speed the country's modernization efforts.

Software companies such as Microsoft face rampant copyright infringement, even in those countries that do extend copyright protection to computer software. A 2001 study by the Business Software Alliance estimated the following software piracy rates:

http://www.
bsa.org

- 63 percent in Eastern Europe
- 58 percent in Latin America
- 57 percent in the Middle East
- 52 percent in Africa
- 51 percent in Asia and the Pacific region
- 34 percent in Western Europe
- 25 percent in North America

Overall, estimates are that 37 percent of business software applications around the world are stolen, with estimated losses to U.S. firms of $11 billion.

The People's Republic of China has been one of the worst offenders. The Business Software Alliance estimates that 92 percent of the installed software in China is illegal. (The only country with a worse record is Vietnam, with a 97 percent piracy rate.) Attempts by the Chinese government to crack down on copyright infringement have met with little success. When piracy operations are shut down in China, they often move to Hong Kong or Macao and continue operations. Since its 2001 entry into the World Trade Organization, the Chinese government has been trying to develop a climate that protects intellectual property rights. However, there is still a long way to go.

Source: Compiled from news reports.

The partners share a common goal and agree on the means for attaining this goal. This seems like an obvious point, but good communication is truly the single most important element of any partnership.

Management must exercise patience in structuring the deal so that the goals of the alliance and the means of obtaining these goals are clearly defined. The more complicated the deal, the more patience is required. Once a partnership is formed, it is important for key executives from both companies to participate in the development and management of the partnership. Opportunism is most likely to raise its ugly head when the partners lose the need or the will to work together. Companies that can master these steps can gain access to new products and technologies, extend the life of their existing products, and reap the benefits of an increasingly integrated global village.

In addition to finding the right partner and working hard (and smart) to nurture the relationship, there are several more explicit ways in which the MNC can limit its exposure to technology loss through international alliances such as license agreements or joint ventures:[6]

- Limiting the scope of the technology transfer to include only nonessential parts of the production process
- Limiting the transferability of the technology by contract
- Limiting dependence on any single partner
- Using only assets near the end of their product life cycle
- Using only assets with limited growth options
- Trading one technology for another
- Removing the threat by acquiring the stock or assets of the foreign partner

These remedies limit the ability and willingness of the foreign partner to behave opportunistically and become a competitor rather than a partner.

14.4 • SUMMARY

Country risk is the risk that the business environment in a host country will unexpectedly change. Country risk includes political and financial risks. Political risk is the risk of unexpected change in the political environment of a host country, whereas financial risk refers more generally to unexpected change in the financial, economic, or business environment of a host country.

A variety of national and supranational agencies and private companies provide assessments of country risk. Macro assessments of a country's overall business climate are often supplemented with a micro assessment of the risk exposures of particular industries or companies operating within the host country.

The multinational corporation's exposures to country risks can be managed in several ways. First, the investment and financial environments should be negotiated with the host government prior to investment to ensure that agreement is reached on each party's rights and responsibilities. This negotiation can take the form of an investment agreement between the host government and the MNC. A formal investment agreement can greatly reduce the risks involved in cross-border investment, allowing the host government and the MNC to strike a deal in which both parties benefit.

Political risk insurance can be used to cover the risks of repatriation restrictions, currency inconvertibility, and expropriation due to war or revolution. Political risk insurers are able to price these risks (and set premiums accordingly) because losses from these events are tied to an identifiable action by the host government. Country risks are also usually diversifiable in a global portfolio, allowing insurers to pool these risks across countries.

The multinational corporation's competitive advantages are based on its intellectual property rights, which include patents, copyrights, trademarks, and trade secrets. The MNC protects and renews its intellectual property rights through investment in its existing core competencies and development of new core competencies. Strategic alliances are one way to obtain access to new core competencies, but they come with the risk of losing control of existing assets.

---

6 See Hamel, Doz, and Prahalad, "Collaborate with Your Competitors—and Win," *Harvard Business Review* (1989).

KEY TERMS

blocked funds

copyright

country risk

discounted payback period

expropriation

financial risk

intellectual property rights

investment agreement

macro and micro country risks

moral hazard

patent

political risk

protectionism

trade secret

trademark

CONCEPTUAL QUESTIONS

14.1   Define country risk. Define political risk. Define financial risk. Give an example of each different type of country risk.

14.2   What factors might contribute to political and financial risk in a country according to the ICRG country risk rating system?

14.3   What is the difference between a macro and a micro country risk? Give an example of each different type of country risk.

14.4   How is expropriation included in a discounted cash flow analysis of a proposed foreign investment? Does expropriation affect expected future cash flows? From a discounted cash flow perspective, is it likely to affect the discount rate on foreign investment?

14.5   What is protectionism, and how can it affect the multinational corporation?

14.6   What are blocked funds? How might they arise?

14.7   What are intellectual property rights? How are they at risk when the multinational corporation has foreign operations?

14.8   What is an investment agreement? What conditions might it include?

14.9   What constitutes an insurable risk? List several insurable political risks.

14.10 What operational strategies does the multinational corporation have to protect itself against political risk?

14.11 How can the MNC protect its competitive advantages in the international marketplace?

PROBLEMS

14.1   In the summer of 1998, Russia suffered a currency and stock market crisis that drove the dollar value of Russian stocks down to 10 percent of their precrash value. The crash caught many investors by surprise, including hedge fund managers specializing in emerging markets. In response to large losses sustained on Russian investments, one hedge fund manager was quoted as saying:[7] "If Russia had taken over a plant belonging to General Motors, the government would have done something about it....Essentially, the Russian government has confis-

---

7 Eaglesham and Martinson, "Funds Suffer 'Confiscated' Russian Assets," *Financial Times* (August 28, 1998), p. 22.

cated Western capital, and nobody is doing anything about it." Is the risk of a market crash in an emerging economy a political risk or a financial risk? Explain.

14.2 Expropriation occurs when a host government confiscates the assets of a corporation doing business in that country. Can expropriation occur in other ways? Explain.

14.3 Suppose the systematic risk of a domestic investment is $\beta_i = \rho_{iW} (\sigma_i / \sigma_W)$, where $\rho_{iW} = 0.4$ is the correlation between domestic asset returns and world market returns, $\sigma_I = 0.2$ is the standard deviation of returns to the domestic asset, and $\sigma_W = 0.10$ is the standard deviation of the world market return. A comparable foreign asset has $\rho_{iW}' = 0.3$ and $\sigma_i' = 0.3$.
a. Is the total risk of the foreign asset more or less than the domestic asset?
b. Is the systematic risk of the foreign asset more or less than the domestic asset?

14.4 Select a country (e.g., Brazil) of interest to you. Perform a search of popular and academic articles using as keywords: "Brazil AND risk." If you find too many entries under this search criterion, try more restrictive keywords such as credit risk, country risk, expropriation, copyright, patent, investment agreement, or protectionism. What types of country risks can you document for multinational corporations doing business in your chosen country?

SUGGESTED READINGS

The effect of political risk on investors' required returns and the cost of capital on foreign investment are discussed in

Claude Erb, Campbell Harvey, and Tadas Viskanta, "Political Risk, Financial Risk and Economic Risk," *Financial Analysts Journal* 52 (November/December 1996), pp. 28–46.

Articles that address protection of intellectual property rights in the context of corporate strategy include

Gary Hamel, Yves L. Doz, and C. K. Prahalad, "Collaborate with Your Competitors— and Win," *Harvard Business Review* 67 (January–February 1989), pp. 133–139.

C.K. Prahalad and Gary Hamel, "The Core Competence of the Corporation," *Harvard Business Review* 68 (May–June 1990), pp. 79–91.

Valuation and the Structure of Multinational Operations

Cross-Border Capital Budgeting

chapter 15

Overview

There is nothing more difficult to take in hand, more perilous to conduct, or more uncertain in its success, than to take the lead in the introduction of a new order of things.

Niccoló Machiavelli, *The Prince*

In principle, capital budgeting for cross-border investments is no different from capital budgeting for domestic investments. From the viewpoint of the parent firm, project value is still equal to the value of expected future cash flows from the investment discounted at an appropriate risk-adjusted discount rate. Projects should be undertaken by the parent firm if and only if the present value of the expected cash flows exceeds the value of the initial investment.

Although the fundamental investment principle is the same, in practice many differences make cross-border investment decisions more interesting than their domestic counterparts.[1] Cross-border investment projects usually involve one or more foreign currencies, multiple tax rates and systems, and foreign political risk. Cross-border projects also can involve capital flow restrictions that block funds in a host country, project-specific subsidies provided by a host government, or project-specific penalties imposed by a host government. To make matters even more complicated, valuing a project in the local currency of the host country provides a different value from valuation in the parent's domestic currency if—as is usually the case—the international parity conditions do not hold. This chapter shows how to apply the discounted cash flow framework to each of these cross-border investment problems.

To simplify the analysis, our discussion assumes that the foreign project is financed with 100 percent equity. This avoids the difficult issue of how the financing of a for-

---

1 As in the Chinese curse "May your life be interesting," the word *interesting* is a euphemism for *difficult.*

eign project affects its value. We'll also assume that tax treatments in the foreign and domestic countries are the same. In practice, cross-border differences in taxes can have a large impact on project value. These topics are left to later chapters in order to focus on the identification and valuation of the expected future cash flows from investment.

15.1 • THE ALGEBRA OF CROSS-BORDER INVESTMENT ANALYSIS

Discounted Cash Flows

In your first course in finance, you learned to value assets using the **discounted cash flow (DCF)** method. Consider a domestic company evaluating an investment proposal in its domestic currency, d. According to the discounted cash flow valuation method, the net present value NPV^d of a domestic project is calculated according to the following procedure:

1. Identify the expected future cash flows $E[CF_t^d]$ generated by the investment.
2. Identify the discount rate i^d appropriate for the risk of the cash flows.
3. Discount the expected future cash flows at the risk-adjusted discount rate.

For a project that lasts T periods, net present value is given by

$$NPV^d = \sum_{t=0}^{T} [E[CF_t^d] / (1+i^d)^t] \qquad (15.1)$$

where CF_0^d is the initial investment. According to the discounted cash flow approach, projects should be undertaken if and only if the net present value is greater than zero.

In this approach, expected future cash flows are estimated according to two rules:

> Include all incremental cash flows and opportunity costs.

- Include only incremental cash flows.
- Include all opportunity costs.

The first rule says to *include only incremental cash flows* that are associated with the project in the capital budgeting analysis. Sunk costs that have already been spent, for instance, should not be included in the analysis. The second rule says to *include all opportunity costs* in the capital budgeting analysis. If building a manufacturing plant in Malaysia reduces sales from your Indonesian plant, then the cash flows associated with the reduction in sales from the Indonesian plant should be incorporated into the decision to invest in Malaysia. Lost sales from the Indonesian plant are an opportunity cost of opening the Malaysian plant.

Note that the discount rate depends on the cash flows. This is a more general and pervasive rule than you might think. In particular, you should

> The discount rate should reflect the riskiness of the cash flows.

- Discount cash flows in a particular currency at a discount rate in that currency.
- Discount nominal (real) cash flows at a nominal (real) discount rate.
- Discount cash flows to equity (debt) at the cost of equity (debt).
- Discount cash flows to debt and equity at a weighted average cost of capital.

For example, discounting dollar cash flows at a Japanese yen discount rate is inappropriate. Similarly, discounting nominal cash flows at a real discount rate makes no

sense. Follow these rules and your valuations will be, if not accurate, at least internally consistent. Violate any one of these rules, and your valuations are guaranteed
to miss the mark.

The Domestic Capital Budgeting Recipe

The domestic capital budgeting recipe assumes that the cash flows and the discount
rate are in the investor's functional currency. This is not generally the case for a cross-
border project. Fortunately, if the international parity conditions hold, discounting
foreign currency cash flows at a risk-adjusted discount rate in the foreign currency is
equivalent to discounting domestic currency cash flows at the domestic discount rate.

   If the international parity conditions do not hold, all bets are off. For example, if
forward exchange rates are biased estimates of future spot rates, so that forward parity does not hold, then the value of a foreign project depends on which currency is used
to discount the expected future cash flows. The case in which the international parity
conditions hold is much easier to handle, so we'll use this equilibrium condition as a
starting point. We'll consider deviations from the international parity conditions in
section 15.3.

The International Parity Conditions and Cross-Border Capital Budgeting

If markets are perfect and PPP holds, then project value doesn't depend on the currency in which cash flows are discounted.

Suppose capital markets are (1) perfect, so there are no barriers to capital
flows between the foreign subsidiary and the parent, and (2) symmetric,
so taxes and investor preferences are identical in each country. In this
(admittedly unlikely) setting, the international parity conditions hold, and
the value of a foreign investment is the same whether discounting is done
in the foreign or in the domestic currency.

   This is easy to demonstrate with a little algebra. First, note that
expected future cash flows in the domestic currency can be rewritten in terms of the
foreign currency by translating at expected future spot exchange rates or, if they are
available, at forward exchange rates:

$$E[CF_t^d] = E[CF_t^f](E[S_t^{d/f}])$$

$$= E[CF_t^f](F_t^{d/f}) \tag{15.2}$$

Interest rate parity allows us to restate nominal domestic currency interest rates in terms
of nominal foreign currency interest rates, forward exchange rates, and the spot rate.

$$\frac{(1+i^d)t}{(1+i^f)t} = \frac{F_t^{d/f}}{S_0^{d/f}} \Leftrightarrow (1+i^d)t = (1+i^f)t\,(F_t^{d/f}/S_0^{d/f}) \tag{15.3}$$

Substituting Equations 15.2 and 15.3 into Equation 15.1, the domestic currency
value of a foreign project can be restated as

$$NPV^d = \sum_{t=0}^{T}[E[CF_t^d]/(1+i^d)t] = \sum_{t=0}^{T}[(E[CF_t^f]\,F_t^{d/f})/((1+i^f)t(F_t^{d/f}/S_0^{d/f}))]$$

After moving the spot exchange rate outside the summation and canceling the forward exchange rates from the numerator and denominator, net present value in the
domestic currency can be rewritten

$$\text{NPV}^d = (S_0^{d/f}) \sum_{t=0}^{T} [E[CF_t^f] / (1+i^f)^t] = (S_0^{d/f}) [\text{NPV}^f] \qquad (15.4)$$

where NPV^f is the value of the foreign project in the foreign currency. Equations 15.1 and 15.4 are equivalent in that they value expected cash flows at an appropriate risk-adjusted discount rate. This suggests two alternative cross-border valuation recipes.

R e c i p e # 1 :   **Project Valuation from the Local (or Foreign) Perspective**
Discount foreign currency cash flows at the foreign currency discount rate.

R e c i p e # 2 :   **Project Valuation from the Parent's (Domestic) Perspective**
Discount domestic currency cash flows at the domestic currency discount rate.

The details of these two equivalent approaches are shown in Figure 15.1.

The good news is that these two methods give identical results when goods markets and financial markets are perfect, so that the international parity conditions hold. The bad news, of course, is that international financial and (especially) goods markets

FIGURE 15.1
Cross-Border Capital Budgeting Recipes

Recipe #1	Recipe #2
$S_0^{d/f}[\sum_{t=0}^{T} E[CF_t^f]/(1+i^f)^t]$	$\sum_{t=0}^{T}[E[CF_t^d]/(1+i^d)^t]$ where $E[CF_t^d] = E[CF_t^f]E[S_t^{d/f}]$
Discounting in the Foreign Currency	*Discounting in the Domestic Currency*

1. Estimate expected future cash flows in the foreign currency.
 	
 2. Identify the foreign discount rate.
 	
 3. Find NPV in the domestic currency.
 	
    a. Discount the foreign currency cash flows at the foreign currency discount rate.
 	
    b. Convert foreign currency NPV to domestic currency at the spot exchange rate.
	1. Convert expected future foreign currency cash flows to the domestic currency.
	
	    a. Estimate cash flows in the foreign currency.
	
	    b. Estimate expected future spot rates of exchange (using forward rates if they are available).
	
	    c. Convert foreign currency cash flows to the domestic currency at the forward exchange rates.
	
	 2. Identify the domestic discount rate.
	
	 3. Find NPV in the domestic currency by discounting domestic currency cash flows at the domestic discount rate.

If the international parity conditions hold,
then these two NPVs are the same.

are far from perfect. With the exception of interest rate parity, the international parity conditions are relatively poor predictors of financial prices. Before we move on to these more difficult issues, let's set the stage by illustrating these two capital budgeting recipes in a world in which there are no market imperfections and the international parity conditions hold.

15.2 • An Example: Wendy's Restaurant in Neverland

Peter Pan and Wendy are considering opening a restaurant in Neverland, an imaginary world in which markets are perfect and the international parity conditions hold.[2] The dreaded pirate Captain Hook, a vindictive tyrant with a consuming jealousy of Peter and Wendy, governs Neverland. We'll deal with Hook's influence on project value in section 15.4 on special circumstances. For now, let's consider Wendy's investment proposal in its most basic form.

Wendy will purchase Captain Hook's ship and convert it into a fast-food restaurant with the appetites of the many pirates on the island as the target market. The ship is shipshape and Wendy (with a little help from Peter) can have the galley ready for business at time t=0. Wendy will invest the necessary equity capital. Peter will invest his own human capital and serve as local manager. The workforce will consist of the local Lost Boys. The details of Wendy's Neverland project are listed in Table 15.1.

The international parity conditions are known to hold (after all, this is an imaginary land), so equivalent assets have the same real required returns wherever they are traded. The real required return (ι_F) on risk-free government bills is 1 percent per year in both British pounds sterling (Wendy's domestic currency) and Neverland crocs (the local currency). Interest and inflation rates as of time t = 0 are shown in Table 15.2.

TABLE 15.1
Details of the Neverland Proposal

- The project lasts four years, at which time Wendy grows up (only Peter stays young forever).
- An initial investment of £10,000 (Cr40,000) will purchase Captain Hook's ship.
- An additional £6,000 (Cr24,000) will be needed for working capital needs (primarily inventory) at that time. Increases in other current asset accounts are offset by increases in current liabilities, so the increase in net working capital (current assets minus current liabilities) is also £6,000.
- Annual sales are expected to be Cr30,000, Cr60,000, Cr90,000, and Cr60,000 in nominal terms over the next four years.
- Variable operating costs (wages to Lost Boys) are 20 percent of sales.
- Fixed maintenance costs on the ship are Cr2,000 at the end of the first year and are expected to increase at the rate of inflation thereafter.
- The ship will be owned by the foreign subsidiary and depreciated on a straight-line basis over four years to a zero salvage value.
- The inventory balance will be sold at the end of the project and is expected to be worth Cr24,000 in real terms.
- The ship is expected to retain its Cr40,000 real value.
- Income taxes are 50 percent in both the United Kingdom and Neverland. Capital gains on the sale of the ship and inventory at the end of the project are also taxed at 50 percent.
- All cash flows occur at the end of the year.

---

2 Can you imagine a world with no hypothetical situations?

TABLE 15.2
Interest and Inflation Rates in Neverland

	United Kingdom			Neverland	
Nominal risk-free government T-bill rate	$i_F^£$	=	10.00%	i_F^{Cr} =	37.05%
Real required return on T-bills	$\iota_F^£$	=	1.00%	ι_F^{Cr} =	1.00%
Expected inflation over each of the next four years	$p^£$	$\approx$	8.91%	p^{Cr} $\approx$	36.14%
Nominal required return on restaurant projects	$i^£$	$\approx$	20.00%	i^{Cr} =	50.00%
Real required return on restaurant projects	$\iota^£$	$\approx$	10.18%	ι^{Cr} $\approx$	10.18%

   According to the Fisher equation, the 20 percent nominal required return on comparable investments in the United Kingdom is composed of an expected inflation rate plus a real required return on restaurant projects according to $i^£ = (1+p^£)(1+\iota^£)-1 = (1.0891)(1.1018)-1 = 0.20$, or 20 percent.[3] Because the parity conditions hold, the real required return of $\iota^£ = 10.18$ percent on restaurant projects in the United Kingdom equals the real required return on restaurant projects in Neverland: $\iota^{Cr} = (1+i^{Cr})/(1+p^{Cr})-1 = (1.50)/(1.3614)-1 = 0.1018$, or 10.18 percent.

   The international Fisher relation ensures that the difference between nominal returns in Neverland and the United Kingdom is driven entirely by the difference in inflation between the two countries. Placing the pound in the denominator of the international Fisher relation, nominal interest rates as well as the expected inflation rate are 25 percent per year higher in Neverland crocs than in pounds:

$$(1+i^{Cr}) / (1+i^£) \quad = \quad (1+i_F^{Cr}) / (1+i_F^£) \quad = \quad (1+p^{Cr}) / (1+p^£)$$
$$= (1.5000) / (1.2000) = (1.3750) / (1.1000) = (1.3614) / (1.0891) = 1.25$$

This implies that the forward premium on the pound and the expected change in the spot exchange rate are also 25 percent per year, so the pound (in the denominator of the foreign exchange rate) is expected to appreciate by 25 percent per year:

$$E[S_t^{Cr/£}] / S_0^{Cr/£} = F_t^{Cr/£} / S_0^{Cr/£} = (1.25)^t$$

The current spot rate of exchange between the pound and the croc is Cr4.00/£. Forward prices at the 25 percent annual forward premium are shown in Figure 15.2.

Recipe #1: Discounting in the Foreign Currency

Table 15.3 presents an overview of the Neverland project's cash flows. As in a domestic capital budgeting problem, the task is made simpler if we view the cash flow stream as being composed of three parts: (1) initial investment cash flows, (2) operating cash flows during the life of the project, and (3) terminal or end-of-project cash flows. The investment cash flows include the Cr40,000 cost of the ship and the Cr24,000 investment in net working capital. After-tax cash flows from operations in this example are straightforward and can be computed from either of the equivalent equations:

$$CF = \text{Net income} + \text{Depreciation}$$
$$= [(\text{Revenues} - \text{Expenses} - \text{Depreciation})(1 - T)] + \text{Depreciation}$$

---

3 This is the weighted average cost of capital in pounds sterling. For an all-equity project, this would be the required return on equity.

FIGURE 15.2
Exchange Rates in Neverland

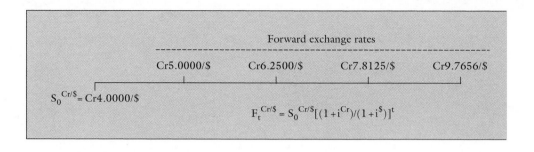

or

$$CF = \text{After-tax operating income} + \text{Depreciation tax shield}$$
$$= [(\text{Revenues} - \text{Expenses})(1 - T)] + [(\text{Depreciation})(T)]$$

where the corporate income tax rate T is assumed to be the same in both countries.[4] Croc operating cash flows from these equations are shown in Table 15.3.

Wendy must recognize the value of the ship and inventory net of capital gains taxes at the end of the project. The value of the ship is expected to grow at the croc inflation rate to $(Cr40,000)(1.3614)^4 = Cr137,400$ in year 4. Because the ship is being depreciated to zero over the life of the project, the entire Cr137,400 amount is a capital gain. Capital gains taxes are 50 percent in Neverland, so a tax payment of Cr68,700 must be made to Hook's treasury at the end of year four. Inventory is also expected to grow in value at the croc inflation rate, so recovery of net working capital yields $(Cr24,000)(1.3614)^4 = Cr82,440$ after four years. If inventory is still carried at its historical cost of Cr24,000, there will be a taxable gain of $(Cr82,440 - Cr24,000) = Cr58,440$ and a capital gains tax of Cr29,220. The resulting stream of nominal cash flows from the Neverland project is

$$\begin{array}{ccccc} & Cr16,000 & Cr27,639 & Cr39,147 & Cr148,397 \end{array}$$

$$-Cr64,000$$

At the croc discount rate of 50 percent on comparable projects, Wendy's investment is worth less than zero; $NPV^{Cr} = -Cr137$. This is worth $NPV^{\pounds} = -\pounds34$ to Wendy at the $Cr4/\pounds$ spot exchange rate.

Recipe #2: Discounting in the Domestic Currency

To discount domestic currency cash flows at the domestic discount rate, foreign currency cash flows should be converted into the domestic currency at forward exchange rates, if forward rates are available. Expected future croc cash flows after converting at the forward rates are shown at the bottom of Table 15.3. The net present value of the Neverland Project from Wendy's perspective is $-\pounds34$, whether the cash flows are discounted in crocs or pounds.

---

4 Tax effects are introduced in Chapter 17.

TABLE 15.3
Valuation of the Neverland Project Cash Flows

Discounting in the Foreign Currency (Neverland crocs)

	t = 0	1	2	3	4
Purchase ship	(Cr40,000)				
Purchase inventory	(24,000)				
(Net working capital)					
Revenues		Cr30,000	Cr60,000	Cr90,000	Cr60,000
– Variable operating costs		(6,000)	(12,000)	(18,000)	(12,000)
– Fixed maintenance cost		(2,000)	(2,723)	(3,707)	(5,046)
– Depreciation		(10,000)	(10,000)	(10,000)	(10,000)
Taxable income		12,000	35,277	58,293	32,954
– Taxes		(6,000)	(17,639)	(29,147)	(16,477)
Net income		6,000	17,639	29,147	16,477
+ Depreciation		10,000	10,000	10,000	10,000
Net cash flow from operations		16,000	27,639	39,147	26,477
Sale of ship					137,400 a
– Tax on sale of ship					(68,700) b
Sale of inventory					82,440 c
– Tax on sale of inventory					(29,220) d
$E[CF_t^{Cr}]$	(Cr64,000)	Cr16,000	Cr27,639	Cr39,147	Cr148,397
NPV^{Cr} (at i^{Cr}=50%)	(Cr137)				

Discounting in the Domestic Currency (British pounds sterling)

	t = 0	1	2	3	4
Expected spot rates	Cr4.0000/£	Cr5.0000/£	Cr6.2500/£	Cr7.8125/£	Cr9.7656/£
$E[CF^£]$	(£16,000)	£3,200	£4,422	£5,011	£15,196
$NPV^£$ (at $i^£$=20%)	(£34)				

Numbers are rounded to the nearest croc or pound depending on the currency of denomination.
a (Cr40,000) (1.3614)^4 = Cr137,400
b (Cr137,400) (0.5) = Cr68,700
c (Cr24,000) (1.3614)^4 = Cr82,440
d (Cr82,440–Cr24,000) (0.5) = Cr29,220

The NPV from the croc and pound perspectives are equal in this example because the international parity conditions hold. Compare this situation to one in which the required croc return on comparable projects in Neverland is 60 percent rather than 50 percent. In that case, NPV depends on whether discounting is done in crocs or in pounds. Tax differences and the size, timing, and form (dividends, interest, management fees) of cash flows back to the parent corporation further distort the picture.

> If PPP holds, then valuation from the project and from the parent perspective are equivalent.

Although the cash flows of this cross-border investment turn out to be quite simple, a multitude of real-world complications can lurk within this simple, imaginary world. In the rest of this section, we will value Wendy's Neverland project in the absence of any real-world complications using Equations 15.1 and 15.4 in turn. Section 15.3 analyzes violations in the international parity conditions and discusses their implications for financial management of the multinational firm. In section 15.4, Captain Hook causes a number of investment and financing nightmares for Wendy and Peter, as well as some business opportunities. These special circumstances are common in cross-border investments.

15.3 • THE PARENT VERSUS LOCAL PERSPECTIVE ON PROJECT VALUATION

The capital budgeting recipes in Equations 15.1 and 15.4 yield consistent values when the international parity conditions hold. They can give conflicting results when the international parity conditions do not hold. Common symptoms of disequilibrium include cross-border differences in real interest rates or in the relative purchasing power of two currencies. Note that these deviations from purchasing power parity can occur even when interest rate parity holds.

This section interprets the two cross-border capital budgeting recipes from the parent's perspective (as in Equation 15.1) and from the project's local perspective (as in Equation 15.4). It concludes with some recommendations for the financial manager when disequilibriums in the international parity conditions give different values depending on one's perspective.

Project Valuation from the Parent's Perspective

The parent's perspective on project valuation is represented in Figure 15.3. A parent corporation's domestic currency is often called its *functional currency* because most of its functions are conducted in that currency. The only relevant cash flows from the parent corporation's point of view are those that are remitted to the parent in its functional cur-

FIGURE 15.3
The Parent's Perspective on Project Valuation

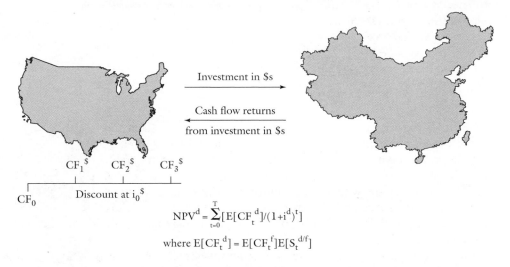

Investment in \$s

Cash flow returns from investment in \$s

$CF_1^{\$}$ $CF_2^{\$}$ $CF_3^{\$}$

CF_0 Discount at $i_0^{\$}$

$$NPV^d = \sum_{t=0}^{T}[E[CF_t^d]/(1+i^d)^t]$$

where $E[CF_t^d] = E[CF_t^f]E[S_t^{d/f}]$

The parent ultimately requires that cash flows be remitted in its functional currency (e.g., dollars for a U.S. parent corporation).

rency. After all, the parent's domestic stakeholders care only about the size, timing, and riskiness of the expected future cash flows that it receives in its functional currency. For this reason, it is important to value foreign investment proposals in the functional currency of the parent and from the perspective of the parent. As a practical matter, this means discounting cash flows at the domestic required return only as they are remitted to the parent in the parent's domestic currency. If cash flows from a foreign project can never be remitted to the parent and the parent's claim on these cash flows cannot be sold, then the project has no value to the parent's stakeholders, and there is no incentive to undertake the project.

> Parent firms want cash flows in their functional currency.

Multinational corporations sometimes do not have a single functional currency. These corporations conduct operations in a variety of countries and currencies and issue debt and equity claims in many countries and in more than one currency. DaimlerChrysler is an example of a multinational corporation that has issued debt and equity securities all over the world including the United Kingdom, the United States, continental Europe, and Asia. To have any value to the parent's debt or equity, foreign cash flows must be convertible into at least one of the corporation's functional currencies. If cash flows from foreign investment cannot ultimately be retrieved from the foreign country and converted into something of value to the firm's stakeholders, then foreign investment has no value.

Project Valuation from the Local Perspective

Initial returns on investment are not necessarily repatriated to the parent in the parent's functional currency. For this reason, it is also useful to compare the value of a foreign project to local alternatives in the foreign market.

> Relevant cash flows from the project's local perspective are those that are earned by the project in the functional currency of the host country.

Consider 3M Corporation's investment in the People's Republic of China. 3M Corporation began as a sandpaper company, and its core competency remains applying coverings to backing materials. Its product line includes a wide assortment of products, ranging from photographic film to their ubiquitous Post-it notes. In the early 1990s, 3M invested a few million dollars in a sales office in Beijing. The company did not expect to immediately recover its Chinese investment. Rather, by gaining a foothold in this huge market of more than 1 billion people, 3M hoped to earn a rate of return on funds invested in China that is above what can be earned elsewhere on projects of similar risk. If funds earned in China can be reinvested profitably in other Chinese investments, then eventually, as repatriation restrictions are eased and the convertibility of the Chinese renminbi improves, these assets will have a large value in dollars (3M's functional currency). This local perspective on project valuation is shown in Figure 15.4.

How to Handle Valuation Differences

Covered interest arbitrage ensures that interest rate parity holds in liquid interbank markets for foreign exchange and Eurocurrency transactions. Cash flows in these markets are contractual, so any disequilibriums result in an arbitrage opportunity. In contrast to the contractual cash flows of the foreign exchange and Eurocurrency markets, the operating cash flows of the multinational corporation's cross-border investments are both contractual and noncontractual in nature. Because the parity conditions do not in general hold for noncontractual cash flows, in practice there can be a substantial difference between project values calculated with the two cross-border capital budgeting recipes.

FIGURE 15.4
The Local Perspective on Project Valuation

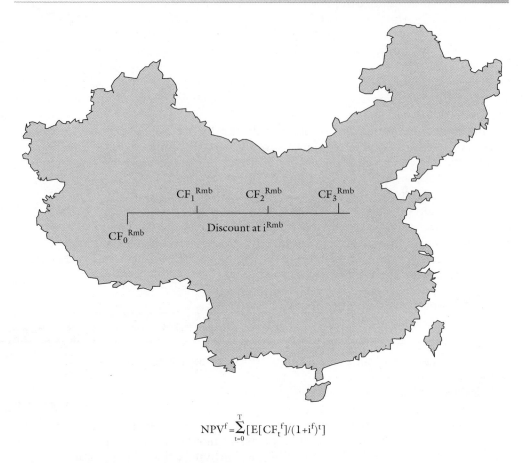

$$\text{NPV}^f = \sum_{t=0}^{T}[E[CF_t^f]/(1+i^f)^t]$$

The parent should not mind blocked funds in a foreign country as long as (1) funds can earn their risk-adjusted rate of return in the local currency (e.g., Chinese renminbi), and (2) funds can be repatriated to the parent sometime in the future.

Consider the classification scheme in Figure 15.5. If both NPV^d and NPV^f are less than zero, then the project clearly should be rejected. Conversely, if both NPV^d and NPV^f are greater than zero, then the project should be accepted. The more ambiguous situations occur in the off-diagonal cells NPV^d > 0 > NPV^f and NPV^f > 0 > NPV^d. The sections that follow provide some guidance on what to do in the "ambiguous" and "accept" situations.

To focus exclusively on disequilibriums in the international parity conditions, these examples assume there are no repatriation restrictions. Special circumstances such as repatriation restrictions are covered in section 15.4.

> Accepting a project for which NPV^d>0 and NPV^f<0 is tantamount to currency speculation.

Positive-NPV for the Parent but Negative-NPV for the Project. If NPV^d > 0 > NPV^f, the project looks attractive when viewed from the parent's perspective but unattractive from the project's local perspective. In this case, the positive expected NPV from the parent's

FIGURE 15.5

Valuation Differences from the Parent and Local Perspectives

		Parent's perspective in domestic currency	
		$NPV^d < 0$	$NPV^d > 0$
Project's perspective in the foreign currency	$NPV^f < 0$	Reject	Look for better projects in the foreign currency
	$NPV^f > 0$	Lock in the local value NVP^f (e.g., through hedging)	**Accept** If $NPV^d > NPV^f$, hedging provides lower risk and lower expected return If $NPV^f > NPV^d$, hedging provides lower risk and higher expected return

perspective may be due to disequilibriums in the international financial markets and owe nothing to the cash flows from the project itself. Indeed, the project is expected to lose value in the local currency. Accepting this type of project is tantamount to speculating on foreign exchange rates.

Suppose real interest rates are higher in renminbi than in dollars, as in the following example:

	United States	China
Nominal risk-free interest rate	$i_F^\$ = 10\%$	$i_F^{Rmb} = 21\%$
Real required return on a risk-free asset	$\iota_F^\$ = 0\%$	$\iota_F^{Rmb} = 10\%$
Expected inflation rate	$p^\$ = 10\%$	$p^{Rmb} = 10\%$
Current spot exchange rate	$S_0^{\$/Rmb} = \$0.20/Rmb$	
Expected future spot rate	$E[S_1^{\$/Rmb}] = \$0.20/Rmb$	

If there are no barriers to cross-border capital flows, investors will prefer to borrow at the low U.S. real interest rate and lend at the high real renminbi rate. In the long term, this will force real interest rates back toward equilibrium, and is likely to lead to a depreciation of the renminbi and an appreciation of the dollar. In the short term, this adjustment in real interest rates and exchange rates may not occur.

Suppose that the spot exchange rate is expected to hold its nominal value; that is, $E[S_1^{\$/Rmb}] = S_0^{\$/Rmb} = \$0.20/Rmb$. According to interest rate parity, renminbi should be selling at a 9.091 percent forward discount to the current spot rate:

$$(F_1^{\$/Rmb}/S_0^{\$/Rmb}) - 1 = [(1+i_F^\$)/(1+i_F^{Rmb})] - 1 = (1.10/1.21) - 1 \approx -0.09091$$

rather than at a forward discount of zero. Thus, the international parity conditions do not hold. If there is no forward exchange market for renminbi, then arbitrage activity will be unable to enforce interest rate parity. The fact that expected future spot exchange rates are not in equilibrium with the interest rate differential provides a financial opportunity (along with some risk) to multinational corporations active in the Chinese market.

Suppose 3M Corporation has identified a riskless investment in China with the following contractual cash flows:

Rmb 605

$NPV^{Rmb} = -Rmb25 \Rightarrow$ Reject (?)

−Rmb 525

$i_F^{Rmb} = 21\%$

At the 21 percent Chinese interest rate, this investment is worth $NPV^{Rmb} =$ (Rmb605/1.21) − Rmb525 = −Rmb25, a negative value in the local currency. Translating the renminbi cash flows into dollars at the expected future spot rate $E[S_1^{\$/Rmb}] =$ \$0.20/Rmb, the project cash flows from the U.S. parent's perspective are

\$121

$NPV^{\$} = +\$5 \Rightarrow$ Accept (?)

−\$105

$i_F^{\$} = 10\%$

Net present value from the U.S. parent's perspective is $NPV^{\$} = \$121/1.10 − \$105 =$ +\$5. This looks like a positive-NPV project from the U.S. parent's perspective.

Should 3M accept this project? The answer is "no" as long as there are better investment opportunities in the local Chinese market. As an alternative to this investment, consider a zero-NPV investment in a Chinese government bond at the 21 percent riskless renminbi interest rate that generates the following renminbi cash flows:

Rmb 635.25

$NPV^{Rmb} = Rmb\ 0$

−Rmb 525

$i_F^{Rmb} = 21\%$

At the expected end-of-period exchange rate of \$0.20/Rmb, this riskless investment provides an expected end-of-period cash flow of (Rmb635.25)(\$0.20/Rmb) = \$127.05. Expected cash flows to the U.S. parent are then

\$127.05

$NPV^{\$} = +\$10.9 \Rightarrow$ Accept !

−\$105

$i_F^{\$} = 10\%$

From the perspective of the U.S. parent, this is a 21 percent expected rate of return on the \$105 investment.

Investing in a zero-NPV government bond rather than a negative-NPV investment project avoids the negative NPV of the project and allows 3M to capture the full benefit of the expected real depreciation of the renminbi. If 3M decides to speculate on this capital market disequilibrium, it should speculate directly in the financial markets rather than through its negative-NPV investment project. For example, by borrowing at $i_F^{\$} = 10\%$ in the United States and investing an equivalent amount at $i_F^{Rmb} = 21\%$ in China, 3M can place a bet that the dollar will not appreciate by more than 10 percent in real terms during the coming year.

If the net present value of a proposed investment is negative when valued in the for-

Reject any project for which $NPV^d > 0$ and $NPV^f < 0$.

eign currency and positive when valued in the domestic currency, the difference in value arises from a disequilibrium in the international parity conditions (or from a repatriation restriction), and not from the project itself. Under these conditions, the parent corporation should continue to look for positive-NPV projects in the foreign currency. If the parent decides to speculate on future exchange rates, there is no reason to use a negative-NPV project as the speculative instrument. A zero-NPV financial transaction allows the corporation to speculate directly and avoid the negative-NPV foreign project.

Positive-NPV for the Project but Negative-NPV for the Parent. If $NPV^f > 0 > NPV^d$, the project looks attractive from the local perspective but not from the parent's perspective. In this case, the foreign investment project is worth more in the local currency than it is worth in the parent's domestic currency. The parent firm should try to realize the value of the project in the foreign currency and capture its positive NPV today. This value can then be transferred to the parent at today's spot rate.

> If $NPV^d < 0$ and $NPV^f > 0$, then the parent firm should try to capture the value of the project in the foreign currency.

Suppose the following rates hold for U.S. dollars and Chinese renminbi:

	United States	China
Nominal risk-free government T-bill rate	$i_F^\$ = 21\%$	$i_F^{Rmb} = 10\%$
Real required return on T-bills	$\iota_F^\$ = 10\%$	$\iota_F^{Rmb} = 0\%$
Expected inflation	$p^\$ = 10\%$	$p^{Rmb} = 10\%$
Current spot exchange rate	$S_0^{\$/Rmb} = \$0.20/Rmb$	
Expected future spot rate	$E[S_1^{\$/Rmb}] = \$0.20/Rmb$	

As before, suppose the current and expected future spot exchange rate is $E[S_t^{\$/Rmb}] = S_0^{\$/Rmb} = \$0.20/Rmb$. Renminbi should be selling at a 10 percent forward premium to the current spot rate based on interest rate parity.

$$(F_1^{\$/Rmb} / S_0^{\$/Rmb}) - 1 = (1+i_F^\$) / (1+i_F^{Rmb}) - 1 = (1.21/1.10) - 1 = +0.10$$

Again, the international markets are not in equilibrium. However, this disequilibrium is in the opposite direction from the previous example.

3M's expected cash flows are the same as in the previous example.

Underlying investment

Rmb 605

$NPV^{Rmb} = +Rmb25 \Rightarrow$ Accept (?)

−Rmb 525

$i_F^{Rmb} = 10\%$

At the 10 percent Chinese interest rate, this investment is worth $NPV^{Rmb} = (Rmb605)/(1.1) - Rmb\ 525 = +Rmb25$. From the U.S. parent's perspective, the project cash flows and net present value at the current and expected future spot rate of $0.20/Rmb are

$121

$NPV^\$ = -\$5 \Rightarrow$ Reject

−$105

$i_F^\$ = 21\%$

This project looks like a winner from the foreign perspective but a loser from the parent's perspective. Should 3M reject this project? Not if it can somehow lock in the value of the project in the foreign currency and then capture this value in its own domestic currency.

Suppose 3M can borrow the initial investment from Chinese investors at the 10 percent renminbi rate. Payoff on this loan will be (Rmb525)(1.10) = Rmb577.5. Cash flows from the local financing are

Local renminbi loan

+Rmb 525

–Rmb 577.5

The cash inflow of the renminbi loan exactly offsets the cash outflow from the investment, leaving a net cash inflow of Rmb25 at time 1.

Resulting position

+Rmb 27.5

$i_F^{Rmb} = 10\%$

$\Rightarrow$ NPV$^\$$ = Rmb25

This has a Rmb25 value when discounted at the 10 percent renminbi interest rate. In dollars, this is worth (Rmb25)($0.20/Rmb) = $5.

If there are no active forward exchange or credit markets in Chinese renminbi, then 3M should try to lock in the positive foreign currency value in some other way. Several alternatives are listed in Figure 15.6. Perhaps the project could be sold to a local investor for whom the project has a positive net present value. By selling the project at its value in the foreign currency (NPV^f > 0), the parent firm could capture this value in its functional currency today. Alternatively, 3M could form a joint venture partnership with a local investor. If the project is attractive in the local currency, a local partner may be willing to form a joint venture partnership on terms that are advantageous to 3M. Each of these alternatives is a way of locking in the positive-NPV value in the local currency while reducing the parent firm's exposure to foreign exchange risk during the life of the project.

In the real world, buying and selling foreign projects to take advantage of disequilibriums in the international parity conditions entails substantial sunk costs that may be difficult to recover.[5] Actively managing the firm's real assets (for example, by selling 3M's Chinese operations and then repurchasing them when exchange rates turn in the other direction) is much more costly than managing currency risk exposure through the financial markets. Moreover, active real asset management can put the multinational corporation's intellectual property rights at risk. For example, if 3M sells its Chinese manufacturing plant to a local investor or shares its knowledge with a local joint venture partner, the local investor may soon become a competitor in other Asian markets.

> If NPV^f > 0 and NPV^d < 0, hedging results in higher return and lower risk.

3M could also use a financial market hedge of currency risk, such as a forward hedge of the renminbi exposure or a local currency (i.e., renminbi) loan. Financial market alternatives have the advantage that they are, by themselves, zero-NPV transactions, and do not involve selling the underlying real asset. When combined with the underlying cash flows, financial market hedges have a double payoff; they both maximize the value of the project and reduce the variability of the outcomes from the project.

---

5 Some of these strategic considerations are addressed in Chapter 18 on real options.

FIGURE 15.6
Alternatives for Capturing the NPV of a Foreign Project

In the asset markets

- Sell the project to a local investor.
- Bring in a joint venture partner from the local market.

In the financial markets

- Hedge the cash flows from the project against currency risk.
- Finance the project with local currency debt or equity.

Positive-NPV for Both the Project and the Parent. Disequilibriums in the international parity conditions can result in valuation differences between the project's foreign currency perspective and the parent's domestic currency perspective. When both net present values are positive, a comparison of the two tells us what to do. When $NPV^d > NPV^f > 0$, the corporation should invest in the foreign project. Depending on the corporate tolerance for currency risk, the corporation may consider leaving its foreign investment unhedged to take advantage of the expected real appreciation of the foreign currency. This is a risky strategy, however, and the corporation and its financial officer must be prepared to accept the consequences of their foreign exchange market speculation.

When $NPV^f > NPV^d > 0$, the corporation should invest in the project. It should then hedge its exposure to currency risk or otherwise try to capture the value of the project in the foreign currency. The value of the project in the foreign currency can then be realized today and passed back to the parent in its domestic (functional) currency. In this case, hedging against currency risk has a double payoff. Hedging maximizes the expected return on the foreign project while minimizing the MNC's exposure to currency risk.

> When $NPV^f > NPV^d > 0$, the corporation should hedge its exposure to currency risk.

15.4 • SPECIAL CIRCUMSTANCES IN CROSS-BORDER INVESTMENTS

Even if the international parity conditions hold, many project-specific circumstances make application of Recipes #1 and #2 difficult. For example, if cash flows are blocked in a foreign country and cannot be freely remitted to the parent, then the equivalence of discounting in either currency may not hold. The act of remitting cash flows to the parent firm is called **repatriation**, and repatriation restrictions can alter the value of foreign projects from the parent's perspective. Other special circumstances include the provision of subsidized financing by a host government or an international agency, negative-NPV tie-in projects required by a host government, and country-specific political risks such as the risk of expropriation.

> Special circumstances in project valuation can often be valued separately as side effects.

Each of these special circumstances can be treated as a **side effect** of the project and valued separately from the project:

$$V_{\text{PROJECT WITH SIDE EFFECT}} = V_{\text{PROJECT WITHOUT SIDE EFFECT}} + V_{\text{SIDE EFFECT}} \qquad (15.5)$$

Identifying a separate value for the project can help decompose the value of a project into its component parts and, hence, identify key value drivers. This in turn can help in negotiating with the host government prior to investment. For example, knowing that a tax holiday is the major source of value in a foreign venture, a multinational corporation can structure the investment in order to minimize the parent's exposure to the risk of a change in the tax rules. This may mean taking profits in the early years of the project before the tax privilege can be revoked. Local debt and equity partners might also be employed, because they are likely to be more effective in lobbying the host government to keep the tax holiday in place. This section uses the Neverland example as a starting point and examines the effect of several special circumstances encountered in cross-border investment.

Blocked Funds

Blocked funds are an example of a repatriation restriction that can cause a discrepancy between the project value from the parent's and local perspectives. **Blocked funds** are cash flows generated by a foreign project that cannot be immediately repatriated to the parent firm because of capital flow restrictions. With blocked funds, the corporation should compare the after-tax returns of local investments to the local required returns. If expected after-tax returns on its local investment alternatives are lower than on comparable alternatives in the local capital markets, then the MNC's investments are negative-NPV compared to local alternatives. In this case, there is a cost to blocked funds. If after-tax returns are greater than local capital costs, then the MNC likely will not change its investment plans and blocked funds do not impose an additional burden.

> Blocked funds cannot be immediately repatriated to the parent firm.

Blocked funds are a classic form of a financial side effect. The loss in value from this side effect can be calculated in a fairly straightforward manner. Suppose that under Neverland law, 50 percent of foreign investor cash flows must be retained within Neverland until the investment is four years old. Blocked funds must be placed in Captain Hook's treasure chest and do not earn interest. Captain Hook has promised to return any blocked funds at the end of the project. Funds not blocked by the good captain can be remitted in the year they are earned. The cash flows of the project are then composed of blocked funds that must be invested in Hook's treasure chest and cash flow that can be repatriated to Wendy and reinvested in an asset of Wendy's choosing. The after-tax cash flows from this situation are shown in Table 15.4.

Suppose you are certain of retrieving funds from Hook's treasure chest. Hook's rules on blocked funds determine the investment's expected return. However, the required return should be the after-tax market rate of interest on a comparable (in this case, riskless) croc investment. Consequently, the appropriate after-tax discount rate on an "investment" in Hook's treasure chest is the $i_F{}^{Cr}(1-T) = (37.5\%)(1-0.5) = 18.75$ percent after-tax riskless rate of interest in crocs.

A Three-Step Procedure for Valuing Blocked Funds. The value of blocked funds can be calculated with a three-step procedure:

- *Step 1: Calculate the after-tax value of blocked funds assuming they are not blocked.*

  Funds are blocked in Neverland in the first three years of the project. They can be freely remitted to Wendy at the end of the project. If blocked funds had been invested at the riskless after-tax croc interest rate of $(37.5\%)(1-0.50) = 18.75$ percent per year, they would have grown to an after-tax value of $(Cr8,000)(1.1875)^3 + (Cr13,819.5)(1.1875)^2 + (Cr19,573.5)(1.1875)^1 \approx Cr56,128$. Discounted

TABLE 15.4
An Example of Blocked Funds in Hook's Treasure Chest

	t = 0	1	2	3	4
Project cash flows without blocked funds[a]					
Sale of ship					137,400.0
Tax on sale of ship					(68,700.0)
Sale of inventory					82,440.0
Tax on sale of inventory					(29,220.0)
CF from operations	(64,000.0)	16,000.0	27,639.0	39,147.0	26,477.0
CF without blocked funds	(64,000.0)	16,000.0	27,639.0	39,147.0	148,397.0
Incremental cash flows from blocked funds					
Blocked by Captain Hook		(8,000.0)	(13,819.5)	(19,573.5)	0.0
Release of blocked funds					41,393.0
Project cash flows with blocked funds					
	(64,000.0)	8,000.0	13,819.5	19,573.5	189,790.0

[a] All cash flows in Neverland crocs

back to time zero at the after-tax rate of 18.75 percent, this has a present value of Cr28,226.

- *Step 2: Calculate the opportunity cost of blocked funds.*

An investment in Hook's treasure chest is assumed to be riskless, so the required return on blocked funds is the market rate of interest on a riskless croc investment. The actual return is 0 percent, because payments into Hook's treasure chest earn no interest. With blocked funds, the accumulated balance as of time 4 is only (Cr8,000+Cr13,819.5+Cr19,573.5) = +Cr41,393. This has a present value of Cr20,816 at the after-tax discount rate of 18.75 percent.

In this example, investment in blocked funds is a negative-NPV investment. The opportunity cost of earning zero interest rather than the market rate is $(Cr28,226–Cr20,816) \approx Cr7,410$.

- *Step 3: Find the value of the project including the opportunity cost of blocked funds.*

  In the original example, the Neverland project is worth $–Cr137$ in the absence of blocked funds. The opportunity cost of the blocked funds is $–Cr7,410$. The value of the project with the blocked funds is then

$$V_{PROJECT\ WITH\ SIDE\ EFFECT} = V_{PROJECT\ WITHOUT\ SIDE\ EFFECT} + V_{SIDE\ EFFECT}$$
$$= -Cr137 - Cr7,410$$
$$= -Cr7,547$$

Blocked funds make this an even worse investment for Wendy.

The Value of Knowing the Value of Blocked Funds. Knowing the value of any side effects of a project, such as the blocked funds in this example, can be important when negotiating the environment with the host government prior to investment. Suppose the value of the project without the blocked funds is $Cr6,000$ rather than $–Cr137$. Adding in the loss in value from blocked funds, $V_{SIDE\ EFFECT}$, the value of the project is

$$V_{PROJECT\ WITH\ SIDE\ EFFECT} = V_{PROJECT\ WITHOUT\ SIDE\ EFFECT} + V_{SIDE\ EFFECT}$$
$$= +Cr6,000 - Cr7,410$$
$$= -Cr1,410$$

Rather than giving up on this negative-NPV project, Wendy should continue to negotiate with Captain Hook and try to structure the deal with the host government (in particular, the blocked funds requirement) so that both parties can benefit. This is still a positive-NPV project for Wendy so long as the loss in value from blocked funds is less than $Cr6,000$. Knowing the value of the project without the blocked funds establishes Wendy's **reservation price**—the price below which she is unwilling to go. Separating the side effect from the project will prove useful to Wendy in her negotiations with Captain Hook. In this example, Wendy may be able to exert some local political pressure on Captain Hook, because employment among Neverland's Lost Boys will increase if this project is approved. Remember, everything is negotiable.

Choice of the Discount Rate for Blocked Funds. In a capital budgeting analysis, after-tax cash flows are discounted at an after-tax discount rate to yield the net present value of the project. Why not discount the blocked funds at Neverland's 50 percent after-tax required return on restaurant projects rather than at the 18.75 percent after-tax riskless croc rate of interest? The answer lies in a fundamental principle of finance:

**The discount rate depends on where funds are going,
not from where they came.**

Project value without the blocked funds reflects the 50 percent required return on restaurant projects in Neverland. Once cash flows from the restaurant project are earned, however, the appropriate discount rate on the next use of the funds depends on where they are invested. Cash flows generated by the project are **free cash flows** in the sense that, in the absence of capital flow restrictions, these cash flows could be invested anywhere and not necessarily in the Neverland project. Because investments in Captain Hook's treasure chest are assumed to be riskless, the riskless croc rate should be used to value the blocked funds. If blocked funds had been invested in another restaurant project in Neverland rather than in Hook's treasure chest, then the appropriate discount rate would be the 50 percent required return on risky Neverland restaurant projects.

Subsidized Financing

The governments of developing countries are sometimes willing to provide loans at subsidized rates in order to stimulate foreign direct investment in key industries. International agencies charged with promoting cross-border trade also occasionally offer financing at below-market rates. As a domestic U.S. parallel, the municipal bond (or "muni") market was born in the United States when the U.S. government allowed tax-free status for municipal debt in order to stimulate local investment.

> Host countries sometimes provide subsidized financing.

Subsidized financing is the mirror image of blocked funds that earn below-market rates of return. In the case of subsidized financing, the multinational pays rather than receives the below-market rate. Suppose that as an investment incentive Captain Hook will provide Wendy with a Cr40,000 nonamortizing loan at a rate of 37.5 percent in Neverland crocs, even though corporate debt yields 40 percent in crocs. Interest payments on Cr40,000 at the 40 percent market rate would have been (Cr40,000)(0.40) = Cr16,000 per year. Hook only requires interest payments of (Cr40,000)(0.375) = Cr15,000 on the subsidized debt. This is a pre-tax savings of Cr1,000 per year, or (Cr1,000)(1–0.5) = Cr500 in after-tax annual interest savings. Discounted at the 40% (1–T) = 20% *after-tax market cost of debt*, this interest subsidy has a value of Cr1,294.

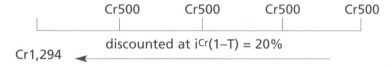

This value is a net gain to Wendy and a net loss to Hook and the taxpayers of Neverland.

An important question for Wendy is whether this interest subsidy is separable from the Neverland project; that is, can it be obtained from Hook regardless of whether the project is accepted? In this example, Hook is likely to require that Wendy invest in the project in order to obtain the subsidy. When the subsidized loan is inseparable from the project, the value of the loan should be added to that of the project in making the investment decision.

When subsidized financing is separable from a project, the additional value from the subsidized financing should not be allocated to the project. In this case, the manager's decision is simple: Take the subsidized loan so long as there are no other strings (such as repatriation restrictions) attached. If the firm can invest the proceeds of subsidized financing at a higher rate in a comparable-risk investment, then borrowing at the subsidized rate and investing at a higher market rate is a positive-NPV strategy.

Negative-NPV Tie-in Projects

Developing countries often require that foreign companies take on additional negative-NPV development or infrastructure projects in order to gain access to positive-NPV investments elsewhere in the economy. By tying approval of a project with a large positive NPV to an otherwise unattractive investment in the local economy, these governments hope to capture at least some of the gain on the lucrative project. In this case, the value of the **negative-NPV tie-in project** should be subtracted from the value of the underlying project when making the investment decision.

> The value of negative-NPV tie-in projects should be subtracted from project value.

Political Risk

Expropriation risk is the most extreme form of political risk.

Political risk is the possibility that political events in a host country or relationships with a host country will affect the value of corporate assets. The most extreme form of political risk is **expropriation** in which a host government seizes a company's assets. Expropriation risk is usually a country-specific risk that is diversifiable in a global portfolio. Hence, it affects expected future cash flows but not the discount rate.

Suppose Wendy estimates that there is an 80 percent chance Hook will seize the ship at the end of the project. Actual and expected cash flows are then as follows:

Incremental cash flows from expropriation

	Actual	Expected
Ship	Cr0	+Cr137,400
Tax on sale of ship	Cr0	−Cr68,700
Total	+Cr0	+Cr68,700

If the ship is expropriated, Wendy no longer has to pay the capital gains tax on its sale. Wendy's incremental after-tax cash flow from expropriation is then (actual minus expected) = −Cr68,700. With an 80 percent probability of expropriation, Wendy's expected after-tax loss is $(0.8)(-Cr68,700) = -Cr54,960$.

The present value of the expected after-tax loss can be found by discounting at the after-tax discount rate in crocs or in pounds.

Alternative #1: Discounting in crocs

$$PV(E[\text{loss from expropriation}]) = [E[CF_4{}^{Cr}]/(1+i^{Cr})^4]/S_0{}^{Cr/\pounds}$$
$$= [Cr54,960 / (1.50)^4]/(Cr4.00/\pounds)$$
$$= Cr10,856/(Cr4.00/\pounds)$$
$$= \pounds2,714$$

Alternative #2: Discounting in pounds

$$PV(E[\text{loss from expropriation}]) = [E[CF_4{}^{Cr}] / E[S_4{}^{Cr/\pounds}]]/(1+i^{\pounds})^4$$
$$= [Cr54,960/(Cr9.7656/\pounds)]/(1.20)^4$$
$$= \pounds5,628/(1.20)^4$$
$$= \pounds2,714$$

Expropriation risk reduces the value of the Neverland project by £2,714.

Tax Holidays

Host countries sometimes provide tax holidays as an inducement to investment.

Developing countries are often willing to offer tax holidays to promote investment. A **tax holiday** usually comes in the form of a reduced tax rate for a period of time on corporate income from a project. As with other subsidies, the project should be valued both with and without the reduced tax rate. Tax holidays are negotiable, and knowing how much the tax holiday is worth is valuable when the corporation negotiates the environment of the project with the host government.

For long-term projects that take awhile before they begin to return positive cash flow, a tax holiday in the project's early years is not worth much. Indeed, if taxable income is expected to be negative for several years and losses can be carried forward, a tax holiday can rob the firm of valuable tax-loss carryforwards. The firm might prefer to be subjected to a high tax rate during the early loss-making (and tax-credit-creating) years of a project. Calculating project value both with and without the tax holiday will help you to uncover situations such as this.

15.5 • SUMMARY

The presentation in this chapter simplified several aspects of cross-border investment and financial analysis. In particular, it developed a discounted cash flow approach to cross-border capital budgeting. In this framework, we know that

- If the international parity conditions hold, discounting foreign currency cash flows at the foreign discount rate is equivalent to discounting domestic currency cash flows at the domestic discount rate.

- If the international parity conditions do not hold, then value depends on your perspective. The multinational firm can sometimes take advantage of market disequilibriums to enhance the value of its foreign investments.

- The discounted cash flow framework can handle many special circumstances commonly found in cross-border investment analysis. These include blocked funds, subsidized financing, negative-NPV tie-in projects, expropriation risk, and tax holidays.

The presentation in this chapter has neglected several important aspects of cross-border investment and financial management. In particular,

- This chapter did not deal with the impact of capital structure on the cost of capital and project value.

- The impact of taxes on cross-border capital budgeting was only superficially covered.

- The discounted cash flow framework does not deal well with dynamic issues such as managerial flexibility in expanding or contracting a project.

- This chapter did not discuss the international market for corporate control. This market can be used (with varying difficulty, depending on the country) to acquire the stock or assets of companies in other countries and provides an alternative to foreign direct investment.

Each of these issues is addressed in the chapters that follow.

KEY TERMS

blocked funds	repatriation
discounted cash flow (DCF)	reservation price
expropriation risk	side effect
free cash flow	subsidized financing
negative-NPV tie-in projects	tax holiday
political risk	

CONCEPTUAL QUESTIONS

15.1 Describe the two recipes for discounting foreign currency cash flows. Under what conditions are these recipes equivalent?

15.2   Discuss each cell in Figure 15.5. What should (or shouldn't) a firm do when faced with a foreign project that fits the description in each cell?

15.3   Why is it important to separately identify the value of any side effects that accompany foreign investment projects?

PROBLEMS

Cross-border capital budgeting when the international parity conditions hold

15.1   An investment in China yields these expected after-tax renminbi cash flows (in millions).

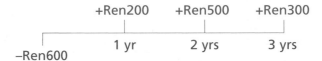

The required return for this risk-class is $i^\$ = 15$ percent in the United States and 11.745 percent in China. Expected inflation is 6 percent in the United States and 3 percent in China. Riskless government bonds in the United States yield 8.12 percent. Chinese government bonds are risky and yield 6.09 percent. The spot exchange rate is $S_0^{\$/Ren} = \$0.5526/Ren$.

a. Assume the international parity conditions hold. Calculate NPV$ by discounting in renminbi and then converting into dollars at the current spot rate.

b. Assume the international parity conditions hold. Calculate NPV$ by converting renminbi to dollars at expected future spot rates and discounting in dollars.

15.2   The following project-specific information is known about investment in a beer brewery in a western European country that uses the euro:

- The project will last two years. Operating cash flows are received at year-end.

- The euro inflation rate is 10 percent per year.

- All cash flows share the same nominal discount rate of 20 percent per year.

- An investment of €100,000 will purchase the land for the brewery. The land is to be sold after two years. The real value of the land is expected to remain constant at €100,000.

- Constructing the brewery will cost €50,000, payable at the start of the project. The brewery will be owned by the foreign subsidiary and depreciated on a straight-line basis over two years to a zero salvage value. The brewery is expected to be sold for its market value of €25,000 after two years.

- An investment in working capital of €50,000 is necessary. No additional investment in working capital is necessary, but the value of this investment is expected to grow at the rate of inflation.

- Annual sales are expected to be 5,000 barrels/year.

- Beer currently sells for €100 per barrel. The price of beer is expected to rise at the euro rate of inflation.

- Variable operating costs are 20 percent of sales.

- Fixed operating costs are currently €20,000 per year and are expected to rise at the rate of inflation.

- Local tax rates on income and capital gains are 40 percent.

a. Identify the expected future euro cash flows of this project and value them at the appropriate euro discount rate.

b. Suppose the current spot exchange rate is $S_0^{\$/€} = \$10/€$. The nominal discount rate on brewery projects in the United States is also 20 percent. Assuming the international parity conditions hold, calculate the dollar value of the brewery project using the capital budgeting recipe in Equation 15.1. Value the project again using Equation 15.4. Are these values the same?

15.3 You currently live in Land-of-Leisure (currency is the leisure-unit L), and you are considering investment in a diploma-printing shop in a foreign country called Land-of-Work (currency is the work-unit W). Financial markets are perfect and the international parity conditions hold in these two countries. The printshop investment will be financed with 100 percent equity. Interest and inflation rates are as follows:

	Leisure	Work
Nominal risk-free government T-bill rate	$i_F^L = 0\%$	$i_F^W = 50\%$
Real required return on T-bills	$\iota_F^L = 0\%$	$\iota_F^W = 0\%$
Expected future inflation	$p^L = 0\%$	$p^W = 50\%$
Real required return on printshop projects	$\iota^L = 10\%$	$\iota^W = 10\%$

The spot exchange rate is W100/L and the following information is known:

- The project will last two years.
- An investment of W200,000 will purchase the land for the printshop. The real value of the land will remain constant throughout the life of the project. The land will be sold at the end of the project.
- Constructing the shop and purchasing the printing press will cost W200,000, payable at the start of the project. The shop and printing press will be owned by the foreign subsidiary and depreciated on a straight-line basis over two years to a zero salvage value. The shop and printing press are expected to have zero market value at the end of two years.
- Just-in-time inventory control will be used. No investment in working capital is necessary.
- Diplomas sell for W200 each in Land-of-Work. The price of a diploma is expected to remain constant in real terms. Annual sales are expected to be 2,000 diplomas per year in each of the next two years.
- Variable operating costs are 20 percent of sales.
- Fixed operating costs will be W45,000 in the first year, and they are expected to grow at the rate of inflation thereafter.
- Income and capital gain taxes are 50 percent in each country.
- Assume all operating cash flows occur at the end of the year.

a. What is the nominal required return on printshop projects in L? In W?

b. Identify expected future exchange rates $E[S_t^{W/L}]$ for each of the next two years.

c. Identify expected future cash flows CF_t^W on this foreign investment project. Discount these cash flows at the work-unit discount rate from part a to find NPV^W.

d. Translate the work-unit cash flows to leisure-units at the expected future spot rates from part b. Discount these cash flows at the leisure-unit discount rate from part a to find NPV^L. Is the answer the same as in part c? Why?

15.4 Toshiyuki Itokazu is production manager for Asahi Chemicals, a Japanese chemical manufacturer operating throughout Southeast Asia. Toshi-san is considering a proposal to build a chemical plant in Thailand to service the growing Southeast Asian market. The attractiveness of the project depends on the following:

- The exchange rate is currently $S_0^{Bt/\yen} = Bt0.2500/\yen$.

- The manufacturing plant will cost Bt4 million and will take one year to construct. Assume the Bt4 million cost will be paid in full at the end of one year.

- The real value of the manufacturing plant is expected to remain at Bt4 million (in time t=1 baht) throughout the life of the project. The plant will be sold at project end.

- Production begins in one year (at time 1) with annual revenues of Bt100 million per year (in nominal terms) over the 4-year life of the project. Fixed expenses are contractually fixed in nominal terms at Bt5 million each year over the 4-year life of the project. Variable costs are 90 percent of gross revenues. Assume end-of-year cash flows.

- The plant will be owned by a subsidiary in Thailand and will be depreciated by one million baht in each year of the project.

- Taxes are 40 percent in Thailand.

- Annual inflation is expected to be 10 percent in Thailand and 5 percent in Japan.

- The required return on similar projects in Thailand is $i^{Bt} = 20$ percent.

- Assume that the international parity conditions hold.

a. Calculate the value of this investment proposal from the local (Thai baht) perspective.
b. What is the nominal required return on similar projects in Japan?
c. Identify the expected future spot exchange rates for each cash flow.
d. Calculate the yen value of the project using capital budgeting Recipes #1 and #2. Are the answers equivalent? Why?

Cross-border capital budgeting when international parity conditions do not hold

15.5 Consider the investment in China from problem 15.1.

a. Suppose that expected future spot rates are
$E[S_1^{\$/Ren}]=\$.5801/Ren$
$E[S_2^{\$/Ren}]=\$.6089/Ren$
$E[S_3^{\$/Ren}]=\$.6392/Ren$

Using a renminbi discount rate of 11.745 percent and the dollar discount rate of 15 percent, calculate NPV using Recipes #1 and #2 from the chapter. Should you invest in the project? How do you respond to this market disequilibrium?

b. Repeat part a using the following expected future spot rates:
$E[S_1^{\$/Ren}]=\$.5575/Ren$
$E[S_2^{\$/Ren}]=\$.5625/Ren$
$E[S_3^{\$/Ren}]=\$.5676/Ren$

Should you invest in the project? How do you respond to this market disequilibrium?

Cross-border capital budgeting when there are investment or financial side effects

15.6   Consider the investment in China from problem 15.1. Suppose each cash flow generated by the project must be loaned to the Chinese government for one year at a zero percent interest rate. At what rate should you discount these blocked funds? What is the present value cost of blocked funds?

15.7   Consider the investment in China from problem 15.1. The Chinese government is willing to provide you with a nonamortizing loan of Ren600 million at the Chinese government borrowing rate of 6.09 percent per annum payable over three years. If you were to finance the project locally in China, your borrowing rate would be 8.15 percent per annum. What is the renminbi value of this subsidized loan? Assume the effective tax rate in both the United States and China is 40 percent.

15.8   Consider the investment in China from problem 15.1. The Chinese government insists that you build an airport near this project at a cost of Ren100 million. Should you still accept the project?

15.9   Consider the investment in China from problem 15.1. Suppose that in any given year there is a 10 percent chance that the Chinese government will expropriate your assets. If your assets are expropriated in a particular year, then you will not receive that year's or any later year's cash flow from your investment. This risk is diversifiable and hence does not change the discount rate. What is the NPV of this asset in dollars, assuming the international parity conditions hold, and the required returns $i^\$ = 15$ percent and $i^{Rmb} = 11.745$ percent are after-tax discount rates?

15.10   Consider the example of blocked funds from the Neverland example in the chapter. As in the example, blocked funds (50 percent of operating cash flow) earn zero interest in Hook's treasure chest. Suppose an investment in Hook's treasure chest is not riskless and that the required return on Neverland bonds issued from Hook's treasury is 40 percent rather than 37.5 percent. What is the opportunity cost of the blocked funds, assuming the international parity conditions hold? What is the value of the project with the blocked funds?

Multinational Capital Structure and Cost of Capital

chapter 16

Overview

Far better an approximate answer to the right question, which is often vague, than an exact answer to a wrong question, which can always be made precise.

John W. Tukey

Capital structure refers to the proportions and forms of long-term debt and equity capital used to finance the assets of the firm. Management must choose the amount of debt, its currency of denomination, maturity, seniority, fixed or floating rates, convertibility or callability options, and other indenture provisions. Capital structure is an important determinant of the firm's overall **cost of capital**; that is, investors' required return on long-term debt and equity capital. Through judicious capital structure choices, the firm can minimize the cost of capital and maximize the value of operating cash flows.

> Capital structure refers to the proportions and forms of long-term capital.

The opportunities as well as the complexities of financial strategy are many times greater for the multinational corporation than for the domestic firm. In particular, the MNC has flexibility in choosing the markets and currencies in which it raises funds. By accessing unsatisfied demand in international capital markets, the MNC can lower its overall cost of capital and thereby increase its value. This chapter describes the multinational corporation's choice of capital structure and its impact on project valuation and the firm's overall cost of capital.

16.1 • CAPITAL STRUCTURE AND THE COST OF CAPITAL

Capital Structure Theory and Practice

Capital Structure in a Perfect World. In 1958, Franco Modigliani and Merton Miller (hereafter MM) identified conditions under which financial policy is irrelevant.[1] MM began with an assumption of **perfect markets**.

- *Frictionless markets*—no transactions costs, government intervention, taxes, costs of financial distress, or agency costs
- *Equal access to market prices*—everyone is a price taker in a barrier-free market
- *Rational investors*—return is good and risk is bad
- *Equal access to costless information*—everyone has instantaneous and costless access to all public information

To these, they added three more assumptions:

- *Homogeneous business risk classes*—there exist perfect substitutes for every asset
- *Homogeneous investor expectations*—so that everyone has the same expectations
- *All cash flows are perpetual*—so that value equals the periodic cash flow divided by the discount rate; $V = CF/i$

In MM's world, the law of one price holds as rational investors will not allow different prices for identical assets.

> If financial markets are perfect, then corporate financial policy is irrelevant.

With equal access to perfect financial markets, individual investors can replicate any financial action that the firm can take. The firm's financial policies and strategies are then irrelevant. This is MM's famous **irrelevance proposition**:

If financial markets are perfect, then corporate financial policy is irrelevant.

The value of an asset is then solely determined by the value of expected future investment cash flows and not by the way in which an investment is financed.

Capital Structure in the Real World. The assumption of perfect financial markets is a far cry from reality. Yet these assumptions provide us with a starting point in understanding the workings of the imperfect and vastly more complex real world. In particular, the converse of MM's irrelevance proposition is that one or more of the perfect market assumptions cannot hold if financial policy is to matter.

If financial policy is to increase firm value, then it must either increase the firm's expected future cash flows or decrease the discount rate in a way that cannot be replicated by individual investors.

MM added corporate taxes to their basic model to illustrate how this imperfection affects the firm's capital structure decision.[2] In particular, financial leverage can add value by reducing taxes through the interest tax shield. Because taxes are assessed at the corporate level, this reduction in corporate taxes cannot be replicated by individual investors.

---

1 Modigliani and Miller, "The Cost of Capital, Corporation Finance and the Theory of Investment," *American Economic Review* (1958).

2 Modigliani and Miller, "Corporate Income Taxes and the Cost of Capital: A Correction," *American Economic Review* (1963).

The MM assumptions can be further relaxed to allow costs of financial distress. **Costs of financial distress** include *direct costs*, such as court costs and attorney fees incurred during bankruptcy or liquidation, and *indirect costs* incurred prior to formal bankruptcy or liquidation. Indirect costs include lower sales and higher operating and financial expenses as managers spend their time and energy on the side effects of financial distress rather than operating the business. Indirect costs also include the agency costs that arise from conflicts of interest between managers and other stakeholders.

Costs of financial distress rise during financial distress as stakeholders contend for the firm's diminishing resources. These costs affect expected future cash flows to debt and equity investors as well as the required returns of these investors. As capital costs begin to rise at higher levels of debt, costs of financial distress eventually begin to dominate the interest tax shields from additional debt. The optimal capital structure includes an amount of debt that minimizes the overall cost of capital and maximizes the value of the firm, given the nature and scale of the firm's investments.

The Capital Structure of Foreign Affiliates. The capital structure of foreign affiliates should be subordinate to the corporation's overall financial goals. Financing should be done with the goal of minimizing the corporation's overall cost of capital, given its assets. To achieve this goal, the parent corporation can shift its financing sources toward those subsidiaries and currencies with relatively low real after-tax borrowing costs.

> Financial policy should minimize the overall cost of capital.

As a part of maximizing firm value, financial managers must pay attention to how they finance individual foreign operations. Although reducing the overall cost of capital is the manager's primary objective, the weight given to local factors is much greater on foreign than on domestic operations. To reduce the costs and risks of foreign operations, financing choices often must be tied to local norms. The risk of expropriation is one of these real-world factors. A MNC's exposure to expropriation risk is greatest when the MNC fails to tie its foreign projects into local communities.

One response is to finance foreign projects with local debt and equity. This reduces the *consequences* of expropriation because less of the corporation's own money is at risk. It also reduces the *probability* of expropriation because locally financed projects belong not just to the foreign subsidiary but to local investors as well.

Foreign currency debt has the additional advantage of providing a "natural hedge" against the currency risk exposures of foreign operations. Offsetting a foreign subsidiary's operating cash flow with local interest expenses reduces the MNC's exposure to currency risk. In a survey of U.S. chief financial officers, Graham and Harvey report more than 85 percent of CFOs believe foreign currency debt provides an important natural hedge against currency risk.[3]

Cost of Capital Theory and Practice

The Cost of Capital in an Integrated Capital Market. The perfect market assumptions applied to international capital markets are sufficient to ensure that markets are integrated. International capital markets are **integrated** when real required returns on assets of equivalent risk are the same everywhere. Because the law of one price holds, in an integrated market the multinational corporation cannot raise funds more cheaply in one location or currency than in another.

> In integrated markets, prices on comparable assets are equal.

---

3 Graham and Harvey, "The Theory and Practice of Corporate Finance: Evidence from the Field," *Journal of Financial Economics* (2001).

In terms of the international parity conditions, an integrated market ensures that *uncovered interest parity* holds on any particular asset:

$$(1+i^d)^t / (1+i^f)^t = E[S_t^{d/f}] / S_0^{d/f}$$

Interest rate differentials equal expected changes in exchange rates because of their joint relation to differences in expected inflation. In equilibrium, this relation ensures that expected and required real returns are equal across currencies.

The Cost of Capital in Segmented Capital Markets. At the other end of the continuum from capital market integration is complete capital market segmentation. A market is **segmented** from other markets if the required rate of return in that market is independent of the required return on assets of equivalent risk in other markets. Similar to complete integration, complete segmentation is not found in practice. Regardless of the ruthlessness with which a government attempts to segment a national financial market, there are invariably some cross-border price leakages. The law of one price is a powerful force, and people will find a way to profit from price disparities.

Factors contributing to capital market segmentation include informational barriers, transactions costs, differing legal or political systems, regulatory interference, differential taxes, and home asset bias (investors' tendency to buy local assets). The extent of national market segmentation depends on the importance of each of these imperfections to cross-border capital flows. Although fewer barriers exist in financial markets than in markets for real goods or services, capital flow barriers nevertheless influence the MNC's financing decisions.

Capital market segmentation can lead to financial opportunities for the MNC if investors in some foreign countries are willing to pay a higher price than domestic investors for securities that provide them with additional investment opportunities or diversification benefits. In these circumstances, MNCs with established reputations in foreign markets can gain access to debt or equity financing at real rates of return that are below those available elsewhere. If other companies cannot gain access to the higher prices paid by foreign investors, then the MNC with access to these markets can obtain a cost of capital advantage.

> Foreigners may pay a higher price than domestic investors for the firm's securities.

Figure 16.1 depicts a situation in which the MNC's cost of capital is below that available domestically. A MNC with a cost of capital advantage over its domestic competitors can squeeze additional value from its projects and even invest in positive-NPV projects that its competitors would reject.

16.2 • PROJECT VALUATION AND THE COST OF CAPITAL

An important input into the MNC's capital budgeting decision is the required return or hurdle rate on foreign investment. Required return on a foreign or domestic project depends on the project's *systematic business risk* and target capital structure. Systematic business risk refers to the systematic risk of the project's operating cash flows. The project's optimal or target capital structure is also important, as higher financial leverage leads to higher required returns on debt and equity capital.

When valuing any real or financial asset, follow one basic valuation rule in determining the required return on investment:

Use an asset-specific discount rate that reflects the opportunity cost of capital.

FIGURE 16.1
The Multinational Corporation's Cost of Capital

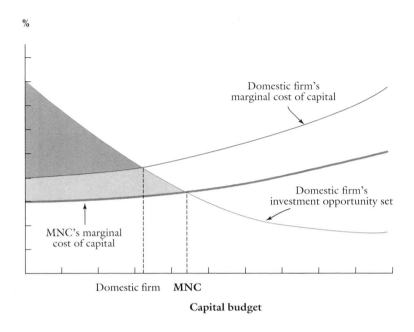

For consistency, the discount rate must match the characteristics of the cash flows:

• Domestic (foreign) currency cash flows should be discounted at a domestic (foreign) discount rate.
• Nominal (real) cash flows should be discounted at nominal (real) discount rate.

The two most popular discounted cash flow valuation methodologies for foreign or domestic projects are the weighted average cost of capital (WACC) and adjusted present value (APV). These two approaches deal with the debt capacity of a foreign project in different but complementary ways. The WACC approach discounts after-tax cash flows to debt and equity at a weighted average of the after-tax required returns of debt and equity. The APV approach separately values operating cash flows and financing side effects. In each method, the discount rate reflects the risk of the cash flows that are being discounted.

It is worthwhile evaluating investment proposals under both methods, as each brings a unique perspective. If the methods yield similar values, you will have confidence that your estimates are in the right ballpark. If the two methods yield vastly different values, you will have less confidence in your estimates. The two methods complement one another, as managers usually prefer to arrive at an approximately correct estimate of project value, rather than a single estimate that is likely to be exactly wrong.

The WACC Approach to Project Valuation

> WACC is the most popular methodology for project valuation.

The most popular valuation methodology is the **weighted average cost of capital (WACC)** approach. According to this approach, expected after-tax cash flows $E[CF_t]$ to debt and equity are discounted at a rate i_{WACC} that reflects the after-tax required returns on debt and equity capital:[4]

$$NPV = \sum_{t=0}^{T} \frac{E[CF_t]}{(1 + i_{WACC})^t} \tag{16.1}$$

The WACC is calculated according to:

$$i_{WACC} = [(B/V_L)i_B(1-T)] + [(S/V_L)i_S] \tag{16.2}$$

where B = the market value of corporate bonds
       S = the market value of common stock
       V_L = B + S = the market value of the firm's long-
             term debt and equity capital
       i_B = the required return on corporate bonds
       i_S = the required return on common stock
       T = the marginal corporate income tax rate

The firm's optimal or target debt capacity is the point at which the weighted average cost of capital is minimized, as shown in Figure 16.2. This target mix of debt and equi-

> Optimal debt capacity is the point at which the cost of capital is minimized.

ty can be measured by the debt-to-value ratio as in Equation 16.2. In a survey of U.S. CFOs, Graham and Harvey report 80 percent of firms have a target capital structure.[5] Whereas most large firms have a fairly narrow target capital structure, only one-third of small firms have a narrow target.

The discount rate i_{WACC} in Equation 16.2 should reflect the target capital structure and not the mix of debt and equity that is actually raised to finance a particular project. The target debt capacity of a foreign project is the amount of debt that the firm would choose to borrow if the project were financed as a stand-alone entity. Corporations do not issue debt or equity on a project-by-project basis, so the proportion of debt that is actually used to finance a project can differ from the debt capacity of the project.

For example, if a MNC borrows £50 million to finance a project in the United Kingdom, the debt capacity of this project is not necessarily £50 million. The corporate treasurer might have used this opportunity to tap the pound sterling debt market for capital to support other assets of the firm. Firms often accumulate several projects under one or more large securities issues to take advantage of the substantial economies of scale in the transactions costs that accompany debt and equity flotations.

> The cost of debt can be estimated by the yield to maturity of similar bonds.

The Cost of Debt. The **yield to maturity** is the discount rate that equates the present value of promised future interest payments to the market value of debt. For a bond issue with maturity T and promised cash flows CF_t, yield to maturity is the rate i_B that satisfies the equality:

$$B = \sum_{t=1}^{T} \frac{CF_t}{(1 + i_B)^t} \tag{16.3}$$

This is just the internal rate of return promised by the bond issue. If the systematic business risk and debt capacity of a foreign project are similar to other assets of the firm, the

---

4 A related method that discounts cash flows to debt and equity (including the interest tax shields) appears in Ruback, "Capital Cash Flows: A Simple Approach to Valuing Risky Cash Flows," *Financial Management* (2002).

5 Graham and Harvey, "The Theory and Practice of Corporate Finance."

F I G U R E   1 6 . 2
The Multinational Corporation's Cost of Capital

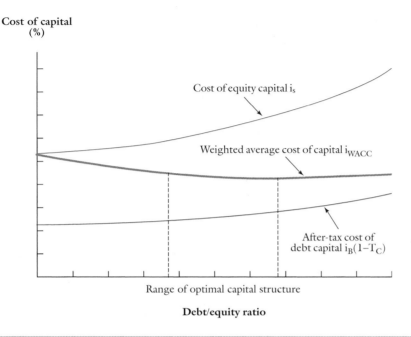

---

yield to maturity on existing debt in a particular currency can be used as the cost of debt on the project. If the corporation's debt is not publicly traded, yield to maturity can be estimated from the yield on publicly traded debt with characteristics (i.e., currency of denomination, debt rating, maturity, seniority, callability, and convertibility) like that of the optimal or target debt structure.

There is one hazard in using yield to maturity as the required return. The calculation is based on promised rather than expected cash flows. In the presence of default risk, expected cash flows are less than promised cash flows, and yield to maturity overstates investors' required return. This, in turn, overstates the firm's cost of debt. The difference between promised and expected cash flows on high-quality debt is small. On low-quality debt, the promised yield to maturity can significantly overstate required return.

International bond issuers sometimes pay Standard & Poor's or Moody's a fee for rating their bonds. These issuers have the option of not publishing bond ratings. MNCs that do publish their bond ratings tend to have high-quality debt. Low-quality issuers often do not have their bonds rated or do not publish their ratings. For these issues, investors must estimate the risks and expected returns themselves.

The Cost of Equity. Graham and Harvey find that large firms overwhelmingly rely on discounted cash flow techniques using cost of capital estimates from the **capital asset pricing model**.[6] The most common way to estimate the required return on the equity of a publicly traded

> Market model betas are used to measure systematic risk.

---

6 Graham and Harvey, "The Theory and Practice of Corporate Finance." Smaller firms and older executives are more likely to use the payback criterion (the expected time until recovery of the initial investment).

firm is to regress the company's stock returns r_i on a stock market index r_M in the **market model regression**:

$$r_i = \alpha_i + \beta_i \, r_M + e_i \tag{16.4}$$

where α_i and β_i are regression coefficients, and e_i represents random error around the regression line. An asset's systematic risk or beta (β_i) is measured by

$$\beta_i = \rho_{i,M} \, (\sigma_i \, / \, \sigma_M) \tag{16.5}$$

where σ_i and σ_M represent the standard deviations of returns on the stock and the market, and ρ_{iM} is the correlation of the stock with the relevant market index.

The regression estimate of equity **beta** β_i is then plugged into the **security market line** to arrive at an estimate of the cost of equity capital i_S or equity required return r_i:

$$r_i = r_F + \beta_i \, (E[r_M] - r_F) \tag{16.6}$$

Pure-plays should match the project's systematic business and financial risks.

where r_F is the riskless rate of interest and $(E[r_M] - r_F)$ is the market risk premium over r_F. Beta represents the sensitivity of equity value to changes in the market portfolio. If a project-specific beta is needed to value a project that differs from other assets of the firm, an estimate can be obtained from the beta of a publicly traded **pure-play** firm; that is, one with the same systematic business risk and debt capacity as the project.

The Market Portfolio. Equation 16.6 cannot provide a hurdle rate for evaluating an investment without first identifying the relevant market portfolio. In an integrated financial market, the appropriate market portfolio is a globally diversified portfolio of securities weighted according to their market values.

In integrated markets, beta is measured against the global market.

The relevant risk in determining the appropriate discount rate on a foreign or domestic project is the beta of the project relative to the world market index. The only role of national market indices in the pricing of systematic risk is through their contribution to the return on a globally diversified portfolio. In contrast, in a completely segmented national market, an asset's risk and required return should depend on its beta relative to the local market.

What does this mean for the choice of the market portfolio in estimating the cost of equity capital? Empirical evidence shows that both global and national factors are important. The world's capital markets are not yet fully integrated, and investors in many countries exhibit strong home asset biases. A

In segmented markets, beta is measured against the local market.

national market index is usually chosen to represent the market portfolio in Equations 16.4 through 16.6 because most investors are domestic. Corporations and institutional investors in the United States tend to use a U.S. market index such as the S&P 500 or the NYSE Composite. Similarly, a Japanese market index such as the Nikkei 225 is commonly used in Japan. With economic and monetary integration and the introduction of the euro, Europeans are switching from national to all-European indices such as Morgan Stanley Capital International's Europe or EMU indices.

Globally diversified corporations that are cross-listed on several stock exchanges sometimes employ a global stock market index in cost of capital estimation. As financial markets become more integrated, cost of capital estimates will increasingly be benchmarked to the world market portfolio or to a mix of global and local factors.

The Market Risk Premium. What equity return would you expect for the stock market of a country that, over the course of 180 years, arose from a backwater nation of

Application

Project Valuation Using the WACC at Phillips NV

The debt of Phillips NV (Netherlands) has a market value of €5 billion and a before-tax cost of $i_B^\varepsilon = 5$ percent. There are 250 million shares outstanding with a share price of €60 on the Amsterdam Stock Exchange and a beta of 1.10. The euro risk-free rate is 4 percent and the market risk premium is estimated to be 5 percent. The tax rate in the Netherlands is 40 percent. A project generates annual cash flows of €100 million in perpetuity, has the same systematic risk and debt capacity as Phillips' average asset, and costs €800 million.

Calculate the equity required return, the WACC, and the NPV of the project:

$$r_i^{\text{€}} = r_F^{\text{€}} + \beta_i\,(E[r_M^{\text{€}}] - r_F^{\text{€}}) = 4\% + 1.10(5\%) = 9.5 \text{ percent}$$

The market value of equity is (€60 per share)(250 million shares) = €15 billion, for a debt-to-value ratio of (€5 billion) / (€5 billion + €15 billion) = 25 percent. Then,

$$
\begin{aligned}
i_{\text{WACC}}^{\text{€}} &= (B/V_L)\, i_B^{\text{€}}\,(1{-}T) + (S/V_L)\, i_S^{\text{€}} \\
&= (\text{€5 billion}/\text{€20 billion})(5\%(1{-}0.4)) + (\text{€15 billion}/\text{€20 billion})(9.5\%) \\
&= 7.875 \text{ percent}
\end{aligned}
$$

$$
\begin{aligned}
\text{NPV} &= V_{\text{PROJECT}} - \text{Initial investment} \\
&= (\text{€100 million}) / (0.07875) - \text{€800 million} \\
&\approx \text{€1,270 million} - \text{€800 million} = \text{€470 million}
\end{aligned}
$$

Note that the after-tax cost of debt is only $(0.06)(1{-}0.4) = 0.36$ or 3.6 percent because every euro of interest expense reduces corporate taxes by 0.4 euros. In the Netherlands, as in most countries, the after-tax cost of equity is the same as the before-tax cost because the corporation's dividend payments, unlike interest payments, are not tax deductible.

---

little international consequence to a position as the foremost economic and military power in the world? Clearly, the question is directed toward the equity risk premium in the United States. Siegel reconstructed U.S. debt and equity returns over the last 180 years and found that the mean U.S. equity premium over T-bills has been 6 percent, as well as about 6 percent during each 60-year subperiod.[7]

Equity investments in most other countries have performed much worse. Jorion and Goetzmann measured real returns to a number of national stock markets.[8] As shown in Table 16.1 and Figure 16.3, U.S. equities had a real return of 5.48 percent from 1921 to 1996. Only Sweden had a higher return (5.60 percent) among the seven countries that had data for the entire period. Capital markets in several countries lost nearly 100 percent of their value at some point, notably in Germany (twice) and Japan. Including these periods, the median annual real equity return across all countries was only 0.75 percent.

> The long-run history of equity returns in non-U.S. markets has been poor.

7 Siegel, "The Equity Premium: Stock and Bond Returns Since 1802," *Financial Analysts Journal* (1992).

8 Jorion and Goetzmann, "Global Stock Markets in the Twentieth Century," *Journal of Finance* (1999).

TABLE 16.1
Return and Risk in Global Equity Markets

		Nominal returns			Real returns		
		Mean	Stdev	Inflation	Mean	Stdev	SI
Australia	1/31–12/96	7.78′	13.49	5.08	2.57	13.94	0.184
Austria	1/25–12/96	6.77′	18.92	4.35	2.32	19.49	0.119
Belgium	1/21–12/96	6.25′	17.92	4.69	1.49	18.97	0.079
Brazil	2/61–12/96	110.69′	68.22	86.58	12.92	51.93	0.249
Canada	1/21–12/96	7.06′	16.81	2.41	4.54′	16.65	0.273
Denmark	1/26–12/96	6.43′	12.04	3.68	2.65	12.69	0.209
Finland	1/31–12/96	10.74′	16.56	7.00	3.50	17.07	0.205
France	1/21–12/96	11.19′	21.57	7.78	3.16	21.25	0.149
Germany	1/21–7/44	10.22	40.24	2.42	7.62	34.26	0.222
	1/50–12/96	9.35′	15.50	2.14	7.06′	15.60	0.453
India	12/39–12/96	6.18′	15.53	7.33	−1.07	16.13	−0.066
Ireland	1/34–12/96	7.88′	14.85	5.16	2.59	15.02	0.172
Italy	12/28–12/96	12.62′	26.01	9.18	3.15	25.66	0.123
Japan	1/21–5/44	2.72	17.51	1.81	0.89	15.79	0.056
	4/49–12/96	9.79′	18.78	2.41	7.21′	18.90	0.381
Mexico	12/34–12/96	21.97′	26.79	15.75	5.37	24.45	0.220
Netherlands	1/21–12/96	4.78′	15.12	1.95	2.78′	14.80	0.188
New Zealand	1/31–12/96	6.20′	12.12	5.62	0.55	12.50	0.044
Norway	1/28–12/96	8.49′	17.90	3.85	4.47′	17.90	0.250
Pakistan	7/60–12/96	7.46′	14.37	8.15	−0.64	15.23	−0.042
Philippines	7/54–12/96	10.62	37.35	9.30	1.21	37.21	0.033
Portugal	12/30–4/74	6.50′	15.16	4.06	2.34	14.69	0.159
	3/77–12/96	27.08′	46.38	10.80	14.69	47.68	0.308
Spain	1/21–12/96	6.77′	18.92	7.32	−0.51	16.00	−0.032
Sweden	1/21–12/96	8.56′	16.61	2.80	5.60′	16.65	0.336
Switzerland	1/26–12/96	5.83′	14.79	1.49	4.28′	14.73	0.291
United Kingdom	1/21–12/96	7.25′	15.43	3.52	3.60′	15.68	0.230
United States	1/21–12/96	8.09′	16.20	2.47	5.48′	15.84	0.346

Nominal and real returns are arithmetic means and standard deviations (stdev) per annum. Inflation is calculated from the mean nominal and real returns as (1+p) = (1+i) / (1+ι). SI, the Sharpe Index, is the mean real return divided by its standard deviation; SI = (μ /σ). An asterisk indicates a difference from zero at a 5 percent significance level.

Source: Compiled from Jorion and Goetzmann, "Global Stock Markets in the Twentieth Century," *Journal of Finance* (June 1999). Countries without inflation data are not reported here.

http://www.
ssrn.com

Choice of the market risk premium is an important input into cost of capital estimates. Therefore, academicians have spent much effort identifying the past and expected future equity premium. In a 1998 survey of academic financial economists, the long-term arithmetic market risk premium was estimated to be 7 percent per year, with a range of 2 to 13 percent.[9] A follow-up survey in 2001 (after the dot.com bust of 2000) produced an estimate of 5 to 5.5 percent.[10] Indeed, some financial economists have estimated the premium to be close to zero.[11]

9 Welch, "Views of Financial Economists on the Equity Premium and on Professional Controversies," *Journal of Business* (2000).

10 Welch, "The Equity Premium Consensus Forecast Revisited," Cowles Foundation Discussion Paper No. 1325 (September 2001); available at http://www.ssrn.com.

11 Arnott and Bernstein, "What Risk Premium Is 'Normal'?" *Financial Analysts Journal* (2002).

FIGURE 16.3
Global Equity Market Returns and Risks

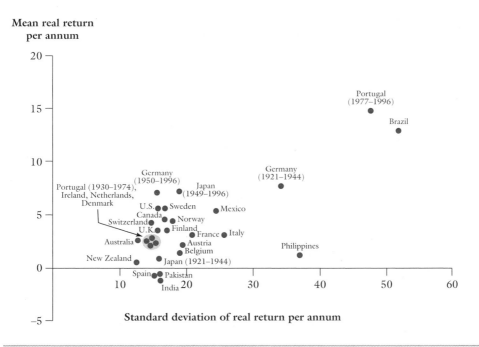

Source: Jorion and Goetzmann, "Global Stock Markets in the Twentieth Century," *Journal of Finance* (June 1999).

The wide variation in national stock market returns and in financial economists' forecasts of the market risk premium should caution us against excessive optimism regarding the market risk premium and the likely returns to equity investments.

The Adjusted Present Value (APV) Approach to Project Valuation

Adjusted Present Value. It is useful to have an idea of how much of the value of a project is from the investment itself and how much is from the way that it is financed. The **adjusted present value (APV)** approach to project valuation separates the net present value of a project into the value of an unlevered project V_U, plus the present value of any financing side effects, minus the initial investment:

> The value of an investment depends on how it is financed.

$$APV = V_U + PV(\text{financing side effects}) - \text{Initial investment} \qquad (16.7)$$

Unlevered project value V_U is simply the present value of after-tax operating cash flows from an unlevered project discounted at the unlevered cost of equity. The most important financial side effects are the interest tax shields and costs of financial distress that accompany debt. The APV approach can be used for valuation of individual projects or the firm itself.

The Unlevered Cost of Equity and Unlevered Project Value. The APV approach begins with an estimate of the value of a project as an all-equity investment. This, in turn, requires an estimate of the unlevered cost of equity.

Business risk is the risk of the firm's operating cash flows, measured by the standard deviation of earnings before interest and taxes (σ_{EBIT}). **Systematic business risk**

is the systematic or nondiversifiable portion of business risk; that is, the portion of σ_{EBIT} that is related to movements in the market portfolio. Systematic business risk is also referred to as the firm's **unlevered beta**, β_U, and represents the beta of an unlevered or all-equity project such that $\beta_U = \beta_{EBIT} = \rho_{EBIT,M} (\sigma_{EBIT} / \sigma_M)$

If a publicly traded pure-play firm can be found with similar systematic business risk and no debt in its capital structure, then the beta of this unlevered pure-play can be used as a proxy for the unlevered beta of the project. Using the unlevered pure-play beta in the security market line of Equation 16.6 yields an estimate of the unlevered cost of equity. As with levered beta, estimation of unlevered beta in Equation 16.6 requires identifying the relevant market portfolio.

The Value of Financing Side Effects. In a perfect capital market with no taxes or costs of financial distress, there are no financing side effects and the value of the levered firm is equal to the value of the unlevered firm. Financial market imperfections introduce a number of financing side effects. In particular, higher levels of debt generate greater interest tax shields but also greater costs of financial distress.

The financial manager's objective is to determine the debt level at which the increase in value from interest tax shields is offset by the decrease in value from costs of financial distress. This optimal capital structure can be difficult to determine because expected future costs of financial distress are not directly observable.[12]

> Knowing the components of project value is useful when negotiating contracts.

Project Valuation and Other Side Effects. Chapter 15 identifies several side effects associated with foreign investments including blocked funds, subsidized financing, negative-NPV tie-in projects, expropriation risk, and tax holidays. Some of these side effects are investment-based

Application

Project Valuation Using APV at Phillips NV

A project at Phillips NV (Netherland) generates annual cash flows of €100 million in perpetuity, has the same systematic business risk and unlevered beta as Phillips' average asset, and costs €400 million. The required return on unlevered Phillips equity based on Equation 16.6 and Phillips' unlevered β_U is $r_U = 0.20$, or 20 percent. The value of financing side effects (the present value of expected future tax shields minus the costs of financial distress) is €154 million.

Calculate the value of the unlevered project and the APV of the project:

$$V_U = (€100 \text{ million}) / 0.20 = €500 \text{ million}$$

$$
\begin{aligned}
APV &= V_U + PV(\text{financing side effects}) - \text{Initial investment} \\
&= €500 \text{ million} + €154 \text{ million} - €400 \text{ million} \\
&= €254 \text{ million}
\end{aligned}
$$

Of this value, €100 million comes from the NPV of the unlevered project and €154 million comes from the project's financial side effects.

---

12 Inselbag and Kaufold apply the APV approach to the present value of interest tax shields in "Two DCF Approaches for Valuing Companies Under Alternative Financing Strategies," *Journal of Applied Corporate Finance* (1997).

and some are financial in nature. The approach to project valuation in Chapter 15 separated the value of the side effect from the project:

$$V_{PROJECT\ WITH\ SIDE\ EFFECT} = V_{PROJECT\ WITHOUT\ SIDE\ EFFECT} + V_{SIDE\ EFFECT} \qquad (15.5)$$

Both APV and Equation 15.5 decompose project value. Whereas APV aggregates all financial side effects into a single term and adds this value to the value of the unlevered project, Equation 15.5 isolates a single side effect from the rest of project. Although this side effect could be all financial side effects as in Equation 16.7, it also could be a single financial side effect, or even an investment side effect such as the threat of expropriation.

16.3 • THE COST OF CAPITAL ON MULTINATIONAL OPERATIONS

An important issue in multinational capital budgeting is whether the additional risks of cross-border operations result in a higher or lower systematic risk on a foreign project. This section discusses factors that influence the cost of capital on foreign projects relative to comparable domestic projects.

Total Versus Systematic Risk

The total operating risks of foreign investment are greater than on similar domestic investments because of the additional cultural, political, and financial risks. These risks increase the variability of outcomes on foreign investment, often to the detriment of the multinational corporation.

Whether higher total risk translates into higher systematic risk, $\beta_i = \rho_{iM}(\sigma_i/\sigma_M)$, depends on the total risk of foreign investment (σ_i) and the correlation of foreign returns with investors' relevant market portfolio (ρ_{iM}). The economies of foreign countries are seldom synchronous with the world stock market or with the MNC's home market. Consequently, an increase in total risk on foreign investment may or may not be offset by a decrease in the correlation of investment returns with market returns.

> Diversifiable risks do not affect the cost of capital.

The diversifiability of country-specific risks, in turn, depends on the extent of capital market segmentation and on whether the firm's investors are locally or globally diversified. To investors diversified only within a local economy, country-specific risks are systematic and cannot be diversified away. This would be the case in markets that are partially segmented from other capital markets. In contrast, globally diversified investors can eliminate many country-specific risks. This would be the case in integrated capital markets.

Consider a local political event that is country-specific and unrelated to events outside the local economy. Local political risks increase the total variability of returns on foreign investment. However, from the perspective of a globally diversified investor, the increase in political risk is exactly offset by a decrease in the correlation with the global market portfolio. From the perspective of investors that confine themselves to the local market, local political risks are not diversifiable and will affect local required returns.

Similarly, currency risks that are specific to a particular country are diversifiable to a global investor, but may not be diversifiable to an investor that holds only local assets. The diversifiability of currency risks within a local portfolio depends on the diversity of a country's industries. In economies that have only a few industries, the value of the local stock market can be strongly related to the local currency value. In

Market Update

The Required Return on Investments in India

Capital flow restrictions have segmented India's stock market from other national and world markets. Except for joint ventures with local partners, foreign direct investment was prohibited until as recently as 1992, when about 25 percent of the stock in individual Indian companies was opened to registered foreign institutional investors.

Union Carbide India Limited (UCIL) is a joint venture between the government of India and the U.S.-based multinational corporation Union Carbide (UC). From the perspective of UCIL, project risk on investments in India should be measured against the Indian stock market. Since the returns on UCIL's investments (e.g., the infamous Bhopal chemical plant) are highly correlated with business activity in India, the covariance of returns and hence the systematic risk or beta of UCIL's investments are close to the risk of the Indian market as a whole.

In contrast, the relevant risk to Union Carbide's investors depends on the covariance of investments in India with alternatives in the equity markets outside India, particularly in the United States. Since business activity in India is only loosely related to business activity elsewhere, the covariance between investments in India and other national or world markets is less than the covariance between investments in India and the stock market in India. This means that the cost of capital of a MNC investing in India is often less than that of its Indian subsidiary. In this case, the MNC is providing indirect diversification benefits to its global investors that might not be available elsewhere in international capital markets.

more diversified economies with importers as well as exporters, the value of the local stock market may be unrelated to local currency value. This can be true in aggregate even though the fortunes of individual importers or exporters are highly sensitive to the value of the local currency.

Returns and Risks in Emerging Markets

Investments in developing or emerging markets can offer higher expected returns than developed markets, but these returns typically come with higher operating risks. Supplier relations, employee relations, distribution channels, business conventions, and private ownership and bankruptcy laws are more standardized in developed markets than in emerging markets. Stable business laws and practices promote predictability in the conduct of business. High political uncertainty and the lack of business and legal conventions in emerging economies lead to some unpredictable returns on investment. If emerging market investments are more risky than developed markets, then one might expect higher returns from these investments. On the other hand, if all of the additional risk is diversifiable, then the required return should be the same as in developed markets.

MNCs are faced with a wide variety of foreign projects. Each foreign project brings its own unique set of risks and potential returns. The preferred alternative for estimating a project's hurdle rate is to identify the systematic risk and required return of a publicly traded pure-play firm with similar investment and financial characteristics. Often, this is the parent firm itself. When the systematic risk of the project differs from that of the parent, another pure-play must be identified. In these cases, the required return and cost of capital of any single project must be determined on a case-by-case basis, perhaps by comparison to a project or firm in the domestic or foreign market. This section offers some guidance in setting required returns in emerging markets.

Empirical Evidence on Country Risks and Equity Returns. Erb, Harvey, and Viskanta found that country risk measures—particularly financial risk measures—are correlated with future equity returns and risks.[13] In particular,

- A decrease (increase) in country risk tends to be followed by a rise (fall) in equity returns in that country.
- Countries with high country risk tend to have more volatile returns than countries with low country risk.
- Countries with high country risk tend to have lower betas (systematic risks) than countries with low country risk.

The first two findings are intuitive. The last finding is somewhat less obvious. Consider the definition of beta, $\beta_i = \rho_{i,M} (\sigma_i / \sigma_M)$, where beta is measured against a globally diversified stock market portfolio. The low correlations of emerging markets with the world market portfolio tend to overcome the high volatilities of emerging markets, resulting in lower systematic risks or betas in emerging markets than on comparable assets in developed markets.

Liberalizations of Emerging Capital Markets. A capital market **liberalization** is a decision by a government to allow foreigners to purchase local assets. Capital market liberalizations can have a significant influence on the cost of capital and on capital investment in emerging markets.

Bekaert and Harvey found that emerging markets vary both cross-sectionally and over time in their extent of integration with the world stock market.[14] Generally, emerging markets tend to become more integrated with other markets with the erosion of barriers to the free flow of capital. As emerging markets are liberalized, local stock market returns tend to become more closely correlated with the global market as international investors enter the previously restricted emerging market. Bekaert and Harvey find that this integration is accomplished without an increase in local market volatility.

> Emerging markets become more integrated as they are liberalized.

In a related article, Bekaert and Harvey determine the affect of liberalizations on emerging markets' capital costs, correlations with the world equity market, and volatilities.[15] Their principal findings are that financial market liberalizations:

- Increase the correlation of emerging stock markets with world markets
- Have little impact on the volatility of emerging stock market returns
- Decrease local firms' cost of capital by up to 1 percent

Although the correlation of an emerging stock market with the world market increases after liberalization, investors' access to the emerging market is limited without the liberalization. Hence, these authors conclude that emerging markets provide valuable diversification benefits to global investors.

---

13 Erb, Harvey, and Viskanta, "Political Risk, Financial Risk and Economic Risk," *Financial Analysts Journal* (1996).

14 Bekaert and Harvey, "Emerging Equity Market Volatility," *Journal of Financial Economics* (January 1997), and "Time-Varying World Market Integration," *Journal of Finance* (1995).

15 Bekaert and Harvey, "Foreign Speculators and Emerging Equity Markets," *Journal of Finance* (2000).

Figure 16.1 suggests that a decrease in capital costs from liberalization should increase private investment, as some previously negative-NPV projects become positive-NPV at the lower cost of capital. Indeed, Henry finds that 9 of 11 emerging market countries that liberalized their stock markets in the late 1980s and early 1990s saw increased investment growth rates after liberalization.[16] The mean investment growth rate in the three years after a liberalization was 22 percent higher than in the year prior to liberalization. This relation persisted after controlling for business cycles, economic reforms, and fundamental variables in the domestic economy. Apparently, stock market liberalizations are good for business.

Estimating the Cost of Capital in an Emerging Market

http://www.
ibbotson.com

National capital markets vary in the extent of their activity, efficiency, capital constraints, and integration with other markets. Moreover, national markets evolve over time. No single theory has been able to successfully model returns in all countries. Firms frequently adjust discount rates for interest rate, currency, or inflation risk.[17] Rather than a single consensus model for cost of capital estimation in emerging markets, there are a number of competing models from which to choose.

Here's an example from Ibbotson Associates' *International Cost of Capital Center*. Ibbotson is a widely used source of financial return data, and offers consulting and investment planning services in asset allocation and forecasting. Ibbotson provides five alternative models for estimating the systematic risk of a single country or a typical asset within a country. (See problem 16.8 for an application.)

- *International CAPM.* The international version of the capital asset pricing model measures systematic risk relative to the world stock market portfolio. It is appropriate in a world in which all capital markets are fully integrated. Some international asset pricing models include currency risk as an additional factor.[18]

- *Globally nested CAPM.* Required returns are a function of a country's systematic risk relative to the world stock market portfolio plus the country's systematic risk relative to regional risk that is not included in the world market portfolio return.[19]

- *Country risk rating model.* Required returns are based on the world stock market portfolio and country credit risk ratings. This model has shown some success in predicting returns in emerging markets.[20]

- *Country spread model.* Required returns are a function of the domestic stock market portfolio plus a country-specific risk adjustment.

- *Relative standard deviation model.* Required returns are a function of a country's standard deviation of return relative to the standard deviation of U.S. returns.

There is no consensus in international cost of capital estimation.

In the absence of a consensus *best practice* in international cost of capital estimation, practitioners select a model that fits the circumstance. For example, a domestic or an international CAPM might be chosen for a developed market. One of the competing models might be chosen for a less developed or emerging market. The point here is that there is no accepted standard for estimating the cost of capital of an emerging market or an investment in an emerging market.

---

16 Henry, "Do Stock Market Liberalizations Cause Investment Booms?" *Journal of Financial Economics* (2000).

17 Graham and Harvey, "The Theory and Practice of Corporate Finance."

18 Adler and Dumas, "International Portfolio Choice and Corporation Finance: A Synthesis," *Journal of Finance* (1983).

19 Clare and Kaplan, "A Macroeconomic Model of the Equity Risk Premium," *Corporate Finance Review* (1999).

20 Erb, Harvey, and Viskanta, "Country Risk and Global Equity Selection," *Journal of Portfolio Management* (1995).

Practitioners sometimes use more than one model to obtain a range of estimates. If the estimates coincide, then managers can proceed with some confidence that the cost of capital estimate is about right. If the estimates diverge substantially, valuation will necessarily be conducted with less confidence.

16.4 • SOURCES OF FUNDS FOR MULTINATIONAL OPERATIONS

Graham and Harvey surveyed U.S. chief financial officers and found that executives rely on informal rules when choosing capital structure, with the firm's financial flexibility and credit rating as the overriding concerns.[21] This suggests that identification of the optimal capital structure, like cost of capital estimation, is at best an inexact science.

Corporations often follow a **pecking order** as they raise funds:

1. Internally generated funds are the preferred source.

2. External sources of funds are accessed only after internal sources are exhausted.

   a. External debt is the preferred external funding source.

   b. New external equity dilutes the ownership and control of existing shareholders and is used only as a last resort.

Figure 16.4 categorizes the financing sources available to the MNC along two dimensions: (1) whether funds are raised from internal or from external sources, and (2) the location of the market in which funds are raised.

Figure 16.5 presents an estimate of the relative importance of each financing source for foreign direct investments by U.S. multinationals.[22] Internally generated funds accounted for 37 percent of U.S. foreign investment, mostly from retained earnings. External debt from foreign sources comprised 47 percent of foreign investment. External equity from foreign sources comprised 16 percent of the total.

Internal Sources of Funds

The preferred source of financing for both domestic and foreign investment is internally generated cash flow from operations, including tax shields from noncash expenses such as depreciation. Internally generated funds can come from existing operations in the parent's home country or the foreign host country.

> Corporations prefer internal funds to finance new investment.

Internally generated funds are preferred because they are **free cash flows**; that is, cash flows in excess of that needed to finance the firm's positive-NPV activities. Free cash flows allow the firm to avoid the transactions costs of external issues. Managers prefer internal funds because they avoid the discipline of the financial markets.

Vehicles for repatriating internal funds from a foreign affiliate to the parent include

- Transfer prices on intracompany sales
- Interest payments on parent loans to foreign affiliates
- Lease payments to the parent on operating and financial lease agreements
- Royalties paid to the parent
- Management fees paid to the parent
- Dividend payments paid to the parent

---

21 Graham and Harvey, "The Theory and Practice of Corporate Finance."

22 Compiled from Feldstein, "The Effects of Outbound Foreign Direct Investment on the Domestic Capital Stock," in *The Effects of Taxation on Multinational Corporations*, pp. 46–48.

FIGURE 16.4
Sources of Funds for Foreign Operations

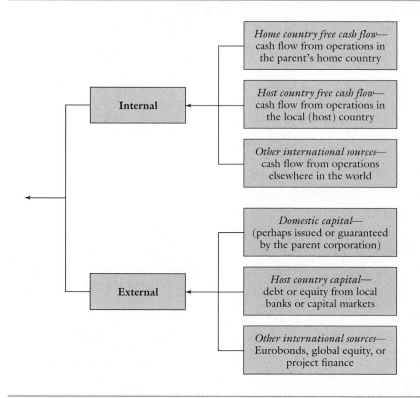

FIGURE 16.5
Sources of Funds for Foreign Operations

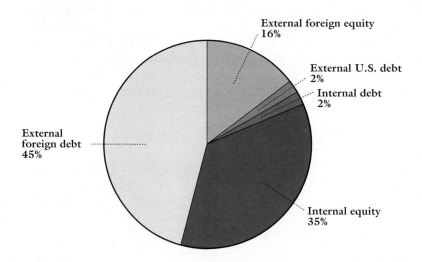

Source: Adapted from Feldstein, "The Effects of Outbound Foreign Direct Investment on the Domestic Capital Stock," in *The Effects of Taxation on Multinational Corporations*, edited by Feldstein, Hines and Hubbard, The University of Chicago Press (1995).

The MNC faces a transfer pricing problem on these repatriation vehicles. If the parent wants to withdraw funds from the foreign subsidiary, it can set high transfer prices on intracompany sales to the subsidiary or low prices on purchases from the subsidiary. Similarly, rates of return must be set on management fees, royalties, interest, and lease payments. The parent can withdraw funds from the foreign subsidiary through high payments to these financial contracts.

To avoid abuses of the tax code, most countries specify that transfer prices be set at arm's-length or market prices. Whether the corporation has flexibility in setting transfer prices depends on applicable tax laws and whether market prices are observable. It is difficult to defend aggressive pricing on debt or lease contracts because market prices are readily observable. The MNC has slightly more discretion in the rates that it sets on royalties and management fees because market prices are not observable for the intellectual property rights that generate these fees. Partly for this reason, many countries place a limit of 5 percent of sales on royalties to the parent.

External Sources of Funds

Firms without internal sources of funds must tap external sources to fund their operations. The MNC has access to international as well as domestic sources of debt and equity capital. In partially segmented markets, the corporation's debt or equity securities can be more attractive to foreign than to domestic investors. In this circumstance, the corporation can reduce its cost of capital by appealing to international investors.

The expanded investor base provided by international sources of funds leads to several potential benefits. These potential benefits include

- Enhanced visibility in foreign markets
- Reduced political risk (greater support from investors in their local markets)
- Greater liquidity for the MNC's debt and equity securities
- Greater access to local companies and assets
- A lower cost of capital

The costs and risks of international sources of funds include

- Language differences and other information barriers
- Capital flow restrictions in some countries
- Greater disclosure requirements on some international exchanges

(e.g., shares listed in the United States must satisfy the SEC's disclosure requirements)

- Filing and listing fees and listing requirements
- Differences in legal systems, and exposure to judicial processes in foreign markets
- Dilution of domestic control

It is difficult for small firms that lack visibility in foreign markets to overcome high information and transactions costs on foreign issues. Percentage issue costs diminish with issue size, so firms with small capital needs are at a disadvantage in both domestic and international markets. Firms with recognizable brand names or copyrights can sometimes leverage their visibility into greater access to international financial markets.

International Bonds. The usual progression of a domestic firm into international capital markets begins with an issuance of debt. Information costs are higher on equity issues, so equity issues usually must wait until the firm has established a foothold into international markets with a debt issue. Although offerings can be privately placed with financial institutions, the ultimate goal is usually to obtain access to the liquidity provided by public capital markets.

> Bonds provide a foothold into international capital markets.

An **international bond** is a bond that is traded outside the country of the issuer. International bonds can be categorized into two types. A **foreign bond** is an international bond issued by a domestic borrower in the internal market of a foreign country and denominated in the currency of that country. A **Eurobond** is traded in a market outside the borders of the country in which the bond is denominated. A Eurobond is called a **global bond** when it trades in one or more internal (foreign or domestic) bond markets as well as in the external Eurobond market.

An advantage of foreign debt is that it ties a foreign subsidiary into the local community. Raising capital in a host country partially insulates the foreign subsidiary from foreign political risk. A disadvantage is that the bond is regulated and taxed by authorities in the foreign market. In contrast, Eurobonds trade outside the jurisdiction of any single nation and are largely exempt from local regulation and taxation.

Eurobonds are issued as fixed-rate (sometimes zero-coupon) bonds or as floating-rate bonds at a spread over an index such as LIBOR or Euribor. Eurobonds are usually bearer bonds with detachable coupons that can be sent in to collect the annual interest payment. There are many variations, such as dual currency Eurobonds that pay interest in one currency and principal in another. Many Eurobonds also involve options, such as

- Equity-linked Eurobonds (convertibles or warrants)
- Eurobonds with call or put options, granted to the issuer or bondholder to buy or sell the bonds at a fixed exercise price
- Currency option Eurobonds (a form of dual currency bond) that give the bondholder or the issuer the option to select the currency of payment at each coupon date

Convertible bonds can be traded for a fixed number of shares of common stock at the option of the bondholder, allowing participation in a company's good fortune while providing a minimum promised return from the bond component. Institutional investors that are prohibited from owning equity sometimes use convertible Eurobonds as an indirect way to participate in an equity market.

> Eurobonds often are convertible or have warrants.

Warrants are detachable options that allow the purchase of additional shares of stock at a fixed exercise price. This allows the debt and equity components of the offering to appeal to different clienteles. For example, prior to 1998 the Japanese Ministry of Finance did not allow options on common stock to be traded on Japanese exchanges. Many Japanese firms issued Eurobonds with detachable warrants that were then purchased by Japanese investors as an indirect way to hold options on Japanese stocks.

Global Equity Issues. Corporations increasingly appeal to investors by offering equity securities directly in foreign markets. Equity issues that are offered directly to investors in international markets are called **Euroequity** or **global equity** issues.

> Global equity issues are sold directly into international markets.

Most securities in the United States are issued in registered form. The convention in most Western European securities markets is to issue securities in bearer form. To permit U.S. corporations to compete for capital in international markets, the 1986 Tax Reform Act (TRA) allowed U.S. corporations to issue securities in bearer form directly to foreign investors.[23] To reduce the costs of

---

23 Prior to the 1986 Tax Reform Act, U.S. corporations could issue bearer securities to foreign investors only through an offshore finance subsidiary.

overseas financing, the U.S. Treasury Department exempted **targeted registered offerings** to foreign financial institutions from the information-reporting and tax-withholding requirements of the 1986 TRA. Four requirements must be satisfied to qualify as a targeted registered offering:

1. The registered owner must be a financial institution in another country.
2. Interest coupons or dividends must be paid to this registered financial institution.
3. The issuer must certify it has no knowledge that a U.S. taxpayer owns the security.
4. The issuer and the foreign institutions must follow SEC certification procedures.

The foreign institution then maintains an over-the-counter secondary market in the securities.

Foreign corporations seeking access to the U.S. stock market typically use foreign shares or depository receipts. **Foreign shares** are shares of a foreign corporation issued directly to domestic investors, usually through an investment bank acting as a transfer agent. Foreign shares are denominated in the currency of the issuing company, so dividends and capital gains are paid to investors in the issuer's currency. The shares of foreign companies that sell directly on U.S. exchanges are called **American shares** and are issued directly to U.S. investors through a transfer agent in accordance with SEC regulations. American shares pay dividends in the currency of the MNC's home country.

Depository receipts are derivative securities that are backed by a pool of foreign shares held in trust by an investment banker or broker. Depository receipts sold in the United States by non-U.S. firms are called **American depository receipts (ADRs)**. ADRs pay dividends in dollars and trade on U.S. exchanges just as other U.S. equities do, but their prices move with the U.S. dollar value of the company's shares in the foreign market. U.S.-based MNCs use depository receipts to appeal to investors in foreign markets.

Part of the reason that external equity is last in the financial pecking order is that domestic markets tend to react negatively to equity issues, such as initial public offerings (IPOs) or seasoned equity offerings (SEOs), in both the short and the long term. For example, studies of the U.S. market have reported negative returns of nearly 3 percent upon the announcement of an equity issue and average annual returns of 7 to 8 percent less than comparable non-issuing companies over the five years following an equity issue.[24] The usual explanation for this negative reaction is that equity issues signal managers' beliefs that equity is overvalued.

In contrast to the domestic evidence, preliminary evidence indicates that international equity issues do not suffer the same degree of post-issuance underperformance. For example, Foerster and Karolyi examine returns to non-U.S. firms when they first cross-list their shares on U.S. exchanges as ADRs.[25] Cross-listing is associated with positive returns of over 20 percent in the year prior to and including the listing week. These same firms average a 14 percent drop in share price during the year after listing.

> First-time issuers of ADRs tend to see a gain in share price.

The net result is an increase in share price, rather than the decrease associated with domestic offerings. Foerster and Karolyi found that non-U.S. firms increased their shareholder base by an average of 28.8 percent. Results for U.S. firms listing on non-U.S. exchanges are qualitatively similar.[26]

24 Loughran and Ritter, "The New Issues Puzzle," *Journal of Finance* (1995).

25 Foerster and Karolyi, "The Effects of Market Segmentation and Investor Recognition on Asset Prices: Evidence from Foreign Stocks Listing in the United States," *Journal of Finance* (1999).

26 Chaplinsky and Ramchand, "The Impact of Global Equity Offerings," *Journal of Finance* (2000).

Market Update

Novo Industri's International Sources of Funds

The impact on the firm's capital costs of moving from domestic to international sources of funds depends on the extent of market segmentation. Consider the emergence of the Danish pharmaceutical and biotechnology firm Novo Industri during the late 1970s.[27] Novo had already internationalized its sales and assets by the late 1970s, with 97 percent of sales outside Denmark and worldwide production and distribution. Despite the international nature of its assets, Novo's debt and equity capital came entirely from Danish sources. Its 1977 rights offering of DKr 56 million ($9.8 million) consumed 25 percent of the Danish new issue market.[28] Saturation of the Danish market meant that Novo's shares sold at a discount in Denmark. As Novo's financing needs outgrew the capacity of the local Danish capital market, Novo implemented a strategy that allowed it to gain access to international sources of funds.

Novo entered international markets in 1978 with a $20 million Eurodollar bond convertible into Novo shares at a price of DKr259 per share, a 10 percent premium to Novo's DKr230 share price. Investors from the United States and the United Kingdom purchased these bonds to diversify their biotech and pharmaceutical holdings. These Eurodollar bonds were converted into common stock during 1980 as Novo's share price rose to DKr300. By the end of 1980, about one-half of Novo's shares were owned by foreign investors. During this period, Novo had been promoting itself to U.S. and European investors through a series of investment seminars, company visits, and press releases. After establishing foreign demand for Novo shares through the convertible Eurobond, Novo appealed directly to U.S. equity investors in the spring of 1981 with a DKr500 million ($65 million) issue of American depository receipts. These sold at a price of $36/ADR, or about DKr1,390/share at the prevailing exchange rate. In this way, Novo was able to escape the confines of the local Danish capital market and ensure their continued access to capital.

Project Financing. **Project financing** allows a project sponsor to raise external funds for a specific project. Three characteristics distinguish this from other forms of financing:

- The project is a separate legal entity and relies heavily on debt financing.
- The debt is contractually linked to the cash flow generated by the project.
- Governments participate in the form of infrastructure support, operating or financial guarantees, rights-of-way, or assurances against political risk.

The hallmark of project financing is that claims on the project are contractually tied to the cash flows of the project. When a corporation finances an investment project using internal funds, cash flows from the project are commingled with those of other projects. Project finance unbundles the project from other assets, allowing the market to value the project as a stand-alone entity. Debt and equity have a claim on project cash flows, but not on the assets or cash flows of the corporation sponsoring the project.

> In project finance, claims are contractually tied to the cash flows of the project.

---

27 Oxelheim, et al., *Corporate Strategies to Internationalize the Cost of Capital* (1998).

28 Rights offerings give current shareholders the option of investing additional funds and maintaining their percentage ownership in the firm or selling the rights to external investors.

Examples of developments funded by project finance include the Channel Tunnel between England and France, the EuroDisney theme park outside Paris, the Orange County (California) and Cuernavaca–Acapulco (Mexico) toll roads, and oil exploration and development in the Forties Field in the North Sea off the coast of England.

Project financing works best for finite-lived, tangible assets that offer stable cash flows that are capable of supporting high debt levels. Ownership of the project is transferred at the end of the project to the sponsor or host government. In a *build-operate-own (BOO)* contract, ownership is transferred to the project sponsor. In a *build-operate-transfer (BOT)* contract, ownership is transferred to the host government.

Natural resource developments, toll roads and bridges, and telecommunication and power generation projects are attractive candidates for project finance because cash flows are relatively stable and tied to a particular location. Reliable cash flows permit the project to borrow against future revenues, which are sometimes guaranteed by selling the output in advance of construction. This allows cash flows to be contractually allocated to those most willing and able to bear the risks of the project.

Quite often, commitments are made by the project sponsor or by supporting governments, suppliers, or customers to ensure that cash flow projections and debt payments are met. Infrastructure projects are high priorities for the governments of developing countries. Government contributions increase the expected return and reduce the risk to other project participants, although these assurances are not always honored. For example, weeks before the planned opening of a project-financed toll road around Bangkok, the Thai government reduced the toll by a third and unilaterally seized control of the highway in violation of the project's 30-year build-operate-transfer agreement. Because of the country-specific political risks of project finance, lenders seek to protect themselves with political risk insurance against expropriation and the imposition of currency or repatriation controls.

Market Update

Project Finance Through the Ages

Suppose you live in Devon, England, and have discovered a rich vein of silver on your property. England is in a recession, and lenders in "The City" (London) are unwilling to lend you money to construct a silver mine. Desperate for funds to invest in your future, you arrange for an Italian bank to finance construction of the silver mine in return for the mine's entire revenue stream for a period of one year. Both parties can benefit from this arrangement. The bank is assured of a good return on its investment through its contractual claim on project cash flows. You get your silver mine after one year, minus a few tons of ore. This example of project finance actually took place . . . in the year 1299.

Project financing was a popular way to fund international ventures throughout the Middle Ages and Renaissance. Oceanic voyages to America and the Far East were financed by governments and merchant banks, with the proceeds distributed to the project sponsor at journey's end. Christopher Columbus's voyage to the New World was financed in this way by the Queen of Spain. As international trade flourished, fleets of ships were eventually brought under one corporate banner, and the need to fund journeys on a trip-by-trip basis declined.

Adapted from Kensinger and Martin, "Project Finance: Raising Money the Old-Fashioned Way," *Journal of Applied Corporate Finance* (1988).

16.5 • THE INTERNATIONAL EVIDENCE ON CAPITAL STRUCTURE

Identifying the determinants of capital structure in an international setting is somewhat more difficult than in a domestic setting. Financial and accounting data are difficult to obtain in many countries and, when available, are subject to widely divergent accounting conventions. There is also great heterogeneity among national taxes, laws, bankruptcy codes, corporate governance, and markets for corporate control. Although variability in business environments limits the inferences that can be drawn from cross-border studies of capital structure, these studies are also potentially more revealing of the underlying determinants of capital structure. This section examines the empirical evidence on the determinants of capital structure choice by domestic and multinational corporations.

Evidence from Developed Capital Markets

Rajan and Zingales studied financial leverage in the G-7 countries (Canada, France, Germany, Italy, Japan, the United Kingdom, and the United States).[29] Rajan and Zingales made adjustments for accounting differences and calculated the average debt-to-capital ratio for each country. With the exception of the United Kingdom and Germany, adjusted debt ratios ranged from 33 to 39 percent. Leverage in Germany and the United Kingdom was somewhat lower than in the other five countries, with debt-to-capital ratios of 18 percent and 16 percent, respectively.

Rajan and Zingales then examined the relation of firm characteristics to financial leverage. The results of their analysis are presented in Table 16.2 and summarized here:

Leverage is positively related to

- Asset tangibility
- Firm size

Leverage is negatively related to

- Growth opportunities
- Profitability

The most striking result in Table 16.2 is the consistency across countries for all variables except firm size.[30]

Leverage is positively related to

- *Asset tangibility.* The ratio of fixed assets to total assets is a measure of asset tangibility. **Tangible assets** can lower the cost of debt by serving as collateral. Secured debt is also less susceptible to agency problems that plague unsecured issues. For example, unsecured debt loses value when the firm shifts into riskier assets. This shifts risk from equity to debt and shifts value from debt to equity. Firms can partially ensure debtholders against opportunistic behavior on the part of managers or equity by securing debt with tangible assets. All else being equal, reductions in agency costs result in increased firm value. Higher leverage is positively associated with asset tangibility in each country and is significant at a 5 percent level in every country except Italy.

---

29 Rajan and Zingales, "What Do We Know About Capital Structure? Some Evidence from International Data," *Journal of Finance* (1995).

30 In a study of U.S. firms, Harris and Raviv ("The Theory of Capital Structure," *Journal of Finance*, 1991), found that leverage is also negatively related to the uniqueness of the firm's products, earnings volatility, advertising and R&D expenditures, and the probability of bankruptcy.

TABLE 16.2
Factors Correlated with Leverage

The estimated model is $Leverage_i = \alpha_i + \beta_1 Tangibility_i + \beta_2 Market\text{-}to\text{-}book_i + \beta_3 FirmSize_i + \beta_4 Profitability_i + \varepsilon_i$.
Leverage is adjusted debt to adjusted debt plus book value of adjusted equity in 1991. All variables are 4-year averages (1987–1990). Standard errors are in parentheses. See the original article for details.

	United States	Japan	Germany	France	Italy	United Kingdom	Canada
Tangibility	0.50[b]	1.41[b]	0.42[a]	0.53[a]	0.36	0.41[b]	0.26[b]
(fixed assets/total assets)	(0.04)	(0.18)	(0.19)	(0.26)	(0.23)	(0.07)	(0.10)
Growth opportunities	−0.17[b]	−0.04	−0.20[b]	−0.17[a]	−0.19	−0.13[b]	−0.11[b]
(asset market-to-book)	(0.01)	(0.04)	(0.07)	(0.08)	(0.14)	(0.03)	(0.04)
Firm size	0.06[b]	0.11[b]	−0.07[b]	0.02	0.02	0.026[b]	0.08[b]
(logarithm of sales)	(0.01)	(0.02)	(0.02)	(0.02)	(0.03)	(0.01)	(0.01)
Profitability	−0.41[b]	−4.26[b]	0.15	−0.02	−0.16	−0.34	−0.46[a]
(EBITDA/total assets)	(0.10)	(0.60)	(0.52)	(0.72)	(0.85)	(0.30)	(0.22)
Number of observations	2079	316	175	117	96	522	264
Pseudo R^2	0.21	0.29	0.12	0.12	0.05	0.18	0.19

[a] Significant at the 5 percent level.
[b] Significant at the 1 percent level.

Source: Rajan and Zingales, "What Do We Know About Capital Structure? Some Evidence from International Data," *Journal of Finance* (December 1995).

- *Firm size.* Large firms are usually more diversified than small firms. Diversification reduces the variability of firm value and can lead to a reduction in costs of financial distress. Consequently, large diversified firms have greater debt capacity, other things constant. In Table 16.2, the relation between firm size and leverage is generally positive and statistically significant. The exception is Germany, where larger firms tend to be less levered.

Leverage is negatively related to

- *Growth opportunities.* Asset market-to-book ratios are a measure of a firm's growth opportunities. Asset market-to-book ratios are negatively related to leverage in each country and are statistically significant in five of seven countries. This negative relation is driven by firms with high market-to-book ratios within each country. The relation is weak or absent in firms with low market-to-book ratios and few growth opportunities. Rajan and Zingales concluded that firms issue stock when they have growth options or real investment opportunities that result in high share prices relative to earnings or book values.

- *Profitability.* The theoretical relation between profitability and leverage is ambiguous. On the one hand, profitable firms can avoid external capital markets and so should have less leverage than unprofitable firms.[31] On the other hand, the larger cash flows of profitable firms can support more debt and generate higher tax

---

31 Myers and Majluf, "Corporate Financing and Investment Decisions When Firms Have Information That Investors Do Not Have" *Journal of Financial Economics* (1984).

shields. Thus, higher debt levels should be forced on managers in countries with efficient markets for corporate control.[32] The evidence in Table 16.2 indicates that profitability and leverage are negatively related in the majority of the G-7 countries. Again, the exception is Germany, although its coefficient is not statistically significant.

Evidence from Emerging Capital Markets

Booth, et al., analyzed the capital structure choices of firms in 10 emerging capital markets.[33] They concluded that capital structure decisions are affected by many of the same variables as in developed markets:

- The influence of asset tangibility, firm size, growth opportunities, and profitability are similar in developed and emerging capital markets.

- The strongest result is that profitable firms use less debt in emerging markets.

These findings hold despite profound cross-country differences in institutional factors

| Profitable firms use less debt in emerging markets. |

such as the relative magnitude of corporate and personal tax rates, regulations governing bankruptcy and reorganization, financial disclosure requirements, and the availability of different forms of financing provided by developed capital markets.

Despite these similarities with developed capital markets, country-specific factors play an important role in emerging markets. In particular, the influences of the various factors are highly variable across the sample countries. Booth, et al., concluded that the country of origin is usually at least as important as the profitability, firm size, or tangibility of assets in explaining capital structures in emerging markets.

16.6 • Summary

In an integrated financial market, real rates of return are equal on equivalent assets. In such a world, MNCs would not enjoy financing advantages over domestic firms. In the real world of partially segmented markets, corporations with access to alternative sources of capital can lower their cost of capital through judicious financing choices.

We began with a description of the two most popular approaches to project valuation:

- The weighted average cost of capital (WACC) method discounts expected after-tax cash flows to debt and equity at a rate that reflects the after-tax required returns on debt and equity capital.

- The adjusted present value (APV) approach separately values the unlevered project and the financing side effects.

A critical input into each of these valuation approaches is the cost of capital. This, in turn, depends on the extent of capital market segmentation:

- In integrated markets, systematic risk should be measured against the world market portfolio.

- In partially segmented markets, systematic risk can depend on a mix of global and local factors.

---

32 Jensen, "Agency Costs of Free Cash Flow, Corporate Financing and Takeovers," *American Economic Review* (1986).

33 Booth, Aivazian, Demirguc-Kunt, and Maksimovic, "Capital Structures in Developing Countries," *Journal of Finance* (2001).

In segmented markets, there is no consensus best practice for cost of capital estimation. In this circumstance, judgment must be used to form an estimate that is at least in the right ballpark.

Finally, we reviewed the international evidence on capital structure. In most countries, firms that are large or have tangible assets tend to use debt as a source of funds. In contrast, firms with growth opportunities or high profitability tend to avoid debt. High-growth firms prefer to fund their growth through external equity issues, and profitable firms are able to fund their operations through internal sources of funds.

KEY TERMS

adjusted present value (APV)	integrated versus segmented capital markets
American depository receipt (ADR)	international bond
American shares	irrelevance proposition
beta (a measure of systematic risk)	liberalization
business risks	market model regression
capital asset pricing model	pecking order
capital structure	perfect markets
convertible bond	project financing
cost of capital	pure-play
costs of financial distress	security market line
depository receipt	systematic business risk or unlevered beta
Eurobond	tangible assets
Euroequity (global equity)	targeted registered offering
foreign bond	warrant
foreign shares	weighted average cost of capital (WACC)
free cash flow	yield to maturity
global bond	

CONCEPTUAL QUESTIONS

16.1 Does corporate financial policy matter in a perfect financial market?

16.2 What distinguishes an integrated from a segmented capital market?

16.3 What factors could lead to capital market segmentation?

16.4 Does the required return on a project depend on who is investing the money or on where the money is being invested?

16.5 Does the value of a foreign project depend on the way it is financed?

16.6 An important input into the required return on equity in the security market line is the market risk premium. How much is the market risk premium?

16.7 When is the adjusted present value approach to project valuation most useful?

16.8 What is the usual consequence of an increase in country risk on a national stock market? Do stock markets in high-risk countries have higher or lower volatility than other markets? Do they have higher or lower betas relative to a world stock index?

16.9 What is a stock market liberalization? What are the usual effects of liberalizations on (a) emerging market correlations with the world stock returns, (b) local market volatility, and (c) the local cost of capital?

16.10 What is a targeted registered offering, and why is it useful to the corporation?

16.11 What is project financing, and when is it most appropriate?

16.12 What evidence is there on the international determinants of corporate capital structure? How is the international evidence similar to the domestic U.S. evidence?

PROBLEMS

16.1 The systematic risk (beta) of France's Oilily Corporation is 1.2 when measured against a world stock market index and 1.4 against a French stock index. The annual risk-free rate in France is 5 percent.
   a. If the required return on the world market index is 12 percent, what is the required return on Oilily stock in an integrated financial market?
   b. Suppose the French financial market is segmented from the rest of the world. If the required return on the French market is 11 percent, what is the required return on Oilily stock?

16.2 The systematic risk (beta) of Grand Pet is 0.8 when measured against the Morgan Stanley Capital International (MSCI) world market index and 1.2 against the London Financial Times 100 (or FTSE 100) stock index. The annual risk-free rate in the United Kingdom is 5 percent.
   a. If the required return on the MSCI world market index is 10 percent, what is the required return on Grand Pet stock in an integrated financial market?
   b. Suppose the U.K. financial markets are segmented from the rest of the world. If the required return on the FTSE 100 is 10 percent, what is the required return on Grand Pet stock?

16.3 Find Oilily's weighted average cost of capital under each of the following scenarios:
   a. Oilily has a market value debt-to-value ratio of 40 percent. Oilily's pretax borrowing cost on new long-term debt in France is 7 percent. Oilily's beta relative to the French stock market is 1.4. The risk-free rate in France is 5 percent and the market risk premium over the risk-free rate is 6 percent. Interest is deductible in France at the marginal corporate income tax rate of 33 percent. What is Oilily's weighted average cost of capital in the French market?
   b. Oilily can borrow in the Europound market at a pretax cost of 6 percent. International investors will tolerate a 50 percent debt-to-value mix. With a 50 percent debt-to-value ratio, the beta of Oilily is 1.2 against the MSCI world index. The required return on the world market portfolio is 12 percent. What is Oilily's weighted average cost of capital under these circumstances?
   c. Suppose Oilily is expected to generate after-tax operating cash flow of $CF_1 =$ BFr10 million in the coming year and that this is expected to grow at 4 percent in perpetuity. The valuation equation $V_0 = CF_1/(i-g)$ can value Oilily's cash flow stream given CF_1 is the coming year's cash flow, i is the weighted average cost of capital, and g is the growth rate of annual cash flow. Find the value of Oilily using the weighted average costs of capital from the scenarios in parts a and b.

16.4 Find Grand Pet's WACC under each of the following scenarios:
   a. Grand Pet has a market value debt-to-equity ratio of 33 percent. Grand Pet's pretax borrowing cost on new long-term debt in the United Kingdom is 6 percent. Grand Pet's beta relative to the Footsie 100 is 1.2. The risk-free rate in the United Kingdom is 5 percent, and the market risk premium over the

risk-free rate is 10 percent. Interest is deductible in the United Kingdom at the marginal corporate income tax rate of 33 percent. What is Grand Pet's weighted average cost of capital in the U.K. market?

b. Grand Pet can borrow in the Europound market at a pretax cost of 5 percent. International investors are willing to tolerate a 50 percent debt-to-equity mix at this cost of debt. With a 50 percent debt-to-equity ratio, the beta of Grand Pet is 0.8 against the MSCI world index. The required return on the world market portfolio is 10 percent. What is Grand Pet's weighted average cost of capital under these circumstances?

c. Suppose Grand Pet is expected to generate after-tax operating cash flow of £1 billion in the coming year, and that this is expected to grow at a g = 3 percent rate in perpetuity. The valuation equation $V_0 = CF_1/(i–g)$ can value Grand Pet's cash flow stream, given CF_1 is the coming year's cash flow, i is the weighted average cost of capital, and g is the growth rate of annual cash flow. Find the value of Grand Pet using the weighted average costs of capital from the scenarios in parts a and b.

16.5 Suppose Oilily uses an APV approach to project valuation.
a. Oilily's latest investment proposal is for a chain of retail stores in the United Kingdom. Initial investment will be BFr100 million and will produce a single after-tax cash flow of BFr12 million after one year. The chain is expected to be sold to a U.K. company for BFr100 million (after tax) at the end of the year. Oilily has an all-equity discount rate of 10 percent. What is the value of Oilily's project as an all-equity investment?

b. Suppose the project can support up to BFr50 million in debt at a pretax cost of 6 percent. Principal and interest (as well as the interest tax shield) are due in one year. Oilily's corporate tax rate is 33 percent. What is the value of the tax shield from the use of debt? Ignoring other financial side effects (i.e., costs of financial distress), what is the value of Oilily's project as a levered investment?

c. Suppose Oilily's project produces after-tax cash flow of BFr12 million per year in perpetuity. What are the unlevered and levered APVs from parts a and b? Assume perpetual debt at an interest rate of 6 percent.

16.6 Suppose Grand Pet uses an APV approach to project valuation.
a. Another Grand Pet investment proposal is to produce nonalcoholic beer for dogs in the United States. Initial investment will be £100 million and will produce a single after-tax cash flow of £8 million after one year. The brewery will be sold for £100 million at the end of the year. Assume there are no tax effects on sale of the brewery. An all-equity company that produces a similar brand of doggy beer trades on the London Stock Exchange and has an all-equity discount rate of 8 percent. What is the value of Grand Pet's project as an all-equity investment?

b. Suppose the project can support up to £25 million in debt at a pretax cost of debt of 6 percent. Principal and interest on the debt (as well as the interest tax shield) are due in one year. Grand Pet's corporate tax rate is 33 percent. What is the value of the tax shield from the use of debt? Ignoring other financial side effects (i.e., costs of financial distress), what is the value of Grand Pet's project as a levered investment?

c. Suppose Grand Pet's project produces after-tax cash flow of £8 million per year in perpetuity. What are the unlevered and levered APVs from parts a and b? Assume perpetual debt at an interest rate of 6 percent.

16.7 As the People's Republic of China evolves toward a market economy, capital markets are likely to replace the government as the firm's primary source of funds for investment. Nevertheless, the Chinese government remains the principal owner of many Chinese firms. Some of these firms use the government's borrowing cost (such as the rate on certificates of deposit from the Industrial Bank of China) as their required return or hurdle rate on new investment.

a. Is it appropriate to use the government's borrowing cost as a required return on investment if a firm is 100 percent owned by the government?

b. Are investments based on this criterion likely to be value-creating or value-destroying from a capital markets perspective? What consequence will the use of this hurdle rate have for the risk of the firm's and the government's asset portfolios. Explain.

c. A Chinese manager is considering an investment of 1.5 million renminbi in a coal mine that generates an expected return of 100,000 renminbi per year in perpetuity. The government's borrowing rate is 5 percent. The project has a beta of 1.0 and a risk-adjusted required return of 10 percent. What is the NPV of this investment using the government's borrowing cost of 5 percent? What is the NPV of this investment using a risk-adjusted return of 10 percent?

d. The Chinese manager expects her division to be privatized in one year. Further, suppose the government does not monitor returns in its investments once they have been made. What will be the likely consequence of accepting the project in part c on the market value of her division after privatization? Does the manager have an incentive to extract as much capital from the government as possible prior to privatization, even at the cost of accepting negative-NPV projects? (*Hint:* Think of the agency conflict between managers and other stakeholders.)

16.8 U.K.'s Vodafone Group needs a cost of capital evaluate to evaluate a proposed investment in Brazil's mobile phone market. Vodafone's experience investing in mobile phone infrastructure in emerging markets suggests that the systematic risk of the investment from the perspective of a U.K. investor is about the same as the average systematic risk of the emerging market. The U.K. risk-free rate is r_F = 3 percent. The world market risk premium is estimated to be $(E[r_W]–r_F)$ = 5 percent. Calculate the expected or required return in pounds sterling on a typical Brazilian investment based on each of the following models:

a. International CAPM: $E[r_{Br}] = r_F + \beta_{Br}(E[r_W]–r_F)$. Vodafone estimates β_{Br} = 1.2 based on a regression of Brazilian returns on world market returns.

b. Globally nested CAPM: $E[r_{Br}] = r_F + \beta_{Br}(E[r_W]–r_F) + \delta_{Br}(E[r_{Region}]–E[r_W])$, where δ_{Br} is Brazil's systematic risk relative to Latin American regional risk that is not included in the world market return. Vodafone estimates β_{Br} = 1.2, δ_{Br} = 1.5, and $(E[r_{Region}]–E[r_W])$ = 4%.

c. Country risk rating model: $E[r_{Br}] = E[r_W] + CR_{Br}$, where CR_{Br} is an adjustment for credit risk in Brazil. Vodafone estimates CR_{Br} = 4%.

d. Country spread model: $E[r_{Br}] = E[r_W] + S_{Br}$, where S_{Br} is the 1-year Brazilian government bond yield minus the 1-year Eurocurrency yield. Currently, this interest rate spread is S_{Br} = 2%.

e. Relative standard deviation model: $E[r_{Br}] = r_F + (0.5)[1+(\sigma_{Br}/\sigma_{UK})](E[r_W]–r_F)$, where $(\sigma_{Br}/\sigma_{UK})$ is based on the standard deviations in Table 16.1.

SUGGESTED READINGS

Capital structure and cost of capital are developed and tested in the following articles:

Milton Harris and Artur Raviv, "The Theory of Capital Structure," *Journal of Finance* 46 (March 1991), pp. 297–355.

Isik Inselbag and Howard Kaufold, "Two DCF Approaches for Valuing Companies Under Alternative Financing Strategies," *Journal of Applied Corporate Finance* 10, No. 1 (1997), pp. 114–122.

Franco Modigliani and Merton Miller, "The Cost of Capital, Corporation Finance, and the Theory of Investment," *American Economic Review* 48 (June 1958), pp. 261–297.

Franco Modigliani and Merton Miller, "Corporate Income Taxes and the Cost of Capital: A Correction," *American Economic Review* 53 (June 1963), pp. 433–442.

Richard S. Ruback, "Capital Cash Flows: A Simple Approach to Valuing Risky Cash Flows," *Financial Management* 31 (Summer 2002), pp. 85–103.

Articles on the multinational corporation's cost of capital include

Michael Adler and Bernard Dumas, "International Portfolio Choice and Corporation Finance: A Synthesis," *Journal of Finance* (June 1983), pp. 925–984.

Claude B. Erb, Campbell R. Harvey, and Tadas E. Viskanta, "Country Risk and Global Equity Selection," *Journal of Portfolio Management* 21 (Winter 1995), pp. 74–83.

Claude B. Erb, Campbell R. Harvey, and Tadas E. Viskanta, "Political Risk, Financial Risk and Economic Risk," *Financial Analysts Journal* 52 (November/December 1996), pp. 29–46.

John R. Graham and Campbell R. Harvey, "The Theory and Practice of Corporate Finance: Evidence from the Field," *Journal of Financial Economics* 61 (2001), pp. 187–243.

The equity risk premium is investigated in

Robert D. Arnott and Peter L. Bernstein, "What Risk Premium Is 'Normal'?" *Financial Analysts Journal* 58 (March/April 2002), pp. 64–85.

Andrew D. Clare and Paul D. Kaplan, "A Macroeconomic Model of the Equity Risk Premium," *Corporate Finance Review* 4 (July/August 1999), pp 26–34.

Philippe Jorion and William N. Goetzmann, "Global Stock Markets in the Twentieth Century," *Journal of Finance* 53 (June 1999), pp. 953–980.

Jeremy Siegel, "The Equity Premium: Stock and Bond Returns Since 1802," *Financial Analysts Journal* 48 (January/February 1992), pp. 28–38.

Ivo Welch, "Views of Financial Economists on the Equity Premium and on Professional Controversies," *Journal of Business* 73 (October 2000), pp. 501–537.

Ivo Welch, "The Equity Premium Consensus Forecast Revisited," Cowles Foundation Discussion Paper No. 1325 (September 2001).

The impact of international financing is investigated in

Susan Chaplinsky and Latha Ramchand, "The Impact of Global Equity Offerings," *Journal of Finance* 55 (December 2000), pp. 2767–2789.

Martin Feldstein, "The Effects of Outbound Foreign Direct Investment on the Domestic Capital Stock," in *The Effects of Taxation on Multinational Corporations*, edited by Martin Feldstein, James R. Hines, Jr., and R. Glenn Hubbard, The University of Chicago Press (1995).

Stephen R. Foerster and G. Andrew Karolyi, "The Effects of Market Segmentation and Investor Recognition on Asset Prices: Evidence from Foreign Stocks Listing in the United States," *Journal of Finance* 54 (June 1999), pp. 981–1013.

John W. Kensinger and John D. Martin, "Project Finance: Raising Money the Old-Fashioned Way," *Journal of Applied Corporate Finance* 1 (Fall 1988), pp. 69–81.

Attempts to document the international determinants of capital structure include

Laurence Booth, Varouj Aivazian, Asli Demirguc-Kunt, and Vojislav Maksimovic, "Capital Structures in Developing Countries," *Journal of Finance* 56 (February 2001), pp. 87–130.

Raghuram G. Rajan and Luigi Zingales, "What Do We Know About Capital Structure? Some Evidence from International Data," *Journal of Finance* 50 (December 1995), pp. 1421–1460.

Agency costs are discussed in

Michael C. Jensen, "Agency Costs of Free Cash Flow, Corporate Financing, and Takeovers," *American Economic Review* 76, No. 2 (1986), pp. 323–339.

Timothy Loughran and Jay R. Ritter, "The New Issues Puzzle," *Journal of Finance* 50 (March 1995), pp. 23–52.

Stewart C. Myers and Nicholas S. Majluf, "Corporate Financing and Investment Decisions When Firms Have Information That Investors Do Not Have" *Journal of Financial Economics* 13, No. 2 (1984), pp. 127–221.

The impact of market segmentation on investment and the cost of capital is examined in

Geert Bekaert and Campbell Harvey, "Time-Varying World Market Integration," *Journal of Finance* 50 (June 1995), pp. 403–444.

Geert Bekaert and Campbell Harvey, "Emerging Equity Market Volatility," *Journal of Financial Economics* 43 (January 1997), pp. 29–77.

Geert Bekaert and Campbell Harvey, "Foreign Speculators and Emerging Equity Markets," *Journal of Finance* 55 (April 2000), pp. 565–613.

Peter Blair Henry, "Do Stock Market Liberalizations Cause Investment Booms?" *Journal of Financial Economics* 58 (October/November 2000), pp. 301–334.

Lars Oxelheim, Arthur Stonehill, Trond Randøy, Kaisa Vikkula, Kåre Dullum, and Karl-Markus Modén, *Corporate Strategies to Internationalise the Cost of Capital* (Copenhagen: Copenhagen Business School Press, 1998).

Taxes and Multinational Corporate Strategy

chapter 17

Overview

The income tax has made more liars out of the American people than golf has.

Will Rogers

This chapter shows how a multinational corporation's foreign income is taxed by foreign and domestic governments. Tax planning and strategy can be a major source of value for the MNC because of national differences in tax rates and systems. Careful planning can lessen the corporation's tax liability and thereby increase after-tax return on investment and corporate value.

Here is a word of caution before we begin. International taxation is an exceedingly technical area that requires a detailed knowledge of two or more (often contradictory) tax systems. If the advice "Consult with your tax accountant" applies to domestic business, it applies tenfold to international business. This chapter is an introduction to international taxation and tax planning. It is not intended to be your sole reference.

17.1 • THE OBJECTIVES OF NATIONAL TAX POLICY

We often hear that the only sure things in life are death and taxes. Taxes are collected to pay for public services, including police and fire protection, roads and infrastructure, social programs, and national defense. **A national tax policy** refers to the way a nation chooses to allocate the tax burden across its residents.

> A neutral tax does not divert capital flows.

Tax Neutrality: A Level Playing Field

A useful starting point in our discussion of national tax policy is the concept of **tax neutrality**. A neutral tax is one that does not divert the natural flow of capital from its most productive uses. Taxes are a form of market friction. As long as taxes fall neutrally on all business activities, they are merely a drain and do not divert capital from its natural destinations.

There are two forms of tax neutrality for multinationals based in the domestic economy:

- *Domestic tax neutrality.* Domestic tax neutrality is a situation in which incomes arising from the foreign and domestic operations of a domestically-based multinational are taxed similarly by the domestic government. Domestic tax neutrality holds if GM's U.S. and European operations are taxed in the same way.

- *Foreign tax neutrality.* Foreign tax neutrality is a situation in which taxes imposed on the foreign operations of domestic companies are similar to those facing local competitors in the foreign countries. Foreign tax neutrality holds from a German perspective if BMW's U.S. operations are taxed in the same way by the U.S. government as GM's U.S. operations are taxed.

Domestic tax neutrality puts the foreign and domestic operations of domestic multinationals on an equal footing. Foreign tax neutrality puts the domestic operations of foreign multinationals and domestic firms on an equal footing. Tax neutrality preserves equality by ensuring that an undue tax burden is not differentially imposed on foreign or domestic operations.

Violations of Tax Neutrality

In practice, tax neutrality is almost impossible to achieve because of cross-border differences in tax rates and systems. If corporate income tax rates are 25 percent in Germany and 35 percent in the United States, then tax rates on the German and U.S. income of a U.S.-based multinational can be consistent either with U.S. or German taxes, but not both. Similarly, tax rates on BMW's U.S. operations can be consistent either with U.S. or German taxes, but not both.

> Cross-border differences in national tax policy make tax neutrality unachievable.

Because taxes are seldom neutral, businesses need tax planning. Multinational corporations are well positioned to take advantage of cross-border differences in tax rates and systems. The remainder of this section describes four deviations from tax neutrality that are important determinants of multinational tax planning and business strategy, based on different tax rates on income from

- Different tax jurisdictions
- Different asset classes
- Different financing instruments
- Different organizational forms of business

Income received from different tax jurisdictions is often taxed at different rates. Some countries, such as Sweden, impose relatively high taxes to finance ambitious social welfare programs. Others, such as Ireland, choose relatively low tax rates to attract foreign capital. Still others, including France and the Netherlands, fully exempt the earnings of foreign operations from domestic taxation. Cross-border differences in tax codes are important considerations in market entry and exit decisions and in how the MNC repatriates income from its foreign operations.

Income received from different types of assets in the same tax jurisdiction, such as active business income versus passive investment income, is often taxed at different rates. In the United States, losses on one type of income cannot be used to offset gains on another type of income. Many countries make a distinction between different forms of income for tax purposes.

Returns on financial securities are taxed differently, depending on whether the security is debt, equity, a debt-equity hybrid (such as preferred stock), or an equity-linked security (such as a stock option or warrant). On the other side of the contract, the tax treatment of financial expenses is different for payments to different classes of creditors, such as employees (wages payable), customers (trade credit), banks (interest), and shareholders (dividends). For example, interest expense is tax deductible in most countries, whereas dividend payments usually are not. Different corporate and personal tax treatments on interest and dividend payments mean that different capital structures might be preferred in different tax jurisdictions.

Income received from different legal organizational forms in the same tax jurisdiction often is taxed at different rates or in different ways. For example, different tax rates apply to corporate and partnership income in the United States and in many other countries. Different tax rules also apply to the foreign branches and subsidiaries of domestic corporations. Foreign branches are legally a part of the parent firm, whereas foreign subsidiaries are incorporated in a foreign country. Many countries (including the United States) tax the foreign branch income of domestic firms as it is received but delay taxes on the foreign subsidiaries until income is repatriated to the parent. Because of cross-border differences in tax rates, a MNC must consider the tax consequences of its choice of organizational form when operating in foreign countries.

National tax policies thus influence the assets held by a MNC, the way in which these assets are financed, and the organizational forms chosen for its operations.

17.2 • TYPES OF TAXATION

National Taxes on Foreign-Source Income

The major issues in international taxation revolve around the fact that **foreign-source income** (that is, income earned from foreign operations) falls under two or more tax jurisdictions. Countries generally apply one of two different tax regimes to income earned by MNCs incorporated within their borders:

- *A worldwide tax system*. In a **worldwide tax system**, foreign-source income is taxed by the home country as it is repatriated to the parent. Income from foreign incorporated subsidiaries usually is not taxed until it is repatriated to the parent, as long as it is reinvested in an active business outside of the home country. Foreign tax credits for income taxes paid to foreign governments prevent double taxation of foreign-source income. This tax regime is used in the United States, the United Kingdom, and Japan.

- *A territorial tax system*. In a **territorial tax system**, only domestic income is taxed. Income from outside the home country is not taxed as long as it is earned in an active business. This tax regime is used in Hong Kong, France, Belgium, and the Netherlands, among others. Still other countries, such as Canada and Germany, use a territorial system for income earned in countries with which they have a tax treaty and a worldwide system for income earned in nontreaty countries. About half of OECD countries have a territorial system, either by statute or treaty with another country.

The intent of both the worldwide and the territorial tax systems is to avoid double taxation of foreign-source income.

Although the details of national income tax systems vary, bilateral tax treaties ensure some consistency in the tax treatment of foreign-source income. Many of these tax treaties follow the *Model Treaty of the Organization for Economic Cooperation and Development.* Tax treaties are intended to ensure foreign tax neutrality; that is, that the foreign operations of each nation's MNCs are not tax-disadvantaged relative to local competitors in the foreign country. Bilateral tax treaties also largely remove the threat of double taxation of foreign-source income.

> Tax treaties promote consistency in the treatment of foreign-source income.

Explicit Versus Implicit Taxes

Explicit Taxes. National governments impose many different kinds of **explicit taxes**:

- Corporate and personal income taxes
- Withholding taxes on dividends, interest, and royalties
- Sales taxes and value-added taxes (VAT)
- Property and asset taxes
- Tariffs on cross-border trade

The costs of doing business in a foreign country depend in large part on the types and levels of explicit taxes imposed by the host government. Table 17.1 lists national tax rates on corporate and personal income, value-added taxes, and withholding tax rates on dividend and interest income.

Local taxes can sometimes be important as well. For example, much of the political and taxing power in Switzerland resides in 25 cantons or provinces. The maximum national corporate income tax rate in Switzerland is 8.5 percent. Each canton then adds its own income tax of between 17 and 35 percent. Municipalities add another small tax.

As might be expected, there is little consistency in the definitions of taxable income. Countries following a territorial tax system typically do not tax foreign-source income. Countries following a worldwide tax system usually tax foreign-source income as it is repatriated to the parent company. Regardless of whether countries follow worldwide or territorial tax systems, the net effect of most bilateral tax treaties is to make foreign-source income taxable at the higher of the two national corporate income tax rates.

Withholding taxes are intended to ensure that residents' taxable income is reported to the tax authorities in the host country. For distributions to nonresidents, withholding taxes also compensate the host government for lost tax revenues from forgone personal income taxes in the host country.

Withholding taxes on dividend distributions are the norm, especially for dividend payments to nonresidents. The dividend withholding tax rate is most frequently 5 percent between countries with bilateral tax treaties, but it varies from 0 percent on cross-border dividend distributions from Hong Kong and the United Kingdom to more than 25 percent on some dividend distributions from Austria and Germany. Some governments impose withholding taxes on interest, royalty payments, and management fees.

As an example of why governments impose withholding taxes, the West German Bundesrechnungshof (or tax court) estimated in the late 1980s that 65 to 70 percent of all interest income received by individuals in Germany went unreported. Germany instituted several tax law changes in the early 1990s in an effort to increase reporting compliance. First, the level at which interest income becomes taxable was raised to several thousand marks in order to help break the tradition of noncompliance. Second, a withholding tax on interest payments by corporations and banks was instituted and

TABLE 17.1
National Tax Rates

| Country | Income tax | | Value-added | Country | Income tax | | Value-added |
	Corporate	Individual	tax (VAT)		Corporate	Individual	tax(VAT)
Argentina	35	35	17	Japan	42	37	0
Australia	30	47	10	Korea	30	44	10
Austria	34	50	20	Malaysia	28	30	14
Belgium	40	55	21	Mexico	35	35	15
Brazil	34	20	0	Netherlands	35	60	19
Canada	26	31	7	Norway	28	28	24
China	33	45	17	Poland	28	40	22
Denmark	30	60	25	Portugal	33	40	17
Finland	29	37	22	Russia	24	30	20
France	34	54	20	Singapore	25	28	0
Germany	25	48	16	South Africa	38	45	14
Greece	35	45	18	Spain	35	56	16
Hong Kong	16	15	0	Sweden	28	56	25
Hungary	18	40	25	Switzerland	25	34	7
India	36	40	0	Taiwan	25	40	5
Indonesia	30	30	10	Thailand	30	37	7
Ireland	16	44	21	Turkey	33	55	15
Israel	36	50	17	United Kingdom	30	40	17
Italy	40	45	20	United States	35	35	0

Source: Corporate income tax rates are from KPMG International, 2002 Corporate Tax Rate Survey (http://www.kpmg.com). The definitions of taxable income vary by country. Some corporate tax rates include local or other taxes. Individual income and value-added tax rates are from World Tax Inc. (http://www.worldwide-tax.com). Tax rates are rounded to the nearest percent.

administered through the banking system. This withholding tax can be partially recovered by those declaring their interest income to the government. Finally, penalties for noncompliance were increased. Prior to these tax law changes, most nonreporters were not discovered until death or divorce brought them before the taxing authority. German taxpayers now have greater incentives to report their interest income.

In lieu of the state sales taxes popular in the United States, many countries around the world use **value-added taxes (VAT)**. Value-added taxes are sales taxes collected at each stage of production in proportion to the value added during that stage. Each of the countries in the European Union uses a value-added tax. Although the merits of value-added taxes are periodically debated in the United States, proposals to institute a value-added tax have met strong resistance in the U.S. Congress.

Tax policy is a competitive tool that local and national governments can use to attract businesses that might not otherwise locate in a particular tax jurisdiction. Developing economies can use tax holidays to attract foreign investment and promote development in key regions and industries. Countries that actively employ tax policy to attract investment include Hong Kong, Hungary, and Ireland. Low taxes or tax subsidies in the form of tax relief or tax holidays allow some locations to overcome the handicaps that make them less desirable than competing locations.

Implicit Taxes. The law of one price requires that equivalent assets sell for the same price. Because investors care about after-tax returns (as opposed to before-tax returns), the law of one price can be restated as follows:

The law of one price requires that equivalent assets sell to yield the same *after-tax* real rate of return.

Not all taxes are neutral. Higher before-tax required returns are demanded in high-tax jurisdictions to compensate for the additional tax burden. Lower expected returns on assets subject to lower tax rates are a form of **implicit tax**.

Suppose a MNC can invest $100,000 in Country H to yield $112,500 for a pretax return of $i_H = 12.5\%$. Corporate income in Country H is taxed at a relatively high rate of $t_H = 60\%$. The after-tax return in Country H is then $i_H(1-t_H) = (0.125)(1-0.60) = 0.05$, or 5 percent. Alternatively, the corporation can invest $100,000 in Country L and face a lower corporate tax rate of $t_L = 40\%$. If a pretax return of $i_L = 12.5\%$ can be earned in this country, then $100,000 can be turned into $107,500 after taxes for an after-tax return of $i_L(1-t_L) = (0.125)(1-0.40) = 0.075$, or 7.5 percent.

The law of one price imposes an implicit tax on assets in low-tax jurisdictions.

This situation cannot persist. Investors will move their investments toward the low-tax country and away from the high-tax country in pursuit of the highest after-tax return. This activity will continue until, in equilibrium, expected after-tax rates of return are equal. In this example, this means that

$$i_H(1-t_H) = i_L(1-t_L)$$
$$\Rightarrow \quad i_H/i_L = (1-t_L)/(1-t_H)$$
$$= (1-0.40)/(1-0.60)$$
$$= 1.50 \tag{17.1}$$

In equilibrium, pretax returns in Country H will be 50 percent higher than pretax returns in Country L to compensate for the higher income tax in Country H. For example, if prices are bid up in the low-tax country until before-tax returns fall to $i_L = 10\%$, then prices in Country H will fall and before-tax expected rates of return will rise until $i_H = 15\%$ in equilibrium. The higher prices and lower expected returns in country L are a form of implicit tax on earnings in that country.

17.3 • U.S. TAXATION OF FOREIGN-SOURCE INCOME

Foreign-source income from a foreign branch is taxed as it is earned.

In the United States, the Internal Revenue Service (IRS) is responsible for collecting taxes and ensuring compliance with the U.S. tax code. The treatment of foreign-source income depends on how foreign operations are organized.

- *Income from foreign corporations.* Depending on the U.S. parent's level of ownership, income from a foreign corporation is treated in one of three ways:
  - *Ownership of 10 percent or less.* Dividends from foreign corporations owned 10 percent or less are placed into a passive income basket (see the "FTC limitations" section) reflecting the U.S. parent's passive stake in the corporation.
  - *Subpart F income.* Income from foreign corporations owned more than 10 percent and up to 50 percent is called **Subpart F income** and is taxed on a pro rata basis according to foreign sales or gross profit.[1]

---

1 Prior to 2003, dividends from *each* 10/50 corporation were treated as a separate income basket, so that losses in one foreign country could not be used to offset gains in another country. In 2003 and beyond, Subpart F dividends are placed in baskets by "looking through" to the character of the underlying income. (See the discussion of income baskets.)

Market Update

Explicit and Implicit Taxes in Puerto Rico

The Commonwealth of Puerto Rico is an example of a location where low taxes have been successfully used as a competitive tool for attracting new businesses. Under the "possessions corporation" provisions of Section 936 of the U.S. Internal Revenue Code, 90 percent of qualified manufacturing income earned in Puerto Rico is exempt from U.S. taxation for the first five years of operations, and 75 percent is exempt for the next five years. Additional tax relief is available for up to 35 years if operations are located in remote regions away from the capital of San Juan. To qualify for exemption from U.S. income taxes, 80 percent of the employees must be Puerto Rican and be employed at least 20 hours per week. A withholding tax of 10 percent discourages U.S. companies from immediately repatriating earnings. The withholding tax falls by 1 percent per year to zero after 10 years if earnings are reinvested in Puerto Rico. These benefits are scheduled to expire after 2005.

These subsidies are an attempt by the U.S. Congress to make investment in Puerto Rico more attractive to U.S. businesses. Tax subsidies were deemed necessary to overcome a history of poor development and a shortage of skilled workers in Puerto Rico and other U.S. possessions. Poor physical infrastructures, undeveloped banking facilities, and a language difference from the mainland (Spanish rather than English) also deterred investment. Tax subsidies have made an important contribution to the Puerto Rican economy. Blessed with some of the best ports in the Caribbean, Puerto Rico is now home to many high-margin manufacturing industries including pharmaceuticals, electronics, and petrochemicals.

Tax subsidies have also spawned a variety of implicit taxes. Demand for local labor has resulted in higher wages than would prevail without the subsidies. Local real estate prices are inflated relative to what they would be without the tax incentives. High operating costs are a form of implicit tax on operations in Puerto Rico. The withholding tax on earnings in Puerto Rico has also contributed to relatively low before-tax returns on Puerto Rican assets.

- *Controlled foreign corporation (CFC) income.* If a U.S. parent owns more than 50 percent of a foreign corporation in terms of market value or voting power, the foreign company is called a **controlled foreign corporation (CFC)**. Income from a CFC is taxed when funds are repatriated to the U.S. parent in the form of dividends, interest, royalties, or management fees.

- *Income from foreign branches.* Foreign branches are treated as a part of the parent, rather than as a separate legal entity in the foreign country. Income earned from a foreign branch is taxed in the United States as it is earned.

The rest of this section describes U.S. taxation of foreign-source income.

Foreign Tax Credits and FTC Limitations

FTCs avoid double taxation of foreign-source income.

Foreign Tax Credits for a Single Foreign Subsidiary. On foreign-source income from a CFC, the United States allows a **foreign tax credit (FTC)** against domestic U.S. income taxes up to the amount of foreign taxes paid on foreign-source income. The amount of the foreign tax credit applied to the U.S. parent's taxable income depends on the amount and form of taxes paid to the foreign government. Foreign taxes used in the computation of the foreign tax credit include foreign income taxes, as well as foreign withholding taxes on dividend distributions to the parent.

Consider the foreign subsidiaries of three different MNCs shown in Table 17.2. The subsidiaries are located in Canada, Israel, and Italy. Suppose that each is the only foreign subsidiary of its U.S. parent, so that we do not have to bother with limitations on foreign-source income pooled across several foreign subsidiaries. (The overall FTC limitation is the topic of the next section.) After translating foreign-source incomes into dollars, each subsidiary has $1,000 of taxable income (line d). Corporate income tax rates are 26 percent in Canada, 36 percent in Israel, and 40 percent in Italy. The highest corporate income tax rate in the U.S. is 35 percent. Withholding taxes on dividend distributions to the U.S. parent of each foreign subsidiary are 5 percent in each foreign country.[2]

The parents' foreign and domestic income tax liabilities shown in the top portion of Table 17.2 assume that all after-tax earnings are repatriated from each subsidiary. The foreign-source income of each controlled foreign corporation is taxed as it is earned in the foreign country (line e). An additional tax on the dividend distribution to the U.S. parent is withheld by each foreign country (line h). The declared dividend net of the dividend withholding tax is available to the U.S. parent (line j). Total foreign tax (line i) is the sum of the foreign income tax (line e) and the foreign dividend withholding tax (line h).

With a 100 percent dividend distribution, 100 percent of foreign-source income is taxed as it is received in the United States (line k). The tentative U.S. income tax on each subsidiary is then $350 (35 percent of $1,000 on line l). This is the amount of tax that would have been due had the income been earned in the United States. With a 100 percent dividend distribution, each subsidiary provides a tax credit equal to total foreign taxes paid (line m). If the tentative U.S. tax is larger than the foreign tax credit, as is the case for the subsidiary in Canada, then the U.S. parent must pay the difference between the tentative U.S. tax and the foreign tax credit (line n). If the foreign tax credit is larger than the tentative U.S. tax, as is the case for the subsidiaries in Israel and Italy, then no additional taxes are due in the United States. If these subsidiaries are the sole foreign operations of their respective parents, then the total foreign and domestic taxes of these three foreign subsidiaries is $1,172.

Multiple Foreign Subsidiaries and the Overall FTC Limitation. The previous example assumed that these were the sole foreign operations of their respective U.S. parent.

> The overall FTC limitation applies to consolidated income.

In this setting, the FTC limitation is simple to apply. The foreign tax credit in any year is the minimum of foreign taxes paid and the U.S. tax that would have been paid if the income was earned in the United States. The net effect is that the U.S. parent pays current-year taxes at the higher of the two rates.

MNCs owning more than one foreign subsidiary face an overall FTC limitation. The total FTC on earnings from active foreign businesses is limited to the amount of U.S. tax attributable to foreign-source income. Total foreign income is pooled or consolidated across all foreign subsidiaries, so that losses in some countries are offset by gains in other countries. When a MNC's domestic income has already placed it in the highest U.S. tax bracket (35 percent), the **overall FTC limitation** is calculated as follows:

Overall FTC limitation = (Total foreign–source income) x (U.S. tax rate)   (17.2)

Total foreign-source income from the three foreign subsidiaries in Table 17.2 is $3,000. At the 35 percent U.S. tax rate, the overall FTC limitation is ($3,000)(0.35) = $1,050

---

2 Withholding taxes for countries with U.S. tax treaties range from 5 to 15 percent.

TABLE 17.2
Repatriation of Active Foreign-Source Income

Tax statements as single foreign subsidiaries		Canada	Israel	Italy
a	Dividend payout ratio	100%	100%	100%
b	Foreign dividend withholding tax rate	5%	5%	5%
c	Foreign tax rate	26%	36%	40%
d	Foreign income before tax	1,000	1,000	1,000
e	less Foreign income tax (d*c)	260	360	400
f	After-tax foreign earnings (d–e)	740	640	600
g	Declared as dividends (f*a)	740	640	600
h	Foreign dividend withholding tax (g*b)	37	32	30
i	Total foreign tax (e+h)	297	392	430
j	Dividend to U.S. parent (d–i)	703	608	570
k	Gross foreign income before tax (d)	1,000	1,000	1,000
l	Tentative U.S. income tax (k*35%)	350	350	350
m	less Foreign tax credit (i)	297	392	430
n	Net U.S. taxes payable [max(l–m, 0)]	53	0	0
o	Total taxes paid (i+n)	350	392	430
p	Net amount to U.S. parent (k–o)	650	608	570
q	Total taxes as separate subsidiaries Σ(o)		1,172	

Consolidated tax statement as subsidiaries of a single U.S. parent

r	Overall FTC limitation (Σk*35%)	1,050
s	Total FTCs on a consolidated basis (Σi)	1,119
t	Additional U.S. taxes due [max(0, r–s)]	0
u	Excess tax credits [max(0, s–r)]	69
	(carried back 2 years or forward 5 years)	

Note: Foreign currency amounts are in U.S. dollar equivalents. Calculations do not include local taxes.

(line r). The $1,119 sum of the foreign tax credits is greater than the tentative U.S. tax of $1,050, so a U.S. MNC owning these three foreign subsidiaries has excess foreign tax credits of $1,119 – $1,050 = $69 (line u). Excess foreign tax credits can be carried back two years or forward five years in the United States.

Other Limitations on Foreign Tax Credits

Income Baskets. The Tax Reform Act (TRA) of 1986 categorized taxable income into a variety of income baskets. The most important income baskets include the following:

> Income baskets limit the value of foreign tax credits to U.S. MNCs.

- *Active income.* Active income is income earned from participation in an active business. This category includes (1) dividends received from active subsidiaries, (2) management fees received from active subsidiaries, (3) interest received from more-than-50-percent-owned subsidiaries, and (4) income from active foreign branches.

- *Passive income.* Passive income is income, such as investment income, that does not come from an active business. This category includes (1) dividends received from less-than-10-percent-owned companies, (2) interest from unrelated parties or less-than-50-percent-owned subsidiaries, (3) rents and royalties not derived from an active business, (4) income from commodity or currency transactions, (5) dividends, interest, rents, royalties, and Subpart F income (discussed in the following paragraphs) to the extent attributable to the passive income of controlled foreign corporations, (6) passive income from the sale of property, and (7) foreign personal holding company income.

- *Financial service income.* Financial service income is derived from financial services, such as banking, insurance, leasing, and financial service management fees. Interest rate, currency, and commodity swap incomes of financial institutions are allocated to this basket. Financial service income is taxed as it is earned.

Additional classifications apply to a wide variety of other forms of income.

Losses in one income basket cannot be used to offset gains in another income basket. For example, passive gains on currency transactions cannot be used to offset losses from an active foreign investment, such as a foreign branch. Because losses in one category could no longer be pooled with gains from another category, the 1986 TRA greatly reduced the value of foreign tax credits to MNCs based in the United States.

Subpart F Income. Taxing foreign-source income only when it is repatriated to the parent corporation allows MNCs to shift sales to foreign subsidiaries and avoid current taxation. To reduce tax-avoidance abuses, Subpart F of the 1962 Revenue Act

> Subpart F income is taxed as it is earned on a pro rata basis.

modified the rule that foreign-source income is taxed only as it is repatriated to the parent. According to Subpart F, shareholders owning more than 10 percent and up to 50 percent of a foreign corporation must include a pro rata share of the Subpart F income of the foreign corporation in their U.S. gross income. This makes Subpart F income taxable when it is earned, whether or not it is remitted to the parent. The most important category of Subpart F income is **foreign base company income**, which includes the following:

- *Foreign base company service income.* Active service income is derived from transactions between related parties when the services are both produced and sold outside the United States. An example is information services sold from a Canadian subsidiary to a Mexican subsidiary of General Motors.

- *Foreign base company sales income.* This is active income derived from transactions between related parties when the goods are both produced and sold outside the United States. An example is sales of auto parts from a Mexican subsidiary of General Motors to an assembly plant owned by a Canadian subsidiary of GM.

- *Foreign holding company income.* This is passive income from dividends, interest, management fees, royalties, rents, net foreign currency and commodity gains, and income from the sale of non–income-producing property. These sources of income do not arise from an active business.

Subpart F includes a number of less common sources of income: (1) income from the insurance of U.S. risks, such as health, life, property, or casualty insurance premiums; (2) any increase in earnings from foreign-source investments in U.S. property; (3) income that is related to international boycotts; and (4) income from illegal foreign bribes.

Once income is identified as belonging to a Subpart F category, gross income net of expenses is "deemed paid" to the parent firm and included in the parent's taxable income, whether or not it is actually repatriated to the parent. Because of the Subpart F rules, active income from related-party transactions that take place outside the United States and all passive foreign-source income are taxed in the U.S. as it is earned.

The Subpart F rules contain several additional provisions. The most important of these is the so-called "5-70 rule":

Market Update

La Mordida—"The Little Bite"

One of the income baskets created under Subpart F of the 1962 Revenue Act is a basket for illegal bribes. Bribery is not commonly practiced in the United States and is illegal in any case, so this income basket seems strange from a U.S. perspective. In many other countries, it is quite common for government bureaucrats and the managers of private businesses to use bribes as they conduct their daily business.

Suppose that you are a sales representative for International Business Machines in the process of negotiating a contract to supply personal computers to the Argentinean government. Competitors from Taiwan are offering to pay the local official in charge of computer acquisitions a modest sum in an effort to secure the contract. If you stick to your (American) principles and refuse to pay *la mordida* (the little bite), there is a good chance that you will lose the contract. On the other hand, you are fairly sure that you can secure the contract if you offer a bribe. What should you do?

A 1999 OECD convention on bribery, signed by 35 countries, states that "enterprises should not, directly or indirectly, offer, promise, give, or demand a bribe or other undue advantage to obtain or retain business." Although this sounds righteous, very few countries have passed antibribery legislation. In the United States, the 1977 Foreign Corrupt Practices Act outlaws bribery as a way to promote the business interests of U.S. corporations or their foreign affiliates. This act requires that U.S. MNCs compete with local firms in foreign markets according to U.S. rules. This can put U.S. firms at a disadvantage in countries where bribery is commonplace.

http://www.oecd.org

Despite good intentions, enforcement of the U.S. Foreign Corrupt Practices Act has been lax. Lockheed Corporation holds the dubious distinction of having paid the largest fine for violating the Foreign Corrupt Practices Act. In 1995, Lockheed admitted that it bribed an Egyptian official to arrange the sale of three aircraft in 1988 and was fined $24.8 million. Very few other fines have been imposed, and most of these have been under $1 million. Further, it is difficult to tell the difference between a bribe and a "facilitation payment" to a local official to expedite a contract. In 2001, British Petroleum testified to the British parliament that they make facilitation payments but would "never offer, solicit or accept a bribe in any form." This is a very slippery slope.

- If Subpart F income is less than the minimum of $1 million or 5 percent of the gross income of the parent firm, then foreign base company income is set to zero.
- If Subpart F income is more than 70 percent of the parent firm's total gross income, the entire gross income of the foreign subsidiary is treated as foreign base company income. This income is then subject to several additional limitations.

Subpart F makes it much more difficult for MNCs to avoid taxes by using tax havens or transfer pricing schemes discussed in section 17.5. Along with the separate income baskets created by the 1986 Tax Reform Act, these changes greatly reduced the ability of U.S. MNCs to shelter foreign-source income from U.S. taxes.

Allocation of Income and Expenses. Another limitation on the usefulness of foreign tax credits comes in the form of **allocation-of-income rules**. When not all profits are repatriated to the parent, the

> Allocation-of-income rules limit FTCs' usefulness.

U.S. tax code applies the allocation-of-income rules to determine what portion of earnings are taxable and how interest, R&D, and other expenses are to be allocated between foreign-source and domestic-source income. The general rule is that income and expenses should be allocated to the tax jurisdiction in which they are earned. These rules are important because of the different tax rates that can apply to foreign and domestic income.

The 1986 TRA allocates interest expense according to the proportion of foreign and domestic assets on the MNC's consolidated financial statements. Thus, regardless of whether the parent or a foreign subsidiary issues debt, the proportion of interest that is allocated to foreign and domestic income depends on the firm's proportion of foreign and domestic assets and not on which entity actually issued the debt.

According to current tax law, 50 percent of R&D expenses are allocated to domestic-source income, with the remainder allocated to foreign- and domestic-source income according to the proportion of either sales or gross income from foreign and domestic sources. Expenses that do not directly arise from an income-related activity (such as general and administrative expenses of the home office) are allocated according to the proportion of either sales or gross income from foreign and domestic sources.

These allocation-of-income rules are important because the size of the MNC's FTC limitation depends on how income and expenses are allocated. Tax shields can be lost altogether if foreign taxing authorities do not follow the IRS's guidelines. For example, allocating home office expenses to a foreign subsidiary reduces the FTC limitation and increases the U.S. tax liability. If the foreign taxing authority does not recognize these as tax-deductible expenses, the FTC limitation is reduced, even though taxes in the foreign country are not reduced. The portion of home office expense that is allocated to the foreign country is simply lost. Along with income baskets and the Subpart F rules, the allocation-of-income rules further limit the usefulness of foreign tax credits.

17.4 • Taxes and Organizational Form

Tax systems influence the choice of organizational form for foreign affiliates, because most nations tax branches and subsidiaries differently. Table 17.3 summarizes the differences between these two organizational forms.

Most U.S.-based MNCs use CFCs for their foreign operations.

Most U.S.-based MNCs conduct their foreign operations through controlled foreign corporations (CFCs). These are foreign corporations owned more than 50 percent either in terms of market value or voting power. CFCs are incorporated in the host country and are governed by the laws and tax rules of the host country. CFC income is not taxed by the IRS until it is repatriated to the parent in the form of dividends, interest, royalties, or management fees. Foreign governments usually impose a withholding tax on dividend distributions to the U.S. parent as compensation for lost tax revenues from forgone personal income taxes in the host country.

Some foreign business is conducted by U.S. MNCs through foreign branches. Foreign branch income is fully taxable in the United States as it is earned. The immediate taxability of foreign branch income is often the overriding tax consideration that leads MNCs to organize foreign operations as incorporated subsidiaries rather than branches, particularly for operations located in low-tax countries. Operating as a foreign branch exposes foreign-source income to the higher domestic tax rates immediately. In contrast, foreign subsidiaries can reinvest abroad without having to pay the higher domestic tax rates until funds are repatriated to the parent.

TABLE 17.3
The Organizational Form of Foreign Operations

	Controlled foreign corporation	**Foreign branch**
Legal	Separate legal entity in the host country	Legally a part of the parent
Tax	U.S. taxes paid as income is repatriated to the parent	U.S. taxes paid as income is earned
Disclosure	Disclosure is limited to local activities in the host country	Disclosure might be required on worldwide operations
Liability	Liability generally limited to assets in the host country	Liability extends to the parent

Foreign branches do have some tax advantages over foreign subsidiaries. Foreign branch income is taxed as it is earned. This creates a tax advantage for the foreign branch organizational form for start-up operations that are expected to lose money. Losses from foreign branch operations are immediately deductible against domestic income, so there is a tax incentive to establish start-up operations that are expected to suffer losses as foreign branches. The foreign branch can be incorporated once operations become profitable, although previously deducted losses must be recaptured as income. Also, there are no withholding taxes on foreign branch income because it is not a dividend distribution. Finally, transfers of property to foreign branches are not a sale to a separate legal entity and, hence, are usually not taxable.

There are several other reasons for incorporating in a host country. First, incorporation limits the liability of the parent company on its foreign operations. The MNC's exposure to the activities of each foreign subsidiary is limited to the assets of that subsidiary. This limit on liability is not absolute, as Union Carbide discovered when its subsidiary in India suffered a major ecological and human disaster at a chemical plant in Bhopal, India. If it can be shown that the parent company had effective control of the subsidiary despite the legal separation of the two, then attorneys can "pierce the corporate veil" and claim that the parent is culpable for the activities of the foreign subsidiary. There is still the difficult issue of which country has jurisdiction over disputes.

Disclosure requirements imposed by a host country also favor incorporating in the host country rather than operating as a foreign branch. Some countries require that firms operating within their borders disclose information on their worldwide operations. The worldwide operations of a foreign subsidiary are limited to those of the subsidiary, but the worldwide operations of a foreign branch include those of the parent. MNCs use incorporated foreign subsidiaries when they would be hurt by publicly disclosing sensitive information on their worldwide operations.

Tax considerations also affect the attractiveness of the international joint venture as an organizational form. The 1986 TRA required that Subpart F dividends received from *each* foreign corporation be treated as a separate income basket. Consequently, excess FTCs from Subpart F income in high-tax countries could not be applied to income from low-tax countries. Desai and Hines found that this greatly reduced the attractiveness of international joint ventures, especially with partners in low-tax countries. Indeed, U.S. participation in international joint ventures fell after 1986, particularly in low-tax countries.[3]

3 Desai and Hines, "Basket Cases: Tax Incentives and International Joint Venture Participation by American Multinational Firms," *Journal of Public Economics* (1999).

17.5 • TRANSFER PRICING AND TAX PLANNING

Transfer prices are prices set on intracompany transfers; that is, on sales from one unit of a company to another. A 2001 Ernst & Young survey of MNCs in 22 countries finds that transfer pricing is the most important tax-related issue facing the MNC.[4] Transfer prices are important both for tax planning and business management purposes, because they allocate taxable income, tax liabilities, and operating profit across business units.

Most national tax codes require that transfer prices be set as **arm's-length prices** that would be negotiated between independent parties. Both Section 486 of the U.S. Internal Revenue Code and Article 9 of the OECD Model Tax Convention call for arms-length pricing. It can be difficult to set defensible transfer prices on assets without observable market prices. The Ernst & Young survey finds the most common method is **cost plus** based on cost plus a profit margin. The second most common method is **comparable uncontrolled price** based on independent market transactions. These methods allow the MNC to defend its transfer prices to domestic and foreign tax authorities.

> Tax codes call for arms-length transfer pricing.

Transfer price management is most effective when intracompany transfers involve

- Business units in more than one tax jurisdiction
- Products with high gross operating margins
- Intermediate or final products for which there are no market prices

Firms with intangible assets such as intellectual property rights (trademarks, trade secrets, copyrights, or patents) are prime candidates for transfer price planning. Products and services based on intangible assets often have high gross margins and no observable market prices. Examples include high-tech electronics and prescription drugs. With wide discretion in setting transfer prices, the MNC can shift expenses toward countries with high tax rates to minimize taxes and maximize firm value.

An Example

Consider the example in Table 17.4. ConAgra, Inc. is a diversified, U.S.-based MNC with operations in Argentina and Hungary. The Argentinean subsidiary of ConAgra exports beef to the ConAgra subsidiary in Hungary. The 18 percent corporate income tax rate in Hungary is less than the 35 percent rate in Argentina. How can transfer prices affect ConAgra's worldwide taxes?

Suppose comparable beef sells in Hungary for $8,000. If ConAgra sets this as the transfer price, it recognizes Argentinean revenues as well as Hungarian expenses of $8,000. The good news is that the $8,000 in Argentinean revenues greatly exceeds the $4,000 production cost. The bad news is that this income in taxed at the relatively high 35 percent Argentinean rate. Relatively little income is exposed to the 18 percent Hungarian tax rate. Table 17.4 shows that worldwide income is effectively taxed at 31.6 percent under this transfer price.

The key to understanding the impact of transfer pricing on worldwide tax liability is to recognize that shifting taxable income toward low-tax jurisdictions reduces worldwide taxes. ConAgra can reduce the transfer price to $5,000 by following the "cost plus" method in the right panel of Table 17.4. This shifts taxable income from Argentina to Hungary, where it is taxed at the lower rate. Under this transfer price, ConAgra's effective tax rate on worldwide operations falls from 31.6 percent to 21.4 percent.

---

4 Ernst & Young, "Transfer Pricing 2001 Global Survey," available from http://www.ey.com.

TABLE 17.4
Transfer Pricing and Tax Planning

	Market-based transfer price			Cost-plus transfer price		
	Argentina	Hungary	Consolidated	Argentina	Hungary	Consolidated
Corporate tax rate	35%	18%		35%	18%	
Revenue	$8,000	$10,000	$10,000	$5,000	$10,000	$10,000
Cost of goods sold	3,000	8,000	3,000	3,000	5,000	3,000
Other expenses	1,000	1,000	2,000	1,000	1,000	2,000
Taxable income	4,000	1,000	5,000	1,000	4,000	5,000
Taxes	1,400	180	1,580	350	720	1,070
Net income	2,600	820	3,420	650	3,280	3,930
Effective tax rate (tax / taxable income)			31.6%			21.4%

Transfer Price Planning

The potential for transfer price abuses by MNCs is high, so tax authorities monitor transfer price policies. Foreign firms in particular are likely to have their transfer prices challenged by domestic tax authorities. The Ernst & Young survey reported that nearly two-thirds of respondents in 22 countries reported an audit related to transfer prices somewhere in the organization. If a tax authority disagrees with a transfer price, it can unilaterally reassess a firm's taxes liability. Appeals of transfer pricing decisions can take years to resolve, and more than one company has gone through Chapter 11 reorganization to avoid the extra tax bite.

> Intangible assets usually have no market prices.

For example, Storage Technology produced disk storage devices in Puerto Rico during the late 1970s to take advantage of Puerto Rico's "possessions corporation" tax status. Most of the company's revenues but none of its R&D expenses were allocated to the Puerto Rican subsidiary. The resulting earnings were exempt from U.S. income tax. The IRS challenged Storage Technology's transfer prices and allocations of R&D expenses. Storage Technology declared bankruptcy in 1983 largely to avoid the back taxes due on earnings from its Puerto Rican manufacturing facilities.

Some transfer price planning is intended to reduce the likelihood of a dispute with tax authorities. Firms follow the IRS's allocation-of-income and allocation-of-expense rules to reduce the likelihood that the IRS will disagree with their transfer prices. Nevertheless, there is room for discretion even within the IRS rules. For example, one input into the allocation rules is a product's manufacturing cost. Firms sometimes choose their investments to increase the manufacturing cost in high-tax jurisdictions and reduce the manufacturing cost in low-tax jurisdictions. This investment-based income shifting toward low-tax jurisdictions can be particularly difficult for the IRS to monitor.[5]

Evidence suggests that large multinationals actively manage their transfer prices to shift income across tax jurisdictions. Collins, Kemsley, and Lang found U.S. MNCs facing foreign tax rates that exceed the U.S. rate exhibit stronger evidence of tax-motivated income shifting than other U.S. multinationals.[6] These authors estimated

---

5 Smith, "Ex Ante and Ex Post Discretion over Arm's Length Transfer Prices," *Accounting Review* (2002).

6 Collins, Kemsley, and Lang, "Cross-Jurisdictional Income Shifting and Earnings Valuation," *Journal of Accounting Research* (1998).

that U.S. MNCs in their sample shifted income worth about $4 billion per year from high-tax countries to the U.S. during 1984–1992. Evidence of income shifting was found for all sample years and for most industries in their study.

Whether it is to reduce the likelihood of a tax audit or to shift income to reduce taxes, transfer price planning is a necessary pursuit for the multinational corporation.

17.6 • Taxes and the Location of Foreign Operations

MNCs have a tax incentive to shift operations toward countries with low income tax rates. For U.S. MNCs, this is particularly true when the overall FTC limitation is binding. If the limitation is binding, unused foreign tax credits from high-tax countries absorb the additional U.S. taxes due on foreign-source income from countries with low tax rates.

> MNCs have an incentive to shift income toward low-tax countries.

The Location of International Operations

An Example. To illustrate the effect of shifting operations toward low-tax foreign jurisdictions, suppose sales are shifted from the Italian to the Canadian subsidiary in the example of Table 17.2. Then Italian taxable income falls to $0 while Canadian taxable income rises to $2,000. This situation is shown in Table 17.5. The overall FTC limitation is still 35 percent of $3,000, or $1,050. Once Italian sales are shifted to Canada, total foreign tax paid ($986) is $64 less than the FTC limitation of $1,050. This means that $64 in additional tax is due to the U.S. tax authorities. Shifting sales from Italy to Canada reduces the U.S. parent's total tax bill in the current fiscal year by $1,119 – $1,050 = $69. Excess foreign tax credits in the U.S. are correspondingly reduced by $69.

In the base case without shifting sales, total taxes depend on whether the $69 excess tax credit can be applied against foreign taxes paid in other years. If the overall FTC limitation is binding in other years, then the $69 excess tax credit cannot be carried backward or forward and would simply be lost to the corporation. Shifting sales to Canada will then capture a $69 reduction in current year taxes.

The Effect of Implicit Taxes. In this example, Canada is the tax-preferred location because of its low tax rates. However, this is not the whole story. Operations in Canada are likely to face implicit taxes as MNCs from around the world shift their operations toward Canada in pursuit of Canada's tax advantages. This flow of foreign capital will squeeze profit margins in Canada, and before-tax expected returns will fall. For example, wine producers flooding the Canadian market in an attempt to reap profits in this low-tax country will drive wine prices down, and profit margins will deteriorate. Falling profit margins mean lower before-tax expected returns on investment in Canada. Conversely, before-tax profit margins in Italy will rise to compensate for the relatively high Italian tax rates. This process will continue until, in equilibrium, after-tax expected returns are equal across all countries.

Explicit taxes are one of many factors to be considered in global location decisions. Implicit taxes also must be taken into account. Minimizing explicit taxes cannot be the overriding criterion in MNC site selection because of the many and subtle forms of implicit taxes faced by the MNC. When governments offer tax incentives to attract foreign investment, it is usually because they cannot compete for capital without these incentives. These countries often have poorly educated workforces, inadequate physical or legal infrastructures, poor communications systems, or other handicaps that lead to higher operating costs or lower final goods prices. MNCs must assess the after-tax, rather than before-tax, expected returns on investment. To the extent that

TABLE 17.5
Effect of Shifting Sales Toward Low-Tax Countries

Tax statements as single foreign subsidiaries		Shift sales from Italy to Canada		
		Canada	Israel	Italy
a	Dividend payout ratio	100%	100%	100%
b	Foreign dividend withholding tax rate	5%	5%	5%
c	Foreign tax rate	26%	36%	40%
d	Foreign income before tax	2,000	1,000	0
e less	Foreign income tax (d*c)	520	360	0
f	After-tax foreign earnings (d–e)	1,480	640	0
g	Declared as dividends (f*a)	1,480	640	0
h	Foreign dividend withholding tax (g*b)	74	32	0
i	Total foreign tax (e+h)	594	392	0
j	Dividend to U.S. parent (d–i)	1,406	608	0
k	Gross foreign income before tax (d)	2,000	1,000	0
l	Tentative U.S. income tax (k*35%)	700	350	0
m less	Foreign tax credit (i)	594	392	0
n	Net U.S. taxes payable [max(l–m, 0)]	106	0	0
o	Total taxes paid (i+n)	700	392	0
p	Net amount to U.S. parent (k–o)	1,300	608	0
q	Total taxes as separate subsidiaries Σ(o)		1,092	

Consolidated tax statement as subsidiaries of a single U.S. parent

r	Overall FTC limitation (Σk*35%)	1,050
s	Total FTCs on a consolidated basis (Σi)	986
t	Additional U.S. taxes due [max(0, r–s)]	64
u	Excess tax credits [max(0, s–r)] (carried back 2 years or forward 5 years)	0

Note: Foreign currency amounts are in U.S. dollar equivalents. Calculations do not include local taxes.

before-tax expected returns are driven down by low explicit tax rates, MNCs may choose to locate elsewhere. The criteria determining site selection for a foreign operation should thus include, but not be dominated by, tax considerations.

The Location of International Debt Issues

> U.S. MNCs tend to issue debt through subsidiaries in high-tax countries.

Tax considerations influence *where* U.S. multinationals issue their debt. Newberry and Dhaliwal examined U.S. multinationals' debt location decisions and found that MNCs tend to issue debt through subsidiaries in countries with higher tax rates than the United States.[7] U.S. multinationals that have reached their FTC limitation have a tax incentive to place debt through foreign subsidiaries in high-tax jurisdictions, because foreign interest deductions in high-tax countries are more valuable than domestic interest deductions. This reduces the foreign tax liability and increases after-tax cash flow to the parent.

Dhaliwal and Newberry also found that U.S. multinationals with domestic tax-loss carryforwards tend to issue bonds through foreign subsidiaries rather than through

---

7 Newberry and Dhaliwal, "Cross-Jurisdictional Income Shifting by U.S. Multinationals: Evidence from International Bond Offerings," *Journal of Accounting Research* (2001).

the U.S. parent. Only 5 percent of their sample of U.S. multinationals reported a domestic tax-loss carryforward. However, 94 percent of the international debt of these firms was issued through a foreign subsidiary. Because they have unused tax-loss carryforwards, these firms are unable to use additional domestic interest deductions to reduce their domestic tax burden. Consequently, these MNCs place debt through foreign subsidiaries in high-tax countries to take advantage of foreign interest deductions. For comparison, firms without tax-loss carryforwards had a 47 percent probability of placing international debt through a foreign subsidiary. Multinationals use their debt location decisions to reduce their worldwide tax liability.

Re-Invoicing Centers

Prior to 1986, U.S. taxes on financial operations did not have to be paid until dividends were remitted to the U.S. parent. U.S.-based MNCs often set up **tax-haven affiliates** in countries with low tax rates, such as Bermuda and the Bahamas, to move capital between their foreign affiliates without triggering the U.S. tax on repatriated dividends. The 1986 TRA categorized offshore banking, shipping, and airline income as financial service income, and required that income taxes be paid as income is earned. This greatly reduced or eliminated the tax benefits of tax-haven affiliates for U.S. MNCs. Tax-haven affiliates are still popular for corporations based in countries with territorial tax systems and in some other countries with worldwide tax systems.

> Many MNCs use offshore re-invoicing centers to redistribute capital.

Nevertheless, MNCs find it convenient to maintain offshore financial affiliates. In many cases, these take the form of **re-invoicing centers** that channel funds to and from the MNC's far-flung operations. Several factors enter the MNC's site location decision for re-invoicing centers. In particular, the location should have

- Low tax rates on foreign-source income and low withholding tax rates on dividends repatriated to the parent firm
- A currency that is not too volatile
- Low political risk, so that the local affiliate and its parent need not be overly concerned about changing local laws and regulations
- Sound physical, legal, and communication infrastructures to support the financial services activities
- A workforce that is sophisticated in the uses of financial products

Re-invoicing centers also often handle cash management and other treasury functions, including currency risk management.

17.7 • TAXES AND CROSS-BORDER MERGERS AND ACQUISITIONS

In equilibrium, after-tax returns should equalize across countries as corporations adapt their investment and financing strategies to take advantage of cross-border tax differentials. Because of higher taxes, equilibrium before-tax returns in high-tax countries should be higher than before-tax returns on similar investments in low-tax countries to compensate for higher taxes. Lower expected and required returns in low-tax countries are a form of implicit tax that cannot be credited against the parent corporation's tax liabilities. The law of one price equalizes after-tax returns so that countries with high (low) explicit taxes have low (high) implicit taxes. In equilibrium, there should be a single worldwide required return on after-tax income of a particular risk.

FIGURE 17.1
Foreign Tax Credits (FTCs) and the Attractiveness of Foreign Investment

Tax status of U.S. buyer	Host country tax rate	
	Low	High
Excess FTCs	neutral	neutral
No excess FTCs	unattractive	attractive

The existence of implicit taxes has an interesting effect on the MNC's incentives to acquire or invest in foreign assets. The effect of implicit and explicit taxes is country-specific in that it depends on how foreign-source income is treated by the MNC's home country. For U.S.-based MNCs, the most important tax variable affecting foreign investment is whether the firm has excess foreign tax credits. Figure 17.1 summarizes the interaction of FTC limitations with the tax rate of the host country.

Table 17.6 illustrates the effect of the FTC limitation on cross-border mergers and acquisitions based on the example in Table 17.2. The bottom panel shows the effect on the worldwide tax liability from an incremental investment in each country.

Overall FTC Limitation Reached (Excess FTCs)

When a U.S. MNC has reached its overall foreign tax credit limitation and has excess FTCs from operations elsewhere in the world, the effective worldwide tax on incremental foreign investment equals the tax rate in the foreign market. Consequently, there is no tax incentive to invest or disinvest internationally. The "excess FTC" panel of Table 17.6 shows the impact of the FTC limitation on the worldwide tax liability of the U.S. parent.

When the MNC has excess FTCs, investments in low-tax countries such as Canada consume some of the FTCs, and the effective tax rate on income from low-tax countries equals the low foreign tax rate. On the other hand, excess FTCs generated on income from high-tax countries such as Italy generally go unused, so the effective tax rate on income from high-tax countries equals the high foreign tax rate. In either case, the effective after-tax rate of return equals the equilibrium after-tax return in the foreign economy. The MNC is in the same competitive position as foreign competitors, and there is no tax incentive to invest or disinvest in the foreign market.

Overall FTC Limitation Not Reached (No Excess FTCs)

An interesting result arises when the MNC has not yet reached its FTC limitation and there are no excess foreign tax credits, as in the bottom panel of Figure 17.6. In this case, foreign-source income from low-tax countries is effectively taxed at the higher U.S. rate. This provides a disincentive toward investing in low-tax countries. Conversely, foreign-source income from high-tax countries generates excess FTCs that can be used to offset the U.S. tax liability on the MNC's existing operations in low-tax countries. This creates an incentive to invest in high-tax countries. The net result is an incentive to invest in high-tax countries and avoid low-tax countries when the MNC has not yet reached its overall FTC limitation.[8]

---

8 Manzon, Sharp, and Travlos find empirical support for this effect in "An Empirical Study of the Consequences of U.S. Tax Rules for International Acquisitions by U.S. Firms," *Journal of Finance* (1994).

TABLE 17.6
Taxes and Cross-Border Mergers and Acquisitions

U.S. parent's consolidated tax statement		Canada	Israel	Italy
Excess FTCs (FTC limitation reached)				
r	Overall FTC limitation (k*35%)	$350	$350	$350
s	Total FTCs on a consolidated basis (i)	297	392	430
t	Additional U.S. taxes due with excess FTCs	0	0	0
v	Total taxes with excess FTCs [s]	297	392	430
No excess FTCs (FTC limitation not yet reached)				
r	Overall FTC limitation (k*35%)	350	350	350
s	Total FTCs on a consolidated basis (i)	297	392	430
t	Additional U.S. taxes due	53	−42	−80
v	Total taxes with excess FTCs [r]	350	350	350

17.8 • SUMMARY

National tax policies play an important role in the business strategies of the multinational corporation. In the absence of other factors, the objective of multinational tax management is to minimize taxes and maximize after-tax earnings. But the MNC does not operate in a vacuum. Although the attractiveness of cross-border investment and financing opportunities depends on national tax policies, it also depends on a host of nontax factors that relegate tax management to an important but ultimately supportive role in the strategies and operations of the MNC. One of these factors is the existence of implicit taxes in the form of lower pretax returns in low-tax countries.

The United States follows a worldwide tax system in which foreign-source income is taxed as it is repatriated to the parent company. Foreign branches are legally a part of the parent company, so income is taxed as it is earned in the foreign country. Income from affiliates that are incorporated in a host country is taxed as it is repatriated to the parent in the form of dividends, interest, management fees, transfer prices, or royalties. The U.S. tax code allows a foreign tax credit (FTC) against domestic U.S. income taxes up to the amount of foreign taxes paid on foreign-source income. Excess FTCs can be carried back two years or forward five years.

Other portions of the U.S. tax code further limit the tax deductibility of business expenses. These limitations include the following:

- Separate income baskets for income from different sources (e.g., active, passive, and financial service income)
- Subpart F rules that specify pro rata taxation based on sales or gross profit for income from foreign corporations that are between 10 percent and 50 percent owned by a U.S. parent
- Allocation-of-income rules that determine how income and expenses are allocated between foreign and U.S. operations

These limitations influence how the overall FTC limitation is applied to different tax jurisdictions, organizational forms, asset classes, and financing instruments.

Although international tax planning is more complicated than domestic tax planning, the opportunities for increasing the value of the firm through tax planning are correspondingly greater. The international business environment provides the MNC with a number of opportunities that are either not available to the domestic firm or available in a greatly diminished form. Because of these opportunities, tax planning is even more important for the MNC than for its domestic counterpart.

KEY TERMS

allocation-of-income rules
arms-length pricing
comparable uncontrolled price
controlled foreign corporation (CFC)
cost plus
explicit tax
foreign base company income
foreign-source income
foreign tax credit (FTC)
implicit tax

national tax policy
overall FTC limitation
re-invoicing centers
Subpart F income
tax-haven affiliates
tax neutrality
territorial tax system
transfer prices
value-added taxes (VAT)
worldwide tax system

CONCEPTUAL QUESTIONS

17.1 What is tax neutrality? Why is it important to the multinational corporation? Is tax neutrality an achievable objective?

17.2 What is the difference between an implicit and an explicit tax? In what way do before-tax required returns react to changes in explicit taxes?

17.3 How are foreign branches and foreign subsidiaries taxed in the United States?

17.4 How has the U.S. Internal Revenue Code limited the ability of the multinational corporation to reduce taxes through multinational tax planning?

17.5 Are taxes the most important consideration in global location decisions? If not, how should these decisions be made?

PROBLEMS

17.1 India imposes a 48 percent tax on corporate income. Thailand's corporate income tax rate is 30 percent. If pretax returns in Thailand are 10 percent, how much must pretax returns be in India for the law of one price to hold?

17.2 Salty Solutions, Inc., has manufacturing facilities in Hong Kong and Japan. Each facility earns the equivalent of $10 million in foreign-source income before tax.
   a. Use Table 17.2 and the tax rates from Table 17.1 to calculate the overall U.S. tax liability (or excess FTC) of Salty Solutions.
   b. Suppose Salty Solutions is able to shift operations so that pretax income is $20 million in Hong Kong and zero in Japan. What is the U.S. tax liability (or excess FTC) under this scenario?
   c. Suppose Salty Solutions is able to shift operations so that pretax income is $20 million in Japan and zero in Hong Kong. What is the U.S. tax liability (or excess FTC) under this scenario?
   d. Is Salty Solutions likely to be able to earn the same pretax return in Hong Kong as in Japan, based on the same effort? Why or why not?

17.3 Quack Concepts, Inc., produces its patented drug Metafour (a duck extract used as an antioxidant) in both Puerto Rico and the United States. The effective marginal tax rate is 35 percent in the United States and 5 percent in Puerto Rico. No additional taxes are due in the United States from Puerto Rican sales. Quack sells Metafour to U.S. consumers for $10 per bottle and has annual sales of 100,000 bottles.

   a. Because the patent is an intangible asset, Quack has wide latitude in the transfer price that it sets on sales from its Puerto Rican manufacturing subsidiary back to the U.S. parent company. Quack's cost of goods sold is $1 per bottle in Puerto Rico. Use Table 17.4 to calculate the effective tax rate on Metafour sales for transfer prices of $1 and $10 per bottle.

   b. Suppose the cost of goods sold is $0.50 per bottle if Metafour is manufactured at Quack's U.S. plant. Where should Quack produce Metafour, based on tax considerations alone? Conduct your analysis using a transfer price of $1 per bottle on sales from Puerto Rico to the U.S. parent.

SUGGESTED READINGS

Articles on how taxes influence the amount and form of foreign operations include

Julie Collins, Deen Kemsley, and Mark Lang, "Cross-Jurisdictional Income Shifting and Earnings Valuation," *Journal of Accounting Research* 36 (Autumn 1998), pp. 209–229.

Mihir Desai and James R. Hines, Jr., "Basket Cases: Tax Incentives and International Joint Venture Participation by American Multinational Firms," *Journal of Public Economics* 71, (March 1999), pp. 379–402.

Gil B. Manzon, Jr., David J. Sharp, and Nickoloas G. Travlos, "An Empirical Study of the Consequences of U.S. Tax Rules for International Acquisitions by U.S. Firms," *Journal of Finance* 49, No. 5 (1994), pp. 1893–1904.

Kaye J. Newberry and Dan S. Dhaliwal, "Cross-Jurisdictional Income Shifting by U.S. Multinationals: Evidence from International Bond Offerings," *Journal of Accounting Research* 39 (December 2001), pp. 643–662.

Michael J. Smith, "Ex Ante and Ex Post Discretion over Arm's Length Transfer Prices," *Accounting Review* 77 (January 2002), pp. 161–184.

Real Options and Cross-Border Investment

chapter 18

Overview

The man with a new idea is a crank until the idea succeeds.

Mark Twain

Chapter 15 introduced the NPV decision rule, "Invest in all positive-NPV projects," and applied this rule to situations encountered in cross-border capital budgeting. In market-based economies, this approach to investment decision making is the overwhelming favorite among companies large and small. Yet companies employing discounted cash flow techniques occasionally make decisions that, at least on the surface, violate the NPV decision rule.

These apparent violations of the NPV rule arise when NPV calculations fail to consider managerial flexibility in responding to changes in an uncertain world. As it is usually applied, NPV is a static calculation that fails to consider the many options that managers have during the life of a project to expand, contract, abandon, accelerate, or delay a project, or develop new products based on knowledge gained from the project. A real options approach to the investment decision accommodates managerial flexibility by viewing the act of investing as the exercise of a **real option**—an option on a real asset.[1]

> A real option is an option on a real asset.

18.1 • TYPES OF OPTIONS

An option conveys the right, not the obligation, to assume a position in the underlying asset at a specific contract (or strike) price at or prior to the time the option expires.

---

[1] Although this chapter illustrates the value of real options, it does so without the use of formal option pricing theory. The appendix to the currency option chapter discusses option pricing models. Interested readers should refer to the suggested readings at the end of this chapter.

Most real options are **American options** that allow exercise any time before the option expires, if it expires at all. This is the case when investment or abandonment of a project could occur at any time.

Simple Options

A **simple option** is an option that has no other options attached. Simple options come in one of two forms—calls or puts. A **call option** is an option to buy an underlying asset at a fixed contractual (exercise or strike) price. Most projects have a deferral call option in which managers can delay the start of the project. The exercise price of the investment option is the initial cost of the project and typically varies over time. Once invested, managers have options to expand or extend the life of the project through additional investment.

A **put option** is an option to sell an underlying asset at a fixed price. An abandonment option can be viewed as a form of put option in which managers can sell or get rid of an existing project for a (perhaps time-varying) price. Similarly, an option to contract can be viewed as a put option in which managers can scale back the project. Although real options are seldom simple in practice, simple options are the starting point for a real options analysis.

Compound Options

A compound option is an option on an option.

Most real options are compound options. A **compound option** is an option on an option. Exercise of a compound option leads to one or more additional options. Decisions to modify a project are compound options because a decision made today affects future opportunities. Because the option to invest and the option to abandon are two sides of the same coin, they are called switching options.[2] A **switching option** is a sequence of alternating call and put options in which one option is exchanged for another upon exercise. A switching option is a special case of a compound option. Many investment decisions can be characterized as switching options, including the invest/abandon, accelerate/delay, expand/contract, suspend/reactivate, and extend/shorten decisions.

Rainbow Options

A **rainbow option** is an option with more than one source of uncertainty. Most real options are of this type, facing uncertainties over future revenues (prices and quantities) and costs, the exercise prices of additional call or put options, interest rates, and even the window of opportunity in which a project has value; that is, the time to expiration. Indeed, most real options are *compound rainbow options* in which managers have flexibility in adapting the firm's marketing, production, and distribution choices to evolving circumstances and new information.

A rainbow option has more than one source of uncertainty.

18.2 • THE THEORY AND PRACTICE OF INVESTMENT

The Conventional Theory of Investment

According to the conventional theory, the value of an investment is determined by discounting expected future cash flows at a risk-adjusted discount rate. The net present value of an investment that has an initial cost CF_0 and lasts T periods can be written as

---

2 See Carr, "The Valuation of Sequential Exchange Opportunities," *Journal of Finance* (1988).

$$NPV = \sum_{t=0}^{T} E[CF_t] / (1+i)^t]$$ (18.1)

According to this approach, a project should be undertaken if and only if the net present value of the project is greater than zero.

Three Puzzles

Financial managers do not always follow the NPV rule, at least not in an obvious way. There are at least three situations in which violations of the NPV rule are likely to occur.

Puzzle #1: The Multinational's Use of Inflated Hurdle Rates. MNCs often impose higher hurdle rates on investments in countries with high political risk despite the fact that country-specific political risk is diversifiable and should not matter to globally diversified investors.

Here is an example of this seemingly irrational managerial behavior. During the 1990s, CMS Energy (NYSE symbol "CMS") had extensive oil and gas exploration and distribution operations and power-generation capacity in North and Latin America, Africa, and Asia. Many of these markets outside North America were expected to experience higher-than-average growth. CMS operations in India, Pakistan, and the Philippines offered the additional attraction of British-based legal systems and dollar-denominated contracts, allowing CMS Energy to operate with a minimum of country risks. Despite the diversifiable nature of many of their country-specific risks, CMS Energy required a higher rate of return on investments in countries with high political risk (such as the Philippines) than in other countries. Management refused to invest in countries with highly unstable environments, such as the People's Republic of China.

Is the use of inflated hurdle rates for investment in some countries and an outright refusal to invest in other countries a violation of the NPV decision rule? Not necessarily. Business practitioners usually have good reasons for the actions they take. Energy production requires large, up-front development costs that cannot be recouped easily should the political situation in a foreign country deteriorate. Many times, investment is not made in apparently positive-NPV projects because those investments are expected to have even higher NPVs if initiated at some later date. During the 1990s, there was a great deal of uncertainty about how the business and investment climate in China would evolve and consequently substantial country risk in China. Even if immediate investment in this uncertain environment yields more than the opportunity cost of capital and a positive expected NPV, investment at some future date might yield even more value to a company like CMS Energy. Exercising a real option today means forgoing investment in the same or similar projects at a future date.

> Investment today must be compared to investment at a later date.

Puzzle #2: The Multinational's Failure to Abandon Unprofitable Investments. Firms often remain in markets even though they are losing money. This frequently happens when real exchange rates move against an exporting firm. For example, Japanese automakers suffered huge losses on their U.S. operations in the mid-1980s as the dollar rose to unprecedented highs against most foreign currencies. The future of U.S. production looked bleak in the face of global overcapacity and an overvalued dollar. Why did Japanese automakers persist in their U.S. operations under these unprofitable circumstances? The hope was that the dollar would fall back to normal

> Abandonment today must be compared to abandonment at a later date.

levels and U.S. operations would return to profitability. The automakers had an option to abandon U.S. production, but once abandoned it would be very difficult for them to reenter this market.

Puzzle #3: The Multinational's Entry into New and Emerging Markets. Firms often make incremental investments into new (especially emerging) markets, even though at any given point in time further investment does not seem warranted according to the "Accept all positive-NPV projects" rule.

Exploratory investments can yield information about future investments.

When a firm enters a foreign market for the first time, the only certainty is that management's initial cash flow forecasts will be wrong. Management often makes incremental investments into foreign markets so that it can assess the viability of the market and determine how to best structure the firm's subsequent investments. In these circumstances, management often states that the investment is being undertaken for "strategic" reasons. Are managers acting irrationally? Are strategic initiatives in violation of the NPV rule? Or, is the conventional application of the NPV rule incomplete? A real option framework brings a new and useful perspective to these issues.

Managerial Flexibility in the Timing and Scale of Investment

Managers behaving in these ways are not acting irrationally. These three puzzles arise because of a failure of naively applied discounted cash flow methods to properly incorporate **managerial flexibility** in the timing and scale of investment.

Real option values reflect managerial flexibility in the timing and scale of investment.

Like financial options, real options give the firm the right but not the obligation to pursue an investment opportunity. Whereas a financial option is based on an underlying financial asset, such as a share of stock or a currency, the value of a real option depends on the (usually uncertain) cash flows generated by the underlying real asset.

In most instances, the risks of cross-border investments exceed those of comparable domestic investments because of the uncertainties of dealing with unfamiliar cultures. This suggests that foreign operations are particularly important to the success or failure of a multinational corporation. Indeed, the share price changes of U.S. multinational corporations are more responsive to changes in their foreign source income than to changes in domestic income.[3]

A real option framework is a useful valuation tool in the presence of uncertainty, as real options gain much of their value from managerial flexibility in moving proactively and reactively in an uncertain world. With the arrival of new information about future investment outcomes, management can make more informed investment choices and modify investment plans to fit the circumstance. This managerial flexibility is difficult to value with traditional discounted cash flow methods. The rest of this chapter shows how the firm's cross-border opportunities can be analyzed in a real options framework.

18.3 • PUZZLE #1: MARKET ENTRY AND THE OPTION TO INVEST

The form and pace of market entry are the biggest concerns of the multinational firm facing uncertain conditions in foreign markets. Market entry is but one of a broader class of investment decisions that can fruitfully be viewed as real options. This section

---

3 Bodnar and Weintrop, "The Valuation of the Foreign Income of U.S. Multinational Firms: A Growth Opportunities Perspective," *Journal of Accounting & Economics* (1997).

presents the decision to invest as a real option and discusses the sources of value in this option.

An Option to Invest in a Natural Resource Project

Crude oil is increasingly being produced from offshore oil wells. Such wells already exist in the North Sea and the Gulf of Mexico. Advances in seismic exploration techniques and drilling and extraction technologies are opening up previously inaccessible regions of the ocean floor. The most promising deep-water prospects are located off the coasts of Angola, Brazil, Malaysia, Mexico, Namibia, the Philippines, the United Kingdom, and the United States.

Governments often lease offshore tracts of land to oil companies for fixed periods of time, such as 10 or 15 years. For our purposes, the lease contract identifies the time to expiration of the oil company's real option. The option to invest expires with the termination of the lease.

Deep-sea oil exploration and extraction is an industry with large sunk costs.[4] For this reason, the value of a given project depends on expectations of oil prices in the years following development. Oil has a very long shelf life when it is stored in the oil field itself. If not for a limited supply of oil reserves and competition for productive capacity in the oil industry, investments in oil wells could be delayed indefinitely.

Uncertainty regarding future prices is called **price uncertainty**. Oil prices are subject to unexpected demand shocks, such as when winter temperatures in the Northern Hemisphere are unusually severe. Oil prices also are subject to unexpected supply shocks as a result of political upheaval. Political events that affected oil prices in the last several decades include the revolution in Iran, the Iran–Iraq War, the Persian Gulf War, and the oligopolistic actions of the Organization of Petroleum Exporting Countries (OPEC).

> Uncertainty about future prices is price uncertainty.

Because of such uncertainties, oil exploration investments are undertaken only when expected returns are substantially higher than required returns. Projects with small positive NPVs relative to the initial sunk costs typically are not undertaken. This is an apparent violation of the conventional "invest in all positive-NPV projects" rule. In fact, the NPV rule still works if (and only if) we include the opportunity cost of investing today and forgoing the option to invest in the future. The following example illustrates the pitfall in applying the "invest in all positive-NPV projects" rule in a naive fashion.

> In the presence of uncertainty, care must be taken in applying the NPV decision rule.

An Example of the Option to Invest

Oil has been found in the deep waters of the Foinaven region west of the Shetland Islands. Suppose British Petroleum (BP) owns a lease to extract crude oil from the region and is considering the construction of a deep-sea oil rig. Construction costs are $I_0 = \$20$ million, and these costs are expected to grow at a constant rate of $g = 10\%$ per year. The risk-free rate of interest is also $i = 10\%$, so the cost of the well is a constant $20 million in present value terms, regardless of when construction begins. Crude oil is priced in dollars throughout the world, and the current price of oil is $P = \$20$ per barrel (bbl). Once a well is set up, BP's variable production costs to extract and refine the crude oil are $V = \$8$ per barrel. For simplicity, assume there are no maintenance or other fixed production costs. The Foinaven well is expected

---

4 Deep sea oil rigs and sunk costs? Sorry about that. Hanging is too good for a man who makes puns; he should be drawn and quoted.

to produce Q = 200,000 barrels per year in perpetuity. All cash flows are assumed to occur at the end of the year. Production can start immediately, in which case the first cash flow will occur at the end of the first year.[5]

OPEC members are currently involved in a heated debate that will determine oil output and prices into the foreseeable future. If OPEC members hold ranks, production will be limited and oil prices will rise to $30/bbl in perpetuity. If the cartel breaks up, production will rise and prices will fall to $10/bbl in perpetuity. This negotiation will be settled within one year. Once the new price is established, it is expected to remain at that level (either $10/bbl or $30/bbl) in perpetuity. BP estimates that an oil price rise and an oil price fall are equally probable.

Suppose there are two investment alternatives in this example: BP can (1) invest today or (2) wait one year and reconsider the investment at that time. If BP invests today, perpetual cash flows begin in one year and the valuation equation is

$$\text{Invest today:} \qquad NPV_0 = \frac{(P-V)Q}{i} - I_0 \qquad (18.2)$$

BP's option to invest expires in one year, and by delaying investment it can reduce uncertainty over future oil prices and make a more informed decision. If BP waits one year before making an investment, the valuation equation as of time t=0 is

$$\text{Wait one year:} \qquad NPV_0 = \left[\frac{(P-V)Q}{i} \Big/ (1+i) \right] - I_0 \qquad (18.3)$$

where the present value of the initial investment is I_0 = $20,000,000 regardless of when investment is made.

To keep matters simple, suppose crude oil prices and production costs are unrelated to changes in the world market portfolio. Hence, the systematic risk of this project is zero and future cash flows should be discounted at the risk-free rate of interest.[6]

The Value of the Option to Invest

Calculation of NPV is least complicated when an investment must be made immediately or lost forever. For such now-or-never projects, there is no chance to wait for additional information, and the value of a project is simply the discounted value of the expected future cash flows net of the initial investment.

Unless a project is a now-or-never proposition, the firm has the option to delay the investment decision so it can obtain more information about future prices, costs,

> Timing is an important part of the option to invest.

and volume. Because of the option to delay investment, projects must compete not only with other projects but also with variations of themselves initiated at each future date. That is, the decision to invest in a project today must be compared with the alternative of investing in the same or similar projects at some future date. Hence, investment in a real asset is equivalent to exercising an investment option. By exercising its option to invest, the firm is forgoing the opportunity to invest in the future. Consequently, a part of the exercise price is the opportunity cost of investing today rather than at

---

5 The assumptions of perpetual cash flows and a constant construction cost in today's dollars are for expositional convenience. Note that the value of a perpetuity that begins in one year and continues forever is equal to the annual cash flow divided by the discount rate (CF/i).

6 Systematic risk has no place in most option pricing models. Instead, a riskless arbitrage position is established with a portfolio that replicates the payoffs of the option. The option position is then valued at the risk-free rate. This topic is discussed in more depth in the chapter on currency options.

some future date. The optimal time to invest is when the value of the forgone future investment becomes less than the value of investing immediately.

The value of a real or financial option can be divided into two distinct parts:

- The **intrinsic value** of the option if exercised today
- The **time value** of the option arising from the fact that the option need not be exercised today

These two components of option value are depicted in Figure 18.1 for British Petroleum's real investment option. The intrinsic and time values of a call option are determined by the five variables listed at the bottom of Figure 18.1. The determinants of the value of BP's investment option are (1) the value of the underlying asset (the oil well), (2) the required investment, (3) the risk-free rate of interest, (4) the time to expiration of the option, and (5) expected future volatility in the value of the oil well.

The Intrinsic Value of the Option to Invest. The intrinsic value of an option depends only on the value of the underlying asset and the exercise price of the option. An **in-the-money option** is an option that would have value if exercised today. The intrinsic value of an in-the-money call option is the value of the underlying asset minus the exercise price. For a real option, the underlying asset is the present value of the proceeds from the project and the exercise price is the cost of the investment.

> The intrinsic value of an option is its value if exercised today.

FIGURE 18.1
BP's Option to Invest

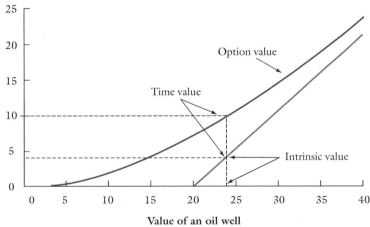

Option value determinant	BP's call option
Value of the underlying asset	$24 million oil well value
Exercise price of the option	$20 million
Risk-free rate of interest	10%
Volatility of the underlying asset	Value of $3.63 million or $40 million with equal probability
Time to expiration of the option	One year

As project value increases, the option to invest falls further in-the-money and the investment becomes more valuable. When the value of the underlying asset is below the exercise price, a call option is **out-of-the-money** and has no value at expiration.

BP's option to invest is an *American call option*, exercisable any time until expiration. The exercise price of BP's investment option is the $20 million initial cost of the project. The expected price level is $20/bbl and variable costs are $8/bbl, so the expected contribution margin is $12/bbl in perpetuity. Expected production is 200,000 barrels per year, so expected cash flows are $2.4 million per year in perpetuity. With an initial investment of $20 million and a 10 percent cost of capital, the value of the oil well if investment is made today is

$$\text{NPV(invest today)} = \left[\frac{(((\$20/\text{bbl}) - (\$8/\text{bbl}))(200{,}000\text{bbl})}{0.10} \right] - \$20{,}000{,}000$$

$$= +\$24{,}000{,}000 - \$20{,}000{,}000$$
$$= +\$4{,}000{,}000 > \$0$$
$$\Rightarrow \text{Invest today (?)}$$

The expected value of the well is $24 million. With a $20 million exercise price, the NPV of the "invest today" alternative is $4 million. Following the conventional "Invest in all positive-NPV projects" decision rule, BP apparently should invest immediately. But, what about the time value of the option to invest?

The Time Value of the Option to Invest. Although tempting, the conclusion of the previous section is incomplete. The "invest today" alternative ignores the firm's **timing option**—the ability of the firm to postpone investment and to reconsider investment at a future date. In the BP example, the value of the well depends on the future price of oil. By delaying the investment decision while OPEC decides on its production quotas, BP can reduce its uncertainty over future oil prices. BP can then make a more informed investment decision based on new information. In particular, BP has an opportunity to avoid the negative outcomes of investment should oil prices fall.

> The timing option reflects managerial flexibility in the timing of investment.

Figure 18.2 shows a decision tree that can help formulate responses to uncertain future events. Our objective is to maximize the value of the oil well by following the optimal decision path. Just as in solving a maze, it is convenient to start at the end and work backward toward the beginning.

The critical uncertainty facing BP is the future price of oil. Let the net present value of investment given an oil price of P_{oil} be written as $\text{NPV}|P_{oil}$. If OPEC can keep production down and prices up, then the price will be $30. If BP postpones the investment decision for one year and oil prices rise to $30, then the expected NPV is

$$\text{NPV} \mid (P_{oil} = \$30) = \left[\frac{(((\$30/\text{bbl}) - (\$8/\text{bbl}))(200{,}000\text{bbl})}{0.10} \Big/ (1.10) \right] - \$20{,}000{,}000$$

$$= \left[\frac{(\$4{,}400{,}000)}{0.10} \Big/ (1.10) \right] - \$20{,}000{,}000$$

$$= \$20{,}000{,}000 > \$0$$
$$\Rightarrow \text{Invest in one period if } P_{oil} = \$30$$

If BP postpones the decision for one year and oil prices fall to $10/bbl, then

FIGURE 18.2
Uncertainty and the Option to Invest

Initial investment	I_0 =	$20,000,000
Price of oil	P_0 =	$20/bbl
	P_1 =	$30 or $10 with equal probability
Variable production cost	$8/bbl	
Expected production	200,000 bbl/year	
Discount rate	i =	10%

Invest today

$$NPV_0 = \left[\frac{(\$20/bbl - \$8/bbl)(200{,}000\ bbls)}{0.10}\right] - \$20{,}000{,}000 \quad \Rightarrow NPV(\text{invest today}) = +\$4{,}000{,}000$$

Invest at P_{oil} = $30

$$NPV_0 = \left[\frac{(\$30/bbl - \$8/bbl)(200{,}000\ bbls)}{0.10}\right]/1.10 - \$20{,}000{,}000 \quad \Rightarrow NPV \mid P_{oil} = \$30 = +\$20{,}000{,}000$$

Invest in one year

Invest at P_{oil} = $10

$$NPV_0 = \left[\frac{(\$10/bbl - \$8/bbl)(200{,}000\ bbls)}{0.10}\right]/1.10 - \$20{,}000{,}000 \Rightarrow NPV \mid P_{oil} = \$10 = -\$16{,}363{,}636$$

$$\Rightarrow NPV\ (\text{wait one year}) = [\text{Prob}(P_{oil} = \$10)]\ (NPV \mid P_{oil} = \$10) + [\text{Prob}(P_{oil} = \$30)](NPV \mid P_{oil} = \$30)$$
$$= (1/2)(\$0) + (1/2)(\$20{,}000{,}000) = +\$10{,}000{,}000$$

Option value	=	Intrinsic value	+	Time value
NPV(wait one year)	=	NPV(invest today)	+	Additional value from waiting one year
$10,000,000	=	$4,000,000	+	$6,000,000

$$NPV \mid (P_{oil} = \$10) = \left[\frac{((\$10/bbl) - (\$8/bbl))(200{,}000\ bbl)}{0.10}\Big/(1.10)\right] - \$20{,}000{,}000$$

$$= \left[\frac{(\$400{,}000)}{0.10}\Big/(1.10)\right] - \$20{,}000{,}000$$

$$= -\$16{,}363{,}636 < \$0$$

$$\Rightarrow \text{Do not invest in one period if } P_{oil} = \$10$$

$$\Rightarrow NPV \mid (P_{oil} = \$10) = \$0$$

By postponing the investment, BP can choose to not invest if oil prices fall to $10/bbl. If BP does not invest, then the net present value of the project is $0.

To determine whether it is worthwhile to wait one year before making its investment decision, BP must consider the probabilities of P_{oil} = $30 and P_{oil} = $10. Prices rise or fall with equal probability, so $\text{Prob}(P_{oil}=\$10) = \text{Prob}(P_{oil}=\$30) = 1/2$. The expected net present value of delaying the decision for one period is an equally weighted average of $NPV \mid (P_{oil} = \$30)$ and $NPV \mid (P_{oil} = \$10)$.

NPV(wait one year)

$$= [\text{Prob}(P_{oil} = \$10)] \,(\text{NPV} \,|\, P_{oil} = \$10) + [\text{Prob}(P_{oil} = \$30)](\text{NPV} \,|\, P_{oil} = \$30)$$
$$= (\tfrac{1}{2})(\$0) + (\tfrac{1}{2})(\$20{,}000{,}000)$$
$$= +\$10{,}000{,}000 > \text{NPV(invest today)} = \$4{,}000{,}000 > \$0$$
$$\Rightarrow \text{Wait one period before deciding to invest}$$

This is $6 million greater than the value of the option to invest today, so BP should wait until OPEC announces its production quotas before making its investment decision. The decision to wait is summarized at the bottom of Figure 18.2.

Consider the components of the value of the option to invest.

Option Value	= Intrinsic Value	+ Time Value	(18.4)
NPV(wait one year)	= NPV(now or never)	+ Opportunity cost of investing today	
$10,000,000	= $4,000,000	+ $6,000,000	

Time value reflects the opportunity cost of investing today.

By investing today, BP forgoes an alternative with an expected value of $10,000,000. The intrinsic value, the "invest today" NPV, does not include the $6 million value of the timing option. The value of this timing option is the opportunity cost of investing today.

Failure to recognize the value of this timing option can result in a firm's investing prematurely and failing to capture the maximum potential value of its real assets. This opportunity cost can be avoided by investing at the most opportune time.

A Resolution of Puzzle #1: Use of Inflated Hurdle Rates

The NPV rule says to accept all positive-NPV projects, which is the same thing as saying, "Accept all projects with expected returns that exceed their required returns." Yet firms in many industries require hurdle rates that are well above their cost of capital before they invest in a new project. At first glance this seems to be at odds with the NPV rule. It is not. The oil well example illustrates why firms require above-market hurdle rates in uncertain environments.

> **The option value of waiting for additional information can lead firms to demand higher hurdle rates in uncertain environments.**

If uncertainty over future oil prices increases, management will demand even higher returns before investing. This is true even if the additional risk is entirely diversifiable and investors' required return does not change. Exercising the investment option means giving up the option of investing at some future date when more information will be known about the likely payoffs on investment. Once exercised, the option to invest cannot be costlessly reversed. This lost option is the opportunity cost of investing today.

18.4 • Uncertainty and the Value of the Option to Invest

The Determinants of Option Value

Reductions in uncertainty allow the firm to avoid making investment decisions that turn out to be wrong. In the BP example, the possibility of a fall in oil prices is behind the incentive to delay investment. British Petroleum can avoid the 50 percent probability of a loss by delaying the investment decision one period. Consider the change in price from \$20/bbl to either \$10/bbl or \$30/bbl. For the "invest now or never" alternative, an increase in oil price from \$20/bbl to \$30/bbl results in an increase in value relative to the expectation. Similarly, a \$10/bbl decrease in price to \$10/bbl results in an offsetting loss in value. Each of these is equally likely to occur, so BP is equally exposed to an increase and to a decrease in oil price if it invests today. If the option to invest is exercised today, BP cannot benefit from new information. The "wait one year" strategy allows BP to forgo investment when oil prices fall. For this reason, the incentive to delay investment is driven entirely by bad news—the size and probability of unprofitable outcomes.

The value of the option to delay investment can be viewed as the value of managerial flexibility. By delaying the investment decision, the firm gains flexibility. In the BP example, if oil prices turn out to be lower than expected, the firm can refuse to invest and avoid the loss in value associated with low oil prices. In option terminology, the option is out-of-the-money, and the firm should leave its option unexercised. If oil prices rise, the firm can exercise its option and capture the NPV arising from high oil prices.

> Time value also reflects managerial flexibility.

The five determinants of the value of BP's investment option are

- The value of the underlying asset (the oil well)
- The required investment
- The risk-free rate of interest
- The time to expiration of the option
- Expected future volatility in the value of the oil well

as shown at the bottom of Figure 18.1.[7] In the BP example, uncertainty affects the time value of the option through oil price volatility and the time to expiration.

In general terms, the time to expiration of the option to invest in a natural resource, such as an oil well, should correspond to the period of the lease on the natural resource. If the option to invest can be extended indefinitely into the future, then the firm has even more flexibility and the investment is likely to have even more time value. Conversely, time to expiration is zero in a now-or-never project. Increases in the ability to delay an investment decision thus increase time value as well as the value of the option to invest, although at a diminishing rate. Changes in option value from changes in time to expiration diminish as the time to expiration is lengthened, so the biggest gains from increases in time to expiration occur in the earliest periods of the investment horizon.

The most important determinant of time value is the degree of uncertainty in the future value of the real asset itself. Uncertainty is the major reason why firms are reluctant to jump wholeheartedly into economies such as Russia and the People's Republic of China. Holding other determinants constant, the value of the option to invest increases with an increase in the volatility of the underlying asset or, equivalently, with an increase in price or input cost uncertainty.

> Time value increases with volatility or time to expiration.

Exogenous Uncertainty

Managers are faced with two types of uncertainty. When price or input cost uncertainty is outside managers' control, it is called **exogenous uncertainty**. Here, information is revealed about price or cost as time

> Uncertainty is endogenous when the act of investing reveals information about price or cost.

---

7 Depletion of the oil reserve has been omitted from our analysis. Depletion of a natural resource is treated in the same way that dividends on a dividend-paying stock are treated in the valuation of a stock option.

unfolds, but the firm cannot uncover new information through its investment activities. In the BP example, oil prices were outside BP's control.

Uncertainty is called **endogenous uncertainty** when the act of investing reveals information about price or cost. Endogenous uncertainty can create an incentive to speed up investment in order to gain more information about likely future prices and costs. Endogenous uncertainty can create an incentive to invest in exploratory projects that, when viewed in isolation, appear to be losers. The examples in the remainder of this section deal with exogenous price and input cost uncertainty. We shall return to endogenous uncertainty in section 18.6.

Exogenous Price Uncertainty. Option values increase with an increase in the volatility of the underlying asset. Greater uncertainty over future oil prices results in a higher time value and a greater incentive to postpone investment. In the BP example, if oil price volatility increases, then BP can gain even more value from rises in price and can still avoid investing if prices fall. Suppose the current price is $20/bbl and that oil prices will either rise to $35/bbl or fall to $5/bbl with equal probability.[8] Based on information available at time t=0, the net present value of the "invest today" alternative is as in the original example:

$$\text{NPV(invest today)} = \left[\frac{(($20/\text{bbl}) - ($8/\text{bbl}))(200{,}000\text{bbl})}{0.10} \right] - $20{,}000{,}000 \quad .$$

$$= +$4{,}000{,}000$$
$$\Rightarrow \text{Invest today (?)}$$

If BP waits one year before making its investment decision, NPV depends on the path of oil prices as follows:

$$\text{NPV} \,|\, (P_{oil} = $35) = \left[\frac{(($35/\text{bbl}) - ($8/\text{bbl}))(200{,}000\text{bbl})}{0.10} \Big/ (1.10) \right] - $20{,}000{,}000$$

$$= +$29{,}090{,}909$$
$$\Rightarrow \text{Invest one period later if } P_{oil} = $35$$

$$\text{NPV} \,|\, (P_{oil} = $35) = \left[\frac{(($5/\text{bbl}) - ($8/\text{bbl}))(200{,}000\text{bbl})}{0.10} \Big/ (1.10) \right] - $20{,}000{,}000$$

$$= -$25{,}454{,}545$$
$$\Rightarrow \text{Do not invest one period later if } P_{oil} = $5$$
$$\Rightarrow \text{NPV} \,|\, (P_{oil} = $5) = $0$$

The NPV of the "wait one year" strategy is then
NPV(wait one year)

$$= [\text{Prob}(P_{oil} = $5)](\text{NPV} \,|\, P_{oil} = $5) + [\text{Prob}(P_{oil} = $35)](\text{NPV} \,|\, P_{oil} = $35)$$
$$= (1/2)($0) + (1/2)($29{,}090{,}909)$$
$$= +$14{,}545{,}455 > \text{NPV(invest today)} > $0$$
$$\Rightarrow \text{Wait one period}$$

The option value is the sum of the intrinsic value and the time value.

---

[8] In this example, we'll assume BP must continue to produce oil even though the $5/bbl price of oil is below the $8/bbl cost of producing and refining the oil. Abandonment options will be discussed shortly.

Option Value	= Intrinsic Value	+ Time Value
NPV(wait one year)	= NPV(invest today)	+ Opportunity cost of investing today
$14,545,455	= $4,000,000	+ $10,545,455

An increase in oil price uncertainty makes the timing option even more valuable and the opportunity cost of investment today even more deleterious than in the original example.

Exogenous Input Cost Uncertainty. Suppose there is exogenous input cost uncertainty in BP's investment option. To focus on one variable at a time, suppose oil prices will remain constant at $20/bbl. Do more volatile production costs increase or decrease the time value of the option to invest?

As with uncertainty over output prices, the value of the option to wait increases with increases in uncertainty over future operating costs. Suppose oil sells for $20 per barrel and that oil processing costs will either rise to $V_{oil} = \$12$/bbl or fall to $V_{oil} = \$4$/bbl with equal probability in one year. The net present value of the "now or never" alternative is still

$$\text{NPV(invest today)} = \left[\frac{((\$20/\text{bbl}) - (\$8/\text{bbl}))(200{,}000\text{bbl})}{0.10} \right] - \$20{,}000{,}000$$

$$= +\$4{,}000{,}000$$
$$\Rightarrow \text{Invest today (?)}$$

If BP waits one year, it can resolve its uncertainty over future operating costs.

$$\text{NPV} \,|\, (V_{oil} = \$12) = \left[\frac{((\$20/\text{bbl}) - (\$12/\text{bbl}))(200{,}000\text{bbl})}{0.10} \Big/ (1.10) \right] - \$20{,}000{,}000$$

$$= -\$5{,}454{,}545$$
$$\Rightarrow \text{Do not invest in one period if } V_{oil} = \$12$$
$$\Rightarrow \text{NPV} \,|\, (V_{oil} = \$12) = \$0$$

BP will not invest if variable processing costs rise to $12 per barrel. If processing costs fall to $4 per barrel, on the other hand, the investment looks attractive:

$$\text{NPV} \,|\, (V_{oil} = \$4) = \left[\frac{((\$20/\text{bbl}) - (\$4/\text{bbl}))(200{,}000\text{bbl})}{0.10} \Big/ (1.10) \right] - \$20{,}000{,}000$$

$$= +\$9{,}090{,}909$$
$$\Rightarrow \text{Invest in one period if } V_{oil} = \$4$$

The NPV of the wait one year strategy is then

NPV(wait one year)

$$= [\text{Prob}(V_{oil} = \$12)](\text{NPV} \,|\, V_{oil} = \$12) + [\text{Prob}(V_{oil} = \$4)](\text{NPV} \,|\, V_{oil} = \$4)$$
$$= (1/2)(\$0) + (1/2)(\$9{,}090{,}909)$$
$$= +\$4{,}545{,}455 > \$0$$
$$\Rightarrow \text{Wait one period}$$

Option value is decomposed as follows:

Option Value	= Intrinsic Value	+ Time Value
NPV(wait one year)	= NPV(invest today)	+ Opportunity cost of investing today
$4,545,455	= $4,000,000	+ $545,455

Exogenous input cost uncertainty has the same effect as exogenous output price uncertainty. As with exogenous price uncertainty, the option's time value derives from

| Exogenous uncertainty creates an incentive to postpone investment. |

the ability to avoid the bad (in this case, high cost) outcome. Uncertainty in either costs or prices creates uncertainty in operating cash flows and an incentive to postpone investment. By waiting for additional information regarding the level of expected future operating cash flows, the firm can choose to either invest or not invest at a later date, depending on new information.

18.5 • PUZZLE #2: MARKET EXIT AND THE ABANDONMENT OPTION

An Example of the Abandonment Option

Abandoning a losing venture is always an option when events do not work out as planned. But abandonment usually entails up-front costs. As an example, suppose British Petroleum invested in an offshore oil well in the Foinaven field and that oil prices subsequently fell to $10/bbl. The well is producing 200,000 barrels per year, as expected. Unfortunately, the oil is of lower quality than expected. Extraction and refinement costs have risen to $12/bbl, so that BP is losing $2 on every barrel it pumps. Her Majesty's Government wants to prevent abandoned oil wells from developing into ecological disasters and requires that any well not producing at capacity be capped and the platform dismantled. BP estimates this abandonment cost at $2 million. For simplicity, let's assume that BP must make the abandonment decision either today or in one period. The risk-free interest rate is 10 percent. The situation is summarized in Figure 18.3.

If oil prices ($10) and production costs ($12) are certain to remain at these levels into the indefinite future, or if BP must make its abandonment decision either now or never, then BP will want to shut down operations as soon as possible. By abandoning the project now, BP can avoid the $2/bbl expected loss. Avoiding this cash outflow provides a net cash inflow of $2/bbl. The expected value of abandoning the well today is

$$\text{NPV(abandon today)} = -\left[\frac{(($10/bbl) - ($12/bbl))(200,000bbl)}{0.10}\right] - $20,000,000$$

$$= +$4,000,000 - $2,000,000$$
$$= +$2,000,000 > $0$$
$$\Rightarrow \text{Abandon immediately (?)}$$

If oil prices and costs are certain to remain at these levels, then the timing option has no value and BP should pay the $2 million abandonment cost to avoid the $4 million loss from operating the well. This is the intrinsic value of the abandonment option.

If there is uncertainty over future prices and costs, then abandoning the project has an opportunity cost. In particular, exercising the abandonment option means losing the ability to continue operations if circumstances change for the better. For instance, if there is an equal probability that oil prices will rise to $15/bbl or fall to $5/bbl and stay at that level in perpetuity, BP may want to continue production for another period and observe the new oil price level before making its abandonment decision. If prices rise to $15 per barrel, the expected net present value of this wait-and-see strategy is

FIGURE 18.3
Uncertainty and the Option to Abandon

Initial investment I_0 = $2,000,000
Price of oil P_0 = $10/bbl
                                       P_1 = $5 or $15 with equal probability
Variable production cost $12/bbl
Expected production   200,000 bbl/year
Discount rate i = 10%

Abandon today

$$\text{NPV}_0 = -\left[\frac{(\$10/\text{bbl} - \$12/\text{bbl})(200{,}000\ \text{bbls})}{0.10}\right] - \$2{,}000{,}000 \qquad \Rightarrow \text{NPV(abandon today)} = +\$2{,}000{,}000$$

Abandon at
P_{oil} = $15

$$\text{NPV}_0 = -\left[\frac{(\$15/\text{bbl} - \$12/\text{bbl})(200{,}000\ \text{bbls})}{0.10}/1.10\right] - \$2{,}000{,}000 \Rightarrow \text{NPV} \mid P_{oil} = \$15 = -\$7{,}454{,}545 \xrightarrow{} \$0$$

Abandon in one year

Abandon at
P_{oil} = $5

$$\text{NPV}_0 = -\left[\frac{(\$5/\text{bbl} - \$12/\text{bbl})(200{,}000\ \text{bbls})}{0.10}/1.10\right] - \$2{,}000{,}000 \Rightarrow \text{NPV} \mid P_{oil} = \$5 = +\$10{,}727{,}273$$

$$\Rightarrow \text{NPV (wait one year)} = [\text{Prob}(P_{oil} = \$15)]\,(\text{NPV} \mid P_{oil} = \$15) + [\text{Prob}(P_{oil} = \$5)](\text{NPV} \mid P_{oil} = \$5)$$
$$= (1/2)(\$0) + (1/2)(\$10{,}727{,}273) = +\$5{,}363{,}636$$

Option value	=	Intrinsic value	+	Time value
NPV(wait one year)	=	NPV(abandon today)	+	Additional value from waiting one year
$5,363,636	=	$2,000,000	+	$3,363,636

$$\text{NPV} \mid (P_{oil} = \$15) = -\left[\frac{((\$15/\text{bbl}) - (\$12/\text{bbl}))(200{,}000\text{bbl})}{0.10}\Big/(1.10)\right] - \$20{,}000{,}000$$

$$= -\$7{,}454{,}545 < \$0$$
$$\Rightarrow \text{Do not abandon in one year if } P_{oil} = \$15$$
$$\Rightarrow \text{NPV} \mid (P_{oil} = \$15) = \$0$$

In this case, BP will continue operating the well and the NPV of this alternative is zero. If prices fall to $5/bbl, however, then BP will want to abandon the well rather than lose $7 on every barrel.

$$\text{NPV} \mid (P_{oil} = \$5) = -\left[\frac{((\$5/\text{bbl}) - (\$12/\text{bbl}))(200{,}000\text{bbl})}{0.10}\Big/(1.10)\right] - \$20{,}000{,}000$$

$$= +\$10{,}727{,}273 > \$0$$
$$\Rightarrow \text{Abandon in one year if } P_{oil} = \$5$$

With an equal probability of prices rising to $15/bbl or falling to $5/bbl, the expected net present value of delaying the abandonment decision for one year is

NPV(wait one year)

$$= [\text{Prob}(P_{oil} = \$5)](\text{NPV} \mid P_{oil} = \$5) + [\text{Prob}(P_{oil} = \$15)](\text{NPV} \mid P_{oil} = \$15)$$
$$= (1/2)(\$10{,}727{,}273) + (1/2)(\$0)$$
$$= +\$5{,}363{,}636 > \$0$$
$$\Rightarrow \text{Wait one period before deciding whether to abandon}$$

This is greater than the abandon today alternative by $3,363,636.

A Resolution of Puzzle #2: Failure to Abandon Unprofitable Investments

Market exit and abandonment decisions can be viewed as *American options.*[9] BP's abandonment decision can be thought of as an American call option in which BP can opt to buy out of the project's negative expected cash flows. The exercise price is the $2 million cost of abandonment. If exercised today, the abandonment option has an intrinsic value of $2 million. Of course, if BP chooses to abandon the well, it forgoes the positive operating cash flows, should oil prices rise. The time value of the option— the value of leaving the abandonment option unexercised and postponing the abandonment decision—is $3,363,636. The total value of the abandonment option is the sum of these two parts.

Option Value	= Intrinsic Value	+ Time Value
NPV(wait one year)	= NPV(abandon today)	+ Opportunity cost of abandoning today
$5,363,636	= $2,000,000	+ $3,363,636

Failure to consider the time value of the option will lead BP to abandon prematurely.

Other exit and abandonment decisions come in the form of American put options. For example, if the oil well can be sold to a competitor for $1 million, then BP holds an American put option to sell the underlying asset (the oil well) at an exercise price of $1 million. As with American call options, the values of American put options depend on the value of the underlying asset and its volatility, the exercise price, the time to expiration of the option, and the time value of money.

The time value of the option to abandon is the flip side of the option to invest. In an uncertain environment, a firm that has control over the timing of its investments

> The option to abandon is the flip side of the option to invest.

will wait until expected returns are well above required returns before it invests. This results in hurdle rates that are well above investors' required returns. Similarly, firms will delay their abandonment decisions until the expected savings from abandonment are well above the up-front costs of abandonment. This is the reason firms continue to operate under adverse conditions.

> **Firms continue to operate in unfavorable environments when there is a chance that prospects will improve and the sunk costs of abandonment can be avoided.**

The time value of the option to invest arises from an ability to avoid negative outcomes, should oil prices fall. Conversely, the time value of an abandonment option arises from an ability to participate in positive outcomes should oil prices rise. That is, real investment options gain value by avoiding bad times, whereas real abandonment options gain value by staying invested during good times. Because of the value of the timing option, firms adopt a wait-and-see attitude before incurring sunk investment or abandonment costs.

> Hysteresis occurs when entry and exit costs are high.

Investment and Disinvestment Strategies in Combination

In the presence of uncertainty, firms impose hurdle rates that are higher than investors' required returns because of the investment timing

---

9 Exit and abandonment options are often valued as put options. See Berger, Ofek, and Swary, "Investor Valuation of the Abandonment Option," *Journal of Financial Economics* (1996).

option. Similarly, once invested, a firm will not abandon investment until the gain from disinvestment is large enough to overcome the alternative of waiting for the situation to improve and thereby avoiding the sunk costs of abandonment. This is a *compound option* in which exercise of an option leads to one or more additional options.

When the investment and abandonment options are considered in combination, the firm faces two thresholds. A sufficiently high level of expected return is necessary to induce the firm to invest. Similarly, a sufficiently high level of expected loss is necessary to induce the firm to disinvest. Because of these twin thresholds, firms' investment behaviors can appear sticky. Firms can forgo investing in markets that appear attractive and, once invested, persist in operating at a loss. This behavior is called **hysteresis** and is characteristic of multinational firms with high entry and exit costs and high uncertainty associated with their foreign operations.

Multinational firms often see the value of their investments rise and fall with changing real exchange rates. An increase in a country's real exchange rate makes goods manufactured in that country relatively more expensive on world markets. A fall in the real value of a currency makes that country's output relatively inexpensive on world markets. When the real value of the dollar was at its peak in the mid-1980s, U.S. manufacturers complained that their products were too expensive relative to foreign competitors' products. Similarly, as the yen appreciated in real terms against other currencies during the mid-1990s, Japanese manufacturers complained that they were losing sales to foreign competitors. Hysteresis arises as changes in real exchange rates drive foreign investments into and then out of profitability, and then back again. The time value of the abandonment option is the reason multinational firms choose to weather the storm and persist in foreign markets despite adverse exchange rate conditions.[10]

More generally, management has flexibility in "rightsizing" projects in the following ways as new information arrives:

- *Invest or abandon the project.* Abandoning a project in a foreign country can spoil the MNC's relationship with the host country and force the firm into forgoing positive-NPV projects later on.

- *Expand or contract the project or extend or shorten its life.* MNCs squeeze additional value out of their products by continuing to fine-tune their marketing, production, and distribution efforts.

- *Suspend (mothball) or reactivate the project.* Suspending or mothballing a project is often less costly than outright abandonment and retains the option to reactivate the project if and when conditions improve.

If conditions improve, the firm can exercise its option to increase investment. If conditions deteriorate, the firm can exercise its option to reduce, mothball, or abandon its investment. These are compound options in that exercising one option brings with it additional flexibility and investment/disinvestment options.

18.6 • PUZZLE #3: THE MULTINATIONAL'S ENTRY INTO NEW MARKETS

When uncertainty is endogenous, real options can create incentives for firms to invest in projects that, at least on the surface, look like negative-NPV projects. When uncertainty is endogenous, the act of

> Endogenous uncertainty creates an incentive to speed up investment.

10 Christophe documents hysteresis in U.S. firms at a time when the dollar was at an all-time high in real terms in "Hysteresis and the Value of the U.S. Multinational Corporation," *Journal of Business* (1997).

investing reveals information about the value of the option. In this case, firms have an incentive to speed up investment in order to gain additional information. Staged investment of this kind is a form of *compound option* in that new information revealed through investing can lead to additional investment options.

Endogenous Price Uncertainty and the Value of Follow-Up Projects

Suppose that the quality of oil produced by the Foinaven oil field cannot be determined until oil production begins. If the oil is high quality, it will sell for $30/bbl in perpetuity. If it is low quality, it will sell for $10/bbl in perpetuity. Again, these two outcomes are equally likely. Variable production costs are $12 per barrel. The present value of investment in the well is $20,000,000, regardless of when the investment is made.

If oil price is $30 per barrel, BP will be glad they invested. If oil price is $10 per barrel, price is less than the $12 variable cost and BP should consider abandoning or mothballing the well. In order not to confound BP's investment option with an abandonment option, let's suppose that BP is contractually required to produce 200,000 barrels per year from the well once they have invested.[11]

Viewed as a now-or-never alternative, the value of investing in an oil well in this setting is less than zero.

$$\text{NPV(invest today)} = \left[\frac{((\$20/\text{bbl}) - (\$12/\text{bbl}))(200{,}000\text{bbl})}{0.10} \right] - \$20{,}000{,}000$$

$$= +\$16{,}000{,}000 - \$20{,}000{,}000$$
$$= -\$4{,}000{,}000 < \$0$$
$$\Rightarrow \text{Do not invest today (?)}$$

If the investment option is viewed as a now-or-never proposition, BP should not invest.

Suppose that this oil well is only the first of ten wells that BP might drill. If constructed, each well will be identical to the others and produce 200,000 barrels of oil per year in perpetuity. If BP were to invest in all ten oil wells today, the expected net present value of all ten wells would be −$40,000,000. Viewed as a now-or-never decision, this is clearly not a good investment.

Uncertainty is said to be *endogenous* when the firm's assessment of the value of a project is influenced by the act of investing. In this example, the act of investing reveals information about the price of oil and the value of the option to invest. BP can gain information about the potential of additional wells by investing in a single exploratory well. For simplicity, assume the quality and market price of the oil will be known one year after the first well is drilled. By investing in an exploratory well, BP can make a more informed decision on the other nine wells.

If the oil is low quality and sells for $10/bbl, BP should not produce oil at a $12 cost that exceeds the $10 price. In this case, the initial investment will be lost and, if it cannot abandon the well, BP will suffer a cash drain with a value of −$4 million. The net present value of this outcome is

$$\text{NPV} \,|\, (P_{oil} = \$10) = \left[\frac{((\$10/\text{bbl}) - (\$12/\text{bbl}))(200{,}000\text{bbl})}{0.10} \right] - \$20{,}000{,}000$$

$$= -\$24{,}000{,}000$$
$$\Rightarrow \text{Do not invest further if } P_{oil} = \$10$$
$$\Rightarrow \text{NPV} \,|\, (P_{oil} = \$10) = \$0$$

---

11 For this example to work, the cost of contracting, abandoning, or mothballing the well must be greater than the loss in value from staying invested. This makes continued production BP's least-cost alternative.

On the other hand, if the oil is high quality, each well has a net present value of

$$\text{NPV} \mid (P_{oil} = \$30) = \left[\frac{((\$30/bbl) - (\$12/bbl))(200{,}000bbl)}{0.10}\right] -\$20{,}000{,}000$$

$$= +\$16{,}000{,}000$$
$$\Rightarrow \text{Invest in additional wells if } P_{oil} = \$30$$

At this price, BP should invest in the nine additional wells. Recalling that the present value cost of investing is $20 million regardless of the timing of investment, each additional well has a value at time t = 0 of

NPV(each additional investment $\mid P_{oil}$=\$30)

$$= \left[\frac{((\$30/bbl) - (\$12/bbl))(200{,}000bbl)}{0.10}\middle/(1.10)\right] -\$20{,}000{,}000$$

$$= +\$12{,}727{,}273$$

The expected value of the decision to drill an exploratory well is then

NPV (invest in exploratory well)
$$= \text{Prob}(P_{oil}=\$10)](\text{NPV} \mid P_{oil}=\$10)+[\text{Prob}(P_{oil}=\$30)](\text{NPV} \mid P_{oil}=\$30)$$
$$= (^1\!/_2)[-\$24{,}000{,}000] + (^1\!/_2)[(1)(\$16{,}000{,}000) + (9)(\$12{,}727{,}273)]$$
$$= +\$53{,}272{,}723 > \$0$$
$$\Rightarrow \text{Invest in an exploratory well}$$

Alternatively, this NPV can be calculated as

$$= \text{NPV(one now-or-never well today)} + [\text{Prob}(P_{oil}=\$30)](\text{NPV} \mid P_{oil}=\$30)$$
$$= -\$4{,}000{,}000 + (^1\!/_2)[(9)(\$12{,}727{,}273)]$$
$$= +\$53{,}272{,}723 > \$0$$

Investing in the exploratory well reveals information about the potential of the oil field and allows BP to make a more informed decision about its other potential investments.

In the original example of the option to invest, uncertainty was exogenous and there was always value in waiting. In this example, there is an incentive to invest early so that BP can determine the quality of the oil. Including the value of follow-up projects can be important when uncertainty is endogenous and the act of investing reveals information that otherwise would remain undiscovered.

A Resolution of Puzzle #3: The MNC's Entry into New Markets

Multinational corporations often make small investments into emerging markets and new technologies, even though the expected return on investment appears to be less than the cost of capital. In option pricing terms, the firm is purchasing an out-of-the-money compound option that entitles it to make further investments if conditions improve.

> **Firms investing in new markets and technologies are purchasing options that entitle them to purchase additional options if conditions warrant further investment.**

By acquiring information that helps it make a better assessment of future opportunities, a firm can withdraw when its experience in a new market or technology suggests a negative outcome, and it can continue and even expand investment when the outlook is positive.

Because the firm's current and future real investments are compound options, asset values are often decomposed as

$$V_{ASSET} = V_{ASSETS\text{-}IN\text{-}PLACE} + V_{GROWTH\ OPTIONS} \qquad (18.5)$$

Assets-in-place are assets in which the firm has already invested. The value of assets-in-place represents the value of operating the firm according to the existing product mix, production levels, marketing and distribution efforts, and cost structures. In this case, valuation of assets-in-place is straightforward, following the NPV rule: Discount expected future cash flows from assets-in-place at the opportunity cost of capital.

Flexibility in the management of existing and future assets can then be viewed as a separate source of value. Valuing managerial flexibility requires that we value many different kinds of options, including the options to enter new markets, exit current and possible future markets, expand or contract the product line, suspend or reactivate existing and possible future investments, and develop follow-up projects to the firm's existing assets. These potential future investments arise because of the firm's unique position in the markets for real goods and services, including its brand names, patents, technological know-how, and managerial culture and expertise. These intangible assets are collectively referred to as **growth options** because they capture the value of managerial flexibility in responding to an uncertain world.

> Growth options reflect managerial flexibility in responding to an uncertain world.

18.7 • THE REAL OPTION APPROACH AS A COMPLEMENT TO NPV

Option pricing models work best for simple options on financial assets such as stocks, commodities, interest rates, or currencies. International markets for these financial assets are competitive, highly liquid, and relatively frictionless. Consequently, financial options have an expected NPV of zero. Real options are another matter entirely. Markets for real assets are less competitive, less liquid, and have higher transactions costs than financial markets. The NPV of a real option can be positive, negative, or zero depending on the particular investment. Indeed, the whole point of performing a capital budgeting analysis is to identify positive-NPV alternatives.

Most real investment opportunities are *compound rainbow options* that provide managerial flexibility and growth options in the presence of multiple sources of uncertainty. The complexity of real investment opportunities can make it difficult to develop realistic valuation models, whether they are based on discounted cash flow or option pricing methods. Although they share this shortcoming, each valuation approach encounters its own unique difficulties in practice.

Why NPV Has Difficulty Valuing Managerial Flexibility

The net present value rule says to accept all positive-NPV projects. Although the NPV rule can faithfully value assets-in-place in the absence of managerial flexibility, it has difficulty valuing the many real options that accompany the firm's real assets. In particular, NPV calculations must include all opportunity costs, including the opportunity cost of investing at a less-than-optimal time.

> NPV requires an estimate of the opportunity cost of capital.

The biggest difficulty in applying discounted cash flow methods to real options lies in identifying the opportunity cost of capital.[12] Identifying the opportunity cost

---

12 Kulatilaka and Marcus, "Project Valuation and Uncertainty: When Does DCF Fail?" *Journal of Applied Corporate Finance* (1992).

of capital in the capital asset pricing model (CAPM) is facilitated by the assumption of normally distributed returns. Normal distributions are completely described by their means, standard deviations, and correlations, and the CAPM takes advantage of this fact. In the CAPM, an asset's opportunity cost of capital is determined by its systematic risk or beta.

The appropriate discount rate for an option is ambiguous because of the peculiar characteristics of the returns to an option position.

- *Degree of option volatility.* Options are always more volatile than the assets on which they are based. Options are levered investments, and small changes in the value of the underlying real or financial asset result in larger changes in option values. Consider BP's oil well investment in section 18.2. The value of the expected cash inflows from the oil well was [($20–$8)(200,000)]/(0.1) = $24 million. The intrinsic value of the option to invest at an exercise price of $20 million was $4 million. Suppose the value of the oil well increases by 50 percent, to $36 million. The intrinsic value of the option increases from $4 million to $16 million (=$36m–$20m), or by ($16m–$4m)/$4m = 300 percent. This illustrates the general rule that the value of an option is more volatile than that of the underlying asset.[13]

- *Changing degree of option volatility.* The volatility of an option changes with changes in the value of the underlying asset. Suppose the value of BP's oil well rises another 50 percent, from $36 million to $54 million. The intrinsic value of the investment call option rises from $16 million to $34 million ($54m–$20m). This is an increase of ($34m–$16m)/$16m = 112.5 percent. Although the option is still more volatile than the underlying asset, the percentage increase in option value at this higher oil price level is less than the percentage increase at the lower oil price level. This illustrates a general rule: The volatility of an option falls as the underlying asset goes deeper in-the-money, although option volatility never falls to the level of volatility in the underlying asset. This changing degree of option volatility has a serious consequence for discounted cash flow valuation methodologies. Because option volatility depends on the value of the underlying asset, no single discount rate reflects the opportunity cost of capital as the value of the underlying asset evolves throughout the life of the option.

- *Distribution of option returns.* Even if returns to the underlying asset are normally distributed, option returns are inherently nonnormal. An easy way to see this is to observe that an option payoff is truncated, or cut off, at the exercise price. Only the in-the-money portion of the distribution of underlying asset value has value to an option. This means that conventional risk measures cannot fully describe the risk of an option. In particular, neither standard deviation of return nor beta captures the asymmetric nature of option risk.

In combination, these three characteristics make determining the opportunity cost of capital on a real option a messy and unrewarding affair.

The Option Pricing Alternative

> A replicating portfolio mimics option payoffs.

Option pricing models circumvent the problem of identifying the opportunity cost of capital by constructing a **replicating portfolio** that mimics the payoffs on the option.[14] The replicating portfolio is composed of a position in the

---

13 It is simplest to focus on the intrinsic value of the option. The general result prevails when the time value is included; the volatility of an option is greater than the volatility of the underlying asset.

14 The appendix to the currency option chapter provides an example of a replicating portfolio.

underlying asset together with riskless borrowing or lending. This portfolio must be continuously rebalanced to reflect changes in the value of the underlying asset. An assumption of costless arbitrage then ensures that the value of the option is equal to the value of the replicating portfolio. Because the combination of an option position and a short position in the corresponding replicating portfolio is riskless, discounting is done at the risk-free rate of interest. This eliminates the need to determine a risk-adjusted discount rate for the option position.

There are two obstacles to costless arbitrage between a real option and its replicating portfolio:

- *Transactions costs.* Arbitrage can only enforce the law of one price within the bounds of transactions costs. Transactions costs are relatively low in financial markets, so arbitrage can ensure that equivalent assets sell for the same price. Transactions costs are much more prominent in real asset markets. Arbitrage cannot ensure the equivalence of the option position and its replicating portfolio.

- *Unobservable prices.* Financial options are contractually written on an asset whose price is readily observable in a competitive financial market. Real assets are less frequently traded and real asset markets are far less competitive than financial markets. When real asset values are unobservable, arbitrage cannot ensure the equivalence of a real option and its replicating portfolio.

In the absence of a viable replicating portfolio, real option values can diverge widely from their theoretical values.

The Real Option Approach and NPV as Complements

Discounted cash flow and option pricing approaches to project valuation should be viewed as complements. Each approach has advantages and disadvantages. Constructing a decision tree of possible future scenarios can assist the financial manager in formulating competitive responses to various situations. Yet a decision tree can only capture a few of the possible future states of the world. Option pricing methods start with an assumption about the distribution of project values and determine the value of the option to invest from this distribution of outcomes.

> NPV and real option methods complement one another.

Applying both valuation methods provides a second opinion regarding the value of an investment. Managers will have confidence in their valuations if the NPV and option value estimates are close. If they differ, viewing the investment as a real option can shed light on possible sources of value from managerial flexibility.

18.8 • SUMMARY

A key variable faced by every cross-border investment is uncertainty. Currency, political, and cultural risks are the most prominent additional risks in cross-border investment, but business risk on foreign projects can also be higher than that of domestic projects. When uncertainty is high, the multinational corporation's real investment opportunities can be viewed as real options. Real options include

- Options to accelerate or delay
- Options to invest or abandon
- Options to expand or contract
- Options to suspend or reactivate

- Options to extend or shorten the life of the project
- Growth options and follow-up projects

Option values can be decomposed into the value of the option if exercised today and the value of waiting.

Option Value	= Intrinsic Value	+ Time Value	(18.4)
NPV(wait)	= NPV(invest today)	+ Opportunity cost of investing today	

Option pricing methods are particularly useful for assessing the time value of a real option.

Conventional discounted cash flow valuation techniques are difficult to apply to real options because

- Options are inherently riskier than the underlying asset on which they are based.
- The risk of an option changes with changes in the value of the underlying asset.
- Returns to options are not normally distributed.

Despite the difficulties of applying discounted cash flow techniques to cross-border valuation, we should not let what we do not know about valuation get in the way of what we do know. Discounted cash flow techniques are useful in many circumstances. They are the valuation tool of choice when an investment decision must be made immediately or forgone entirely. When used with decision trees, discounted cash flow techniques are also useful in formulating competitive strategy in the timing and scale of investment.

Option valuation is simplest to implement when option values are contingent on a single financial price variable. Even when project value depends on many complex and interacting variables, viewing the project as a package of real options can begin to account for managerial flexibility in the face of an uncertain world and help you realize the asset's full value.

KEY TERMS

American option	out-of-the-money option
assets-in-place	price uncertainty
call option	put option
compound option	rainbow option
endogenous uncertainty	real option
exogenous uncertainty	replicating portfolio
growth option	simple option
hysteresis	switching option
in-the-money option	time value
intrinsic value	timing option
managerial flexibility	

CONCEPTUAL QUESTIONS

18.1 What is a real option?

18.2 In what ways can managers' actions seem inconsistent with the "accept all positive-NPV projects" rule? Are these actions truly inconsistent with the NPV decision rule?

18.3   Are managers who do not appear to follow the NPV decision rule irrational?

18.4   Why is the timing option important in investment decisions?

18.5   What is exogenous uncertainty? What is endogenous uncertainty? What difference does the form of uncertainty make to the timing of investment?

18.6   In what ways are the investment and abandonment options similar?

18.7   What is a switching option? What is hysteresis? In what way is hysteresis a form of switching option?

18.8   What are assets-in-place? What are growth options?

18.9   Why does the NPV decision rule have difficulty in valuing managerial flexibility?

18.10   What are the shortcomings of option pricing methods for valuing real assets?

PROBLEMS

Exogenous uncertainty and the investment and abandonment options

18.1   A proposed brewery in the East European country of Dubiety will produce a beer—dubbed the "Dubi Dubbel"—for Grolsch N.V. of the Netherlands. A number of other West European brewers have announced plans to produce and sell beer in the Dubi market. If too many breweries open, beer prices will fall. If some of these investment plans do not materialize, prices are likely to rise. The price of beer is determined exogenously and will be known with certainty in one year. Grolsch management must decide whether to begin production today or in one year. The following facts apply:

Initial investment	I_0 = D200,000,000; rises by 10% each year
Actual price of beer in a year	P_1 = either D25 or D75 with equal probability
Expected price of beer	$E[P_1]$ = D50 per bottle in perpetuity
Variable production cost	D10 per bottle
Fixed production cost	D10,000,000 per year
Expected production	1,000,000 bottles per year forever
Tax rate	0%
Discount rate	i = 10%

a. Draw a decision tree that depicts Grolsch's investment decision.
b. Calculate the NPV of investing today as if it were a now-or-never alternative.
c. Calculate the NPV (at t = 0) of waiting one year before making a decision.
d. Calculate the NPV of investing today, including all opportunity costs.
e. Should Grolsch invest today or wait one year before making a decision?

18.2   Grolsch management has gone ahead with the brewery investment in problem 18.1. The market has grown increasingly competitive, and nearly all of the brewery investments in Eastern Europe are losing money. To make matters worse, variable production costs of D20/bottle are higher than expected. To its dismay, Grolsch has discovered that employment laws in Dubiety state employees cannot be laid off so long as the brewery is open. Grolsch must either produce at capacity or close the brewery. A major competitor is considering abandoning the market. If this brewer does not abandon, price will remain constant at D15/bottle. If the brewer abandons, price immediately will rise to D35/bottle. Assume Grolsch's abandonment decision does not influence competitor's decision, so price uncertainty is exogenous. The following facts apply to the abandonment decision:

Cost of abandoning brewery	I_0 = D10,000,000; rises by 10% each year
Current price of beer	P_0 = D15 per bottle in perpetuity
Price of beer in a year	P_1 = either D15 or D35 with equal probability
Fixed production costs	D10,000,000 per year
Variable production cost	D20 per bottle
Expected production	1,000,000 bottles per year forever
Tax rate	0%
Discount rate	i = 10%

a. Draw a decision tree that depicts Grolsch's investment decision.
b. Calculate the NPV of abandoning today as if it were a now-or-never alternative.
c. Calculate the NPV (as of $t = 0$) of waiting one year before making a decision.
d. Calculate the NPV of abandoning today, including all opportunity costs.
e. Should Grolsch abandon this losing venture today?

Endogenous uncertainty and growth options

18.3 The "Dubi Dubbel" investment of problem 18.1 is one of five brewery investments that Grolsch is considering in Eastern Europe. The quality of the beer produced by the Dubi brewery will provide Grolsch with information on the quality of beer that it can expect from the other five investments. Grolsch will not know the quality of beer and, hence, the price at which the beer will sell until production begins. The situation is similar to problem 18.1:

Initial investment	I_0 = D200,000,000; rises by 10% each year
Expected price of beer	P_0 = D50 per bottle in perpetuity
Actual price of beer in a year	P_1 = either D25 or D75 with equal probability
Fixed production cost	D10,000,000 per year
Variable production cost	D10 per bottle
Expected production	1,000,000 bottles per year forever
Tax rate	0%
Discount rate	i = 10%

a. Draw a decision tree that depicts Grolsch's investment decision.
b. Calculate the NPV of investing today as if it were a now-or-never alternative.
c. Calculate the NPV (as of $t = 0$) of investing in an exploratory brewery today and then reconsidering investment in the additional four breweries after one year (i.e., after the price of beer is revealed by the initial investment).
d. Calculate the NPV of investing today, including all opportunity costs.
e. Should Grolsch invest today? What is different in this problem from the setting in problem 18.1, and how does it affect Grolsch's investment decision?

18.4 A proposed automotive plant in South America will produce automobiles in Brazil. The Brazilian currency is the real. The following facts apply:

Initial investment	CF_0 = R100,000,000; rises by 20% each year
Price of automobile	P_0 = R18,000 per vehicle
Expected production cost	$E[C_1]$ = R15,000 per vehicle
Actual cost per vehicle	C_1 = R12,000 or R18,000 with equal probability
Production	10,000 vehicles per year forever
Tax rate	0%
Discount rate	i = 20%

a. (Exogenous cost uncertainty and the option to invest)
Suppose production costs are determined exogenously by government fiat and will be known with certainty in one year. Management must decide whether to begin production today or in one year. Calculate (1) the NPV of investing today as if it were a now-or-never alternative, (2) the NPV (at t = 0) of waiting one year before making a decision, and (3) the NPV of investing today, including all opportunity costs.

b. (Endogenous cost uncertainty and growth options)
Suppose this investment is one of ten auto plants with identical characteristics that could be built in Brazil. The outcome from your initial investment will provide information about the production costs that will be incurred at other sites. Calculate (1) the NPV of investing today in all ten sites as if it were a now-or-never alternative, (2) the NPV (at t = 0) of investing in one factory today and then waiting one year before making a decision on the other nine factories, and (3) the NPV of investing today including all opportunity costs.

18.5 You have discovered a mountain of guano in Japan. Up to five guano mines could be constructed on the mountain. Each guano mine costs ¥600,000 today and is expected to yield 150 ounces of guano in one year. The actual yield of each mine will be either 100 ounces or 200 ounces with equal probability. All of the guano will be extracted from the mine in the first year of operation and sold to the government at a guaranteed price of ¥5,000 per ounce. (It's high quality guano.) According to your contract with local miners, variable production costs are ¥1,000 per ounce. The nominal yen discount rate is 0% per year. The guano mines will be worthless after the guano is extracted. Because of the importance of guano to Japanese politics, the government has agreed to provide you with a tax-free holiday on the proceeds of the mine. (Note that non-cash depreciation or depletion allowances have no effect on cash flow when the tax rate is zero.) You can invest in a single exploratory mine today and then base subsequent investment on the outcome of the first mine. Once you know the yield of the first mine, you will know the yield of the other four mines with certainty. Each additional mine costs ¥600,000 in nominal terms. Price and variable cost will remain constant at ¥5,000 and ¥1,000 per ounce, respectively.

a. Calculate the NPV of investing in all five mines as a "now-or-never" alternative.

b. Calculate the NPV (as of t = 0) of investing in a single mine and then waiting one year before considering investment in the other 4 mines.

c. Should you invest in the exploratory mine?

18.6 Solve problem 18.5 assuming a nominal yen discount rate of 10 percent per year and a corporate tax rate of T = 30 percent. The initial cash outflow of ¥600,000 will be capitalized on the balance sheet and depleted during the year. At the end of the year, you will receive a depletion tax shield of ¥600,000(0.30) = ¥180,000. Note that taxes will also reduce your operating cash flow by 30 percent.

A thought-provoking problem in competitive strategy

18.7 In problems 18.1 through 18.3, how might Grolsch's decisions be different if its actions influence competitors' actions, and vice versa?

SUGGESTED READINGS

Useful textbook references on real options and strategy include

Martha Amram and Nalin Kulatilaka, *Real Options: Managing Strategic Investment in an Uncertain World* (Cambridge, MA: Harvard Business School Press, 1999).

Michael J. Brennan and Lenos Trigeorgis (editors), *Project Flexibility, Agency, and Product Market Competition* (London: Oxford University Press, December 1999).

Thomas Copeland, *Real Options: A Practitioner's Guide* (Texere, 2001).

Avinash K. Dixit and Robert S. Pindyck, *Investment Under Uncertainty* (Princeton: Princeton University Press, 1994).

Financial Management devoted an entire special issue (Vol. 22, No. 3, Autumn 1993) to real options. The following articles in this issue are particularly illustrative:

"Real Options and Interactions with Financial Flexibility," by Lenos Trigeorgis

"Reversion, Timing Options, and Long-Term Decision Making," by David G. Laughton and Henry D. Jacoby

"Creating Value by Spawning Investment Opportunities," by Eero Kasanen

"Case Studies in Real Options," by Angelien G.Z. Kemna

Valuation of off-shore oil leases is developed in

James L. Paddock, Daniel R. Siegel, and James L. Smith, "Option Valuation of Claims on Real Assets: The Case of Offshore Petroleum Leases," *Quarterly Journal of Economics* 103 (August 1988), pp. 479–508.

Daniel R. Siegel, James L. Smith, and James L. Paddock, "Valuing Offshore Oil Properties with Option Pricing Models," *Midland Corporate Finance Journal* 5 (Spring 1987), pp. 22–30.

Growth options in foreign operations are compared to those of domestic investments in

Gordon M. Bodnar and Joseph Weintrop, "The Valuation of the Foreign Income of U.S. Multinational Firms: A Growth Opportunities Perspective," *Journal of Accounting & Economics* 24 (December 1997), pp. 69–97.

When and why discounted cash flow methods prove insufficient to value real options is discussed in

Nalin Kulatilaka and Alan J. Marcus, "Project Valuation and Uncertainty: When Does DCF Fail?" *Journal of Applied Corporate Finance* 5, No. 3 (1992), pp. 92–100.

Other useful references on options include

Philip G. Berger, Eli Ofek, and Itzhak Swary, "Investor Valuation of the Abandonment Option," *Journal of Financial Economics* 42, (October 1996), pp. 257–287.

Peter Carr, "The Valuation of Sequential Exchange Opportunities," *Journal of Finance* 43, No. 5 (1988), pp. 1235–1256.

Stephen E. Christophe, "Hysteresis and the Value of the U.S. Multinational Corporation," *Journal of Business* 70 (July 1997), pp. 435–462.

Corporate Governance and the International Market for Corporate Control

chapter 19

Overview

"O world! world! world! Thus is the poor agent despised."

William Shakespeare

Corporate governance refers to the ways in which major stakeholders exert control over the modern corporation and assure themselves a return on their investment. Each nation's laws, legal institutions and conventions, and regulatory framework determine stakeholder rights in corporate governance. These national systems influence many aspects of economic life:[1]

> Legal systems manifest themselves in corporate ownership and control.

- The way in which capital is allocated within and between national economies
- The opportunities available to borrowers and investors
- Ownership and control of corporations

Although national legal systems share many common elements, they are shaped by unique political, social, and economic forces. These forces manifest themselves in country-specific differences in corporate governance systems that have a profound influence on the ways in which corporations are governed and perform. This in turn affects the frequency and form of cross-border mergers, acquisitions, and divestitures.

Dispersed equity ownership, a large proportion of public debt and equity issues, and a relatively independent management team characterize the **market-based** corporate governance systems of the United Kingdom and the United States. The **bank-based** system used in Germany relies on concentrated bank ownership of debt and equity capital and a management team that is closely monitored by the lead bank. Other nations have their

---

1 An excellent survey appears in Shleifer and Vishny, "A Survey of Corporate Governance," *Journal of Finance* (1997).

own unique mechanisms for corporate governance, with varying powers being wielded by equityholders, debtholders, managers, employees, suppliers, customers, prominent (perhaps royal) families, and governments.

Disparate national systems of corporate governance result in dissimilar markets for corporate control. Corporate control contests in the United States and the United Kingdom tend to be large-scale, aggressive, financially motivated deals that involve private investors or other corporations. Hostile acquisitions in these markets prompt equally forceful defensive maneuvers by the management of target firms. In Germany, change in ownership or management is often initiated, facilitated, or managed by the company's lead bank. In Japan, the corporation's main bank and business partners typically manage corporate takeovers.

After presenting some merger and acquisition (M&A) terminology and a review of the major corporate stakeholders, this chapter examines national differences in corporate governance using the United States, Germany, and Japan for illustration. The pace and form of cross-border M&A activity are then examined in the context of these national differences in corporate governance. The chapter concludes with a review of the domestic and international evidence on factors related to M&A activity.

19.1 • THE TERMINOLOGY OF MERGERS AND ACQUISITIONS

A firm can obtain control over the assets of another firm in three direct ways:[2]

- Through acquisition of another firm's assets
- Through merger or consolidation
- Through acquisition of another firm's stock

Chapter 15 covered acquisition of another firm's assets. This chapter concentrates on mergers and acquisitions of stock.

In a **merger**, one firm absorbs another. The acquiring firm usually retains its name and legal status. All assets and liabilities of the target firm are merged into the acquiring firm. A **consolidation** is like a merger, except that an entirely new firm is created. When firms merge or consolidate, one firm usually serves as the dominant or acquiring firm, with the other firm as a target firm. The acquiring firm's management usually retains its management role in the merged firm. In an **acquisition of stock**, the acquiring firm purchases some or all of the equity of another firm. A merger sometimes follows an acquisition, after the acquiring firm obtains a controlling interest in the target firm. An acquisition of stock can be in any amount up to 100 percent of the acquired firm's stock. Acquisitions of stock of 50 percent or less are referred to as partial acquisitions. In each of these transactions, the target firm's management may or may not be retained.

> Synergy occurs when the whole is greater than the sum of the parts.

Firms are acquired or merged in the hope that the combined entity will have more value than the sum of the parts (as in $2 + 2 = 5$). Cross-border mergers and acquisitions derive their value from more efficient utilization of the competitive advantages of the acquiring or acquired firm. This additional value is called **synergy** and is measured as

$$\text{Synergy} = V_{AT} - (V_A + V_T) \qquad (19.1)$$

where V_A and V_T are the values of the acquiring firm (A) and the target firm (T) prior to the announcement of the merger or acquisition, and V_{AT} is the postacquisition

---

2 A joint venture provides an indirect way of obtaining control over the assets of another firm.

value of the combined firm. Note that synergy in Equation 19.1 is not constrained to be positive, although value-destroying combinations are not considered synergistic.

The purchase price paid to the shareholders of the target firm includes the preacquisition value V_T of the target and an **acquisition premium** paid to target shareholders. The acquisition premium is the difference between the purchase price and the preacquisition market value:

$$\text{Acquisition premium} = \text{Purchase price} - V_T \qquad (19.2)$$

If the target is publicly traded, target shareholders will never sell for less than their preacquisition market value, so the acquisition premium to preacquisition price is always positive. If the target firm is not publicly traded, the preacquisition value V_T is not easily identified, and target firm shareholders may end up selling for more or less than the fair market value.

Whether the acquiring firm wins or loses depends on whether the synergies created by the merger or acquisition outweigh the acquisition premium paid to the target firm:

$$
\begin{aligned}
\text{Gain to acquiring firm} &= V_{AT} - (V_A + V_T + \text{Acquisition premium}) \\
&= \text{Synergy} - \text{Acquisition premium}
\end{aligned}
\qquad (19.3)
$$

Acquiring shareholders win if the synergy created through the acquisition is greater than the acquisition premium paid to target shareholders. If only one or a few target firms offer the competitive advantages that acquiring firms desire, then the target firm's position will be enhanced as it negotiates with its suitors. The bargaining position of an acquiring firm is greatest when there are many potential targets but only a few acquiring firms in a position to make an offer.

Cross-border mergers and acquisitions are conducted within the rules and conventions established by national governments and their regulatory bodies. Consequently, it is useful to describe how financial markets and institutions and the regulations that govern them affect corporate ownership and corporate governance in different countries.

19.2 • CORPORATE GOVERNANCE

Corporate governance systems can be characterized according to the group or groups exercising control over the corporation. Control of large corporations tends to be dominated by one of the following parties:

- Prominent families (as in Mexico)
- The State (as in China and Singapore)
- Commercial banks (as in Germany)—perhaps in combination with a group of business partners (as in Japan)
- A dispersed set of equity shareholders (as in the United Kingdom, the United States, and Ireland)

Figure 19.1 displays the corporate governance systems of the United States, Germany, Japan, and China in three dimensions by combining families and the State into a single dimension.

In nearly all countries, small businesses are founded and controlled by individuals or families.[3] The way that small businesses grow to become larger companies depends on

---

3 La Porta, Lopez-de-Silanes and Shleifer, "Corporate Ownership Around the World," *Journal of Finance* (1999).

FIGURE 19.1
Corporate Governance Systems

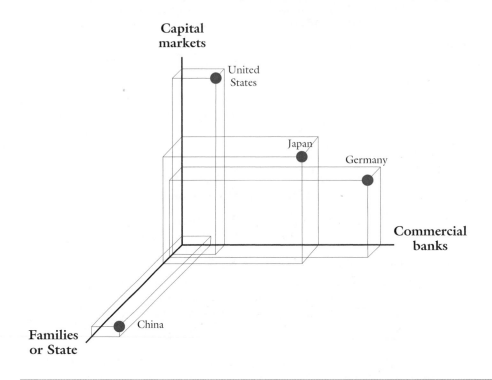

a nation's corporate governance system. In some countries, families retain their position at the center of business life in even the largest businesses. Powerful families sometimes even control the government, such as in Saudi Arabia, the Philippines, and Indonesia (especially under Suharto's rule). At their best, these family-based systems serve as benevolent dictatorships that develop local industries and promote the welfare of local residents. At their worst, national resources are exploited for the benefit of a few through corruption, nepotism, and crony capitalism.

> Capital markets are growing in importance.

Many corporate governance systems are migrating upward in Figure 19.1 toward a capital market-based system. Strong global growth in capital markets is reducing the influence of governments, founding families, and commercial banks in many corporate boardrooms. Capital markets are the most important providers of capital to large businesses in the United States, the United Kingdom, Canada, and Australia. Although commercial banks continue to be major players in continental Europe and parts of Asia (particularly Japan and Korea), capital market growth in these countries is gradually eroding the influence of commercial banks, prominent families, and governments.

One of the driving forces toward a global equity culture has been rapid **privatization** of state-owned enterprises. Figure 19.2 shows the value of privatizations by region during the 1990s. Sales of telecommunication assets have been especially popular in developed countries, mostly through initial public offerings. These have included Japan's NTT (1986), Italy's STET (1995), Spain's Telefonica de España (1995), the Netherlands' KPN (1995), Deutsche Telekom (1996), France Telecom (1997), Brazil's

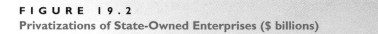

FIGURE 19.2
Privatizations of State-Owned Enterprises ($ billions)

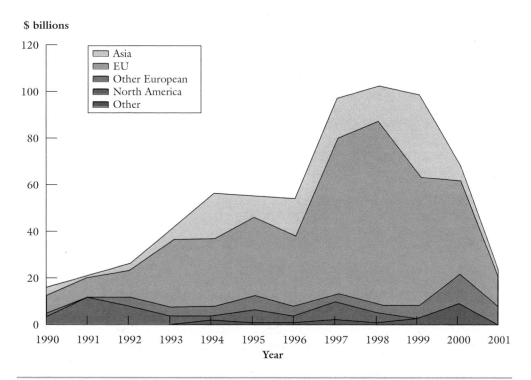

Source: *OECD Financial Market Trends,* June 2002 (World Bank and OECD estimates).

Telebras (1998), and Swisscom (1998). Although the largest privatizations have been from developed countries, privatizations in Central and Eastern Europe, Russia, South America, and Asia have been an important stimulus to capital market growth in these markets. The market for privatizations has been less active since 1999, reflecting a diminishing supply of large government-owned monopolies and a slowdown in M&A activity.

During the 1990s, Russia and its allies used voucher or mass privatization programs to create their equity markets with varying degrees of success. In contrast, China is taking a staged approach to capital market development. The Chinese government needs money to fund economic development and the transition to capitalism. Although privatizations offer a quick source of funds, the Chinese equity market is still in its infancy and cannot easily absorb large offerings. At the same time, the government wants control of Chinese enterprises to remain within China and so does not want to offer too many shares on international markets. The Chinese strategy is to gradually privatize state-owned enterprises as the capacity of China's capital market grows.

> Russia used a voucher system to privatize state-owned firms.

Despite the growing influence of capital markets, family or state ownership and control remain widespread in both developing and developed economies.

Examples of Market-Based and Bank-Based Systems

This section tours the corporate governance systems of the United States, Germany, and Japan to demonstrate how a nation's unique history, culture, legal system, and regulation

Market Update

Privatization in Transition Economies
(Or, the only thing worse than having to take a capitalist's money is not being offered a capitalist's money.)

Privatizations provide an important stimulus for growth in economies that are making the transition from a state-controlled to a market-based economy. Privatizations force firms to become more efficient in both developed and emerging markets.[4]

Privatizations are conducted either as voucher programs, management buyouts (MBOs), or mass privatization programs (MPPs). Recent privatizations programs include:

Armenia—voucher	Bulgaria—MPP	Croatia—MBO
Czech Republic—voucher	Estonia—MPP	Georgia—voucher
Hungary—MPP	Kazakhstan—voucher	Kyrgyz Republic—voucher
Latvia—MPP	Lithuania—voucher	Macedonia—MBO
Moldova—voucher	Poland—MPP	Romania—MBO
Russia—voucher	Slovakia—MPP	Slovenia—MBO

These privatizations often have been poorly managed and led to opportunistic behavior on the part of insiders including illegal takeovers, asset stripping, and outright theft and fraud. The keys to a successful transition include enforceable contracts and institutions that allow monitoring of insiders by key stakeholders. Here are three examples.

Russia. From 1992 to 1994, Russia privatized more than 16,000 state-owned enterprises by distributing vouchers to Russian citizens in the world's largest and fastest privatization scheme. Inside managers and workers repurchased most of these shares and retained controlling interests. In the absence of business laws and a corporate governance system, fraud was commonplace. Foreign investors often complained that their stake was being illegally diluted or even eliminated. By 1996, a small group of politically-connected financial oligarchs had established control of Russian commercial banks and privately arranged to buy natural resource-based firms from the government at deeply discounted prices. Russian privatization failed because it was conducted without concurrent reforms in Russia's legal, regulatory, and administrative structures.

Poland. Poland began a slow privatization of state-owned enterprises beginning in 1991. Although there were a few prominent public offerings, most asset sales were private transactions with other domestic and international buyers. At the same time, Poland introduced free trade and promoted the growth of new private firms that have been a driving force in Poland's transition to a market economy. Strong labor unions ensured that managers did not abuse their positions. Consequently, Poland's transition to a market economy has been relatively successful.

Czech Republic. From 1991 to 1995, the Czech Republic privatized 1,800 medium-to-large firms through a voucher program and sold the assets of another 350 firms to international investors. In contrast to Russia, nearly two-thirds of these vouchers were reinvested in investment funds that diversified shareholder risk and promised to monitor managers. This led to a relatively successful privatization, as the funds limited the opportunities for managers to expropriate assets. Industrial production remained strong and unemployment remained under control throughout this transition.

These countries are continuing to develop their legal, regulatory, and administrative framework to ensure transparency and protections for minority shareholders.

---

4 Megginson and Netter, "From State to Market: A Survey of Empirical Studies on Privatization," *Journal of Economic Literature* (2001).

environment influence its financial markets and institutions. Although each of these nations has a highly developed system for assuring investors a return on their investment, there are nevertheless significant differences in their corporate governance systems. Table 19.1 provides an overview of the three corporate governance systems.

The Market-Based System in the United States. In most industrialized economies, corporations have a **supervisory board** charged with supervising the management team on behalf of the stakeholders. The composition of the supervisory board and its powers and responsibilities vary widely across countries. In the United States, this supervisory board is called the *board of directors* and is usually controlled by management. The typical NYSE/AMEX firm has about 12 board members, more than half of whom are outsiders who have no other direct affiliation with the corporation.

> U.S. banks do not have a strong voice in corporate boardrooms.

In the United States, commercial banks have little influence in corporate boardrooms except when firms are in financial distress. Relative to banks in many other countries, commercial banks in the United States have been constrained in where and in how they have conducted their business. As to the *where*, the National Banking Act of 1863 confined national commercial banks to a single location. The McFadden Act of 1927 later allowed bank branches only to the extent permitted by state law. Only within the last 30 years have state laws allowed entry to out-of-state banks. Branches of foreign banks are an even more recent innovation in the United States.

Banks in the United States have also been restricted in *how* they conduct their business. The Glass-Steagall Banking Act of 1933 imposed the following prohibitions on the equity-related activities of commercial banks:

- Banks could not actively vote shares held in trust for their banking clients.
- Banks could not own stock for their own account.
- Banks could not make a market in equity securities.
- Banks could not engage in investment banking activities.

Glass-Steagall barred commercial banks from "engaging principally" in underwriting or dealing in equity securities. This prevented banks from operating as investment bankers, brokers, or equity market makers. Glass-Steagall also barred commercial banks from owning stock except in trust for their banking clients. The Bank Holding Company Act

TABLE 19.1
Cross-Border Differences in Corporate Governance Systems

Country and system	Equity concentration	Bank ownership of equity	Supervisory board	Hostile acquisitions
Germany (bank-based)	High—lead bank	Unlimited equity ownership	Outside directors, bankers, labor representatives	Rare—approval of lead bank and 75% of shareholders
Japan (bank-based)	High—main bank; keiretsu or business partners	Limited equity ownership (5% maximum)	Inside managers, bankers, keiretsu members, business partners	Rare—blocked by cross-holdings with keiretsu or business partners
United States (market-based)	Low	No direct equity ownership	Inside managers, outside directors	Common through proxy contests and tender offers

of 1956 later limited banks' trust activities to passive ownership in no more than 5 percent of a corporation's stock. These geographic and product market restrictions permitted the growth of only small, regional banks with limited product lines. These limitations largely removed commercial banks from corporate boardrooms and prohibited banks from taking an active role in corporate governance except during bankruptcy.

In the 1980s and 1990s, the Federal Reserve Board gradually relaxed the Glass-Steagall restrictions on underwriting and dealing activities by commercial banks. This process culminated in 1999, when the Financial Services Modernization Act (FMA) formally repealed Glass-Steagall and allowed commercial banks, investment banks, brokers, insurers, investment companies (pension and mutual funds), and other financial companies (mortgage, finance, and leasing companies) to affiliate through a holding company structure. This allowed U.S. and foreign banks to compete as investment bankers, brokers, and insurers in the U.S. market.

Despite deregulation of the U.S. financial services industry, banks still do not have a strong voice in corporate boardrooms. The FMA left in place many restrictions, including the prohibition against banks owning stock for their own account and firewalls between commercial banking, investment banking, and brokerage activities. The U.S. banking industry has lagged many of its international competitors because of this history of limited bank involvement in corporate boardrooms.

Germany's universal banking system allows banks to have an active role in corporate governance.	**Germany's Universal Banking System.** Commercial banking in Continental Europe has evolved along quite different lines from the Anglo-American model used in the United Kingdom and the United States. Germany provides an example of universal banking found on the Continent. In **universal banking**, banks offer a full range of banking and financial services to their individual and corporate customers. This

provides banks with a strong voice in corporate governance as they provide debt and equity financing, brokerage and investment banking activities, insurance underwriting, and consulting.

German banks influence corporate boardrooms in four ways:

- Banks are the primary suppliers of debt capital to German businesses of all sizes.
- Banks are equity owners through their own direct investments.
- Banks serve as Germany's investment bankers.
- Banks actively vote the shares of their trust (pension fund) and brokerage customers.

Banks also are involved in the operation of German stock exchanges, including the largest exchange in Frankfurt. Because they control the votes on existing equity capital as well as corporate access to new capital, commercial banks dominate corporate governance in Germany.

In contrast to U.S. law, German law gives banks *Vollmachtstimmrecht*—the authority to vote on behalf of their brokerage clients. German banks obtain revocable proxies from their brokerage customers that allow banks to vote their shares. Banks advise the shareholders of their intentions prior to voting and, unless instructed otherwise, vote the shares on behalf of their brokerage customers. German banks also manage most of Germany's pension fund assets. This near monopoly on trust and brokerage activities provides German banks a dominant role in German corporate governance.

Large publicly traded corporations in Germany are called *Aktiengesellschaft (AG)*.[5] The German equivalent of the U.S. board of directors is the *Aufsichtsrat*, which means

---

5 Small corporations in Germany are called *Gesellschaft mit beschränkter Haftung (GmbH)*, or "corporation with limited liability." *Aktiengesellschaft* are allowed to issue securities to the public, whereas GmbH are not. The GmbH form is much less popular in Switzerland, where the acronym GmbH is jokingly referred to as *Gesellschaft mit beschränkter Hoffnung*, or "corporation with limited hope."

"supervisory board." German corporations also have a management board, or *Vorstand*, that reports to the supervisory board. German law stipulates the representation of various stakeholders on the supervisory board. There are 21 seats on the supervisory board for most corporations with over DM20 million in equity capitalization. If there are at least 2,000 employees in the company, then employees elect 10 seats and shareholders elect 11 seats. The chairman of the supervisory board represents shareholders and has the twenty-first vote. The number of seats and the proportion held (by equity and by employees) vary for smaller companies and for companies in different industries. German banks control the Aufsichtsrat in large part through their dominance of the equity seats on the supervisory board.

The control of German banks over the equity portion of the Aufsichtsrat also allows them to control the proxy mechanism by which shares are voted. In the United States, the chief executive officer (CEO) controls the proxy mechanism, especially if the CEO serves as chairperson of the board of directors. In Germany, the CEO is prohibited from serving on the supervisory board. Without a corporate insider at the head of the board, German managers must filter their requests to shareholders through a board that is controlled by the company's bankers. This allows banks to control both the equity portion of the Aufsichtsrat and the proxy mechanism by which equity shares are voted.

Some German corporations have sought debt and equity financing through the capital markets specifically to break the hegemony of banks over corporate affairs. Transaction volume on the Deutsche Börse is growing, and an emerging market in the equity issues of high-growth and technology companies is providing capital to small and medium-sized businesses. Investment banks from other countries have captured a share of the new issue market, but the market is still dominated by German banks.

One last characteristic of the German system of corporate governance should be noted. Publicly held companies account for about 20 percent of sales by German companies, and about one-fifth of these are exchange-listed. The vast majority of German businesses are unincorporated small- to medium-sized *Mittlestand* companies. These are often controlled by a single family and maintain a close relationship with a single bank.

Japan's Keiretsu System. Japan's corporate governance system can be classified as bank-based, although the role of commercial banks in Japan is somewhere between that of the U.S. and German systems. Banks have less influence in Japan than in Germany, but a far greater role than in the United States. Their role is more that of partner than banker, at least from a Western perspective.

Prior to World War II, Japan was dominated by family-controlled business groups called *zaibatsu*. At the start of the war, four zaibatsu (Mitsubishi, Mitsui, Sumitomo, and Yasuda) controlled one-third of banking and foreign trade, half of all shipbuilding and maritime shipping, and most heavy industry. Group members were linked through extensive share cross-holdings led by a family-controlled main bank.

Zaibatsu were instrumental in the Japanese war effort, so the allied powers imposed American-style Glass-Steagall limitations on Japan's banking system to limit their influence. Banks were prohibited from owning more than 5 percent of any nonbank company, and investment and commercial banking activities were separated. Despite this constraint on equity participation, banks retained an active role in corporate governance.

After the war, the traditional zaibatsu reemerged in a Japanese institution called the keiretsu. **Keiretsu** are collaborative groups of horizontally or vertically integrated companies with extensive share cross-holdings. Each keiretsu has a small group of core members and a number of more loosely affiliated companies. About one-half of publicly traded firms in Japan are formal or informal members of a keiretsu.

> Keiretsu are characterized by extensive share cross-holdings.

There are two types of keiretsu. **Vertical keiretsu** (sangyô) are led by large manufacturers such as Hitachi, Sony, and Toshiba in electronics and automakers Honda, Nissan, and Toyota. These industrial groups connect the manufacturers to their suppliers through share cross-holdings, personnel swaps, and strategic coordination. Although the suppliers benefit from the security of a guaranteed business partner, the lead firm can be in a position to dictate prices to the suppliers. These closely linked vertical keiretsu make it difficult for non-Japanese suppliers to gain a foothold in these industries.

Horizontal keiretsu (kinyû) are centered on a main bank and feature extensive share cross-holdings between firms in different industries. Prior to 1999, there were six major horizontal keiretsu in Japan. These keiretsu and their most recognizable members were

- Mitsubishi   Bank of Tokyo-Mitsubishi (Mitsubishi, Nikon, Kirin Beer)
- Sumitomo   Sumitomo Bank (NEC)
- Mitsui   Sakura Bank (Toshiba)
- Fuyo   Fuji Bank (Marubeni)
- Dai-Ichi   Dai-Ichi Kangyo Bank (Nissan, Canon)
- Sanwa   Sanwa Bank (Kobe Steel)

The first three of these were prewar zaibatsu that reemerged after the 1946–1952 allied occupation of Japan. The last three were collaborations that emerged after the war. These keiretsu tried to avoid direct competition between member firms by having only one company in each industry. Each keiretsu had between 20 and 50 primary members and several hundred more loosely linked affiliates. Figure 19.3 shows the members of the Mitsubishi keiretsu, the most powerful keiretsu.

Their main bank and keiretsu partners closely monitor Keiretsu members. The Japanese custom is for the senior officers of the companies in each keiretsu to meet in a monthly "president's council." At these meetings, top managers discuss topics of mutual interest and formulate business strategy. Keiretsu members frequently exchange employees on temporary assignments, to learn the other's business and promote interaction among the partners. Although banks are restricted to no more than 5 percent ownership of any single stock, the accumulation of cross-holdings by other keiretsu members means control effectively resides within the keiretsu.

The board of a typical large corporation listed on the Tokyo Stock Exchange has 23 board members but only one outsider.[6] It is rare for a member of the supervisory board to come from a group other than management, the main bank, or a closely affiliated company. An inner circle of inside managers, their bankers, and their major business partners thus dominates governance of large Japanese corporations.

The Japanese stock market and real estate crash of 1990 put enormous pressure on the Japanese economy and has stimulated change in the keiretsu system. As asset prices fell during the early 1990s, commercial banks found themselves with large portfolios of nonperforming loans. At the same time, the government lowered the barriers between commercial banks, investment banks, securities firms, and insurance companies. The culmination of this process was a series of bank mergers during 1999–2002 that produced four new megabanks:

- Mitsubishi Tokyo Financial Group   Bank of Tokyo-Mitsubishi and Mitsubishi Trust
- Sumitomo Mitsui Banking Corp.   Sumitomo Bank and Sakura Bank

---

6 Kang and Shivdasani, "Firm Performance, Corporate Governance, and Top Executive Turnover in Japan," *Journal of Financial Economics* (1995).

FIGURE 19.3
The Mitsubishi Keiretsu

Mitsubishi Corporation	Bank of Tokyo—Mitsubishi	Mitsubishi Heavy Industries

Automotive
Mitsubishi Fuso Truck and Bus
Mitsubishi Motors
Shin Caterpillar Mitsubishi

Finance and insurance
DC Card
Diamond Lease
Meiji Life
Mitsubishi Auto Credit-Lease
Mitsubishi Securities
Mitsubishi Trust & Banking
Tokio Marine and Fire

Industrial equipment
Mitsubishi Electric
Mitsubishi Kakoki
Mitsubishi Precision
Toyo Engineering Work

Electronics and telecommunications
IT Frontier
Mitsubishi Research Institute
Mitsubishi Space Software
Nikon
Space Communications

Transportation and distribution
Mitsubishi Logistics
Mitsubishi Ore Transport
NYK Line

Industrial materials and textiles
Asahi Glass
Dai Nippon Toryu
Mitsubishi Aluminum
Mitsubishi Cable Industries
Mitsubishi Materials
Mitsubishi Plastics
Mitsubishi Rayon
Mitsubishi Shindoh
Mitsubishi Steel

Consumer goods and foods
Kirin Beverage
Kirin Brewery
Ryoshoku

Chemicals and pharmaceuticals
Dai Nippon Toryo
Mitsubishi Chemical
Mitsubishi Gas Chemical
Mitsubishi Petrochemical

Resources and energy
Nippon Oil
Mitsubishi LPG
Mitsubishi Nuclear Fuel
Mitsubishi Paper Mills

Real estate and construction
Mitsubishi Estate
P.S. Mitsubishi

Source: Mitsubishi Public Affairs Commission (http://www.mitsubishi.or.jp), April 2003.

- Mizuho Holding Financial Group   Fuji Bank, Dai-Ichi Kangyo Bank, and
  Industrial Bank of Japan
- United Financial of Japan (UFJ)   Sanwa Bank, Tokai Bank, and Tokyo Trust

How these changes will influence the traditional keiretsu structure is difficult to foresee. The Mitsubishi keiretsu remains intact and seems determined to maintain its traditional structure. The Sumitomo-Mitsui and Mizuho combinations realigned companies from previously exclusive keiretsu groups. Some of these competing firms are merging, such as a proposed merger of Sumitomo Chemical and Mitsui Chemical that would create Japan's largest chemicals company. At the same time, realignments have also weakened traditional ties within the keiretsu. Indeed, the proportion of share cross-holdings in Japan has fallen dramatically since the early 1990s. Despite these recent changes, the keiretsu system still commands a prominent role in Japanese corporate governance and business life.

Market Update

Korea's Chaebol

Many Korean firms belong to a **chaebol**, a horizontally diversified group of firms that bears some resemblance to a Japanese keiretsu.[7] The major chaebol were founded after the Korean War and rose to power through government protections and subsidies. The five major postwar chaebol, founding families, and most recognizable corporations are

- Samsung   Lee   Samsung Electronics
- LG (Lucky-Goldstar)   Koo, Huh   LG Electronics (partial spinoff in 1999)
- SK (Sunkyong)   Chey   SK Telecom
- Hyundai   Chung   Hyundai Motors (spun off in 2001)
- Daewoo   Kim   Daewoo Motors (acquired by GM in 2001)

> Chaebol are diversified (often family-controlled) Korean business groups.

The biggest difference between a chaebol and a keiretsu is that each chaebol had a single founder. With centralized ownership, the Korean chaebol have formal organizational structures and centralized control. This is in contrast to the informal network of control in a Japanese keiretsu. Another difference is that chaebol are not allowed to own financial institutions and so do not have a main bank at the center of the group.

Following the currency crisis of 1997, the Korean government instituted reforms aimed at greater openness, efficiency, and competitiveness. Chaebol were encouraged to focus on their key businesses and divest themselves of peripheral operations. Several prominent bankruptcies hastened this process. The Daewoo chaebol was divided into several small business groups in 1999 following the bankruptcy of Daewoo Motors. General Motors acquired two-thirds of Daewoo for $400 million in 2001. Similarly, in 2001 financial difficulties forced the Hyundai group to spin off Hyundai Motors. Other chaebol are restructuring as well.

Characteristics of Market-Based and Bank-Based Systems

There is general consensus that a well-developed banking sector is essential to economic growth and prosperity.[8] However, there is much variation in the importance and structure of the banking sector within domestic economies.

Banking outside the United States tends to be more concentrated in a few large banks than in the United States because of the historical constraints of the Glass-Steagall Act. Table 19.2 compares the relative importance of the largest banks in the United States, Germany, Japan, the United Kingdom, and China. In 2001, the five largest U.S. banks controlled assets worth $3,005 billion. Gross domestic product (GDP) in the United States during 2002 was $10,366 billion. The five largest banks in the United States thus held a stake in assets equal to 29 percent of United States gross domestic product. The ratio of assets controlled by the five largest German banks ($2,711 billion) to German GDP ($1,975 billion) was 1.37, or nearly five times the comparable U.S. ratio. In Japan,

---

7 Bae, Kang, and Kim study the winners and losers in mergers and acquisitions by chaebol in "Tunneling or Value Added? Evidence from Mergers by Korean Business Groups," *Journal of Finance* (2002).

8 Cetorelli and Gambera, "Banking Market Structure, Financial Dependence, and Growth: International Evidence from Industry Data," *Journal of Finance* (2001).

TABLE 19.2
The Importance of Commercial Banking to the Domestic Economy

	United States	Japan	Germany	United Kingdom	China
GDP (2002, U.S. $ billions)	10,366	3,936	1,975	1,548	1,232
Assets of the five largest banks	3,005	3,849	2,711	2,399	1,527
Bank assets / GDP	0.29	0.98	1.37	1.55	1.24
Bank assets / GDP relative to the United States	—	3.37	4.74	5.35	4.28

Sources: Bank assets at year-end 2001 from the July 2002 issue of *The Banker.* Gross domestic products (GDP) for 2002 from *International Financial Statistics,* a publication of the International Monetary Fund. China's GDP is an estimate.

the ratio of assets ($3,849 billion) to GDP ($3,936 billion) was 0.98, or more than three times the ratio in the United States. Banks are also important in the United Kingdom and the People's Republic of China, with assets-to-GDP ratios of 1.55 and 1.24, respectively.

High concentration in the banking sector may or may not be a good thing. On the one hand, a powerful bank can foster close relationships with its client firms, monitor the performance of these firms, and facilitate the growth of young firms. Because of their informational advantage over financial markets, banks also can be in a better position than markets to fund projects that require staged financing.

> Banks can help firms grow, but can impede growth if they become too powerful.

On the other hand, banks can impede economic growth if they become too powerful. If banks are able to extract monopoly rents from their clients, they reduce the incentives for firms to pursue new and profitable projects. Similarly, banks that focus too much on debt repayment will favor conservative investments and may forego riskier, possibly positive-NPV projects. In these situations, financial markets may be better at allocating capital, funding risky projects, and promoting economic growth.

Beck and Levine examine the influence of market-based and bank-based financial systems on industrial growth, the establishment of new firms, and the efficiency of capital allocation.[9] They find that whether a financial system is market-based or bank-based matters less than whether the country has effective legal protections for minority investors against expropriation by managers and controlling shareholders.

The Legal Environment and Investor Protection. The legal environment determines who exercises control over the firm's voting and cash flow rights. This is important because separation of ownership and control of the firm is difficult when there are inadequate legal safeguards to ensure minority investors a return on their investment. Legal protections thus influence the ways in which publicly traded and privately held firms raise external capital, the concentration of equity ownership, and the turnover in top management during financial distress.

> Separation of ownership and control is difficult without legal safeguards to protect minority investors.

There are considerable cross-country differences in the legal protections afforded minority investors.[10] Legal protections are highest in *common law* countries such as the United Kingdom and the United

---

9 Beck and Levine, "Industry Growth and Capital Allocation: Does Having a Market- or Bank-Based System Matter," *Journal of Financial Economics* (2002).

10 Legal protections around the world are surveyed in La Porta, Lopez-de-Silanes, Shleifer, and Vishny's "Investor Protection and Corporate Governance," *Journal of Financial Economics* (2000).

States. With strong protection and enforcement of their legal rights, minority investors can afford to have their ownership claims separated from control of the firm. Legal protections ensure a return commensurate with their claim on the firm. Consequently, these countries tend to have a higher proportion of small, diversified investors.

Civil law countries (including most European and Latin American countries) tend to have weak legal protections for minority investors. In these countries, controlling managers and shareholders sometimes opportunistically seize the voting and cash flow rights of minority investors. Investors in these countries avoid minority positions and ownership tends to be concentrated in the hands of one or a few investors.

Legal protections for minority investors are weakest in countries in the Napoleonic sphere, such as France and Italy. Corporate governance can suffer in these countries, as minority shareholders are unable to exercise their voting and cash flow rights. Volpin studied Italian firms in which the top executive is the largest shareholder and yet had less than a 50 percent claim on the firm's cash flows.[11] In these firms, Tobin's q (equity market-to-book) ratios are relatively low and executive turnover tends not to be closely related to performance. Each of these is an indicator of poor corporate governance.

Civil law countries in the Germanic and Scandinavian spheres tend to have legal protections that are intermediate between the Napoleonic and Anglo-American systems.

The euro has stimulated growth in European capital markets.

Studies find that firm performance in Germany is positively related to the concentration of equity ownership, particular if a bank exercises control.[12] However, there is also evidence that the gains associated with transfers of ownership accrue primarily to large stakeholders, and not to minority investors.[13] The rapid growth of European capital markets following the introduction of the euro is changing the balance of power in European boardrooms, and is likely to lead to changes in investor protections as well.

The Concentration of Equity Ownership. An important consequence of a nation's relative emphasis on a market-based or bank-based system is the concentration of ownership in the firm. In the market-based system of corporate governance used in

Equity ownership tends to be dispersed in market-based governance systems.

the United States and United Kingdom, ownership is diffusely held across a large number of outside investors. In Germany's bank-based system, ownership and control are concentrated in the hands of a single institution. In Japan's bank-based system, ownership and control rest with a small group of business partners through reciprocal relationships and equity cross-holdings within the keiretsu. In many other countries, control rests with families or the state.

The automobile industry is at the heart of the national economies of Germany, Japan, and the United States, so it is interesting to compare ownership structures in this industry across these countries. Table 19.3 lists the largest automaker in each country along with the percentage of shares controlled by the largest institutional shareholders in the early 1990s. These ownership patterns are typical of large firms in Germany, Japan, and the United States, and they illustrate the relative power of commercial banks in these countries.

The largest institutional owner of General Motors was the Michigan State Treasury, which owned only 1.4 percent of GM's outstanding shares. Without banks to supply equity capital, U.S. corporations rely heavily on public issues of stock. This has fragmented the ownership of large U.S. corporations among many individual and institutional investors.

---

11 Volpin, "Governance with Poor Investor Protection: Evidence from Top Executive Turnover in Italy," *Journal of Financial Economics* (2002).

12 Gorton and Schmid, "Universal Banking and the Performance of German Firms," *Journal of Financial Economics* (2000).

13 Franks and Mayer, "Ownership and Control of German Corporations," *Review of Financial Studies* (2001).

TABLE 19.3
Institutional Ownership of Public Corporations[1]

	United States	**Japan**	**Germany**
Largest domestic automaker	General Motors	Toyota	Daimler-Benz[2]
Largest institutional owner	State of Michigan Treasury	Sakura Bank	Deutsche Bank
Percent owned by largest institutional owner	1.4%	4.9%	41.8%
Percent owned by five largest institutional owners	5.7%	21.6%	78.4%

1 From Mark J. Roe, "Some Differences in Corporate Structure in Germany, Japan, and the United States," *The Yale Law Journal*, Vol. 102 (1993), pp. 1927–2003. Reprinted by permission of *The Yale Law Journal* and Fred B. Rothman & Company. Reprinted by permission of The Yale Law Journal company and Fred B. Rothman & Company.

2 Daimler-Benz merged with Chrysler Corporation of the United States in a 1998 stock swap to form DaimlerChrysler A.G., incorporated in Germany and with an equity capitalization of $40 billion at the time of the deal. Deutsche Bank's ownership fell from about 40 percent of Daimler-Benz to 29 percent of DaimlerChrysler.

In Germany, Deutsche Bank directly or indirectly controlled more than 40 percent of Daimler-Benz's outstanding shares. Direct control arises through ownership of Daimler-Benz stock and through bank-controlled mutual funds and investment companies. Indirect control springs from the bank's power to vote the shares owned by its brokerage customers. Along with its services as lender and investment banker, this concentration of equity ownership provides Deutsche Bank with a singularly powerful voice in company affairs. In recognition of this position, Deutsche Bank is considered Daimler-Benz's *Hausbank* (house bank), and the chair of the supervisory board is customarily a Deutsche Bank executive. The next two largest investors in Daimler-Benz (Dresdner Bank and Commerzbank) together control an additional 36 percent of outstanding shares.

Although no single shareholder owns more than 5 percent of Toyota, Table 19.3 shows that the five largest shareholders owned more than 20 percent of Toyota's outstanding shares. This is typical of the ownership structure of large Japanese corporations. Japanese banks are prohibited from owning more than 5 percent of the equity of any single company, but in combination with other keiretsu members they typically control up to one-third of the equity of each keiretsu member. Because of reciprocal trade and reciprocal equity ownership, Japanese managers must seek the blessing of other keiretsu members before undertaking major new projects. The primary role served by banks in the Japanese keiretsu and in Japanese corporate governance places their corporate governance system closer to that of Germany than the United States, although Japanese banks by themselves are not necessarily the dominant keiretsu member, as the Hausbank is in Germany.

Top Executive Turnover and Firm Performance. There is a built-in tension between stakeholders in the corporation. Each stakeholder has an incentive to pursue his or her own selfish interest. These interests are often in conflict with those of other stakeholders, especially during times of financial distress. Different corporate governance systems manage these tensions and their attendant costs differently.

Debt and equity shareholders, in effect, hire management to run the corporation through the mechanism of the supervisory board. In this principal-agent relationship, management serves as an agent of the principal stakeholders. This requires that other stakeholders monitor the

> Agency costs are the costs of ensuring that managers act in the best interests of other stakeholders.

activities and performance of management. The costs of monitoring management and ensuring that it acts in the best interest of other stakeholders are called **agency costs**.

Concentrated ownership of public corporations in Germany and Japan provides a strong incentive for financial institutions in those countries to monitor management performance. Corporate management is more easily monitored by the lead bank in Germany or by closely affiliated members of the keiretsu in Japan than by a dispersed set of equity owners, as in the United States. Control of the supervisory board provides institutional owners in Germany and Japan with the means by which to monitor management. Consequently, bank-based systems can reduce the agency costs that arise between managers and other stakeholders.

Without a single source of capital such as in Germany and Japan, corporations in the United States and the United Kingdom rely much more extensively on public capital markets. Without equity capital from commercial banks and with dispersed institutional ownership, managers in these countries do not often have to face a dominant stakeholder and can operate more independently than managers in Germany and Japan.

One test of a corporate governance system is in how well it deals with poorly performing managers. Replacing inefficient managers should increase the value of poorly performing firms. In market-based governance systems, corporate control is contested either as a proxy fight over seats on the supervisory board or through the public takeover markets. In bank-based governance systems, top executive turnover is much more likely to be initiated by the lead bank in Germany or by the firm's business partners in Japan.

The empirical evidence suggests that there are similarities in *why* and *when* top management is replaced in developed countries such as the United States, Germany, and Japan. In each country, the likelihood that top management will be replaced is greater for firms reporting poor earnings performance or a recent decline in share price. Further, empirical evidence indicates that firm performance tends to improve after turnover in the top management of poorly performing companies.

The major difference among these countries is in the mechanism by which top management is replaced—the *how* of top executive turnover. Turnover in the ranks of top executives is usually initiated by the supervisory board. In each country, the likelihood of top executive turnover in poorly performing firms is positively related to the concentration of equity ownership and to the proportion of outsiders on the board.

> There are national differences in *how* top executives are replaced.

In the United States, any attempt to replace top management must be channeled through the board of directors. The board represents shareholders and is responsible for initiating any change in top management. Corporate control contests occur either as proxy contests for seats on the board or as hostile takeover contests. These contests are conducted in the financial markets between unrelated investors. Corporate control contests are highly public and receive a great deal of coverage in the press.

In the Japanese keiretsu, the main bank or corporation takes the initiative in replacing the management of poorly performing keiretsu members.[14] Turnover in the ranks of the firm's top executives tends to be greater in bank-dominated keiretsu than in keiretsu that do not include a main bank. Announcements of top executive turnover often increase share price, particularly when turnover is forced because of a performance decline or when the successor is appointed from outside the firm.

In Germany, the lead bank usually takes the initiative in replacing top executives. As in Japan and the United States, poor earnings or stock price performance is likely to lead to a turnover in top management and an improvement in firm performance. In contrast

---

14 Kang and Shivdasani, "Firm Performance," and Kang and Shivdasani, "Does the Japanese Governance System Enhance Shareholder Wealth? Evidence from the Stock-Price Effects of Top Management Turnover," *Review of Financial Studies* (1996).

to the United States, the gains associated with transfers of ownership often accrue only to large blockholders and not to minority investors.[15]

These empirical findings suggest that there is more than one way for a corporate governance system to successfully deal with underperforming managers and to resolve the agency problems that exist between managers and other stakeholders in the firm.

19.3 • THE INTERNATIONAL MARKET FOR CORPORATE CONTROL

A Recent History of Cross-Border M&A Activity

Cross-border mergers and acquisitions were rare as recently as 1970. For example, during 1968 there were only 16 cross-border deals out of more than 4,000 deals involving U.S. firms. Cross-border deals became more common during the 1980s and 1990s, although most of these were small acquisitions rather than blockbuster megamergers. Large cross-border deals occurred with increasing frequency in the late 1990s and early 2000s, as shown in Table 19.4. The first cross-border deal to exceed $10 billion in value was as recently as 1998.

TABLE 19.4
Cross-Border M&A over $10 Billion in Value

Year	Acquirer (country)	Target (country)	Value ($ billions)	Industry
2002	Vivendi Universal S.A. (France)	USA Networks, Inc. (U.S.)	10.7	Entertainment
2001	Deutsche Telekom AG (Germany)	VoiceStream Wireless (U.S.)	29.4	Telecom
2001	Citigroup (U.S.)	Grupo Financiero (Mexico)	12.8	Banking
2001	Fortis (Belgium)	Fortis (Netherlands)	12.5	Insurance
2001	BHP Ltd (Australia)	Billiton PLC (U.K.)	11.5	Mining
2001	DB Investments (U.K.)	De Beers Mines Ltd (S Africa)	11.1	Mining
2001	Nestlé SA (Switzerland)	Ralston Purina (U.S.)	10.5	Pet foods
2000	Vodaphone AirTouch PLC (U.K.)	Mannesmann (Germany)	202.8	Telecom
2000	France Telecom SA	Orange PLC unit of Vodaphone (U.K.)	46.0	Telecom
2000	HSBC Holding (Hong Kong)	Credit Commercial de France	11.1	Banking
2000	BP Amoco PLC (U.K.)	Atlantic Richfield (U.S.)	27.2	Oil and gas
2000	Unilever PLC (U.K.)	Bestfoods (U.S.)	25.1	Food
2000	UBS AG (Switzerland)	PaineWebber Group (U.S.)	16.5	Investment bank
2000	Credit Suisse Group (Switzerland)	Donaldson, Lufkin & Jenrette (U.S.)	13.5	Investment bank
1999	Vodaphone Group PLC (U.K.)	AirTouch Comm (U.S.)	60.3	Telecom
1999	Zeneca Group PLC (U.K.)	Astra AB (Sweden)	34.6	Pharmaceuticals
1999	Mannesmann AG (Germany)	Orange PLC (U.K.)	32.6	Telecom
1999	Rhone Poulenc SA (France)	Hoechst AG (Germany)	21.9	Textiles, drugs
1999	Deutsche Telekom AG (Germany)	One 2 One (U.K.)	13.6	Telecom
1999	Scottish Power PLC (U.K.)	PacifiCorp (U.S.)	12.6	Electric
1999	Aegon NV (Netherlands)	TransAmerica (U.S.)	10.8	Insurance
1999	Wal-Mart Stores (U.S.)	ASDA Group PLC (U.K.)	10.8	Retaining
1999	Global Crossing Ltd (Bermuda)	Frontier Corp (U.S.)	10.1	Telecom
1998	BP Amoco PLC (U.K.)	Amoco Corp (U.S.)	48.2	Oil and gas
1998	Daimler-Benz AG (Germany)	Chrysler Corp (U.S.)	40.5	Automobiles
1998	Texas Utilities (U.S.)	Energy Group PLC (U.K.)	10.9	Oil and gas
1998	Allianz AG Holding (Germany)	Assurances Generales de France	10.0	Insurance

Source: *Mergers and Acquisitions*, various issues.

---

15 Franks and Mayer, "Ownership and Control."

Japanese companies went on an international buying spree in the late 1980s, gobbling up foreign companies at an unprecedented rate. At least part of the reason for this acquisition binge was the run-up in Japanese real asset and share prices during the 1980s that left Japanese corporations and banks with a great deal of buying power on international markets. The rise in the value of the yen during the late 1980s also reduced the cost of foreign assets relative to Japanese assets. The subsequent fall in Japanese share and currency values during the 1990s resulted in a financial crisis that drastically curtailed the overseas acquisitions of Japanese corporations. In combination with a gradual liberalization of Japanese financial markets, lower Japanese share prices have at least partially opened the door to foreign acquisitions within Japan.

In Europe, the pace of mergers and acquisitions increased in the 1980s and 1990s as businesses responded to political efforts to increase European integration and harmonization. Survival strategies in a unified Europe are focused on cross-national alliances to take advantage of price and cost differences, diversify operations, reduce operating risk, and gain footholds in new markets. Buying an existing business in another location is often easier than establishing a new investment from scratch. The signing of the Maastricht Treaty in December 1991 provided impetus to activity in the European market for corporate control, culminating with the introduction of the euro in 2001. European M&A activity has been dominated by the telecommunications and insurance industries. The number and value of cross-border deals involving European companies is now about the same as those of intra-national deals in Europe.

Figures 19.4 and 19.5 display the number and market values of mergers and acquisitions since 1988. M&A activity grew throughout the 1990s, riding on the crest of a

FIGURE 19.4
Volume of Mergers and Acquisitions Activity, Number of Deals 1989–2002

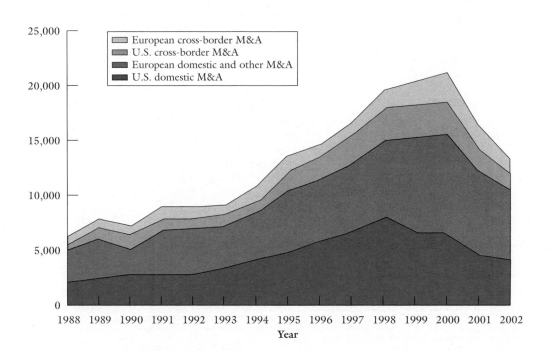

Source: Compiled from *Mergers and Acquisitions,* various issues.

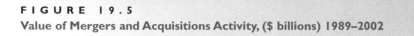

FIGURE 19.5
Value of Mergers and Acquisitions Activity, ($ billions) 1989–2002

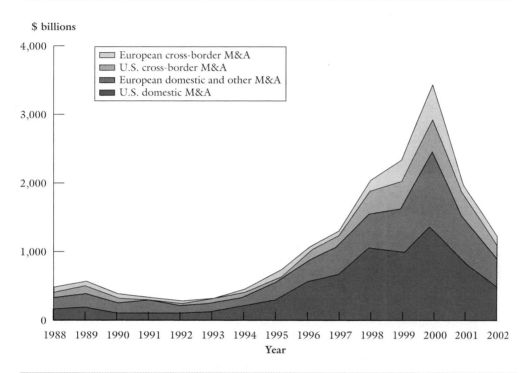

Source: Compiled from *Mergers and Acquisitions*, various issues.

prolonged boom in the developed stock markets of Europe and North America. This merger wave came to a crashing halt in the spring of 2000 with the burst of the technology stock bubble. As companies focused on consolidation rather than expansion, domestic and cross-border M&A activity during 2002 fell to about half of its 2000 level.

Regulation of Mergers and Acquisitions

In many countries, corporate takeovers are regulated separately from competitive and antitrust considerations. Many countries also regulate foreign and domestic takeovers separately from one another. Foreign ownership of key industries, such as national defense, can be barred outright or subjected to closer scrutiny than domestic acquisitions.

In the United States, the Securities and Exchange Commission (SEC) regulates takeovers. The Federal Trade Commission (FTC) and the Justice Department regulate economic and antitrust issues. Many industries also have their own regulatory bodies, such as the Federal Reserve Board (banking) and the Federal Communications Commission (broadcasting and communications).

The City Panel on Takeovers, a self-regulatory agency of the London Stock Exchange, determines takeover rules in the United Kingdom. The Monopolies and Mergers Commission handles antitrust issues and has the power to stop mergers and acquisitions that it considers anticompetitive. Rather than having a separate regulatory body for each industry, the Secretary of State for Trade and Industry regulates all U.K. commerce. Governmental policies are more likely to be consistent across industries with a single regulatory body, but the cost of this regulatory consistency is a lower level of regulatory expertise in any single industry.

Takeover conduct in Germany is governed by the Stock Exchange Commission, which is dominated by bankers. The German Antitrust Authority has jurisdiction over competitive issues. Major changes require approval of 75 percent of shareholders, and golden parachutes (lucrative severance packages) for managers are not allowed.

In Japan, the Fair Trade Commission has jurisdiction whenever 10 percent or more of a company changes hands. A registration statement must be filed with the Japanese Ministry of Finance on any offer of more than 10 percent of a company's shares. Bidders must wait a minimum of 10 days after official acceptance of the registration statement before an offer can be made. For a cash offer to be approved, funds in the amount of the offer must be on deposit at a Japanese bank.

Hostile Acquisitions

The Anglo-American tradition of the United States and the United Kingdom (as well as Australia and Canada) is to trust the *invisible hand* of the marketplace. In these economies, dispersed equity ownership has led to price-oriented, arm's-length transactions in a relatively competitive marketplace. Public proxy contests are much more common in U.S. and U.K. equity markets than in countries with bank-based governance systems. Control contests are also much more likely to be hostile in countries with market-based systems. Well-developed capital markets and dispersed equity ownership make hostile acquisitions relatively easy to accomplish in these markets.

> Hostile acquisitions are more common in the United Kingdom and the United States than in Germany or Japan.

Although there are several thousand takeovers annually in Japan, most of these are friendly acquisitions between related companies. The sums involved are usually small relative to the size of the Japanese market. A small number of private investors engage in **greenmail**—buying shares on the open market in the hope that the corporation or its business partners will buy back the shares at inflated prices. Sometimes these investors—called *sokaiya*—threaten to disrupt annual stockholder meetings. Although Japan's Commercial Law prohibits payments to sokaiya, payoff scandals continue to surface.

Foreign acquisitions of Japanese firms are relatively rare. Typically, there are only around 50 foreign acquisitions of Japanese companies in any given year. This is a small fraction of the level of acquisition activity in other large economies. About half of these foreign acquisitions are friendly takeovers of Japanese joint venture partners or transfers of control from one non-Japanese company to another.

Three impediments make a hostile foreign acquisition of a Japanese company difficult. The first and weakest barrier is a requirement that foreign bidders notify the Japanese Ministry of Finance of their intention to acquire a Japanese company. The Ministry of Finance and the Japanese Fair Trade Commission can delay acquisitions (especially foreign acquisitions) for a "suspense period" that can last for several months. This allows target management time to erect takeover defenses.

A second barrier to hostile foreign acquisitions is a cultural aversion to hostile and aggressive social behavior. Japanese business practices place a heavy emphasis on reciprocity and cooperation. Keiretsu members strive for harmony within the keiretsu group, and they prize trust, loyalty, and friendship in their business dealings. Consequently, many Japanese find American-style takeovers to be offensive. Keiretsu members, business partners, and other institutional owners strongly resist foreign intrusion into their keiretsu relationships.

> In Japan, the keiretsu structure makes hostile acquisitions difficult.

The third and most powerful barrier to a hostile foreign acquisition of a Japanese firm is the convention of reciprocal share cross-holdings among keiretsu members and business partners. These cross-holdings ensure that a large proportion of outstanding shares are in friendly hands, including a company's main bank. When faced with a hostile acquisition,

Japanese managers rely on the shares held by their business partners or keiretsu as a source of stability during turbulent times.

Each of these barriers is weakening as regulations are liberalized, share cross-holdings are unraveled, and cross-border acquisitions become more common. Nevertheless, mergers and acquisitions of Japanese companies by foreign companies are still the exception rather than the rule.

Hostile takeovers in Germany are also rare, but for different reasons than in Japan. The largest impediment to a hostile acquisition in Germany is the structure of the German supervisory board. The corporation's Hausbank controls a majority of the stock in large public corporations, so the cooperation of this bank is essential. Support of the labor force is also necessary, because employees control nearly one-half of the seats on the boards of large corporations. This makes it difficult for a hostile bidder to gain control of a German corporation with the expressed intention of cutting the workforce or moving production to a foreign site.

> The German supervisory board makes hostile acquisitions difficult.

German laws also serve to block hostile acquisitions. Takeover guidelines are enforced by commercial banks, which also control corporations through their extensive stock holdings and through the supervisory board. German corporation law requires that a supermajority of 75 percent of shareholders approve a takeover and prohibits paying golden parachutes (lucrative severance packages) to management. Takeover guidelines also require that all shareholders must be paid the same price even if they have previously accepted a lower bid for their shares. For all of these reasons, hostile takeovers in Germany are rare. Friendly takeovers account for a large proportion of corporate M&A activity.

19.4 • THE INTERNATIONAL EVIDENCE ON MERGERS AND ACQUISITIONS

The U.S. market for corporate control has been more closely studied than other national markets because of its international prominence and the fact that information is more readily available in the United States than in other countries. Although other national markets have been studied less extensively, some common themes have emerged.

The Winners and Losers

First and foremost, shareholders of acquired firms capture large gains at the time of an acquisition or merger announcement. Acquisition premiums in the United States typically range from 20 to 55 percent when measured from share price one month prior to the acquisition announcement.[16] In the United States, returns to target firm shareholders tend to be larger in acquisitions than in mergers. Returns to target firms are also larger when there are multiple bidders, suggesting that an increase in competition for target firms drives up acquisition premiums.

> Target shareholders gain in M&As.

Although the shares of target firms rise in price at the time of an acquisition or merger announcement, returns to the shareholders of bidding firms are mixed. In the United States, most studies find that bidding firms either receive no net gain or slightly overpay for target firms. This is consistent with a competitive U.S. market for corporate control in which bidding firms are forced to pay nearly full value for target firms.[17]

---

16 Jensen and Ruback report gains to target firms of 29 percent for acquisitions versus 16 percent for mergers in "The Market for Corporate Control," *Journal of Financial Economics* (1983).

17 Bradley, Desai, and Kim, "Synergistic Gains from Corporate Acquisitions and Their Division Between the Stockholders of Target and Acquiring Firms," *Journal of Financial Economics* (1988).

In contrast to the U.S. evidence, mergers and acquisitions in other countries are likely to result in announcement period gains to bidding shareholders. Kang, Shivdasani, and Yamada documented a 1.2 percent announcement period return to bidding shareholders in mergers within Japan and a 5.4 percent cumulative return for the duration of the mergers.[18] Gains for bidders in domestic mergers also have been identified in Canada and some countries in Europe and the Far East.[19]

> M&As outside the United States are more likely to result in gains to bidders.

Cross-border mergers and acquisitions often result in wealth gains for both targets and bidders even if they involve a U.S. firm. For example, Kang found wealth gains for Japanese firms acquiring U.S. firms of about one-half percent.[20] Markides and Ittner found similar wealth gains for U.S. acquisitions of foreign firms.[21]

Why are bidding firm shareholders more likely to gain outside the United States? Perhaps international markets for corporate control are less competitive than the market in the United States. Alternatively, it is possible that synergistic gains are greater in non-U.S. and cross-border mergers and acquisitions, leaving more value for bidding firm shareholders. A final answer must await further research.

Contributing Factors

Gains or losses are related to several factors, including the method of payment, the free cash flow or profitability of the acquiring firm, the tax environment, and the real exchange rate.

Method of Payment. In both domestic and international mergers and acquisitions, announcement period returns to acquiring firms are related to the **method of payment**

> Bidding firm shareholders are more likely to gain when offering cash.

used to finance the acquisitions. In domestic U.S. acquisitions, offers of stock are associated with negative returns to acquiring firms, whereas cash offers generate little share price movement on average.[22] The commonly accepted explanation for this phenomenon is that offers of stock signal that management believes the stock is overvalued. Offers of cash do not send the same signal to the market.

Franks and Harris found shareholder wealth and method of payment effects in the United Kingdom.[23] On average, U.K. target firms receive large premiums, but the share prices of U.K. acquiring firms either do not change or change only slightly during announcement periods. Returns to both acquiring and target firms within the United Kingdom are comparable in size to those in the United States after controlling for the method of payment. As in the United States, returns to target firms are higher when there are multiple bidders for the target firm.

Free Cash Flow. Managers with a substantial ownership stake in the firm are much more likely to use cash or debt to finance an acquisition than stock. Owner-managers have two reasons for avoiding new stock offers to finance acquisitions. First, their large

---

18 Kang, Shivdasani, and Yamada, "The Effect of Bank Relations on Investment Decisions: An Investigation of Japanese Takeover Bids," *Journal of Finance* (2000).

19 Eckbo and Thorburn, "Gains to Bidder Firms Revisited: Domestic and Foreign Acquisitions in Canada," *Journal of Financial and Quantitative Analysis* (2000).

20 Kang, "The International Market for Corporate Control," *Journal of Financial Economics* (1993).

21 Markides and Ittner, "Shareholder Benefits from Corporate International Diversification: Evidence from U.S. International Acquisitions," *Journal of International Business Studies* (1994).

22 Travlos, "Corporate Takeover Bids, Methods of Payment, and Bidding Firms' Stock Return," *Journal of Finance* (1987).

23 Franks and Harris, "Shareholder Wealth Effects of Corporate Takeovers: The U.K. Experience 1955–1985," *Journal of Financial Economics* (1989). In contrast, Eckbo and Thorburn ("Gains to Bidder Firms Revisited") found acquiring firms experienced positive gains with stock offers in Canada.

equity shareholdings are prima facie evidence that they believe their shares to be undervalued by the market. If they believe that their shares are undervalued, then a stock offer would dilute their ownership stake and rob them of some of this latent value. Second, financing acquisitions with stock dilutes their ownership position in the firm. With a smaller vote in company affairs, managers risk loss of control.

Jensen suggested that losses to acquiring firm shareholders are related to free cash flow.[24] **Free cash flow** is defined as cash flow that is available to the firm after all positive-NPV investments have been exhausted in the firm's main line of business. According to Jensen's hypothesis, managers with control over large amounts of free cash flow are more likely to spend it on wasteful investments, such as overpriced acquisitions, rather than paying these surplus funds as a dividend or repurchasing the firm's debt or equity securities. The U.S. evidence is consistent with Jensen's hypothesis. Firms with higher free cash flow are more likely to engage in acquisitions that destroy rather than create value for their shareholders.

> Firms with lots of cash are more likely to waste it.

Similarly, returns to acquiring firms are negatively correlated with the profitability of the acquiring firm in mergers and acquisitions that cross the U.S. border.[25] That is, the higher the acquiring firm's profitability, the lower the return to the shareholders of the acquiring firm. This is consistent with Jensen's free cash flow hypothesis and the U.S. evidence. The international evidence substitutes *profitability* for *free cash flow* because of the difficulty in identifying the free cash flow of firms with accounting rules that are, in most cases, less transparent than U.S. accounting principles.

The Tax Environment. Tax laws can influence the pace and profitability of merger and acquisition activity. Tax laws influence the treatment of carryforwards and carrybacks, such as operating losses, capital losses, investment tax credits, and foreign tax credits. The value of unused carryforwards can be realized more quickly and more fully through merger with a profitable firm than if the firm with unused carryforwards is left to generate taxable income on its own. Mergers and acquisitions also can facilitate asset sales to change to a more accelerated depreciation schedule, step up the book value of an asset to its fair market value and thus increase the depreciation deduction, or realize taxable losses and generate an immediate tax deduction.

> M&A gains are sensitive to tax laws.

Empirical evidence shows that changes in U.S. tax laws influence domestic acquisitions of U.S. companies.[26] In particular, the Economic Recovery Tax Act of 1981 encouraged asset sales by allowing acquiring firms to step up the depreciable basis and to change the depreciation schedule to an accelerated cost recovery system. The Tax Reform Act (TRA) of 1986 later removed these tax incentives. Provisions of the 1986 TRA on asset purchases went into effect on January 1, 1987. The last quarter of 1986 saw a surge in merger and acquisition activity as corporations scrambled to consummate their acquisitions under the old, more favorable tax rules.

If taxes play a role in domestic mergers and acquisitions, then they should play an even greater role in cross-border mergers and acquisitions. National taxes on foreign-source income are complex and vary by country. Cross-border differences in tax rates and tax regimes allow MNCs with geographically diversified operations to arbitrage across tax jurisdictions. In turn, the ability of the MNC to arbitrage tax asymmetries depends on how foreign-source income is taxed in the parent's home country.

---

24 Jensen, "Agency Costs of Free Cash Flow, Corporate Financing, and Takeovers," *American Economic Review* (1986).

25 See, for example, Markides and Ittner, "Shareholder Benefits."

26 Scholes and Wolfson, "The Effects of Changes in Tax Laws on Corporate Reorganization Activity," *Journal of Business* (1990).

The empirical evidence suggests that markets do react to firm-specific tax-related factors around the time of cross-border acquisition announcements. In particular, returns to the foreign targets of U.S. firms and to the U.S. targets of foreign firms are sensitive to changes in U.S. tax laws.[27] The evidence suggests that the market responds favorably to a foreign acquisition that enhances a multinational corporation's ability to repatriate after-tax funds and unfavorably to an acquisition that is likely to trigger additional taxes.

It is important not to overemphasize the importance of tax considerations to M&A returns and the pace of M&A activity. Taxes are but one of many factors that influence reorganization activity. Nevertheless, mergers and acquisitions can facilitate the transfer and realization of tax benefits.

Real Exchange Rates. Intuition suggests that foreign acquisitions of domestic assets should increase when the real value of the foreign currency is high relative to the domestic currency. The conventional wisdom is that a real depreciation of the domestic currency increases the purchasing power of foreign residents relative to domestic residents, which results in a competitive advantage in corporate control contests. This conception of the impact of purchasing power on M&A activity is intuitively appealing. Anyone who has traveled to a foreign country has felt the impact of real exchange rate changes on purchasing power.

Yet finance theory asserts that corporate financial policy is irrelevant in a perfect capital market. This irrelevance proposition has an interesting consequence for the relation between exchange rates and the pace of cross-border mergers and acquisitions. In a perfect capital market, all corporations have equal access to frictionless capital markets and costless information. This means that there is no innate advantage to a foreign (or domestic) bidder in corporate control contests. For example, changes in the real exchange rate may mean that foreign bidders are wealthier than domestic bidders. But the fact that either firm can gain access to additional capital at prevailing market prices means that it is no easier for one firm than another to raise funds in international capital markets. Consequently, neither foreign nor domestic bidders have an advantage in takeover contests in a perfect capital market.

One or more market imperfections must preferentially benefit a firm for that firm to have an advantage in raising capital. Several capital market imperfections can lead to an advantage, depending on the MNC's country of residence. Froot and Stein suggest that such an advantage can arise when there is an informational asymmetry between corporate insiders and outside investors that makes outside capital more expensive than internally generated funds.[28] According to their theory, a fall in the value of the domestic currency results in an increase in the cash position of foreign corporations relative to domestic corporations. Foreign firms have additional cash on hand, so they need not raise additional capital through the external markets to mount a bidding campaign. Domestic firms, on the other hand, suffer a decrease in their relative wealth and must tap the external markets if they want to initiate or join a bidding contest. The lower cost of internal funds confers an advantage on foreign firms over domestic firms in bidding contests when the domestic currency falls in value.

The converse occurs when a foreign currency falls against the domestic currency. To the extent that domestic firms enjoy a relative wealth increase, they will have more cash on hand and will not have to tap the external capital markets to mount an acquisition

---

27 Manzon, Sharp, and Travlos, "An Empirical Study of the Consequences of U.S. Tax Rules for International Acquisitions by U.S. Firms," *Journal of Finance* (1994); and Servaes and Zenner, "Taxes and the Returns to Foreign Acquisitions in the United States," *Financial Management* (1994).

28 Froot and Stein, "Exchange Rates and Foreign Direct Investment: An Imperfect Capital Markets Approach," *Quarterly Journal of Economics* (1991).

Market Update

The Creation of DaimlerChrysler

On May 6, 1998 (a Wednesday), Germany's Daimler-Benz A.G. announced a merger with Chrysler Corporation of the United States to create the world's fifth largest automaker. Chrysler shareholders were offered a stock swap worth $38.3 billion. The new company, DaimlerChrysler A.G., is now incorporated in Stuttgart, Germany. Returns to Daimler-Benz and Chrysler stock and to the German and U.S. stock markets over the weeks surrounding the announcement are shown in the following graph.

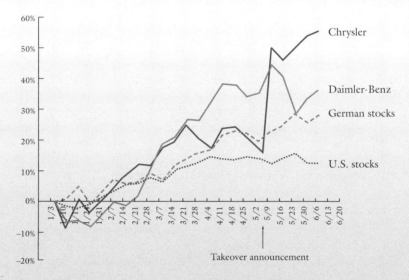

Merger and acquisition activity tends to increase with increases in equity values. Many national stock markets rose during early 1998, including Germany and the United States. At the time of the announcement, shares of both Daimler-Benz and Chrysler were also well above their levels at the start of the year.

Chrysler shareholders were the clear winners in this merger, with a 34.1 percent gain during the announcement week. Daimler-Benz' share price rose 9.3 percent during the week, although 3.2 percent of this gain was attributable to a general rise in the value of German stocks. This increase in both acquiring and target firm share prices is not unusual in a cross-border merger or acquisition. The long-term gain or loss to Daimler-Benz's shareholders is more difficult to determine. After an initial rise, Daimler-Benz stock fell by 15.3 percent during the subsequent two weeks, despite a 5.8 percent overall gain in German stock values.

Rarely are the partners in a merger or acquisition equal. One management team usually retains the upper hand. American managers have taken a back seat to their German counterparts in the DaimlerChrysler merger. The melancholy joke at Chrysler headquarters after the merger was: "How do you pronounce DaimlerChrysler in German?" The answer: "The 'Chrysler' is silent."

bid. Foreign firms are relatively cash constrained and will be more likely to need to access external capital before they can mount a bidding contest. A fall in the foreign currency thus benefits the domestic acquirer relative to its foreign competitors.

An informational asymmetry between inside and outside stakeholders is not the only capital market imperfection that results in an advantage to the foreign firm when the domestic currency falls in value. Any capital market imperfection that results in higher costs on external capital will result in a competitive advantage for the firm that has access to internally generated funds. Underwriting fees and transactions costs on new debt and equity issues are other examples of imperfections that raise the cost of external capital.

Empirical studies generally confirm that the level of foreign acquisitions is positively related to the value of the domestic currency.[29] Moreover, gains to bidding firms are pos-

> A strong domestic currency leads to more foreign acquisitions and higher bidder returns.

itively related to the strength of the domestic currency. For example, acquiring firms based in the United States gain from an appreciation of the dollar. Similarly, gains to Japanese bidders rise with an appreciation of the yen. When the domestic currency is strong, domestic firms are more likely to acquire foreign companies, and shareholders are more likely to benefit from the acquisition.

A relative corporate wealth effect similar to that proposed by Froot and Stein may be the dominant effect. Dewenter found that the exchange rate has no power to explain foreign direct investment beyond that explained by change in the relative corporate wealth of foreign and domestic firms and the overall level of investment.[30] Dewenter measured relative corporate wealth as the value of a foreign stock market divided by the value of the U.S. market. The relative corporate wealth variable dominated the exchange rate variable in her sample of foreign acquisitions of U.S. target firms. A firm with high relative corporate wealth was both more likely to acquire a foreign firm and more likely to see a share price appreciation upon announcing an acquisition.

The Advantages of Multinationality

A growing body of literature examines factors related to the success of the multinational corporation in its forays into cross-border mergers and acquisitions. In general, the empirical findings are consistent with the eclectic paradigm.[31] The **eclectic paradigm** categorizes competitive advantages into ownership-specific, location-specific, and market internalization advantages. According to this theory of the firm, multinational corporations are successful when they can do the following:

- Create and maintain intangible *ownership-specific advantages*, such as brand names, patents, copyrights, proprietary technology or technological processes, or marketing or management expertise

- Obtain privileged access to *location-specific advantages*, such as natural or manufactured resources, low taxes or wage costs, markets for the firm's products, or high labor productivity

- Successfully exploit their ownership-specific and location-specific advantages through *market internalization advantages*

For cross-border mergers and acquisitions to make sense, the MNC must enjoy advantages over local firms in capitalizing on the firm-specific and location-specific advantages of its foreign acquisitions. Of course, even if an MNC can identify a foreign acquisition that possesses firm-specific or location-specific advantages, these advantages are of no use if the purchase price is too high.

29 Harris and Ravenscraft, "The Role of Acquisitions in Foreign Direct Investment: Evidence from the U.S. Stock Market," *Journal of Finance* (1991).

30 Dewenter, "Do Exchange Rate Changes Drive Foreign Direct Investment?" *Journal of Business* (1995).

31 Dunning, *Multinational Enterprises and the Global Economy* (1993); and Caves, *Multinational Enterprise and Economic Analysis* (1996).

Multinationality and Intangible Firm-Specific Assets. Multinational corporations tend to spend more heavily than domestic firms on research and development (R&D) and on advertising to create and promote intangible firm-specific advantages. International expansion benefits the MNC by allowing it to exploit these intangible assets on a larger scale and across a greater range of markets than its domestic competitors.

> MNCs spend more heavily on R&D and advertising to create and promote their products.

Using Tobin's q (the market value of firm assets divided by their replacement cost) as a measure of firm value, Morck and Yeung found that the positive impact of spending to create and promote the firm's intangible assets increases with a firm's multinationality.[32] Morck and Yeung found that multinationality itself has little relationship to the returns of acquiring firms after controlling for R&D and advertising expense. These authors concluded that multinationality has little value in and of itself. Multinationality must be accompanied by intangible firm-specific assets to be of value to the corporation.

Multinationality and the Relatedness of the Target Firm. Multinationality also benefits the MNC by providing access to a more diverse stock of assets and, therefore, better prepares the MNC to seize opportunities as they arise. Markides and Ittner found that cross-border acquisitions of companies in related businesses result in large gains to acquiring firms, whereas acquisitions of unrelated businesses result in shareholder losses, on average.[33] As in the domestic market, these authors found horizontal acquisitions into unrelated businesses in other countries result in losses for the shareholders of acquiring firms. This result is consistent with Morck and Yeung in that international diversification per se does not appear to be of value. MNCs need intangible advantages such as patents to be able to increase their market values through international acquisition.

> Acquisitions in related businesses lead to bigger gains than unrelated businesses.

Prior International Experience. The experience gained through multinational operations can itself be of value if it increases the efficiency with which the MNC internalizes product and factor markets and exploits its ownership and locational advantages. As an example, the international scope of the MNC can confer advantages in manufacturing industries such as electronics and semiconductors as the MNC shifts production to the lowest cost plants. The international scope of the MNC also can confer market power if it preempts competitors from gaining sufficient scale to compete on an international level or exploiting their own intangible assets in new locations. Consequently, firms that expand their multinational network through mergers and acquisitions should see their share prices increase when these deals are announced.

> Prior international experience is a valuable asset.

Doukas and Travlos examined the gains to U.S.-based MNCs acquiring foreign assets through international acquisition.[34] They found that shareholder gains are largest for MNCs entering foreign markets in which they are not already operating. Returns are especially large for MNCs entering emerging markets through acquisition. Returns are not significantly different from zero for firms entering foreign markets in which they are already operating or for the first time.

> Gains are largest for MNCs entering foreign markets in which they are not already operating.

In a similar vein, Harris and Ravenscraft found that the premiums paid to the U.S. targets of foreign acquirers (40 percent) are almost double those paid to the U.S. targets of U.S. acquirers (26 percent).[35] This is presumably because the non-U.S. acquirers can

---

32 Morck and Yeung, "Why Investors Value Multinationality," *Journal of Business* (1991).

33 Markides and Ittner, "Shareholder Benefits."

34 Doukas and Travlos, "The Effect of Corporate Multinationalism on Shareholders' Wealth: Evidence from International Acquisitions," *Journal of Finance* (1988).

35 Harris and Ravenscraft, "The Role of Acquisitions."

exploit the assets of the U.S. targets better than the U.S. acquirers can exploit these same assets in foreign markets. This additional value is then reflected in the higher price that the non-U.S. acquirers are willing to pay for the U.S. targets.

The Benefits and Costs of Cross-Border Diversification

An objective of financial strategy is to minimize the firm's overall cost of capital given its investment policy. If investors already have access to international markets, then the MNC cannot provide diversification benefits that investors cannot already capture through portfolio investment. In this case, corporate diversification into international markets cannot reduce investors' required returns or the firm's cost of capital. The MNC might be able to better employ its intangible assets in international markets than in domestic markets, but the added value arises from the investment itself and not from a lower cost of capital.

If investors are restricted from some national markets, then the MNC can provide **indirect diversification benefits** through corporate investment into restricted markets.

> MNCs can provide indirect diversification benefits into restricted markets.

Cross-border portfolio investment is restricted in many emerging markets, and even in some developed markets. MNCs can invest in these countries directly or through joint ventures with local partners, acquiring foreign assets and diversification benefits that are not available to individual investors or portfolio managers. These indirect diversification benefits then can lead to a lower cost of capital in the MNC's own national market.

Possibly offsetting this benefit is the **diversification discount** faced by industrially and globally diversified firms. The market values of diversified MNCs are about 15 percent less than portfolios of single-segment firms operating in the same industries in the United States,[36] and in the United Kingdom and Japan.[37] The diversification discount appears to be related to the corporate governance system, but not in any obvious way.[38] Indeed, there is not yet consensus in the literature that the diversification discount even exists.[39]

Managers have an incentive to diversify even at the expense of shareholder value because it can increase their compensation (through control of a larger firm) and decrease their risk (through increased corporate diversification). The common explanation for the diversification discount is that it is an agency cost of inefficient investment by managers attempting to limit their risks and maximize their wealth.

A Caveat

Theoretical and empirical research into the international market for corporate control is still in its infancy. Ongoing research will surely modify and extend the conclusions reported here. Moreover, academic research is most likely shooting at a moving target, as the factors that influence the winners and the losers in corporate control contests will surely evolve as markets are integrated across national borders.

---

36 Berger and Ofek, "Diversification's Effect on Firm Value," *Journal of Financial Economics* (1995); and Denis, Denis, and Yost, "Global Diversification, Industrial Diversification, and Firm Value," *Journal of Finance* (2002).

37 Lins and Servaes, "International Evidence on the Value of Corporate Diversification," *Journal of Finance* (1999).

38 In "International Evidence," Lins and Servaes found a diversification discount in Japan only for firms with links to an industrial group. In contrast, Khanna and Palepu found that association with an industrial group in India enhances value in "Is Group Affiliation Profitable in Emerging Markets? An Analysis of Diversified Indian Business Groups," *Journal of Finance* (2000).

39 Graham, Lemmon, and Wolf, "Does Corporate Diversification Destroy Value?" *Journal of Finance* (2002); and Mansi and Reeb, "Corporate Diversification: What Gets Discounted?" *Journal of Finance* (2002).

19.5 • SUMMARY

International markets for corporate control provide the multinational financial manager with exciting and challenging opportunities to consolidate existing operations, preempt competitors from entry into existing and future markets, and protect and expand the value of current and future operations.

This chapter described corporate governance and the markets for corporate control with an emphasis on Germany, Japan, and the United States. Corporate governance systems share many common elements, but they have unique features as well. For example, the supervisory board represents the major stakeholders in each country. Yet the composition, powers, and responsibilities of the board vary across countries. In the U.S. market-based system, the board is elected by a diverse set of shareholders and operates relatively independently. In Germany's universal banking and Japan's keiretsu systems, banks supply both debt and equity capital. Through their equity stake in the firm, bankers in Germany and Japan maintain a prominent position on the supervisory board and closely monitor the management team.

There are important differences even within the bank-based corporate governance systems of Germany and Japan. In Germany, the lead bank supplies both debt and equity capital and serves as investment banker and market maker for public equity offerings. Because the lead bank controls the mechanisms by which the corporation raises capital, the bank plays a very powerful role in corporate affairs. The role of commercial banks in Japan is intermediate between that in Germany and the United States. In Japan, power is shared within the keiretsu, a network of companies linked through business partnerships that share cross-holdings and that have a major bank or corporation at the center.

The structure of these corporate governance systems influences top executive turnover and the market for corporate control. In the United States, management is much more likely to be disciplined through the public equity markets through (possibly hostile) corporate takeovers. Hostile acquisitions are much less common in Germany and are almost nonexistent in Japan because of the concentration of equity ownership in the hands of the lead bank in Germany and in other keiretsu members in Japan. A hostile acquisition is simply not possible in Germany or Japan without the cooperation of the major stakeholder or stakeholders.

Acquisition premiums paid to target firm shareholders are roughly comparable in domestic and in cross-border acquisitions. However, the shareholders of acquiring firms are much more likely to gain in a cross-border acquisition than in a domestic acquisition, especially when the acquiring firm

- Has intangible, firm-specific assets such as patents or trademarks
- Is acquiring a firm in a related line of business
- Has prior international experience
- Is entering a market for the first time

Finally, a firm is much more likely to acquire foreign assets when there has been a recent appreciation of its domestic currency.

KEY TERMS

acquisition of stock	consolidation
acquisition premium	corporate governance (family-, state-,
agency costs	bank-, or market-based)
chaebol	diversification discount

eclectic paradigm   method of payment
free cash flow   privatization
greenmail   supervisory board
indirect diversification benefits   synergy
keiretsu (horizontal or vertical)   universal banking
merger

CONCEPTUAL QUESTIONS

19.1   Define corporate governance. Why is it important in international finance?

19.2   In what ways can one firm gain control over the assets of another firm?

19.3   What is synergy?

19.4   What is the difference between a private and a public capital market? Why is this difference important in corporate governance?

19.5   Describe several differences in the role of commercial banks in corporate governance in Germany, Japan, and the United States.

19.6   Why are hostile acquisitions less common in Germany and Japan than in the United Kingdom and the United States?

19.7   How is turnover in the ranks of top executives similar in Germany, Japan, and the United States? How is it different?

19.8   Who are the likely winners and losers in domestic mergers and acquisitions that involve two firms incorporated in the same country?

19.9   In what ways are the winners and losers in cross-border mergers and acquisitions the same as in domestic mergers and acquisitions? In what ways do they differ?

19.10 Why might the shareholders of bidding firms lose when the bidding firm has excess free cash flow or profitability?

19.11 How are gains to bidding firms related to exchange rates?

PROBLEMS

19.1   Connect each term to its definition or description.

a. Acquisition of assets   A. Creation of an entirely new firm

b. Acquisition of stock   B. A combination of the assets and liabilities of two firms

c. Acquisition premium   C. The difference between the value of a combination and the sum of the parts

d. Consolidation   D. An acquisition in which one firm buys an equity interest in another

e. Merger   E. An acquisition in which none of the liabilities supporting an asset are transferred to the purchaser

f. Method of payment   F. The difference between the purchase price and the preacquisition value of the target firm

g. Synergy   G. The way in which a merger or acquisition is financed

19.2 Suppose Agile Corporation of the United States acquires Mobile Plc of the United Kingdom. The value of Agile stock on the Nasdaq in the United States is $3 billion. Mobile sells on the London Stock Exchange for the pound sterling equivalent of $1 billion. Agile pays a 20 percent acquisition premium to acquire Mobile. The synergy created through the combination of Agile and Mobile adds 10 percent to the value of the combined firm. How much are Agile's shareholders likely to gain or lose through this acquisition?

19.3 The British Petroleum acquisition of U.S.-based Amoco was the largest cross-border acquisition during 1998. Were BP and Amoco a good fit? Did Amoco shareholders gain or lose when the acquisition was announced on August 11, 1998? How did BP shareholders fare relative to other oil companies? How do these shareholder returns compare to other international acquisitions and to the typical domestic acquisition?

19.4 You are the CEO of XO, a bulk chemical producer and processor. XO is generating quite a lot of free cash flow that cannot be profitably invested domestically. You are looking to expand XO's operations abroad through acquisition, despite having no international operations or experience.
   a. Is the existence of free cash flow a benefit or a hindrance to your international expansion plans? How might shareholders view your plans to spend free cash flow on an international investment or acquisition?
   b. How might your lack of international experience influence your international acquisition plans?
   c. Your VP of New Product Development points out that this is an opportunity to get into the automotive supply business that you've always wanted to enter. Her friend, an executive at Ford Motor Company's new plant in Brazil, is looking for a company to supply seats to the Brazilian plant. What does academic research say about the value that is likely to be added by a cross-border investment in an unrelated business?
   d. Suppose one of your lines of business—specialty chemicals—has been operating in southern Europe. Your VP of New Product Development suggests expanding operations in South America. Does this proposal make sense?

19.5 You are the chairman of Tres Equis, a beverage manufacturer based in Mexico City. For years, you have harbored ambitions of expanding operations into other Latin American countries and perhaps even into the United States. The Mexican peso has recently risen in real terms against most foreign currencies. Is now a good time to expand internationally through acquisition? Describe the influence of exchange rates on cross-border merger and acquisition activity.

19.6 Chronic overcapacity in the global automotive industry has forced automakers to reexamine their long-term strategic options. The industry sells around 50 million vehicles in a good year, but global capacity is about 70 million vehicles. Automakers with free cash flow are looking to acquire other automakers rather than build new capacity. Distressed automakers are looking for new investors.
   a. At the time this book went to press, both Volvo (Sweden) and Nissan (Japan) were actively courting investments from other automakers. Use your library database to identify what became of these efforts.
   b. Have any other automotive assets changed hands recently?

19.7 A continuing recession has forced many changes on financial institutions and the market for corporate control within Japan. Use your library database to identify recent changes in each of the following:

a. Have there been any recent mergers or consolidations in Japanese banking?
b. Have there been any recent breaks in the keiretsu system within Japan?
c. Are there recent changes to the Japanese practice of lifelong employment?

SUGGESTED READINGS

Corporate governance systems in various countries are discussed in the following:

Thorsten Beck and Ross Levine, "Industry Growth and Capital Allocation: Does Having a Market- or Bank-Based System Matter," *Journal of Financial Economics* 64, No. 2 (2002).

Nicola Cetorelli and Michele Gambera, "Banking Market Structure, Financial Dependence and Growth: International Evidence from Industry Data," *Journal of Finance* 56, No. 2 (2001), pp. 617–648.

Gary Gorton and Frank A. Schmid, "Universal Banking and the Performance of German Firms," *Journal of Financial Economics* 58 (October 2000), pp. 29–80.

William L. Megginson and Jeffry M. Netter, "From State to Market: A Survey of Empirical Studies on Privatization," *Journal of Economic Literature* 39 (June 2001), pp. 326–389.

Rafael La Porta, Florencio Lopez-de-Silanes, and Andrei Shleifer, "Corporate Ownership Around the World," *Journal of Finance* 54 (April 1999), pp. 471–517.

Rafael La Porta, Florencio Lopez-de-Silanes, Andrei Shleifer. and Robert Vishny, "Investor Protection and Corporate Governance," *Journal of Financial Economics* 58 (October/November 2000), pp. 3–27.

Mark J. Roe, "Some Differences in Corporate Structure in Germany, Japan, and the United States," *Yale Law Journal* 102 (1993), pp. 1927–2003.

Andrei Shleifer and Robert Vishny, "A Survey of Corporate Governance," *Journal of Finance* 52 (June 1997), pp. 737–783.

Paolo F. Volpin, "Governance with Poor Investor Protection: Evidence from Top Executive Turnover in Italy," *Journal of Financial Economics* 64 (April 2002).

Domestic mergers and acquisitions have been studied in

Kee-Hong Bae, Jun-Koo Kang, and Jin-Mo Kim, "Tunneling or Value Added? Evidence from Mergers by Korean Business Groups," *Journal of Finance* 57, (December 2002), pp. 2695–2740.

Michael Bradley, Anand Desai, and E. Han Kim, "Synergistic Gains from Corporate Acquisitions and Their Division Between the Stockholders of Target and Acquiring Firms," *Journal of Financial Economics* 21, No. 1 (1988), pp. 3–40.

B. Espen Eckbo and Karin S. Thorburn, "Gains to Bidder Firms Revisited: Domestic and Foreign Acquisitions in Canada," *Journal of Financial and Quantitative Analysis* 35 (March 2000), pp. 1–25.

Julian R. Franks and Robert S. Harris, "Shareholder Wealth Effects of Corporate Takeovers: The U.K. Experience 1955–1985," *Journal of Financial Economics* 23, No. 2 (1989), pp. 225–250.

Michael C. Jensen, "Agency Costs of Free Cash Flow, Corporate Financing, and Takeovers," *American Economic Review* 76, No. 2 (1986), pp. 323–339.

Jun-Koo Kang, Anil Shivdasani, and Takeshi Yamada, "The Effect of Bank Relations on Investment Decisions: An Investigation of Japanese Takeover Bids," *Journal of Finance* 55 (October 2000), pp. 2197–2218.

Michael C. Jensen and Richard S. Ruback, "The Market for Corporate Control," *Journal of Financial Economics* 11, No. 1 (1983), pp. 5–50.

Nickolaos G. Travlos, "Corporate Takeover Bids, Methods of Payment, and Bidding Firms' Stock Return," *Journal of Finance* 62, No. 4 (1987), pp. 943–963.

The gains to shareholders in cross-border mergers/acquisitions are discussed in

John Doukas and Nickolaos G. Travlos, "The Effect of Corporate Multinationalism on Shareholders' Wealth: Evidence from International Acquisitions," *Journal of Finance* 63, No. 5 (1988), pp. 1161–1175.

Robert S. Harris and David Ravenscraft, "The Role of Acquisitions in Foreign Direct Investment: Evidence from the U.S. Stock Market," *Journal of Finance* 66, No. 3 (1991), pp. 825–845.

Jun-Koo Kang, "The International Market for Corporate Control," *Journal of Financial Economics* 34, No. 3 (1993), pp. 345–371.

Gil B. Manzon, Jr., David J. Sharp, and Nickolaos G. Travlos, "An Empirical Study of the Consequences of U.S. Tax Rules for International Acquisitions by U.S. Firms," *Journal of Finance* 49 (December 1994), pp. 1893–1904.

Constantinos C. Markides and Christopher D. Ittner, "Shareholder Benefits from Corporate International Diversification: Evidence from U.S. International Acquisitions," *Journal of International Business Studies* 25, No. 2 (1994), pp. 343–366.

Randall Morck and Bernard Yeung, "Why Investors Value Multinationality," *Journal of Business* 64, No. 2 (1991), pp. 165–187.

Henri Servaes and Marc Zenner, "Taxes and the Returns to Foreign Acquisitions in the United States," *Financial Management* 23, No. 4 (Winter 1994), pp. 42–56.

The impact of the macroeconomic environment on cross-border acquisitions and foreign direct investment is discussed in

Kathryn L. Dewenter, "Do Exchange Rate Changes Drive Foreign Direct Investment?" *Journal of Business* 68, No. 3 (1995), pp. 405–433.

Kenneth A. Froot and Jeremy C. Stein, "Exchange Rates and Foreign Direct Investment: An Imperfect Capital Markets Approach," *Quarterly Journal of Economics* 106 (November 1991), pp. 1191–1217.

Myron S. Scholes and Mark A. Wolfson, "The Effects of Changes in Tax Laws on Corporate Reorganization Activity," *Journal of Business* 63, No. 1, Part 2 (1990), pp. S141–S164.

Top executive turnover as a means of restructuring poorly performing companies is discussed in

Julian Franks and Colin Mayer, "Ownership and Control of German Corporations," *Review of Financial Studies* 14 (Winter 2001), pp. 943–977.

Jun-Koo Kang and Anil Shivdasani, "Firm Performance, Corporate Governance, and Top Executive Turnover in Japan," *Journal of Financial Economics* 38 (May 1995), pp. 29–58.

Jun-Koo Kang and Anil Shivdasani, "Does the Japanese Governance System Enhance Shareholder Wealth? Evidence from the Stock-Price Effects of Top Management Turnover," *Review of Financial Studies* 9 (Winter 1996), 1061–1095.

The eclectic paradigm (a theory of the multinational enterprise) is developed in

Richard E. Caves, "International Corporations: The Industrial Economics of Foreign Investment," *Economica* (February 1971), pp. 1–27.

John H. Dunning, "Reappraising the Eclectic Paradigm in an Age of Alliances," *Journal of International Business Studies* 26, No. 3 (1995), pp. 461–491.

The global diversification discount is investigated in

Philip G. Berger and Eli Ofek, "Diversification's Effect on Firm Value," *Journal of Financial Economics* 37 (January 1995), pp. 39–66.

David J. Denis, Diane K. Denis, and David Yost, "Global Diversification, Industrial Diversification, and Firm Value," *Journal of Finance* 57 (October 2002), pp. 1951–1979.

John R. Graham, Michael L. Lemmon, and Jack G. Wolf, "Does Corporate Diversification Destroy Value?" *Journal of Finance* 57 (April 2002), pp. 695–720.

Tarun Khanna and Krishna Palepu, "Is Group Affiliation Profitable in Emerging Markets? An Analysis of Diversified Indian Business Groups," *Journal of Finance* 55 (April 2000), pp. 867–892.

Karl Lins and Henri Servaes, "International Evidence on the Value of Corporate Diversification," *Journal of Finance* 54 (December 1999), pp. 2215–2239.

Sattar A. Mansi and David M. Reeb, "Corporate Diversification: What Gets Discounted?" *Journal of Finance* 57 (October 2002), pp. 2167–2183.

International Portfolio Investment and Asset Pricing

International Portfolio Diversification

chapter 20

Overview

We are so small between the stars, so large against the sky.

Leonard Cohen

Foreign investments have great appeal for investors and portfolio managers. The primary appeal lies in their potential for higher returns. Although much of the world's wealth resides in developed countries, emerging markets are more likely to experience above-average economic growth. This can lead to higher returns in emerging markets.

The other appeal of foreign investments is their potential for lowering portfolio risk. National economies do not move in unison, and stock and bond returns vary widely across national markets. Diversifying across national markets can greatly reduce portfolio risk because of the relatively low correlations between national markets.

This chapter provides the theoretical rationale for diversifying investment portfolios across national borders. Despite the predictions of theory, investors exhibit a strong preference for assets from their home market. This home asset bias is at least partly due to the many barriers that investors face in distant and unfamiliar markets. As barriers to cross-border trade progressively fall, international portfolio diversification is increasingly accessible to individual investors and fund managers.

> Risk depends on an asset's contribution to the risk of a portfolio.

20.1 • THE ALGEBRA OF PORTFOLIO DIVERSIFICATION

In 1990, Harry Markowitz and William Sharpe were awarded the Nobel Prize in economics for their work in portfolio theory and asset pricing.[1] The insight at the heart

---

1 Merton Miller shared the 1990 Nobel Prize for his work in continuous time finance.

of their work is quite simple. Markowitz and Sharpe observed that investors are concerned with the expected return and risk of their portfolio of assets, not with the return or risk of any single asset in isolation. Consequently, the characteristics of an asset that are important to investors are the asset's contributions to the expected return and risk of the portfolio. To appreciate the implications of this insight for asset prices in a global marketplace, we first need to develop a little algebra.

The Mean-Variance Framework

Let's start with two simplifying assumptions:

- Nominal returns are normally distributed.
- Investors want more nominal return and less risk in their functional currency.

The normal distribution is completely described by its mean and standard deviation (or variance). Faced with normally distributed returns, investors will want to maximize expected return and minimize the standard deviation of return on their portfolio.

Like the perfect market conditions, these assumptions are invoked more for convenience than for the way in which they represent the real world. We know, for instance, that equity returns are leptokurtic or fat-tailed relative to the normal distribution. Because exchange rate changes are also leptokurtic, returns on foreign stocks and bonds are even less normal than returns on comparable domestic assets. Investors with obligations in more than one currency also may want returns in more than one currency. Nevertheless, an assumption of normally distributed returns in a single functional currency is a convenient starting point. It greatly simplifies the algebra of portfolio diversification and captures most of what is important to investors.

The Expected Return on a Portfolio

The return on a portfolio of assets is a weighted average of the returns on the individual assets in the portfolio. Algebraically, this can be expressed as $r_P = \sum_i x_i r_i$ where the weights x_i represent the proportion of wealth devoted to asset i such that $\sum_i x_i = 1$. For example, the expected return on a two-asset portfolio of assets A and B is

> Portfolio return is a weighted average of asset returns.

$$E[r_P] = x_A\, E[r_A] + x_B\, E[r_B] \qquad (20.1)$$

subject to $x_A + x_B = 1$. The expected return on a portfolio of N assets is a linear function of the expected returns $E[r_i]$ on the individual assets in the portfolio and the weight given to each asset:

$$E[r_P] = \sum_i x_i\, E[r_i] \qquad (20.2)$$

subject to $\sum_i x_i = 1$. Each weight is constrained to $0 \leq x_i \leq 1$ if **short selling** (that is, selling an asset you do not own) is not allowed.

Table 20.1 presents the performance of the G-7 stock markets based on data from Morgan Stanley Capital International (MSCI). The performance of markets identified by MSCI as developed markets is presented in Figure 20.1 and Table 20.2. Emerging market returns are presented in Table 20.3. These are value-weighted nominal dollar returns from the perspective of a U.S. investor.

http://www.msci.com

Nominal returns in different currencies are not directly comparable because of cross-currency differences in inflation. One solution is to present real (inflation-adjusted) returns to each market. Another solution is to calculate returns in a common currency, such as the U.S. dollar. Nominal returns can then be compared because they are stated in the same units. We'll follow this convention.

TABLE 20.1

International Stock and Government Bond Returns, in U.S. Dollars

Stock Returns (1970–2002)

	Mean (%)	Stdev (%)	β_W	SI	Can	Fra	Ger	Japan	Swiss	U.K.	U.S.	World
Canada	10.4	18.8	0.79	0.17								
France	14.0	29.1	1.09	0.23	0.472							
Germany	12.5	30.0	1.05	0.18	0.388	0.645						
Japan	15.4	36.5	1.39	0.23	0.320	0.399	0.364					
Switzerland	14.2	25.5	0.98	0.28	0.464	0.618	0.670	0.430				
United Kingdom	14.6	29.4	1.14	0.25	0.513	0.559	0.451	0.369	0.569			
United States	11.8	17.8	0.87	0.26	0.727	0.482	0.443	0.304	0.504	0.522		
World	11.2	17.6	1.00	0.23	0.735	0.657	0.618	0.671	0.674	0.685	0.855	
U.S. T-bills	7.2	3.3	–0.01	0.00	–0.055	–0.071	–0.041	–0.059	–0.119	–0.061	–0.042	–0.068

Based on dollar returns to U.S. investors from Morgan Stanley Capital International (MSCI). "Mean" and "Stdev" represent the mean (μ_i) and standard deviation (σ_i) of annual returns, respectively. Correlations and betas are measured against monthly changes in the MSCI world stock market portfolio. The Sharpe index SI = $(\mu_i - \mu_F)/\sigma_i$ is based on annual returns to 30-day U.S. T-bills.

Suppose investments in American and British equities have return distributions as in Table 20.1.[2] If history were to repeat itself, then the mean annual return would be 11.8 percent on American (A) and 14.6 percent on British (B) equities. Of course, history is unlikely to repeat itself in precisely this way. We'll use these numbers as expected returns for convenience and not necessarily as indicators of future mean returns. Applying Equation 20.1, the expected return on an equally weighted portfolio of American and British equities is $E[r_P] = (1/2)(0.118) + (1/2)(0.146) = 0.132$, or 13.2 percent.

Portfolio risk is measured by the variance or standard deviation of return.	### The Risk of a Two-Asset Portfolio

If an asset's returns are distributed as normal $N(\mu, \sigma^2)$, then its return distribution can be completely described by its mean and standard deviation (or variance) of return. The variance of return on a portfolio of two assets A and B, $\text{Var}(r_P) = \sigma_P^2$, is found by substituting for $r_P = x_A r_A + x_B r_B$:

$$\text{Var}(r_P) = \text{Var}(x_A r_A + x_B r_B)$$
$$= \text{Var}(x_A r_A) + \text{Var}(x_B r_B) + 2\text{Cov}(x_A r_A, x_B r_B)$$

where Cov(.) is a covariance term. Because the weights x_A and x_B are constants, they can be extracted from the variance and covariance terms:

$$\text{Var}(r_P) = x_A^2 \text{Var}(r_A) + x_B^2 \text{Var}(r_B) + 2x_A x_B \text{Cov}(r_A, r_B)$$
$$= x_A^2 \sigma_A^2 + x_B^2 \sigma_B^2 + 2x_A x_B \sigma_{AB} \tag{20.3}$$

where $\sigma_{AB} = \text{Cov}(r_A, r_B)$ is the **covariance** of returns between assets A and B. Variance is in units of percentage squared ($\%^2$), so it is often more convenient to use the standard deviation σ of return. This is in the same units (%) as expected return.

---

2 Although the term *American* should properly refer to all of the Americas (North, South, and Central), it is myopically used here to refer to U.S. equities.

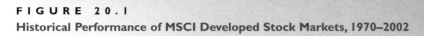

FIGURE 20.1
Historical Performance of MSCI Developed Stock Markets, 1970–2002

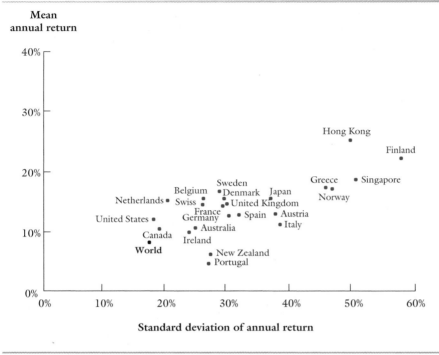

The covariance term can alternatively be stated in terms of the **correlation** ρ_{AB} and standard deviations σ_A and σ_B of assets A and B:

$$\sigma_{AB} = \sigma_A \sigma_B \, \rho_{AB} \quad \Leftrightarrow \quad \rho_{AB} = \sigma_{AB}/\sigma_A \sigma_B$$

The correlation is simply the covariance scaled by the standard deviations of assets A and B. Dividing the percentage-squared units of covariance by the product of two standard deviations (each with units in percent) results in a unitless correlation measure bounded on the interval $-1 \le \rho_{AB} \le +1$.

Correlation and covariance measure the extent of comovement between two assets. They are important measures because of this rule:

**The extent to which risk is reduced by portfolio diversification
depends on how highly the individual assets in the portfolio
are correlated.**

If the correlation between assets is equal to one, then diversifying across assets is ineffective in reducing portfolio risk. If the correlation is less than one, then diversifying across assets results in portfolio risk that is less than a simple average of the variances of the individual assets in the portfolio.

For illustration, let's calculate the standard deviation of an equally weighted portfolio of American (A) and British (B) equities using the standard deviations $\sigma_A = 17.8\%$ and $\sigma_B = 29.4\%$ from Table 20.1. To demonstrate the impact that correlation has on portfolio risk, we'll perform this calculation under three assumptions: (1) a perfect positive correlation ($\rho_{AB} = +1$), (2) a perfect negative

Diversification relies on low correlations between assets.

TABLE 20.2
Returns to MSCI Developed Stock Markets, in U.S. Dollars (1970–2002)

	Principal exchange	U.S. dollar returns		Correlation with world	Beta vs. world	Sharpe index
		Mean	Std dev			
Australia	Sydney	10.4%	24.5%	0.572	0.960	0.124
Austria	Vienna	12.8%	37.1%	0.325	0.462	0.147
Belgium	Brussels	15.3%	25.7%	0.615	0.803	0.208
Canada	Toronto	10.4%	18.8%	0.735	0.971	0.153
Denmark	Copenhagen	15.3%	29.0%	0.526	0.679	0.201
Finland	Helsinki	22.1%	57.7%	0.572	1.331	0.140
France	Paris	14.0%	29.1%	0.657	1.028	0.160
Germany	Frankfurt	12.5%	30.0%	0.618	0.898	0.150
Greece	Athens	17.4%	45.6%	0.266	0.695	0.117
Hong Kong	Hong Kong	25.1%	49.6%	0.447	1.168	0.164
Ireland	Dublin	9.9%	23.6%	0.686	0.966	0.129
Italy	Milan	11.1%	38.0%	0.462	0.817	0.101
Japan	Tokyo	15.4%	36.5%	0.671	1.040	0.157
Netherlands	Amsterdam	15.1%	20.0%	0.756	0.953	0.222
New Zealand	Wellington	5.9%	26.9%	0.466	0.765	0.066
Norway	Oslo	17.0%	46.2%	0.532	0.959	0.143
Portugal	Lisbon	4.6%	26.6%	0.505	0.810	0.050
Singapore	Singapore	18.6%	50.2%	0.546	1.132	0.138
Spain	Madrid	12.6%	31.5%	0.547	0.849	0.138
Sweden	Stockholm	16.6%	28.3%	0.614	1.004	0.183
Switzerland	Zurich	14.2%	25.5%	0.674	0.868	0.197
United Kingdom	London	14.6%	29.4%	0.685	1.090	0.161
United States	New York	11.8%	17.8%	0.855	0.919	0.202
World	—	11.2%	17.6%	1.000	1.000	0.204

Source: Based on the Morgan Stanley Capital International (MSCI) gross indices, representing pre-tax returns with dividends. Means and standard deviations are based on annual U.S. dollar returns. All series are over 1970–2002 except Finland (1982–2002), Greece (1988–2002), Ireland (1988–2002), New Zealand (1982–2002) and Portugal (1988–2002). Correlations and betas are measured against monthly changes in the MSCI world stock index. The Sharpe index SI = $(\mu_i - \mu_F)/\sigma_i$ is based on monthly returns to 30-day U.S. T-bills. World is a value-weighted float-adjusted index of 23 developed stock markets.

correlation ($\rho_{AB} = -1$), and (3) the historically observed correlation of $\rho_{AB} = 0.522$ between American and British equities from Table 20.1. Remember, the expected return on an equal-weighted portfolio of American and British equities is $E[r_P] = (1/2)(0.118)+(1/2)(0.146) = 0.132$, or 13.2 percent, regardless of the correlation of return between these assets.

Case 1: Perfect Positive Correlation. If returns in these two markets are perfectly positively correlated ($\rho_{AB} = +1$), then the standard deviation of portfolio return is

$$\sigma_P = (x_A^2\sigma_A^2 + x_B^2\sigma_B^2 + 2x_Ax_B\rho_{AB}\sigma_A\sigma_B)^{1/2}$$
$$= (x_A^2\sigma_A^2 + x_B^2\sigma_B^2 + 2x_Ax_B\sigma_A\sigma_B)^{1/2}$$
$$= [(x_A\sigma_A + x_B\sigma_B)^2]^{1/2}$$
$$= x_A\sigma_A + x_B\sigma_B$$

The standard deviation of return on an equal-weighted portfolio of American and British stocks is then

TABLE 20.3
Returns to MSCI Emerging Stock Markets, in U.S. Dollars

	Principal exchanges	U.S. dollar returns		Correlation with world	Beta vs. world	Sharpe index
		Mean	Std dev			
Argentina	Buenos Aires	36.9%	111.1%	0.142	0.598	0.267
Brazil	São Paolo, Rio de Janeiro	28.1%	62.4%	0.384	1.556	0.335
Chile	Santiago	21.1%	38.2%	0.352	0.614	0.364
China	Shanghai, Shenzhen	−12.0%	29.9%	0.366	1.034	−0.642
Columbia	Bogotá	5.6%	33.1%	0.145	0.319	−0.047
Czech Republic	Prague	4.7%	22.8%	0.250	0.517	−0.109
Egypt	Cairo, Alexandria	10.5%	47.8%	0.223	0.431	0.069
Hungary	Budapest	22.9%	51.5%	0.506	1.333	0.305
India	Mumbai, others...	5.6%	35.1%	0.256	0.511	−0.046
Indonesia	Jakarta	25.2%	84.3%	0.217	0.848	0.214
Israel	Tel Aviv	5.0%	30.8%	0.531	1.001	−0.073
Jordan	Amman	2.6%	19.2%	0.100	0.103	−0.239
Korea	Seoul	16.3%	58.0%	0.424	1.214	0.158
Malaysia	Kuala Lumpur	15.0%	48.6%	0.411	0.941	0.160
Mexico	Mexico City	31.1%	50.2%	0.469	1.119	0.477
Morocco	Casablanca	7.5%	23.8%	−0.027	−0.030	0.011
Pakistan	Karachi	14.3%	62.0%	0.106	0.307	0.115
Peru	Lima	12.1%	26.1%	0.340	0.733	0.186
Philippines	Makati, Pasig City	11.2%	52.0%	0.408	0.970	0.078
Poland	Warsaw	72.8%	241.4%	0.393	1.574	0.272
Russia	Moscow, St. Petersburg	55.4%	109.7%	0.490	2.369	0.440
South Africa	Johannesburg	12.1%	35.0%	0.536	1.015	0.141
Taiwan	Taipei	14.8%	52.1%	0.318	0.903	0.145
Thailand	Bangkok	13.9%	52.7%	0.448	1.302	0.127
Turkey	Istanbul	55.2%	168.4%	0.263	1.156	0.285
Venezuela	Caracas	8.5%	48.6%	0.245	0.816	0.026
Average		19.1%	61.3%	0.319	0.894	0.116
EMF (Emerging Market) Free index		15.0%	36.0%	0.652	1.051	0.216
All-Country World index		7.9%	17.1%	1.000	1.000	0.040

Source: Based on the Morgan Stanley Capital International gross (pre-tax returns with dividends) indices. Means and standard deviations are based on annual U.S. dollar returns. All series are over 1988–2002 except China, Columbia, India, Israel, Pakistan, Peru, Poland, S. Africa, and Venezuela (1993–2002) and the Czech Republic, Egypt, Hungary, Morocco, and Russia (1995–2002). Correlations and betas are against the monthly MSCI all-country index, a value-weighted float-adjusted index of 23 developed and 26 emerging markets. Averages are equal-weighted means. EMF Free is a value-weighted float-adjusted index of the 26 emerging markets.

$$\sigma_P = (1/2)(0.178) + (1/2)(0.294)$$
$$= 0.236, \text{ or } 23.6 \text{ percent}$$

When $\rho_{AB} = +1$, portfolio standard deviation is a simple weighted average of the individual standard deviations. Combining assets A and B in different proportions results in a straight line that runs between points A and B, as shown in Figure 20.2. Both the expected return and the standard deviation of the portfolio change linearly as wealth is shifted from one asset to another. In this case, there are no risk reduction benefits from portfolio diversification.

FIGURE 20.2

Portfolio Diversification and the Correlation Coefficient

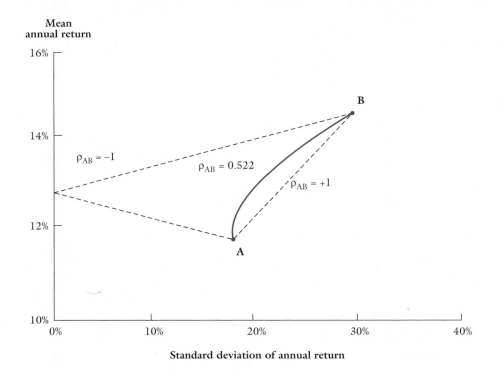

Case 2: Perfect Negative Correlation. If two markets are perfectly negatively cor-related ($\rho_{AB} = -1$), then the standard deviation of portfolio return is

$$\sigma_P = (x_A^2\sigma_A^2 + x_B^2\sigma_B^2 + 2x_Ax_B\rho_{AB}\sigma_A\sigma_B)^{1/2}$$
$$= (x_A^2\sigma_A^2 + x_B^2\sigma_B^2 - 2x_Ax_B\sigma_A\sigma_B)^{1/2}$$
$$= [(x_A\sigma_A - x_B\sigma_B)^2]^{1/2}$$
$$= |x_A\sigma_A - x_B\sigma_B|$$

The risk reduction benefits of portfolio diversification are at their greatest when two assets are perfectly negatively correlated. If $\rho_{AB} = -1$, then the standard deviation of an equal-weighted portfolio of American and British stocks is equal to

$$\sigma_P = |(^1/_2)(0.178) - (^1/_2)(0.294)|$$
$$= 0.058, \text{ or } 5.8 \text{ percent}$$

When $\rho_{AB} = -1$, the losses on one asset can be exactly offset by gains on the other asset through a judicious choice of portfolio weights. In this example, if you pick $x_A = (0.294)/(0.178 + 0.294) \approx 0.623$ and $x_B = (1 - x_A) = 0.377$, portfolio risk falls to $\sigma_P = 0$ and losses (or gains) on A are exactly offset by gains (or losses) on B.[3] Expected return on this portfolio is $E[r_P] = (0.623)(0.118) + (0.315)(0.146) \approx 0.129$, so you can capture a risk-less return of about 12.9 percent as in Figure 20.2. Progressively varying the weights on

---

3 As an exercise, verify that $\sigma_P = 0$ using these weights and Equation 20.3.

A and B defines a straight line that begins at point A, bounces off the vertical axis, and continues to point B.

Case 3: Correlations Between −1 and +1. Most correlations between international stock markets range between 0.3 and 0.8. Substituting $\sigma_{AB} = \rho_{AB}\sigma_A\sigma_B$ into Equation 20.3, the equation for the standard deviation of a portfolio of assets A and B is

$$\sigma_P = (x_A^2\sigma_A^2 + x_B^2\sigma_B^2 + 2x_Ax_B\rho_{AB}\sigma_A\sigma_B)^{1/2}$$

Using the historically observed correlation of 0.522 between American and British equities in Table 20.1, the standard deviation of an equal-weighted portfolio is

$$\sigma_P = [(1/2)^2(0.178)^2 + (1/2)^2(0.294)^2 + 2(1/2)(1/2)(0.522)(0.178)(0.294)]^{1/2}$$
$$= 0.208, \text{ or } 20.8 \text{ percent}$$

This is less than halfway between the standard deviation of return on American ($\sigma_A = 17.8\%$) and British ($\sigma_B = 29.4\%$) equities. By varying the proportion of wealth invested in each asset, investors can obtain any point (that is, any portfolio) along the curved line from A to B in Figure 20.2. Although a correlation of $\rho_{AB} = 0.522$ does not yield the same reduction in risk as a perfect negative correlation, it does provide a noticeable improvement in portfolio risk over the straight line between A and B corresponding to $\rho_{AB} = 1$. Again, the general rule is: The lower the correlation between two assets, the greater the potential for risk reduction through portfolio diversification.

Portfolios of Many Securities

The variance of a portfolio with N securities is calculated as a weighted average of the N^2 cells in the variance-covariance matrix:

$$\begin{aligned}
\text{Var}(r_P) &= \sigma_P^2 \\
&= \sum_i\sum_j x_ix_j\sigma_{ij} \\
&= \sum_i x_i^2\sigma_i^2 + \sum_i\sum_{\substack{j \\ i \neq j}} x_ix_j\sigma_{ij}
\end{aligned} \tag{20.4}$$

where the weights sum to one ($\sum_i x_i = 1$) across the N assets. The double summation $\sum_i\sum_j x_ix_j\sigma_{ij}$ has a total of N^2 terms including N variance terms along the diagonal of the covariance matrix and $N^2 - N$ covariance terms in the off-diagonal elements.

As an example, suppose we extract the variance-covariance matrix of a three-asset portfolio of American, British, and Japanese stocks from Table 20.1. Each term in the variance-covariance matrix is calculated as $\sigma_{ij} = \rho_{ij}\sigma_i\sigma_j$.

	America	Britain	Japan
America	0.0317	0.0273	0.0198
Britain	0.0273	0.0864	0.0396
Japan	0.0198	0.0396	0.1332

The variance-covariance matrix for a three-asset portfolio has $N^2 = 9$ cells including $N = 3$ variances and $N^2 - N = 6$ covariances. The diagonal cells represent national return variances because $\sigma_{ii} = \sigma_i^2$ for $i = j$. For example, the bottom-left cell is the variance of Japanese equity returns: $\sigma_J^2 = (0.365)^2 = 0.1332$. The off-diagonal covariances $\sigma_{ij} = \rho_{ij}\sigma_i\sigma_j$ are symmetric around the diagonal. For example, the covariance of the American and British equity markets is $\sigma_{AB} = \sigma_{BA} = \rho_{AB}\sigma_A\sigma_B = (0.522)(0.178)(0.294) = 0.0273$. An equal-weighted portfolio of all three equity indices has a return variance of

$$\sigma_p{}^2 = (1/3)^2[(0.0317)+(0.0864)+(0.1332)]+2(1/3)^2[(0.0273)+(0.0198)+(0.0396)]$$
$$= 0.0472$$

The standard deviation of return is $\sigma_P = (0.0472)^{1/2} = 0.217$, or 21.7 percent.

The covariance terms begin to dominate the portfolio variance calculation as the number of assets held in a portfolio increases. The ratio of variance cells to total cells in the variance-covariance matrix is $N/N^2 = 1/N$, whereas the ratio of covariance cells to total cells is $(N^2–N)/N^2$. For $N = 2$, there are $N = 2$ variance terms and $N^2–N = 4\text{-}2 = 2$ covariance terms, so half of the cells are variances. For $N = 3$, one-third of the ($N^2 = 9$) cells are variances, and two-thirds of the cells are covariances ($N^2–N = 6$). For $N = 100$, only 1 percent of the ($N^2 = 10,000$) cells in the variance-covariance matrix are variances, and 99 percent ($N^2–N = 10,000\text{-}100 = 9,900$) are covariances. This is summarized in the following rule:

**As the number of assets in a portfolio increases,
portfolio variance becomes more dependent on the covariances
between the individual securities and less dependent on the variances
of the individual securities.**

This is the large-portfolio analog of our rule from earlier in the chapter, "The extent to which risk is reduced by portfolio diversification depends on how highly the individual assets in the portfolio are correlated." In a large portfolio, portfolio variance depends on the covariances between the individual assets and not on the individual asset variances.

This rule has an interesting consequence for the risk of an asset when it is held as a part of a portfolio. If an investor is concerned with the risk of his or her total portfolio, then the characteristic of an individual asset that matters is the asset's return covariance with other assets in the portfolio and not its return variance:

**The risk of an individual asset when it is held in a portfolio with
a large number of securities depends on its return covariance with
other securities in the portfolio.**

This concept is the key to understanding the benefits of portfolio diversification. It is also central to what should be included in (and excluded from) an international asset pricing model.

Of course, an investor can't pick the correlation between two assets. This is determined in the capital markets. However, through a judicious selection of assets with low correlations, the risk reduction benefits of portfolio diversification can be used to maximize a portfolio's return-risk performance.

20.2 • MEAN-VARIANCE EFFICIENCY

The popular press often claims that investor behavior is driven by "fear and greed." Portfolio theory is based on these two fundamental human motives. If asset returns are distributed as normal, then investors' objective is to maximize the expected return and minimize the standard deviation of return in their portfolios. Investors want to be as far up and to the left as possible in Figure 20.2. When an asset has higher mean return at a given level of risk than other assets (or, lower risk at a given level of return), it is said to be **mean-variance efficient**.[4]

---

4 Don't confuse mean-variance efficiency with market efficiency. Mean-variance efficiency refers to the return/risk performance of an asset or portfolio. Market efficiency refers to how well the market performs its operational, allocational, or informational (pricing) functions.

Consider what happens when assets are combined to form a portfolio. Let's start with the American and British assets as in Figure 20.2. Given a correlation of $\rho_{AB} = 0.522$, an investor can reach any point along a curved line from A to B by varying the weight assigned to each asset. As additional assets are added to the set of possible investments, these new assets can be combined with A, B, or any combination of A and B.

> Mean-variance efficient assets have higher returns than other assets at a given risk.

Suppose there is an asset J (for Japan) with $E[r_J] = 15.4\%$, $\sigma_J = 36.5\%$, and correlations $\rho_{AJ} = 0.304$ and $\rho_{BJ} = 0.369$. Combining assets A and J in various weights results in a curved line between A and J, as shown in Figure 20.3. Combining B with J allows an investor to achieve any point along a curved line between B and J. The three assets can be combined, as in the thin black line that falls between point A and the minimum-variance point along line BJ.

As additional assets are added, the set of possible investments will move even farther up and to the left. By examining all possible combinations of assets, investors can identify the **investment opportunity set** bounded by the outside border in Figure 20.3. Investors must select from this menu. As in any decision, once investors have identified the available alternatives they must choose from these alternatives based on their individual preferences. This choice depends on the investor's level of risk aversion; that is, how much risk the investor is willing to accept in order to capture a given level of expected return. Investors want the most return at the least risk. These sought-after portfolios lie

FIGURE 20.3
Mean-Variance Efficiency

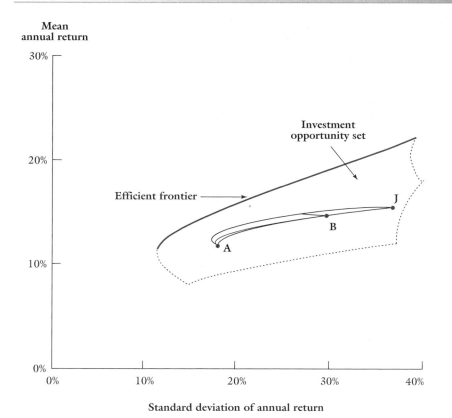

along the **efficient frontier**, the upper-left border of the investment opportunity set in Figure 20.3. These portfolios are efficient in a return-risk (or mean-variance) sense in that they provide the most expected return for a given level of risk, or the least risk at a given level of expected return.

A straightforward way to measure an asset's return-risk performance is to divide the asset's excess return (return in excess of the risk-free rate r_F) by its standard deviation. Called the **Sharpe index** (SI), this performance measure is appropriate when comparing realized returns to investors whose entire wealth is invested in one asset or another:

> The Sharpe index is a measure of excess return per unit of risk.

$$\text{Sharpe index (SI)} = (r_P - r_F)/\sigma_P$$

Sharpe indices are reported in Tables 20.2 and 20.3 for the MSCI developed and emerging markets. These are dollar returns from a U.S. investor's perspective, so the mean U.S. T-bill rate of 7.2 percent is used as the risk-free rate. The United States has the smallest standard deviation of all the markets, reflecting the diversified U.S. economy and the additional currency risk of foreign returns to U.S. investors. The relatively low 11.8 percent U.S. mean return resulted in a return-risk performance of 0.202, or 0.202 percent in excess return for every 1 percent of standard deviation.

Systematic Versus Unsystematic Risk

> Systematic risk cannot be eliminated through portfolio diversification.

The portion of an individual asset's risk that cannot be diversified away by holding the asset in a large portfolio is called **systematic risk**. Systematic risk is also called **nondiversifiable risk** or **market risk** because it is a risk that is shared by all assets in the market. Systematic risks arise through market-wide events, such as real economic growth, a rise in government spending, or changing investor sentiment regarding asset values.

The portion of an individual asset's risk that can be diversified away by holding a portfolio with many securities is called **unsystematic risk**. Unsystematic risk is also called **nonmarket risk** or **diversifiable risk**. If the asset is a share of stock in a company, then that part of total risk that is diversifiable is also called company-specific risk. Unsystematic risks include labor strikes, changes in top management, company-specific sales fluctuations, or any other event that is unique to a single company.

The total risk (or variance) of an asset's returns can be decomposed into systematic and unsystematic risk:

$$\text{Total Risk} = \text{Systematic Risk} + \text{Unsystematic Risk}$$

In Chapter 21, we will see that only systematic risk matters to well-diversified investors in a perfect market. Unsystematic risk can be diversified away in a large portfolio, so it does not command a risk premium and is not priced in the marketplace.

The relative proportion of systematic and unsystematic risk in an individual asset's returns depends on the asset's correlations or covariances with other assets in the portfolio. If an asset's return is highly correlated with the returns on other assets, then total risk will be largely composed of systematic risk. If an asset's returns have relatively low correlations with returns on other assets in the portfolio, then the algebra of portfolio diversification results in a relatively large proportion of unsystematic risk and a smaller proportion of systematic risk.

Return Distributions in Emerging Capital Markets

Table 20.3 presents return statistics, measured in U.S. dollars, for the MSCI emerging stock market indices. Note that the reliability of these statistics is only as good as the length of the time series. Return statistics for markets with a short history, such as China and Russia, are less reliable than statistics for markets with a longer history. Mean returns of –12.0 percent in China and +55.4 percent in Russia should not be expected to persist. As the investments industry warns, past performance is no guarantee of future results.

The algebra of portfolio diversification in sections 20.2 and 20.3 presumes normally distributed returns. In fact, returns in emerging markets are not normally distributed.[5] Twenty of the 26 emerging markets in Table 20.3 exhibit positive **skewness** over 1988–2002, indicating more large positive returns than large negative returns.[6] Twenty-five of the 26 markets (all except India) exhibit excess **kurtosis**, or leptokurtosis, with fatter tails than the normal distribution. Bekaert, et al., find similar results in local currency returns to 20 emerging markets.[7]

As an example, monthly returns to the MSCI-Argentina index over 1988–2002 are displayed relative to the normal distribution in Figure 20.4. This period saw U.S. dollar returns of 96, 95, 65, 54, 53, and 52 percent to Argentina's stock market. The biggest loss was only 38 percent. This asymmetry resulted in positive skewness of 1.95, compared to zero skewness in the normal distribution. The extreme observations in the right tail resulted in excess kurtosis of 8.03, or 8.03 greater than the normal distribution.

Some of the nonnormality in emerging capital markets may be a temporary phenomenon caused by opening segmented markets to international investors. Many emerging capital markets—as well as some developed capital markets—saw regulatory changes during the 1980s and 1990s that allowed greater access to local assets by international investors. Removing investment barriers typically increases local values, as international investors seek the diversification benefits (and possibly high returns) of assets in these markets. A one-time shock can conceal normality in the underlying returns.[8]

20.3 • THE BENEFITS OF INTERNATIONAL PORTFOLIO DIVERSIFICATION

The risk-reduction benefits of international portfolio diversification arise from two sources. First, because many national economies are dominated by only a few industries, stock markets retain a distinctive national character and are only loosely linked to other markets. It is easy to find examples of national markets with firms concentrated in a few industries. Oil and construction companies dominate the economies of Saudi Arabia and its Persian Gulf neighbors. The economies of Brazil and Indonesia are similarly dependent on their natural resources. Stock markets in these countries reflect international commodity prices and hence the fortunes of the local economy.

The second reason that returns to foreign investments differ from those of comparable domestic investments is because of the influence of exchange rates. From a domestic investor's perspective, the return on a foreign investment derives partly from the foreign market return and partly from the change in the spot rate of exchange. Domestic stock markets are further isolated from foreign markets by the low comovement of stock markets and exchange rates.

---

5 Bekaert, Erb, Harvey, and Viskanta, "Distributional Characteristics of Emerging Market Returns and Asset Allocation," *Journal of Portfolio Management* (1998).

6 This tendency toward positive skewness disappears when returns are measured with continuous compounding. Leptokurtosis remains. See Appendix 20-A.

7 Bekaert, Erb, Harvey, and Viskanta, "Distributional Characteristics of Emerging Market Returns and Asset Allocation," *Journal of Portfolio Management* (1998).

8 See Bekaert and Harvey, "Time-Varying World Market Integration," *Journal of Finance* (1995).

FIGURE 20.4
Monthly Stock Returns to Argentina Relative to the Normal Distribution, in U.S. Dollars

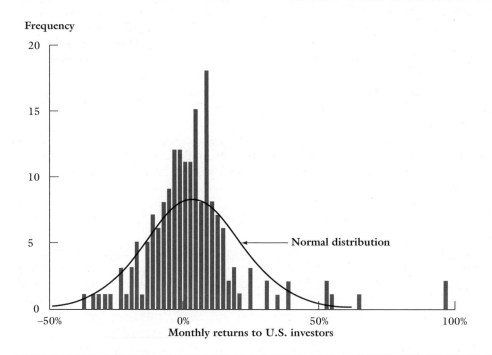

Returns on Foreign Investments

Here's how these two sources of return can be decomposed using the law of one price. Let the foreign currency price of a foreign asset at time t be given by P_t^f. The domestic currency price of the foreign asset P_t^d is

$$P_t^d = P_t^f \, S_t^{d/f} \qquad (20.5)$$

This is simply the price of the foreign asset in the foreign currency translated back into the domestic currency at the spot exchange rate. If the euro value of a French asset is €500 and the spot rate is \$1.10/€, then according to the law of one price the value of the asset in dollars is $P_t^\$ = P_t^\text{€} S_t^{\$/\text{€}} = (\text{€}500)(\$1.10/\text{€}) = \$550$. The percentage change $s^{d/f}$ in the spot exchange rate over period t is given by

$$(1+s^{d/f}) = (S_t^{d/f}/S_{t-1}^{d/f}) \qquad (20.6)$$

where the time index on $s^{d/f}$ is dropped for notational convenience. Let the foreign and domestic currency returns on the foreign asset over period t be denoted r^f and r^d, respectively. The domestic currency return on the foreign asset is then

$$\begin{aligned}
r^d &= (P_t^d/P_{t-1}^d)-1 = [(P_t^f S_t^{d/f})/(P_{t-1}^f S_{t-1}^{d/f})]-1 = (P_t^f/P_{t-1}^f)\,(S_t^{d/f}/S_{t-1}^{d/f})-1 \\
&= (1+r^f)(1+s^{d/f})-1 \qquad\qquad (20.7) \\
&= r^f+s^{d/f}+r^f\, s^{d/f}
\end{aligned}$$

The domestic currency return on a foreign asset arises from foreign market returns, spot rate changes, and their interaction.

Suppose the Paris Bourse appreciates 20 percent while the euro depreciates by 10 percent against the U.S. dollar. The total return to a U.S. investor in the French market is

Application

Portfolio Theory and Hedging with Derivative Securities

The algebra of portfolio diversification applies to all assets, including derivative securities such as forwards, futures, options, and swaps. Consider a U.S. resident with an obligation of 100,000 euros ($€$) due in six months. At a spot exchange rate of $S^{\$/€} = \$1.20/€$, the $€100,000$ payment costs $\$120,000$. This unhedged *short* position results in a negative exposure to the euro, as shown in the risk profile at left.

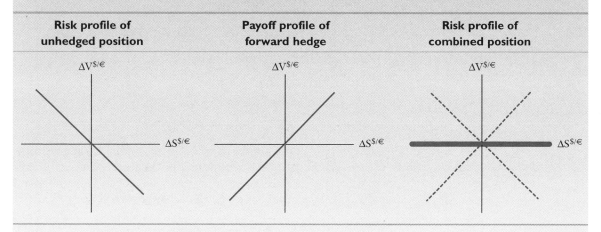

Risk profile of unhedged position	Payoff profile of forward hedge	Risk profile of combined position

For every $+\$0.01/€$ change in the spot rate, there is a $(-€100,000)(+\$0.01/€) = -\$1,000$ change in the value of the unhedged position. For example, if the spot rate goes to $S^{\$/€} = \$1.25/€$, then $€100,000$ will cost $\$125,000$.

The payoff profile of a forward contract to buy euros and sell dollars is shown in the middle figure. The dollar value of this *long* euro forward hedge is positively related to the value of the euro. The correlation between the short (S) underlying position and the long (L) forward hedge is $\rho_{SL} = -1$. Although these exposures are in opposite directions, the return variabilities are identical so that $\sigma_S = \sigma_L = \sigma$. If portfolio weight $x_S = x_L = 1/2$ is invested in each position, then the standard deviation of portfolio return is $\sigma_P = |x_S\sigma_S - x_L\sigma_L| = |1/2\sigma - 1/2\sigma| = 0$. When combined with the underlying position, the forward contract results in a fully hedged position.

$r^{\$} = (1+r^{€})(1+s^{\$/€})-1 = (1.20)(0.90)-1 = 0.08$, or 8 percent. The 20 percent rise in the Bourse is offset by a 10 percent fall in the value of the euro, and U.S. investors see an 8 percent rise in the dollar value of the French market.

Expected Return on a Foreign Asset

The expected return on a foreign asset is given by

$$E[r^d] = E[r^f] + E[s^{d/f}] + E[r^f s^{d/f}] \tag{20.8}$$

Equation 20.8 states that the expected domestic currency return on a foreign asset is composed of the expected return on the foreign asset in the foreign currency, the expected change in the value of the foreign currency, and the expectation of the cross-product.[9]

---

[9] Continuous compounding eliminates the cross-product term: $E[r^d] = E[\ln(1+r^d)] = E[\ln((1+r^f)(1+s^{d/f}))] = E[\ln(1+r^f)] + E[\ln(1+s^{d/f})] = E[r^f] + E[s^{d/f}]$, where r^f and $s^{d/f}$ are continuously compounded foreign asset returns and changes in the spot exchange rate, respectively. See Appendix 20-A.

The algebra of Equations 20.7 and 20.8 is the same as that of the Fisher equation that relates nominal interest rates i to real rates ɩ and inflation p according to $(1+i) = (1+ɩ)(1+p)$. If the real interest rate is 1 percent and inflation is 10 percent, then the nominal interest rate is $i = (1+ɩ)(1+p)–1 = (1.01)(1.10)–1 = 0.111$, or 11.1 percent. Similarly, if the foreign market goes up $r^f = 1\%$ in the foreign currency and the foreign currency value rises by $s^{d/f} = 10\%$, then the domestic currency return on the foreign asset is $r^d = (1+r^f)(1+s^{d/f})–1 = (1.01)(1.10)–1 = 0.111$, or 11.1 percent.

Variance of Return on a Foreign Asset

The general case for the variance of a random variable $r = a+b+c$ is

$$Var(r) = Var(a)+Var(b)+Var(c)+2Cov(a,b)+2Cov(b,c)+2Cov(a,c)$$

Similarly, the variance of $r^d = r^f+s^{d/f}+r^f s^{d/f}$ is given by

$$Var(r^d) = Var(r^f)+Var(s^{d/f})+Var(r^f s^{d/f})$$
$$+ 2Cov(r^f,s^{d/f})+2Cov(r^f, r^f s^{d/f})+2Cov(s^{d/f}, r^f s^{d/f}) \qquad (20.9)$$

Let's consider riskless and then risky foreign currency cash flows in turn.

Riskless Foreign Currency Cash Flows. Suppose a U.S.-based multinational is promised a riskless cash flow of 100,000 euros in six months from the French government. Spot and 6-month forward exchange rates are $S^{\$/€} = F^{\$/€} = \$1.20/€$. This unhedged cash flow is fully exposed to changes in the spot rate of exchange, as follows:

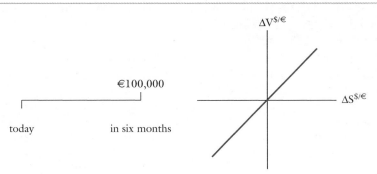

Risk profile of unhedged position

For every $\$0.01/€$ change in the value of the euro there is a $(\$0.01/€)(€100,000) = \$1,000$ change in the value of the unhedged position. If the euro falls to $S^{\$/€} = \$1.19/€$, then €100,000 will convert to only $\$119,000$ rather than the $\$120,000$ expected value.

This is both good news and bad news for riskless cash flows denominated in euros. The bad news is that the value of the cash flow in dollars depends on the spot exchange rate. The good news is that the dollar value of the euro cash flow depends *only* on the spot exchange rate. Because the euro payment is guaranteed by the French government, it has a certain nominal return $r_F^{€}$ in euros. This means that $Var(r_F^{€})$ and all of the interaction terms in Equation 20.9 are equal to zero. Moreover, $Var(r_F^{€} s^{\$/€}) = (r_F^{€})^2 Var(s^{\$/€})$ for a constant $r_F^{€}$. Variability of return in dollars on this riskless euro cash flow then reduces to

$$\begin{aligned} Var(r^\$) &= Var(r_F^{€})+Var(s^{\$/€})+Var(r_F^{€}s^{\$/€})+\text{(covariance terms)} \\ &= 0+Var(s^{\$/€})\ (r_F^{€})^2 Var(s^{\$/€})+0+0+0 \\ &= [1+(r_F^{€})^2]\ Var(s^{\$/€}) \\ &\approx Var(s^{\$/€}) \end{aligned}$$

when the riskless rate $r_F{€}$ is small. For riskless foreign currency cash flows, the primary source of variability in domestic currency nominal return is exchange rate volatility.

To hedge against unanticipated changes in the spot rate, the MNC should sell €100,000 for (€100,000)($1.20/€) = $120,000 at the forward exchange rate $F^{\$/€}$ = $1.20/€:

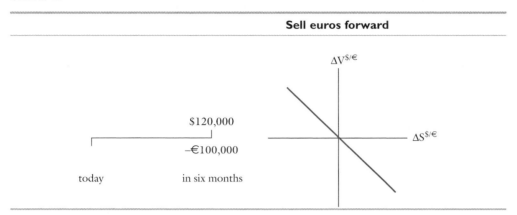

Sell euros forward

The riskless euro cash flow can be converted into a riskless dollar cash flow in this way.

Is this "riskless" dollar cash flow truly riskless? As a general rule, both domestic and foreign cash flows (even riskless ones) are exposed to purchasing power or inflation risk. In real terms, the purchasing power of a nominal cash flow to be received in the future depends on whether domestic inflation is as expected. In the previous example, the real future value of the nominally riskless $120,000 cash flow may be more or less than $120,000, depending on realized inflation during the period. Hedging foreign currency risk does not completely eliminate risk. It merely substitutes exposure to domestic purchasing power (inflation) risk for exposure to currency risk.

> Hedging an exposure to currency risk substitutes domestic purchasing power risk for currency risk.

To hedge against domestic purchasing power risk, contracts must be signed in real, not nominal, terms. This means pegging all contracts to an inflation index, such as a consumer price index (CPI). This hedges against domestic purchasing power risk to the extent that changes in the CPI approximate changes in prices actually faced by the hedger. Contracts pegged to an inflation index are common in high-inflation countries. An approximation to this hedge can be obtained using contracts with rates that float according to the level of nominal interest rates. To the extent that nominal interest rate changes reflect only changes in inflation and not changes in the real rate of return, floating rate contracts hedge against purchasing power risk.

Risky Foreign Currency Cash Flows. As the planning horizon is extended farther into the future, cash flows become less certain. Suppose a U.S. multinational exports computers to France through a French partner. The actual level of sales in France will depend on the firm's pricing decisions as well as on the product, its promotion in France, and its distribution channels.

> Risky foreign cash flows are exposed to foreign market returns and exchange rates.

Risky foreign currency cash flows are exposed to each of the terms in Equation 20.9. As with riskless cash flows, the dollar value of a euro cash flow depends on the level of exchange rates, so the exchange rate term $Var(s^{\$/€})$ contributes to dollar return variability. Because the actual return earned on the investment in euros is uncertain, the term $Var(r^{€}) > 0$ also contributes to dollar return variability.

Exchange rate and foreign currency changes interact through the $Var(r^{€}s^{\$/€})$ and covariance terms in Equation 20.9, because the actual level of sales and profits in France

Market Update

Financial Contracts in High-Inflation Countries

The convention in many high-inflation countries is to link financial contracts to a local price index. To deal with high and volatile inflation during the 1970s and 1980s, the Brazilian government constructed a variety of consumer and producer price indices for different sectors of the economy. Brazilian financial contracts, such as savings deposits and bank loans, were conventionally indexed to one of these price indices. Pegging financial contracts to a representative inflation index reduces exposure to inflation risk for both borrowers and lenders.

depends on the value of the euro. This is easiest to see if we consider two pricing alternatives for the French market. Pricing the computers in euros makes it easier to forecast the euro return $r^€$, but the dollar value of these sales will depend on the exchange rate. Pricing the computers in dollars can reduce uncertainty over the exchange rate, but sales in France will fall (rise) as the value of the dollar goes up (down). This influences the euro returns $r^€$. In the typical case, risky foreign currency cash flows cannot be perfectly hedged against currency risk when foreign market returns are uncertain.

20.4 • VARIANCES ON FOREIGN STOCK AND BOND INVESTMENTS

> Foreign stock returns are dominated by variability in the foreign markets, and not by currency risk.

The top half of Table 20.4 uses Equation 20.9 to decompose the return variance of foreign stock investments from the perspective of a U.S. investor. The variance of foreign stock returns to U.S. investors arises primarily from return variance in the foreign markets, $Var(r^f)$. Foreign stock market variability accounts for an average of 91.1 percent of total return variance. On average, exchange rate variability $Var(s^{\$/f})$ accounts for 16.4 percent of total variance. The average effect of the interaction terms (–7.4 percent) is small, although in some countries the interaction terms are a major contributor. It is clear that the dominant risk of foreign equity investments is return variability in the national stock markets themselves. Exchange rate risk is of secondary importance.

The bottom half of Table 20.4 decomposes the variance of foreign government bond returns from the perspective of a U.S. investor. In contrast to foreign stock returns, returns to foreign bonds are dominated by currency risks. On average, exchange rate variability accounted for 67.7 percent of total return variability. The average contribution of foreign market return variability was 25.3 percent. The average contribution of the interaction terms was only 7.0 percent of total return variability.

The influence of exchange rates on the return variance of foreign investments suggests that it may be useful to hedge foreign investments against currency risk. We'll return to this issue in the following two chapters.

Diversifying with International Equity Investments

Solnik was the first to formally quantify the risk reduction benefits of international portfolio diversification.[10] Figure 20.5 presents Solnik's estimate of the gain from equity

---

10 Solnik, "Why Not Diversify Internationally," *Financial Analysts Journal* (1974). Reprinted in 1995.

TABLE 20.4
Decomposition of Return Variance on Foreign Investments from the Perspective of a U.S. Investor

Stock Returns

	Var(r^f)	+	Var(s^{$/f})	+	Interaction terms	=	Var(r^$)
Canada	91.5%		3.3%		5.3%		100.0%
France	93.7%		14.9%		−8.6%		100.0%
Germany	97.3%		19.4%		−16.7%		100.0%
Japan	81.3%		18.2%		0.5%		100.0%
Switzerland	92.8%		29.8%		−22.5%		100.0%
United Kingdom	90.2%		12.7%		−2.9%		100.0%
Average	91.1%		16.4%		−7.5%		100.0%

Bond Returns

	Var(r^f)	+	Var(s^{$/f})	+	Interaction terms	=	Var(r^$)
Canada	60.1%		18.4%		21.5%		100.0%
France	24.2%		82.3%		−6.5%		100.0%
Germany	12.4%		81.8%		5.8%		100.0%
Japan	17.2%		70.1%		12.6%		100.0%
Switzerland	9.0%		93.6%		−2.6%		100.0%
United Kingdom	28.7%		59.9%		11.4%		100.0%
Average	25.3%		67.7%		7.0%		100.0%

Source: Stock returns are based on the Morgan Stanley Capital International (MSCI) gross indices, representing pre-tax dollar returns with dividends, over 1971–2002. Bond returns are based on long-term government bond monthly returns from Ibbotson Associates over 1970–1998.

diversification for a U.S. resident. The graph depicts the reduction in portfolio variance as additional assets are added to a portfolio. The y-axis is the ratio of portfolio variance to the variance of a typical U.S. stock. As Solnik added more stocks to a domestic U.S. portfolio, portfolio variance fell to 27 percent of the variance of a typical U.S. stock. This means that 73 percent of the variance of a typical U.S. stock can be eliminated through diversification within a large U.S. portfolio. The systematic risk that remains cannot be eliminated through diversification within the U.S. stock market. As the opportunity set was expanded from domestic U.S. stocks to international equities, systematic risk fell to 12 percent of the variance of a typical stock. This is less than half of the systematic risk in a fully diversified domestic U.S. stock portfolio.

> Systematic risk falls as portfolios are diversified across national borders.

The benefits of international equity diversification are even greater for residents of countries with smaller and less diversified markets. Solnik estimated that systematic risk comprised 35 percent of total variance for a typical stock in the United Kingdom, 33 percent in France, 44 percent in Germany, and 44 percent in Switzerland. If systematic risk comprises 12 percent of total risk within a globally diversified portfolio, investors in each of these countries would benefit from international diversification. Investors from smaller and less diversified markets are likely to capture even greater diversification gains.

Diversifying with International Bond Investments

Diversification into foreign bond markets can substantially reduce the risk of a bond portfolio. Indeed, the potential for risk reduction through international portfolio

---

FIGURE 20.5
Risk Reduction Through International Diversification

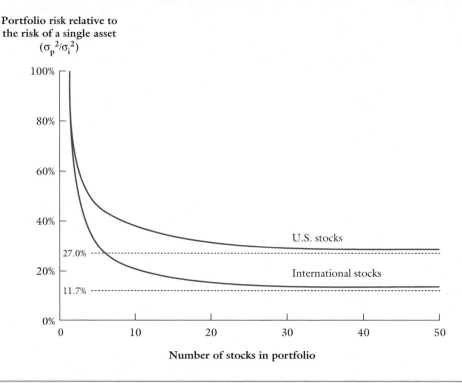

Source: Adapted from "Why Not Diversify Internationally Rather Than Domestically?" by Bruno Solnik, *Financial Analysts Journal* (July/August 1974). Reprinted in 1995.

diversification with bonds is often greater than with stocks.[11] For U.S. investors, foreign bonds have had the additional benefit of higher mean returns as well.

The prices of fixed rate bonds are determined by nominal interest rates. Changes in nominal interest rates are in turn determined by changes in anticipated inflation and to a lesser extent by changes in real required returns. Although stock values also vary with macroeconomic factors such as expected inflation, there is a much bigger asset-specific component to stock returns than to bond returns.

Because the variability of foreign stock returns is greater than the variability of foreign bond returns, currency risk is a much larger percentage of total variance for bonds than for stocks. In Table 20.4, exchange rate variability accounts for 67.7 percent of the variance on a typical bond portfolio and only 24.1 percent of the variance on a typical stock portfolio. Consequently, the risk reduction benefits of hedging foreign bonds against currency risk are even greater than for hedging foreign stocks. Fortunately, bonds have contractual payoffs that are simple to hedge against currency risk using currency forwards, futures, options, or swaps.

Diversifying with International Stocks and Bonds

When combined with stocks, bonds can further improve the return-risk efficiency of a globally diversified portfolio. Figure 20.6 presents Jorion's estimate of the gains

---

11 See Levy and Lerman, "The Benefits of International Diversification in Bonds," *Financial Analysts Journal* (1988).

FIGURE 20.6
Efficiency Gains Through International Stock and Bond Diversification

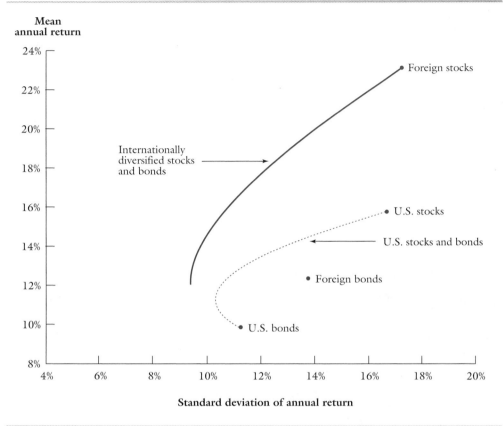

Source: Adapted from "Asset Allocation with Hedged and Unhedged Foreign Stocks and Bonds" by Philippe Jorion, *Journal of Portfolio Management* (Summer 1989), pp. 49–54. Reprinted with permission.

from international stock and bond diversification from the perspective of a U.S. investor.[12] This figure shows that investing in foreign stocks can improve the return-risk performance of an equity portfolio. Similarly, investing in foreign bonds can improve the return-risk performance of a bond portfolio. Further gains can be obtained by combining stocks and bonds, because the correlation between stock and bond returns is low.

20.5 • HOME BIAS

> Investors exhibit home bias, favoring local assets.

Despite the compelling logic of portfolio theory, few investors fully diversify their portfolios across national borders. Instead, investors tend to invest in assets from their own country. This tendency to invest in local assets is called **home asset bias**, or simply **home bias**. Home bias exists in many different markets, including stock and bond markets, commercial lending, and real estate.

12 Jorion, "Asset Allocation with Hedged and Unhedged Foreign Stocks and Bonds," *Journal of Portfolio Management* (1989).

Table 20.5 presents home bias in the equity portfolios of investors from several developed countries. U.S. investors were among the least diversified internationally, with a very high percentage of their equity portfolios held in domestic equities. This is in part because the investment opportunities of investors in the large and diversified U.S. market are greater than the opportunities of investors in less diversified economies. U.S. investors held only 2 percent of their equity portfolios in foreign stocks during the 1980s and only about 10 percent by the year 2003. This percentage is increasing over time, but is still a small fraction of U.S. pension assets. Investors in Western Europe have more of a tradition of international diversification, as reflected in their lesser degree of home bias. Home bias is evidence that national financial markets are not yet fully integrated.

What could account for this strong home bias in equity portfolios? Two classes of explanations have been suggested:

- Explanations based on international asset pricing models
- Explanations based on market imperfections

Both types of explanations are likely at work.

Explanations Based on International Asset Pricing Models

International asset pricing models (Chapter 21) send mixed signals as to whether investors should prefer local assets or an internationally diversified portfolio.

Home bias may serve to hedge against domestic inflation risk.

Domestic Assets as a Hedge of Domestic Inflation Risk. Investors in different countries have different consumption baskets and are exposed to inflation risk in their domestic currencies. In most models of international portfolio choice, home bias arises from the ability of domestic assets to hedge domestic inflation risk.[13]

The high levels of domestic liabilities at insurance companies and pension funds also warrant a strong home bias on the asset side of the balance sheet.[14] Insurance compa-

TABLE 20.5
Home Bias in International Equity Portfolios

	Market cap as a percentage of the total	Percentage of portfolio held in domestic equities	Difference
France	2.6%	64.4%	61.8%
Germany	3.2%	75.4%	72.2%
Italy	1.9%	91.0%	89.1%
Japan	43.7%	86.7%	43.0%
Spain	1.1%	94.2%	93.1%
Sweden	0.8%	100.0%	99.2%
United Kingdom	10.3%	78.5%	68.2%
United States	36.4%	98.0%	61.6%

Source: Ian Cooper and Evi Kaplanis, "Home Bias in Equity Portfolios, Inflation Hedging, and International Capital Market Equilibrium," *Review of Financial Studies* 7, No. 1 (Spring 1994). Statistics are from 1989 and are not adjusted for share crossholdings or free float.

---

13 See Adler and Dumas, "International Portfolio Choice and Corporation Finance: A Synthesis," *Journal of Finance* (1983).

14 Griffin, "Why Do Pension and Insurance Portfolios Hold So Few International Assets?" *Journal of Portfolio Management* (1997).

nies are not diversified on the liability side of the balance sheet because of product market imperfections. In particular, it is difficult to maintain an agent base that can sell property, casualty, life, and other insurance contracts in multiple national markets. Domestic assets allow insurance companies to reduce their exposures to currency and interest rate risks by matching the currencies and maturities of their assets to those of their liabilities. This asset-liability match also reduces their exposures to domestic and foreign inflation risks.

Human Capital and the Incentive to Diversify. Other portfolio-related factors suggest that investors should be more diversified internationally, not less. In particular, people have a large stake of human capital through their labor income. Although an individual can borrow against his or her own income, labor income itself is a nontraded asset. Because the value of this nontraded asset is more highly correlated with domestic assets than with foreign assets, a diversified world portfolio should hold even more foreign assets when human capital is considered than when it is not. This suggests investors should be even more internationally diversified than they are.[15]

Explanations Based on Imperfect Markets

Financial market imperfections are becoming less important as markets are progressively opened to foreign capital. Nevertheless, there are still many barriers to international investment. This section discusses real-world market imperfections and the way that they influence international asset prices and portfolio choices.

> Market frictions impede cross-border capital flows.

Market Frictions. Market frictions impede cross-border capital flows. Frictions include:

- *Government controls.* Governments sometimes try to stabilize cross-border financial flows through currency controls (such as fixed exchange rates or currency boards) or limitations on foreign ownership of domestic assets. These market frictions tend to keep capital at home.

- *Taxes.* Taxes are sometimes imposed on two types of cross-border financial transactions: share purchases, and dividend or interest distributions:

  - *Taxes on cross-border share purchases.* Some countries impose taxes on cross-border share purchases. These are sometimes called stamp taxes. Some stamp taxes are proportional to the amount of the transaction, such as in Switzerland where there is a federal stamp tax equal to 0.09 percent of the transaction amount. Some other European countries apply a value-added tax based on the size of the broker's commission. Still other countries charge a flat fee per transaction.

  - *Withholding taxes.* Many countries also impose withholding taxes on dividend or interest paid from within their borders. Investors can usually claim withholding taxes on foreign shares as a domestic tax deduction or credit up to the amount of their domestic tax liability. Nontaxable investors, such as pension funds, typically cannot recover withholding taxes, although the size of the loss is usually small. For example, unrecoverable withholding taxes of 15 percent on a stock with a 2 percent dividend yield result in a loss of $(0.15)(0.02) = 0.003$, or 0.3 percent.

- *Transactions costs.* The level of transactions costs in a market is an important measure of the market's operating efficiency and also influences the market's informational

---

15 Baxter and Jermann, "The International Diversification Puzzle Is Worse Than You Think," *American Economic Review* (1997).

and allocational efficiency. In the United States, transactions costs can be less than 0.1 percent for large transactions in actively traded stocks. In developing markets, direct trading costs often exceed 1 percent.

These market frictions discourage international portfolio diversification by reducing the expected returns and increasing the perceived risks of foreign investments.

> Behavioral finance does not assume that investors always act rationally.

Investor Irrationality. The traditional paradigm in finance and economics rests on an assumption that rational investors price assets with a dispassionate eye toward expected returns and risks. Psychological factors do not enter into valuation except insofar as they affect perceived risks and returns and the cost of acquiring information. Unfortunately for the traditional model, individuals often act in irrational ways.

Behavioral finance studies the impact of psychological or behavioral factors on asset prices. Behavioral finance does not presume markets are always rational, so prices can diverge from fundamental values. Here are two behaviors that can appear irrational:[16]

- *The use of heuristics.* Heuristics are rules-of-thumb or shortcuts used to simplify the decision-making process. Although heuristics can save time and simplify decisions, they can also lead to cognitive biases. In particular, people tend to place too much weight on recent, negative, or frequently received information.
- *Frame dependence.* The form in which a problem is presented can influence decisions. Here are two examples of frame dependence:
  - *Overconfidence and trading volume.* Individuals are typically overconfident about their knowledge, abilities, and future prospects. Overconfidence can lead investors to trade more than rational investors with unbiased forecasts, even when excessive trading lowers their expected returns.[17] Interestingly, both trading behavior and overconfidence appear to be gender-related.[18]
  - *The desire to avoid recognizing losses.* Humans have an innate desire to avoid regret. In financial markets, regret avoidance causes investors to hold onto their losing investments and sell their winners early.[19]

The cognitive biases associated with heuristics and frame dependence can result in inefficient markets; that is, in prices that deviate from fundamental values.

Behavioral finance does not yet have an agreed or comprehensive model of investor behavior and asset prices. Nevertheless, it can provide insights into behaviors and prices that do not fit traditional theories. There is a healthy debate in the literature between the two sides. Proponents of the traditional view strive to explain or incorporate the insights of behavioral finance using a rational expectations framework.[20] Proponents of the behavioral view dismiss the beliefs of traditionalists as frame dependent; that is, as overconfidence in their beliefs and an unwillingness to recognize their losses.[21] As they say: "Let's get ready to rumble!"

---

16 An important early paper in the field of behavioral finance is Kahneman and Tversky, "Prospect Theory: An Analysis of Decision Under Risk," *Econometrica* (1979).

17 Odean, "Do Investors Trade Too Much?" *American Economic Review* (1999).

18 Barber and Odean, "Boys Will Be Boys: Gender, Overconfidence, and Common Stock Investment," *Quarterly Journal of Economics* (2001).

19 Shefrin and Statman, "The Disposition to Sell Winners Too Early and Ride Losers Too Long: Theory and Evidence," *Journal of Finance* (1985).

20 For example, see Fama, "Market Efficiency, Long-Term Returns, and Behavioral Finance," *Journal of Financial Economics* (1998).

21 The November/December 1999 issue of *Financial Analysts Journal* is devoted to behavioral finance.

Unequal Access to Market Prices. In perfect financial markets, large numbers of buyers and sellers ensure that no single player can influence prices. Consequently, market participants have equal access to market prices.

- *Governments and other price makers.* Equal access to market prices presumes all investors are "price takers," so that no one can directly influence prices. In the real world, wealth and power are not equally distributed across market participants. The most powerful actors are governments, international cartels such as the Organization of Petroleum Exporting Countries (OPEC), investment banks, large corporations, corporate and securities industry insiders, and wealthy individuals.

- *The availability of shares.* Another contributor to home bias is the fact that one or a few large shareholders, such as a founding family, control many firms outside the United States. Controlling shareholders usually do not trade their shares, so not all market capitalization is available to investors. Dahlquist, Pinkowitz, Stulz, and Williamson estimate that 32 percent of shares worldwide are closely held.[22] Shares that are available for trade are referred to as **free float** (or **float**).

Table 20.6 presents these authors' estimate of the impact of float on the portfolio holdings of U.S. investors. The first column lists the capitalization of several national markets as a percent of world stock market capitalization. The second column shows the 1997 weight of each market in the portfolio of a typical U.S. investor. The third column shows the percent of each nation's shares that are closely held. Closely held shares are prominent in most countries, such as in Brazil (67.13 percent), Argentina (52.68 percent), and Canada (48.82 percent). The fourth column lists the weight of each market in the world portfolio based on available, rather than issued, shares. These free float weights would be the optimal portfolio weights for an internationally diversified investor based on available shares.

Based on total market capitalization, internationally diversified investors should have held 49.6 percent of their portfolio in U.S. equities. Based on available shares, this weight should have been 58.32 percent. Although this is closer to the observed portfolio weight of 91.29 percent, home bias nevertheless remains large.

Unequal Access to Information. It can be difficult to obtain and interpret information from distant markets and monitor the actions of distant managers. Here is some evidence:

- *Distance and portfolio choice.* Grinblatt and Keloharju found investors in Finland are more likely to own firms that are located nearby.[23] Coval and Moskowitz found U.S. mutual fund managers similarly prefer local firms, especially small and highly levered firms that produce nontraded goods.[24] Information and monitoring costs are particularly high for these firms.

- *Language, culture, and portfolio choice.* Grinblatt and Keloharju found that Finnish investors are more likely to own firms that communicate in their native language (Swedish versus Finnish) or have CEOs of the same cultural background.[25] This suggests that language and culture influence investors' portfolio choices.

---

22 Dahlquist, Pinkowitz, Stulz, and Williamson, "Corporate Governance and the Home Bias," *Journal of Financial and Quantitative Analysis* (2003).

23 Grinblatt and Keloharju, "How Distance, Language, and Culture Influence Stockholdings and Trades," *Journal of Finance* (2001).

24 Coval and Moskowitz, "Home Bias at Home: Local Equity Preference in Domestic Portfolios," *Journal of Finance* (1999).

25 Grinblatt and Keloharju, "How Distance, Language, and Culture."

TABLE 20.6
Home Bias in U.S. Equity Portfolios (selected countries)

	Market cap	U.S. shareholdings	Closely held	Free float cap
	Market cap as a percentage of the total	Percentage of a U.S. investor's portfolio	Percentage of market cap closely held	Available cap as a percentage of available shares
Argentina	0.26	0.10	52.68	0.16
Australia	1.30	0.24	24.85	1.25
Brazil	1.12	0.24	67.13	0.47
Canada	2.49	0.54	48.82	1.63
Finland	0.32	0.11	23.49	0.31
France	2.96	0.65	37.98	2.34
Germany	3.62	0.49	44.74	2.55
Hong Kong	1.81	0.21	42.73	1.32
Ireland	0.22	0.11	13.06	0.24
Italy	1.51	0.32	37.54	1.21
Japan	9.72	1.04	38.38	7.65
Mexico	0.69	0.27	26.15	0.65
Netherlands	2.05	0.81	33.74	1.74
Sweden	1.20	0.30	20.99	1.21
Switzerland	2.53	0.47	25.73	2.39
United Kingdom	8.76	1.66	9.93	10.07
United States	49.60	91.29	7.64	58.32

Source: Magnus Dahlquist, Lee Pinkowitz, René M. Stulz, and Rohan Williamson, "Corporate Governance and the Home Bias," *Journal of Financial and Quantitative Analysis* 38, Special Issue on International Corporate Governance (March 2003).

- *The cross-country holdings of multinational corporations.* Kang and Stulz found that Japanese multinationals with a greater international presence (i.e., ADRs or large export volume) have greater foreign ownership.[26] Conversely, those with less of an international presence are more likely to be owned by Japanese investors.

These studies conclude that investors prefer to hold local assets because of their greater access to information and familiarity with local assets.

There is conflicting evidence on whether local investors enjoy an informational advantage over more distant investors. Coval and Moskowitz found local investments by U.S. fund managers outperformed passive benchmark portfolios by almost 2 percent per year.[27] Local holdings generated 3 percent more return than local stocks that were not held by local fund managers. This is in sharp contrast to most studies of mutual fund performance, in which mutual funds tend to underperform benchmark portfolios. In contrast to these U.S. results, Grinblatt and Keloharju found that foreign investors out-

---

26 Kang and Stulz, "Why Is There a Home Bias? An Analysis of Foreign Portfolio Equity Ownership in Japan," *Journal of Financial Economics* (1997). ADRs are American depository receipts, a form of international equity sold to U.S. investors.

27 Coval and Moskowitz, "The Geography of Investment: Informed Trading and Asset Prices," *Journal of Political Economy* (2001).

perform local investors in Finland.[28] Because of these and other conflicting findings, the jury is still out on whether local or foreign investors achieve higher returns.

20.6 • SUMMARY

Assuming nominal returns are normally distributed, the expected return and variance of a portfolio are given by

$$E[r_p] = \sum_i x_i E[r_i] \qquad (20.2)$$

and

$$\begin{aligned}
Var(r_p) \quad &= \sigma_p^2 \\
&= \sum_i \sum_j x_i x_j \sigma_{ij} \\
&= \sum_i x_i^2 \sigma_i^2 + \sum_{\substack{i \ j \\ i \neq j}} x_i x_j \sigma_{ij}
\end{aligned} \qquad (20.4)$$

The variance calculation has three implications for portfolio risk and return:

- The extent to which risk is reduced by portfolio diversification depends on how highly the individual assets in the portfolio are correlated.
- As the number of assets held in a portfolio increases, the variance of return on the portfolio becomes more dependent on the covariances between the individual securities and less dependent on the variances of the individual securities.
- The risk of an individual asset when it is held in a portfolio with a large number of securities depends on its return covariance with other securities in the portfolio and not on its return variance.

According to the algebra of portfolio theory, the total risk of an asset can be decomposed into systematic and unsystematic components. Systematic risks are related to risks in other stocks and cannot be diversified away in a large portfolio. Unsystematic risks are unrelated to risks in other stocks and are diversifiable in a large portfolio.

Returns on foreign investments are given by

$$r^d = r^f + s^{d/f} + r^f s^{d/f} \qquad (20.7)$$

Equation 20.7 has expected return

$$E[r^d] = E[r^f] + E[s^{d/f}] + E[r^f s^{d/f}] \qquad (20.8)$$

and variance

$$\begin{aligned}
Var(r^d) = Var(r^f) + Var(s^{d/f}) + Var(r^f s^{d/f}) \\
+ 2Cov(r^f, s^{d/f}) + 2Cov(r^f, r^f s^{d/f}) + 2Cov(s^{d/f}, r^f s^{d/f})
\end{aligned} \qquad (20.9)$$

The principal determinants of return variance on a foreign asset are the variance of return in the foreign market and the variance of foreign exchange rates. The cross-product terms are relatively minor contributors to portfolio risk.

---

28 Grinblatt and Keloharju, "The Investment Behavior and Performance of Various Investor Types: A Study of Finland's Unique Data Set," *Journal of Financial Economics* (2000).

International stock and bond investments differ in the relative contribution of each source of variability. The largest source of variability in international stock returns comes from return variance in the foreign market. Variability in foreign exchange rates plays a lesser role. In contrast, international bond returns are influenced both by bond price variability in the foreign markets and by exchange rate variability.

Despite the logic of portfolio theory, few investors fully diversify their portfolios across national borders. Instead, investors tend to invest in local assets. This home bias exists in most asset markets, including stocks, bonds, currencies, and real estate.

KEY TERMS

behavioral finance	mean-variance efficiency
correlation and covariance	Sharpe index
efficient frontier	short selling
free float (or float)	skewness
home asset bias (or home bias)	systematic, market, or nondiversifiable risk
investment opportunity set	unsystematic, nonmarket, or diversifiable risk
kurtosis	

CONCEPTUAL QUESTIONS

20.1   How is portfolio risk measured? What determines portfolio risk?

20.2   What happens to portfolio risk as the number of assets in the portfolio increases?

20.3   What happens to the relevant risk measure for an individual asset when it is held in a large portfolio rather than in isolation?

20.4   In words, what does the Sharpe index measure?

20.5   Name two synonyms for systematic risk.

20.6   Name three synonyms for unsystematic risk.

20.7   Is international diversification effective in reducing portfolio risk? Why?

20.8   What is a perfect financial market?

20.9   Are real world financial markets perfect? If not, in what ways are they imperfect?

20.10 Describe some of the barriers to international portfolio diversification.

20.11 What is home asset bias? What might be its cause?

PROBLEMS

20.1   Based on the historical returns in Table 20.1, calculate the mean and standard deviation of return in dollars for an equally weighted portfolio of French and German stocks. Calculate the Sharpe index for this portfolio using the historical mean return on U.S. T-bills as the risk-free rate.

20.2   Based on the historical returns in Table 20.1, calculate the mean and standard deviation of return in dollars for an equally weighted portfolio of German and Japanese stocks. Calculate the Sharpe index for this portfolio using the historical mean return on U.S. T-bills as the risk-free rate.

20.3 The correlation between dollar returns to the MSCI world stock and bond market indices listed in Table 20.1 is 0.360. Calculate the expected return and standard deviation of return in dollars to an equally weighted portfolio of stocks and bonds. Calculate the Sharpe index for this portfolio using the historical mean return on U.S. T-bills as the risk-free rate.

20.4 Based on the historical returns in Table 20.1, calculate the expected return and standard deviation of return in dollars to an equally weighted portfolio of U.S., U.K., and Japanese stocks. Calculate the Sharpe index for this portfolio using the historical mean return on U.S. T-bills as the risk-free rate.

20.5 Suppose expected returns in the United States and Germany are 10 percent and 20 percent, respectively. Standard deviations are also 10 percent and 20 percent, respectively. Calculate the standard deviation of an equally weighted combination of the two assets under the following four cases: a) perfect positive correlation, b) perfect negative correlation, c) zero correlation, and d) a correlation of 0.3.

20.6 A portfolio consists of three assets: A, B, and C. Portfolio weights are $x_A = 20\%$, $x_B = 30\%$, and $x_C = 50\%$. Expected returns are $E[r_A] = 8\%$, $E[r_B] = 10\%$, $E[r_C] = 13\%$. What is the expected return on the portfolio?

20.7 Suppose you calculated a Sharpe index for every security in the world over the most recent year. Are any of these securities likely to exhibit performance (measured as excess return per unit of risk) that is superior to that of the world market portfolio? Why or why not?

20.8 Suppose that an asset, A, earns 16 percent in the United States over the period of one year. If the cost of a dollar to a resident of the European Union goes from €0.7064/$ at the beginning of the year to €0.7182/$ at the end of the year, what is the euro return on the U.S. asset?

20.9 The Philippine stock market in Makati rises 12 percent in Philippine pesos. During the same period, the peso rises from $0.0425/Peso to $0.0440/Peso. By how much does the Philippine stock market rise in U.S. dollars?

20.10 What is the standard deviation of return on the Philippine stock market to a U.S. investor if the standard deviation of the local stock market is 24.8 percent, the standard deviation of the dollar-per-peso exchange rate is 32.7 percent, and the interaction terms involving local market returns and the exchange rate are negligible?

20.11 How much of the return variance on a foreign stock investment is likely to come from variation in the foreign stock market and how much from the variation in the exchange rate? What are the proportions for a foreign bond investment?

20.12 Suppose you replicate Solnik's experiment in Figure 20.5 for Greenland. What percent of the variance on a typical Greenland stock do you think would be eliminated within a portfolio of domestic stocks? What percent of the variance of a typical stock is likely to be diversifiable within a globally diversified portfolio?

SUGGESTED READINGS

The algebra of international portfolio diversification is developed and tested in

Michael Adler and Bernard Dumas, "International Portfolio Choice and Corporation Finance: A Synthesis," *Journal of Finance* 38 (June 1983), pp. 925–984.

Geert Bekaert and Campbell Harvey, "Time-Varying World Market Integration," *Journal of Finance* 52, No. 2 (June 1995), pp. 403–444.

Geert Bekaert, Claude Erb, Campbell Harvey, and Tadas E. Viskanta, "Distributional Characteristics of Emerging Market Returns and Asset Allocation," *Journal of Portfolio Management* 21 (Winter 1998), pp. 102–116.

Articles that make a case for international portfolio diversification include

Bruno Solnik, "Why Not Diversify Internationally?" *Financial Analysts Journal* 30 (July/August 1974), pp. 48–54. Reprinted in *Financial Analysts Journal* 51 (January/February 1995), pp. 89–94.

Haim Levy and Zvi Lerman, "The Benefits of International Diversification in Bonds," *Financial Analysts Journal* 44 (September/October 1988), pp. 56–64.

Philippe Jorion, "Asset Allocation with Hedged and Unhedged Foreign Stocks and Bonds," *Journal of Portfolio Management* 15 (Summer 1989), pp. 49–54.

Home asset bias is investigated in

Marianne Baxter and Urban J. Jermann, "The International Diversification Puzzle Is Worse Than You Think," *American Economic Review* 87 (March 1997), pp. 170–180.

Joshua D. Coval and Tobias J. Moskowitz, "Home Bias at Home: Local Equity Preference in Domestic Portfolios," *Journal of Finance* 53 (December 1999), pp. 2045–2074.

Joshua D. Coval and Tobias J. Moskowitz, "The Geography of Investment: Informed Trading and Asset Prices," *Journal of Political Economy* 109 (August 2001), pp. 811–841.

Ian Cooper and Evi Kaplanis, "Home Bias in Equity Portfolios, Inflation Hedging, and International Capital Market Equilibrium," *Review of Financial Studies* 7, No. 1 (Spring 1994), pp. 45–60.

Magnus Dahlquist, Lee Pinkowitz, René M. Stulz, and Rohan Williamson, "Corporate Governance and the Home Bias," *Journal of Financial and Quantitative Analysis* 38, Special Issue on International Corporate Governance (March 2003).

Mark W. Griffin, "Why Do Pension and Insurance Portfolios Hold So Few International Assets?" *Journal of Portfolio Management* 23 (Summer 1997), pp. 45–50.

Mark Grinblatt and Matti Keloharju, "How Distance, Language, and Culture Influence Stockholdings and Trades," *Journal of Finance* 56 (June 2001), pp. 1053–1073.

Mark Grinblatt and Matti Keloharju, "The Investment Behavior and Performance of Various Investor Types: A Study of Finland's Unique Data Set," *Journal of Financial Economics* 55 (January 2000), pp. 43–67.

Jun-Koo Kang and René M. Stulz, "Why Is There a Home Bias? An Analysis of Foreign Portfolio Equity Ownership in Japan," *Journal of Financial Economics* 46 (1997), pp. 43–67.

Behavioral finance is discussed in

Brad M. Barber and Terrance Odean, "Boys Will Be Boys: Gender, Overconfidence, and Common Stock Investment," *Quarterly Journal of Economics* 116 (February 2001), pp. 261–292.

Eugene F. Fama, "Market Efficiency, Long-Term Returns, and Behavioral Finance," *Journal of Financial Economics* 49 (September 1998), pp. 283–306.

Daniel Kahneman and Amos Tversky, "Prospect Theory: An Analysis of Decision Under Risk," *Econometrica* 47 (March 1979), pp. 263–292.

Terrance Odean, "Do Investors Trade Too Much?" *American Economic Review* 89 (December 1999), pp. 1279–1298.

Hersh Shefrin and Meir Statman, "The Disposition to Sell Winners Too Early and Ride Losers Too Long: Theory and Evidence," *Journal of Finance* 40 (July 1985), pp. 777–782.

Continuous Compounding and Emerging Market Returns

Returns measured with periodic compounding are asymmetric, with losses limited to 100 percent and potentially infinite gains. Appendix 5-A introduced continuous compounding in which a periodic or holding period return r is transformed into a continuously compounded rate r according to $r = \ln(1+r)$ or, equivalently, $(1+r) = e^r$. Continuously compounded returns are convenient because they are additive rather than multiplicative over time. They are also symmetric, in that a percentage increase from P_0 to P_1 is exactly offset by a percentage decrease from P_1 back to P_0.

> Returns are additive over time with continuous compounding.

Consider an index that begins at 100, rises to 200, and then falls back to 100. The algebra of this movement in holding period returns is multiplicative over time. The geometric mean return over T periods with periodic compounding is the solution to

$$(1+r_{geo})^T = (1+r_1)(1+r_2)...(1+r_T) \tag{20A.1}$$

or $r_{geo} = (P_T/P_0)^{1/T}-1$ The geometric mean return for the two-period example is $r_{geo} = [(1+r_1)(1+r_2)]^{1/2}-1 = [(1+1)(1-1/2)]^{1/2}-1 = 0$. In contrast, continuously compounded returns are additive according to

$$r_{avg} = \frac{1}{T}(r_1 + r_2 + ... + r_T) \tag{20A.2}$$

In the example, a continuously compounded return of $r_1 = \ln(1+1) = +0.6931$ in the first period is exactly offset by a continuously compounded return of $r_2 = \ln(1-1/2) = -0.6931$ in the second period. The mean return is simply $r_{avg} = 1/2(0.6931-0.6931) = 0$. This symmetry makes statistics such as the mean and standard deviation more meaningful for continuously compounded returns than for returns with periodic compounding.

Returns to Emerging Capital Markets. Annual returns to the MSCI stock market index for Argentina are shown in Table 20A.1. The level of this index is graphed in the top panel of Figure 20A.1. With annual compounding, the arithmetic average of the 1-year returns is $r_{avg} = 0.36853$. This is not an entirely satisfactory measure because 36.853 percent earned every year for 15 years does not yield the observed return of $(647.26/100)-1 = 5.7426$, or 574.26 percent. On the other hand, the geometric mean of $r_{geo} = (674.26/100)^{(1/15)}-1 = 0.21027$ is not as good as the arithmetic mean $r_{avg} = 0.36853$ at describing a typical 1-year return.

Continuous compounding removes this inconsistency. In continuously compounded returns, Argentina has a mean 1-year return that is 1/15 of the 15-year return; $r_{avg} = \ln(674.26/100)/15 = 0.12723$, or 12.723 percent. This continuously compounded annual return is the arithmetic mean, as well as the return that yields the value of the index after 15 years; $(T)r_{avg} = (15)(0.12723) = 1.9084$, or 190.84 percent. This is equal to the holding period return of $r = e^r-1 = e^{1.9084}-1 \approx 5.7426$, or 574.26 percent. The continuously compounded mean is thus both the arithmetic mean and the return that yields the end-of-period return after T periods.

Observed Returns Relative to the Normal Distribution. The normal distribution is more likely to fit continuously compounded returns than periodic returns because of this symmetry. Figure 20A.4 presents Argentina's return distribution with monthly com-

TABLE 20A.1
Annual Returns to Argentina's Stock Market, in U.S. Dollars

Year end	MSCI index level	Percentage return	
		Periodic compounding	Continuous compounding
1987	100.00	—	—
1988	202.62	102.62	70.61
1989	367.12	81.19	59.44
1990	344.72	–6.10	–6.29
1991	1740.84	405.00	161.94
1992	1070.56	–38.50	–48.62
1993	1695.67	58.39	45.99
1994	1294.95	–23.63	–26.96
1995	1461.54	12.86	12.10
1996	1757.83	20.27	18.46
1997	2190.17	24.59	21.99
1998	1657.90	–24.30	–27.84
1999	2226.42	34.29	29.48
2000	1668.23	–25.07	–28.86
2001	1363.43	–18.27	–20.18
2002	674.26	–50.55	–70.41
Arithmetic mean annual return		36.853	12.723
Standard deviation of annual return		111.075	57.554
Ten-year total return		574.26	190.84
Geometric mean annual return		21.027	—

MSCI index level is the level of the Morgan Stanley Capital International (MSCI) gross market index for Argentina, representing pre-tax returns with dividends.

pounding. The two extreme values at +95 percent make the normal distribution a poor fit. Continuously compounded monthly returns are plotted against the normal distribution in the top panel of Figure 20A.2. This distribution is more symmetric than the periodic return distribution. There remains some leptokurtosis, with more observations in the center and in the tails (and fewer in the shoulders) than in the normal distribution.

This general result holds for other emerging markets. Although 20 of the 26 emerging markets have positive skewness with holding period returns, about half (10 of 26) have positive skewness in continuously compounded returns. Evidence of leptokurtosis remains strong; 25 of the 26 distributions are leptokurtic using either measure.

The Lognormal Distribution and the Logarithmic Scale. If continuously compounded returns have a normal distribution, then prices and returns have lognormal distributions. The bottom (logarithmic) panel of Figure 20A.2 plots periodic returns against lognormal probabilities based on the mean and standard deviation of Argentina's monthly returns. Asymmetry in the lognormal probability density matches the asymmetry in the periodic return distribution.

Long-term charts that cover a wide range of prices are often displayed on a logarithmic scale, such as in the bottom panel of Figure 20A.1.[29] On a log scale, the distance on the y-axis is proportional to the percentage change in the index regardless of the

---

29 A word of caution: The logarithmic scaling option in many spreadsheet programs uses base 10 rather than base e (~2.71828). Base 10 logs are defined by $10^x = y$ rather than $e^x = y$.

FIGURE 20A.1
The MSCI–Argentina Index, in U.S. Dollars

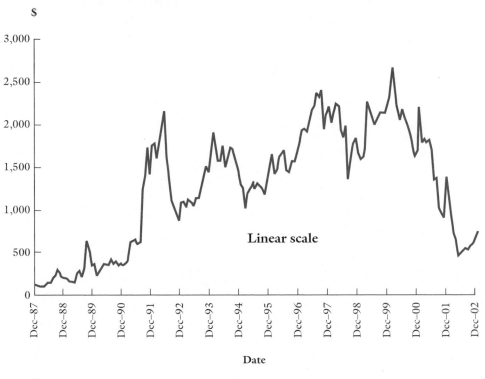

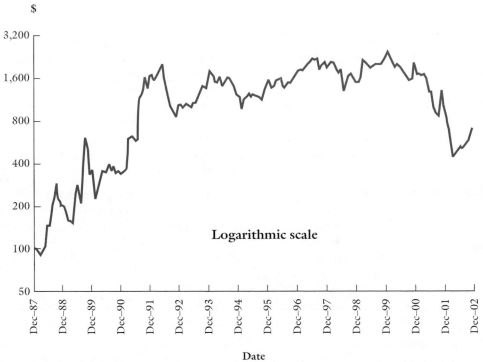

FIGURE 20A.2
Argentina's Monthly Return Distribution, in U.S. Dollars

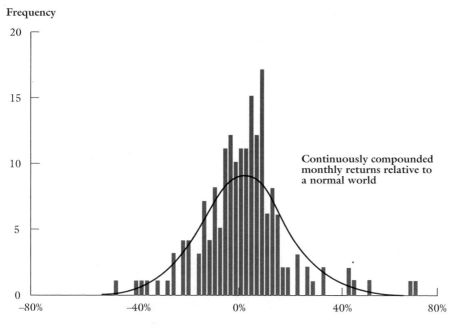

Continuously compounded monthly returns relative to a normal world

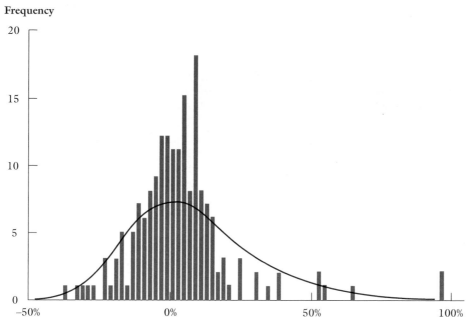

starting point. A doubling of an index from 100 to 200 results in the same distance along the y-axis as a doubling from 200 to 400 or from 400 to 800. In contrast, linear scales exaggerate the movements of prices at higher levels. On the linear scale in Figure 20A.1, Argentina appears to have had low volatility in the 1980s and higher volatility

Distance is proportional to percentage change on a log scale.

during the 1990s. Measured in proportional changes on the logarithmic scale, volatility was in fact relatively low during the mid to late 1990s. The log scale allows a comparison of percentage movements in the index at different price levels.

Measures, Correlations, Betas, and Risk. Table 20A.2 compares holding period return statistics to continuously compounded return statistics for the MSCI emerging market indices. Compared to continuously compounded returns, periodic compounding exagger-

TABLE 20A.2
Returns in Emerging Stock Markets, in U.S. Dollars

	Holding period returns				Continuously compounded returns			
	Mean	Std dev	Correlation	Beta	Mean	Std dev	Correlation	Beta
Argentina	36.9%	111.1%	0.142	0.598	12.7%	57.6%	0.177	0.665
Brazil	28.1%	62.4%	0.384	1.556	13.0%	52.1%	0.404	1.681
Chile	21.1%	38.2%	0.352	0.614	14.8%	30.4%	0.369	0.639
China	−12.0%	29.9%	0.366	1.034	−17.7%	32.6%	0.373	1.021
Columbia	5.6%	33.1%	0.145	0.319	0.4%	34.8%	0.145	0.317
Czech Republic	4.7%	22.8%	0.250	0.517	2.6%	21.3%	0.278	0.578
Egypt	10.5%	47.8%	0.223	0.431	1.4%	45.1%	0.235	0.432
Hungary	22.9%	51.5%	0.506	1.333	13.7%	38.9%	0.542	1.426
India	5.6%	35.1%	0.256	0.511	1.1%	30.0%	0.263	0.520
Indonesia	25.2%	84.3%	0.217	0.848	2.2%	68.0%	0.243	0.868
Israel	5.0%	30.8%	0.531	1.001	0.8%	30.3%	0.538	1.017
Jordan	2.6%	19.2%	0.100	0.103	1.0%	18.1%	0.100	0.103
Korea	16.3%	58.0%	0.424	1.214	2.8%	53.3%	0.434	1.183
Malaysia	15.0%	48.6%	0.411	0.941	5.0%	46.0%	0.422	0.951
Mexico	31.1%	50.2%	0.469	1.119	19.6%	41.3%	0.476	1.148
Morocco	7.5%	23.8%	−0.027	−0.030	5.0%	22.4%	−0.020	−0.021
Pakistan	14.3%	62.0%	0.106	0.307	1.3%	51.3%	0.102	0.290
Peru	12.1%	26.1%	0.340	0.733	8.4%	27.4%	0.363	0.783
Philippines	11.2%	52.0%	0.408	0.970	−0.2%	49.5%	0.415	0.969
Poland	72.8%	241.4%	0.393	1.574	13.9%	78.2%	0.444	1.563
Russia	55.4%	109.7%	0.490	2.369	13.4%	95.7%	0.498	2.459
S. Africa	12.1%	35.0%	0.536	1.015	7.2%	30.6%	0.545	1.054
Taiwan	14.8%	52.1%	0.318	0.903	3.9%	46.5%	0.334	0.928
Thailand	13.9%	52.7%	0.448	1.302	0.7%	55.8%	0.460	1.338
Turkey	55.2%	168.4%	0.263	1.156	4.8%	84.8%	0.293	1.227
Venezuela	8.5%	48.6%	0.245	0.816	0.7%	39.3%	0.250	0.854
Average	19.1%	61.3%	0.319	0.894	5.1%	45.4%	0.334	0.923
EMF Free	15.0%	36.0%	0.652	1.051	9.6%	30.4%	0.665	1.087
All-country world	7.9%	17.1%	1.000	1.000	6.3%	16.7%	1.000	1.000

Source: Based on the Morgan Stanley Capital International gross (pre-tax returns with dividends) indices. Means and standard deviations are based on annual U.S. dollar returns. All series are over 1988–2002 except China, Columbia, India, Israel, Pakistan, Peru, Poland, S. Africa, and Venezuela (1993–2002) and the Czech Republic, Egypt, Hungary, Morocco, and Russia (1995–2002). Correlations and betas are against the monthly MSCI all-country index, a value-weighted float-adjusted index of 23 developed and 26 emerging markets. Averages are equal-weighted means. EMF Free is a value-weighted float-adjusted index of the 26 emerging markets.

ates the arithmetic means and standard deviations. Continuous compounding has much less of an effect on correlations and betas. For example, the average beta across the 26 emerging markets is 0.894 with monthly compounding and 0.923 with continuous compounding. The correlation between the betas measured with periodic and with continuous compounding is 0.998.

Continuous compounding also provides insight into the return-risk trade-off. With periodic compounding, there is an apparent relation in Figure 20.1 between mean and standard deviation suggesting that risk is a function of variability. This apparent relation is even more visible when emerging markets are included, as in the top panel of Figure 20A.3. However, there is no obvious relation between the mean and standard deviation of continuously compounded returns, as shown in the bottom panel of Figure 20A.3. This suggests that risk is not a simple function of the standard deviation of return. The next chapter investigates the nature of risk for an individual asset within a large and diversified portfolio.

PROBLEMS

20A.1 The MSCI index levels for Hungary and Russia are listed here:

	Index level	
Date	**Hungary**	**Russia**
12/31/94	100.00	100.00
12/31/95	82.87	72.91
12/31/96	171.73	184.40
12/31/97	335.22	391.16
12/31/98	307.86	66.53
12/31/99	343.75	230.89
12/31/00	251.61	161.57
12/31/01	228.57	251.81
12/31/02	298.71	291.36

a. Calculate the mean and standard deviation of each series using annual holding period returns, and again with continuously compounded returns. How different are these measures?
b. Calculate the correlation coefficient between the two series using both periodic and continuous compounding. How different are these measures?
c. Display each series over time on a linear and on a natural logarithmic scale using 100 as the base. (For the natural log scale, calculate $\ln(P_t/P_{t-1})$ times 100 and add the result to the previous level using 100 as P_0. Plot this value over time.)

FIGURE 20A.3
Annual Returns to Developing and Emerging Stock Markets, in U.S. Dollars

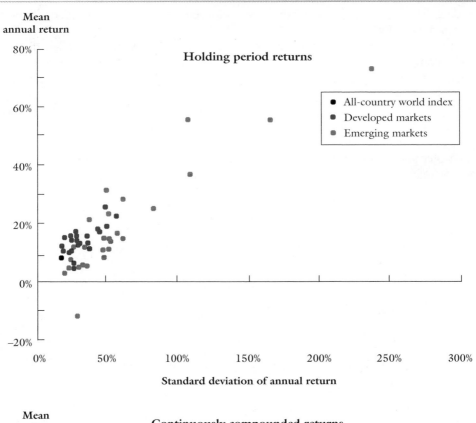

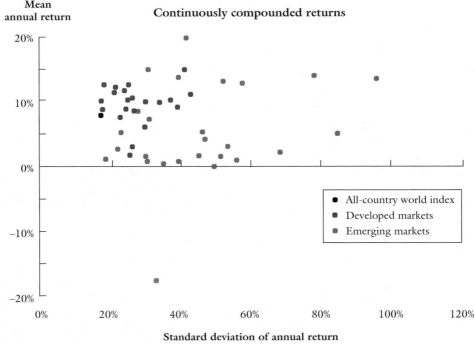

International Asset Pricing

chapter 21

Overview

We dance round in a ring and suppose, But the Secret sits in the middle and knows.

Robert Frost

This chapter develops several models for pricing international assets. We begin our discussion with the single-currency capital asset pricing model (CAPM). With a few additional assumptions, the algebra of portfolio diversification leads to an international version of the CAPM called the international asset pricing model (IAPM). The appeal of these asset pricing models is that an asset's risk is uniquely identified by its systematic risk or beta measured against a broadly diversified market portfolio. Unfortunately for the CAPM and IAPM, empirical evidence shows that betas have almost no relation to mean returns. In the absence of a relation between mean returns and beta, finance has resorted to factor models (also called arbitrage pricing theory, or APT) to identify the fundamental determinants of returns to domestic and international assets. The chapter concludes with a discussion of the contribution of currency risk to equity return and its interaction with the multinational corporation's currency risk hedging activities.

21.1 • THE TRADITIONAL CAPITAL ASSET PRICING MODEL (CAPM)

Before we move on to the international asset pricing model, we need to complete the development of the traditional, single-currency version of the **capital asset pricing model (CAPM)**. Let's again start with the **perfect market assumptions**:

- Frictionless markets
- Rational investors
- Equal access to market prices
- Equal access to costless information

Two more assumptions are necessary to complete the traditional version of the CAPM:

- Investors have homogeneous expectations regarding future expected returns and risks.
- Everyone can borrow and lend at the risk-free rate of interest r_F.

The first is an assumption that all investors have the same expectations. In such a world, every investor faces the same investment opportunity set in Figure 21.1. An assumption of homogeneous expectations is out of place in a book founded on differences among the people of the world, but it is necessary for the traditional version of the CAPM.

The risk-free asset yields a nominal rate r_F at which any party can borrow or lend. Nominal returns to this asset are certain ($\sigma_F=0$), so the covariance or correlation of the risk-free asset with any risky asset A is zero ($\sigma_{F,A}=\rho_{F,A}=0$). The standard deviation of a portfolio of the risk-free asset F and any risky asset A, $\sigma_P=[x_A^2\sigma_A^2]^{1/2}=x_A\sigma_A$, is proportional to the percentage invested in the risky asset A. A combination of the risk-free asset and any risky asset forms a straight line between the two points in $E[r]$–σ space.

The **capital market line (CML)** extends from the risk-free asset to point M in Figure 21.1. Along this tangency line, investors achieve the highest level of expected return per unit of risk of any combination of assets in the opportunity set. That is, investors receive the biggest "bang for the buck" along this line. There is a single tangency point, so portfolio M is unique. Point M is called the **market portfolio** and is a portfolio of all assets in the investment opportunity set weighted according to their market values.

> The CML describes the most efficient combination of risky and riskless assets.

FIGURE 21.1
The Capital Market Line

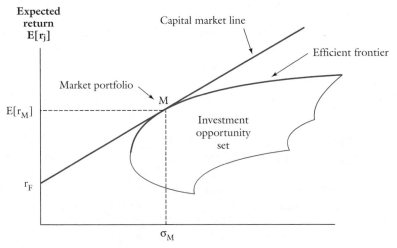

Standard deviation of return

Under the assumptions of the CAPM, each investor choosing to invest in a risky asset will hold the market portfolio. The **systematic risk** (also called *nondiversifiable risk* or *market risk*) of an individual asset can then be measured by how its returns covary with those of the market portfolio. This allows us to shift the focus from capital market equilibrium depicted in Figure 21.1 to the expected return and risk of a single asset in the market portfolio shown in Figure 21.2.

Systematic (Nondiversifiable) Risk and the Security Market Line

Assets are correctly priced in efficient financial markets, so the expected net present value of any financial investment is zero. This means that the expected return on each asset must equal that asset's required return. In the CAPM, required return is determined by the **security market line (SML)**. The equation of the SML is

> The SML describes the relation between systematic risk and required return.

$$r_j = r_F + \beta_j \, (E[r_M] - r_F) \tag{21.1}$$

The SML is graphed in Figure 21.2. This relation states that the required return on an individual asset is equal to the risk-free rate r_F plus a risk premium appropriate for the systematic risk of the asset. The risk premium is the product of the **market risk premium** (that is, the risk premium on an average stock, $E[r_M]-r_F$) and the firm's systematic risk, or beta (β_j). **Beta** is a measure of systematic risk and reflects the sensitivity of an asset's price to changes in the value of the market portfolio. Systematic risks arise through market-wide events, such as unexpected changes in real economic activity or in investor sentiment regarding asset values. Systematic risk cannot be diversified away by holding assets in larger portfolios because it is already measured against the market portfolio (the largest portfolio of all).

FIGURE 21.2
The Security Market Line

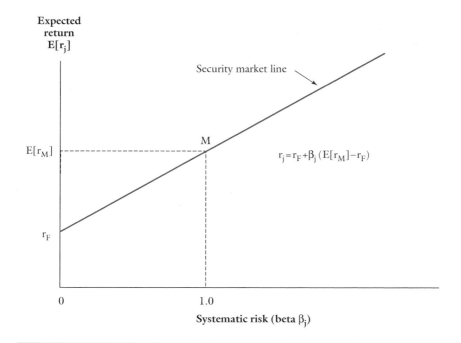

Risk-adjusted investment performance is measured in the CAPM by the difference between actual return and the expected return from Equation 21.1:

$$e_j = r_j - E[r_j] = rj - [(r_F + \beta_j(r_M - r_F)] \tag{21.2}$$

where r_j is the observed return to asset j and $E[r_j]$ is the expected (and required) return from the SML. Using the current T-bill rate as r_F and the observed excess return of the market portfolio over the risk-free rate $(r_M - r_F)$, the residual return e_j measures risk-adjusted performance over the period. Because $E[e_j] = 0$, abnormal (positive or negative) investment performance is measured by the difference of e_j from zero.[1]

Beta is estimated by regressing security return on the return of the market index using the following regression equation:

$$r_j = \alpha_j + \beta_j r_M + e_j \tag{21.3}$$

This **market model** regression is depicted in Figure 21.3. The slope coefficient β_j captures that part of the variation in an individual stock that is linearly related to the market return.

As with any regression coefficient, beta can be restated as a correlation coefficient scaled by the standard deviations of r_j and r_M:

$$\beta_j = \rho_{j,M} (\sigma_j / \sigma_M) \tag{21.4}$$

> Market model beta measures an asset's sensitivity to changes in the market.

In this way, beta measures the asset's sensitivity to returns on the market portfolio; that is, the asset's systematic risk. The beta of the market itself is $\beta_M = \rho_{M,M} (\sigma_M/\sigma_M) = 1$. The beta of the risk-free asset is $\beta_F = \rho_{F,M}(\sigma_F/\sigma_M) = 0$. Firms with betas greater than 1 have more systematic risk than the average firm in the market. These stocks tend to perform better than the average when the overall market is up and worse than the average when the market is down. Another way of stating this is that firms with betas greater than 1 are more sensitive to changes in the market index than the average firm. Conversely, firms with betas less than 1 have less systematic risk than the average.

FIGURE 21.3
Beta as a Regression Coefficient

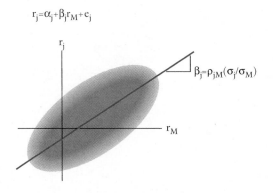

---

[1] A t-test comparison of means is used as a test of statistical significance.

Sources of Unsystematic (Diversifiable) Risks

The residual term e_j captures all return variation in r_j that is unrelated to the market portfolio. The residual term captures that portion of individual security risk that can be diversified away by holding the security in a portfolio with many securities. Such risk is called **unsystematic risk**. It is also called *nonmarket risk* or *diversifiable risk*. If returns are normally distributed, then the residual term is also distributed as normal with zero mean ($E[e_j] = 0$), and it is uncorrelated with other securities ($Cov(e_i,e_j) = 0$ for $i \neq j$) and with the market portfolio ($Cov(e_j,r_M) = 0$). If the asset is a share of stock in a company, then the portion of risk that is diversifiable is also called *company-specific risk*. Unsystematic risks include labor strikes, changes in top management, company-specific sales fluctuations, and any other events that are unique to a single company.

> Unsystematic risks are eliminated in a diversified portfolio.

An important source of risk on a foreign investment is **political risk**—the risk of unexpected political events in a host country affecting the value of an investment. Many types of political risk are country-specific. To assess the importance of a country-specific risk, investors weigh the probability of an adverse country-specific event by the consequences of that event. Political risks that have a low probability but are catastrophic in nature include the risk of expropriation. **Expropriation** occurs when a government seizes foreign assets within its borders.

A political risk of particular importance to MNCs is the risk of unexpected changes in the operating environment, such as the risk of an unexpected change in tax laws and regulations. This type of political risk is much more common than a catastrophic event, such as expropriation. The consequences of unexpected changes in the operating environment can be nearly as profound as those of expropriation. The uncertain operating environments in the republics of the former Soviet Union and in the People's Republic of China have kept many multinational corporations from investing in these potentially lucrative markets.

To the extent that country-specific political risks can be diversified away by holding country-specific investments within a globally diversified portfolio, these risks are unsystematic and, hence, should not be reflected in the required return from the security market line. The theoretically correct way to handle country-specific political risks is to incorporate them into the expected future cash flows from investment (see Chapter 15).

21.2 • THE INTERNATIONAL ASSET PRICING MODEL (IAPM)

One way to generalize the CAPM to accommodate the fact that investors have different functional currencies is to create a world in which the international parity conditions always hold.[2] In addition to the assumptions of the traditional CAPM, two more conditions are necessary to ensure that the international parity conditions hold:

- Purchasing power parity holds, so prices and real interest rates are the same in every country and for every individual.

- Investors have the same consumption basket, so inflation is measured against the same benchmark in every country.

If the international parity conditions hold, then changes in exchange rates simply mirror inflation differentials. In this world, the exchange rate is nothing more than a device for translating between currencies and holds no real power over investors.

---

2 Adler and Dumas, "International Portfolio Choice and Corporation Finance: A Synthesis," *Journal of Finance* (1983).

Once these conditions are imposed, extension of the CAPM to a world of many functional currencies is straightforward. The resulting model is called the **international asset pricing model (IAPM)**. Just as in the traditional CAPM, all investors hold their funds at risk in a single, mean-variance efficient market portfolio of risky assets. In the IAPM, the market portfolio is a globally diversified portfolio comprised of all risky assets weighted according to their market values at prevailing exchange rates. In the IAPM, investors also hold a currency-specific **hedge portfolio** that serves a role similar to that of the risk-free asset in the traditional CAPM. This hedge portfolio consists of risk-free domestic and foreign assets and is held for two reasons:

> In the IAPM, investors hold a market portfolio and a hedge portfolio.

- As a store of value (like the risk-free asset in the traditional CAPM)
- To hedge the currency risk of the market portfolio

If inflation is a constant in each currency, then the hedge portfolio held by each investor reduces to the investor's home-currency risk-free asset as in the CAPM.

Financial Market Segmentation and Choice of the Market Portfolio

The assumptions of the IAPM are sufficient to ensure that financial markets (including national stock and bond markets, spot and forward currency markets, and Eurocurrency interest rate markets) are integrated. In an **integrated** market, prices are simultaneously established across all markets so that required returns on assets of the same risk are the same in all locations. Because markets are integrated in the IAPM, the world market portfolio is a fully diversified set of risky international assets that is shared by investors in every country. Risk-averse investors hold a hedge portfolio that includes riskless domestic and foreign bills. In the IAPM, the systematic risk of an asset reflects the asset's sensitivity to changes in the value of the world market portfolio. Industry and national market indices are of importance only in that they reflect the sensitivity of the industry or national market to changes in the value of the world market portfolio.

> Purchasing power parity in frictionless markets ensures that markets are integrated.

In completely **segmented** markets, prices are set independently in each national market. In this case, purchasing power parity will not hold across national markets even though it might hold within each national market. Without access to international markets, investors hold their own national market portfolio of risky assets. The systematic risk of an asset in a segmented national market then depends on its sensitivity to national market movements and not on its sensitivity to world market movements.

The reality of present-day financial markets lies somewhere between these two extremes.[3] Investors exhibit a strong **home asset bias**, favoring their own domestic market portfolio rather than choosing to be fully diversified internationally. For example, less than 5 percent of pension assets in the United States are invested in foreign markets, despite the fact that more than half of the world's publicly traded assets reside outside the United States. Home asset bias is also prevalent in smaller, less-diversified economies. Because of this segmentation, the market portfolio is often proxied by a domestic portfolio. As an example, the *Value Line Investment Survey* reports betas measured with weekly returns over a 5-year window against the value-weighted New York Stock Exchange (NYSE) Composite Index. Other information services calculate and report betas relative to other domestic market indices. With the increasing inte-

---

3 Bekaert and Harvey discuss the integration/segmentation debate and estimate how market integration evolves over time in "Time-Varying World Market Integration," *Journal of Finance* (1995).

gration of European capital markets and the introduction of the euro, many European investors now choose an all-European stock index as their market portfolio.

Choice of a benchmark portfolio against which to measure systematic risk has an important consequence for the measurement and evaluation of investment performance, as we shall see in the next section.

Roll's Critique

The intuition behind the CAPM is simple—higher risks demand higher expected returns. This intuition suggests that there should be a relation between mean returns and betas. In fact, if the ex post efficient market portfolio is used as the performance benchmark, then the algebra of the CAPM requires that beta and only beta explains an asset's mean return. There is no systematic portion of return left to be explained by any other variable.

Unfortunately for proponents of the CAPM, empirical tests commonly find no relation between mean returns and betas. In an influential study, Fama and French found that "the relation between market beta and average return is flat, even when beta is the only explanatory variable."[4] This is a curious and unsettling finding for the CAPM. If beta is unrelated to return, then it makes no sense to use beta in estimating the cost of capital, constructing investment portfolios, or measuring investment performance.

> Empirical tests often find no relation between mean returns and betas.

The heart of the problem was identified by Roll and is called **Roll's critique**.[5] In theory, the CAPM market portfolio is a value-weighted index of all assets, including frequently traded assets such as stocks and bonds, less frequently traded assets such as real estate, and nontraded assets such as human capital. In practice, a proxy for the market portfolio must be constructed from assets with observable returns, such as a stock market index. Roll made the following observations:

- If performance is measured relative to an index that is ex post *efficient*, then the algebra of the CAPM says that no security can have abnormal performance when measured as a departure from the security market line.

- If performance is measured relative to an index that is ex post *inefficient*, then any ranking of portfolio performance is possible depending on which inefficient market index has been chosen as the standard for comparison.

Mean-variance efficiency is like pregnancy—a woman can't be a little bit pregnant, and a market index can't be a little bit efficient. It either is or isn't.

Roll and Ross investigated how far off the efficient frontier an index must be to produce betas that have no relation to returns.[6] They found that indices lying only a small distance inside the efficient frontier can produce betas that are unrelated to mean returns. They concluded that "the almost pathological knife-edged nature of the expected return-beta OLS cross-sectional relation . . . is a shaky base for modern finance."

> Roll's critique also applies to the international version of the CAPM.

Roll's critique was originally aimed at the single-currency CAPM. Because of barriers to cross-border portfolio investment, it is just as relevant for the IAPM. Impediments to holding the world market portfolio include restrictions on cross-border capital flows, differences in tax rates and regimes, high and differential transactions costs, and information costs. The resulting

---

4 Fama and French, "The Cross-Section of Expected Stock Returns," *Journal of Finance* (1992). Fama and French found other variables play a role in explaining returns. We'll return to this topic later in the chapter.

5 Roll, "A Critique of the Asset Pricing Theory's Tests," *Journal of Financial Economics* (1977).

6 Roll and Ross, "On the Cross-Sectional Relation Between Expected Stock Returns and Betas," *Journal of Finance* (1994).

Market Update

The Relevance of Market Indices

The fact that a particular market index is not mean-variance efficient does not mean that indices have no use. Although inefficient indices are unlikely to yield meaningful measures of systematic risk, returns to an index reflect averages of investor holdings and provide a performance benchmark for the asset class included in the index. Comparison of investment returns to those of an index with the same target weights has become the most widely accepted criterion of investment performance.

Financial newspapers such as *The Wall Street Journal* and the *London Financial Times* report global, regional, local, and industry indices on a broad range of portfolios. National market indices, such as the S&P 500 and London's FTSE All-Shares 750, provide performance benchmarks for equity investments in these national markets. Regional indices track stock returns in broad geographic regions such as the Americas, Europe, Nordic, or Asia/Pacific. Some industry indices are local in scope, such as the Dow Jones Utilities Index. Others are transnational, such as Morgan Stanley Capital International's industry indices for aerospace, automobiles, and banking. These stock market indices provide performance benchmarks for investments in these asset classes.

home asset bias ensures that the multicurrency IAPM is even less likely to hold than the single-currency CAPM. For this reason, the world market portfolio is a pedagogical ideal and not a fully operational instrument.

Roll's critique tells us that we need to look elsewhere for meaningful measures of systematic risk and an explanation of why mean returns differ across assets in international markets.

21.3 • FACTOR MODELS AND ARBITRAGE PRICING THEORY (APT)

The CAPM and IAPM have great intuitive and practical appeal because they suggest a simple measure of systematic risk (beta) and a simple linear relation (the security market line) between systematic risk and expected return. The finding that beta has little relation to ex post mean return is a critical failure of the models. This is perhaps not surprising given (1) the sensitivity of tests of the CAPM and IAPM to the market portfolio proxy and (2) the fact that there is not a single world market portfolio held by all investors.

> APT assumes a linear relation between required return and one or more systematic risk factors.

In response to these criticisms of the CAPM, Ross proposed **arbitrage pricing theory (APT)**.[7] Like the CAPM, APT assumes a linear relation between systematic risk and expected return. A security's risk in the CAPM depends on its sensitivity to changes in the value of the market portfolio. The APT takes a more general view

---

7 Ross, "The Arbitrage Theory of Asset Pricing," *Journal of Economic Theory* (1976).

of the types of risks that might be priced in the market. In the APT, a security's rate of return is a linear function of K systematic risk factors:

$$r_j = \mu_j + \beta_{1j}F_1 + \dots + \beta_{Kj}F_K + e_j \tag{21.5}$$

where r_j = the random rate of return on asset j
μ_j = the mean or expected return on asset j
β_{kj} = the sensitivity of asset j's return to factor k where k=1,...,K
F_k = systematic risk factor k
e_j = a random error or noise term specific to asset j

Factor models such as Equation 21.5 are based on the idea that the actual return on an individual security can be decomposed into an expected part and an unexpected part. The expected return $E[r_j] = \mu_j$ is common to all assets. The unexpected part of the return contains a systematic risk component $(\sum_k \beta_{kj}F_k)$ and an unsystematic risk or error component e_j. The systematic factors F_k are risks that affect a large number of assets. The systematic risk and, hence, the return of an individual security j, depend on the K systematic risk factors and the asset's sensitivities to those factors.

As in the CAPM and IAPM, unsystematic risk e_j is specific to a single asset and depends on such asset-specific events as management changes, research breakthroughs, labor strife, and retainment or retirement of key personnel. The APT's linear structure ensures that firm-specific error e_j is unrelated to the systematic risk factors as well as to other firms' error terms, so that $E[e_j] = Cov(e_i,e_j) = 0$ for $i \neq j$.

The major drawback of the APT is that the factors that might be priced in the market are not identified a priori by the model. In the CAPM and the IAPM, the one and only systematic risk factor is the market portfolio return. This is the major appeal of the CAPM and IAPM. In the APT, the systematic risk factors must be either empirically identified from the data (for example, through factor analysis) or independently identified through another asset pricing theory that guides the search for factors that might be priced in the market.

> APT does not identify the factor(s) that might matter to the market a priori.

A prominent special case of the APT is the **one-factor market model**. Figure 21.4 presents this model in graphical form. This is the same market model that was used in Equation 21.3 to estimate beta in the CAPM, although it will be developed in a little more detail here. The model is as follows:

$$r_j = \alpha_j + \beta_j r_M + e_j \tag{21.3}$$

The expectation of this equation is $E[r_j]=\alpha_j+\beta_j E[r_M]$. Substituting observed means μ_j and μ_M for the expectations and subtracting the resulting equation $(\mu_j=\alpha_j+\beta_j\mu_M)$ from the one-factor market model in Equation 21.3 results in a one-factor market model in *excess return* form:

$$r_j = \mu_j + \beta_j F_M + e_j \tag{21.6}$$

The systematic risk factor in this model is the difference between actual market index returns and the mean market return: $F_M = r_M - \mu_M$. Equation 21.6 is the APT equivalent of the one-factor (CAPM or IAPM) market model in Equation 21.3. The measure of systematic risk, $\beta_j = \rho_{j,M} (\sigma_j/\sigma_M)$, captures the sensitivity or exposure of security return to unexpected changes in the market index.

FIGURE 21.4

Factor Models

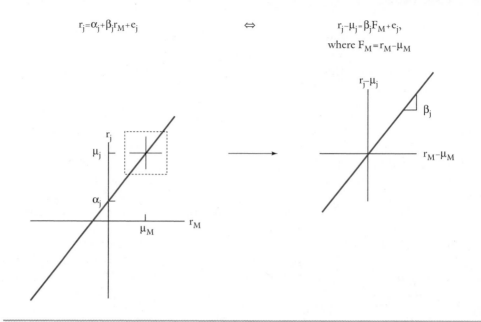

$$r_j = \alpha_j + \beta_j r_M + e_j \qquad\qquad \Leftrightarrow \qquad\qquad r_j - \mu_j = \beta_j F_M + e_j,$$

$$\text{where } F_M = r_M - \mu_M$$

21.4 • APPLICATIONS OF ARBITRAGE PRICING THEORY

Macroeconomic Factors Associated with Domestic Stock Returns

One of the first applications of APT was Chen, Roll, and Ross's study of U.S. stocks.[8] Through a simple discounted cash flow model, these authors identified several macroeconomic factors that ought to be sources of systematic risk. Roll and Ross later simplified this model to include the following factors:[9]

F_1 = unanticipated changes in inflation
F_2 = unanticipated changes in industrial production
F_3 = unanticipated changes in the slope of the term structure of interest rates (measured by the spread between long-term and short-term bonds)
F_4 = unanticipated changes in risk premiums (measured by the spread between low-grade and high-grade bonds)

The factor model for estimating the relation of these factors to an asset's mean return is

$$r_j = \mu_j + \beta_{1j}F_1 + \beta_{2j}F_2 + \beta_{3j}F_3 + \beta_{4j}F_4 + e_j \qquad\qquad (21.7)$$

Each factor is constructed in excess return form, such that $E[F_k] = 0$. Subtracting the mean return μ_j from both sides of Equation 21.7 results in

---

8 Chen, Roll, and Ross, "Economic Forces and the Stock Market," *Journal of Business* (1986).

9 Roll and Ross, "The Arbitrage Pricing Theory Approach to Strategic Portfolio Planning," *Financial Analysts Journal* (1995).

$$r_j - \mu_j = \beta_{1j}F_1 + \beta_{2j}F_2 + \beta_{3j}F_3 + \beta_{4j}F_4 + e_j \qquad (21.8)$$

Equation 21.8 centers the regression on an asset's mean return μ_j.

Coefficients on each of the factors were statistically significant. The influence of these fundamental economic factors was especially strong for the industrial production, risk premium, and term structure indices. Moreover, when a market portfolio index was included along with the economic factors, the market factor had an insignificant coefficient, whereas the economic factors were undiminished. These authors concluded that any explanatory power of the market factor is a statistical artifact—a consequence of the fact that all stocks are exposed to fundamental economic risks that underlie returns to the market portfolio. That is, the stock market factor does not explain movements in individual stocks or cross-sectional differences in mean returns once these fundamental economic factors have been included.

The Relative Importance of Global, National, and Industry Factors

International asset pricing models such as the IAPM predict that an asset's systematic risk and required return should depend on its covariance with the world market portfolio. If national markets are segmented, then an asset's return should depend on its covariance with the local market. While increasing integration in the world's equity markets suggests that returns should depend on global factors, persistent home asset bias suggests that local factors should be important. Which factor—local or global—is dominant?

Confounding this question is the possible influence of industry factors. Managers of international equity funds often allocate their assets across industry sectors rather than national markets in the belief that international returns are driven by industry rather than national factors. Managers following this approach believe that the benefits of international portfolio diversification derive from industry diversification rather than geographic diversification.

Beckers, Connor, and Curds investigated the relative importance of global, national, and industry factors with the following factor model:

$$r_j = \mu_M + \beta_{Cj}F_{Cj} + \beta_{Ij}F_{Ij} + e_j \qquad (21.9)$$

where r_j = local currency excess return to stock j
μ_M = return to the global market factor
F_{Cj} = return to stock j's country factor
and F_{Ij} = return to stock j's industry factor

Their sample included over 2,000 stocks from 19 developed countries and 36 industries.[10] Each stock was assigned to a single country and industry. To reduce the influence of currency risk, returns were measured in the local currency and in excess of the local risk-free rate. From the perspective of an international investor, these correspond to excess returns that are fully hedged against currency risk.

The industry and country factors were measured net of the global market return by constraining the average global effects of the industry and country factors to zero across sample firms. To assess the relative contribution of each factor, Equation 21.9 was estimated by omitting the industry factor, the country factor, and both industry

---

10 Beckers, Connor, and Curds, "National Versus Global Influences on Equity Returns," *Financial Analysts Journal* (1996). See also Heston and Rouwenhorst, "Does Industrial Structure Explain the Benefits of International Diversification?" *Journal of Financial Economics* (1994); and Griffin and Karolyi, "Another Look at the Role of the Industrial Structure of Markets for International Diversification Strategies, *Journal of Financial Economics* (1998).

and country factors. The explanatory power of the global, national, and industry factors in Equation 21.9 was measured with an EP (explanatory power) statistic that is related to the regression's coefficient of determination.[11]

Average EP statistics are reported in Table 21.1 for each of the estimated models. When the model included only the global stock market factor, the regression explained 21.07 percent of the variation in individual stock returns. Because it is the only factor present, this factor includes any information in the national stock market and industry factors that is related to the global factor.

| Global and national factors dominate industry factors. |

Adding the industry factor F_{Ij} to the model with only a global factor μ_M captures the contribution of industry-specific information that is unrelated to the global factor. The industry factor added only 4.3 percent (from 21.07 to 25.37) to the explanatory power of the model. This relatively small increase in explanatory power suggests that most of the information in the industry factor is already included in the global stock market factor.

In contrast to the relatively small contribution of the industry factor, the national stock market factor F_{Cj} increased the explanatory power of the regression by 15.13 percent (from 21.07 to 36.20 percent). Because the information in the national market return that is related to the global stock market factor is already included in the global factor, this increase in explanatory power reflects the contribution of country-specific variation in national stock market returns.

Both global and national stock market factors play important roles in explaining stock return variability. The exposure of stocks to industry-specific factors is low, so industrial structure explains very little of the cross-sectional difference in return variability. This suggests that the low correlation between country stock market indices is due to country-specific (rather than industry-specific) sources of return variation. For the portfolio manager seeking to take advantage of the risk reduction benefits of international portfolio diversification, these findings suggest that geographic diversification is more effective in reducing portfolio risk than diversification across industries.

Low correlations between national market indices can arise from several sources:

- *Cross-country differences in industrial structure.* Low correlations might arise from national differences in industrial structure. For example, electronics accounts for

---

T A B L E   2 1 . 1

Contribution of Global, National, and Industry Factors

Global factor alone	Global and industry factors
0.2107	0.2537
Global and national stock market factors	Global, industry, and national stock market factors
0.3620	0.3970

From Beckers, Connor, and Curds, "National Versus Global Influences on Equity Returns," *Financial Analysts Journal* (March/April 1996).

---

11 The percent of the variation in r_j that is explained by variation in the factor(s) is called the coefficient of determination or r-square. With a single independent variable, r-square equals the square of the correlation between the dependent and independent variables. The EP statistic differs from r-square in that it includes the explanatory power of the global stock market factor μ_M.

over 50 percent of manufacturing in Singapore's highly industrialized economy. In contrast, Argentina's economy is based on agriculture and natural resource development. Returns to assets in Singapore and Argentina will have a low correlation simply because of these different industrial structures.

- *Country-specific shocks.* Many fiscal and monetary shocks are country-specific. Changes in a nation's fiscal or monetary policies have profound effects on local inflation and economic activity, and will decrease cross-country correlations.

- *Home asset bias.* Investors prefer to hold local assets, which increases the importance of local factors relative to global factors. If investor sentiment also differs across countries, national factors will assume an even greater significance.

As investors increasingly diversify across national borders and markets become further integrated, national factors might eventually assume a lesser role in the variation of portfolio returns. Correspondingly, global factors and perhaps even industry factors might play an increasing role. Indeed, many practitioners recently have moved away from international and toward industry-based investment strategies. This is particularly true within the European Union, where increasing integration, harmonization, and cross-border mergers and acquisitions are reducing the importance of national factors.[12] Which of these factors will dominate in the future? Stay tuned.

The International Value Premium

In which type of firm would you rather invest—a firm in financial distress with a track record of low earnings growth and poor stock price performance, or a firm that has recently experienced high earnings growth and stock price appreciation? Alternatively, would you rather invest in a large blue-chip company or in a small company with volatile earnings and uncertain return prospects?

Keep in mind that a well-run company does not necessarily make a good investment. If investors correctly anticipate the firm's growth prospects, then each of these firms should be properly priced in the marketplace according to its expected cash flows and systematic risk. However, if investors fail to incorporate information into share price, savvy investors might be able to identify bargain stocks.

> Good companies are not necessarily good stocks.

Fama and French fit the following three-factor model:[13]

$$r_j = \mu_j + \beta_j F_M + \beta_{Zj} F_Z + \beta_{Dj} F_D + e_j \qquad (21.10)$$

The coefficient β_j is stock j's sensitivity to the domestic market factor $F_M = (r_M - \mu_M)$. The coefficients β_{Zj} and β_{Dj} reflect the sensitivity of stock j to a firm size and a relative financial distress factor. In combination, these three factors explain a significant proportion of mean returns in stocks around the world.

Fama and French model the firm size factor F_Z as the difference in mean return between the smallest 10 percent of firms and the largest 10 percent of firms. Smaller firms tend to have higher mean returns than larger firms in both U.S. and non-U.S. markets. In Fama and French's study of NYSE and AMEX stocks in the United States over 1965–1990, small firms averaged over 7 percent higher annual returns than large stocks. Many developed and emerging markets exhibit a similar **size effect**—a tendency for small firms in a national market to outperform large firms in that market.

---

12 Rouwenhorst, "European Equity Markets and the EMU," *Financial Analysts Journal* (1999).

13 Fama and French, "The Cross-Section." Also, "Multifactor Explanations of Asset Pricing Anomalies," *Journal of Finance* (1996).

Relative Financial Distress and the Value Premium. Fama and French constructed their relative financial distress factor F_D by taking the difference in mean return between portfolios of firms with high and low ratios of book-to-market equity (equity book value divided by equity market value). Stocks were first ranked into deciles according to each firm's equity book-to-market ratio. Firms with high book-to-market ratios are called **value stocks** and firms with low book-to-market ratios are called **growth stocks**. Value stocks have depressed share prices due to low expected earnings growth or financial distress. Low prices on value stocks result in relatively high ratios of earnings-to-price, cash-flow-to-price, dividend-to-price, and equity book-to-market. Conversely, growth stocks have low earnings-to-price, cash-flow-to-price, dividend-to-price, and book-to-market ratios. Fama and French model relative financial distress as the difference in mean return between value and growth stock portfolios

Figure 21.5 shows average annual returns to Fama and French's ten portfolios of U.S. companies ranked on equity book-to-market. Value stocks outperformed growth stocks by an average of 12 percent per year. According to Fama and French, this **value premium** reflects a systematic risk—relative financial distress—that is not captured by the traditional CAPM or one-factor APT.

> Value premiums exist in developed and emerging markets.

The International Evidence. Fama and French found evidence of a value premium (that is, value stocks outperformed growth stocks) in 12 of 13 national stock markets over 1975–1995 (see Figure 21.6).[14] The value premium was statistically significant in about half of these devel-

FIGURE 21.5
The Value Premium: Equity Book-to-Market as a Predictor of Return

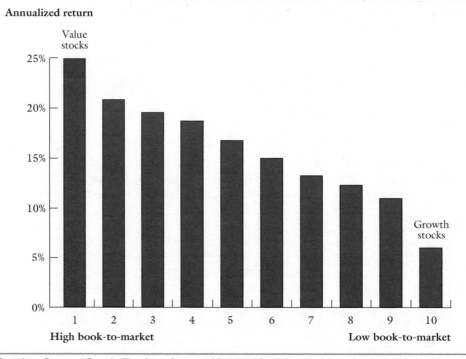

Data from Fama and French, "The Cross-Section of Expected Stock Returns," *Journal of Finance*, (June 1992), Table IV.

---

14 Fama and French, "Value Versus Growth: The International Evidence," *Journal of Finance* (1998).

FIGURE 21.6
The Difference in Annual Dollar Returns in Excess of the U.S. T-Bill Rate for Value and Growth Stock Portfolios

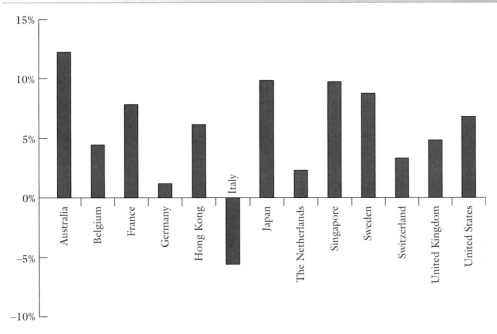

Data from Fama and French, "Value Versus Growth: The International Evidence," *Journal of Finance*, (December 1998), Table III.

oped markets. The difference between average annual returns on global portfolios of value and growth stocks was 7.60 percent. Fama and French found similar value premiums when international stocks were sorted on earnings-to-price, cash-flow-to-price, and dividend-to-price.

Fama and French also found evidence of a value premium in emerging stock markets. Rouwenhorst and others have corroborated the existence of a value premium, as well as a size effect, in a majority of emerging markets.[15] These risk factors are negatively related to market turnover, with small firms and value stocks having lower turnover than large firms and growth stocks.

Are the Size and Distress Factors Global or National? Griffin examined whether global or national factors are more useful in explaining average returns in the three-factor model of Equation 21.10:[16]

> Size and distress factors are best estimated on a country-specific basis.

$$r_j = \mu_j + \beta_j(r_M - \mu_M) + \beta_{Zj} F_Z + \beta_{Dj} F_D + e_j \qquad (21.10)$$

Griffin estimated this equation with global factors, as well as with country-specific factors for the United States, the United Kingdom, Japan, and Canada. Domestic factors explained much more of the variation in returns than global factors. Moreover, adding

---

15 Rouwenhorst, "Local Return Factors and Turnover in Emerging Stock Markets," *Journal of Finance* (1999); Chui and Wei, "Book-to-Market, Firm Size, and the Turn-of-the-Year Effect: Evidence from the Pacific-Basin Emerging Markets," *Pacific Basin Finance Journal* (1998); Barry, et al., "Robustness of Size and Growth-Value Effects: Evidence from Emerging Equity Markets," *Emerging Markets Review* (2002).

16 Griffin, "Are the Fama and French Factors Global or Country Specific?" *Review of Financial Studies* (2002).

the global factors to the domestic model resulted in more pricing errors than the domestic model alone.

It is important to choose the correct factor model. For U.S. stocks, Griffin estimated a difference of 8.41 percent per year between expected returns in the domestic and global models. A difference of this magnitude can result in vastly different investment decisions when investors estimate required returns or when managers estimate the cost of capital. Griffin's results indicate that size and relative financial distress factors should be estimated with country-specific factors, rather than with global factors.

So, would you rather invest in a value stock or in a growth stock? Value stocks have higher expected returns than growth stocks, but their higher expected returns could reflect exposures to a systematic risk factor such as relative financial distress. If markets are efficient, then you are merely getting what you pay for. If markets are inefficient, then this might represent an investment opportunity. We'll return to the issue of whether the value premium represents rational asset pricing or irrational investor behavior after discussing momentum-based investment strategies.

Momentum Strategies

Here's another puzzle. Would you rather invest in a firm that has recently risen in price or one that has recently fallen in price? In an efficient capital market, rational investors react instantaneously and without bias to new information and stocks are correctly priced. Ex ante, it won't matter which stock you buy—you'll get what you pay for.

The U.S. Evidence. In a widely cited article, Jegadeesh and Titman studied momentum in U.S. stocks.[17] **Momentum** (or *relative strength*) **strategies** selectively buy or sell securities based on their recent return performance. These authors categorized firms into ten equal-sized portfolios according to return over the preceding six months. Stocks in the portfolio with the highest returns over a particular 6-month measurement period were called *Winners* and stocks in the portfolio with the lowest returns were called *Losers.* After forming portfolios of past Winners and Losers, returns were examined over the subsequent 36 months. The 6-month measurement period was then moved forward one month and the procedure repeated.

> Momentum strategies buy Winners and sell Losers.

The top panel of Figure 21.7 shows the difference in monthly returns to the Winner and Loser portfolios in Jegadeesh and Titman's sample of U.S. stocks over holding periods of up to 36 months. The cumulative difference between the two portfolios is displayed in Figure 21.8. Over the first 12 months, portfolios formed on past Winners realized cumulative returns that were 9.5 percent greater than returns to the portfolio of Losers. This Winner-over-Loser pattern subsequently reversed itself, with the Winners giving up more than half of their accumulated gain over Losers during the next 24 months.

The International Evidence. Rouwenhorst replicated Jegadeesh and Titman's study on 12 European stock markets over 1980–1995.[18] The bottom panel of Figure 21.7 shows the difference in monthly returns to the European Winner-minus-Loser portfolios over Rouwenhorst's holding periods of up to 24 months (the maximum period reported by Rouwenhorst). Figure 21.8 displays the cumulative difference between the Winner and Loser portfolios. Figure 21.9 shows that momentum was present in each of the 12 European markets, even after controlling for country, market risk, and firm size effects. Momentum was strongest in smaller firms, although it was present in all size deciles.

---

17 Jegadeesh and Titman, "Returns to Buying Winners and Selling Losers: Implications for Stock Market Efficiency," *Journal of Finance* (1993).

18 Rouwenhorst, "International Momentum Strategies," *Journal of Finance* (1998).

FIGURE 21.7
Monthly Return Difference Between Winner and Loser Portfolios

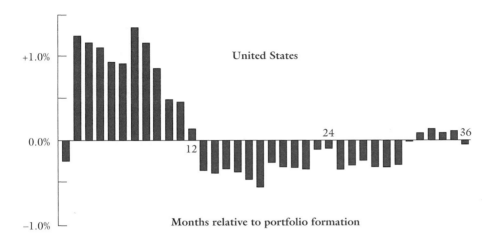

Data from Jegadeesh and Titman, "Returns to Buying Winners and Selling Losers: Implications for Stock Market Efficiency, *Journal of Finance* (March 1993), Table VII.

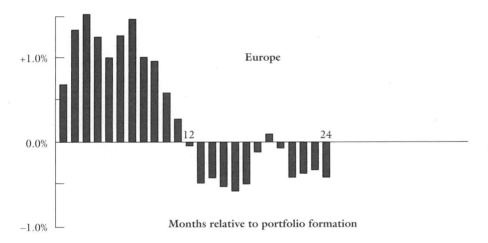

Data from Rouwenhorst, "International Momentum Strategies," *Journal of Finance* (February 1998), Table VI. Returns are in local currency and adjusted for market and size factors. Rouwenhorst does not report returns beyond 24 months.

As in the U.S. stock market, positive abnormal returns were present for about one year in the European markets with cumulative returns of about 12 percent. As in Jegadeesh and Titman's study of U.S. stocks, returns to a Winner-minus-Loser strategy turned negative after about 12 months. Momentum has also been found in international stock market indices.[19] Momentum in emerging stock markets appears to be qualitatively similar to momentum in developed markets.[20]

> Momentum appears in developed and emerging markets.

---

19 Chan, Hameed, and Tong, "Profitability of Momentum Strategies in the International Equity Markets," *Journal of Financial and Quantitative Analysis* (2000).

20 Rouwenhorst, "Local Return Factors and Turnover in Emerging Stock Markets," *Journal of Finance* (1999).

FIGURE 21.8
Cumulative Return Difference Between Winner and Loser Portfolios

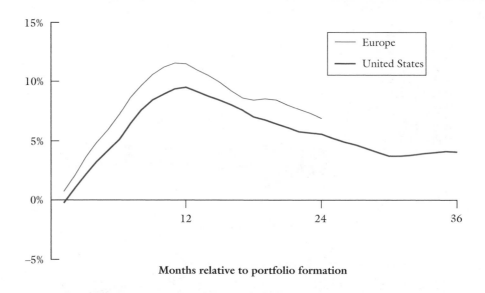

Months relative to portfolio formation

United States returns are from Jegadeesh and Titman, "Returns to Buying Winners and Selling Losers: Implications for Stock Market Efficiency," *Journal of Finance* (March 1993), Table VII. European returns are from Rouwenhorst, "International Momentum Strategies," *Journal of Finance* (February 1998), Table VI. All returns are in local currency. European returns are adjusted for market and size factors, but are not reported beyond 24 months.

FIGURE 21.9
The Momentum Effect in European Stocks: A Country-by-Country Comparison

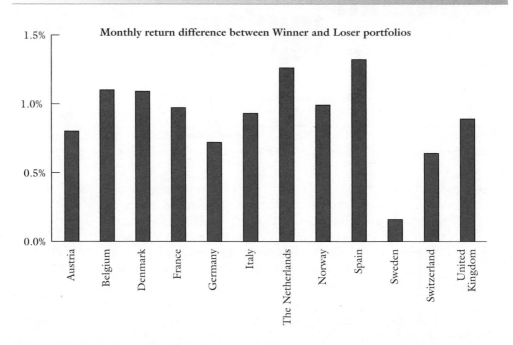

Monthly return difference between Winner and Loser portfolios

Data from Rouwenhorst, "International Momentum Strategies," *Journal of Finance* (February 1998).

Application

Get a Job!

Suppose you are interviewing for a job in the investments industry and a potential employer asks whether you believe in stock market efficiency. What should you say?

Answer an emphatic "No!" The job opening probably wouldn't exist if the employer believed in market efficiency. You might further improve your job prospects by referring to the international evidence on momentum trading.

Rational Asset Pricing or Irrational Investor Behavior?

Views on the efficiency of capital markets tend to be held as deeply as religious beliefs. If one accepts the premise that capital markets are efficient, then the profitability of investing in size, value, or momentum strategies can be explained as compensation for risk. In this view, these are systematic risk factors that must be included in asset pricing models in order to correctly price risk. If a new anomaly is found that does not fit the prevailing wisdom, then a new factor must be added to capture this previously unidentified systematic risk. If one is unwilling to accept market efficiency, then anomalies such as the size effect and the value premium are prima facie evidence of mispriced assets. Like religious convictions, the truth of a particular set of beliefs becomes self-evident once you accept a particular point of view.

The challenge for a factor model explanation of momentum is the curious reversal in the Winner-minus-Loser returns that occurs in both U.S. and European stocks after about one year. If the superior return performance of Winners over Losers did not reverse itself, an omitted risk factor could plausibly have driven the return difference between the two portfolios. For example, the Winners portfolio could have contained smaller firms, stocks with high relative financial distress, or stocks with some other omitted systematic risk factor.[21] However, the subsequent reversal in return performance suggests that investors react slowly to information or that their reactions are biased.[22] In either case, momentum effects promise above-average returns to savvy investors.

> Momentum reversals are difficult to reconcile with market efficiency.

21.5 • The Currency Risk Factor in Stock Returns

Portfolio Theory and the Irrelevance of Hedging in a Perfect World

In the perfect capital market of the CAPM and IAPM, the firm cannot do anything through diversification that investors cannot already do for themselves. Hedging a risk that is not priced by investors is a waste of managers' time and shareholders' money.

> Hedging does not add value to the firm in a perfect capital market.

Here's an example that illustrates how currency risks might be irrelevant to globally diversified investors. Consider two companies, L and S. Each company resides in the United States and uses the dollar as its functional currency. A European

---

21 As an example, Chordia and Shivakumar relate momentum to a set of lagged macroeconomic variables in "Momentum, Business Cycle, and Time-Varying Expected Returns," *Journal of Finance* (2002).

22 Jegadeesh and Titman, "Profitability of Momentum Strategies: An Evaluation of Alternative Explanations," *Journal of Finance* (2001).

subsidiary of Company S has promised to make a payment of €100,000 to Company L in one year. Company L is long the euro (and short the dollar). Company S is short the euro (and long the dollar). Figure 21.10 shows the risk profile of each company with respect to the euro.

A well-diversified U.S. investor owning shares in each company faces no net exposure to this transaction. Changes in the value of Company L in response to changes in the spot rate $S^{\$/€}$ are exactly offset by changes in the value of Company S. To a well-diversified investor owning shares in each company, exposures to currency risks such as these are diversifiable and result in the risk profile shown at the right in Figure 21.10.

In a globally integrated marketplace, currency risks such as these are diversifiable and hence should not be priced in required return. If the managers of either firm hedge these risks, any hedging costs incurred will be a deadweight loss to the firm with no reduction in shareholders' risk or expected return.

Measuring Currency Risk Exposure

Because investors do not operate in perfect capital markets, the magnitude and relevance of exposure to currency risk is an empirical question. Like other risk factors, exposure to currency risk can be measured in a regression framework. In the previous example, exposure to the euro can be modeled as

$$r_j^{\$} = \alpha_j^{\$} + \beta_j^{€}s^{\$/€} + e_j^{\$} \qquad (21.11)$$

where $r_j^{€}$ = return on asset j in euros

$s^{\$/€}$ = percentage change in the dollar/euro spot exchange rate $S^{\$/€}$

$r_j^{\$} = (1+r_j^{€})(1+s^{\$/€}) - 1$

= dollar-denominated return on the euro-denominated asset j

FIGURE 21.10
The Diversifiability of Exposure to Currency Risk

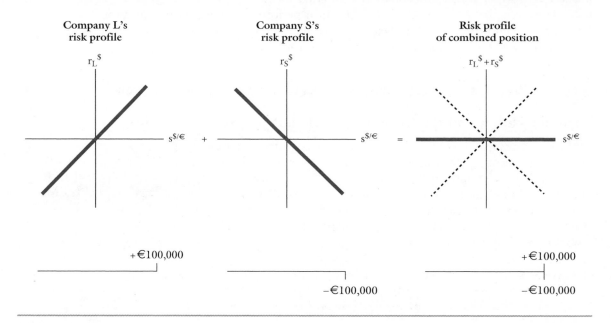

In its APT form, Equation 21.11 becomes

$$r_j^\$ = \mu_j^\$ + \beta_j^{\text{€}} (s^{\$/\text{€}} - \mu_s) + e_j^\$$$
$$= \mu_j^\$ + \beta_j^{\text{€}} s^{\$/\text{€}} + e_j^\$ \qquad (21.12)$$

If exchange rates are a random walk, then the mean change μ_s in the spot exchange rate is zero. This is why the mean exchange rate change does not appear in Equation 21.12; that is, $(s^{\$/\text{€}} - \mu_s) = s^{\$/\text{€}}$ for $\mu_s = 0$. The unexpected change in the spot rate is simply $s^{\$/\text{€}}$.

These regression equations decompose the variability of dollar returns on the euro-denominated asset into the part associated with exchange rate changes (measured by $\beta_j^{\text{€}}$) and the part that is unrelated to currency movements ($e_j^\$$). Euro returns $r_j^{\text{€}}$ are exposed to currency risk if $Cov(r_j^{\text{€}}, s^{\$/\text{€}}) \neq 0$, so the euro exposure coefficient $\beta_j^{\text{€}}$ depends in general on changes in both the spot rate and the value of the asset in the local currency. The error term $e_j^\$$ is denominated in dollars and includes all sources of variability in dollar returns that are unrelated to currency fluctuations, such that $Cov(e_j^\$, s^{\$/\text{€}}) = 0$. The expectation of the error term is simply $E[e_j^\$] = 0$.

Currency risk hedging cannot, in general, completely eliminate risk. Rather, hedging merely removes that part of the variation in $r_j^\$$ that is linearly related to changes in the spot exchange rate $s^{\$/\text{€}}$. The remaining uncertainty is independent of the exchange rate. There is still risk if there is uncertainty in the local (euro) value of the foreign asset.

Is Currency Risk Priced in Financial Markets?

If currency risk is diversifiable, then currency risk exposure should not be reflected in expected returns. On the other hand, if currency risk is systematic to a large number of stocks, then investors should price this risk in their expected and required returns.

Currency Risk in the Unconditional IAPM. Classic or *unconditional* asset pricing models assume that returns have constant means, variances, and covariances. These models often find that currency risk is not priced in mean returns, especially in the broadly diversified U.S. stock market. For example, Jorion studied the diversifiability of currency risk in a sample of U.S. multinational corporations by combining the one-factor market model from Equation 21.3 with the currency factor $s^{\$/f}$ from Equation 21.12:[23]

$$r_j^\$ = \mu_j^\$ + \beta_{1j} F_M^\$ + \beta_{2j}^f s^{\$/f} + e_j^\$ \qquad (21.13)$$

The $ superscripts indicate that the returns and factors are denominated in dollars. Jorion also added an exchange rate factor to the economic factors of Equation 21.8:[24]

$$r_j^\$ = \mu_j^\$ + \beta_{1j} F_1^\$ + \beta_{2j} F_2^\$ + \beta_{3j} F_3^\$ + \beta_{4j} F_4^\$ + \beta_{6j}^f s^{\$/f} + e_j^\$ \qquad (21.14)$$

The exchange rate factor was insignificant in each regression, suggesting that exposure to currency risk was subsumed into the market index in Equation 21.13 and into the economic factors in Equation 21.14. Jorion concluded that exchange rate risk is diversifiable and is not priced in aggregate in the U.S. stock market.

Currency Risk in the Conditional IAPM. In contrast to unconditional asset pricing models, *conditional* asset pricing models allow risks—such as currency and market risks—

---

23 Jorion, "The Pricing of Exchange Rate Risk in the Stock Market," *Journal of Financial and Quantitative Analysis* (1991).

24 Jorion included a factor for expected inflation, following Chen, Roll, and Ross, "Economic Forces."

to vary over time. These models sometimes yield different conclusions than unconditional asset pricing models. In particular, the market risk factor is insignificant in most unconditional tests, but is often significant in conditional asset pricing models.

De Santis and Gérard estimated conditional and unconditional versions of the international CAPM with a sample of stocks from Germany, Japan, the United Kingdom, and the

> Currency risk appears to be priced in international markets.

United States.[25] When the authors applied an unconditional IAPM that constrained currency and market risk to be constant over time, neither risk appeared to be priced by investors. These risks were detected in a conditional IAPM that allowed risks and required returns to vary over time. After estimating their conditional model, these authors concluded that both market risk and currency risk are priced in international stock markets.

Different national markets had different exposures to these risks. Currency risk was a small fraction of total risk in the U.S. market, but a significant percentage of total risk in the stock markets of Germany, Japan, and the United Kingdom. Other studies have similarly found that currency risk is more important in markets outside the United States than in the U.S. market.[26] Currency risk is likely to be especially important in the emerging capital markets of Southeast Asia, Latin America, Eastern Europe, and Africa.

21.6 • CURRENCY RISK EXPOSURE AND MNC HEDGING ACTIVITIES

The Exposure of Multinational Corporations to Currency Risk

Whether or not currency risk affects required returns, there is considerable cross-sectional variation in the exchange rate exposure of individual firms and industries. A stylized characterization of the currency risk exposure of exporters and importers appears in Figure 21.11. Exporters, such as mining and manufacturing firms, tend to benefit from a depreciation of the domestic currency. Importers, such as textile and apparel firms, tend to benefit from an appreciation of the domestic currency.

FIGURE 21.11
The Currency Risk Exposure of Importers and Exporters

$$r_j^d = \mu_j^d + \beta_j^f s^{d/f} + e_j^d$$

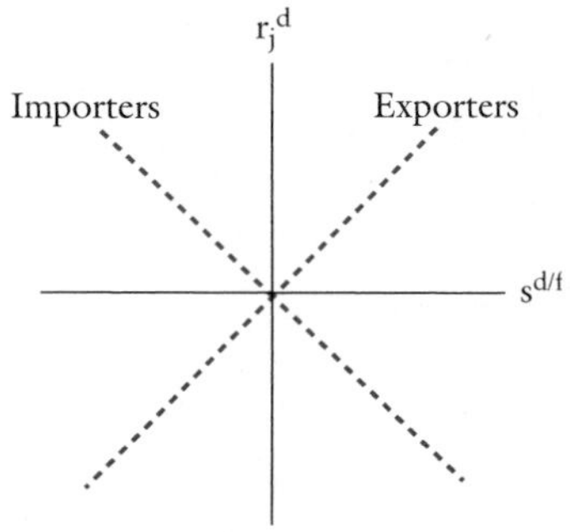

25 De Santis and Gérard, "How Big Is the Premium for Currency Risk," *Journal of Financial Economics* (1998).

26 See Dumas and Solnik, "The World Price of Foreign Exchange Risk," *Journal of Finance* (1995); and Cheung, Kwan, and Lee, "The Pricing of Exchange Rate Risk and Stock Market Segmentation: The Canadian Case," *Review of Quantitative Finance and Accounting* (1995).

Consider the currency risk exposure of General Motors Corporation. GM exports a large number of cars from its U.S. manufacturing facilities. When the dollar appreciates in real terms against foreign currencies, GM's production costs rise relative to those of its non-U.S. competitors. Conversely, when the dollar depreciates in real terms, GM's production costs fall relative to those of non-U.S. automakers. A real depreciation of the dollar allows GM to either earn higher profits per car or lower its prices and sell more cars. Hence, the value of a U.S. exporter such as GM is negatively related to the value of the dollar or, as in Figure 21.11, positively related to foreign currency values.

Importers are likely to benefit from a real appreciation of the domestic currency. Consider Payless Shoe Stores, a Kansas-based importer that accounts for about one in ten pairs of footware sold in the United States. Payless benefits from an appreciation of the dollar because it costs fewer dollars to purchase shoes from its Southeast Asian suppliers. This, in turn, results in higher profit margins on U.S. sales. As the dollar depreciates, these foreign inputs cost more in dollars. The value of an importer such as Payless is positively related to the value of the domestic currency or, as in Figure 21.11, negatively related to foreign currency values.

Just as currency risk seems to be less of a consideration for firms in the United States, the proportion of firms with exposures to currency risk is also smaller in the United States than in other national markets. Jorion found that around 5 percent of a sample of U.S. MNCs had significant foreign exchange exposures.[27] At a 5 percent significance level, this is just what you'd expect from chance. In contrast, about one-quarter of Japanese firms, two-thirds of Canadian firms, and nearly all of large German firms have significant exposures to currency risk.[28] The magnitude of exposure is positively related to the proportion of international operations or sales. Firms with a high proportion of international operations or sales tend to have a high degree of exposure to currency risk.

> Firms with international activities are likely to be exposed to currency risk.

The Managers' Perspective

In contrast to other stakeholders, managers have a huge incentive to hedge the firm's exposure to currency risk. A manager's livelihood depends on the health and continued existence of the company. Managers are overinvested in the firm and are unable to fully diversify their wealth. Further, the performance evaluation and compensation of a divisional manager is tied to divisional performance. The performance assessment of divisional managers can be sensitive to exchange rate fluctuations. In these circumstances, managers have an incentive to hedge against currency risk even if this risk is diversifiable from the perspective of shareholders.

> Managers have a huge incentive to hedge against currency risks.

Corporate Hedging Activities

Firms can change their underlying currency risk exposures through operating and financial market hedges. For example, even though the operations of a U.S. exporter may be hurt by a real appreciation of the dollar, the exporter can mitigate this operating risk by hedging with currency forwards, futures, options, or swaps. Unfortunately for the outside observer, many corporate hedging activities are not observable by investors unless and until they are disclosed in the financial statements. Even then, only a portion of the firm's hedging activities are typically reported. The sensitivity of

---

27 Jorion, "Pricing." Also, "The Exchange-Rate Exposure of U.S. Multinationals," *Journal of Business* (1990).

28 He and Ng, "The Foreign Exchange Exposure of Japanese Multinational Corporations," *Journal of Finance* (1998); Booth and Rotenberg, "Assessing Foreign Exchange Exposure: Theory and Application Using Canadian Firms," *Journal of International Financial Management and Accounting* (1990); and Glaum, Brunner, and Himmel, "The DAX and the Dollar: The Economic Exchange Rate Exposure of German Corporations," *Journal of International Business Studies* (2000).

stock prices to foreign exchange rates reflects the market's best guess of a firm's net exposures to currency risks; that is, net of the firm's hedges of currency risks.

21.7 • SUMMARY

Assumptions necessary to develop the capital asset pricing model (CAPM) are (1) perfect financial markets (frictionless and competitive with equal access to information), (2) normally distributed nominal returns, (3) rational investors (return is good and risk is bad), (4) homogeneous expectations, and (5) equal access to the risk-free rate r_F. These assumptions allowed us to complete our development of the CAPM. A fundamental result of this model is the security market line (SML):

$$r_j = r_F + \beta_j \, (E[r_M] - r_F) \tag{21.1}$$

which states that the required return on an asset j is a linear combination of the expected market risk premium and the asset's sensitivity to changes in market returns. Market model beta, $\beta_j = \rho_{j,M} \, (\sigma_j/\sigma_M)$, is a measure of the sensitivity of security j's returns to market returns and is estimated with the regression equation:

$$r_j = \alpha_j + \beta_j r_M + e_j \tag{21.3}$$

Roll identified a critical weakness of the CAPM. If performance is measured relative to an ex post efficient market index, then the algebra of the CAPM ensures that measuring performance relative to an ex post *efficient* index results in all assets falling on the security market line. In this case, beta is the only measure of systematic risk and all securities are correctly priced by the model. On the other hand, measuring performance against an ex post *inefficient* index yields almost no information regarding risk-adjusted return and any ranking of investment performance is possible.

We then developed an international pricing model by extending the CAPM to a multicurrency setting. Two additional assumptions were necessary: (1) purchasing power parity holds, and (2) investors in each country have the same consumption basket. This ensures that the international parity conditions hold. The resulting model is called the international asset pricing model, or IAPM. The market portfolio is a globally diversified portfolio of risky assets in the IAPM, and the risk-free asset is replaced by a hedge portfolio of riskless domestic and foreign assets. Roll's critique is just as relevant for the IAPM as for the CAPM, because world market portfolios are even more difficult to construct than domestic market portfolios.

Factor models offer a partial remedy to Roll's critique. In these models, returns are assumed to be a linear function of K systematic risk factors F_K:

$$r_j = \mu_j + \beta_{1j}F_1 + \dots + \beta_{Kj}F_K + e_j \tag{21.5}$$

where μ_j is the expected return on asset j, the β_{kj} are the asset's sensitivities to the K factors, and e_j is firm-specific random error. Studies of domestic and international stock returns have identified macroeconomic factors such as industrial production, inflation, risk premia on corporate over government bonds, and the term structure of interest rates. Other well-documented factors in international stock returns include global, national, and industry stock indices, and size and value premiums. Momentum or relative strength effects are also present.

The chapter concluded with an investigation of the currency risk factor in international stock returns. Exposure to currency risk appears to be more important in non-U.S. markets than in the U.S. market, both in the percentage of firms that are exposed to currency risk and the effect on investors' required returns. It also appears to be important to recognize the conditional or time-varying nature of currency risk exposure in international markets. This is an area of active academic and professional inquiry, so stay tuned for further developments.

KEY TERMS

arbitrage pricing theory (APT)
beta (β)
capital asset pricing model (CAPM)
capital market line (CML)
expropriation
factor models
growth stock
hedge portfolio
home asset bias
integrated market
international asset pricing model (IAPM)
market model (one-factor market model)
market portfolio

market risk premium
momentum strategies
one-factor market model
perfect market assumptions
political risk
Roll's critique
security market line (SML)
segmented market
size effect
systematic versus unsystematic risk
value premium
value stock

CONCEPTUAL QUESTIONS

21.1   What is the capital market line? Why is it important?

21.2   What is the security market line? Why is it important?

21.3   What is beta? Why is it important?

21.4   Does political risk affect required returns?

21.5   What assumptions must be added to the traditional CAPM to derive the international version of the CAPM?

21.6   What is the hedge portfolio in the international version of the CAPM?

21.7   What is the difference between an integrated and a segmented capital market?

21.8   What is home asset bias?

21.9   What is Roll's critique of the CAPM? Does it apply to the IAPM? Does it apply to APT?

21.10 What is the APT? In what ways is it both better and worse than the IAPM?

21.11 What four factors did Roll and Ross [1995] identify in their study of U.S. stocks?

21.12 Are individual stock returns more closely related to national or industry factors? What implication does this have for portfolio diversification?

21.13 What is the value premium? What is the size effect? Do international stocks exhibit these characteristics? Are these factors evidence of market inefficiency?

21.14 What is momentum? Can it lead to profitable investment opportunities for international investors?

21.15 Are individual stocks exposed to currency risk? Does currency risk affect required returns?

PROBLEMS

21.1 Calculate the required return on equity under each of the following conditions, assuming the CAPM holds.
   a. The risk-free rate is 8 percent, beta is 1.5, and the market risk premium is 8.5 percent.
   b. The risk-free rate is 4 percent, beta is 1.2, and the market risk premium is 8.5 percent.

21.2 The correlation between returns to DaimlerChrysler (DC) stock on the Frankfurt Stock Exchange and to the Morgan Stanley Capital International (MSCI) German stock market index is 0.44 when all returns are calculated in euros. The standard deviations of monthly returns to DC stock and to the German stock market index are 10.5 percent and 4.6 percent, respectively.
   a. What is the beta of DC relative to the German domestic stock market index?
   b. If the risk-free rate in euros is 5 percent and the market risk premium on the German stock index is 6 percent, what is the required return on DC stock when measured against the German stock market index?
   c. The correlation between the German and world stock market indices is 0.494. The standard deviation of monthly returns to the German and world indices are 4.13 percent and 5.26 percent, respectively. What is the beta of the German stock market index relative to the MSCI world stock market index?

21.3 As a security analyst for the London branch of Merrill Lynch, you have identified the following factors and factor sensitivities for British Petroleum (BP):

$$E[r] = \mu + \beta_{Prod} F_{Prod} + \beta_{Oil} F_{Oil} + \beta_{Spot} F_{Spot}$$

Factors and factor sensitivities are as follows:

Factors		Betas	
F_{Prod}:	change in world industrial production	β_{Prod}	= +1.50
F_{Oil}:	change in crude oil prices	β_{Oil}	= –0.80
F_{Spot}:	change in the exchange rate (s£/f) against a basket of foreign currencies f with which BP trades	β_{Spot}	= +0.01

BP's expected return if all factors are equal to their expectation is $\mu = 14\%$.
   a. All else constant, are BP's shares likely to go up or down with an increase in world industrial production? With an increase in crude oil prices? With an increase in the value of the pound?
   b. What is the expected return on BP stock in a year when world industrial production is 2 percent above the expectation, oil prices rise unexpectedly by 10 percent, and the spot rate $S^{£/f}$ goes down by 5 percent?
   c. If BP stock rises by 4 percent during this period, by how much does BP over- or underperform its expectation?

21.4 As a security analyst for the Paris branch of Morgan Stanley Dean Witter, you've identified the following factors and factor sensitivities for Elf Acquitaine ("Elf"):

$$E(r) = \mu + \beta_{Prod} F_{Prod} + \beta_{Oil} F_{Oil} + \beta_{Term} F_{Term} + \beta_{Risk} F_{Risk} + \beta_{Spot} F_{Spot}$$

Elf's functional currency is the euro. Factors and factor sensitivities in euros are

Factors		Betas	
F_{Prod}:	change in world industrial production	β_{Prod}	= +1.10
F_{oil}:	change in crude oil prices	β_{Oil}	= +0.60
F_{Term}:	long minus short government bonds	β_{Term}	= −0.05
F_{Risk}:	corporate minus government bonds	β_{Risk}	= −0.10
F_{Spot}:	change in the euro value of a basket of foreign currencies (s€/f) with which Elf trades	β_{Spot}	= −0.02

Elf's expected return is $\mu = 12$ percent if all factors are equal to their expectation.
a. Are Elf's shares likely to go up or down with an increase in world industrial production? With an increase in crude oil prices? With an increase in the slope of the term structure? With an increase in the risk premium on corporate bonds? With an increase in the value of the euro?
b. Given these parameters, what is the expected return on BP stock in a year when each factor is 10 percent higher than its expectation?
c. If Elf stock falls by 12 percent during this period, by how much does Elf over- or under-perform its expectation?

21.5 As a security analyst for the New York branch of Deutsche Bank, you have identified the following factors and factor sensitivities for Amazon.com:

$$r = \mu + \beta_M F_M + \beta_Z F_Z + \beta_D F_D$$

Amazon.com's factor sensitivities in dollars are

Factors		Betas	
F_M:	market factor ($r_M - \mu_M$)	β_M	= +1.00
F_Z:	firm size factor (small minus large stocks)	β_Z	= +0.10
F_D:	relative financial distress (value minus growth stocks)	β_D	= +0.05

Amazon.com's expected return is $\mu = 10$ percent if all factors are equal to their expectation.
a. What is Amazon.com's expected return in a year when each factor is 1 percent lower than its expectation?
b. If Amazon.com's stock price rises by 12 percent during this period, by how much does Amazon.com over- or under-perform its expectation?

21.6 Two mutual fund managers are discussing their investment strategies over lunch. The first manager follows a value-oriented strategy of selectively buying stocks with high book-to-market value equity ratios. The second prefers firms with high earnings growth that will hopefully lead to high stock price appreciation.
a. Which manager is likely to see higher returns over a 1-year investment horizon? Why?

b. Which manager is likely to see higher returns over a 10-year investment horizon? Why?

c. Which manager is likely to see higher returns on a risk-adjusted basis over a 10-year investment horizon? Explain your answer.

21.7 The regional directors of a major investment bank are discussing investment strategies for their respective countries.

a. As director of North American investments, describe an investment strategy based on momentum to your foreign colleagues.

b. As director of European investments, do you think such a momentum-based strategy will work in your markets? Why or why not?

c. As director of Latin American investments, do you think a momentum-based strategy will work in your markets? Why or why not?

Suggested Readings

The traditional capital asset pricing model (CAPM) and the international CAPM (IAPM) are developed and tested in the following article:

Michael Adler and Bernard Dumas, "International Portfolio Choice and Corporation Finance: A Synthesis," *Journal of Finance* 38 (June 1983), pp. 925–984.

Arbitrage pricing theory (APT) is developed and tested in the following articles:

Nai-Fu Chen, Richard Roll, and Stephen A. Ross, "Economic Forces and the Stock Market," *Journal of Business* 59 (July 1986), pp. 383–404.

Richard Roll and Stephen A. Ross, "The Arbitrage Pricing Theory Approach to Strategic Portfolio Planning," *Financial Analysts Journal* 51 (January/February 1995), pp. 122–132.

Stephen A. Ross, "The Arbitrage Theory of Asset Pricing," *Journal of Economic Theory* 13 (December 1976), pp. 341–360.

Arbitrage pricing theory is applied to international assets in the following:

C. Sherman Cheung, Clarence C.Y. Kwan, and Jason Lee, "The Pricing of Exchange Rate Risk and Stock Market Segmentation: The Canadian Case," *Review of Quantitative Finance and Accounting* 5, No. 4 (1995), pp. 393–402.

Bernard Dumas and Bruno Solnik, "The World Price of Foreign Exchange Risk," *Journal of Finance* 50 (June 1995), pp. 445–479.

International capital market integration/segmentation is discussed in

Geert Bekaert and Campbell R. Harvey, "Time-Varying World Market Integration," *Journal of Finance* 50 (June 1995), pp. 403–444.

The cross-sectional relation between betas and mean returns is discussed in

Richard Roll, "A Critique of the Asset Pricing Theory's Tests," *Journal of Financial Economics* 4 (March 1977), pp. 129–176.

Richard Roll and Stephen A. Ross, "On the Cross-Sectional Relation Between Expected Returns and Betas," *Journal of Finance* 49 (March 1994), pp. 101–121.

The relative importance of global, national, industry and currency factors is assessed in

Stan Beckers, Gregory Connor, and Ross Curds, "National Versus Global Influences on Equity Returns," *Financial Analysts Journal* 52 (March/April 1996), pp. 31–39.

Laurence Booth and Wendy Rotenberg, "Assessing Foreign Exchange Exposure: Theory and Application Using Canadian Firms," *Journal of International Financial Management and Accounting* 2 (Spring 1990), pp. 1–22.

Giorgio De Santis and Bruno Gérard, "How Big Is the Premium for Currency Risk?" *Journal of Financial Economics* 49 (September 1998), pp. 375–412.

Martin Glaum, Marko Brunner, and Holger Himmel, "The DAX and the Dollar: The Economic Exposure of German Corporations," *Journal of International Business Studies* 31, No. 4 (2000), pp. 715–724.

John M. Griffin, "Are the Fama and French Factors Global or Country Specific?" *Review of Financial Studies* 12 (Summer 2002), pp. 783–803.

John M Griffin and G. Andrew Karolyi, "Another Look at the Role of the Industrial Structure of Markets for International Diversification Strategies, *Journal of Financial Economics* 50 (December 1998), pp. 351–373.

Jia He and Lilian K. Ng, "The Foreign Exchange Exposure of Japanese Multinational Corporations," *Journal of Finance* 53 (April 1998), pp. 733–753.

Steven L. Heston and K. Geert Rouwenhorst, "Does Industrial Structure Explain the Benefits of International Diversification?" *Journal of Financial Economics* 36 (August 1994), pp. 3–27.

Philippe Jorion, "The Exchange-Rate Exposure of U.S. Multinationals," *Journal of Business* 63, No. 3 (1990), pp. 331–346.

Philippe Jorion, "The Pricing of Exchange Rate Risk in the Stock Market," *Journal of Financial and Quantitative Analysis* 26 (September 1991), pp. 363–376.

K. Geert Rouwenhorst, "European Equity Markets and the EMU," *Financial Analysts Journal* 55 (May/June 1999), pp. 57–64.

Asset pricing and its relation to value stocks, firm size, and momentum are developed in the following articles:

Christopher B. Barry, Elizabeth Goldreyer, Larry J. Lockwood, and Mauricio Rodriguez, "Robustness of Size and Growth-Value Effects: Evidence from Emerging Equity Markets," *Emerging Markets Review* 3 (Winter 2002), pp. 1–30.

Kalok Chan, Allaudeen Hameed, and Wilson Tong, "Profitability of Momentum Strategies in the International Equity Markets," *Journal of Financial and Quantitative Analysis* 35 (June 2000), pp. 153–172.

Tarun Chordia and Lakshmanan Shivakumar, "Momentum, Business Cycle, and Time-Varying Expected Returns," *Journal of Finance* 57 (April 2002), pp. 985–1019.

Andy Chui and K.C. John Wei, "Book-to-Market, Firm Size, and the Turn-of-the-Year Effect: Evidence from Pacific-Basin Emerging Markets," *Pacific-Basin Finance Journal* 6 (August 1998), pp. 275–293.

Eugene F. Fama and Kenneth R. French, "The Cross-Section of Expected Stock Returns," *Journal of Finance* 47 (June 1992), pp. 427–465.

Eugene F. Fama and Kenneth R. French, "Multifactor Explanations of Asset Pricing Anomalies," *Journal of Finance* 51 (March 1996), pp. 55–84.

Eugene F. Fama and Kenneth R. French, "Value Versus Growth: The International Evidence," *Journal of Finance* 53 (December 1998), pp. 1975–1999.

Narasimhan Jegadeesh and Sheridan Titman, "Returns to Buying Winners and Selling Losers: Implications for Stock Market Efficiency," *Journal of Finance* 48 (March 1993), pp. 65–91.

Narasimhan Jegadeesh and Sheridan Titman, "Profitability of Momentum Strategies: An Evaluation of Alternative Explanations," *Journal of Finance* 56 (April 2001), pp. 699–720.

K. Geert Rouwenhorst, "International Momentum Strategies," *Journal of Finance* 53 (February 1998), pp. 267–284.

K. Geert Rouwenhorst, "Local Return Factors and Turnover in Emerging Stock Markets," *Journal of Finance* 54 (August 1999), pp. 1439–1464.

Managing an International Investment Portfolio

chapter 22

Overview

If a man takes no thought about what is distant, he will find sorrow close at hand.

Confucius *(551–479 B.C.)*

Why diversify an investment portfolio internationally? First, although much of the world's wealth resides in developed countries, developing countries are more likely to experience above-average economic growth. Second, international diversification results in lower portfolio risk because of the relatively low correlations between national stock market returns. As information and transactions costs fall, investors in search of higher returns or lower portfolio risk are increasingly investing in foreign markets.

Many roads lead to Rome—and there are many alternatives for investing in foreign securities. This chapter begins with a review of the alternatives for diversifying an investment portfolio internationally. The rest of the chapter focuses on the practical issues of managing an internationally diversified investment portfolio.

22.1 • VEHICLES FOR OVERCOMING CAPITAL FLOW BARRIERS

Chapter 20 discussed some of the barriers to international portfolio diversification. These barriers can be overcome by diversifying investment portfolios internationally through ownership in multinational corporations, direct purchase of foreign securities in domestic or foreign markets, or indirectly through professionally managed funds. Each of these alternatives is described here, along with some more exotic forms of entry into international markets.

Invest in Domestic-Based Multinational Corporations

A convenient alternative for investors in countries with developed capital markets is to invest in domestic firms that do business internationally. The diversification benefits of a multinational corporation depend on the type of foreign operations conducted by the company. Classic exporters have foreign revenues and domestic expenses. Classic importers have domestic revenues and foreign expenses. Diversified multinationals have a geographic balance in revenues and expenses. The diversification benefits brought by each type of firm depend on the nature and extent of their international involvement, and on whether their stock returns move more closely with domestic or foreign markets.

MNCs might provide some international diversification benefits.

The returns of large U.S. multinationals are much more closely related to the U.S. stock market than to foreign markets. The correlation of the 50 largest U.S. multinationals with the MSCI U.S. index is about 0.9, whereas the correlation of these same U.S. multinationals and the MSCI world-ex-U.S. index is closer to 0.6. Consequently, an investment in large U.S. multinationals does not provide the same diversification benefits to U.S. investors as direct ownership of foreign assets.[1]

Multinational corporations in less diversified economies or in countries with controls on cross-border portfolio investment provide greater diversification benefits to their residents than U.S. multinationals provide to U.S. investors. More than 90 percent of the revenues of Royal Dutch Petroleum, Unilever, and Phillips come from outside the Netherlands. The Swiss giants Nestle, Ciba-Geigy, and Sandoz similarly derive the bulk of their revenues from outside Switzerland. Returns to these multinationals often move more closely with international markets than with other domestic stocks. In these cases, multinationals based in the domestic market can provide international diversification benefits to domestic residents.

Invest in Individual Foreign Securities

Investors can buy foreign debt and equity securities directly in many national markets. The costs and benefits of this direct route to international diversification depend on the particular assets and investment vehicles chosen, and on capital flow barriers in the domestic and foreign markets. The rest of this section describes several ways that foreign securities can be purchased by domestic investors.

Direct Purchase in the Foreign Market. The most straightforward way to diversify internationally is to buy foreign securities directly in a foreign market. Unfortunately for the small investor, there are several impediments to direct purchase in foreign markets:

- Higher information costs on foreign assets
  - Geographic distances
  - Language and cultural differences
  - Differences in taxation, accounting measurement, and disclosure conventions
- Higher transactions costs on foreign assets
  - Commissions on foreign trades are often higher than on domestic transactions
  - Dividends and capital gains received in a foreign currency must be converted from the foreign currency into investors' domestic currencies
  - Differences in tax systems and tax rates

---

1 See Jacquillat and Solnik, "Multinationals Are Poor Tools for International Diversification," *Journal of Portfolio Management* (1978).

Market imperfections can impose formidable barriers to international diversification for small investors. They are less of a problem for professional fund managers with experience in international markets.

Direct Purchase in the Domestic Market. A growing number of foreign corporations are issuing common stock directly in the well-developed financial markets of Europe, North America, and Southeast Asia. Similarly, global bond markets are increasingly being used to satisfy the borrowing needs of national governments, multinational corporations, and transnational agencies such as the IMF and the World Bank. The market for euro-denominated bonds in particular has seen a surge in popularity and an increase in liquidity with the conversion of Emu-zone currencies to the euro.

Companies can list their shares on foreign exchanges in two ways—through foreign shares or depository receipts. **Foreign shares** are shares of a foreign corporation issued directly to domestic investors through a transfer agent in accordance with local (domestic) regulations. **Depository receipts** are derivative securities that represent a claim on a block of foreign stock held by a domestic trustee. Depository receipts are sold through a domestic broker, regulated by domestic authorities, and denominated in the domestic currency.

> Foreign companies list as depository receipts or foreign shares.

A non-U.S. company can list shares on a U.S. exchange through American shares or American depository receipts. **American shares** are foreign shares issued directly to U.S. investors by a foreign corporation through a transfer agent in accordance with Securities and Exchange Commission (SEC) regulations. American shares are denominated in the currency of the issuing company, so dividends and capital gains are received in the foreign currency. Because they are denominated in foreign currencies, American shares are an inconvenient way for small investors to achieve international diversification. Foreign shares that list on more than one foreign market (e.g., DaimlerChrysler) are sometimes called **global shares**.

The inconvenience of foreign currency receipts is less of an impediment to large mutual funds that can convert dividends and capital gains into dollars at low cost. For these investors, American shares can be effective vehicles for achieving international diversification. The convenience of American shares to U.S. portfolio managers must be weighed against their liquidity in the U.S. market. When stocks are more liquid in their home market, institutional investors often prefer to invest directly in the foreign markets rather than through American shares.

American depository receipts (ADRs) are denominated in dollars and trade on a U.S. exchange, just like any other U.S. share. To issue an ADR, a foreign company employs an investment banker to purchase a block of shares. The investment banker then issues dollar-denominated stock certificates called ADRs in the U.S. market with the foreign shares as collateral. The underlying asset is a portfolio of foreign shares held by the investment banker as trustee. Dividends are converted into dollars and distributed by the trustee. Depository receipts that trade in more than one foreign

> Foreign firms list in the United States as American shares or as American depository receipts.

market (e.g., Switzerland's UBS) are sometimes called **global depository receipts**.

The prices of depository receipts depend on the value of the foreign shares in the foreign currency and the exchange rate according to $P^d = P^f S^{d/f}$. When transactions costs and capital flow barriers are small, arbitrage ensures that the law of one price holds and the value of a depository receipt is the foreign currency value translated into the domestic currency at the prevailing exchange rate. If there are large transactions costs or capital flow barriers, depository receipts can sell at slight premiums or discounts to their foreign market value. Because the ADRs move in price with the dollar

Market Update

Share Classes in China

China is rapidly developing its equity markets under the direction of the China Securities Regulatory Commission (CSRC), with active stock exchanges in Shanghai and Shenzhen. The shares of public listed companies in China fall into the following categories:

Domestic shares:

- *State shares.* Held by the central or local government or a government-owned institution. State shares are not publicly traded, but can be transferred to another domestic institution with the approval of the CSRC.
- *Legal person shares.* Shares owned by domestic institutions. A legal person is a nonindividual legal entity. Legal person shares are not tradable, but can be transferred into other domestic institutions upon approval from the CSRC.
- *Employee shares.* Offered to employees, usually at a discount to market value. Employees can sell their shares with the approval of the CSRC, although top management cannot sell shares during their term of office.
- *A-shares.* Traded on Chinese exchanges and held by domestic individuals and institutions. There is no restriction on the number of shares traded, but there is a requirement that A-shares account for no less than 25 percent of total outstanding shares at the time of an initial public offering.

Shares available to foreign investors:

- *B-shares.* Traded on Chinese stock exchanges, but available only to foreign investors and some selected domestic securities firms with the approval of the CSRC. B-shares are denominated in U.S. dollars on the Shanghai Stock Exchange and Hong Kong dollars on the Shenzhen Stock Exchange.
- *H-shares.* Traded on the Hong Kong Stock Exchange with the same rights and privileges as A-shares. H-shares cannot be traded on domestic exchanges.
- *N-shares.* Traded on the New York Stock Exchange with the same rights and privileges as A-shares. N-shares cannot be traded on domestic exchanges.

State ownership is central to management and control of Chinese firms, as the government is the largest—and often the majority—shareholder in nearly half of Chinese listed stocks.

value of the foreign shares, ADRs have the same foreign exchange exposure as the underlying shares.

More than 400 firms from over 30 countries list ADRs on the New York, American, or Nasdaq stock exchanges in the United States. Approximately half of these are Canadian firms. The United Kingdom has more than 50 firms listed in the United States. Well-known foreign companies trading on the NYSE include the Royal Dutch/Shell Group (Netherlands), DaimlerChrysler (Germany), British Petroleum (United Kingdom), and Matsushita Electric (Japan). Foreign listings (either as foreign shares or depository receipts) are also common on the London, Tokyo, Hong Kong, and Singapore exchanges.

Mutual Funds Specializing in International Assets

Small investors buying individual foreign shares face formidable information and transactions costs. These costs can be reduced by concentrating funds from many small investors in the hands of one or a few professional portfolio managers.

> Mutual funds pool investment funds from many investors.

Mutual Funds. In an **open-end mutual fund**, the amount of money under management grows (or shrinks) as investors invest in (or disinvest from) the fund. Management expenses on open-end mutual funds typically fall in the range of 0.5 to 3 percent per year. In a **closed-end mutual fund**, total funds under management are fixed and shares are traded in the market like a depository receipt. Closed-end funds have a front-loaded sales charge or a back-loaded charge that is due upon sale of the fund, as well as an annual charge for management expenses.

Mutual funds are most popular in the United States, although their popularity is increasing in other countries. Many global, regional, and country funds are available, as are a variety of sector and industry funds. Many of the largest mutual funds are index funds that follow a passive buy-and-hold strategy in an attempt to mimic an equity index, such as the United Kingdom's FTSE ("footsie") 100 or Germany's DAX index. Other international funds are actively managed, either through security selection (stock picking) or asset allocation (shifting funds across asset classes in the hope of hitting the winners).

Mutual fund families provide menus of global, regional, country, and sector (or industry) funds. Several members of the NYSE-listed Franklin Templeton Investments family of funds, along with their recent asset allocations, are listed here:

> http://www.
> franklin
> templeton.com

- *Templeton World Fund*. North America 33%, Asia 28%, Europe 26%, Latin America 5%, Australia and New Zealand 2%, Cash 6%
- *Templeton Developing Markets*. Asia 54%, Latin America 16%, Middle East and Africa 14%, Europe 13%, Cash 3%
- *Templeton Global Smaller Companies Fund*. Europe 40%, Asia 29%, North America 24%, Latin America 4%, Middle East and Africa 1%, Cash 2%
- *Templeton Global Bond Fund*. Europe 51%, Latin America 20%, North America 11%, Asia 7%, Australia and New Zealand 6%, Cash 5%
- *Latin America*. Mexico 53%, Brazil 35%, Chile 3%, Peru 1%, Spain 1%, United States 1%, Cash 6%
- *Pacific Growth Fund*. Japan 30%, South Korea 14%, Hong Kong 13%, India 6%, Australia 6%, Taiwan 5%, Singapore 4%, China 3%, New Zealand 2%, Philippines 2%, Thailand 1%, Cash 16%

All large brokerage firms maintain a similar set of funds in their product mix.

Country Funds. Closed-end country funds (CECFs) invest in assets—typically shares of stock—from a single country. Many emerging markets have CECFs or CECF-like vehicles trading on stock exchanges around the world:

- *New York Stock Exchange*. Closed-end country funds trading on the NYSE include Brazil, Germany, India, Indonesia, Italy, Japan, Korea, Mexico, Malaysia, South Africa, Spain, Switzerland, Taiwan, Thailand, and the United Kingdom. The NYSE also lists global, regional, and specialty funds, such as Morgan Stanley Dean Witter's Emerging Markets Fund (ticker "MSF").

Market Update

Debt of Developing Countries

During the 1960s and 1970s, commercial banks made huge loans to the governments of developing nations to fund infrastructure development and foreign aid. By the 1980s, many of these loans had soured, and commercial banks were faced with the uncomfortable task of writing down the value of their loan portfolios. The largest losses were suffered on loans to Mexico, Brazil, and Argentina. For example, Citibank set aside $3 billion in 1987 as a reserve after Brazil ceased making interest payments on its debt. Although smaller in magnitude, percentage losses were even larger on loans to smaller countries such as Cuba, Nicaragua, and the Sudan. The debt of these countries is referred to as *exotics* by commercial and merchant bankers.

Exotics are traded by commercial and merchant banks at a discount to face value. Institutional investors (such as hedge funds) willing to tolerate large risks and illiquidity can occasionally pick up exotics at bargain-basement prices and capture huge returns. Equally likely, of course, are huge losses.

Exotics fluctuate in value with political events. For example, Sudanese debt went from 1/2 percent of face value in 1993 to 6 percent of face value in 1994 (a return of 1,100 percent) on rumors of a debt-reduction deal. Prices fell back down to 11/2 percent of face value when the rumored deal fell apart. This was still a 200 percent return on the pre-deal price.

- *American Stock Exchange.* The Amex trades more than 100 closed-end index funds called *iShares* that track corporate and government bonds, industry sectors, international stocks, and broad market indices.
  - Country funds track MSCI indices of Australia, Austria, Belgium, Brazil, Canada, France, Germany, Hong Kong, Italy, Japan, Malaysia, Mexico, the Netherlands, Singapore, South Korea, Spain, Sweden, Switzerland, Taiwan, and the United Kingdom.
  - Regional funds track MSCI's EMU, Pacific-ex-Japan, and Europe Asia and Far East (EAFE); plus S&P's Europe 350, Latin America 40, and TSE 60 indices.

Similar investment vehicles trade on many other stock exchanges around the world.

Hedge Funds

Hedge funds are private investment partnerships with a general manager and a small number of limited partners. A typical hedge fund pays the general partner a 1 or 2 percent management fee and 5 to 25 percent of annual profits. Given these lucrative compensation packages, it is not surprising that each year the top money winners on Wall Street are hedge fund managers. Hedge fund manager George Soros (Quantum Fund) set an all-time record in 1995 with earnings of $1.5 billion.

Hedge funds became popular in the United States during the 1950s. The first hedge funds specialized in equity short sales. Today, hedge funds invest in a wide array of assets, from low-risk government bonds to high-risk emerging markets. There are upwards of 1,000 hedge funds in the United States with several hundred billion dollars under management. Hedge funds are increasingly popular in Europe, with more than 100 hedge funds currently in operation.

> Hedge funds are private investment partnerships.

The principal investors in hedge funds are large pension funds and wealthy investors that can afford the partnership fee—often a minimum investment of $1 million and a minimum investment period of several years.[2] Invested funds cannot be easily liquidated because of the partnership organization. In the United States, the SEC does not regulate hedge funds as long as there are fewer than 100 partners and each partner passes the SEC's accreditation process (individuals must have a net worth of $1 million or income of $200,000 in the year prior to investment). This is in contrast to publicly traded mutual funds, which are regulated by the SEC. Hedge funds are frequently criticized in the popular press because of the lucrative compensation packages paid to management, their unregulated status, and the huge speculative positions taken by some of the more aggressive funds.

Hedge funds range from very low risk to very high risk, depending on the investment objectives and trading strategies of individual fund managers. These managers have wide latitude in the positions that they take and often use specialized trading strategies such as borrowing on margin, short selling, or derivative market transactions. *MAR Hedge*, a newsletter that follows the industry, categorizes hedge fund strategies as (1) arbitrage, (2) emerging markets, (3) market-neutral (indexed), (4) opportunistic, (5) short selling (the traditional favorite), (6) small cap, (7) special situations, (8) value, and (9) yield-curve arbitrage. There are also "funds of funds"—hedge funds that diversify across other hedge funds. Clearly, not all hedge funds are created equal.

Other International Investment Vehicles

Equity-Linked Bonds. Many domestic and international bonds are sold with an equity option, typically in the form of a convertibility option or warrant. **Convertible bonds** are bonds with a conversion feature that allows the holder to convert the bond into common stock on or prior to a conversion date and at a prespecified conversion price.

> Bonds often have equity options such as warrants or convertibility into common stock.

If the stock price rises above the conversion price, then it is worthwhile converting the bond into stock. The conversion option cannot be detached from the underlying bond. Convertible bonds provide individuals and institutional investors an equity option while promising a fixed return on the bond portion of the instrument.

Warrants are long-term options to buy stock in the issuing company at a prespecified exercise price. The exercise date is usually several years in the future. Warrants are detachable so that the option can sell separately from the bond. Warrants often find their way back to the issuer's domestic market if that country does not allow stock option trading on its local exchanges. For example, the Japanese Ministry of Finance did not allow stock option trading on Japanese exchanges until the summer of 1997. For many years, Japanese companies filled this gap by issuing Eurobonds with detachable warrants. These warrants were then purchased by Japanese investors. The demand of Japanese investors for options on Japanese equities was partially satisfied in 1997 when the Tokyo and Osaka exchanges began trading stock options on Japanese corporations.

Index Futures, Options, or Swaps. Investments in foreign stock indices can be purchased or sold through **stock index futures**.[3] The London Stock Exchange trades futures contracts on several national market indices, including the French CAC-40, the German DAX, the Nikkei 225, and the S&P 500. Like currency futures, stock index futures are marked

> Index futures, options, and swaps are available on country stock indices.

2 Investing in a hedge fund is like buying a yacht. If you have to ask how much it costs, you can't afford it.

3 For details, see Jorion and Roisenberg, "Synthetic International Diversification: The Case for Diversifying with Stock Index Futures," *Journal of Portfolio Management* (1993).

to market daily. Futures exchanges require an initial margin of 5 to 10 percent of the face value of the contract, depending on the volatility of the underlying index and the exchange on which the futures contract is traded.

A number of **index options** are traded on national stock indices. In the United States, the Chicago Board of Trade lists near-term and long-term options (called *leaps*) on a Mexican stock index. The American Stock Exchange lists short-term options on Mexican and Japanese indices and long-term options on a Hong Kong stock index. Index options have asymmetric payoffs that can be used for hedging against, or speculating on, changes in a particular national market.

A **stock index swap** is possible if a counterparty can be found that wants to swap into or out of a foreign market for a period of time. For example, a long position in a foreign market index could be swapped for a short position in a domestic (or another foreign) stock index. This would be a stock-for-stock swap. An investor wanting to swap into a long position in the foreign market index also could construct a debt-for-equity swap with a short position in foreign bonds (perhaps hedging the foreign bond investment in the spot and forward currency markets), a short position in domestic bonds, or any other position that a counterparty might accept. The major disadvantage of a stock index swap is that it can be difficult and costly to find a counterparty with the opposite investment preferences. Stock index swaps can be arranged through an investment banker.

22.2 • SHARE PRICES IN INTERNATIONAL MARKETS

Share Prices in Segmented Markets

Governments restrict access to their domestic capital markets in several ways. Closed-end country funds and restricted/unrestricted shares allow the premiums investors are willing to pay for international portfolio diversification to be measured directly.

CECF Prices in Restricted Markets. The governments of emerging markets sometimes limit access to their capital markets through closed-end country funds. Governments impose restrictions on cross-border capital flows as a way of protecting and controlling their capital markets. Capital outflow controls intended to preserve scarce capital can reduce foreign investments because investors cannot freely withdraw their funds. Capital inflow controls intended to preserve local ownership prevent investors from freely investing in local assets. Closed-end country funds provide a way for small investors to access these restricted markets.

Net asset value (NAV) refers to the market value of a mutual fund's underlying assets. Because closed-end country fund shares sell in a different market than the fund's underlying assets, capital flow barriers prevent arbitrage from forcing CECF share price to net asset value. Consequently, the CECF shares of restricted markets can trade at substantial premiums (or discounts) to their net asset value in the foreign market. As capital flow controls are removed, cross-market arbitrage becomes possible and CECF prices converge toward their net asset values according to $P^d = P^f S^{d/f}$.[4]

> The CECFs of restricted markets often trade at a premium to NAV.

Two explanations have been offered as to why the CECFs of restricted markets sell at premiums to their net asset values:

- International asset pricing models with investment restrictions

---

[4] Domestic closed-end funds usually sell at a slight discount to NAV. CECFs that have been open-ended and CECFs of countries that have no restrictions on foreign investment also tend to sell at or slightly below net asset value. A comprehensive review appears in "Closed-End Fund Discounts and Premiums" by Rozeff, *Pacific-Basin Capital Markets Research* II (1991).

- Investor sentiment

The first school takes a classic portfolio maximization approach, assuming rational investors with homogeneous expectations attempting to maximize the mean-variance efficiency of their portfolios. The effect of ownership restrictions on the actions of foreign and domestic investors is then derived using methods such as those of the capital asset pricing model.[5] Investment restrictions in these models result in different required returns for investors of different nationalities, and consequently a different share price for domestic assets and their corresponding CECF. Bonser-Neal, Brauer, Neal, and Wheatley found empirical evidence consistent with this approach in a study of the relation between announcements of changes in CECF ownership restrictions and CECF share prices.[6]

The investor sentiment school does not assume rationality, instead taking a behavioral finance approach that emphasizes heterogeneous investor expectations and potential inefficiencies in asset pricing. Based on the observation that the principal owners of closed-end funds are individual small investors, Lee, Shleifer, and Thaler argued that the sentiment of small investors should systematically affect the prices of closed-end funds selling in the domestic market.[7] These authors hypothesized the following:

- Institutional investors have rational and unbiased expectations of the expected future returns and risks of closed-end country funds.
- Individual investors trade on their (possibly irrational) sentiment regarding the future returns and risks of closed-end country funds.

In this setting, if domestic individual investors are more bullish on foreign stocks than their foreign counterparts, they can bid up the price of CECF shares relative to their net asset values. According to this view, a premium or discount to NAV reflects the differential between domestic and foreign sentiment regarding the assets underlying the closed-end country fund. Changes in the expectations of domestic individual investors regarding foreign stocks relative to domestic stocks result in changes in CECF premiums/discounts that are common to all closed-end country funds.

Consistent with this story, a study by Bodurtha, Kim, and Lee found the following to be true for CECFs selling in the United States:[8]

1. CECF premiums/discounts move together in the U.S. market.
2. Domestic closed-end fund premiums/discounts are not correlated with the U.S. stock market, whereas closed-end country fund premiums/discounts are positively correlated with the U.S. stock market.
3. Changes in NAV are positively correlated with returns in the foreign (or local) market, but are not correlated with U.S. stock market returns.

The anticipated diversification benefits of entry into restricted foreign markets are not realized if CECFs move with the domestic market rather than with the foreign market. Because CECF shares trading in a domestic market are more highly correlated with other domestic stocks than they are with their own net asset values, CECFs tend to be poor vehicles for international portfolio diversification.[9]

5 See, for example, Eun and Janakiramanan, "A Model of International Asset Pricing with a Constraint on the Foreign Equity Ownership," *Journal of Finance* (1986).

6 Bonser-Neal, Brauer, Neal, and Wheatley, "International Investment Restrictions and Closed-End Country Fund Prices," *Journal of Finance* (1990).

7 Lee, Shleifer, and Thaler, "Investor Sentiment and the Closed-End Fund Puzzle," *Journal of Finance* (1991).

8 Bodurtha, Kim, and Lee, "Closed-End Country Funds and U.S. Market Sentiment," *Review of Financial Studies* (1995).

9 See Bailey and Lim, "Evaluating the Diversification Benefits of the New Country Funds," *Journal of Portfolio Management* (1992).

The Prices of Restricted and Unrestricted Shares. Many countries maintain legal limits on foreign ownership of domestic companies by maintaining different classes of stock for domestic and foreign investors. Typically, **restricted shares** may be held only by domestic residents and **unrestricted shares** may be held by anyone. When the supply of unrestricted shares is greater than the quantity demanded by foreign investors, unrestricted shares can sell at premiums to restricted share prices of up to 100 percent.

> Premiums are highest for large, liquid stocks from creditworthy countries.

Bailey, Chung, and Kang compare the prices of restricted and unrestricted shares in 11 national markets.[10] These authors were unable to find evidence that premiums were related to cross-border differences in required returns, as suggested by international asset pricing models with investment restrictions. However, premiums were positively related to two proxies for foreign investor demand:

- Investor sentiment
  - Premiums were positively related to CECF premiums, suggesting that the sentiment of foreign investors affects both CECF and unrestricted share premiums.
- Fund flows
  - Premiums were positively related to the flow of funds into internationally-oriented U.S. mutual funds, so that premiums increase when foreign investor demand is high.

Premiums were also positively related to the firm's information environment and the liquidity of the firm's unrestricted shares:

- Information
  - Premiums were positively related to country credit ratings and firm size, suggesting that foreign investors value reliable information.
- Liquidity
  - Premiums were positively related to the relative liquidity of unrestricted shares, suggesting that foreign investors value liquidity.

These results suggest that foreign investors are willing to pay a premium for large, liquid stocks in countries with low country risk. Premiums are likely to be particularly large when foreign investor demand is high.

The Effectiveness of Homemade International Diversification

Errunza, Hogan, and Hung have tested whether U.S. investors can achieve international diversification through securities traded in the United States.[11] These authors found that U.S. investors can replicate the diversification benefits of foreign market returns by augmenting domestic stocks with U.S.-based multinationals, American depository receipts, and closed-end country funds. In particular, the market values of portfolios augmented with MNCs, ADRs, and CECFs moved more closely with foreign markets than with the U.S. market. These authors also found that the need for direct purchase in foreign markets has diminished with the increasing availability of assets representing claims on foreign assets. These authors concluded that U.S. investors no longer need to trade abroad to achieve a portfolio that is internationally mean-variance efficient.

The benefits of direct share purchases in foreign markets are likely to be greater for investors in smaller, less developed countries. First, the benefits of international diver-

---

10 Bailey, Chung, and Kang, "Foreign Ownership Restrictions and Equity Price Premiums: What Drives the Demand for Cross-Border Investments?" *Journal of Financial and Quantitative Analysis* (1999).

11 Errunza, Hogan, and Hung, "Can the Gains from International Diversification Be Achieved Without Trading Abroad?" *Journal of Finance* (1999).

sification are greater in small countries than in large countries because small countries tend to be less diversified. Second, larger markets such as the United States tend to offer a wider selection of assets representing claims on foreign assets than smaller markets. Investors without access to these securities will find it harder to achieve international diversification through domestically traded assets.

22.3 • ASSET ALLOCATION POLICY AND INVESTMENT STYLE

Asset allocation policy refers to the target weights given to various asset classes in an investment portfolio. A mutual fund's asset allocation policy is the most important decision made by fund management. Nobel Prize winner William Sharpe estimates that 90 percent of a portfolio's return is determined by the asset allocation decision.[12] Mutual funds' asset allocation policies also determine how they are marketed to the public.

> Asset allocation policy sets target weights for various asset classes.

A fund manager's **investment style** or **investment philosophy** refers to the investment objectives pursued by the manager, including whether the manager follows an active or passive investment approach. Individual investors tend to migrate toward either a passive buy-and-hold approach or a more active approach based on their beliefs about market efficiency or the lack thereof. Mutual funds cluster into active or passive funds to appeal to these two distinct clienteles.[13]

Mutual funds describe their investment philosophy and asset allocation policy in the fund **prospectus**. The prospectus identifies whether the fund primarily invests in stocks, bonds, derivatives, real estate, or some combination of assets. The prospectus sets limits on the proportions of various assets held in the fund, and states whether the fund engages in derivative transactions to reduce exposure to financial price risks or take advantage of speculative opportunities. Finally, the prospectus provides information on past and expected future commission charges incurred in managing the assets of the fund.

Passive Fund Management

The advantages of a passive buy-and-hold approach to portfolio management are that it is less costly to implement and less risky than an actively managed portfolio invested in similar assets, at least for the investor without above-average skill. The disadvantage of the passive approach is that returns are likely to be no better (and yet no worse) than returns on benchmark portfolios of comparable risk.

> Some passively managed funds try to track a particular market index.

The logic of passive fund management comes from the algebra of portfolio diversification and the literature on market efficiency. The efficient markets hypothesis suggests that financial markets are informationally efficient. Active fund management in such a market is futile because consistently successful market timing or security selection is not possible. If financial markets are perfect and efficient and asset returns are normally distributed, then the world market portfolio should be mean-variance efficient. An internationally diversified mutual fund that holds individual assets according to their market value weight in the world market portfolio should provide better return-risk performance over the long run than other portfolios.

http://www.msci.com

http://www.ftse.com

http://www.smithbarney.com

---

12 Sharpe, "Asset Allocation: Management Style and Performance Measurement," *Journal of Portfolio Management* (1992).

13 Some fund managers try to "game" the system by claiming one style and following another so that their performance is benchmarked to a lower standard. See Brown and Goetzmann, "Mutual Fund Styles," *Journal of Financial Economics* (1997).

Following this logic, passively managed global funds are often diversified across countries and asset classes to exploit the ability of portfolio diversification to improve return-risk performance. Fund managers use the low correlations between national markets to achieve mean-variance efficient returns given the investment objectives of the fund. Many passively managed funds are index funds that try to hold the same proportion of stocks as a major market index. Commonly tracked global stock indices include the MSCI World Index (Morgan Stanley Capital International) and the FTSE All-World Index. The most widely tracked global bond index is Salomon Smith Barney's World Government Bond Index. Each of these indices weights assets according to their market capitalization.

Many investors build diversified portfolios using index funds as building blocks. To appeal to this clientele, some index funds specialize in particular countries, regions, or industries. Individual investors may either passively or actively manage these portfolios of index funds, and the funds themselves might be passively or actively managed. Regional and national funds are often set up to track the regional or national indices published by Morgan Stanley, FTSE, or Salomon Smith Barney. Commonly tracked national indices include the NYSE Composite and the S&P 500 in the United States, Tokyo's Nikkei 225, Frankfurt's DAX, Paris' CAC 40, Hong Kong's Hang Seng, and London's FTSE 30 and 100 stock indices. Financial newspapers such as the *London Financial Times* and *The Wall Street Journal* publish national and international indices in the consumer products, energy, financial, industrial, materials, and technology industries.

Active Fund Management

Successful active management holds out the promise of higher portfolio return and, by avoiding assets that fall in value, lower portfolio risk as well. For an actively managed portfolio, long-run asset allocation refers to the average proportion of each asset class in the portfolio over the long run. The extent to which a particular portfolio manager diverges from these long-run target weights reflects the manager's style. Aggressively managed funds can diverge quite a bit from their long-run target weights. Less aggressive funds tilt their portfolios away from long-run targets to a lesser degree. Passively managed funds maintain their asset allocations close to their long-run targets.

Active strategies include asset allocation and security selection.

Actively managed funds follow one or both of the following investment strategies:

- **Active asset allocation** (or **market timing**) strategies, in which funds are shifted between asset classes in anticipation of market events
- **Active security selection** (e.g., stock picking) strategies, in which funds are selectively invested in stocks or bonds that are underpriced by the marketplace and not invested (or sold short) in those securities that are overpriced by the marketplace

Each of these active investment strategies presumes an ability to anticipate next period's returns and shift funds accordingly.

Active Asset Allocation Strategies. National economies seldom move in phase with each other, and stock returns vary widely across national markets in both the short run and the long run. The lure of potentially higher returns and lower portfolio risk entices many investors into diverging from passive diversification into a market timing strategy of shifting among asset classes. Successful market timing strategies rely on correctly predicting which asset classes will appreciate during the coming period. By allocating funds into the right assets at the right time, successful market timing can increase expected returns and reduce portfolio risk.

Unfortunately for market timers without timing skill, randomly shifting between assets results in higher portfolio risk than a buy-and-hold strategy at the same level of expected return.[14] With transactions costs, timing strategies executed without timing skill result in lower expected returns as well. This return-risk penalty for ineffective market timing means that investors without timing skill are better off with a buy-and-hold strategy than with an active market timing strategy.

The penalty for ineffective market timing is the flip side of the portfolio diversification benefit. Figure 22.1 shows the portfolios attainable by combining U.S. and Hong Kong stocks in various combinations, based on observed returns from 1970–2002. A diversified portfolio benefits from the low correlation of 0.39 between these markets, as indicated by the line bowed to the left in Figure 22.1. The line to the right in Figure 22.1 shows the expected return and standard deviation for a market timer randomly switching between these markets. Whereas the passive buy-and-hold investor benefits from low correlations between assets, the ineffective market timer forgoes these diversification benefits. This additional risk is indicated in Figure 22.1 as the market timer's penalty.

FIGURE 22.1

The Market Timer's Penalty for Random Switches Between the U.S. and Hong Kong Stock Markets

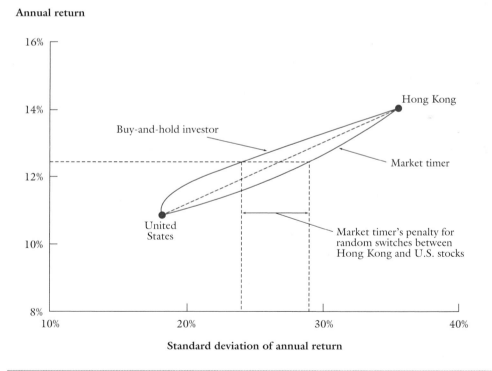

Source: Based on continuously compounded monthly returns over 1970–2002. For a discussion, see Butler, Domian, and Simonds, "International Portfolio Diversification and the Magnitude of the Market Timer's Penalty," *Journal of International Financial Management and Accounting* 6 (Winter 1995).

---

14 See Sharpe, "Are Gains Likely from Market Timing?" *Financial Analysts Journal* (1975).

Butler, Domian, and Simonds estimated that a market timer randomly switching between U.S. and Japanese stocks faces 26 percent more standard deviation of return than a comparable buy-and-hold investor at the same level of expected return.[15] Randomly switching between stocks and T-bills is an even worse strategy, with a 50 percent higher standard deviation at the same level of expected return.

Evidence on the market timing performance of fund managers is mixed. Although some studies have found evidence of timing ability on the part of fund managers in the U.S. market,[16] most studies fail to find evidence of market-timing ability.[17] Even if some fund managers are able to consistently outperform a buy-and-hold strategy, it may be difficult to identify these superior market timers with any degree of confidence. Even the most widely regarded market timers (such as George Soros of the hedge fund *Quantum Fund*) have achieved average annual returns only slightly higher than competing benchmark portfolios, and their performance is quite variable from year to year.

Active Security Selection. Managers following an active security selection strategy attempt to identify individual securities that are mispriced relative to other securities in a market or industry. Proponents of active security selection do not believe that assets are correctly priced in an informationally efficient market. To identify mispriced

Market Update

Mark Mobius and Templeton Investments

Perhaps the best-known international stock picker is Mark Mobius of Franklin Templeton Investments. With a PhD in economics and political science from MIT, Mobius travels the world on his Gulfstream IV jet in search of investment opportunities in emerging markets. Templeton's emerging market funds have more than $10 billion under management.

Mobius is a vocal advocate of transparent accounting and good corporate governance practices. After more than 30 years of investing in emerging markets, he has seen more than his share of fraud and crony capitalism. He states:[18]

> "Apologists in many countries retreat to the defense of cultural differences as an excuse for not implementing good corporate governance. But it is basically about fair play, and fairness has no regional, national, cultural or ethnic boundaries. It's best for everyone to level the playing fields and to make business dealings transparent. Only then will confidence in these markets fully return, and only then will investors benefit fully from the potential that is in global markets."

Mobius's point is that the risks of investing in emerging markets are directly related to accounting transparency and the fairness of local legal systems.

---

15   Butler, Domian, and Simonds, "International Portfolio Diversification and the Magnitude of the Market Timer's Penalty," *Journal of International Financial Management and Accounting* (1995).

16   Lee and Rahman, "Market Timing, Selectivity, and Mutual Fund Performance: An Empirical Investigation," *Journal of Business* (1990).

17   Becker, Ferson, Myers, and Schill, "Conditional Market Timing with Benchmark Investors," *Journal of Financial Economics* (1999); and Goetzmann, Ingersoll, and Ivkovic, "Monthly Measurement of Daily Timers," *Journal of Financial and Quantitative Analysis* (2000).

18   *Asiaweek, London Financial Times* (November 30, 2001), p.1.

securities, these strategies require accurate and detailed information on a firm's investments and investment opportunities, new product development, and possible changes in capital structure or corporate governance. Needless to say, it is much more difficult to acquire and interpret such information from a distant market than from one's local market. Successful investing in international markets (whether through passive investing, active security selection, or market timing) also requires familiarity with the cross-border differences that exist in financial measurement and disclosure. These issues are discussed in the next section.

22.4 • CROSS-BORDER FINANCIAL STATEMENT ANALYSIS

There are many barriers to obtaining and interpreting information on foreign firms. The most obvious barrier is language. Yet learning the local idiom can be a problem even for investors that share a common tongue because of differences in accounting measurement and disclosure. For example, in the United States the term *stock* refers to common equity. In the United Kingdom, the term refers to an inventory of unsold goods. In the United States, firms with large amounts of debt in their capital structures are *highly levered*. In the United Kingdom, this is referred to as *gearing*. This is enough to make you want to table the entire issue of international accounting diversity.[19]

> Differences in accounting measurement and disclosure impose added costs on international investments.

Language barriers can be overcome with the help of an interpreter familiar with the business culture and accounting conventions of the foreign country. More difficult to overcome are cross-country differences in accounting measurement and disclosure that spring from each country's unique history, political system, cultural environment, and legal, tax, and institutional structures.

The rest of this section examines international differences in the measurement and disclosure of financial information. This is not intended to be a comprehensive guide to cross-border financial statement analysis. It is only intended to make you aware of some of the difficulties encountered by financial analysts on their forays into the financial accounting conventions of other countries.

International Differences in Financial Accounting Measurement

You work in commercial credit and have just received your dream assignment—a 1-year posting to Citigroup's London office. This should be a lark, you think.

Your first assignment is to review a proposed loan to a Chelsea microbrewery called Brown Bog Brewery. Brown Bog provides you with the following current accounts:

Cash	£20,000		
Accounts receivable	£40,000	Wages payable	£40,000
Inventory	£40,000	Taxes payable	£20,000
Total current assets	£100,000	Total current liabilities	£60,000

As a seasoned loan officer, you calculate a current ratio (current assets divided by current liabilities) to measure Brown Bog's liquidity:

Brown Bog (U.K. accounting): current ratio = current assets / current liabilities
= £100,000 / £60,000 = 1.67

---

19 Here we go again. To a U.S. resident, the term *table* means to "discontinue discussion" of a topic. To a U.K. resident, it means to "put it on the table" and open the topic for discussion. What a bloody mess.

Is this current ratio high or low relative to firms in the same industry? Fortunately, you remember that you performed a credit analysis last year on Red Dog Brewery in the United States. You retrieve Red Dog's credit analysis from your computer. Here are the U.S. microbrewer's current accounts:

Cash	$60,000	Bank overdrafts	$30,000
Accounts receivable	$60,000	Wages payable	$60,000
Inventory	$60,000	Taxes payable	$30,000
Total current assets	$180,000	Total current liabilities	$120,000

You calculate Red Dog's current ratio:

Red Dog (U.S. accounting): current ratio = current assets / current liabilities
= $180,000 / $120,000 = 1.5

The U.K. firm appears to be more liquid than its U.S. counterpart. You might as well make the loan, right?[20]

Wait a moment. By whose standards should you judge this measure of liquidity? The United Kingdom follows the *Statements of Standard Accounting Practice*, which do not always coincide with the generally accepted accounting principles (GAAP) of the Financial Accounting Standards in the United States. For example, the United States and the United Kingdom do not share a common accounting definition of cash. According to U.S. GAAP, *cash* is defined as cash, demand deposits, and highly liquid investments. In the United Kingdom, *cash* is defined as cash, demand deposits, and highly liquid investments *less bank overdrafts.*

Let's restate Red Dog's accounts after adjusting for the U.K. definition of cash:

Cash (less overdrafts)	$30,000		
Accounts receivable	$60,000	Wages payable	$60,000
Inventory	$60,000	Taxes payable	$30,000
Total current assets	$150,000	Total current liabilities	$90,000

Under this convention, Red Dog's current ratio is exactly the same as Brown Bog's:

Red Dog (U.K. accounting): current ratio = current assets / current liabilities
= $150,000 / $90,000 = 1.67

After adjusting for this accounting difference, the current ratio of Red Dog turns out to be identical to that of Brown Bog.

Cash would seem to be the least ambiguous of the financial accounts. If the definition of cash can make such a big difference, just think what the U.K.'s conventions are doing to your U.S.-based notions of accounting for inflation, depreciation, and pension liabilities! Maybe this assignment won't be the lark that you had envisioned. Off you go to the pub to drown your troubles with a pint of Brown Bog ale.

---

20 If you are from the United Kingdom, you should reverse the perspective in this example. Assume that you have been assigned to the U.S. branch of Standard Chartered Bank in (pick a U.S. city) and have been asked to review Red Dog's loan application. From the U.S. perspective, Red Dog appears to lack liquidity.

International Differences in Financial Disclosure

The multinational corporation can respond in several ways to a demand on the part of foreign stakeholders for financial accounting information:

- *Do nothing.* Small companies that have few dealings with the outside world have neither the need nor the resources to prepare supplementary financial statements.

- *Prepare convenience translations.* Under this alternative, the firm translates the names of the financial accounts into another language but does not change the accounting conventions used to construct the accounts. Large U.S. multinationals seldom go beyond preparing convenience translations for foreign investors, relying instead on foreign investors to understand and interpret the financial statements according to U.S. accounting conventions.

- *Prepare supplementary financial statements using different accounting principles.* Many MNCs based outside the United States restate their financial statements according to U.S. standards or the International Accounting Standards (IAS) of the International Accounting Standards Board, an international organization devoted to harmonizing accounting standards.

The response chosen by a particular firm reflects the importance of international investors and the costs of conformance with foreign or international accounting standards.

International differences in the market for corporate control are reflected in differences in public disclosure requirements. Disclosure requirements are most common in countries with active financial markets, such as in the United States and the United Kingdom. In many developing countries, the majority of funds are still privately raised through banks, wealthy investors, or the government. In these countries, there are likely to be few public disclosure requirements.

Accounting standard setters around the world are attempting to harmonize their national conventions, often through the adoption or adaptation of U.S. or IAS standards. For example, China is promoting IAS standards for Chinese companies that want to raise capital in international markets. Japanese multinationals frequently prepare secondary financial statements according to U.S. GAAP. Beginning in 2005, the European Union plans to accept various combinations of IAS, U.S., and local standards. In the United States, the SEC requires that foreign firms follow IAS or U.S. standards. If firms use IAS standards, they must provide a statement that reconciles their use of IAS accounts with U.S. accounting standards. International accounting standards will make it easier for a firm from Milan or Shanghai, say, to crosslist on other international exchanges.

Despite this effort to harmonize accounting standards, there remain many differences between IAS and domestic standards. In particular, IAS measurement and disclosure requirements are frequently more restrictive than domestic standards.[21] Table 22.1 lists some of the differences between IAS and domestic standards in accounting for depreciation, lease and pension liabilities, and research and development expense. As a practical matter, U.S. and IAS standards are similar.

---

21 See Ashbaugh and Pincus, "Domestic Accounting Standards, International Accounting Standards, and Predictability of Earnings," *Journal of Accounting Research* (2001).

T A B L E   2 2 . 1
Variation in Measurement Methods of IAS and Domestic GAAP

	Measurement method restrictions			
	Additional depreciation	Accounting for leases	Accounting for pensions	Research and development
Australia			X	X
Canada				
Denmark		X		X
Finland	X	X	X	X
France	X	X	X	
Hong Kong				X
Japan		X	X	
Malaysia				
Norway			X	
Singapore				
Spain			X	
Sweden		X	X	
Switzerland	X	X	X	X

An "x" indicates that International Accounting Standards (IAS) restrict accounting measurement methods relative to those under domestic GAAP.

Source: Ashbaugh and Pincus, "Domestic Accounting Standards, International Accounting Standards, and Predictability of Earnings," *Journal of Accounting Research* 39 (December 2001).

22.5 • THE SHIFTING SANDS OF PORTFOLIO ANALYSIS

The Inputs to Portfolio Analysis

Quantitative inputs to portfolio analysis include expected returns, variances, and covariances or correlations for global and national stock and bond markets, industries, and—for active security selection—individual companies. Consider the expected return and variance of return on a diversified portfolio of international securities.

$$E[r_p] = \sum_i x_i \, E[r_i] \tag{22.1}$$

and

$$Var(r_p) = \sigma_p^2 = \sum_i x_i^2 \sigma_i^2 + \sum_i \sum_{\substack{j \\ i \neq j}} x_i x_j \sigma_{ij} \tag{22.2}$$

Estimates of portfolio return and risk will be only as good as the inputs to Equations 22.1 and 22.2. Chapter 20 provided historical measures of expected return $E[r_i] = \mu_i$, standard deviation of return σ_i, and cross-market correlation ρ_{ij} for global and national stock and bond market indices. If the expected returns or standard deviations of national market indices change, or if the correlations change, then historical estimates will not accurately predict the distribution of future returns. For this reason, mutual fund prospectuses prominently display the disclaimer "past returns are no guarantee of future performance." There ain't no such thing as easy money.

Time-Varying Expected Returns and Volatilities

A growing body of evidence finds that stocks' expected returns and volatilities vary over time and that these variations are related to business cycles. Here is a summary:

> Expected returns and volatilities are related to business cycles.

- Expected stock and bond returns are low when economic conditions are strong and high when conditions are weak.
- Expected stock return and volatility are positively related.
- Stock return volatility depends on the volatility of returns in the recent past.

Fama and French found that expected returns on U.S. stocks and long-term bonds contain a default premium that is low near peaks and high near troughs of the business cycle.[22] For example, stock and bond prices were low and expected returns were high during the Great Depression in the 1930s. In contrast, prices were high and expected returns were low during the relatively strong economy of the 1950s and 1960s. Similar evidence has been found in other developed capital markets.

Expected returns are also related to volatility, which is itself time-varying. Figure 22.2 plots local currency monthly returns to Morgan Stanley's (MSCI) Canadian, Japanese, U.K., and U.S. stock indices over 1970–2002. Monthly returns are displayed as gray shading. Conditional volatility based on the *RiskMetrics* model of Chapter 4 appears as

FIGURE 22.2
Volatility in National Stock Markets, 1970–2002

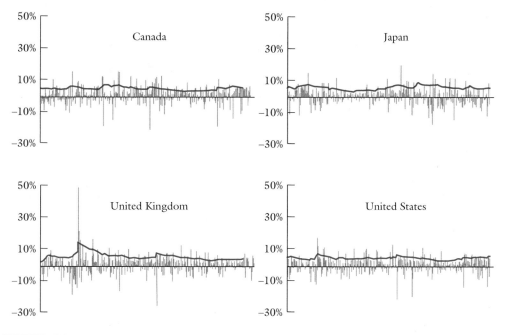

Note: RiskMetrics conditional volatility appears as a dark line, based on monthly returns to MSCI indices (shaded in gray).

---

22 See Fama and French, "Business Conditions and Expected Returns on Stocks and Bonds," *Journal of Financial Economics* (1989). Fama and French also found evidence of a term or maturity premium.

a solid line.[23] Local currency returns correspond to returns to a nonlocal investor that have been fully hedged against currency risk. The international stock market crash of October 1987 appears as a large downward spike in each market. October 1987 was the largest monthly drop in all but the Japanese market, which suffered even larger losses during several months in 1990. Each market had periods of high and low volatility. Although the empirical evidence is just beginning to accumulate, expected returns also appear to vary over time.[24] Instability in expected returns and volatilities across national indices make the portfolio manager's job more difficult, but also more interesting.

Correlations Between National Stock Markets: When It Rains, It Pours

Figure 22.3 plots 60-month "rolling correlations" between the U.S. stock market and the national stock markets of Canada, Japan and the United Kingdom using the MSCI local-currency indices. Each point on the graph represents a correlation with the U.S. market based on returns from the previous 60 months. Canada has the highest correlation with the U.S. market (0.74) over 1975–2002 because of its geographic proximity and high level of cross-border trade. Because of their greater distance and lower levels of trade, correlations with the U.S. market are lower for Japan (0.35) and the United Kingdom (0.58).

FIGURE 22.3
60-Month Rolling Correlations with the U.S. Stock Market

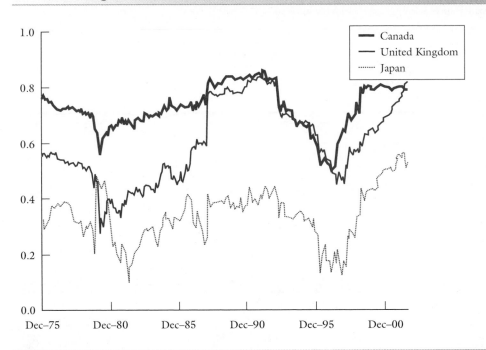

Source: Based on monthly returns to MSCI indices.

---

23 *RiskMetrics* conditional volatility estimate puts a 97% weight on the previous month's conditional volatility and a 3% weight on the square of the most recent spot rate change: $\sigma_t = \sqrt{(0.97\sigma_{t-1}^2 + 0.03s_{t-1}^2)}$.

24 See Lin, Engle, and Ito, "Do Bulls and Bears Move Across Borders? International Transmission of Stock Returns and Volatility," *Review of Financial Studies* (1994); Lewellen, "The Time-Series Relations Among Expected Return, Risk, and Book-to-Market," *Journal of Financial Economics* (1999).

The instability of these rolling correlations is striking. For example, the 60-month rolling correlation of the U.K. market with the U.S. market varies from a low of 0.27 in February 1980 to a high of 0.84 in December 2002. Because of instability in cross-market correlations, it is difficult to predict the risk reduction effects of international portfolio diversification. Portfolio weights that optimize mean-variance performance based on historic correlations are unlikely to deliver the same risk-reduction benefits in the future.

> Diversification benefits cannot be precisely estimated with historical data.

All is not lost, however. The Canadian market typically moves more closely with the U.S. market than Japan or the United Kingdom. Just as clearly, the Japanese stock market is likely to provide more diversification benefits than the other markets to a U.S. investor because of its lower average correlation with the U.S. market. Instability in the correlations between these national markets simply serves to caution us that the *future* risk reduction benefits of international portfolio diversification cannot be precisely estimated using historical data.

The International Stock Market Crash of October 1987. Stock markets around the world dropped in unison following the weekend of October 17–18, 1987. No stock markets were spared from this international crash. Local currency losses ranged from 16.3 percent in Italy to 45.8 percent in Hong Kong. Most major markets lost between 20 and 25 percent of their value during the month. Figure 22.4 displays daily returns during October 1987 to the stock markets of Japan, the United Kingdom, and the United States

FIGURE 22.4
National Stock Market Indices During the Crash of October 1987

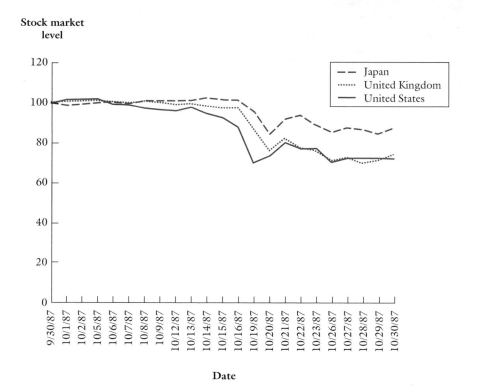

Source: MSCI.

using a level of 100 as the beginning-of-month base. Note the extent to which these markets moved together during this extraordinary period of stock market history.

Pundits around the world searched for local reasons for the stock market crash. In the United States, the crash was blamed on everything from a perceived change in Federal Reserve policy to a shift in U.S. investor sentiment. (Quite a shift!) Similarly parochial explanations were seen in other countries, with local politicians as common scapegoats. Regardless of the cause, the crash of 1987 was a truly international event.

Roll examined the international determinants of the crash and found that the size of each market's movement during the crash was related to that market's systematic risk (market model beta) relative to a world market portfolio.[25] National markets with higher betas measured against a world market index tended to fall further than markets with low betas during the month of the crash.

The after-effects of the crash of 1987 will be seen in stock market data for decades to come. Evidence of the crash appears in Figure 22.3 as an upward shift in the correlations of each of the national stocks with the U.S. stock market beginning in October 1987 and continuing for 60 months. Once October 1987 falls off the tail end of the 60-month rolling correlations, cross-market correlations return to near their former levels.

Market crashes have an important impact on mutual fund performance. Mutual funds report their performance over 1-, 5-, and 10-year horizons. Portfolio managers breathed a sigh of relief on January 1, 1998, when the 1987 crash no longer appeared in their 10-year return performances. Managers of portfolios specializing in Asian stocks will be similarly elated once the 1997–1998 Asian contagion falls off of their 5- and 10-year performance figures.

Higher Correlations in Volatile Markets. Figures 22.3 and 22.4 suggest that national markets moved together to a greater degree than usual during the 1987 crash. If correlations are higher than normal during bear markets such as October 1987, then the actual gains from international portfolio diversification might not be as great as promised by the algebra of portfolio diversification.

> International stock market correlations increase in bear markets.

Butler and Joaquin examined international stock market correlations from the perspective of domestic investors from Australia, Europe, Japan, Switzerland, the United Kingdom, and the United States, as shown in Table 22.2.[26] Months were categorized as bear, calm, or bull markets according to the level of domestic return, such that one-third of all months fell into each category. The correlation between domestic and international returns within each category was then calculated. Observed correlations within each category were then compared to bear, calm, and bull market correlations from a normal distribution with the same means, variances, and correlation as observed returns. Confidence intervals were generated from the normal distribution using Monte Carlo simulation. Figure 22.5 graphs the correlations in Table 22.2 against mean returns to the domestic market in bear, calm, and bull market periods. The dark lines represent the observed correlations. The dotted lines are correlations at the $2^{1/2}$, 50, and $97^{1/2}$ percentiles from the normal distribution.

Correlation profiles produced by the normal distribution are u-shaped and symmetric, with higher correlations in bear and bull markets than in calm markets. This characteristic of the normal distribution is at least partially responsible for the popular notion that international stock market correlations increase during volatile periods.

---

25 Roll, "The International Crash of October 1987," *Financial Analysts Journal* (September/October 1988).

26 Butler and Joaquin, "Are the Gains from International Portfolio Diversification Exaggerated? The Influence of Downside Risk in Bear Markets," *Journal of International Money and Finance* (2002).

TABLE 22.2
International Stock Market Correlations in Bear, Calm, and Bull Markets

Domestic		Partitioned correlations			
		Bear markets	Calm markets	Bull markets	Overall correlation
Australia–World	Observed	0.597″	0.128	0.256	
	Normal	0.350	0.172	0.350	0.576
Europe–World	Observed	0.667″	0.074′	0.485	
	Normal	0.449	0.229	0.449	0.689
Japan–World	Observed	0.387′	0.109	0.199	
	Normal	0.244	0.116	0.244	0.428
Switzerland–Europe	Observed	0.722″	0.449″	0.570	
	Normal	0.501	0.262	0.501	0.739
U.K.–World	Observed	0.574″	0.227	0.295	
	Normal	0.381	0.189	0.381	0.614
U.S.–World	Observed	0.633″	0.018″	0.194″	
	Normal	0.398	0.198	0.398	0.633

Source: Butler and Joaquin, "Are the Gains from International Portfolio Diversification Exaggerated? The Influence of Downside Risk in Bear Markets," *Journal of International Money and Finance* (December 2002). Double (or single) quotes indicate statistical significance at a 95 (or 90) percent confidence level.

High correlations during volatile (bear or bull market) times are only inconsistent with the normal distribution if observed correlations are higher than normal; that is, higher than predicted by a normal distribution with means, variances, and correlation equal to observed returns.

Table 22.2 and Figure 22.5 show that this is indeed the case. Observed correlations during bear markets are significantly higher than normal in each stock market pair. Observed correlations during calm and bull markets are unexceptional compared to the normal distribution. Qualitatively similar results were found when the normal distribution was replaced with *RiskMetrics*' GARCH(1,1) distribution or a Student-t distribution with four degrees of freedom.

Although international portfolio diversification is valuable, these findings indicate that the gains from international diversification are weakest just when these benefits are most needed.

22.6 • PORTFOLIO HEDGING STRATEGIES

In Chapter 21, we found that changes in currency values are largely unrelated to changes in national market indices. This suggests that we should be able to improve the mean-variance efficiency of an internationally diversified portfolio of stocks and bonds by hedging the additional layer of currency risk on foreign investments.

Currency Risk and the IAPM

In the international asset pricing model (IAPM), each investor's optimal portfolio is a combination of the world market portfolio, riskless foreign and domestic currency bonds, and a currency-specific **hedge portfolio** that strips foreign bonds of their currency risk.

FIGURE 22.5

Stock Market Correlations in Bear, Calm, and Bull Markets

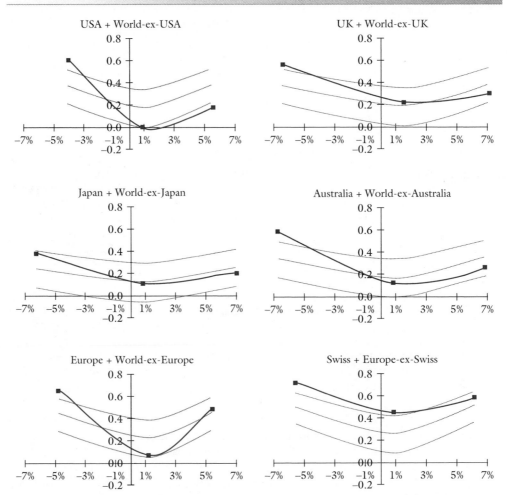

The y axis is a bear, calm, or bull market correlation between a domestic and an international-ex-domestic (i.e, excluding the domestic) index. The x axis is the mean domestic return in the bear, calm, or bull market. Dotted lines show $2^{1/2}$, 50, and $97^{1/2}$ percentiles from the normal distribution based on the overall sample means, variances, and correlation. Lines are drawn between the bear, calm, and bull market observations (from Table 22.2) for visual effect only.

Source: Butler and Joaquin, "Are the Gains from International Portfolio Diversification Exaggerated? The Influence of Downside Risk in Bear Markets," *Journal of International Money and Finance* (December 2002).

All investors hold individual stocks in proportion to their market value weights in a globally diversified equity portfolio. The composition of the hedge portfolio depends on the investor's functional currency.

In a one-period international asset pricing model world, interest rate parity tells us that an investment in a riskless foreign bond is equivalent to a combination of a riskless domestic bond along with a long forward position in the foreign currency:

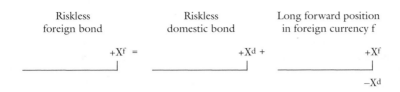

Riskless foreign bond	Riskless domestic bond	Long forward position in foreign currency f
$+X^f =$	$+X^d +$	$+X^f$
		$-X^d$

Mean-variance efficient portfolios in the IAPM are internationally diversified combinations of stocks and bonds that have been hedged against currency risk.

The Benefits of Hedging Currency Risk

In practice, there are many ways to construct a hedge portfolio. One alternative is to hedge the entire amount of funds exposed to currency risk.[27] Figure 22.6 presents Jorion's estimate of the additional benefit from hedging 100 percent of the currency

FIGURE 22.6
The Benefits of Hedging Currency Risk

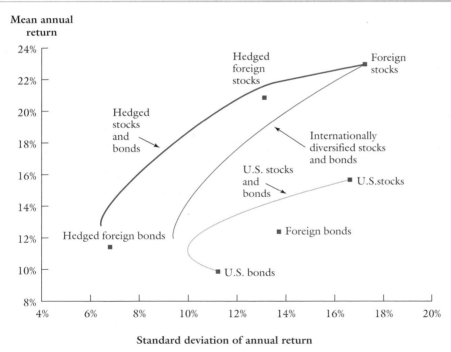

Source: Adapted from "Asset Allocation with Hedged and Unhedged Foreign Stocks and Bonds" by Philippe Jorion, *Journal of Portfolio Management* (Summer 1989), pp. 49–54. Reprinted with permission.

---

27 One approach is to construct a minimum-variance hedge using a form of the hedge ratio of Chapter 7, preferably allowing the hedge ratio to vary over time. See Adler and Jorion, "Universal Currency Hedges for Global Portfolios," *Journal of Portfolio Management* (1992); and Glen and Jorion, "Currency Hedging for International Portfolios," *Journal of Finance* (1993).

risk of the world market portfolio.[28] The leftmost line represents the return-risk performance possible by hedging the currency risk of the combined stock-bond portfolio. To obtain Figure 22.6, Jorion uses a rolling 1-month forward hedge of the full amount of the investment in each foreign currency. With a 1-month rolling foreign currency hedge, the amount invested in each foreign market is sold forward at the start of each month with a 1-month forward contract. As Figure 22.6 shows, the potential gains in return-risk efficiency from hedging the currency risk in an internationally diversified portfolio can be substantial.

22.7 • SUMMARY

This chapter described several ways to diversify into international stocks and bonds:

- Invest in multinational corporations based in the domestic economy
- Invest in foreign securities directly in the foreign market
- Invest in foreign assets through securities traded in the domestic market
  - Foreign shares
  - Depository receipts
  - Mutual funds
  - Hedge funds

Open-ended mutual funds provide an excellent vehicle for international portfolio diversification. Investors with the means and inclination to invest in individual foreign companies can purchase them directly in the foreign market or, when available, through foreign shares or depository receipts in their own domestic market. Hedge funds are appropriate only for wealthy investors.

We looked at passive and active portfolio management styles and how they are implemented on a global scale. The benefits of international investments are difficult to estimate for several reasons. First, obtaining and interpreting financial information on foreign companies can be difficult. Individual investors and portfolio managers investing in individual companies must be aware of international differences in financial accounting measurement and disclosure. Second, there is considerable randomness in foreign market returns and exchange rates themselves. Third, inputs to portfolio analysis include expected returns, variances, and correlations or covariances. Each of these inputs exhibits instability over time.

Finally, we examined the gains in return-risk efficiency that can be obtained by hedging the currency risk of foreign investments. Reducing the currency risk of an internationally diversified portfolio can greatly reduce the variability of return without a corresponding decrease in expected return.

KEY TERMS

active security selection
American depository receipts (ADRs)
American shares
asset allocation policy

closed-end country funds (CECFs)
closed-end funds
convertible bonds
depository receipts (e.g., ADRs)

---

28 Jorion, "Asset Allocation with Hedged and Unhedged Foreign Stocks and Bonds," *Journal of Portfolio Management* (1989).

foreign shares	net asset value (NAV)
global depository receipts	open-end funds
global shares	prospectus
hedge funds	restricted shares
hedge portfolio	stock index futures
index options	stock index swaps
investment style or philosophy	unrestricted shares
market timing (active asset allocation)	warrants

CONCEPTUAL QUESTIONS

22.1 List the various ways in which you might invest in foreign securities.

22.2 Do MNCs provide international portfolio diversification benefits? If so, do they provide the same diversification benefits as direct ownership of companies located in the countries in which the MNC does business?

22.3 What is the difference between a passive and an active investment philosophy?

22.4 What makes cross-border financial statement analysis difficult?

22.5 What alternatives does a MNC have when investors in a foreign country demand accounting and financial information?

22.6 You are planning for retirement and must decide on the inputs to use in your asset allocation decision. Knowing the benefits of international portfolio diversification, you want to include foreign stocks and bonds in your final portfolio. What statistics should you collect on the world's major national debt and equity markets? Can you trust that the future will be like the past?

22.7 Which portfolio has the most to gain from currency hedging—a portfolio of international stocks or a portfolio of international bonds? Why?

PROBLEMS

22.1 You are a U.S.-based investor evaluating a closed-end country fund called Korea Foods. Korea Foods' sole assets are the following three South Korean investments:

	Share price (Millions of won)	Shares held by Korea Foods	Portfolio weight
Chop Chae Corporation	8,000	1,000,000	1/2
Bulgogi Business Machines, Inc.	4,000	1,000,000	1/4
Yuk Gae Jong International Corp.	8,000	500,000	1/4

The current spot exchange rate is W800/$. The fund sells for $22 per share on the NYSE. There are one million shares outstanding.

a. What is the net asset value (NAV) of this fund in South Korean won?

b. What is the NAV in U.S. dollars?

c. Is this a good investment?

22.2 A portfolio manager gathers monthly stock returns going back to the year 1901 and estimates mean returns, variances, and cross-market correlations for 50 countries. She identifies the efficient frontier (that is, the set of mean-variance efficient combinations of the national markets) and then invests in the portfolio that is mean-variance efficient relative to the U.S. risk-free rate. Is this fund manager's performance over the coming year likely to be similar to the historical record? Over the next five years? Over the next ten years? Explain.

22.3 There is a continuing debate in the United States over whether hedge funds should be more closely regulated or required to report their holdings and investment performance to the public. Search your library for recent articles discussing the pros and cons of hedge fund regulation. Answer the following questions after researching this issue:
a. Do you think hedge funds should be more closely regulated?
b. Should hedge funds be required to report their holdings and investment performance to the Securities and Exchange Commission?

Suggested Readings

Articles that examine various investment vehicles for diversifying internationally include

Warren Bailey and Joseph Lim, "Evaluating the Diversification Benefits of the New Country Funds," *Journal of Portfolio Management* 18 (Spring 1992), pp. 74–80.

Vihang Errunza, Ked Hogan, and Mao-Wei Hung, "Can the Gains from International Diversification Be Achieved Without Trading Abroad?" *Journal of Finance* 54 (December 1999), pp. 2075–2107.

Bertrand Jacquillat and Bruno Solnik, "Multinationals Are Poor Tools for International Diversification," *Journal of Portfolio Management* 4 (Winter 1993), pp. 65–74.

Philippe Jorion and Leonid Roisenberg, "Synthetic International Diversification: The Case for Diversifying with Stock Index Futures," *Journal of Portfolio Management* 19 (Winter 1993), pp. 65–74.

Michael S. Rozeff, "Closed-End Fund Discounts and Premiums," *Pacific-Basin Capital Markets Research* II (1991), pp. 503–522.

Articles that investigate the causes of closed-end country fund (CECF) premiums to net asset value include

Warren Bailey, Y. Peter Chung, and Jun-Koo Kang, "Foreign Ownership Restrictions and Equity Price Premiums: What Drives the Demand for Cross-Border Investments?" *Journal of Financial and Quantitative Analysis* 34 (December 1999), pp. 489–511.

James N. Bodurtha, Dong-Soon Kim, and Charles Lee, "Closed-End Country Funds and U.S. Market Sentiment," *Review of Financial Studies* 8 (Fall 1995), pp. 879–918.

Catherine Bonser-Neal, Greggory Brauer, Robert Neal, and Simon Wheatley, "International Investment Restrictions and Closed-End Country Fund Prices," *Journal of Finance* 45 (June 1990), pp. 523–548.

Cheol Eun and S. Janakiramanan, "A Model of International Asset Pricing with a Constraint on the Foreign Equity Ownership," *Journal of Finance* 41 (September 1986), pp. 897–914.

Charles Lee, Andrei Shleifer, and Richard Thaler, "Investor Sentiment and the Closed-End Fund Puzzle," *Journal of Finance* 46 (March 1991), pp. 75–110.

Articles that review the performance of market timing and security selection across domestic and/or international markets include

Connie Becker, Wayne Ferson, David H. Myers, and Michael J. Schill, "Conditional Market Timing with Benchmark Investors," *Journal of Financial Economics* 52 (April 1999), pp. 119–148.

Stephen J. Brown and William N. Goetzmann, "Mutual Fund Styles," *Journal of Financial Economics* 43 (March 1997), pp. 373–399.

Kirt C. Butler, Dale L. Domian, and Richard R. Simonds, "International Portfolio Diversification and the Magnitude of the Market Timer's Penalty," *Journal of International Financial Management and Accounting* 6 (Winter 1995), pp. 193–206.

William N. Goetzmann, Jonathan Ingersoll, Jr., and Zoran Ivkovic, "Monthly Measurement of Daily Timers," *Journal of Financial and Quantitative Analysis* 35 (September 2000), pp. 257–290.

Cheng-Few Lee and Shafiqur Rahman, "Market Timing, Selectivity, and Mutual Fund Performance: An Empirical Investigation," *Journal of Business* 63 (April 1990), pp. 261–278.

William F. Sharpe, "Are Gains Likely from Market Timing?" *Financial Analysts Journal* 31 (March/April 1975), pp. 60–69.

William F. Sharpe, "Asset Allocation: Management Style and Performance Measurement," *Journal of Portfolio Management* 18 (Winter 1992), pp. 7–19.

International accounting measurement and disclosure practices and their impact on earnings predictability is investigated in

Hollis Ashbaugh and Morton Pincus, "Domestic Accounting Standards, International Accounting Standards, and Predictability of Earnings," *Journal of Accounting Research* 39 (December 2001), pp. 417–434.

The literature on time-varying expected returns, volatilities, and covariances and on the international transmission of stock market prices tends to be rather technical.

Kirt C. Butler and Domingo Castelo Joaquin, "Are the Gains from International Portfolio Diversification Exaggerated? The Influence of Downside Risk in Bear Markets," *Journal of International Money and Finance* (December 2002).

Eugene F. Fama and Kenneth R. French, "Business Conditions and Expected Returns on Stocks and Bonds," *Journal of Financial Economics* 25 (November 1989), pp. 23–50.

Jonathan Lewellen, "The Time-Series Relations Among Expected Return, Risk, and Book-to-Market," *Journal of Financial Economics* 54 (October 1999), pp. 5–43.

Weng-Ling Lin, Robert F. Engle, and Takatoshi Ito, "Do Bulls and Bears Move Across Borders? International Transmission of Stock Returns and Volatility," *Review of Financial Studies* 7 (Fall 1994), pp. 507–538.

Richard Roll, "The International Crash of October 1987," *Financial Analysts Journal* 44 (September/October 1988), pp. 19–35.

Articles that discuss currency hedging of internationally diversified portfolios include

Michael Adler and Philippe Jorion, "Universal Currency Hedges for Global Portfolios," *Journal of Portfolio Management* 18 (Summer 1992), pp. 28–35.

Jack D. Glen and Philippe Jorion, "Currency Hedging for International Portfolios," *Journal of Finance* 48 (December 1993), pp. 1865–1887.

Philippe Jorion, "Asset Allocation with Hedged and Unhedged Foreign Stocks and Bonds," *Journal of Portfolio Management* 15 (Summer 1989), pp. 49–54.

Appendix 22-A

Keeping Track of an International Investment Portfolio

It is difficult to track the value of a portfolio of international investments because of exchange rate translation. Nevertheless, it's not too onerous.

In answering the following exercise, note that the meanings of decimal points and commas are reversed in the United States and continental Europe. For example, "one thousand" is written "1.000" in Europe and "1,000" in the United States. "One and a quarter" is written "1,25" in Europe and "1.25" in the United States. Accounts can appear odd when stated from someone else's perspective.

Here's an exercise that illustrates the issues involved in tracking an international portfolio of stocks, bonds, and cash.

PROBLEM

22A.1 Frau Gatti's beginning-of-year account balances with her Zurich bank are shown here. (Note the Swiss convention for commas and periods. For example, "one thousand shares" is written "1.000 shares" and "twelve and three-tenths percent" is written "12,3 percent" in this statement.)

Gnomes of Zurich Bank—Account of Frau Gatti

1 Jan., 200x

Security (dividend yield or interest rate)	Number of shares or par value	Local price (local)	Capital amount (local)	Dividends or accrued interest (local)	Spot rate (SF/f)	Capital amount (SF)	Div or accr int (SF)	Market value (SF)	Sub-totals %
Equities									
Foster's Ltd. (1,6%)	1.000 shs	692	A$692.000	A$11.072	SF0,836/A$	SF578.512	SF9.256	SF587.768	12,3
Mazda Motors (0,0%)	50.000 shs	380	¥19.000.000	¥0	SF0,01315/¥	SF249.850	SF0	SF249.850	5,2
General Motors (2,4%)	2.000 shs	52¹⁄₂	$105.000	$2.520	SF1,168/$	SF122.640	SF2.943	SF125.583	2,6
Bonds									
French Gov (6% 2007)	1.000.000	89,00	€890.000	€60.000	SF1,550/€	SF1.379.500	SF93.000	SF1.472.500	30,8
Australian Gov (6.875% 2008)	1.000.000	100,95	A$1.009.500	A$68.750	SF0,836/A$	SF843.942	SF57.475	SF901.417	18,9
U.S. Gov (6.5% 2008)	1.000.000	102,08	$1.020.800	$65.000	SF1,168/$	SF1.192.294	SF75.920	SF1.268.214	26,6
Cash									
Swiss Francs (1,5%)	SF168.000		SF168.000	SF2.520		SF168.000	SF2.520	SF170.520	3,6
Total						SF4.534.738	SF241.115	SF4.775.853	100,0

Beginning cash balance	SF168.000
Deduct divs & accrued int (SF)	(SF241.115)
Add to cash balance (SF)	+SF241.115
Ending cash (SF)	SF409.115

Given the following end-of-year figures, compute the returns that Frau Gatti has earned on her various investments including dividends and accrued interest. Note that the Swiss money market interest rate has fallen to 1.4 percent per year.

Gnomes of Zurich Bank—Account of Frau Gatti

31 Dec., 200x

Security (dividend yield or interest rate)	Number of shares or par value	Local price (local)	Capital amount (local)	Dividends or accrued interest (local)	Spot rate (SF/f)	Capital amount (SF)	Div or accr int (SF)	Market value (SF)	Sub-totals %
Equities									
Foster's Ltd. (1,6%)	1.000 shs	704			SF0,842/A$				
Mazda Motors (0,0%)	50.000 shs	372			SF0,01152/¥				
General Motors (2,4%)	2.000 shs	58¼			SF1,204/$				
Bonds									
French Gov (6% 2007)	1.000.000	90,20			SF1,560/				
Australian Gov (6.875% 2008)	1.000.000	101,05			SF0,842/A$				
U.S. Gov (6.5% 2008)	1.000.000	102,42			SF1,204/$				
Cash									
Swiss Francs (1,5%)	SF409.115		SF409.115						
Total									

Beginning cash balance	SF409.115	
Deduct divs & accrued int (SF)		(SF)
Add to cash balance (SF)	+SF	
Ending cash balance (SF)	SF	

Glossary

A

Accounting (translation) exposure: Changes in a corporation's financial statements as a result of changes in currency values. (Contrast with *economic exposure*.)

Acquisition: Acquiring control of an asset through purchase of the asset or the equity that controls the asset.

Acquisition of assets: In an acquisition of assets, one firm acquires the assets of another company. None of the liabilities supporting that asset are transferred to the purchaser.

Acquisition of stock: In an acquisition of stock, one firm buys an equity interest in another.

Acquisition premium: In a merger or acquisition, the difference between the purchase price and the preacquisition value of the target firm.

Active fund management: An investment approach that actively shifts funds either between asset classes (asset allocation) or between individual securities (security selection).

Active income: In the U.S. tax code, income from an active business as opposed to passive investment income.

Active security selection: An investment strategy that attempts to identify individual securities that are underpriced relative to other securities in a particular market or industry.

Adjusted present value: A valuation method that separately identifies the value of an unlevered project from the value of financing side effects.

Agency costs: The costs of monitoring management and ensuring that it acts in the best interest of other stakeholders.

Agent: Someone who represents another. In corporate governance terminology, management is the agent of the principal stakeholders in a principal-agent relationship.

All-in cost: The percentage cost of a financing alternative, including any placement fees.

Allocation-of-income rules: Rules that define how income and deductions are to be allocated between domestic-source and foreign-source income.

Allocational efficiency: The efficiency with which a market channels capital toward its most productive uses.

American depository receipt: A derivative security issued by a non-U.S. borrower through a U.S. trustee representing ownership in the deposit of non-U.S. shares held by the trustee.

American option: An option that can be exercised anytime until expiration. (Contrast with *European option*.)

American shares: Shares of a foreign corporation issued directly to U.S. investors through a transfer agent in accordance with SEC regulations.

American terms: A foreign exchange quotation that states the U.S. dollar price per foreign currency unit. (Contrast with *European terms*.)

Andean Pact: A regional trade pact that includes Venezuela, Colombia, Ecuador, Peru, and Bolivia.

Appreciation: An increase in a currency value relative to another currency in a floating exchange rate system.

Arbitrage: Simultaneous purchase and sale of the same or equivalent security in order to ensure a profit with no net investment or risk.

Arbitrage Pricing Theory (APT): An asset pricing model that assumes a linear relation between required return and systematic risk as measured by one or more factors according to $r_j = \mu_j + \beta_{1j}F_1 + ... + \beta_{Kj}F_K + e_j$.

Arbitrage profit: Profit obtained through arbitrage.

Arms-length pricing: Prices that would be negotiated between independent parties. Arms-length transfer prices are required by Section 486 of the U.S. Internal Revenue Code, Article 9 of the OECD Model Tax Convention, and other national and international tax standards.

Asia-Pacific Economic Cooperation Pact (APEC): A loose economic affiliation of Southeast Asian and Far Eastern nations. The most prominent members are China, Japan, and Korea.

Ask (offer) rates: The rate at which a market maker is willing to sell the quoted asset.

Asset allocation policy: The target weights given to various asset classes in an investment portfolio.

Assets-in-place: Those assets in which the firm has already invested. (Compare to *growth options*.)

Association of Southeast Asian Nations (ASEAN): A loose economic and geopolitical affiliation that includes Singapore, Brunei, Malaysia, Thailand, the Philippines, Indonesia, and Vietnam. Future members are likely to include Burma, Laos, and Cambodia.

At-the-money option: An option with an exercise price that is equal to the current value of the underlying asset.

B

Balance-of-payments (BoP) statistics: The International Money Fund's accounting system that tracks the flow of goods, services, and capital in and out of each country.

Bank-based corporate governance system: A system of corporate governance in which the supervisory board is dominated by bankers through their equity ownership in the firm.

Banker's acceptance: A time draft drawn on and accepted by a commercial bank.

Basis: The simple difference between two nominal interest rates.

Basis point: Equal to 1/100 of one percent.

Basis risk: The risk of unexpected change in the relationship between futures and spot prices.

Basis swap: A floating-for-floating interest rate swap that pairs two floating rate instruments at different maturities (such as 6-month LIBOR versus 30-day U.S. T-bills).

Bearer bonds: Bonds that can be redeemed by the holder. The convention in most West European countries is to issue bonds in registered form. (Contrast with *registered bonds*.)

Behavioral finance: The study of the impact of psychological factors on investor behavior and asset prices.

Beta (β): A measure of an asset's sensitivity to changes in the market portfolio (in the CAPM) or to a factor (in the APT). The beta of an asset j is computed as $\beta_j = \rho_{j,k} (\sigma_j/\sigma_k)$, where k represents a market factor (such as returns to the market portfolio in the *capital asset pricing model*).

Bid rate: The rate at which a market maker is willing to buy the quoted asset.

Bid-ask spread: The dealer's profit margin on currency transactions, equal to the ask price minus bid price.

Blocked funds: Cash flows generated by a foreign project that cannot be immediately repatriated to the parent firm because of capital flow restrictions imposed by the host government.

Bond equivalent yield: A bond quotation convention based on a 365-day year and semiannual coupons. (Contrast with *effective annual yield*.)

Bretton Woods Conference: An international conference held in 1944 at Bretton Woods, New Hampshire, that established the International Monetary Fund and the World Bank.

Business risk: The risks of operating cash flows.

C

Call option: The right to buy the underlying currency at a specified price and on a specified date.

Capital account: A measure of change in cross-border ownership of long-term financial assets, including financial securities and real estate.

Capital asset pricing model (CAPM): An asset pricing model that relates the required return on an asset to its systematic risk.

Capital market line: The line between the risk-free asset and the market portfolio that represents the mean-variance efficient set of investment opportunities in the CAPM.

Capital markets: Markets for financial assets and liabilities with maturity greater than one year, including long-term government and corporate bonds, preferred stock, and common stock.

Capital (financial) structure: The proportion of debt and equity and the particular forms of debt and equity chosen to finance the assets of the firm.

Cash in advance: Payment for goods prior to shipment.

Chaebol: A Korean business conglomerate, sometimes controlled by a single family.

CHIPS (Clearing House Interbank Payments System): Financial network through which banks in the United States conduct their financial transactions.

Closed-end fund: A mutual fund in which the amount of funds under management is fixed and ownership in the funds is bought and sold in the market like a depository receipt.

Commodity price risk: The risk of unexpected changes in a commodity price, such as the price of oil.

Commodity swap: A swap in which the (often notional) principal amount on at least one side of the swap is a commodity such as oil or gold.

Comparable uncontrolled price: A transfer pricing method based on independent market transactions.

Comparative advantage: The rule of economics that states that each country should specialize in producing those goods that it is able to produce relatively most efficiently.

Compound option: An option on an option.

Consolidated income: The sum of income across all of the multinational corporation's domestic and foreign subsidiaries.

Consolidation: A form of corporate reorganization in which two firms pool their assets and liabilities to form a new company.

Continuous quotation system: A trading system in which buy and sell orders are matched with market makers as the orders arrive, ensuring liquidity in individual shares.

Controlled foreign corporation (CFC): In the U.S. tax code, a foreign corporation owned more than 50 percent either in terms of market value or voting power.

Convertible bonds: Bonds sold with a conversion feature that allows the holder to convert the bond into common stock on or prior to a conversion date and at a prespecified conversion price.

Convex tax schedule: A tax schedule in which the effective tax rate is greater at high levels of taxable income than at low levels of taxable income. Such a schedule results in progressive taxation.

Copyright: A government-approved protection against the unauthorized reproduction of creative works, such as books, paintings, video recordings, and computer software.

Corporate governance: The way in which major stakeholders exert control over the modern corporation.

Correlation: A measure of the comovement of two assets that is scaled for the standard deviations of the assets ($\rho_{AB} = \sigma_{AB}/\sigma_A\sigma_B$ such that $-1 < \rho_{AB} < +1$).

Cost plus: The most common transfer pricing method, based on cost plus a profit margin.

Costs of financial distress: Costs associated with financial distress, including direct costs such as court costs and attorney fees incurred during bankruptcy or liquidation and indirect costs incurred prior to formal bankruptcy or liquidation.

Countertrade: Exchange of goods or services without the use of cash.

Country risk: The political and financial risks of conducting business in a particular foreign country.

Coupon swap: A fixed-for-floating interest rate swap.

Covariance: A measure of the comovement of two assets ($\sigma_{AB} = \sigma_A\sigma_B\,\rho_{AB}$).

Covered interest arbitrage: Arbitrage that takes advantage of a disequilibrium in interest rate parity.

Cross exchange rates (cross rates): Exchange rates that do not involve the domestic currency.

Cross hedge: A futures hedge using a currency that is different from, but closely related to, the currency of the underlying exposure.

Cumulative translation adjustment (CTA): An equity account under FAS #52 that accumulates gains or losses caused by translation accounting adjustments.

Currency coupon swap: A fixed-for-floating rate nonamortizing currency swap traded primarily through international commercial banks.

Currency of reference: The currency that is being bought or sold. It is most convenient to place the currency of reference in the denominator of a foreign exchange quote (see Rule #2 in Chapter 4).

Currency option: A contract giving the option holder the right to buy or sell an underlying currency at a specified price and on a specified date. The option writer (seller) holds the obligation to fulfill the other side of the contract.

Currency (foreign exchange) risk: The risk of unexpected changes in foreign currency exchange rates.

Currency swap: A contractual agreement to exchange a principal amount of two different currencies and, after a prearranged length of time, to give back the original principal. Interest payments in each currency are also typically swapped during the life of the agreement.

Current account: A measure of a country's international trade in goods and services.

Current account balance: A broad measure of import-export activity that includes services, travel and tourism, transportation, investment income and interest, gifts, and grants along with the trade balance on goods.

Current rate method: A translation accounting method, such as FAS #52 in the United States, that translates monetary and real assets and monetary liabilities at current exchange rates. FSA #52 places any imbalance into an equity account called the "cumulative translation adjustment."

Current/noncurrent method: A translation accounting method that translates current assets and liabilities at current exchange rates and all other accounts at historical rates.

D

Day count: The day count defines the way in which interest accrues on a bond.

Dealing desk (trading desk): The desk at an international bank that trades spot and forward foreign exchange.

Debt capacity: The amount of debt that a firm chooses to borrow to support a project.

Debt-for-equity swap: A swap agreement to exchange equity returns for debt returns over a prearranged length of time.

Decision trees: A graphical analysis of sequential decisions and the likely outcomes of those decisions.

Deliverable instrument: The asset underlying a derivative security. For a currency option, the deliverable instrument is determined by the options exchange and is either spot currency or an equivalent value in futures contracts.

Delta-cross hedge: A futures hedge that has both currency and maturity mismatches with the underlying exposure.

Delta hedge: A futures hedge using a currency that matches the underlying exposure and a maturity date that is different from, but preferably close to, the maturity of the underlying exposure.

Depository receipt: A derivative security issued by a foreign borrower through a domestic trustee representing ownership in the deposit of foreign shares held by the trustee.

Depreciation: A decrease in a currency value relative to another currency in a floating exchange rate system.

Derivative security: A financial security whose price is derived from the price of another asset.

Devaluation: A decrease in a currency value relative to another currency in a fixed exchange rate system.

Difference check: The difference in interest payments that is exchanged between two swap counterparties.

Direct costs of financial distress: Costs of financial distress that are directly incurred during bankruptcy or liquidation proceedings.

Direct terms: The price of a unit of foreign currency in domestic currency terms, such as $1.10/€ for a U.S. resident. (Contrast with *indirect quote.*)

Discounted cash flow: A valuation methodology that discounts expected future cash flows at a discount rate appropriate for the risk, currency, and maturity of the cash flows.

Discounted payback: The length of time needed to recoup the present value of an investment; sometimes used when investing in locations with high country risk.

Discounting: A form of factoring in which a trade acceptance is sold at a discount to face value.

Discretionary reserves: Balance sheet accounts that are used in some countries to temporarily store earnings from the current year or the recent past.

Diversification discount: Diversified (both industrially and globally) firms usually sell at a discount to portfolios of single-segment firms operating in the same industries.

Domestic bonds: Bonds issued and traded within the internal market of a single country and denominated in the currency of that country.

Domestic International Sales Corporation: In the U.S. tax code, a specialized sales corporation whose income is lumped into the same income basket as a foreign sales corporation.

Draft (trade bill, bill of exchange): A means of payment whereby a drawer (the importer) instructs a drawee (either the importer or its commercial bank) to pay the payee (the exporter).

E

Earnings response coefficient: The relation of stock returns to earnings surprises around the time of corporate earnings announcements.

Eclectic paradigm: A theory of the multinational firm that posits three types of advantage benefiting the multinational corporation: ownership-specific, location-specific, and market internalization advantages.

Economic exposure: Change in the value of a corporation's assets or liabilities as a result of changes in currency values.

Economic value added: A method of performance evaluation that adjusts accounting performance with a charge reflecting investors' required return on investment.

Economies of scale: Achieving lower average cost per unit through a larger scale of production.

Economies of vertical integration: Achieving lower operating costs by bringing the entire production chain within the firm rather than contracting through the marketplace.

Effective annual yield: Calculated as $(1+i/n)^n$, where i is the stated annual interest rate and n is the number of compounding periods per year. (Contrast with *bond equivalent yield* and *money market yield*.)

Efficient frontier: The mean-variance efficient portion of the investment opportunity set.

Efficient market: A market in which prices reflect all relevant information.

Efficient market hypothesis: A supposition that a market is informationally efficient.

Emerging stock markets: The stock markets of emerging economies. These markets typically have higher expected returns than established markets but also higher risk.

Endogenous uncertainty: Price or input cost uncertainty that is within the control of the firm, such as when the act of investing reveals information about price or input cost.

Equity-linked Eurobonds: A Eurobond with a convertibility option or warrant attached.

Euro Interbank Offered Rate (Euribor): The offer rate on euro-denominated term deposits between major banks within the euro zone.

Eurobonds: Bonds that trade in external markets; that is, outside the borders of the country in which the bond is denominated.

Eurocurrencies: Deposits and loans denominated in one currency and traded in a market outside the borders of the country issuing that currency (e.g., Eurodollars).

Eurodollars: Dollar-denominated deposits held in a country other than the United States.

Euroequity (or global equity) issues: Equity issues offered directly to investors in international markets.

European currency unit (ECU): A trade-weighted basket of currencies in the European Exchange Rate Mechanism (ERM) of the European Union.

European exchange rate mechanism (ERM): The exchange rate system used by countries in the European Union in which exchange rates were pegged within bands around an ERM central value.

European Monetary System (EMS): An exchange rate system based on cooperation between European Union central banks.

European option: An option that can be exercised only at expiration. (Contrast with *American option*.)

European terms: A foreign exchange quotation that states the foreign currency price of one U.S. dollar. (Contrast with *American terms*.)

European Union (EU): Formerly the European Economic Community, a regional trade pact that includes Belgium, France, Germany, Italy, the Netherlands, Portugal, Spain, and the United Kingdom (England, Wales, Northern Ireland, and Scotland).

Exercise price: The price at which an option can be exercised (also called the *striking price*).

Exogenous uncertainty: Price or input cost uncertainty that is outside the control of the firm.

Expiration date: The date on which an option (such as a currency call option) expires.

Explicit tax: A tax that is explicitly collected by a government; includes income, withholding, property, sales, and value-added taxes and tariffs.

Export: An entry mode into international markets that relies on domestic production and shipments to foreign markets through sales agents or distributors, foreign sales branches, or foreign sales subsidiaries.

Export financing interest: In the U.S. tax code, interest income derived from goods manufactured in the United States and sold outside the United States as long as not more than 50 percent of the value is imported into the United States.

Export management company: A foreign or domestic company that acts as a sales agent and distributor for domestic exporters in international markets.

Expropriation: A specific type of political risk in which a government seizes foreign assets.

External market: A market for financial securities that are placed outside the borders of the country issuing that currency.

F

Factor model: A model that assumes a linear relation between an asset's expected return and one or more systematic risk factors.

Factoring: Sale of an accounts receivable balance to buyers (factors) that are willing and able to bear the costs and risks of credit and collections.

Financial engineering: The process of innovation by which new financial products are created.

Financial innovation: The process of designing new financial products, such as exotic currency options and swaps.

Financial markets: Markets for financial assets and liabilities.

Financial policy: The corporation's choices regarding the debt-equity mix, currencies of denomination, maturity structure, method of financing investment projects, and hedging decisions with a goal of maximizing the value of the firm to some set of stakeholders.

Financial price risk: The risk of unexpected changes in a financial price, including currency (foreign exchange) risk, interest rate risk, and commodity price risk.

Financial risk: Financial risk refers to unexpected events in a country's financial, economic, or business life.

Financial service income: In the U.S. tax code, income derived from financial services such as banking, insurance, leasing, financial service management fees, and swap income.

Financial (capital) structure: The proportion of debt and equity and the particular forms of debt and equity chosen to finance the assets of the firm.

Financial strategy: The way in which the firm pursues its financial objectives.

Fixed exchange rate system: An exchange rate system in which a government maintains an official exchange rate.

Floating exchange rate system: An exchange rate system in which currency values are allowed to fluctuate according to supply and demand forces in the market without direct interference by government authorities.

Foreign base company income: In the U.S. tax code, a category of Subpart F income that includes foreign holding company income and foreign base company sales and service income.

Foreign bonds: Bonds that are issued in a domestic market by a foreign borrower, denominated in domestic currency, marketed to domestic residents, and regulated by the domestic authorities.

Foreign branch: A foreign affiliate that is legally a part of the parent firm. In the U.S. tax code, foreign branch income is taxed as it is earned in the foreign country.

Foreign direct investment (FDI): The act of building productive capacity directly in a foreign country.

Foreign exchange broker: Brokers serving as matchmakers in the foreign exchange market that do not put their own money at risk.

Foreign exchange dealer: A financial institution making a market in foreign exchange.

Foreign exchange (currency) risk: The risk of unexpected changes in foreign currency exchange rates.

Foreign sales corporation (FSC): In the U.S. tax code, a specialized sales corporation whose income is lumped into the same income basket as that of a domestic international sales corporation.

Foreign shares: Shares of a foreign corporation issued directly to domestic investors through a transfer agent in accordance with local (domestic) regulations.

Foreign-source income: Income earned from foreign operations.

Foreign tax credit (FTC): In the U.S. tax code, a credit against domestic U.S. income taxes up to the amount of foreign taxes paid on foreign-source income.

Forfaiting: A form of factoring in which large, medium- to long-term receivables are sold to buyers (forfaiters) that are willing and able to bear the costs and risks of credit and collections.

Forward contract: A commitment to exchange a specified amount of one currency for a specified amount of another currency on a specified future date.

Forward discount: A currency whose nominal value in the forward market is lower than in the spot market. (Contrast with *forward premium*.)

Forward market: A market for forward contracts in which trades are made for future delivery according to an agreed-upon delivery date, exchange rate, and amount.

Forward parity: When the forward exchange rate is an unbiased predictor of future spot rates.

Forward premium: A currency whose nominal value in the forward market is higher than in the spot market. (Contrast with *forward discount*.)

Forward premium anomaly: The widespread empirical finding that the slope coefficient in a regression of the change in the spot exchange rate on the forward premium is less than unity (as suggested by forward parity), and is often negative.

Franchise agreement: An agreement in which a domestic company (the franchisor) licenses its trade name or business system to an independent company (the franchisee) in a foreign market.

Free cash flow: Cash flow after all positive-NPV projects have been exhausted in the firm's main line of business.

Free float (or float): Shares available for trade. Free float capitalization based on available shares differs from market capitalization based on issued shares when controlling shareholders (such as a founding family) do not trade their shares.

Freight shippers (freight forwarders): Agents used to coordinate the logistics of transportation.

Fundamental analysis: A method of predicting exchange rates using the relationships of exchange rates to fundamental economic variables such as GNP growth, money supply, and trade balances.

Futures commission merchant: A brokerage house that is authorized by a futures exchange to trade with retail clients.

Futures contract: A commitment to exchange a specified amount of one currency for a specified amount of another currency at a specified time in the future. Futures contracts are periodically marked to market, so that changes in value are settled throughout the life of the contract.

G

General Agreement on Tariffs and Trade (GATT): A worldwide trade agreement designed to reduce tariffs, protect intellectual property, and set up a dispute resolution system. The agreement is overseen by the World Trade Organization (WTO).

Generalized autoregressive conditional heteroskedasticity (GARCH): A time series model in which returns at each instant of time are normally distributed but volatility is a function of recent history of the series.

Global bond: A bond that trades in the Eurobond market as well as in one or more national bond markets.

Global depository receipt: A depository receipt that trades in more than one foreign market.

Global share: A foreign share that trades in more than one foreign market.

Gold exchange standard: An exchange rate system used from 1925 to 1931 in which the United States and England were allowed to hold only gold reserves while other nations could hold gold, U.S. dollars, or pounds sterling as reserves.

Gold standard: An exchange rate system used prior to 1914 in which gold was used to settle national trade balances. Also called the "classical gold standard."

Goodwill: The accounting treatment of an intangible asset such as the takeover premium in a merger or acquisition.

Greenmail: Buying shares on the open market in the hope that the target's business partners will buy back the shares at inflated prices.

Growth options: The positive-NPV opportunities in which the firm has not yet invested. The value of growth options reflects the time value of the firm's current investment in real assets as well as the option value of the firm's potential future investments.

Growth stocks: Stocks with high equity price/book or price/earnings ratios.

H

Hedge: A position or operation that offsets an underlying exposure. For example, a forward currency hedge uses a forward currency contract to offset the exposure of an underlying position in a foreign currency. Hedges reduce the total variability of the combined position.

Hedge funds: Private investment partnerships with a general manager and a small number of limited partners.

Hedge portfolio: The country-specific hedge portfolio in the international asset pricing model serves as a store of value (like the risk-free asset in the CAPM) as well as a hedge against the currency risk of the market portfolio.

Hedge quality: Measured by the r-square in a regression of spot rate changes on futures price changes.

Hedge ratio: The ratio of derivatives contracts to the underlying risk exposure.

Home asset bias: The tendency of investors to over-invest in assets based in their own country.

High-withholding-tax interest income: In the U.S. tax code, interest income that has been subject to a foreign gross withholding tax of 5 percent or more.

Historical volatility: Volatility estimated from a historical time series.

Horizontal keiretsu (kinyû): Japanese industrial groups, typically centered on a main bank and featuring extensive share cross-holdings between firms in different industries.

Hysteresis: The behavior of firms that fail to enter markets that appear attractive and, once invested, persist in operating at a loss. This behavior is characteristic of situations with high entry and exit costs along with high uncertainty.

I

Implicit tax: Lower (higher) before-tax required returns on assets that are subject to lower (higher) tax rates.

Implied volatility: The volatility that is implied by an option value given the other determinants of option value.

Income baskets: In the U.S. tax code, income is allocated to one of a number of separate income categories. Losses in one basket may not be used to offset gains in another basket.

Index futures: A futures contract that allows investors to buy or sell an index (such as a foreign stock index) in the futures market.

Index option: A call or put option contract on an index (such as a foreign stock market index).

Index swap: A swap of a market index for some other asset (such as a stock-for-stock or debt-for-stock swap).

Indirect costs of financial distress: Costs of financial distress that are indirectly incurred prior to formal bankruptcy or liquidation.

Indirect diversification benefits: Diversification benefits provided by the multinational corporation that are not available to investors through their portfolio investment.

Indirect terms: The price of a unit of domestic currency in foreign currency terms such as €0.9091/$ for a U.S. resident. (Contrast with *direct terms.*)

Informational efficiency: Whether or not market prices reflect information and thus the true (or intrinsic) value of the underlying asset.

Integrated financial market: A market in which there are no barriers to financial flows and purchasing power parity holds across equivalent assets.

Intellectual property rights: Patents, copyrights, and proprietary technologies and processes that are the basis of the multinational corporation's competitive advantage over local firms.

Interbank spread: The difference between a bank's offer and bid rates for deposits in the Eurocurrency market.

Interest rate parity: The forward premium or discount between two currencies is determined by the nominal interest rate differential between those currencies.

Interest rate risk: The risk of unexpected changes in an interest rate.

Interest rate swap: An agreement to exchange interest payments for a specific period of time on a given principal amount. The most common interest rate swap is a fixed-for-floating coupon swap. The notional principal is typically not exchanged.

Intermediated market: A financial market in which a financial institution (usually a commercial bank) stands between borrowers and savers.

Internal market: A market for financial securities that are denominated in the currency of a host country and placed within that country.

International asset pricing model (IAPM): The international version of the CAPM in which investors in each country share the same consumption basket and purchasing power parity holds.

International Bank for Reconstruction and Development: Also called the World Bank, an international organization created at Bretton Woods in 1944 to help in the reconstruction and development of its member nations.

International bonds: Bonds that are traded outside the country of the issuer. International bonds are either foreign bonds trading in a foreign national market or Eurobonds trading in the international market.

International Fisher relation: The nominal interests rate i is related to the real (or inflation-adjusted) interest rate ι and inflation rate p according to $(1+i) = (1+ι)(1+p)$.

International Monetary Fund (IMF): An international organization that compiles statistics on cross-border transactions and publishes a monthly summary of each country's balance of payments.

International monetary system: The global network of governmental and commercial institutions within which currency exchange rates are determined.

International parity conditions: Fundamental macroeconomic relations that link spot and forward exchange rates, Eurocurrency interest rates, and inflation.

In-the-money option: An option that has value if exercised immediately.

Intrinsic value of an option: The value of an option if exercised immediately.

Investment agreement: An agreement specifying the rights and responsibilities of a host government and a corporation in the structure and operation of an investment project.

Investment opportunity set: The set of possible investments available to an individual or corporation.

Investment philosophy: The investment approach—active or passive—pursued by an investment fund and its managers.

Investment Securities Directive (ISD): The so-called European "passport" that allows investment services companies based in EU member states to operate in other EU countries so long as they have the approval of regulatory authorities in their home country.

Irrelevance proposition: The proposition (following Miller-Modigliani) that corporate financial policy is irrelevant if financial markets are perfect. The corollary is: If financial policy is to increase firm value, then it must either increase the firm's expected future cash flows or decrease the discount rate.

J

Joint venture: An agreement of two or more companies to pool their resources to execute a well-defined mission. Resource commitments, responsibilities, and earnings are shared according to a predetermined contractual formula.

K

Keiretsu: Collaborative groups of vertically or horizontally integrated firms with extensive share cross-holdings. Horizontal keiretsu have a major Japanese bank or corporation at the center.

Kurtosis: Kurtosis is a measure of the size or probability mass of a distribution's tails. Distributions with fat tails relative to the normal distribution are said to be leptokurtic. Thin-tailed distributions are called platykurtic. Most assets have return distributions that are leptokurtic.

L

Law of one price (purchasing power parity): The principle that equivalent assets sell for the same price. The law of one price is enforced in the currency markets by financial market arbitrage.

Lead manager: The lead investment bank in a syndicate selling a public securities offering.

Leading and lagging: Reduction of transaction exposure through timing of cash flows within the corporation.

Less developed country (LDC): A country that has not yet reached the level of industrial organization attained by developed countries.

Letter of credit (L/C): A letter issued by an importer's bank guaranteeing payment upon presentation of specified trade documents (invoice, bill of lading, inspection and insurance certificates, etc.).

Liberalization: A decision by a government to allow foreigners to purchase local assets.

License agreement: A sales agreement in which a domestic company (the licensor) allows a foreign company (the licensee) to market its products in a foreign country in return for royalties, fees, or other forms of compensation.

Liquid market: A market in which traders can buy or sell large quantities of an asset when they want and with low transactions costs.

Liquidity: The ease with which an asset can be exchanged for another asset of equal value.

Loanable funds: The pool of funds from which borrowers can attract capital; typically categorized by currency and maturity.

Locational arbitrage: Arbitrage conducted between two or more locations.

Location-specific advantages: Advantages (natural and created) that are available only or primarily in a single location.

London Interbank Bid Rate (LIBID): The bid rate that a Euromarket bank is willing to pay to attract a deposit from another Euromarket bank in London.

London Interbank Offer Rate (LIBOR): The offer rate that a Euromarket bank demands in order to place a deposit at (or, equivalently, make a loan to) another Euromarket bank in London.

Long position: A position in which a particular asset (such as a spot or forward currency) has been purchased.

M

Macro country risks: Country (or political) risks that affect all foreign firms in a host country.

Management contract: An agreement in which a company licenses its organizational and management expertise.

Managerial flexibility: Flexibility in the timing and scale of investment provided by a real investment option.

Margin requirement: A performance bond paid upon purchase of a futures contract that ensures the exchange clearinghouse against loss.

Market-based corporate governance system: A system of corporate governance in which the supervisory board represents a dispersed set of largely equity shareholders.

Market failure: A failure of arms-length markets to efficiently complete the production of a good or service. In the eclectic paradigm, the multinational corporation's market internalization advantages take advantage of market failure.

Market internalization advantages: Advantages that allow the multinational corporation to internalize or exploit the failure of an arms-length market to efficiently accomplish a task.

Market maker: A financial institution that quotes bid (buy) and offer (sell) prices.

Market model (one-factor market model): The empirical version of the security market line: $r_j = \alpha_j + \beta_j r_M + e_j$, or $r_j = \alpha_j + \beta_j F_M + e_j$ where $F_M = (r_M - \mu_M)$.

Market portfolio: A portfolio of all assets weighted according to their market values.

Market risk premium: The risk premium on an average stock; $(E[r_M]-r_F)$.

Market timing: An investment strategy of shifting among asset classes in an attempt to anticipate which asset class(es) will appreciate or depreciate during the coming period.

Marking to market: The process by which changes in the value of futures contracts are settled.

Mean-variance efficient: An asset that has higher mean return at a given level of risk (or lower risk at a given level of return) than other assets.

Mercosur: The "common market of the South," which includes Argentina, Brazil, Paraguay, and Uruguay in a regional trade pact that reduces tariffs on intrapact trade.

Merger: A form of corporate acquisition in which one firm absorbs another and the assets and liabilities of the two firms are combined.

Method of payment: The way in which a merger or acquisition is financed. Gains to acquiring firm shareholders are related to the method of payment.

Micro country risks: Country risks that are specific to an industry, company, or project within a host country.

Ministry of Finance (MoF): The regulatory body that oversees securities regulation in Japan.

Momentum (or relative strength) strategy: An investment strategy that selectively buys or sells securities based on their recent return performance.

Monetary assets and liabilities: Assets and liabilities with contractual payoffs.

Money market hedge: A hedge that replicates a currency forward contract through the spot currency and Eurocurrency markets.

Money market yield: A bond quotation convention based on a 360-day year and semiannual coupons. (Contrast with *bond equivalent yield*.)

Money markets: Markets for financial assets and liabilities of short maturity, usually defined as less than one year.

Moral hazard: The risk that the existence of a contract will change the behaviors of parties to the contract.

Multinational corporation: A corporation with operations in more than one country.

Multinational netting: Elimination of offsetting cash flows within the multinational corporation.

N

National tax policy: The way in which a nation chooses to allocate the burdens of tax collections across its residents.

Nationalization: A process whereby privately owned companies are brought under state ownership and control. (Contrast with *privatization*.)

Negative-NPV tie-in project: A negative-NPV infrastructure development project that a local government requires of a company pursuing a positive-NPV investment project elsewhere in the economy.

Negotiable acceptance: A banker's acceptance that is (1) in writing, (2) signed by a bank representative, (3) an unconditional payment guarantee once trade documents are received, (4) a sight or time draft, and (5) payable either to order or bearer.

Net asset value (NAV): The sum of the individual asset values in a closed-end mutual fund. Closed-end funds can sell at substantial premiums or discounts to their net asset values.

Net currency exposure: Exposure to foreign exchange risk after netting all intracompany cash flows.

Net exposed assets: Exposed assets less exposed liabilities. The term is used with market values or, in translation accounting, with book values.

Net monetary assets: Monetary assets less monetary liabilities.

Net position: A currency position after aggregating and canceling all offsetting transactions in each currency and maturity.

Newly industrializing country (NIC): A country that has recently industrialized its economy. Examples include Argentina, Brazil, Mexico, Singapore, South Korea, and Taiwan. The economy is referred to as a newly industrializing economy (NIE).

No-arbitrage condition: An absence of arbitrage opportunities, so that the law of one price holds within the bounds of transactions costs.

Nonintermediated debt market: A financial market in which borrowers (governments and large corporations) appeal directly to savers for debt capital through the securities markets without using a financial institution as intermediary.

Nonmonetary assets and liabilities: Assets and liabilities with noncontractual payoffs.

North American Free Trade Agreement (NAFTA): A regional trade pact among the United States, Canada, and Mexico.

Notional principal: In a swap agreement, a principal amount that is only "notional" and is not exchanged.

O

Offer (ask) rates: The rate at which a market maker is willing to sell the quoted asset.

Offering statement: In the United States, a shortened registration statement required by the Securities and Exchange Commission on debt issues with less than a 9-month maturity.

Official settlements balance (overall balance): An overall measure of a country's private financial and economic transactions with the rest of the world.

Open account: The seller delivers the goods to the buyer and then bills the buyer according to the terms of trade.

Open-end fund: A mutual fund in which the amount of money under management grows/shrinks as investors buy/sell the fund.

Operating exposure: Changes in the value of real (nonmonetary) assets or operating cash flows as a result of changes in currency values.

Operating leverage: The trade-off between fixed and variable costs in the operation of the firm.

Operational efficiency: Market efficiency with respect to how large an influence transactions costs and other market frictions have on the operation of a market.

Opportunity set: The set of all possible investments.

Options: Contracts giving the option holder the right to buy or sell an underlying asset at a specified price and on a specified date. The option writer (seller) holds the obligation to fulfill the other side of the contract.

Out-of-the-money option: An option that has no value if exercised immediately.

Outright quote: A quote in which all of the digits of the bid and offer prices are quoted. (Contrast with *points quote*.)

Overall balance: (See *official settlements balance*.)

Overall FTC limitation: In the U.S. tax code, a limitation on the FTC equal to foreign-source income times U.S. tax on worldwide income divided by worldwide income.

Ownership-specific advantages: Property rights or intangible assets, including patents, trademarks, organizational and marketing expertise, production technology and management, and general organizational abilities, that form the basis for the multinational's advantage over local firms.

P

Parallel loan: A loan arrangement in which a company borrows in its home currency and then trades this debt for the foreign currency debt of a foreign counterparty.

Passive income: In the U.S. tax code, income (such as investment income) that does not come from active participation in a business.

Patent: A government-approved right to make, use, or sell an invention for a period of time.

Payoff profile: A graph with the value of an underlying asset on the x-axis and the value of a position taken to hedge against risk exposure on the y-axis. Also used with changes in value. (Contrast with *risk profile*.)

Pecking order: A frequently observed preference for financing assets with internally generated funds, followed in order by external debt and equity.

Pension liabilities: A recognition of future liabilities resulting from pension commitments made by the corporation. Accounting for pension liabilities varies widely by country.

Perfect market assumptions: A set of assumptions under which the law of one price holds. These assumptions include frictionless markets, rational investors, and equal access to market prices and information.

Periodic call auction: A trading system in which stocks are auctioned at intervals throughout the day.

Points quote: An abbreviated form of the outright quote used by traders in the interbank market.

Political risk: The risk that a sovereign host government will unexpectedly change the rules of the game under which businesses operate. Political risk includes both macro and micro risks.

Price elasticity of demand: The sensitivity of quantity sold to a percentage change in price; $-\%\Delta Q/\%\Delta P$.

Price uncertainty: Uncertainty regarding the future price of an asset.

Private placement: A securities issue privately placed with a small group of investors rather than through a public offering.

Privatization: A process whereby publicly owned enterprises are sold to private investors. (Contrast with *nationalization*.)

Progressive taxation: A convex tax schedule that results in a higher effective tax rate on high income levels than on low income levels.

Project financing: A way to raise nonrecourse financing for a specific project characterized by the following: (1) the project is a separate legal entity and relies heavily on debt financing and (2) the debt is contractually linked to the cash flow generated by the project.

Prospectus: A description of a mutual fund's investment objectives, strategies, and position limits.

Protectionism: Protection of local industries through tariffs, quotas, and regulations that discriminate against foreign businesses.

Public securities offering: A securities issue placed with the public through an investment or commercial bank.

Purchasing power parity (law of one price): The principle that equivalent assets sell for the same price. Purchasing power parity is enforced in the currency markets by financial market arbitrage.

Pure-play firm: A firm with the same systematic business risk and debt capacity as a project.

Put option: The right to sell the underlying asset at a specified price and on a specified date.

Put-call parity: The relation of the value of a long call, a short put, the exercise price, and the forward price at expiration; $\text{Call}_T^{d/f} - \text{Put}_T^{d/f} + K^{d/f} = F_T^{d/f}$.

R

Rainbow option: An option with multiple sources of uncertainty.

Random walk: A process in which instantaneous changes in exchange rates are normally distributed with a zero mean and constant variance.

Real appreciation/depreciation: A change in the purchasing power of a currency.

Real exchange rate: A measure of the nominal exchange rate that has been adjusted for inflation differentials since an arbitrarily defined base period.

Real interest parity: Real required returns on equivalent foreign and domestic assets are equal; $\imath^d = \imath^f$.

Real options: An option or optionlike feature embedded in a real investment opportunity.

Reciprocal marketing agreement: A strategic alliance in which two companies agree to comarket each other's products in their home market. Production rights may or may not be transferred.

Registered bonds: Bonds for which each issuer maintains a record of the owners of its bonds. Countries requiring that bonds be issued in registered form include the United States and Japan. (Contrast with *bearer bonds*.)

Registration statement: In the United States, a statement filed with the Securities and Exchange Commission on securities issues that discloses relevant information to the public.

Reinvoicing centers: An offshore financial affiliate that is used to channel funds to and from the multinational's foreign operations.

Relative purchasing power parity: Expected change in the spot exchange rate is determined by the inflation rate differential according to $E[S_1^{d/f}]/S_0^{d/f} = (1+p_d)/(1+p_f)$.

Repatriation: The act of remitting cash flows from a foreign affiliate to the parent firm.

Replicating portfolio: A portfolio that mimics the payoffs on an option. Replicating portfolios are used in option pricing models to circumvent the problem of identifying the opportunity cost of capital.

Reservation price: The price below (above) which a seller (purchaser) is unwilling to go.

Restricted shares: Shares that may be held only by domestic residents.

Revaluation: An increase in a currency value relative to other currencies in a fixed exchange rate system.

Rights of set-off: An agreement defining each party's rights should one party default on its obligation. Rights of set-off are used in parallel loan arrangements.

Risk: The possibility that actual outcomes might differ from expectations.

Risk exposure: Changes in the value of the firm's assets or liabilities as a consequence of unexpected changes in some underlying factor, such as general business conditions or a financial price variable (exchange rates, interest rates, or commodity prices).

Risk profile: A graph with the value of an underlying asset on the x-axis and the value of a position exposed to risk in the underlying asset on the y-axis. Also used with changes in value. (Contrast with *payoff profile*.)

Roll's Critique: The CAPM holds by construction when performance is measured against a mean-variance efficient index. Otherwise, it holds not at all.

R-square (the coefficient of determination): The percent of the variation in a dependent variable that is "explained by" variation in an independent variable.

Rule #1: Always keep track of your currency units.

Rule #2: Always think of buying and selling the currency in the denominator of a foreign exchange quote.

S

Scenario analysis: A process of asking "What if?" using scenarios that capture key elements of possible future realities.

Securities and Exchange Commission (SEC): The regulatory body that oversees securities regulation in the United States.

Security market line (SML): In the CAPM, the relation between required return and systematic risk (or beta): $r_j = r_F + \beta_j (E[r_M] - r_F)$.

Segmented market: A market that is partially or wholly isolated from other markets by one or more market imperfections.

Semi-strong form efficient market: A market in which prices fully reflect all *publicly* available information.

Sharpe index: A measure of risk-adjusted investment performance in excess return per unit of total risk: $SI = (r_P - r_F)/(\sigma_P)$.

Short position: A position in which a particular asset (such as a spot or forward currency) has been sold.

Short selling: Selling an asset that you do not own.

Side effect: Any aspect of an investment project that can be valued separately from the project itself.

Sight draft: A draft that is payable on demand.

Signaling: The use of observable managerial actions in the marketplace as an indication of management's beliefs concerning the prospects of the company.

Simple option: An option that has no other options attached.

Size effect: The finding that small firms tend to have higher mean returns than large firms.

Skewness: Skewness is a measure of asymmetry around a sample mean. The normal distribution is symmetric and has zero skewness.

Positive skewness is an indication of large positive returns. Conversely, negative skewness is an indication of large negative returns.

Special drawing right (SDR): An international reserve created by the International Monetary Fund and allocated to member countries to supplement foreign exchange reserves.

Spot market: A market in which trades are made for immediate delivery (within two business days for most spot currencies).

Stakeholders: Those with an interest in the firm. A narrow definition includes the corporation's debt and equity holders. A broader definition includes labor, management, and perhaps other interested parties, such as customers, suppliers, and society at large.

Stamp tax: A tax on a financial transaction.

Stationary time series: A time series in which the process generating returns is identical at every instant of time.

Stock index futures: A futures contract on a stock index.

Stock index swap: A swap involving a stock index. The other asset involved in a stock index swap can be another stock index (a stock-for-stock swap), a debt index (a debt-for-stock swap), or any other financial asset or price index.

Strategic alliance: A collaborative agreement between two companies designed to achieve some strategic goal. Strategic alliances include international licensing agreements, management contracts, and joint ventures.

Striking price: The price at which an option can be exercised (also called the *exercise price*).

Subpart F income: In the U.S. tax code, income from foreign subsidiaries owned more than 10 percent and controlled foreign corporations that is taxed on a pro rata basis as it is earned.

Subsidized financing: Financing that is provided by a host government and that is issued at a below-market interest rate.

Sunk costs: Expenditures that are at least partially lost once an investment is made.

Supervisory board: The board of directors that represents stakeholders in the governance of the corporation.

Swap: An agreement to exchange two liabilities (or assets) and, after a prearranged length of time, to reexchange the liabilities (or assets).

Swap book: A swap bank's portfolio of swaps, usually arranged by currency and by maturity.

Swap pricing schedule: A schedule of rates for an interest rate or currency swap.

Swaption: A derivative contract granting the right to enter into a swap.

SWIFT (Society for Worldwide Interbank Financial Transactions): Network through which international banks conduct their financial transactions.

Switching options: A sequence of options in which exercise of one option creates one or more additional options. Investment-disinvestment, entry-exit, expansion-contraction, and suspension-reactivation decisions are examples of switching options.

Syndicate: The selling group of investment banks in a public securities offering.

Synergy: In an acquisition or merger, when the value of the combination is greater than the sum of the individual parts: Synergy $= V_{AT} = V_A + V_T$.

Synthetic forward position: A forward position constructed through borrowing in one currency, lending in another currency, and offsetting these transactions in the spot exchange market.

Systematic business risk (unlevered beta): The systematic risk (or beta) of a project that is financed with 100 percent equity.

Systematic risk: Risk that is common to all assets and cannot be diversified away (measured by beta).

T

Tangibility: Tangible assets are real assets that can be used as collateral to secure debt.

Targeted registered offerings: Securities issues sold to "targeted" foreign financial institutions according to U.S. SEC guidelines. These foreign institutions then maintain a secondary market in the foreign market.

Tax arbitrage: Arbitrage using a difference in tax rates or tax systems as the basis for profit.

Tax clienteles: Clienteles of investors with specific preferences for debt or equity that are driven by differences in investors' personal tax rates.

Tax-haven affiliate: A wholly owned affiliate that is in a low-tax jurisdiction and that is used to channel funds to and from the multinational's foreign operations.

Tax holiday: A reduced tax rate provided by a government as an inducement to foreign direct investment.

Tax neutrality: Taxes that do not interfere with the natural flow of capital toward its most productive use.

Tax preference items: Items such as tax-loss carryforwards and carrybacks and investment tax credits that shield corporate taxable income from taxes.

Technical analysis: Any method of forecasting future exchange rates based on the history of exchange rates.

Temporal (and monetary/nonmonetary) method: A translation accounting method (such as FAS #8 in the United States) that translates monetary assets and liabilities at current exchange rates and all other balance sheet accounts at historical exchange rates.

Territorial tax system: A tax system that taxes domestic income but not foreign income. This tax regime is found in Hong Kong, France, Belgium, and the Netherlands.

Time draft: A draft that is payable on a specified future date.

Time value: The difference between the value of an option and the option's intrinsic value.

Timing option: The right to choose when to exercise an option, In particular, the ability of the firm to postpone investment (or disinvestment) and to reconsider the decision at a future date.

Total risk: The sum of systematic and unsystematic risk (measured by the standard deviation or variance of return).

Trade acceptance: A time draft that is drawn on and accepted by an importer.

Trade balance: A country's net balance (exports minus imports) on merchandise trade.

Trade secret: An idea, process, formula, technique, device, or information that a company uses to its competitive advantage.

Trademark: A distinctive name, word, symbol, or device used to distinguish a company's goods or services from those of its competitors.

Trading desk (dealing desk): The desk at an international bank that trades spot and forward foreign exchange.

Transaction exposure: Changes in the value of contractual (monetary) cash flows as a result of changes in currency values.

Transfer prices: Prices set on intracompany sales.

Translation (accounting) exposure: Changes in a corporation's financial statements as a result of changes in currency values.

Triangular arbitrage: Arbitrage conducted between three exchange rates.

U

Unbiased expectations hypothesis: The hypothesis that forward exchange rates are unbiased predictors of future spot rates. (See *forward parity*.)

Uncovered interest parity (UIP, or *Fisher Open*): The nominal interest rate differential equals the expected change in the exchange rate.

Universal banking: A banking system (such as Germany's) in which banks offer a full range of banking and financial services to their individual and corporate clients.

Unlevered beta (systematic business risk): The beta (or systematic risk) of a project as if it were financed with 100 percent equity.

Unlevered cost of equity: The discount rate appropriate for an investment assuming it is financed with 100 percent equity.

Unrestricted shares: Shares that may be held only by anyone, including foreigners.

Unsystematic risk: Risk that is specific to a particular security or country and that can be eliminated through diversification.

V

Value premium: The finding that value stocks tend to have higher mean returns than growth stocks.

Value stocks: Stocks with low equity price/book ratios or price/earnings ratios.

Value-added tax (VAT): A sales tax collected at each stage of production in proportion to the value added during that stage.

Value-at-risk (VaR): Value-at-risk is an estimate of potential loss with a certain level of confidence and over a certain time horizon due to adverse price movements in an underlying asset.

Vertical keiretsu (sangyô): Japanese industrial groups with extensive cross shareholdings in related businesses. Vertical keiretsu are led by a major manufacturer in electronics (Hitachi, Sony, Toshiba) or automotive (Honda, Nissan, Toyota).

W

Warrant: An option issued by a company that allows the holder to purchase equity from the company at a predetermined price prior to an expiration date. Warrants are frequently attached to Eurobonds.

Weak form efficient market: A market in which prices fully reflect the information in past prices.

Weighted average cost of capital (WACC): A discount rate that reflects the after-tax required returns on debt and equity capital.

Withholding tax: A tax on dividend or interest income that is withheld for payment of taxes in a host country. Payment is typically withheld by the financial institution distributing the payment.

World Bank: See *International Bank for Reconstruction and Development.*

World Trade Organization (WTO): Created in 1994 by 121 nations at the Uruguay Round of the General Agreement on Tariffs and Trade (GATT). The WTO is responsible for implementation and administration of the trade agreement.

Worldwide tax system: A tax system that taxes worldwide income as it is repatriated to the parent company. Used in Japan, the United Kingdom, and the United States.

Y

Yield to maturity: The discount rate that equates the present value of promised future interest payments to the current market value of the debt.

Z

Zaibatsu: Large family-owned conglomerates that controlled much of the economy of Japan prior to World War II.

Name Index

Subject Index